Augsburg Seminary
Library

A SURVEY OF INTERNATIONAL RELATIONS BETWEEN THE UNITED STATES AND GERMANY

AUGUST 1, 1914—APRIL 6, 1917

BASED ON OFFICIAL DOCUMENTS

BY

JAMES BROWN SCOTT

Doctor of Jurisprudence of the University of Heidelberg; Technical Delegate of the United States to the Second Hague Peace Conference; Member of the Institute of International Law; President of the American Institute of International Law, Major and Judge Advocate, United States Reserves

---

Know once and for all that in the matter of kingcraft we take when we can, and that we are never wrong unless we have to give back what we have taken.
—FREDERICK THE GREAT: *Les Matinées Royales*, circa 1764.

The true honor and dignity of the Nation are inseparable from justice.
—ALBERT GALLATIN: *Peace with Mexico*, 1847.

NEW YORK
OXFORD UNIVERSITY PRESS
AMERICAN BRANCH: 35 WEST 32ND STREET
LONDON, TORONTO, MELBOURNE, AND BOMBAY

1917

COPYRIGHT 1918
BY THE
OXFORD UNIVERSITY PRESS
AMERICAN BRANCH

THE QUINN & BODEN CO. PRESS
RAHWAY, N. J.

RESPECTFULLY DEDICATED TO THE HONORABLE ROBERT LANSING,
SECRETARY OF STATE OF THE UNITED STATES, AND
THROUGH HIM TO HIS COUNTRYMEN AND TO ALL
PARTISANS OF JUSTICE BETWEEN NATIONS,
WHOSE CAUSE HE HAS FINELY STATED
AND FAITHFULLY SERVED

PUBLISHERS' PREFACE

The publishers announce, separate and distinct from, but to be used in connection with the present volume, the Diplomatic Correspondence between the United States and Germany from August 1, 1914, to April 6, 1917, the date of the declaration of a state of war by the Congress of the United States against the Imperial German Government, and President Wilson's Messages, Addresses, and Papers on Foreign Policy. These volumes are of the same format as the Survey of International Relations between the United States and Germany, 1914-1917, and they are edited by its author.

The differences of opinion, crystallizing into opposition, and resulting eventually in war between the United States and Germany, are stated clearly, unmistakably, and officially in the Diplomatic Correspondence between the two Governments since the outbreak of the European War in 1914, and up to the declaration of war by the United States because of the controversies between the two countries. The Diplomatic Correspondence makes the case of the United States, just as the Diplomatic Correspondence is the defense of Germany. Upon this Correspondence each country rests its case, and upon this Correspondence each is to be judged. It is thought best to present it in a volume by itself, disconnected from narrative or from correspondence with other belligerent nations, which would indeed have been interesting but not material to the present case.

President Wilson's views upon foreign policy were important during the neutrality of the United States, and it is even more important to understand them now, inasmuch as they are the views of the United States at war and indicate in no uncertain way the attitude which the United States under President Wilson's guidance may be expected to assume in the negotiations which must one day bring about peace to a long-suffering and war-ridden world. This volume is of interest to Mr. Wilson's countrymen; it is of interest to the belligerents; it is of interest to the neutrals, whose cause Mr. Wilson has championed.

The publishers have pleasure in announcing that the author of "A Survey of International Relations between the United States and Germany" and editor of "President Wilson's Messages, Addresses, and Papers on Foreign Policy" and of the "Diplomatic Correspondence," has directed that the royalties due him be presented to the Department of State War Relief Work Committee, of which Mrs. Robert Lansing is President.

OXFORD UNIVERSITY PRESS
American Branch

September 16, 1917.

TABLE OF CONTENTS

INTRODUCTION

                                                        PAGE

1. Address to the Congress by the President of the United States, April 2, 1917, recommending a declaration of war against the Imperial German Government xiii

2. Joint Resolution of Congress declaring a state of war to exist between the United States and the Imperial German Government, April 6, 1917 xxi

3. German Conceptions of the State, International Policy, and International Law xxii
    - (a) Frederick the Great xxii
    - (b) Georg Wilhelm Friedrich Hegel xxxv
    - (c) Karl von Clausewitz xxxix
    - (d) Ernst Moritz Arndt xli
    - (e) Frederick William IV, King of Prussia . . . xlii
    - (f) Theodor Mommsen xlii
    - (g) Prince Otto von Bismarck xliii
    - (h) Count Helmuth von Moltke xlvii
    - (i) Adolf Lasson l
    - (j) Gustav Rümelin lxx
    - (k) Heinrich von Treitschke lxxiii
    - (l) *Kriegsbrauch im Landkriege* xci
    - (m) Friedrich von Bernhardi xcii
    - (n) Theobald von Bethmann-Hollweg cxii
    - (o) William II, German Emperor and King of Prussia . . cxiv

4. Declarations of a State of War cxv

CHAPTER I
Genesis of the War of 1914 1

CHAPTER II
The Neutrality of the United States 43

CHAPTER III
German Charges of Unneutral Conduct. 54

CHAPTER IV
Censorship of Communications 57
    Section 1. Cable and Wireless 57
    Section 2. Mail 59

CONTENTS

CHAPTER V

	PAGE
Unlawful Seizure of Persons upon the High Seas	66
Section 1. Searching of American Vessels for German and Austrian Subjects	66
Section 2. Arrest of Americans on Neutral Vessels	72

CHAPTER VI

Restraints on Commerce	74
Section 1. Contraband	74
Section 2. Copper	77
Section 3. Trade with Neutral Countries	79
Section 4. Trade with Germany	91
Section 5. Summary	96

CHAPTER VII

Sale of Munitions of War	98

CHAPTER VIII

Miscellaneous Complaints	106
Section 1. Sale of Dumdum Bullets	106
Section 2. Hovering of British Warships off American Ports	110
Section 3. Disregard of American Citizenship Papers and Passports	116
Section 4. Change of Policy in regard to Loans to Belligerents	118
Section 5. Indifference to Confinement of Noncombatants in Detention Camps in England and France	119
Section 6. Failure to Prevent Transshipment of British Troops and War Material Across the Territory of the United States	120
Section 7. Internment of German Steamship *Geier* and the collier *Locksun* at Honolulu	121
Section 8. Coaling of Warships in Panama Canal Zone	128
Section 9. Failure to Protest against Modification of the Declaration of London by the British Government	130
Section 10. General Unfriendly Attitude of United States toward Germany and Austria	132
Section 11. Summary	134

CHAPTER IX

Submarine Warfare	136
Section 1. *The Lusitania*	149
Section 2. *The Arabic*	168
Section 3. *The Sussex*	169

CHAPTER X

Reprisals, Retaliation, Necessity	177

CHAPTER XI

Belligerent Use of Neutral Flag	197

CHAPTER XII

Mines, War Zones, and Blockade	205

CONTENTS

CHAPTER XIII

	PAGE
Status of Merchant Vessels	216
Section 1. The Right of Merchant Vessels to Arm	216
Section 2. Visit and Search	230
Section 3. Destruction of Prizes	234
Section 4. Treatment of Armed Merchant Vessels in the Present War	247

CHAPTER XIV

The Accepted Rules of Maritime Warfare	265
Section 1. Views of German Publicists	265
Section 2. The German Prize Ordinance	280
Section 3. The Prussian-American Treaties	285

CHAPTER XV

Renewal of Submarine Warfare 290

CHAPTER XVI

Severance of Diplomatic Relations and Proclamation of Armed Neutrality . 295

CHAPTER XVII

The Declaration of War 298

CHAPTER XVIII

Why Not Arbitration?	311
Section 1. The Origin and Extent of the Modern Practice of Arbitration	311
Section 2. The German Attitude towards Arbitration	314
Section 3. The *Frye* Case	326

CHAPTER XIX

The Freedom of the Seas	336
CONCLUSION	360

POST SCRIPTUM

1. Reply of the President of the United States to the Peace Appeal of the Pope, August 27, 1917 361
2. Address of the President of the United States Delivered at a Joint Session of the Two Houses of Congress, December 4, 1917 . . . 364
3. War with the Imperial and Royal Austro-Hungarian Government . 372
4. Joint Resolution Declaring that a State of War Exists between the Imperial and Royal Austro-Hungarian Government and the Government and the People of the United States, and Making Provision to Prosecute the Same 379

INDEX 381

NOTE.—In Chapter I the references to the official correspondence of the European Powers regarding the outbreak of the war of 1914 are made to *Diplomatic Documents Relating to the Outbreak of the European War*, a work in two volumes edited by the author of the present volume and issued by the Oxford University Press in 1916. The references in parentheses are to the pages of that publication, but the titles of the memoranda and the numbers of the documents are given in each case, so that the reader can locate them in other collections.

The references to The Hague Conventions and Declarations are made throughout to a work entitled *The Hague Conventions and Declarations of 1899 and 1907*, edited by the author of this volume and issued by the Oxford University Press in 1915, as this publication gives the reservations, signatures and ratifications of the Powers, certified to by the Department of State of the United States and the Netherland Government.

INTRODUCTION

INTRODUCTION

1. ADDRESS OF THE PRESIDENT OF THE UNITED STATES DELIVERED AT A JOINT SESSION OF THE TWO HOUSES OF CONGRESS APRIL 2, 1917:

Gentlemen of the Congress:

I have called the Congress into extraordinary session because there are serious, very serious, choices of policy to be made, and made immediately, which it was neither right nor constitutionally permissible that I should assume the responsibility of making.

On the third of February last I officially laid before you the extraordinary announcement of the Imperial German Government that on and after the first day of February it was its purpose to put aside all restraints of law or of humanity and use its submarines to sink every vessel that sought to approach either the ports of Great Britain and Ireland or the western coasts of Europe or any of the ports controlled by the enemies of Germany within the Mediterranean. That had seemed to be the object of the German submarine warfare earlier in the war, but since April of last year the Imperial Government had somewhat restrained the commanders of its undersea craft in conformity with its promise then given to us that passenger boats should not be sunk and that due warning would be given to all other vessels which its submarines might seek to destroy, when no resistance was offered or escape attempted, and care taken that their crews were given at least a fair chance to save their lives in their open boats. The precautions taken were meager and haphazard enough, as was proved in distressing instance after instance in the progress of the cruel and unmanly business, but a certain degree of restraint was observed. The new policy has swept every restriction aside. Vessels of every kind, whatever their flag, their character, their cargo, their destination, their errand, have been ruthlessly sent to the bottom without warning and without thought of help or mercy for those on board, the vessels of friendly neutrals along with those of belligerents. Even hospital ships and ships carrying relief to the sorely bereaved and stricken people of Belgium, though the latter were provided with safe conduct through the proscribed areas by the German Government itself and were distinguished by unmistakable marks of identity, have been sunk with the same reckless lack of compassion or of principle.

I was for a little while unable to believe that such things would in fact be done by any government that had hitherto subscribed to the humane practices of civilized nations. International law had its origin in the attempt to set up some law which would be respected and observed upon the seas, where no nation had right of dominion and where lay the free highways of the world. By painful stage after stage has that law been built up, with meager enough results, indeed, after all was accomplished that could be accomplished, but always with a clear view, at least, of what the heart and conscience of mankind demanded. This minimum of right the German Government has swept aside under the plea of retaliation and necessity and because it had no weapons which it could use at sea except those which it is impossible to employ as it is employing them without throwing to the winds all scruples of humanity or of respect for the understandings that were supposed to underlie the intercourse of the world. I am not now thinking of the loss of property involved, immense and serious as that is, but only of the wanton and wholesale destruction of the lives of noncombatants, men, women, and children, engaged in pursuits which have always, even in the darkest periods of modern history, been deemed innocent and legitimate. Property can be paid for; the lives of peaceful and innocent people cannot be. The present German submarine warfare against commerce is a warfare against mankind.

It is a war against all nations. American ships have been sunk, American lives taken, in ways which it has stirred us very deeply to learn of, but the ships and people of other neutral and friendly nations have been sunk and overwhelmed in the waters in the same way. There has been no discrimination. The challenge is to all mankind. Each nation must decide for itself how it will meet it. The choice we make for ourselves must be made with a moderation of counsel and a temperateness of judgment befitting our character and our motives as a nation. We must put excited feeling away. Our motive will not be revenge or the victorious assertion of the physical might of the nation, but only the vindication of right, of human right, of which we are only a single champion.

When I addressed the Congress on the twenty-sixth of February last I thought that it would suffice to assert our neutral rights with arms, our right to use the seas against unlawful interference, our right to keep our people safe against unlawful violence. But armed neutrality, it now appears, is impracticable. Because submarines are in effect outlaws when used as the German submarines have been used against merchant shipping, it is impossible to defend ships against their attacks as the law of nations has assumed that merchantmen would defend themselves against privateers or cruisers, visible craft giving chase upon the open sea. It is common prudence in such circumstances, grim necessity indeed, to endeavor to destroy them before they have shown their own intention. They must be dealt with upon sight, if dealt with at all. The German Government denies the right of neutrals to use arms at all within the areas of the sea which it has proscribed, even in the defense of rights which no modern publicist has ever before questioned their right to defend. The intimation is conveyed that the armed guards which we have placed on our merchant ships will be treated as beyond the pale of law and subject to be dealt with as pirates would be. Armed neutrality is ineffectual enough at best; in such circumstances and in the face of such pretensions it is worse than ineffectual: it is likely only to produce what it was meant to prevent; it is practically certain to draw us into the war without either the rights or the effectiveness of belligerents. There is one choice we cannot make, we are incapable of making: we will not choose the path of submission and suffer the most sacred rights of our nation and our people to be ignored or violated. The wrongs against which we now array ourselves are no common wrongs; they cut to the very roots of human life.

With a profound sense of the solemn and even tragical character of the step I am taking and of the grave responsibilities which it involves, but in unhesitating obedience to what I deem my constitutional duty, I advise that the Congress declare the recent course of the Imperial German Government to be in fact nothing less than war against the government and people of the United States; that it formally accept the status of belligerent which has thus been thrust upon it; and that it take immediate steps not only to put the country in a more thorough state of defense but also to exert all its power and employ all its resources to bring the Government of the German Empire to terms and end the war.

What this will involve is clear. It will involve the utmost practicable coöperation in counsel and action with the governments now at war with Germany, and, as incident to that, the extension to those governments of the most liberal financial credits, in order that our resources may so far as possible be added to theirs. It will involve the organization and mobilization of all the material resources of the country to supply the materials of war and serve the incidental needs of the nation in the most abundant and yet the most economical and efficient way possible. It will involve the immediate full equipment of the navy in all respects but particularly in supplying it with the best means of dealing with the enemy's submarines. It will involve the immediate addition to the armed forces of the United States already provided for by law in case of war at least five hundred thousand men, who should, in my opinion, be chosen upon the principle of universal liability to service, and also the authorization of subsequent additional increments of equal force so soon as they may be needed and can be handled in training. It will involve also, of course, the granting of adequate credits to the government, sustained, I hope, so far as they can equitably be sustained by the present generation, by well conceived taxation.

I say sustained so far as may be equitable by taxation because it seems to me that it would be most unwise to base the credits which will now be necessary entirely on money borrowed. It is our duty, I most respectfully urge, to protect our people so far as we may against the very serious hardships and evils which would be likely to arise out of the inflation which would be produced by vast loans.

In carrying out the measures by which these things are to be accomplished we should keep constantly in mind the wisdom of interfering as little as possible in our own preparation and in the equipment of our own military forces with the duty,—for it will be a very practical duty,—of supplying the nations already at war with Germany with the materials which they can obtain only from us or by our assistance. They are in the field and we should help them in every way to be effective there.

I shall take the liberty of suggesting, through the several

executive departments of the government, for the consideration of your committees, measures for the accomplishment of the several objects I have mentioned. I hope that it will be your pleasure to deal with them as having been framed after very careful thought by the branch of the government upon which the responsibility of conducting the war and safeguarding the nation will most directly fall.

While we do these things, these deeply momentous things, let us be very clear, and make very clear to all the world what our motives and our objects are. My own thought has not been driven from its habitual and normal course by the unhappy events of the last two months, and I do not believe that the thought of the nation has been altered or clouded by them. I have exactly the same things in mind now that I had in mind when I addressed the Senate on the twenty-second of January last; the same that I had in mind when I addressed the Congress on the third of February and on the twenty-sixth of February. Our object now, as then, is to vindicate the principles of peace and justice in the life of the world as against selfish and autocratic power and to set up amongst the really free and self-governed peoples of the world such a concert of purpose and of action as will henceforth insure the observance of those principles. Neutrality is no longer feasible or desirable where the peace of the world is involved and the freedom of its peoples, and the menace to that peace and freedom lies in the existence of autocratic governments backed by organized force which is controlled wholly by their will, not by the will of their people. We have seen the last of neutrality in such circumstances. We are at the beginning of an age in which it will be insisted that the same standards of conduct and of responsibility for wrong done shall be observed among nations and their governments that are observed among the individual citizens of civilized states.

We have no quarrel with the German people. We have no feeling towards them but one of sympathy and friendship. It was not upon their impulse that their government acted in entering this war. It was not with their previous knowledge or approval. It was a war determined upon as wars used to be determined upon in the old, unhappy days when peoples were nowhere consulted by their rulers and wars were provoked and waged in the interest of dynasties or of little groups of ambitious men who were accustomed to use their fellowmen as pawns and tools. Self-governed nations do not fill their neighbor states with spies or set the course of intrigue to bring about some critical posture of affairs which will give them an opportunity to strike and make conquest. Such designs can be successfully worked out only under cover and where no one has the right to ask questions. Cunningly contrived plans of deception or aggression, carried, it may be, from generation to generation, can be worked out and kept from the light only within the privacy of courts or behind the carefully guarded confidences of a narrow and privileged class. They are happily impossible where public opinion commands and insists upon full information concerning all the nation's affairs.

A steadfast concert for peace can never be maintained except by a partnership of democratic nations. No autocratic government could be trusted to keep faith within it or observe its covenants. It must be a league of honor, a partnership of opinion. Intrigue would eat its vitals away; the plottings of inner circles who could plan what they would and render account to no one would be a corruption seated at its very heart. Only free peoples can hold their purpose and their honor steady to a common end and prefer the interests of mankind to any narrow interest of their own.

Does not every American feel that assurance has been added to our hope for the future peace of the world by the wonderful and heartening things that have been happening within the last few weeks in Russia? Russia was known by those who knew it best to have been always in fact democratic at heart, in all the vital habits of her thought, in all the intimate relationships of her people that spoke their natural instinct, their habitual attitude towards life. The autocracy that crowned the summit of her political structure, long as it had stood and terrible as was the reality of its power, was not in fact Russian in origin, character, or purpose; and now it has been shaken off and the great, generous Russian people have been added in all their naïve majesty and might to the forces that are fighting for freedom in the world, for justice, and for peace. Here is a fit partner for a League of Honor.

One of the things that has served to convince us that the Prussian autocracy was not and could never be our friend is that from the very outset of the present war it has filled our unsuspecting communities and even our offices of Government with spies and set criminal intrigues everywhere afoot against our national unity of counsel, our peace within and without, our industries and our commerce. Indeed it is now evident that its spies were here even before the war began; and it is unhappily not a matter of conjecture but a fact proved in our courts of justice that the intrigues which have more than once come perilously near to disturbing the peace and dislocating the industries of the country have been carried on at the instigation, with the support, and even under the personal direction of official agents of the Imperial Government accredited to the Government of the United States. Even in checking these things and trying to extirpate them we have sought to put the most generous interpretation possible upon them because we knew that their source lay, not in any hostile feeling or purpose of the German people towards us (who were, no doubt as ignorant of them as we ourselves were), but only in the selfish designs of a government that did what it pleased and told its people nothing. But they have played their part in serving to convince us at last that that government entertains no real friendship for us and means to act against our peace and security at its convenience. That it means to stir up enemies against us at our very doors the intercepted note to the German Minister at Mexico City is eloquent evidence.

We are accepting this challenge of hostile purpose because we know that in such a government, following such methods, we can never have a friend; and that in the presence of its organized power, always lying in wait to accomplish we know not what purpose, there can be no assured security for the democratic governments of the world. We are now about to accept gauge of battle with this natural foe to liberty and shall, if necessary, spend the whole force of the nation to check and nullify its pretensions and its power. We are glad, now that we see the facts with no veil of false pretense about them, to fight thus for the ultimate peace of the world and for the liberation of its peoples, the German peoples included: for the rights of nations great and small and the privilege of men everywhere to choose their way of life and of obedience. The world must be made safe for democracy. Its peace must be planted upon the tested foundations of political liberty. We have no selfish ends to serve. We desire no conquest, no dominion. We seek no indemnities for ourselves, no material compensation for the sacrifices we shall freely make. We are but one of the champions of the rights of mankind. We shall be satisfied when those rights have been made as secure as the faith and the freedom of nations can make them.

Just because we fight without rancor and without selfish object, seeking nothing for ourselves but what we shall wish to share with all free peoples, we shall, I feel confident, conduct our operations as belligerents without passion and ourselves observe with proud punctilio the principles of right and of fair play we profess to be fighting for.

I have said nothing of the governments allied with the Imperial Government of Germany because they have not made war upon us or challenged us to defend our right and our honor. The Austro-Hungarian Government has, indeed, avowed its unqualified indorsement and acceptance of the reckless and lawless submarine warfare adopted now without disguise by the Imperial German Government, and it has therefore not been possible for this government to receive Count Tarnowski, the Ambassador recently accredited to this government by the Imperial and Royal Government of Austria-Hungary; but that government has not actually engaged in warfare against citizens of the United States on the seas, and I take the liberty, for the present at least, of postponing a discussion of our relations with the authorities at Vienna. We enter this war only where we are clearly forced into it because there are no other means of defending our rights.

It will be all the easier for us to conduct ourselves as belligerents in a high spirit of right and fairness because we act without animus, not in enmity towards a people or with the desire to bring any injury or disadvantage upon them, but only in armed opposition to an irresponsible government which has thrown aside all considerations of humanity and of right and is running amuck. We are, let me say again, the sincere friends of the German people, and shall desire nothing so much as the early re-establishment of intimate relations of mutual advantage between us,—however hard it may be for them, for the time being, to believe that this is spoken from our hearts. We have borne with their present government through all these bitter months because of that friendship,—exercising a patience and forbearance which would otherwise have been impossible. We shall, happily, still have an opportunity to prove that friendship in our daily attitude and actions towards the millions of men and women of German birth and native sympathy who live amongst us and share our life, and we shall be proud to prove it towards all who are in fact loyal to their neighbors and to the government in the hour of test. They are, most of them, as true and loyal Americans as if they had never known any other fealty or allegiance. They will be prompt to stand with us in rebuking and restraining the few who may be of a different mind and purpose. If there should be disloyalty, it will be dealt with with a firm hand of stern repression; but, if it lifts its head at all, it will lift it only here and there and without countenance except from a lawless and malignant few.

It is a distressing and oppressive duty, Gentlemen of the Congress, which I have performed in thus addressing you. There are, it may be, many months of fiery trial and sacrifice ahead of us. It is a fearful thing to lead this great peaceful people into war, into the most terrible and disastrous of all wars, civilization itself seeming to be in the balance. But the right is more precious than peace, and we shall fight for the things which we have always carried nearest our hearts,—for democracy, for the right of those who submit to authority to have a voice in their own governments, for the rights and liberties of small nations, for a universal dominion of right by such a concert of free peoples as shall bring peace and safety to all nations and make the world itself at last free. To such a task we can dedicate our lives and our fortunes, everything that we are and everything that we have, with the pride of those who know that the day has come when America is privileged to spend her blood and her might for the principles that gave her birth and happiness and the peace which she has treasured. God helping her, she can do no other.

2. JOINT RESOLUTION DECLARING THAT A STATE OF WAR EXISTS BETWEEN THE IMPERIAL GERMAN GOVERNMENT AND THE GOVERNMENT AND THE PEOPLE OF THE UNITED STATES AND MAKING PROVISION TO PROSECUTE THE SAME.

Whereas the Imperial German Government has committed repeated acts of war against the Government and the people of the United States of America; Therefore be it

Resolved by the Senate and House of Representatives of the United States of America in Congress assembled, That the state of war between the United States and the Imperial German Government which has thus been thrust upon the United States is hereby formally declared; and that the President be, and he is hereby, authorized and directed to employ the entire naval and military forces of the United States and the resources of the Government to carry on war against the Imperial German Government; and to bring the conflict to a successful termination all of the resources of the country are hereby pledged by the Congress of the United States.

CHAMP CLARK,
Speaker of the House of Representatives.

THOS. R. MARSHALL,
Vice President of the United States and President of the Senate.

Approved, April 6, 1917,
WOODROW WILSON."

3. GERMAN CONCEPTIONS OF THE STATE, INTERNATIONAL POLICY, AND INTERNATIONAL LAW.

Because the good old rule
Sufficeth them,—the simple plan,
That they should take who have the power,
And they should keep who can.

(a) *Frederick the Great* (1712-1786)

To keep up the rôle of an honest man with knaves is very perilous; to play a sharp game in the company of cheats is desperate. Success in such an attempt is very doubtful. What, then, is to be done? Either war or negotiation, just as your very humble servant and his minister are now doing. If there is anything to be gained by it, we will be honest; if deception is necessary, let us be cheats.[1]

Since it has been agreed upon among men that cheating one's fellowmen is a cowardly act, an expression has been sought for which might soften this act and the word Politics has been chosen to that end. This word has most certainly been employed only in favor of sovereigns, because in decency we cannot be treated as rogues and rascals.

But be that as it may, here is what I think of politics. My dear nephew, by the word Politics I understand that we must seek to deceive others; it is a means of having the advantage, or at least

---

[1] Frederick the Great to Minister de Podewils, dated the Camp at Mollwitz, May 12, 1741. (*Politische Correspondenz Friedrichs des Grossen* [Berlin, 1879], vol. 1, pp. 244-245.)

of being on a par with the rest of mankind; for you may be absolutely certain that all the states of the world run the same career and that it is the hidden goal at which the high and the lowly of the world aim.

This principle having been stated, never blush for making alliances with a view to your being the only one to draw advantage from them. Do not commit the stupid mistake of not abandoning them whenever you believe that your interests are at stake, and especially maintain vigorously this maxim, that to despoil your neighbors is to take away from them the means of doing you injury.

Properly speaking, it is politics which founds and preserves kingdoms. Therefore, my dear nephew, you must understand politics thoroughly and conceive of it in the clearest light. To this end I shall divide it into Politics of the State and into Private Politics. The former concerns only the great interests of the kingdom; the latter concerns the particular interests of the Prince.[1]

Politics of the State reduces itself to three principles: the first, to preserve, and, according to circumstances, to aggrandize one's self; the second, not to make any alliance except for one's own advantage;

---

[1] *Les Matinées Royales, ou l'Art de Régner. Opuscule inédit de Frédéric II, dit le Grand, roi de Prusse.* London, Williams and Norgate, 1863, pp. 18-19.

General Savary, Duke of Rovigo, who accompanied Napoleon in his visit to Sans Souci in 1806, purloined from Frederick's desk a copy of the *Matinées Royales*, said to be in Frederick's own handwriting. A copy of this was made in 1816 by one C. Whittall, with the Duke's permission and was published in 1901 by the copyist's grandson, Sir James William Whittall, in a book entitled *Frederick the Great on Kingcraft. From the original MS.* (London: Longmans, Green & Co., 1901), pp. 15-16.

The French text of *Les Matinées Royales, ou l'Art de Régner*, to which references are made, was edited in 1863 by the late Lord Acton from a copy made at Sans Souci in 1806 by Baron de Méneval, Private Secretary to Napoleon. It contains five of the seven *Matinées* and fills the thirty-five pages of this little volume.

In 1870 an English translation of Lord Acton's edition was issued in Boston in a pamphlet of fifty-two pages, under the highly significant and accurate title of "Origin of the Bismarck policy; or, *The Hohenzollern doctrine and maxims described and defined by . . . Frederick the Great; his opinions on religion, justice, morals, politics, diplomacy, statesmanship, the German people, etc., etc. Written by himself expressly for the use of his successor to the throne.*" Carefully translated from an authentic copy of the original manuscript by M. C. L. Boston; Crosby & Damrell, 1870.

For the origin, nature, and authenticity of the *Matinées Royales*, see an article entitled *The Confessions of Frederick the Great*, and a review of *Buffon; sa famille, ses collaborateurs et ses familiers. Mémoires par M. Humbert-Bazile, son Secrétaire; mis en ordre, annotés et augmentés de documents inédits par M. Henri Nadault de Buffon.* Paris: Renouard (1863), in *Home and Foreign Review* for 1863, vol. 2, pp. 152-171; vol. 3, pp. 704-711, both written by Lord Acton, the most critical and painstaking of historians, commonly called "the most erudite man of his generation." (See *A Bibliography of the Historical Works of Dr. Creighton, Dr. Stubbs, Dr. S. R. Gardiner, and the Late Lord Acton.* Edited for the Royal Historical Society by U. A. Shaw, London, 1903, pp. 45, 47, 53.)

and the third, to make one's self feared and respected in the most untoward times.

When I ascended the throne I visited the coffers of my father; his great economy enabled me to form great projects. Some time afterwards I reviewed my troops, and I found them superb. After this review, I returned to my coffers and found the wherewith to double my military force. As I had just doubled my power, it was natural that I should not limit myself to preserving what I already had. Thus I had soon resolved to profit by the first opportunity that should offer. Meanwhile I thoroughly trained my troops and made every effort to keep the eyes of all Europe riveted upon my *manœuvers*. I renewed them every year, in order to appear the more thoroughly versed in the art, and finally I attained my purpose. I turned the head of all the Powers. Everyone considered himself lost, if he could not move arms, feet and head in the Prussian style. All my soldiers came to think that they were twice the men they had been before when they saw that they were everywhere aped.

When my troops had thus acquired an advantage over all other troops, I was busy only with examining what pretensions I could lay to various provinces. Four principal points offered themselves to my view, Silesia, Polish Prussia, Dutch Gueldre, and Swedish Pomerania.

I limited myself to Silesia, because that object deserved more of my attention than all the others, and also because the circumstances were more favorable to me. I left to time the care of the execution of my projects upon the other points, and I shall not undertake to prove to you the validity of my pretensions upon that province. I have had these pretensions established by my orators; the Empress opposed them with her own and the case was ended by cannon, sabre and rifle. . . .

From all this there results that we must always be attempting something, and be thoroughly persuaded that all available means are proper to our purpose. But it is good policy to be careful not to announce one's pretensions with too much vanity, and especially to maintain at your court two or three eloquent men, and to leave it with them to justify your acts.[1]

Posterity will perhaps be surprised to find in these memoirs

---

[1] *Les Matinées Royales*, pp. 29-32.
"The matter of right is the business of the ministers; it is your business; it is time to work it up in secret, for the troops have received their orders." (Frederick the Great to Minister de Podewils, November 7, 1740; *Politische Correspondenz Friedrichs des Grossen* [Berlin, 1879], vol. 1, p. 91.)

accounts of treaties entered into and broken; although such examples are common in history, the author of this work could not justify himself, if he had no better reasons for excusing his conduct.

The interest of the State must serve as the rule for the conduct of sovereigns. Cases when alliances must be broken are the following: (1) When the ally fails to fulfill his engagements; (2) when the ally plans to deceive one, and when one has no other means to prevent him; (3) when *force majeure* hangs over one and compels one to break one's treaties; (4) finally, when one lacks the means for continuing the war. By a sort of fatality, which I cannot explain, wealth of resources exercises an influence upon everything, and princes are the slaves of their means; the interest of the State is a law unto them, and this law is inviolable. If the prince is under obligation to sacrifice his very self for the salvation of his subjects, he must *a fortiori* sacrifice engagements, the continuation of which might become harmful to them. Examples of treaties of this nature which have been broken are commonly met with in history; it is not our intention to justify all such cases; I venture, however, to affirm that there are such treaties which necessity, wisdom, prudence, or the welfare of the people compel sovereigns to break, because there is no other means left by which to avoid ruin. . . . It appears to me clear and obvious that a private individual must scrupulously observe his pledged word, even if he should have inconsiderately made such a pledge: if another private individual fails to observe his given word, the person against whom such violation is committed can have recourse to the protection of the laws, and, whatever may be the result of such an act, it is only an individual who suffers; but to what tribunals can a sovereign have recourse if another prince violates engagements entered into with him? The word of a private individual involves but the misfortune of one man; the word of sovereigns may lead to calamities involving entire nations. This matter may, therefore, be stated as follows: Is it better that a people should perish, or that a prince should break his treaty? Where would one find the imbecile who would hesitate in answering this question?[1]

In this work you will meet with treaties entered into and broken; and I must tell you, in regard to this matter, that we are subordinated to our means and to our capacities: when our interests change, we must change our actions accordingly. We are employed to watch

[1] *Histoire de mon temps*, tome i, avant-propos (1775), pp. xxvi-xxvii; *Œuvres de Frédéric le Grand*, tome ii.

over the happiness of our peoples: therefore, as soon as we realize that danger or risk are involved for them in an alliance, it is our duty to break such alliance, rather than to expose them to the evil effects thereof; in such case the sovereign sacrifices himself for the good of his subjects. The annals of the whole world furnish such examples; and in truth, one can hardly act otherwise. Those who are so severe in condemning such conduct are people who regard the pledged word as something sacred; they are right, and as a private individual, I think as they do, for a man who pledges his word to another, even although he promised inconsiderately something which might turn out to his greatest prejudice, must keep his word, because honor is above interest; but a prince who gives his word, does not commit only himself; for if he did commit only himself, the case would be the same as that of a private individual; but he exposes great states and great provinces to a thousand and one misfortunes: it is better, therefore, that the sovereign should break his treaty rather than that the people should perish. What would we say of a ridiculously scrupulous surgeon, unwilling to amputate the gangrenous arm of a man, because it is an evil act to cut off a man's arm? Is it not readily seen that it would be by far a greater evil to let a citizen perish who might have been saved? I venture to state that it is the circumstances of an act, that which accompanies and flows from such act, by which one is to judge whether or not it is a good or an evil act; but there are few people able to judge of such cases in full knowledge of the facts; men are like sheep and blindly follow their leader: let a wit deliver himself of a catchy phrase, and a thousand fools will repeat him.[1]

To form alliances for one's own advantage is a maxim of the State, and there are no powers which are warranted in neglecting to observe it. Thus results this consequence, that an alliance must be broken whenever it becomes prejudicial. During my first war with the Queen, I forsook the French at Prague, because in doing so I acquired Silesia. If I had taken the French to Vienna, they would never have given me so much. Some years afterwards, I concluded a new alliance with France, because I desired to attempt the conquest of Bohemia, and because I wished to treat them generously for the possible need I might have of them. Since then I have neglected this nation in order to go into closer relations with the one that offered me more. When Prussia, dear nephew, shall have made her fortune, she will then be able to assume an air of good faith and of

[1] *Histoire de mon temps*, tome i, avant-propos (1746), pp. xvi-xvii; *Œuvres de Frédéric le Grand, roi de Prusse*, tome ii.

constancy such as, at the most, becomes only great states and little sovereigns. I have told you, dear nephew, politics and rascality are synonymous, and this is true; still, you will find in this respect, some people of good faith who have formed for themselves certain systems of probity. Thus, you may chance anything with your ambassadors. I have found some who have served me faithfully, and who, in order to uncover a mystery would have rifled the pockets of a king. Attach yourselves especially to those possessing the talent of expressing themselves in vague, ponderous, or ambiguous phrases. You will make no mistake in keeping some political locksmiths and doctors; they may be of great use to you. I know from experience all the advantages to be derived through them.[1]

One of the first principles of politics is to endeavor to become an ally of that one of one's neighbors who may deal the most dangerous blows to one's state. It is for this reason that we have an alliance with Russia, because as long as the alliance lasts, Prussia's rear will have nothing to fear from Russia.[2]

It has been said, and the phrase has been thoughtlessly reëxpressed that treaties are useless because all their stipulations are hardly ever fulfilled, and because men are no more scrupulous in our century than they have been in other centuries. I answer to those who think in this way that I have no doubt whatever that there have been, in ancient and even in very recent times, Princes who have not exactly fulfilled their engagements; but that it is always most advantageous to conclude treaties. For every ally one secures there will be in each case an enemy the less, and, if one's allies are of no assistance, still they always ought to observe an exact neutrality.[3]

Nothing was more contrary to the welfare of the Prussian state than to allow the formation of an alliance between Saxony and Russia, and nothing would have seemed more unnatural than to sacrifice a Princess of the royal blood in order to dislodge the Saxon Princes. Another expedient was resorted to. Of all the German Princesses of marriageable age none but the Princess of Zerbst was more suitable to Russia and more likely to serve the Prussian interests. . . .

When the Empress had made up her mind to choose the Princess of Zerbst for marriage with the Grand Duke, less difficulty was met

---

[1] *Les Matinées Royales*, pp. 32-33.
[2] *Exposé du gouvernement prussien—Œuvres philosophiques*, tome ii, p. 187; *Œuvres de Frédéric le Grand*, tome ix.
[3] *L'Antimachiavel—Œuvres philosophiques*, tome i, p. 94; *Œuvres de Frédéric le Grand*, tome viii.

with to secure her consent for the marriage of the Prussian Princess Ulrica with the new royal Prince of Sweden. It was upon these two alliances that Prussia relied for her security: a Prussian Princess near the Swedish throne could not be the enemy of the king, her brother, and a Russian Grand Duchess educated and brought up on Prussian Territory and who owed her fortune to the king, could not be hostile to him, without being ungrateful.[1]

By careful management and intrigue the king succeeded in inducing the Russian Czarina to choose the Princess of Darmstadt, the sister of the Princess of Prussia, as a wife for her son, the Grand Duke Paul. In order to have influence in Russia it was necessary for Prussia to place there persons who were likely to favor Prussia. It was to be hoped that the Prince of Prussia, when succeeding King Frederick, would be able to draw great advantage from the fact that his wife's sister had married the heir to the Russian throne.[2]

Natural allies are those States the interests of which are identical with our own. Nevertheless alliances may be concluded among nations the interests of which differ, although they will be only short-lived.

In the present position of Europe all States are strongly armed, and as a Power of superior strength can destroy the weaker ones, it is necessary to conclude alliances either for mutual defense or for foiling the plans of one's enemies. However, alliances by themselves do not suffice. It is necessary to have in one's neighbor States, and especially among one's enemies, agents who report faithfully all they see and hear. Men are bad. It is most necessary to protect one's self against being surprised. . . .[3]

It is a well-known fact in politics that the most natural and hence, the best allies are those whose interests are identical with our own. . . . Strange events sometimes lead to extraordinary combinations . . . between nations that have at all times been inimical and hostile to each other; . . . such alliances can be only short-lived. . . . In the present position of Europe when all the princes are armed and when from their midst there may arise preponderating powers capable of crushing weaker ones, prudence requires that one enter into alliance with other powers, either to

[1] *Histoire de mon temps,* tome ii, pp. 29-31; *Œuvres de Frédéric le Grand,* tome iii.
[2] *Memoirs depuis la paix de Hubertsbourg, jusqu'à la paix de Teschen—Œuvres de Frédéric le Grand,* tome vi, p. 57.
[3] *Essai sur les formes de gouvernement et sur les devoirs des souverains—Œuvres philosophiques,* tome ii, pp. 201-202; *Œuvres de Frédéric le Grand,* tome ix.

insure to one's self assistance in case of attack or to foil the dangerous projects of one's enemies. . . . But this is not enough; it is necessary to have in one's neighbor state, especially among one's enemies, open eyes and ears that will faithfully report that which they have seen and heard.

If the Cabinet in Vienna can be gained to Prussia's interests by bribery, my Ambassador, von Borcke, had instructions given him on the 7th of this month to offer up to 200,000 thalers to the Grand Chancellor, Count Zinzendorff, and 100,000 thalers to the Secretary of State, Toussaint. If others have to be bribed, Count Gotter should let me know, and I will give my orders. . . .[1]

Thus, you will skillfully throw an apple of discord among the ministers, in order that we may play an easy game and realize our main object; and I leave you full liberty to employ, besides flatteries and promises, as much money as you may judge proper, and Major Winterfeld may draw on the treasury of the company.[2]

The situation in which the King found himself was delicate and embarrassing. It might have become dangerous if he had not had the good luck to corrupt two persons, by means of whom the King was informed of the most secret plans of his enemies. One was named Weingarten, the secretary to the Count de La Puebla, envoy of Austria to the Court of Berlin; the other, a clerk [Frederick William Menzel] in the secret chancellery of Dresden. The secretary furnished copies of all the dispatches which the minister received from Petersburg, Vienna, and London; the clerk of the secret chancellery at Dresden supplied a copy of the treaties between Russia and Saxony and of the correspondence which Count Brühl carried on with Bestusheff as well as of the dispatches of Count Fleming of Vienna. . . . Thus, through the agency of these two men whom we have just mentioned, there was nothing hidden from the King, and their frequent reports were to him as a compass to direct his course between the rocks which he had to avoid, and prevented him from having recourse to open measures against a plan devised to declare war upon him immediately.[3]

Religion is absolutely necessary to a state. This is a maxim which it would be foolish to dispute. A king is very foolish to permit his subjects to make ill use of it; on the other hand, a king is

---

[1] *Politische Correspondenz Friedrichs des Grossen* (Berlin, 1879), vol. 1, p. 134.
[2] *Ibid.*, vol. 1, p. 172.
[3] *Histoire de la guerre de sept ans*, tome i, pp. 18-19; *Œuvres de Frédéric le Grand*, tome iv.

unwise in having any religion. Listen well to this, my dear nephew: there is nothing that tyrannizes the mind and the heart more than religion, because it agrees neither with our passions, nor with those great political views which a monarch must have. The true religion of a prince consists in desiring the interests of men and his own glory because of his station; he must be dispensed from having any other; he must have maintained a respectable outward appearance in order to conform himself to those who notice and surround him. If he fears God, or, to speak as women and priests do, if he fears hell, as did Louis XIV in his old age, he becomes timid and worthy of being a Capuchin.

If we are desirous of entering into a treaty with other powers and we remember that we are Christians, we are undone, we are always duped. As regards war, it is a trade in which the least scrupulous would spoil everything. Indeed, what man of honor would ever wage war, if he had not the right to make those rules permitting of plunder, fire, and carnage?[1]

A celebrated author has compared the military to bulldogs which it was necessary to chain up carefully, and who must not be loosed except when necessary. This comparison is carried too far, but, in spite of that fact, it will serve you not as a maxim, but as a warning. . . .

By its nature my kingdom is military, and, properly speaking, it is only by its help that you must hope to maintain and aggrandize yourself; it is necessary, therefore, that your mind should ever be fixed upon this. . . .[2]

A Prince who rules independently and has formed his own political system will never be placed in an embarrassing situation when a prompt decision must be made; for all his acts are directed to the finer object he has set unto himself. He must especially have acquired the greatest imaginable knowledge with regard to the details of army organization. Seated by the green table a man devises but unsatisfactory plans for military campaigns; and what can be the use of the finest plans for a campaign when they break down through the ignorance of those who are intrusted with their execution? The man who does not know the needs of an army, who does not concern himself with the innumerable details of its commissariat, who does not know how an army is mobilized, who does not understand the rules of the art of war and who does not

---

[1] *Les Matinées Royales*, pp. 6-7.
[2] Whittall, *Frederick the Great on Kingcraft* (London; Longmans, Green & Co., 1901), pp. 97-98.

know how to train soldiers while in garrison nor how to lead them in the field, such a man will never accomplish great things, if he is not himself a military leader, even although he were a most intellectual and a most skillful statesman. Unreservedly, the King of Prussia must make war his principal study and inspire the zeal of those who have chosen the noble and dangerous profession of arms.

Prussia is surrounded by mighty neighbors. You must, therefore, be prepared to face many wars. From this there follows that the military in Prussia must occupy the first position even as was the case with the old conquering Romans during the period of their ascendency, and as was also the case in Sweden, when Gustavus Adolphus, when Charles X and Charles XII filled the world with their fame and the glory of Sweden's name penetrated into the remotest lands. Offices, honors, and rewards conferred each in turn, stimulate and inspire talent. Praise bestowed for merit arouses noble emulation in the heart of the nobility, encourages its members to enter the profession of arms, to acquire knowledge and leads them to distinction and fortune. To show contempt toward officers and to require of them at the same time that they serve with honor, is a paradox. You must encourage a profession which forms the power of the kingdom; you must respect the pillars of the state (if I may so express myself with regard to that profession), and prefer it to the effeminate and weak-hearted race of men who are only fit as a decoration for an ante-chamber. . . .

Finally I venture to assert that the ruler himself alone can introduce and maintain this wonderful discipline in the army. For he must frequently assert his authority; some he must blame severely without distinction of person or rank; others he must reward liberally; he must, as frequently as possible, review the troops and he must not allow the slightest negligence to escape his attention. The King of Prussia must, therefore, of necessity be a soldier and the commander-in-chief. . . .[1]

To make one's self respected and feared by one's neighbors is the very summit of high politics. One may attain this object in two ways: first, to have real power and actual resources; second, to know how to make the most of one's available strength. We are not within the first case. For this reason I have neglected nothing that might put me in the second case. There are powers that imagine that an embassy must always be carried on with great pomp. . . .

[1] Bolz, *Ausgewählte Werke Friedrichs des Grossen* (Berlin, 1916), vol. 2, pp. 69-71.

Never ask for anything in half-hearted fashion. Rather, have the air of exacting it. If anyone fail you, reserve your vengeance until the moment when you can get complete satisfaction, and, above all, do not fear reprisals. Your glory will never suffer from them; so much the worse for your subjects upon whom these reprisals will fall. But here is the real point. All your subjects should be convinced that you suspect nothing and that nothing can astonish you.

Above all, endeavor to pass with them for a dangerous man who knows no other principles but those that lead to glory. Act in such a manner that they will certainly feel that you would rather lose two kingdoms than not to play a rôle for posterity. As these sentiments demand an uncommon soul, they strike, they bewilder the greater part of men, and it is this which constitutes the greatest monarch in this world.

If a stranger should come to your court, shower civilities upon him, and especially endeavor to have him always near you; this is the true means of concealing from him the vices of your government. If he is a soldier, make your regiment of guards manœuver before him, and let it be yourself who is in command. If he is a wit who has composed a work, let him see it lying on your table and talk with him of his talents. If he is a merchant, listen to him with kindness, flatter him and try to get him to establish himself in your country.[1]

The number of troops maintained by a State must be in proportion to the troops of its enemies; . . . it may be said perhaps that the prince must rely upon the help of his allies . . .; this would be true if the allies were what they should be; but their zeal is but lukewarmness, and we are certainly deceiving ourselves if we rely upon other than ourselves. . . .[2]

I give you a problem to solve. When one has the advantage, should he or should he not avail himself of it? I am ready with my troops and all else; if I do not make use of them, I hold within my hands a good thing which I fail to use; if I do make use of them, it will be said that I have the skill to avail myself of the superiority which I have over my neighbors.[3]

The politics of invasion has established as its principle that the first step for the conquest of a country is to get a footing upon it,

---

[1] *Les Matinées Royales*, pp. 33-35.
[2] *Essai sur les formes de gouvernement—Œuvres philosophiques*, tome ii, p. 203; *Œuvres de Frédéric le Grand*, tome ix.
[3] *Politische Correspondenz Friedrichs des Grossen*, vol. 1, p. 84.

and it is this which offers the greatest difficulty; the rest is decided by the fate of arms and by the right of the stronger. . . .[1]

The permanent principle for Princes is to aggrandize their dominions as far as their power permits them to do so; and although such aggrandizement be subject to different and infinitely varied modifications, either in view of the geographic position of the states, or of the strength of one's neighbors, or again as the constellations are of good augury, the principle is none the less invariable, and Princes never depart from it; their pretended fame is at stake; in other terms, it is necessary for them to extend their dominions.[2]

Politics must look as far as possible into the future, and calculate the political affairs of Europe, either with a view to forming alliances or to thwart the plans of one's enemies. It is wrong to believe that politics can create the desired events; but when they present themselves, it must seize them in order to profit by them. This is the reason for keeping one's finances in good order. It is also for this reason that money must always be kept in reserve, in order that the government may be ready to act as soon as political reasons make it clear that the moment for action has come. War itself must be waged in accordance with the principles of politics, in order to deal the most sanguinary blows to one's enemies.[3]

When sovereigns wish to come to a break, they are not restrained by the form of the manifesto which is to make the matter public; they make up their minds to that effect, wage war, and leave to some painstaking jurisconsult the trouble of justifying them.[4]

There are wars of precaution which it is wise for princes to undertake. In truth, such wars are offensive wars, but they are nevertheless just wars.

When the excessive greatness of a state seems on the point of overflowing its boundaries and threatening to swallow up the world, it is prudent to oppose dykes against it and to stop the tempestuous course of a torrent while there is still time to make one's self master of it. Clouds are gathering, a tempest is on the rise and lightning announces its coming; and the sovereign threatened by this danger—if alone he cannot control the tempest—will, if he be wise, combine with all those imperiled alike and whose interests are identical.

---

[1] *Considérations sur l'Etat présent du corps politique de l'Europe—Œuvres philosophiques*, tome i, p. 10; *Œuvres de Frédéric le Grand*, tome viii.
[2] *Ibid.*, p. 15.
[3] *Exposé du Gouvernement prussien—Œuvres philosophiques*, tome ii, p. 190; *Œuvres de Frédéric le Grand*, tome ix.
[4] *Histoire de la guerre de sept ans*, tome i, p. 25; *Œuvres de Frédéric le Grand*, tome iv.

If the kings of Egypt, of Syria, and of Macedonia had united against the power of Rome, the latter would never have been able to overthrow them; a carefully devised alliance and a vigorously prosecuted war would have thwarted those ambitious plans whose realization enslaved the world. . . .

It is better, therefore, that a prince engage in an offensive war while he is still free to choose between the olive branch and the laurel wreath, than that he should wait until times become desperate and when a declaration of war could but postpone for a short while his enslavement and ruin. It is an accepted maxim that it is better to anticipate than to be anticipated; all great men have fared well in following it. . . .[1]

As the state is not rich care must be had, above all, not to have anything to do with wars where nothing is to be gained, because one's strength becomes exhausted to no purpose, and also because if a good opportunity should present itself afterward, one could not take advantage of it. All distant acquisitions are a burden to the state. A village on the frontier is more important than a principality sixty leagues away. It is necessary to conceal, as far as possible, one's designs of ambition, and, if possible, to awaken the envy of Europe against other powers, under the auspices of which one strikes the intended blow. . . . Secrecy is an essential virtue both in politics and in the art of war.[2]

Politics, the army, and the finances are branches so closely bound together that they cannot be separated; all three must be carefully attended to, and from their combination, controlled by the rules of sound politics, there result the greatest advantages for the states.[2]

The prince, therefore, is not a despot, whose only rule is caprice, who must be looked upon as the central point where all the lines of the circumference unite. This government maintains in its deliberations the secrecy which is absent in republics, and the various branches of the administration being coördinated, can get together like the ancient Roman quadriga, mutually coöperating for the general public welfare. Furthermore, you will find less party spirit and less strife in monarchies than in republics, provided the former have a strong sovereign at their head, it being a fact that republics

---

[1] *L'Antimachiavel ou Examen du Prince de Machiavel*—*Œuvres philosophiques*, tome i, p. 159; *Œuvres de Frédéric le Grand*, tome viii

[2] *Exposé du Gouvernement prussien*—*Œuvres philosophiques*, tome ii, p. 190; *Œuvres de Frédéric le Grand*, tome ix.

are frequently torn asunder by the citizens who are intriguing and caballing to overthrow one another.[1]

Sweden, which under rulers like Gustavus Adolphus and Charles XII had been regarded as the home of valor, became in these times a model of cowardice and infamy; . . . thus, kingdoms and empires, after having risen to the greatest glory, may grow weak and rush to their fall. . . .

The political reason for these changes may probably be found in the different forms of government through which the country passed. While Sweden was a monarchy, the army was held in honor; it was useful for the defense of the state, and could never have become a danger to it. In a republic we witness the opposite conditions; by its very nature the government must be peaceful and the army must be held under; one has everything to fear from generals to whom the troops are devoted; it is such generals who may bring about a revolution. In republics ambition and intrigue combine if one would achieve success; corruption gradually debases them, and the true sense of honor is lost sight of, because success may be attained through means which do not require any merit on the part of the office seeker. Furthermore, secrecy is never observed in the republics; the enemy knows their plans in advance and can thwart them.[2]

(b) *Georg Wilhelm Friedrich Hegel* (1770-1831)[3]

In that which has just been stated we have discovered the ethical motive of war, which is not to be regarded as an absolute evil or as a mere external accident which may have its own accidental ground, no matter where it may be met with, either in the passions of those wielding power or of peoples, in injustice, etc., or generally speaking in anything which ought not to be. . . . War regarded as the state in which the vanity of temporal goods and things is taken seriously—a view frequently expounded with impressive eloquence—is therefore the motive by which the idealization of that which is particular receives its right and becomes an actuality;—it has this higher significance, in that through war, as

---

[1] *Exposé du Gouvernement prussien—Œuvres philosophiques*, tome ii, p. 216; *Œuvres de Frédéric le Grand*, tome ix.

[2] *Histoire de mon temps*, tome i, p. 139; *Œuvres de Frédéric le Grand*, tome ii.

[3] *Grundlinien der Philosophie des Rechts* (von Georg Wilhelm Friedrich Hegel; Berlin, 1821); neu herausgegeben von Georg Lasson; (Leipzig, Felix Meiner, 1911).

I have elsewhere expressed it, "the moral soundness of peoples is preserved in their indifference toward the stability of the finite certainties, even as the movement of the winds preserves the ocean from foulness, into which a perpetual calm would place it, and even as a lasting or even a perpetual peace would corrupt the nations."[1]

In peace the civic life develops constantly; all the divisions of this life become exclusive and at length society becomes stagnant; the peculiarities of men become more and more fixed and ossified. But the health of the body demands the unity of the body, and where the parts thereof become hardened, then death ensues. Eternal peace is frequently proclaimed as an ideal towards which mankind shall steer its course. Therefore, Kant proposed the alliances of princes which should settle the disputes between states, and the Holy Alliance probably purposed to become an institution of this kind. But the state is an individual, and in individuality negation is essentially contained. Hence, if a number of states form themselves into a family, this union, as an individuality, must therefore create an opposition, and thus beget an enemy. Peoples not only issue from wars as strengthened bodies, but nations which by their nature cannot get on with one another, secure peace within their boundaries by means of wars which they wage abroad. It is true that property is made insecure through war, but this real insecurity is a moving action which is necessary. From the pulpits we hear much about the insecurity, the vanity and instability of temporal things; though the speakers may be stirred to the depths of their hearts by the expression of such thought, they nevertheless think at the same time that they will somehow manage to hold on to what they have. But when this insecurity comes in the form of hussars with glistening sabers and is made manifest in vigorous fashion, then that stirring eloquence which prophesied everything, turns its shafts and hurls curses at the conquerors. In spite of this, wars are being waged when they lie in the nature of the matter; the seeds sprout again, and all idle talk is silenced in the presence of the earnest repetitions of history.[2]

States are not private persons, but in themselves completely independent entities, and, hence, their relation presents itself other than one merely of morality and of private right. It has often been desired to regard states from the viewpoint of private right and of morality, but in the case of private persons, the position is such that

[1] Hegel, *Grundlinien der Philosophie des Recht*, p. 263.
[2] *Ibid.*, pp. 368-369.

they have over them a tribunal which realizes that which is right. To be sure, a relation between states should also be in itself one of right, but in the affairs of the world that which exists in itself, that is to say, right, should also have power. But as there is no power which shall decide with regard to the state, to wit, that which in itself is right, and which shall realize this decision, the question in regard to this matter, therefore, must be left in suspense until such time as that power shall be evolved. The relation of states to one another is one of independence; they stipulate between themselves, but at the same time these stipulations are held in abeyance.[1]

The people considered as the state are the spirit in its substantial reasonableness and immediate reality, hence, it is the absolute power on earth; consequently, each state in relation to other states exercises sovereign independence.[2]

Between states there is no judge, at most only an arbitrator or mediator, and the latter only as an accidental thing, that is to say, chosen according to particular needs. The Kantian concept of an eternal peace is an alliance between states which would settle every dispute, and which as a power recognized by each individual state would adjust every misunderstanding and thus make impossible the resort to arms for a decision. It assumes a unanimous accord of the states which, strengthened by moral, religious, or other reasons and considerations, rests, nevertheless, and always, on the special will of the sovereign and therefore is liable to be disturbed by the element of chance.

So far as the particular wills can come to no agreement, the dispute between states can therefore be settled only through war. Because of the widely expanding realm and the multitudinous relations of the citizens of different states to one another, offenses occur easily and frequently. Thus, these offenses which are to be viewed as a definite breach of a treaty or as a violation of recognition and honor, cannot, in their very nature, but remain indefinite, for a state may introduce its infinitude and honor into every one of its separate compartments. It is more inclined to this irritability, in proportion as a powerful individuality feels itself impelled by a long internal rest to seek and find abroad an object on which to exercise its activity.[3]

The European nations form one family in accordance with the

---

[1] Hegel, *Grundlinien der Philosophie des Rechts*, p. 370.
[2] *Ibid.*, p. 266.
[3] *Ibid.*, p. 268.

general principle of their legislation, of their customs, and of their civilization, and their international conduct is accordingly being improved, while elsewhere mutual infliction of evils is the rule. The relation of states to other states is inconstant; there is no judge to settle disputes. The higher judge is alone the general and absolute spirit: the world spirit.[1]

As states are particular, there is manifested in their relation to one another a shifting play of internal particularity of passions, interests, aims, talents, virtues, force, wrong, vice, and external contingency on the very largest scale. In this play even the ethical whole,—national independence,—is exposed to chance. The spirit of a nation is an existing individual having in particularity its objective actuality and self-consciousness. Because of this particularity it is limited. The destinies and deeds of states in their connection with one another are the visible dialectic of the finite nature of these spirits. Out of this dialectic the universal spirit, the spirit of the world, the unlimited spirit, produces itself. It has the highest right of all, and exercises its right upon the lower spirits in world-history. The history of the world is the world's court of judgment.

In the mutual relations of the states—because in these relations they appear as distinct entities—there manifests itself on a very large scale, the extremely shifting play of the respective inner particularity of passions, of interests, of aims, of talents and virtues, of force, wrong, vice and external adventitiousness,—a play wherein the ethical whole and the independence of the state are exposed to chance. Because of the particularity of each respective national spirit, the principles in virtue of which, as an existing individual, it has its objective actuality and self-consciousness, are limited; the destinies and acts in the mutual relations of the states constitute the visible dialectic of the finitude of the different national spirits; from this dialectic issues the general spirit, the *spirit of the world:* a spirit unlimited in its essence; and this spirit which possesses the highest right, applies this right in the history of the world, *which is the tribunal of humanity.*[2]

---

[1] Hegel, *Grundlinien der Philosophie des Rechts,* p. 371.
[2] *Ibid.,* pp. 270-271.

INTRODUCTION

(c) *Karl von Clausewitz* (1780-1831)[1]

We shall not, by way of preliminaries, here enter into a ponderous definition of war such as is given by publicists, but we shall confine ourselves to the element of war itself, which is a duel. War is nothing but an extended duel. If we would represent to ourselves as a unit the numberless duels in which war consists, we had better think of two wrestlers. By physical force, each seeks to compel the other to submit to his will; his immediate object is to throw his opponent and thereby to render him incapable of further resistance.

War, therefore, is an act of force intended to compel the opponent to fulfill our will.

Force arms itself with the inventions of the arts and sciences for the purpose of contending against violence. Under the term of international customs, force imposes upon itself limits imperceptible and hardly worth mentioning, without essentially impairing its power. Force, that is to say, physical force (for there is no moral force without the conception of state and law), is therefore the *means;* and the *object* of force is to impose our will upon the enemy. To make sure of attaining this object, we must disarm the enemy, and disarmament is the real aim of the act of war. It takes the place of the object and somehow puts it aside as something not pertaining to war itself.

Now, altruistic souls might readily believe that there is a skillful method for disarming and throwing the opponent without occasioning overmuch bloodshed, and that this is the true tendency of the art of war. Plausible though this may appear, it is an error which must be done away with, for in such dangerous things as war, errors which proceed from gentleness of spirit are the worst. As the use of physical force to the utmost extent does in no manner exclude the coöperation of the intelligence, it follows that he who uses this force unsparingly, without regard to the bloodshed involved, must secure a superiority, if his opponent uses that force less vigorously. Thereby he imposes his law upon his opponent, and both thus resort to the extremest measures limited only by the immanent countervailing forces.

The matter must, therefore, be viewed in this light, and it is a useless, even an ill-judged effort, to disregard the real nature of the thing because its horrors are repugnant.[2]

---

[1] *Vom Kriege—Hinterlassenes Werk des Generals Karl von Clausewitz* (Berlin; Ferdinand Dümmler, 1832-1834; 3 vols.).
[2] *Ibid.*, vol. 1, pp. 3-5.

The war of a community—of whole peoples—and especially of *civilized peoples,* always arises from a political condition, and it is called forth only by a political motive. It is, therefore, a political act. . . . Now, if we bear in mind that war arises from a political object, it is quite natural, therefore, that this first motive which called it into being, must remain the first and highest consideration in its conduct. Still, the political object is no despotic lawgiver on that account; it must conform to the nature of the means, and while the object is frequently modified by the latter, still it must always have first consideration. Policy is, therefore, interwoven with the entire act of war and must exercise a continuous influence upon it, as far as the nature of the forces liberated by it will permit.

We see, therefore, that war is not merely a political act, but a true political instrument, a continuation of political intercourse, a carrying out of this intercourse by other means. All else which remains peculiar to war relates merely to the peculiar nature of its means . . . but, however powerfully this may react on political views in particular cases, still it must always be regarded as a modification of them, for the political intention is the object, war is the means, and the means can never be thought of without including the object.[1]

We maintain . . . that war is nothing but a continuation of political intercourse with a mixture of other means. We say with a mixture of other means in order thereby to maintain at the same time that this political intercourse does not cease through the war itself, that it has not changed into something entirely different, but, that in its essence, it continues to exist, in whatever form the means which it uses may appear, and that the chief lines along which the events of the war progress and to which they are bound, are the only lines along which the war is prosecuted until peace is concluded. And how could we imagine it to be otherwise? Have the political relations of different nations and governments ever ceased with the cessation of diplomatic notes? Is not war merely another kind of writing and of language of their political thoughts? It has, to be sure, its own grammar but not its own logic.[2]

Therefore, once more, war is an instrument of policy; it must necessarily bear its character and measure with its scale; the conduct of war in its general features, is therefore, policy itself, which

---

[1] Clausewitz, *Vom Kriege*, vol. 1, pp. 26-28.
[2] *Ibid.,* vol. 3, p. 140.

the pen exchanges for the sword, but which has not on that account ceased to think according to its own laws.¹

(d) *Ernest Moritz Arndt* (1769-1860)²

If it was impossible to restore the union between Belgium and Holland, the next thing was a union of the land with Germany, an ancient right, hence an old and new duty, and at the same time the most obvious advantage to England.³ For on the fields of Belgium Germany and England will of necessity be everlastingly at war for the possession of the Rhine and the supremacy of the Channel. . . .⁴

This neutrality belongs to the many expedients of the London protocols. It was the apparent desire to stop the turning of a wheel which threatened much destruction. Belgium can never be that which Switzerland was: a land well situated to face the enemy but not a land for battlefields; and it is even doubtful if Switzerland can long continue to bask in its earlier good fortune. But as for Belgium, the granary and armory, it is predestined to be the battlefield in the struggle for the Meuse and the Rhine. I ask any general or statesman who has seriously considered the problems of war and politics, whether Belgium can remain neutral in a European war—that is to say, can be respected as neutral any longer than may appear expedient to the power which feels itself possessed of the best advantages for attack. . . .⁵

---

¹ Clausewitz, *Vom Kriege*, vol. 3, p. 150.
² *Schriften für und an seine lieben Deutschen* (von Ernst Moritz Arndt; Leipzig, 1845; 3 vols.).
³ Arndt here had in mind the fear in England that France would acquire Belgium. On the other hand, the union of Belgium with Germany would have removed this fear, and at the same time taken the question of conflict between England and Germany out of the realm of possibility; for as long as that question was not so settled, the possibility of conflict was ever present.
⁴ Arndt, *Schriften für und an seine lieben Deutschen*, vol. 3, p. 164.
⁵ *Ibid.*, p. 178. Arndt's vision was not confined solely to the neutralized states. He knew and appreciated England and ventured a prediction which has not been hailed with enthusiasm, as in the case of Belgium, but which might well have been pondered by his countrymen, for in the same volume he thus writes of England:

" That which you will certainly have on your hands and the weight of which you will find a heavy burden to bear, if you nevertheless itch to wage war and reap misfortune, listen to what I here state: old England, which will not sit quiet for a moment, will in the first place be roused as soon as you venture to reach out for Antwerp, Mainz, and Coblenz. You know what that means. All your calculations about Ireland, about unrest in England her-

(e) *Frederick William IV, King of Prussia* (1795-1861)

All written constitutions are only scraps of paper.[1]

The plaintiff states that he is absolute monarch of the kingdom of Prussia, and as king thereof is the sole government of that country; that he is unrestrained by any constitution or law, and that his will, expressed in due form, is the only law of that country, and is the only legal power there known to exist as law. . . .[2]

(f) *Theodor Mommsen* (1817-1903)[3]

When from the miserable monotony of political selfishness which fought its battles in the Curia and in the streets of the capital, the course of history again turns to matters which are of greater importance than the question as to whether or not the first monarch of Rome should be called Gnaeus, Gaius, or Marcus, we may well be granted, on the threshold of an event whose effects influence even now the destinies of the world, to look about us for a moment and to characterize the connection of things under which the conquest of the present France by the Romans, and the latter's first contact with the inhabitants of Germany and of Great Britain are to be viewed in their bearing upon the history of the world.—By virtue of the law that a people which has developed into a state gathers within its limits all neighbors politically immature and the civilized people absorbs all neighbors who are in intellectual nonage—by virtue of this law which is as generally valid and as much a law of nature as the law of gravitation, the Italian nation, the only one of antiquity which was able to combine the higher political development and the higher civilization, although it appropriated the latter

self will go for naught. That great people has such a thorough appreciation for real freedom and lawfulness, that it does not, as you and your ilk are wont to do, impatiently fly into a passion at sight of every evil; through its sensible and equable nature it has learned the meaning of the proverb, time brings counsel; and even though some local troubles should break out, it will have them put down by its own citizens, and be able to overwhelm you with the fearful power of its fleets and armies." (*Ibid.*, pp. 120-121.)

[1] Speech from the throne, April 11, 1847. In *L'Intermédiare des Chercheurs et Curieux* for May 30, 1915, at p. 371, the reader will find an interesting comment, under the caption "Scraps of Paper," upon this famous statement of Frederick William IV.

[2] King of Prussia, Plaintiff in Error, *v.* Kuepper's Administrator, Defendant in Error, 22 *Missouri Reports* (1856), p. 550.

[3] *Römische Geschichte*, von Theodor Mommsen (Berlin; Weidmanische Buchhandlung, 1889), 5 vols.; vol. 4 not published.

in only an imperfect and external manner, the Italian nation was entitled to reduce to its subjection the Greek states of the East which were on the decline, and by means and through its settlers to crowd out the peoples of a lower grade of culture in the West, such as the Libyans, Iberians, Kelts, and Germans, even as England has with equal right, in Asia, subjected to its authority a civilization of equal rank, but politically impotent, and in America and Australia characterized and ennobled, and still continues to characterize and ennoble extensive barbarian countries with the stamp of its nationality. The Roman aristocracy had fulfilled the preliminary condition of this task: the union of Italy; however, it never solved the task itself; it regarded the extra-Italian conquests either as a necessary evil or as a fiscal possession without the pale of the state. It is the imperishable glory of the Roman democracy or monarchy—for the two coincide—to have correctly understood and vigorously realized that highest destination.[1]

(g) *Prince Otto von Bismarck* (1815-1898)[2]

Prussia must brace herself up for the fitter moment which has already more than once been missed; Prussia's borders are not favorable to the development of a healthy state. Not by speechifying and majorities can the great questions of the time be decided—that was the mistake of 1848 and 1849—but by blood and iron.[3]

On July 12 [1870], I decided to leave Varzin for Ems to persuade His Majesty to convoke the Reichstag for the purpose of mobilization. As I passed through Wussow, my friend Mulert, the old preacher, stood before the door of the parsonage and greeted me in friendly manner; my answer from the open carriage was a thrust in quart and tierce in the air, and he understood that I believed I was going to war. When I drove into the court of my Berlin home, and even before I had left the carriage, I received telegrams informing me that the king continued to negotiate with Benedetti, even after the French threats and offenses in parliament and in the press, instead

---

[1] Mommsen, *Römische Geschichte*, vol. 3, pp. 220-221.
[2] Quotations from Bismarck, with the exception of the first, are taken from *Gedanken und Erinnerungen*, von Otto Fürst von Bismarck (New York and Stuttgart, I. G., Gotta'sche Buchhandlung Nachfolger, 1898).
[3] In Military Committee of Prussian Chamber of Deputies [1862]. *Prince Bismarck*. By Charles Lowe. (New York and London; Cassell & Co., Ltd.), vol. 1, p. 290.

of referring him with calm reserve to his ministers. During the meal at which Moltke and Roon were present, announcement arrived from the ambassador in Paris that the Hohenzollern prince had renounced his candidature in order to prevent the war with which France had threatened us. My first thought was to sever my connection with the service, because, after all the offensive provocations which had gone before, I perceived in this extorted yielding a humiliation of Germany for which I did not wish to be held officially responsible.[1]

Having decided to resign in spite of the remonstrances addressed to me in the matter by Roon, I invited him and Moltke to dine with me alone on the 13th, when I communicated to them my views and intentions. Both were greatly depressed and indirectly reproached me for selfishly availing myself of my greater facility, as compared with theirs, for leaving the service. I told them that I could not sacrifice my sense of honor to politics, and that both of them, as professional soldiers, unable to decide because not free to do so, need not take the same view. During the conversation announcement was made to me that a telegram from Ems, in cipher (if I remember correctly) of about 200 groups, signed by Privy Councilor Abeken, was being translated. When the copy had been handed to me, it showed that Abeken had drafted and signed the telegram at His Majesty's command. I read it to my guests, whose depression became so great that they turned away from food and drink. Upon reëxamining the document I gave my particular attention to the authorization of His Majesty, including an order immediately to communicate Benedetti's new demand and its rejection both to our ambassadors and to the press. I put a few questions to Moltke with regard to the measure of his confidence in the state of our armaments, especially as to the time they might yet require in order to meet the danger of war, which had so suddenly arisen. He answered that if there was to be war, he would expect no advantage to us by deferring its outbreak; even if we should not be strong enough immediately to protect all the territory on the left bank of the Rhine against a French invasion, our preparations would soon overtake the French, while at a later period this advantage would decrease; on the whole, he regarded an immediate outbreak of war as more advantageous for us, than delay.

The dispatch handed in at Ems on July 13, 1870, at 3:50 p. m., and received at Berlin at 6:09, read, when deciphered, as follows:

[1] Bismarck, *Gedanken und Erinnerungen*, p. 434.

His Majesty writes to me: "Count Benedetti joined me on the promenade, finally to request me in a very urgent manner, to authorize him to telegraph forthwith that I pledge myself for all future time, never again to give my consent if the Hohenzollerns should again present their candidature. I declined somewhat brusquely to do so for the reason that I neither could nor would enter into engagements of this kind *à tout jamais*. I told him, of course, that I had received no news as yet, and as he would receive earlier news from Paris and Madrid than myself, he could readily see that my Government again had no hand in the matter." His Majesty has since received a letter from the Prince. As His Majesty had told Count Benedetti that he was expecting news from the Prince, His All-Highest Majesty had decided, in reference to the above presumption, upon the proposal of Count Eulenburg and myself, not to receive Count Benedetti again, but to have him informed through an adjutant: that His Majesty had now received from the Prince confirmation of the news which Benedetti had already received from Paris, and that he had nothing further to communicate to the Ambassador. His Majesty requests the opinion of Your Excellency as to whether Benedetti's new demand and its rejection should not be communicated forthwith to our Ambassador and to the press.[1]

All these considerations, conscious and unconscious, strengthened my feeling that the war could be avoided only to the detriment of our Prussian honor and of the national confidence in it.

Under this conviction I made use of the royal authorization sent to me by Abeken, to publish the contents of the telegram, and in the presence of my two table guests I reduced the telegram through omissions, but without adding or changing one word, so that it read as follows:

"After the news of the renunciation of the hereditary prince of Hohenzollern had been officially communicated to the Imperial French Government by the Royal Spanish Government, the French Ambassador at Ems further demanded of His Majesty, the King, that he would authorize him to telegraph to Paris that His Majesty the King pledged himself for all future time never again to give his consent if the Hohenzollerns should again present their candidature. His Majesty the King thereupon declined to receive the French Ambassador again and had him informed through the adjutant on duty, that His Majesty had nothing further to communicate to the Ambassador." The difference in the effect of the condensed text

[1] Bismarck, *Gedanken und Erinnerungen*, pp. 436-437.

of the Ems dispatch as compared with that produced by the original was not the result of stronger words, but of the form which made this announcement appear as final, while the wording of Abeken would only have appeared as a fragment of negotiations still pending and to be continued at Berlin.

After I had read the condensed text to my two guests, Moltke remarked: "In this form, it has a different ring; it sounded before like a parley; now it sounds like a flourish in answer to a challenge." I went into details: "If in execution of the All-Highest's order I forthwith communicate this text which contains no alterations in and no additions to the telegram, not only to the newspapers, but as well by telegraph, to all our embassies, it will be known in Paris before midnight, and there, not only on account of its contents, but also because of the manner of its distribution, it will have the effect of a red rag upon a Gallic bull. We must fight if we do not want to appear in the rôle of the vanquished without a battle. Success depends essentially upon the impression which the origin of the war produces upon ourselves and others; it is important that we should be the party attacked, and Gallic conceit and excitableness will make of us the party attacked if through a *European-wide publicity* we announce, so far as we can do so without using the speaking-tube of the Reichstag, that we fearlessly meet the public threats of France.[1]

The durability of all treaties between great states is conditional as soon as it is put to the test "in the struggle for existence." No great nation can ever be induced to sacrifice its existence on the altar of faithfulness to contract, if it is compelled to choose between the two. The *ultra posse nemo obligatur* cannot be made ineffective through any contractual clause; nor can any treaty guarantee the measure of zeal and force by which the obligation is fulfilled when the private interest of him who is to fulfill the provisions of the treaty no longer reinforces the text to which he put his signature, and its earlier interpretation. Therefore, if changes occur in the currents of European politics, such as would make an anti-German policy appear *salus publica* for Austria-Hungary, self-immolation for the sake of faithfulness to treaty could be as little expected as was gratitude in the Crimean War, though the obligation was perhaps stronger than the provisions recorded on the parchment of a political treaty.[2]

International policy is a fluid element which under certain

[1] Bismarck, *Gedanken und Erinnerungen*, pp. 439-440.
[2] *Ibid.*, p. 588.

INTRODUCTION
xlvii

circumstances becomes a solid for the time being, but in atmospheric changes reverts to its original state. In political treaties which require the fulfillment of certain obligations, the *clausula rebus sic stantibus* tacitly is accepted. The Triple Alliance is a strategic position which, in view of the perils threatening at the time of its conclusion, was advisable, and feasible under the then prevailing conditions. . . .[1]

The Triple Alliance which I originally sought to bring about after the Frankfort Peace and about which I had already sounded Vienna and St. Petersburg in September, 1870, from Meaux, was an alliance of the three emperors with the further thought of persuading monarchical Italy to join it, and directed to the struggle which, I feared in some form or other confronted the two European tendencies, which Napoleon called the Republican and the Cossack, and which, according to present concepts, I would designate on the one hand as the system of organization on a monarchical basis, and on the other, as the social republic to the level of which, either gradually or by leaps, the anti-monarchical development usually sinks, until the unbearable conditions created under its sway dispose the disappointed people to return, through violence, to monarchical institutions of a Cæsarean form. . . . Since 1871 I have sought for immediate security against those struggles in the alliance of the three emperors and in the effort to secure a firm support in that alliance for the monarchical principle in Italy. . . .[2]

Treaties are scraps of paper. All depends upon the manner of turning them to account. Even an excellent weapon, in inexperienced hands, may cause more damage than good. . . .[3]

(h) *Count Helmuth von Moltke* (1800-1891)[4]

You have been kind enough to transmit to me the *Manual* which the Institute of International Law has published, and you wish my approval of the work.

In the first place, I fully honor the humane endeavor to alleviate the sufferings which war carries in its train.

Eternal peace is a dream, not even a beautiful dream; war is a

---

[1] Bismarck, *Gedanken und Erinnerung*, pp. 596-597.
[2] *Ibid.*, pp. 560 570.
[3] Chiala, *Pagine di storia contemporanea* (Torino, 1898), vol. 3, p. 498.
[4] *Schriften und Denkwürdigkeiten des General-Feldmarschalls Grafen Helmuth von Moltke* (Berlin, 1892), 8 vols. in 7.

part of God's cosmic system. Man's noblest virtues: courage and self-denial, loyalty to duty, and self-sacrifice even to the staking of his life, are developed through war. Without war the world would sink into materialism. I perfectly agree with that sentence of the preface which announces that advancing civilization will also improve warfare, but I go farther in believing that it alone, and not a codified military law, will be able to attain this goal.

Every law requires an authority to supervise and enforce its execution, and there is no such authority with regard to the observance of international agreements. What third state will take up arms because of two belligerents, one—or both—have violated the *lois de la guerre?* For such cases, there is no judge on earth. Success can only be expected from the religious and moral education of the individuals, from the sense of honor and from the sense of justice of the leaders who are a law unto themselves and act accordingly, in so far as the abnormal conditions of the war permit.

It cannot be denied that humaneness in the conduct of war has really kept pace with the general progress of morality.

One need but compare the lawlessness of the Thirty Years' War with the wars of modern times.

An important thing for the realization of the desired goal has been found in our day in the introduction of a universal military service which has incorporated the educated classes in the armies. To be sure, the rough and violent elements have also remained in them, but, they are not, as in former times, the only elements constituting the armies.

Two other effectual means remain in the hands of the governments, in order to prevent the worst excesses. On the one hand, the strict discipline introduced and maintained in the armies even in times of peace, and on the other, the administrative foresight for the maintenance of the troops in the field.

Without this foresight, discipline can be maintained in only a limited degree. The soldier who is exposed to suffering and privation, to exertion and danger, cannot be satisfied *en proportion avec les ressources du pays;* he must seize everything that is necessary to his existence. We cannot demand the impossible of him.

The greatest good in war is its quick termination, and to this end all means, not directly reprehensible, must be used. I can in no manner agree with the *Déclaration de St. Pétersbourg* that the "weakening of the hostile fighting power, etc.," is the only justified proceeding in the war. No; all auxiliary resources of the hostile government must be seized: its finances, railroads, necessaries of life, and even its prestige.

With this energy, and yet with more moderation than ever before, the last war against France was waged. After two months of fighting the campaign was decided, and only when a revolutionary government continued it for four months to the detriment of its own country, did the battles assume an embittered character.

I readily acknowledge that the *Manual* defines in clear and short sentences, in a higher degree than has been the case in former attempts, the necessities of war. But even the recognition by governments of the rules which it lays down, does not insure their execution. It has long since been a universally recognized usage of war not to fire at the bearer of a flag of truce, and yet this usage was repeatedly violated during the last campaign. No paragraph which has been learned by heart will convince the soldier that the unorganized population which (*spontanément*, that is to say, of its own impulse) takes up arms and from which he is not safe a moment by day or night, is not a regular enemy (§§ 2 and 43). Specific demands of the *Manual* are, to my mind, impossible in practice, for instance, the identifying of the fallen after a great battle. Other demands of the *Manual* would give rise to serious doubt if the insertion of "*Lorsque les circonstances le permettent, s'il se peut, si possible, s'il-y-a nécessité*, etc.," did not give them an elasticity without which the bitter earnestness of reality would break the chains which they impose.

In war everything must be looked at from its own distinct point of view; I believe that only those paragraphs of the *Manual* which refer essentially to the leaders, can become effective. The same is true of those parts of the *Manual* dealing with the wounded, the sick, the physicians and the sanitary materials. General recognition of these principles, as well as those in reference to the treatment of the prisoners would mark real progress towards the aim which the institute of international law is striving for, with such praiseworthy perseverance. . . .[1]

---

[1] Moltke, *Gesammelte Schriften und Denkwürdigkeiten*, vol. 5, pp. 194-197.
This was in reply to a letter from Professor Bluntschli, who, under date of November 19, 1880, wrote as follows:

Herewith, the undersigned has the honor, respectfully to transmit some copies of the Manual *Les Lois de la Guerre sur terre*, prepared and published by the Institute of International Law, in conformity with the Brussels Declaration, with the instructions recently issued by some European states and with scientific literature. The Commission has sincerely endeavored to harmonize the practices and the interests of the army with the necessary

INTRODUCTION

(i) *Adolf Lasson* (1832-)[1]

We, especially in Prussia, are still under the immediate impression of events which, only two years ago, passed before our very eyes, and whose world-transforming importance is every day more and more revealed to the intelligent mind. At the same time everyone realizes the possibility that the great war movement has not even been brought to a momentary conclusion, and that the successes so suddenly obtained must first be secured through new tests. The iron age demands an iron generation. . . .[2]

If war is to be done away with, *all* states must in that case submit to the judgment of a higher court, that is to say, they must renounce being states. This would mark the end of the plurality of states; the universal state would arise and the whole of mankind, at least the civilized part of mankind, would be subject to it. Actual force would be resorted to only against the savages who might perhaps not be forced into the paths of civilization. Removal of war means therefore abrogation of all states and transformation of the whole of civilized mankind into a single political being. . . .

Even as the necessity of doing away with war means the doing away with the plurality of the states, even so does the continuance of the plurality of the states mean that war is unavoidable. For a state cannot exist without a supreme will which wills for the entirety of the state; but between two wills of which each wills for itself, the conflict is ever imaginable and possible, and as long as two states differ from one another, that is to say, as long as they have no common law, no common judge, and are subject to no common compulsion, there is no other means to settle the conflict, except by mutual resort to force, that is to say, to war. . . .[3]

Force *per se* may be regarded as absolutely justified whenever recalcitrant arbitrariness will not submit to law; but force, before

---

principles of right and the needs of the civilian world, and to state the laws of warfare in a form fundamentally correct, and comprehensible to the plain mind of any layman and of the ordinary soldier.

The undersigned, and especially the reporter and the other members of the Institute of International Law, would feel much requited and very pleased, if the work, intended for practical use, were to meet with the approval of your Excellency. (Moltke, *Schriften und Denkwürdigkeiten*, p. 193.)

[1] *Das Culturideal und der Krieg*, von Adolf Lasson (Berlin, 1868), and *Princip und Zukunft des Völkerrechts*, von Adolf Lasson (Berlin, 1871).
[2] Lasson, *Das Culturideal und der Krieg*, p. 1.
[3] *Ibid.*, p. 5.

the decision upon the legal question involved, appears thoroughly appropriate to such a case; and it does indeed seem unreasonable that he exercise the force which law lays claim upon and which is disputed by the opponent. The real question is as to whether there can be a law in regard to the relations between states, as there is in regard to the relations of the nationals of one and the same state? The question seems a quite different one; . . . for there is no international law. . . .

Right exists by the limitation of the activity of the will through law; it is through the law that that which is right is judged and the exercise of right is secured through force. Force is the characteristic feature of right. In international intercourse, in consequence, there are and there can be no laws. Supposing, however, that there were laws, the transgressor would then have to be subject to the superior force; one to whom such force were applied, he would have to be extremely weak and incapable of resistance. In that case he would be living only by the grace of the mightier; the state would not be sufficient unto itself and thus would be no state. A state exists only where there is present the unconditional possibility of resistance to the consciousness of capacity to resist. A so-called small state is no state at all, but a community that is suffered to exist, which in risible fashion pretends to be a state, but without being able to exercise the most essential function of the state, without being able to ward off force through force. . . . A minor state resting its existence upon the hope that for fear of another state it will not be attacked, is no state at all, but the vassal of the one which is to protect it, on whose generosity its existence depends. Between states there can be no thought of superior force, and hence there can be no thought of law and right. . . . Between states there can be but one form of right: the right of the strong; and because, as long as there are states, there will be conflicts between states which must be decided, it is therefore conformable to reason that war will be waged between states. . . .[1]

There is no right where there is no law, no judge, no superior compelling force. All these matters in the relations between states, are not open to discussion; hence, the relations of states to one another are not based upon right. . . .

States have absolutely no mutual duties, because as between them, there is no law or right. . . . There is no commandment of right to observe political treaties; but to observe political treaties is a com-

[1] Lasson, *Das Culturideal und der Krieg*, p. 7.

mandment of circumspect sagacity. Whenever a state breaks a treaty, it must expect to have each of its treaties broken in turn; any state resorting to deceit must expect everywhere to be repaid in kind. Infraction of the right by force is a crime in civil life; a state can commit no crime. The greatest mistake a state can be guilty of is lack of circumspect sagacity. . . .

The state breaking a treaty enters into a state of war; it acts unwisely whenever it challenges a decision through the force of arms, unless it is sure of its superior force. If it has this force, then it may do whatever it pleases; for between states the right of the strong alone prevails. . . .

If the state is to endure, its first task is to husband its force; for the weaker is, in spite of any and all treaties, the prey of the stronger, whenever the latter wills to and can prey upon it.

Because every state seeks only its own advantage, war is therefore the natural condition between states. But it is also this advantage which induces the state not to live in constant warfare. As long as a state is a real state, no other state can attack it without at the same time staking its own existence. Success in war cannot be mathematically established. The reasonable state risks its existence only in case of extreme necessity. . . .[1]

Every civilized state is a peace-loving state; but it can, of course, not escape the necessity of war. Riches that have been amassed by a state rouse envy on the part of other states; they confer superior influence and hence, awaken the natural effort of every other state not to be obscured, not to lose in position of power. The further civilization progresses, and the success of the laboring masses has been realized, the more it becomes necessary to insure real protection of it through strong military defensive force against foreign encroachments, against hatred and envy which, to be sure, may have sprung not from certain viewpoints of civilization, but from quite different ones, from political causes, but which, nevertheless, first and mainly, with all the might and all the fury of the attack, are directed against civilization. . . .[2]

The will of the state is bound and restricted by the will of some other state. This condition predicates the conflict, and the ability militarily to meet attack and offer defense becomes the fundamental condition for the existence of the state. For it is untenable for one to argue for a legal organization, for a court and force whereby to

[1] Lasson, *Das Culturideal und der Krieg*, pp. 8-9.
[2] *Ibid.*, p. 10.

control the relations between states. Between states as intelligent beings the conflict can be decided only through actual force. War is therefore included in the concept of the word "state." . . .

Without the state, man cannot be man; without war, the state would not be a state; hence war is included in the concept of the word "mankind," not simply as mankind was or now is, but as it will be ever more. Once the fire ceases to burn, once the light ceases to illumine and matter ceases to move, then war will also cease. . . .

War necessarily completes all the other institutions. . . . The state when at peace is no real state; it is only when in war that the state reveals its complete significance. . . .

"Law is the friend of the weak"; but the strong also becomes weak when it is deprived of the burden to put its strength to the test. . . . Peace organization and all regulations to curb impulse are the tomb of courage. Peace is intended to generate a busy, patient, and an amiable race; . . . war, on the other hand, rouses the slumbering demon in the breast of man: great deeds are then accomplished; the eye feasts on brave feats; the ruder and the highly developed qualities of man perform in the service of the highest purposes; . . .[1]

War demands all there is in man. Contempt for death is the first proof of the right appreciation of life. . . .

In the state everything must be done to meet the possibility of war, everything must be appointed in such manner that in war there shall be the greatest possible fullness of strength. . . . There is no greater drama than to see a people who wage a war in a manner worthy of the war. . . .

If the state is capable of existing, it must train its citizens or a part of its citizens to be able to bear arms, that is to say, the state must rear them for war. . . . A state without the institution of war would be no state at all because it fails to meet the most important part of its task. . . .

Hence there must be an inexorably strict law of subordination, and for each man the feeling that he is but an infinitesimal atom in the aggregate, but a cog in the machinery, a means for the great purpose of the totality of its people. . . . He deserves to be free who, conscious of the purpose in question, is willing blindly to obey the man higher up; and he is a real man who in the midst of danger, quietly and thoughtfully, makes, in the higher one's place, the best use of the gift granted to him for the great purpose. . . .

[1] Lasson, *Das Culturideal und der Krieg*, pp. 15-17.

A people that makes light of its oath and whose warriors, instead of obeying, want to guide and direct the action of the state, is without the slightest doubt on the brink of ruin, and when the moment of danger approaches, becomes the prey of destruction.

Military training is a health bath for any people, and a rejuvenating bath for a people that is growing old. Without such training any people will degenerate physically, even as it must morally degenerate when those psychic activities which find their sufficient excitement in war only, are stunted in permanent peace. . . .[1]

When in an atmosphere of freedom, people are but talking of rights and not of obligations, there can be no idea of what freedom is and such people are not ripe for it. . . . The real warrior is the best citizen; a people militarily trained can best bear and thrive in the atmosphere of freedom. . . .[2]

War is but the natural condition between states. Between states there is no friendship, only a community of interests which in turn may develop into a conflict of interests. For as a reasonable natural being, the state is an absolutely selfish being, and like any other mere natural being, it is everywhere completely justified in its selfishness; no one has a right to demand anything else of it; no one may expect anything else from it. . . .

It is not society, but the state that wages war. The state is not society; nor does it exist in the interest of society. . . . From the point of view of the state, the progress of civic society is merely to increase the power of taxation and the military power of the state. . . .

A small state has no honor because it has no mission. In the true state, however, all living forces serve the honor of the state as the simple expression of its fully justified historic existence. The poet is therefore right in saying that that nation is unworthy to exist which does not stake its all for the sake of its honor. . . .[3]

The peculiar culture of a people is its highest possession, at least the form in which the highest possession exists for that people. Its honor, its human dignity depends thereon. Where the condition of this culture is threatened by the foreigner, there the elemental state of things reasserts itself, and the eternally indestructible and sound natural basis of the human being, the physical power of the body, directed by the intellectual power and by the resolve of the will, seeks to ward off this foreign encroaching invasion through war.

---

[1] Lasson, *Das Culturideal und der Krieg*, pp. 18-21.
[2] *Ibid.*, p. 22.
[3] *Ibid.*, pp. 26-28.

INTRODUCTION
lv

Every reasonable war is a war in behalf of the form of culture, though it may even develop into a war for the existence of the state.

Once a war has broken out, then all is at stake; for every war postulates the "to be or not to be." Each of the belligerents means to strike at the heart of his opponent and seek out his most vulnerable spots, that the intended blows may strike the more effectively. In war, a state must be ready for the worst; it would therefore be weak, to exercise any sympathy before the decision has been brought about, and it would be miserable on the part of either of the belligerents to count upon sympathy. . . . Where there is an aggregate compound that feels itself as such, it must have room to labor to obtain the material positions and the ideal purposes of culture, in its own peculiar outer organization of right, in conformity with its own peculiar moral ethics; this free action must not be denied it. Such is the all comprehensive concept of popular freedom; that which is contrary thereto is servitude.

One can never tell in advance what tremendous dimensions a war may assume, even when it has an apparently trifling beginning. . . . To begin a war without real necessity is to tempt Providence.

A people may never cease to be warlike. Where extreme necessity does not force the sword into the hand of the opponent, a people of culture will with noble resignation avoid entering into war. And even though the opportunity were ever so favorable and its superiority over the opponent undoubted: war must not be waged so long as it can be avoided. There is but one thing that justifies war: the freedom of the people must be indirectly or directly threatened. Every reasonable war is a war for freedom or for the necessary conditions of freedom, and a war for freedom is alone moral and rational. . . .[1]

It is mere idiocy to preach against wars of conquest as such. . . . An industrial state which has an insufficient coast outlet, a people distant from the seas, a state whose territory lacks natural connection because of territories lying between it and the seas, or other states lacking the controlling heights or river courses and the natural points of support for their own defense, or which are excluded from the use of the most important lines of communication: all such states have the natural and absolutely justified right to supplement the necessary conditions for their existence, to secure that which they need

---

[1] Lasson, *Das Culturideal und der Krieg*, pp. 29-31.

and that which they must necessarily have in order to be able to exist in safety. Through generosity they may secure it in rare cases only; they must therefore obtain it through force by clearly and forcibly profiting by the most favorable opportunity. . . .[1]

It is clear that the ideal effort must react against the real forms historically evolved. Wherever culture has risen to a high level and the impulse for freedom has become strong, the people look to the national state to secure that which has been established, because only in the state is there a real preserver through which the most precious treasure of the cultural people, its peculiar form of culture, its language, its rights, its poetry, its science and its schools can thrive and develop. While this looked-for state is being created, other states which oppose this ideal, must be destroyed. This question, of course, can be settled through force only; for no state is generous enough to be willing, for the sake of sentimental reasons, to permit of its disintegration. . . .[2]

Any wholesome culture is characterized by a strong, sufficient, proud, and glorious state which in case of need, may through energetic action, prove to the other states its greatness and its right.

The right to exist in national independence is not the innate right of a people; rather, it must be acquired through high endeavor. Only a people which actually develops the necessary power for the defense of its independence has thereby shown its right to such independence, and such right will remain secured to it if the people do not grow debilitated. . . .

Whoever wishes to realize his desire, must will to have the means to bring it about; whoever desires independent development, must adequately organize the powers to safeguard it. . . . It is the mission of culture to make itself felt as a power. If culture neglects this mission, it shows itself thereby a one-sided feature in the life of mankind, and another people must take in hand the mission it has failed to fulfill; the former people must in such case eat the *hard* bread of servitude, *a bread which is enjoyed the less,* if in spiritual development the people feel themselves superior to their ruler.

No one is compelled to be a serf. Whoever is not able to bear servitude, may escape it by surrendering his life. Let war in such case decide, a war in which each of the serfs is ready to surrender his life in order to save freedom. . . . From the generosity and

---

[1] Lasson, *Das Culturideal und der Krieg*, p. 32.
[2] *Ibid.*, p. 35.

considerateness of people of high culture, people of a lesser culture must not expect anything; that which they wish to obtain let them obtain it in battle with the watchword: Freedom or Death.

The builders of new worlds upon the ruins of decayed races are appointed to take in tow those other peoples unable to develop independently and to establish things perpetually valuable, and to appropriate their physical powers for their own purposes, so that they may not be wholly wasted to mankind. A war waged by an active people in order to subject a passive people, is a rational war.[1]

Every nation is justified in hating any other nation; it is compelled to do so whenever the foreign nationality threatens its own existence; the word nation is here to be understood in its most strict sense; individuals as such are not referred to. To curb or to loosen this hatred, as circumstances may require, is the task of statecraft, according to the prevailing inferior or superior interests of national egotism and of the general human movement of culture.

National hatred fosters the durable possibility of war; the conflicting interests of national cultures bring it ever and anon into the realm of reality. For there is always a moment when foreign culture is not furthering the national culture, but obstructs it, and then is the time, under any and all conditions to stand for the national culture and to combat the foreign influences if unavoidable, by means of the physical force organized by the state.[2]

Whoever possesses the power, let him use it; whoever does not trust his power, let him be careful not to interfere in matters where might only confers upon him the right to enforce his advice and his judgment. . . .[3]

In war, . . . strength is ineffectual if it is not accompanied by skill and readiness to act, if it is not supported by the clever use of the moment, through the ever ready presence of mind, through the true love for the duty and the cause for which one fights, through the sacrificial enthusiasm for the whole; for any war, when the struggle for life and death is being waged, when at the same time victory means immortal glory and defeat endless disgrace, an irreparable loss, all minor and base motives are lost sight of and the vast purpose of mankind discovers its well appointed arena.

The outcome of war is therefore always righteous; it is a true judgment of God. The highest right, the last right depends on the sword. The weak succumbs to the strong; in the political realm this

---

[1] Lasson, *Das Culturideal und der Krieg*, pp. 37-40.
[2] *Ibid.*, p. 42.
[3] *Ibid.*, p. 45.

means that wrong succumbs to right or the lesser right to the higher right. . . .

No state which itself is powerful doubts the right of might.

The small state finds comfort in the feeling that that which has been agreed upon through treaty shall not be violated, because it will guarantee its wretched existence. . . . A treaty as a result of which a state can no longer exist nor fulfill its mission, is null and void, for the simple reason that the state is strong enough to tear it to pieces. A contractual right between states is guaranteed in only one way: through a sufficient military power to compel the observance of the treaty.

We must learn to distinguish between the letter of the contractual right and right in its true sense. The treaty at some time may have been a righteous treaty; but it will certainly become unrighteous, for the conditions, under which it was held to be righteous, change. . . .[1]

Important as is the security of the status of peace for peaceful labor, it is destructive of all real virility. War, therefore is a liberating element and rejuvenates a civilized people. . . .[2]

Under certain conditions, the state demands war as an extreme necessity; in such case no subjective disinclination must prevent it from taking such action. It would be highly immoral, it would be an evident violation of primordial ethical principles for kindly and humanitarian reasons and the like, not to wage the war that must be waged. . . . A king shall not be a lover of peace, nor shall he, of course, be a lover of war; he must love peace when the state needs peace, and he must not avoid war, when war is necessary for the state. . . .[3]

The fact that states practice self-seeking, . . . and are not willing to enter into strict legal relations, appears to be the constant cause for those fearful hostilities which, recurring intermittently, threaten with ruin all that has been established by cultural labor through the years, and force at times the people of different states to think out in what manner they may inflict upon one another as much evil as possible.

Can it be said that man has to perform a duty where his willpower cannot exert itself? and can it be a matter of practical reason to endeavor to ameliorate things upon which reason is denied the power to act? Let us suppose that human will-power were able to

---

[1] Lasson, *Das Culturideal und der Krieg*, pp. 50-52.
[2] *Ibid.*, p. 55.
[3] *Ibid.*, p. 63.

establish those conditions of social life which eternal peace postulates: would eternal peace be a matter of practical reason if, together with its conditions, it (eternal peace) presented a much greater evil than that which it is to do away with?

The average man means to do away with the evils that arise in the community of mankind by establishing everywhere a thoroughgoing legal organization. By such a super-state organization it is thought that the painful and destructive conflicts between the states may be removed. . . .[1]

That the right is intended to prevail within the state, lies within the concept itself of the state; but it is not quite so clear that without and between states a legal organization is possible: the question seems appropriate as to whether states can be subjects of a legal organization and whether a legal organization is possible where there are no subjects.

The power of the state seems immeasurable, its ways and means seem inexhaustible; but that both these attributes have their limit, and that the state possesses nothing except it be given to it, these are matters which the average man has difficulty in comprehending.

Of all things existing on this earth, the existence of the state is most confronted with danger, ever full of fear and compelled to infuse fear, and therefore, with all its power, the state is the most necessitous of all beings. . . . Its needs are indeed infinite, and the means offered it to meet these needs are limited, even under the most favorable circumstances. The state must secure these means by force, for it possesses nothing itself, and without force it obtains nothing. . . . Thus it has ever been, thus it is even now, and thus it shall ever essentially remain, as long as man is man and state is state. Only the visionary . . . can deceive himself upon this matter. . . .[2]

The eternal laws of nature are, however, an irremovable barrier to the power of will, and this power of will cannot but let these laws have their course. . . . From the beginning of time, even to the present day, it has been a fact without exception that hostility rules between state and state, between people and people; an absolutely unfeeling relation exists between state and state, between people and people for the acquisition of all things of the earth and their existence itself; there are passing moments of friendship between them, but in the background of it all there lurks naked selfishness; and in every moment there lies the possibility of a fearful outbreak into extreme

[1] Lasson, *Princip und Zukunft des Völkerrechts* (Berlin, 1871), pp. 2-3.
[2] *Ibid.*, pp. 4-7.

hostility which means to rob the other party of this or that position or this or that comfort of life, because each has to fear the same from the other, and, with all means of destruction and the loosing of the fiercest hatred, would deprive one another of the roots of their existence. It is this fact which in all its causes and inner necessity we must realize and understand.

1.—*The plurality of states cannot be done away with.* Where there are men, there must be a legal organization protected by force. But men are not free so long as the legal organization which compels them to submission does not meet their inner nature and consciousness, but is imposed upon them as a yoke. But men are intended to be free; it would therefore be unreasonable to subject different peoples to one and the same law of right, because in such case only one of the peoples thus united, or even none at all would find the road open to free development in accordance with its own inner principle of life, and because those would not be free to whom this road were closed.

It would be an unreasonable state of affairs if national natures, so different in their inner being, did not, so far as possible, have their own appropriate national boundaries. . . . A people stakes its honor to preserve its culture; it would incur the stigma of self-contempt, it would dishonor itself and become enslaved if it could no longer uphold its own peculiar culture; and along with the people as a whole, each single component individual of it would become dishonored and rob itself of its better self. . . .[1]

The universal state as a legal organization binding upon all men alike, is impossible so long as there are different national natures in which, in part, the outward circumstances of existence establish fundamentally different needs and require institutions of different outward organization, and in which, on the other hand, peculiar currents of the activity of the will are reflected in the mind in an essentially different form. The universal state would therefore be against the nature of things and of man; it would lead to an extreme despotism and to the forcible servility of the peoples, and quite apart from the evident outward impossibility of its realization when once incorporated into the life of mankind, it would not present a higher and more complete organization of things than the present organization does, but it would merely serve to debase mankind and throw into chaos all the constitutive elements of the present organization.

The will which we call state, has its inner limitation only in the

[1] Lasson, *Princip und Zukunft des Völkerrechts*, pp. 8-10.

INTRODUCTION lxi

positiveness of its purpose; but it extends unlimited over all things in the entire realm of nature that can serve that purpose. Hence it is possible that the will of different states is directed to one and the same object and that between them the conflict may arise even as, under like conditions, it may arise between the will of the individual human beings. . . .[1]

A tremendous step in advance was made when a bold mind dared to free statecraft unceremoniously from all theological notions and to build it up on its own peculiar principles. Statecraft is really ruled by the principle of interest. For the state is essentially a purpose, a definite final purpose; that is to say, it does not will merely the good, but the really useful in this respect; in all its activities it is guided by its interest and by nothing else. . . . To succeed in establishing a real state, a temporary despotism of the strongest was the inevitable means, and for this purpose, that is to say, to build the national state, Machiavelli advocates in the deed the uttermost inconsiderate use of lawless force. . . .[2]

Machiavelli is indeed right when he asserts that the standard of the outward activity of the state is not controlled by morality, not by right, but by shrewdness. Yet when he explains how this shrewdness proceeds, he teaches indeed how one can, with calculated cunning, obtain momentary and transitory successes, but not how durable and permanently insured things are created. . . . To awaken and to foster confidence is therefore the first commandment of shrewdness, and confidence one secures only through honesty. If durable peace is to be acquired by the state, honesty is therefore the best means to secure it, and institutions must be created which are the expression of this mutually prevailing honesty between state and state. Such institutions are, however, made impossible by a statecraft such as is taught by Machiavelli; he falsifies that which is in itself a correct principle when he regards shortsighted faithlessness, baseness of mind, absence of all moral viewpoints—all attributes which in many ways characterize his own nation and his entire generation, but especially the statesmen of those times,—as the logical consequence of the shrewd selfishness which is the rule of the political activity of the state; and those institutions which are based upon honesty have their source in selfishness. . . .[3]

The state which is not controlled by the idea of that which is right is not in any way whatever bound by anything but its own

---

[1] Lasson, *Princip und Zukunft des Völkerrechts*, pp. 12-13.
[2] *Ibid.*, p. 15.   [3] *Ibid.*, p. 17.

purposes; hence, everywhere and in any manner it sees fit, it seeks that which is useful to it, and it is its nature to be shrewd and nothing but shrewd in pursuing its selfish interests.

All that which may be required of the person of the statesman is that he understand this will of the state and that he carry it out regardless of his own will and his own interest. . . .[1]

By nature and independent of his own will and choice, the individual being is the subject of a legally organized community; the state, however, can never be a subject, not even if it wanted and desired to be a subject, unless it surrendered itself completely and ceased to be a state. A legal organization with compulsory force at its command and to which the states were subject, would itself be a state, and the states subject to it would no longer be states, but subjects. Instead of the many states we would therefore have a universal state, and such a state cannot and shall not be. With such a state all freedom would vanish from the earth, and to mankind there would be nothing else in store except general decay and decomposition. . . .

Therefore, a state can never submit to a judicial decision. . . .[2]

This treatment of a legal organization to be established over and between states is an idle and senseless dream, born of cowardice and false sentimentalism surrounded with a halo of possible realization and reasonableness through the misuse of words and through conflicting and confused pictures. . . .[3]

In the first place, the state must protect the interests of its people which in part are its own interests as well; at the same time, however, the state has its own peculiar interests which it must guard and which command it to secure, wherever it may find it, that which is useful for its existence.

Wherever on earth there may be goods accessible to two states, the latter may come into conflict and will most certainly get into conflict. . . .[4]

Antipathy exists between peoples differently constituted at heart, regardless even of the danger which mutually confronts one another, and regardless of the mutual fear arising therefrom. . . . One people is unfriendly to another people; in the conflict of interests this aversion develops into an embittered deadly hatred, and this repulsive power of the consciousness of one's own worth and of one's

---

[1] Lasson, *Princip und Zukunft des Völkerrechts*, p. 21.
[2] *Ibid.*, p. 23.   [3] *Ibid.*, p. 26.   [4] *Ibid.*, pp. 31-32.

INTRODUCTION lxiii

own nature belongs inseparably to and forms a part and parcel of the healthiness of a people's life. A people that cannot hate what is alien to it, are a wretched people, unworthy of independence and destined to be plundered and robbed. It is a repulsive picture for a people which has been scorned and mistreated, "to do penance in sackcloth and ashes" and to live in shame, instead of striking the violator to the earth, at the risk of their own existence, or of going down in defeat with honor.

The state itself is, of course, unable, on its part, to share in this hatred of the peoples; for the state is a thoroughly heartless being; its egotism is, for that very reason, all the more inconsiderate in the interests of others. It is the task of the state to safeguard the legal organization adequate for the people and at the same time to realize and secure those conditions making for the development of the peculiar culture of the people. To this end, it resorts to any and all means at its disposal. In the hatred of peoples it finds such a means for safeguarding the treasured possessions of the Fatherland. . . .[1]

Right and morality do not bind the will of the state. There is but one thing which may hinder the state in the pursuit of its selfish interests, namely, fear of a foreign power. It is only toward the weak that a state acts boldly and dares to do what it pleases; uneasiness and fear compel the state to act considerately toward the strong; for the issue of the battle would be uncertain, and the danger for success and existence alone would be evident. Hence, all international relations are controlled by the point of the sword; might alone decides; the strong alone can exist; and the weak, because of their very weakness, are destined to succumb.

The state of self-defense excludes any and all consideration, and it is a war of all against all, if not a war of open violence, yet the latent war of cunning and prudence. A right without guarantees is no right at all. For lack, therefore, of a guaranteeing force, the states are engaged in an incessant warfare. . . .[2]

There is a system of provisions which is closely related to the legal organization established within the states, and which system, in contradistinction to the system of laws prevailing within a state, has been called the *law* of *nations,* international law, public law. But along with the similarity existing between these two systems we must not lose sight of the differences between them in order that we may

---

[1] Lasson, *Princip und Zukunft des Völkerrechts,* pp. 33-34.
[2] *Ibid.,* pp. 35-36.

not confound the two and not attribute to this law of nations the qualities of the real law, with which, in the nature of the things, international law has nothing to do. For such a confusion would lead not only to a grievous political error, since in our everyday life we can see how through such a confusion of different conceptions in the one indistinct representation of the law, consequences most inimical to the practical treatment of political relations arise and misrepresent the sentiments of the people. . . .[1]

International institutions have no guarantees of a legal nature. Their observance cannot be compelled; for there is no greater power than the power of the state. . . . The state will observe stipulations which are not causing it essential injury so long as urgent interests do not compel it to disregard such stipulations; it will observe its word and an obligation which it has taken upon itself as long as it can continue to exist under these limitations and fulfill its purposes; and it will do so the more certainly, if it comprehends thoroughly its interests. For the state must wish that another state observe its given faith and meet it in honesty, so that it may enjoy some security and some peace, and it can secure these only provided it keep faith itself. But in case of an urgent necessity, the state will of course not be able to observe this honesty altogether, especially so when reciprocity cannot be depended upon. *It will suffice that other states know that it means to observe its given faith up to the point where its own self-preservation might be endangered, that is to say, where a compelling necessity will force it to break its faith.* . . .[2]

Through historic evolution and without any ill-will, conflicts about vital interests of the states will always occur and cannot be settled except by force. . . . It is of the nature of things that where blind, barbarous passion does not govern, but where the interest of the state comes to expression, this part of international law is able to lead to a lasting and certain peaceful intercourse. And something precarious is even involved in this matter because it can never be certainly determined in advance as to whether along with the progress of things in general, something agreed upon may become so fraught with contingencies as will directly threaten the prosperity of the state. In such case, and in the nature of things, the state cannot, under the pressure of its urgent interests, keep from violating its given word or the regulation agreed upon, provided it cannot free

---

[1] Lasson, *Princip und Zukunft des Völkerrechts*, p. 43.
[2] *Ibid.*, p. 45.

INTRODUCTION lxv

itself of this obligation in any other way. The state itself must, however, decide when such urgency has arisen; no other state can pass judgment upon such a matter, because it does not comprehend the situation and the needs of the former or because it is not impartial, but prejudiced against it. All rules of international law, both those that immediately concern the self-preservation of the state and those directed to the regulation of less important relations, are valid only upon certain conditions, namely, only as long as a state believes that its self-preservation is not threatened by such stipulations. In the latter case, the will of the state cannot be controlled by outer barriers; it will do what it pleases to do without regard for anything else whatever. This is the nature of the matter, and in this sense every rule of international law should be understood, that is to say, never should the state be required to observe the rule absolutely, nor should the state itself make such a promise.

Because of this precariousness, the law of nations is no law. . . . International law is a voluntary agreement between coördinate powers which the latter cannot be compelled to observe. . . .[1]

International law is a means of progress for the states. These could of course exist in unrestricted independence without it; but international law is of advantage to them in order that in time of peace they may the more easily and more safely realize their purposes. And even if here and there the rules of international law assume the form of legal principles, yet according to the tenor and the form of obligation, they are principles of quite a different kind. They constitute rules of shrewdness; they are not commandments of law. . . .[2]

All barriers are rendered powerless under the pressure of necessity: we know of what little use has been the promise between states affirmed under oath with regard to the observance of the promise itself. . . .[3]

The unrestricted sovereignty of the state freely to dispose of itself and to direct its actions in accordance with the necessities of its situation cannot be impaired through international law.

In dire necessity, the state will not observe agreements, and nobody must complain about the unexpected or hateful when the state, driven by necessity, does not keep the faith of obligations which it has taken upon itself. . . . We must be on our guard against the state; it can never be bound absolutely, and any obligations it takes

---
[1] Lasson, *Princip und Zukunft des Völkerrechts*, p. 47.
[2] *Ibid.*, p. 49.   [3] *Ibid.*, p. 51.

upon itself, it goes without saying, have but a relative value, though this may nowhere be expressed, even in the face of the most explicit assurance to the contrary. . . .[1]

An agreement entered into between the strong and the weak has no sense at all. As soon as the strong is confronted by a pressing interest to break such an agreement, the latter is by that fact abrogated and destroyed as though it had never existed. . . . Only he who has sufficient force to threaten the other party to the same extent as he himself is threatened, may on the basis of treaties entered into expect in some measure a lasting state of peace.

Smaller states can therefore exist in complete independence by the side of the larger ones, only in case they can find confederates who can reënforce their power of resistance. But he alone can secure confederates if his existence is of value to others. Hence, the smallness of states is reasonably limited by this consideration. For, a state whose worthlessness for the entire system is plainly evident, which as a confederate is of no importance in the general scheme and in whose existence no one takes an interest, such a state cannot really continue in independence; and as soon as it is drawn into a crisis of conflicting interests of the strong states, it will completely disappear. A relatively small state can prove its right to its existence only in case its existence is an essential advantage in the balance of the entire system. . . .[2]

A further question is as to what significance political treaties may have with regard to the matters therein agreed upon. In view of what we have already said it must be evident that they have not the strict effect of legal obligation.

By nature every state is so constituted that it cannot accept any fetters to its will except on the condition that by its own volition it may cast them off again, of course not whenever it may see fit to do so,—for the state possesses no such arbitrary and unfounded right,—but only in case its pressing interests demand that it do so.[3]

A treaty will be observed only so long as it is advantageous, and it is not advantageous so long as there is a force at hand by which its observance may be compelled. . . . Whoever concludes a treaty must realize that he cannot rely upon its being observed.[4]

War is waged with a view to the treaty of peace which is to be concluded; . . . war has a political aim in view, namely, to

---

[1] Lasson, *Princip und Zukunft des Völkerrechts*, pp. 53-54.
[2] *Ibid.*, p. 58.   [3] *Ibid.*, pp. 60-61.   [4] *Ibid.*, p. 65.

reorganize on a new and reasonable basis all the mutual relations between the states.

War is therefore, in effect, merely a continuation of the usual negotiations between states, but carried on in different form and with different means.

States are not subject to a law of right, and it is vain to attempt to control their action by a so-called law. There is no praetor above them who might sit in judgment upon them; rather war is the only praetor which does not render its judgment with regard to the states according to a code of laws, but according to justice. This praetor is inexorable; he cannot be bribed; there can be no appeal nor escape from his sentence.

The power of the state lies in the discipline, in the virility, in the manliness and in the education of its citizens; the powerful state is the better state; its people are the better people; its culture is the more valuable culture. Whoever succumbs must acknowledge that he has deserved his fate; the victor may say unto himself, not that he was good, but that he was the better one as between himself and his opponent. Chance cannot decide a fight or battle, nor a war. For no defeat, no victory is definitive. All international relations are in constant flux and undergoing a constant change. The defeated party, however low he has fallen, may rise again; the victor, however great his victory may have been, may sink into ignominy. A people must constantly assert itself; it must not permit the fountain of its strength to run dry; on the contrary, it must ever enrich and increase the flow of its strength. . . . The state *must* be strong. This is its mission and its duty; woe to the state if it neglects this first duty and chases after other possessions at the cost of its might! In the great historic world process that which is weak succumbs because it is worthless, and that which is strong maintains itself because in particular events and at a particular time it is able better to serve the great mission of mankind. Such is the eternal impartiality of world history. . . .[1]

The nature of things is mightier than mere vain wishes; it neither permits now, nor will it ever permit that the states shall live in friendship and mutual love or that they shall be restricted in their actions by obedience to a compulsory legal organization. From a greater perfection of international law we can, therefore, not expect that international relations could ever be regulated on the basis of right or morality; from such perfection we may however expect

[1] Lasson, *Princip und Zukunft des Völkerrechts*, pp. 72-75.

that, more than hitherto, the true interests of the states will be safeguarded and that the relations of honesty and mutuality, based upon a justified self-interestedness will be further developed and strengthened. . . .[1]

The international law of contract has no absolute value for the simple reason that no impartial decision and no absolutely correct interpretation of it can be expected. . . .[2]

The states do not fight for the "right," nor yet for "ideas," but for their interests, and they bind themselves to "right" in so far as their interests permit. . . . Truth and simplicity alone can ameliorate human institutions and ennoble mankind; if things on earth are to be made better, it will be necessary in the first place to rid international relations of the hypocritical phrase of "right" and of the "sacredness of treaties"; in the second place it will be necessary to recognize expressly that international law has no other guarantees than its own inner worth and its conformity to that which is advantageous for the self-preservation of the states. It can be of value only in case statesmen comprehend the true interests of their states and in case the propositions of international law correspond to these interests. . . .[3]

All civilized peoples wishing to live in peace have evident need of a code of international law, generally recognized, and apt to cover any and all cases of disputes that may arise between them. But such a code must be restricted to the field within which falls the real international law in its narrower sense, and not attempt to reach, in each concrete case, into the field governed by temporary treaties. It is difficult to draw the line of demarcation in this matter; . . . such a code must not lose sight of the fact that international law is a very precarious thing; it must not attempt to bind the states absolutely and for every case that may arise; for in the presence of the necessity of self-preservation, all rules of international law disappear.

There is no promising prospect that war can be certainly prevented once and for all; this can be accomplished neither by a law, nor by the discretion or the goodwill of a person, nor by any institution, however excellent it may be. It is however a reasonable and most important aim of all human endeavor to prevent wars, except where they cannot be avoided. . . .[4]

The weak neighbor sharpens the appetite of the stronger and he

---

[1] Lasson, *Princip und Zukunft des Völkerrechts*, p. 84.
[2] *Ibid.*, p. 89.   [3] *Ibid.*, p. 91.   [4] *Ibid.*, pp. 93-94.

will certainly disappear if he is in the way of the stronger and if the proper opportunity to attack presents itself. Small states,—we do not even refer to minor states, for minor states have never been real states, but have always, through a fiction, been merely looked upon as such,—small states should not exist at all; they are a danger to peace; they are the bone of contention of the strong states; they are the natural cause and theaters of wars and through their desire to exist, they are constantly engaged in intrigues to keep apart from one another and in constant conflict all other great states which might do injury to them.

All there is left for the small states to do is to get together and constitute themselves into a federation on the basis of equality, or to join a stronger state under whose hegemony, or even, when the existence of such a state in full independence is by exception a need of the entire system of states, to surrender a part of its political sovereignty and become neutralized, in other words, to renounce foreign politics. Neutralization, moreover, is something precarious; the ever present question in this respect is as to whether or not in a pressing conflict, its recognition can be safeguarded.

It is necessary, therefore, that the states should, as far as possible, do everything to develop their power. An army as large as possible, with soldiers as intelligent as can be, with the best trained officers and disposing of all auxiliary means procurable through science, worth, and practice, all these are an assurance to the state that it will not be heedlessly attacked. Rid the world of all the armies which are now ready to do battle, and social life will be the same as in the middle ages, before there were standing armies, and war will incessantly govern between the states, as feud reigned between the members of the state in the middle ages. Standing armies alone are a guarantee for a lasting state of peace; without them the balance of power is not possible, and therefore no real negotiations, no honesty and reciprocity can prevail. The institution of the standing armies alone saves the world from barbarism. In the world of culture, armies can only be increased, never diminished. They will increase to the uttermost limits of possibility, even to the point when it will no longer be possible to secure the means for their maintenance and when their existence will sap rather than protect the productive strength of the nation. Hence, to make war the exception and peace the general rule is a problem which is identical with that other problem: to make the armies as large as possible and as inexpensive as possible. This problem can be solved only with a standing army just large enough to furnish the framework for its enlargement, with the entire population armed back of it, so that all who are physically fit may be disciplined in the use of arms from their youth up and for a short time trained in real military technique, and able through the years of vigorous manhood to strengthen, in case of war, the power of the Fatherland.

The actual facts of history go to prove that, other conditions being equal, the people which possesses the better universities, the better scientific laboratories and public schools is, in a military sense, the fitter and stronger. The strength of people in war is in general only the expression for its moral and intellectual capacity and for the healthiness of its institutions, in the home, in the community, and in the state.

An army of professional soldiers or an army of mercenaries is ever at the command of the caprice of the ruler; an armed people can be put into action only for the true and for the highest interests of the Fatherland.

Even as a military organization which permits of the highest development of power is the surest guarantee for peace, so the realization of the ever recurring project of a general disarmament is the greatest imaginable danger for the peace of the world. For, taking things as they are, it is a fact that might can be held in check only through might; so soon as the fear of a foreign might ceases the possibility of negotiation for peace also ceases. The voice of the negotiator exerts a proper influence only in case it is backed by the necessary number of bayonets and guns in order to make it respected. . . . Mirabeau justly answered a deputation of Quakers who came to him with a petition seeking to secure peace through disarmament: "It is weakness which causes war; universal resistance would mean universal peace." . . .[1]

(j) *Gustav Rümelin* (1815-1889)[2]

Is politics, that is to say, is the self-determined administration of all the affairs of the state subordinated to the law of morality, or shall it follow independent laws of its own? And, accordingly, are their actions permissible in politics, but forbidden by moral law, and *vice versa?*[3]

---

[1] Lasson, *Princip und Zukunft des Völkerrechts*, pp. 109-114.
[2] *Ueber das Verhältniss der Politik zur Moral—Reden und Aufsätze* von Gustav Rümelin, vol. 1. (Freiburg, n. d.).
[3] *Ibid.*, p. 144.

We praise and honor the men who have freed their people from servitude, from degradation and from impotency, and raised them to a higher plane of welfare, power, and liberty, without our losing sight of or being misled in our judgment by the fact that they have accomplished those things by intrigue, by force, by blood and iron, and by other means which, under other circumstances, we would condemn.[1]

The universal validity of the moral requirements is beyond all question. There can be absolutely no individual nor any class of free human actions that might be regarded as beyond or even above the law of morality.[2]

In consequence, if politics is the handiwork of man and the result of his free resolve, it must, of necessity, and to its full extent, become subject to conscience and to the control of moral laws. The statesman cannot be separated into two beings, of which the one, the non-politician, would possess a conscience, and the other, the politician, none. . . .[3]

Now, it would be just as illogical as it is impracticable, to demand from the community itself the same course of action as from those of its members who are in its employ. The injunctions "Thou shalt" and "Thou shalt not" of the ten commandments and of all legal language, have their proper sense only when the state is the party which commands, and the individual the party upon whom the command is enjoined. The state, as we well know, has no parents to honor; it has contracted no union which it might break. The injunction "Thou shalt not kill" cannot be directed against him who alone wields the sword, in order to punish the murderer, and who must spend millions for the purpose of preparing the most effective instruments of death, should it become necessary to resort to their use in self-defense. In order to accomplish its purpose, the state must likewise covet our houses and fields, our oxen and asses and any other of our property, without asking the individual how he likes it. . . .[4]

It may well be asked how the injunction "Love thy neighbor as thyself" could be practicable in the relations of one state to other states? None of all the ties which bind man to man, can bind the states one to another. Even although, in this respect, more ideal aims should be considered and striven for, still nations actually confront one another as in the state of nature, that is to say, they

---

[1] Rümelin, *Ueber das Verhältniss der Politik zur Moral—Reden und Aufsätze*, vol. 1, p. 145.
[2] *Ibid.*, p. 147.   [3] *Ibid.*, pp. 147-148.   [4] *Ibid.*, pp. 149-150.

are strangers to each other, and are compelled to observe foresight and mistrust, even as wanderers meeting one another in the desert. Over them there is no higher power than their own to regulate and settle their relations. "Love thy neighbor as thyself" cannot be applied here.[1]

In short the entire chapter of the duties of love, hence the chief part of all morality, is not practicable for the states. . . . Nations must not depend upon the love of others, but upon love of self, upon the preservation and development of their own power and welfare. It may not be maintained that it is the unconditional duty of the state to observe treaties into which it has entered or which it may have recognized. . . .[2]

Thus, with regard to the duties of justice, we have finally reached the same conclusion as with regard to the duties of love. Even as all human actions, politics is subject to a moral duty; but a morality which prescribes virtues and duties for the individual, cannot be made use of in the administration of the affairs of the state. In their very roots, morality and politics differ from each other.[3]

In this sense, we must answer No, to our first question—Is politics subordinated to the moral law? And we must answer Yes, to our second question—Does politics bear within itself a self-governing and independent principle for its actions? By these answers we merely repeat the true sense of the old maxim: *salus publica suprema lex esto,* that is to say, every other consideration is subordinated to the preservation and welfare of the community. . . .[4]

The interests of an individual or of a minority are subordinated to those of a majority or of the whole community. Individual liberty is subject to the limitations required by the general well-being. . . .[5]

The interests of a foreign state can be considered only in so far as they are compatible with our own. The preservation of the state justifies every sacrifice and is superior to every commandment.[5]

The principle of self-abnegation applies to the individual citizen; the principle of self-preservation applies to the state. The individual is a servant of the law which the state creates, directs, and executes. The individual is only a transient member of the moral organism; the state, if not this organism itself, is nevertheless its real regulating force; the state is immortal and sufficient unto itself. . . .[6]

In cases of political actions of an extraordinary character which

---

[1] Rümelin, *Ueber das Verhältniss der Politik zur Moral—Reden und Aufsätze,* vol. 1, pp. 149-150.
[2] *Ibid.,* p. 150.   [4] *Ibid.,* pp. 156-157.   [6] *Ibid.,* p. 156.
[3] *Ibid.,* p. 156.   [5] *Ibid.,* p. 161.

no individual is *compelled* to perform, introspection and wisdom are a bounden duty, and stupidity becomes a criminal offense. For the politician, caution is not only an intellectual but a moral quality, and whoever lacks this quality, or even whoever is incapable of sound judgment, commits a sin by the fact that he aspires to a position for which he is unfit and by virtue of which he is called upon to consider interests other than his own. . . .[1]

But the condition of moral politics of the state is the moral sense of the peoples themselves. Only if among the German people the receptivity for ideal possessions maintains its preponderance over the desire for gain and enjoyment, over indifference to the activities of the community, over narrow prejudices,—can the politics of a national administration, based on an equal suffrage, be administered in a similar spirit. The morality of the people and that of their statesmen go hand in hand. It is but the passing good fortune when, in free states, the government of a people is better than their own standard of morality. And only in this constant and living reciprocal action lies the ultimate solution of the riddle considered in this address. . . .[2]

(k) *Heinrich von Treitschke* (1834-1896)[3]

The state is the people legally united as an independent power. Briefly speaking, by the word "people" we understand a number of families permanently living side by side. This judgment implies that the state is primordial and necessary, that it exists as long as there is a history of mankind and that it is no less essential to mankind than speech itself.[4]

The state is power for the sole purpose of asserting itself toward other powers, equally independent. War and the administration of justice are the first tasks of even the most barbaric state. . . .[5]

In history we meet throughout with only virile characters; history is not for sentimental or feminine natures. Only brave peoples have a secure existence, a future, an evolution; weak and cowardly

---

[1] Rümelin, *Ueber das Verhältniss der Politik zur Moral—Reden und Aufsätze*, vol. 1, p. 166.
[2] *Ibid.*, pp. 170-171.
[3] *Politik* (Vorlesungen gehalten an der Universität zu Berlin von Heinrich von Treitschke). Zweite, durchgesehne Auflage (Leipzig: G. Hirzel, 1899-1900, 2 vols.).
[4] Treitschke, *Politik*, vol. 1, p. 13.
[5] *Ibid.*, p. 29.

peoples perish, and justly so. In this eternal conflict of different states, we find the grandeur of history; it is an evident un-reason to wish to do away with this world struggle. Mankind has at all times found this to have been so.[1]

If we examine more closely our definition, that "a state is the people legally united as an independent power," we will find that we may shorten this definition to read as follows: "The state is the public power for defense and offense." Above all, the state is power in order to assert itself; it is not the totality of the people themselves as Hegel assumed in his deification of the state.[2]

The state is not an academy of fine arts; if it neglects its power in favor of the ideal pursuits of mankind, it repudiates its own nature and perishes. Repudiation of its own power is, indeed, so far as the state is concerned, equivalent to the sin against the Holy Ghost; to follow, from purely sentimental reasons, in the train of a foreign state, as we Germans have so frequently done with regard to England, is indeed a mortal sin. . . .[3]

The real nature of the state is characterized by the fact that it cannot suffer to have a higher power over itself. How proudly and truly statesmanlike Gustavus Adolphus has expressed this thought when he said: "I recognize no one over me except God and the sword of the victor." This is so unreservedly true that again we see forthwith that it cannot be the view of mankind to form a single political power, but that the ideal toward which we are striving is a harmonious society of peoples, who, by means of treaties which they freely conclude among themselves, set restrictions upon their sovereignty without abrogating it.

Nor can the spirit of sovereignty be inelastic; it is flexibly relative like all political conceptions. For its own sake, every state will by means of treaties limit its sovereignty in certain directions. When states enter into treaties with one another, they restrict somewhat their absolute power. But the rule will still hold, for every treaty is a voluntary restriction upon individual power, and all international treaties contain the clause: *"rebus sic stantibus."* No state can bind its will for the future to another state. The state has no higher judge than itself, and, therefore, it will conclude all its treaties with the above tacit reservation. For it is true that as long as there shall be an international law, all treaties between the belligerent states lapse with the moment of declaration of war; as sovereign,

---

[1] Treitschke, *Politik*, vol. 1, p. 30.
[2] *Ibid.*, p. 32.
[3] *Ibid.*, p. 34.

each state has, however, the indubitable right to declare war whenever it sees fit, and in consequence, every state is then entitled to abrogate any treaties it may have concluded. Upon this constant change of treaties rests the progress of history; every state must see to it that no other power will denounce them with a declaration of war. For treaties which have ceased to be useful, must be denounced, and new ones, consonant with the new circumstances, must take their places.

All this makes it clear that the international treaties which limit the power of a state are not absolute, but voluntary self-restrictions. From this we conclude that the organization of an international arbitral court, as a durable institution, is incompatible with the nature of the state. At all events, only in matters of second or third rate importance could the state submit to such arbitral court. There is, moreover, no impartial outside power to judge of vital matters. If we were to commit the folly of treating the Alsace-Lorraine matter as an open question and to submit it to an arbitrator, who would really believe that such an arbitrator could be impartial? It is, furthermore, a matter of honor for a state to settle such questions for itself. Therefore, it will be impossible to constitute a court that shall sit in judgment over peoples. The only thing we may look forward to is that international treaties may become more frequent. But until the end of history, the appeal to arms will maintain its right; and therein lies precisely the sacredness of war.

We have, therefore, seen that the concept of sovereignty is flexible; but we are not to infer from this that this concept is a non-sense. We are rather to determine in what consists the inalienable kernel of sovereignty! Legally, this kernel lies in the authority to determine the scope of one's own rights of sovereignty, and politically in the appeal to arms. An unarmed state which is not in a position to draw the sword when it sees fit, is subject to the higher power, which, in its stead, has the right to declare war. To speak of a war sovereignty in times of peace implies an obvious *contradictio in adjecto*. A state admitting the claim to such a sovereignty may still be called a kingdom for conventional reasons and from pure flattery, but science, whose first duty is to ascertain the truth, shall boldly speak out and declare that in the nature of the thing itself such a country is no longer a state.

This, therefore, is the one essential criterion: the right of arms distinguishes the state from all other corporate bodies, and whoever cannot take up arms for himself cannot be regarded as a state, but only as a member of a federated organization of states. Already we perceive the difference between the crown of Prussia and the other German states, namely, that the King of Prussia is himself the war lord, and therefore, that Prussia has not lost its sovereignty, as the other states have lost theirs.[1]

In matters of this kind we may not follow the guidance of scholars, but that of statesmen. When, one day, Bismarck observed to William I that the empire would not give its consent in the matter of a certain political decision, the latter, in a moment of indignation, replied: "What, the empire! The empire, as you know, is merely an extended Prussia." This expresses the thing in trooper fashion, but it is true.[2]

When we look more closely into the matter, it becomes quite evident, that if the state is power, then only that state which is really powerful, meets that idea. Thence we get the undeniably ridiculous phase which we perceive in the existence of a small state. Weakness is, of course, not itself ridiculous; but that other weakness which demeans itself as power, is ridiculous. In small states there develops that beggarly spirit which judges the state by the taxes which it levies; a spirit which feels that if the state does not repress as an egg-shell, it will not be able to afford protection, and that the moral possessions which we owe to the state are inestimable. The small state exercises a destructive influence upon the spirit of its citizens, because it generates that kind of materialism.

Moreover, the small state lacks absolutely the capacity of administering justice which characterizes the great state. . . .

Therefore, when all things have been considered, we come to the conclusion that the large state possesses the nobler parts. This is especially true with regard to the great fundamental functions of the state, such as the protection afforded through its arms, and the protection of right. Both can be much better accomplished by the great than by the small state. The small state cannot wage war with any prospect of success. . . .[3]

Furthermore, the economic superiority of great states is an obvious fact. In organizations on a vast scale greater security is also found. More easily than the small state, a big state can successfully meet economic crises; for instance, a failure of crops can hardly extend over all of its parts. Only in great states can there develop a real national pride which is a mark of the moral thoroughness of a

---

[1] Treitschke, *Politik*, vol. 1, pp. 37-39.
[2] *Ibid.*, p. 40.
[3] *Ibid.*, pp. 43-44.

people; in aggregations on a large scale the world-view of the citizens becomes freer and greater.¹

When we see the state as a personality, it becomes evident that it must seek its goal within itself. . . . On sight of a living being, we shall not confine ourselves to inquire: What is the purpose of that being? But we must put to ourselves the further question: What is the moral task of this personality? And in the case of the state, we shall, therefore, have to inquire: What is its task in the world of civilization? And first of all: What are the national boundaries of its activity?²

The second essential function of the state is the conduct of war. That this should have been left unconsidered for such a long time, is proof of the fact that the science of government, evolved by civilian minds only, had thoroughly degenerated. In our century, since the time of Clausewitz, this sentimental conception has vanished; its place was, however, taken by a one-sided materialistic conception, which, after the fashion of the Manchester school, looks upon man as a two-legged being whose destiny it is to buy cheap and to sell dear. That this conception is likewise incompatible with war, can be readily explained; only after the experiences of the later wars, a more wholesome view of the state and of its military power has gradually arisen. Without war there would be no state. All states we have any knowledge of came about as the result of wars; the protection of its citizens by armed force remains the first and most essential task of the state. Therefore, wars there will be to the end of history, as long as there is a multiplicity of states. That the course of history should, in this respect, ever change, is neither to be inferred from the loss of human thought or of human nature, nor is it in any manner whatever to be wished for. The blind worshipers of an eternal peace commit an error of thought when they isolate the state or when they dream of a universal state, which we have already found to be against reason.

As we have furthermore seen that it is impossible to conceive even of a higher judge over the states, which in their very essence are sovereign, it is likewise impossible to conceive of the world as without the condition of war. It is the favorite fashion of our time to point to England as especially ready for peace. But England, as we well know, is perpetually waging war; there is hardly a moment to which we may point in modern history when England has not

¹ Treitschke, *Politik*, vol. 1, pp. 44-45.
² *Ibid.*, pp. 68-69.

been obliged to fight somewhere. The great cultural progress of mankind can be realized by the sword only against the resistance of barbarism and unreason. Between civilized peoples, war remains, likewise, the form of the process by which the claims of the states are made valid. The proofs evidenced in these terrible conflicts between peoples are compelling to a greater extent than the proofs evidenced in civil processes. In theory we have frequently endeavored to convince the small states that Prussia alone can be the leader in Germany; we were compelled to furnish the really convincing proof of this on the battlefields of Bohemia and by the Main. . . .[1]

We must not consider all these things by the light of the student's lamp only; the historian who lives in the world of the Will sees forthwith that the demand for an eternal peace is in its essence reactionary; he sees that if war disappears, all movement and all growth will disappear from history. The really spiritless degenerate times have ever been the only ones in which men have toyed with the dream of an eternal peace. There have been three such periods in modern history. In the first place, we have the dismal time after the peace of Utrecht, after the death of Louis XIV. The world seemed to be breathing afresh; but Frederick the Great pointedly declared that these years were a period of general degeneracy in European politics. The Holy Roman Empire in its then ridiculous position, the unfinished Prussia faced with the problem of growth or decline—all these immature conditions were declared moral conditions by the apostles of reason. The elder Rousseau, the Abbé Castel de Saint Pierre, and still others came forthwith and wrote their foolish books about eternal peace. The second epoch during which the pipe of peace was again being smoked generally, arose under similar conditions. After the Congress of Vienna the Viennese treaties were looked upon as *ratio scripta;* it was held to be reasonable and moral to cripple for all eternity, two noble peoples, the Italians and the Germans. We are living now in the third epoch, again after a great war which seems to have destroyed idealism in Germany. Does not the neighing laughter of vulgarity resound loud and shameless when anything of all that which has made Germany great, is destroyed? The foundations of our old and noble culture are now being destroyed; all that which once made us an aristocracy among the peoples, is being scoffed at and trampled upon. This, then, is certainly the proper time to toy once more with the concept of an eternal peace. As for the rest, it is scarcely worth

[1] Treitschke, *Politik*, vol. 1, pp. 72-73.

the trouble further to consider this matter; the living God will see to it that war shall ever return as a terrible medicine for mankind.¹

And the economic ravages of war play also greater havoc with civilized peoples than with barbarians. In our day, a war may have especially hard and fearful consequences in destroying the artificial system of credit. If a conqueror should ever enter London, the effect would be terrible beyond anything we can imagine. The threads which bind the credit of millions are gathered together there, and a conqueror as inconsiderate as Napoleon might there perpetrate devastations of which we can altogether have no idea. From the natural repugnance of mankind against bloodshed and from the size and quality of modern arms, there necessarily follows that wars must become rarer and shorter, for it is impossible to understand how the burdens of a great war can long be borne in their present-day conditions. It is, however, illusory to conclude from all of this that wars will ever entirely cease. Wars cannot and should not cease so long as the state is sovereign and confronted by other sovereign states.²

As contrasted with the conception of antiquity, our modern views of individualism, adorned with various appellations, are as great as the difference between night and day. The modern view of individualism starts with the idea that the state should be satisfied with protecting life and property at home and abroad, and to this restricted state it applies the name of "constitutional state." This doctrine is the legitimate child of the doctrine of the old natural law. According to this doctrine, the state can only be a means for the purposes of the existence of the individuals, something which we have already shown to be contrary to reason.³

The complicated activity of our state results from our world position, from our history and geographical situation, through all of which we are pursuing aims which, in the opinion of other peoples, are incompatible with each other. . . . Moreover, we are the most monarchical people of Europe; at the same time, however, we must endeavor to harmonize with that fact a respectable popular representation. We have solved the riddle of how a civilized people can also be a people in arms; and we desire to solve the even greater riddle of how a rich people can preserve the moral benefits of an army and of a military service.⁴

When we look upon a state as a moral community which from

---

¹ Treitschke, *Politik*, vol. 1, pp. 75-76.
² *Ibid.*, p. 77.   ³ *Ibid.*, pp. 78-79.   ⁴ *Ibid.*, p. 86.

its appointed place shall coöperate in the education of mankind, the state must then undoubtedly be subject to the general law of morality. Still, we constantly hear about the conflict between politics and morality. This general aspect of the matter shows clearly that the relation between the two cannot be so very simple and evident. . . . [1]

It was Machiavelli who gave expression to the thought that in case the salvation of a state was at stake one should not stop to inquire if the means resorted to are or are not permissible; that the state must be preserved and that afterwards everybody would justify their use. . . . It will ever remain Machiavelli's glory, first, for having put the state upon its own feet, and in questions of morality, for having freed it from the influence of the church, but above all, for having been the first to declare that the state is power. . . .

This genial Florentine was the first, with the mighty force of his intellect, to put into the center of all politics this great thought that the state is power. For this is the truth; and whoever is not virile enough to look this truth squarely in the face would better leave politics alone.[2]

Now, if we apply this standard of a deeper, and really Christian morality to the state, and we will remember that the nature of this great collective personality is power, we realize at once that it is the highest moral duty of the state to uphold its power. The individual must sacrifice himself for a higher community of which he is a member; the state itself is, however, the highest in the external community of man; hence, the duty of self-effacement cannot apply to it. The Christian duty of self-sacrifice for something higher does not apply to the state, because in the history of the world there is nothing whatever that is superior to it; in consequence it cannot sacrifice itself to something which is higher than itself. Only the state clearly beholds its destruction, yet we give it praise, when it succumbs with sword in hand. Sacrifice for a foreign people is not only not moral, but is contrary to the idea of self-assertion, which is the highest volition of the state.

From all of this there results that it becomes necessary to differentiate between public and private morality. As the state is power, the rank of its different duties must necessarily be different from the rank of the duties of the individual man. A number of these duties which devolve upon the individual cannot be considered at all

[1] Treitschke, *Politik*, vol. 1, p. 87.
[2] *Ibid.*, pp. 89-91.

with reference to the state. Its highest command is to assert itself; for the state this is absolutely moral. It must therefore be said that of all political sins, the sin of weakness is the most reprehensible and the most despicable. It is the sin against the Holy Ghost of politics. In private life there are excusable weaknesses of character. There can be no question of such weaknesses in a state; the state is power, and if it repudiates this which is its nature, it cannot be too thoroughly judged. . . .

From the nature of the state as a sovereign power, it further follows that it can recognize no arbitrary authority over it and, therefore, that in the last analysis, its legal obligations are subject to its own decision. This we must clearly bear in mind, so that in great crises we may not judge from the advocate's philistine point of view. When Prussia broke the treaty of Tilsit, Prussia was wrong from the point of view of the civil law. But who would have the brazen affront to assert now that it did wrong? The French themselves no longer do so. This is likewise true of international treaties which are not quite as unmoral as that which was forced upon Prussia and France. Every state, therefore, reserves to itself the right to be the judge of its own treaties, and the historian cannot in such cases content himself with a merely formal standard. He must put to himself the deeper question whether the unconditional duty of self-preservation does not justify the state.[1]

Everyone knows that the well known Jesuit expression is raw and radical in its crudity; but no one can deny that it contains a modicum of truth. Unfortunately, in public as in private life there are numberless cases when the use of absolutely irreproachable means is impossible. And if the use of irreproachable means is possible and a moral goal can be attained through moral means, the latter are to be preferred, even when they lead more slowly and more uncomfortably towards the goal.[2]

Political history begins with a system of small states. The next development witnesses the conflict between these tribes and the combination of larger masses into a common organization; thus, conquest and subjugation become the real active motive for the building of larger states. The states have not issued from the sovereignty of the people, but were created against their will; the state is the self-determined power of the strongest tribe.

There is nothing in all this to complain of. In such simple

---

[1] Treitschke, *Politik*, vol. 1, pp. 100-102.
[2] *Ibid.*, p. 105.

conditions of life, the physical power must decide, and this power of the victor is morally justified, because it makes for protection, and in this way it works beneficially. . . . Through the subsequent course of history we find that, of all the powers of which we know, war is the mightiest and the most efficient for building up nations. In war alone a people is woven together into a people, and the extension of existing states results in most cases through conquest, even if subsequently the results of the armed conflict are confirmed by treaty. . . .[1]

That federalistic atmosphere from which have issued political organizations such as Switzerland and the North American Union could, therefore, not be generated within our territorial possessions. Rather, in the whirl of forces and counter-forces, but one has finally remained as the real and living force: "Any impartial judge cannot but agree that ever since the days of the Great Elector the political history of Germany has been wholly and absolutely the history of Prussia. Every clod of land which had been lost through the sins of the ancient empire, and has been won back, has been won back through Prussia. Thenceforth, the political strength of the German nation lay in that state as surely as that same state had failed for a long time to accept its ideal forces, nay, had almost repelled them. . . . Against the will of all Germany, the Prussian state created with its faithful sword a constitution which, of course, could be nothing else except a complete subordination of the smaller states, a subordination of the conquered to the victor, although the constitution expressed this fact in generous and friendly forms. . . . Prussia was not swallowed up in Germany. This expression which is still current in our own day, states the very opposite of that which is palpable to our hands: Prussia extended its own institutions over the rest of Germany.

It is a fact that it required all of the fatuous forces of the learned German pedagogy to establish the theory which may be found in nearly every manual of German constitutional law, to the effect, that Prussia, in order to reserve itself for its victories in Bohemia and by the Main, has committed suicide and placed itself in the same situation as the states which it conquered. It is said that Prussia, along with all the other individual German states, has been swallowed up in the new empire. This idea is so extremely ridiculous that it would have been impossible to evolve it in any

---

[1] Treitschke, *Politik*, vol. 1, pp. 113-114.

other country of the world but our own, because we are so frequently engulfed by the flood of theory. . . .[1]

What would become of Germany if the Prussian state ceased to be? The German Empire, in such case, could not continue to exist. From this results a truth unpleasant to most people, yet not at all offensive to non-Prussian people, to the effect, that within this German Empire, Prussia alone of the former German states has preserved its sovereignty. Prussia alone has remained a sovereign state. Prussia has not lost the right of arms; nor need Prussia permit other states to curtail its sovereign rights. The German Emperor is also the King of Prussia; he is the military leader of the nation, and we are indulging in unavailing hair-splitting when we imagine cases in which the German Emperor and the King of Prussia might come into conflict with one another.[2]

It was an error of the old political science when it regarded the army merely as an instrument of diplomacy, and when in the chapter dealing with foreign politics, it assigned to the army a subordinate place in its system. It was purely and simply regarded as a means of diplomacy. But in our age of universal military service this idea about the army has vanished. Everyone now feels that the army is not merely a means for attaining the aims of diplomacy, but that the very constitution of a state rests upon the nation's share in bearing arms. For the state is maintained by the physical strength of the nation, which is represented by the army. If power, within and without, is the nature of the state then the organization of the army must be one of the first constitutional questions of the state. The state's innermost character is determined by the organization of the army, dependent on whether the constitution will prescribe universal service, organize a territorial militia, or establish conscription with substitution. . . .[3]

Even those who look upon the army as an evil, must in any case regard it as a necessary evil. If the existence of the state itself is necessary and reasonable, it follows, of course, that it must assert itself towards other states. . . .[4]

It is an advantage to a nation to have a strong and well organized army, for the very reason that the army is not only intended as a means which shall serve its foreign policy, but because a noble nation with a glorious history can for a long time use the army as a weapon for maintaining order, and because it forms a school for

---

[1] Treitschke, *Politik*, vol. 2, pp. 338-340.
[2] *Ibid.*, pp. 343-344. [3] *Ibid.*, p. 355. [4] *Ibid.*, p. 357.

the really virile virtues of the people which are so easily lost in an age bent on gain and luxury.¹

It is, therefore, normal and reasonable when, by its physical strength, a great nation embodies and develops the essence of the state, which is power, through an organized military system. And, as we have lived in a warlike age, the very sentimental and philanthropic way of looking at these things has passed more and more into the background, so that, even as Clausewitz, we regard war as the continuation of politics by force. All the peace-pipe smokers in the world will never succeed in bringing the political powers into agreement, and if these powers are not agreed among themselves, then the sword alone can decide between them. We have learned to know the moral majesty of war in the very things which to the superficial observer seem brutal and inhuman. That for the sake of the Fatherland we must overcome our natural feeling of humanity, that men shall murder one another who never before have done one another an injury and perhaps respect one another as chivalrous enemies, it is this which at first sight seems to constitute the abhorrent part of war, but at the same time its grandeur as well. Man shall not merely sacrifice his life, but even natural, deeply justified instincts of the human soul; he shall sacrifice his whole soul for the sake of a great patriotic idea; and it is this which constitutes the morally sublime part of war. When we further examine this thought, we will see how, with all its hardness and brutality, war weaves a bond of love between men, how in war the difference between classes disappears, how the peril of death links man to man. He who understands history knows full well that when scholars study these matters, they start out with the idea that the state is only intended to be an academy of arts and sciences. And it shall be this also, but it is not its primary profession. When a state neglects its physical strength for the sake of promoting its intellectual strength, then it perishes.²

If the army is the organized political power of the state, this organization can be nothing but power and can have no will of its own, for it is intended for the carrying out with unconditional obedience the will of the supreme authority of the state.³

. . . Since that time (after the peace of the Pyrenees), the map of our hemisphere has become much more natural; its center has been strengthened, and the brilliant thought that the center of gravity of Europe should be found in the middle of it, has become a reality.

¹ Treitschke, *Politik*, vol. 2, p. 360.
² *Ibid.*, pp. 361-362.   ³ *Ibid.*, p. 365.

INTRODUCTION   lxxxv

Through the establishment of the German Empire a calmer atmosphere has prevailed within the system of states inasmuch as Prussia may now repress its ambition; in all essentials, Prussia has attained all the power it needs.[1]

When we ask, is there really an international law? we are confronted with two contradictory, and at the same time extreme and untenable, conceptions of the international life of states. The first, the naturalistic, whose chief representative we have already found in Machiavelli, starting with the idea that the state is power, purely and simply, and that it may do anything which may be useful to it; it can, therefore, not bind itself to an international law; its position towards other states is mechanically determined by the mutual relations of strength. . . .

Alongside of this view we meet with the equally false and moralizing conception of liberal theorists. It regards the state as a good youngster to be washed and combed and sent to school, and he should have his ears boxed so that he may be obedient; he is expected to be grateful and just, and God knows what else besides. . . . The theoretical German teacher of international law thinks that he need only formulate a few principles and that the nations, as reasonable beings, will then be obligated to observe them. Ever and anon he forgets that stupidity and passion are great powers in history. Who cannot see what a real force nationalistic passions have become again in this our century! And whence do individual men, such as Rotteck, Bluntschli, and Heffter, derive their authority toward states in such a thing as "Thou shalt"? There is no human being placed so high that he could impose binding prescriptions upon all states; he must expect to find that his arguments are overcome and modified by the living life. The idea that there is some imaginary law is brought to naught in that living life. Only a positive law exists, and no theorist can invent principles which shall forthwith pass as positive law. As long as the conviction about the truth and the reasonableness of certain legal principles has not become a life conviction among the people, the labor of science can only be preparatory and break the way. If we carry the abstract conception of a state to its last analysis a supreme power on earth, endowed with extraordinary authority, would be necessary. . . . But there shall be no such authority on earth, for our fair world shall be a world of freedom as well. . . .

If then we have established the fact that these two extreme views

[1] Treitschke, *Politik*, vol. 2, p. 540.

cannot be carried out in practice, it is, on the other hand, quite possible to establish a doctrine of international law, based upon history and, therefore, a doctrine which can be put into practice. . . .

We must, therefore, go to work with history as our basis and regard the state as that which it really is: physical power, but at the same time, as an institution which shall coöperate in the education of the human race. As physical power, the state will naturally be inclined to appropriate unto itself as many necessaries of life as it may regard as useful, for in its essence the state is an intruder. But every state will, of course, of its own accord, have certain considerations for the neighboring powers. From reasonable considerations and from the mutual recognition of personal advantage, a more definite feeling of law will in time be evolved. It will be found that a state is bound to the communal life of all the states within which it is situated, and that it must in one way or another be able to adapt itself to this communal life. This consideration rests upon the very real sentiment of reciprocity, and not upon love for mankind.[1]

Gortschakow was right in saying that neither the nations constantly fearing attack, nor the very powerful nations believing themselves at all times ready to attack, would take up the time of the last conference on international law. The expression was to the point and can be reinforced by living examples. In countries like Belgium and Holland, which, to the great detriment of the science of international law, have unfortunately been for a long time the home of the theories of international law, a sentimental conception of international law has arisen because these countries are in constant fear of being attacked; it is customary in the name of humanity to present to the victor demands which are contrary to the power of the state, which are unnatural and unreasonable. . . . As it is certain that public law has its roots in practice, it is equally certain that a state placed in an abnormal position will occasion an abnormal misconstruction of international law. Belgium is a neutral state; in its essence it is a crippled state; and how then could sound principles of international law be evolved in such a state? I beg you to bear that fact in mind when later on you are confronted by the voluminous Belgian literature upon this subject. . . .

If we do not wish to be mistaken as to the real meaning of international law, we must constantly bear in mind the fact that all the paraphernalia of international law cannot put an end to the essence

[1] Treitschke, *Politik*, vol. 2, pp. 542-546.

of the state. Never can the state regard as reasonable any demand made upon it which would lead, if carried out, to its suicide. Likewise, every state must remain a sovereign in the society of nations; in international relations as well, the preservation of its sovereignty is its highest duty. The best principles of international law are those which do not touch upon the matter of sovereignty, that is to say, principles of international etiquette and of international private law.[1]

From all these considerations there results further that all the restrictions which the states impose upon themselves by treaties, are voluntary and concluded on the tacit reservation: *rebus sic stantibus*. There has never been a state and there never will be a state which upon concluding a treaty really intends to preserve it throughout all time. No state will ever be in position to conclude for perpetuity a treaty containing a restriction in its own sovereignty. It always reserves unto itself the right to annul such a treaty; it will be valid only so long as the present circumstances have not been completely changed. This is a principle which has been looked upon as inhuman, but which in its last analysis will prove to be the contrary. When the state realizes that all its treaties possess only a conditional validity then it will conclude treaties with the greatest prudence. History is not meant to be looked at from the point of view of a judge of a civil suit. . . .

Politics must never neglect to take account of the free moral powers of the people's life. No state in the world is able to renounce the "I" of its sovereignty. When conditions are imposed upon it which cripple it and which it cannot prevent, then "the breach brings it more honor than the observance of it." It is, indeed, one of the fine things about history, that a state would rather suffer material losses than to allow things which would do injury to its honor.[2]

When a state realizes that existing treaties no longer express the real relations of power and it cannot, by peaceful negotiation, persuade the other state to yield, then the international suit, that is to say, war sets in. The declaration of war by a state in such position follows from the consciousness of a necessary duty. There is no personal greed whatever involved, but the parties interested realize that the existing treaties no longer express the real relations of power, and because we cannot agree peacefully, the great international suit must decide.[3]

[1] Treitschke, *Politik*, vol. 2, pp. 548-549.
[2] *Ibid.*, pp. 550-551.
[3] *Ibid.*, p. 552.

No international court of arbitration will ever succeed in removing war from the world. In the great vital questions of a nation, impartiality on the part of the other members of the society of states is absolutely impossible. They must take sides, precisely because they form a living community, and because of the manifold and mutual interests they are either bound together or driven apart. If Germany were foolish enough to allow the Alsace-Lorraine question to be decided by a court of arbitration, what European power could be impartial in the matter? We cannot think of a single one which could be impartial. Thence results the well known fact that international congresses are indeed capable of putting the results of war into formulas and of clothing them in juridical phrases, but that they cannot prevent a threatening outbreak of war. A foreign state can be impartial in matters of third-rate importance only.

We have already seen that war can be justified and that it is moral; we have seen also that the thought of an eternal peace is an impossible, and at the same time, an immoral idea. It is unworthy of man to regard the impracticable as practicable; but a purely intellectual activity has only too often an enervating influence upon the thinker. War cannot be banished from the earth so long as the human race with its foibles and passions remains what it is. . . . Once more, it must be repeated that the violent form of the international conflict results from the nature of the state itself. In the multiplicity of states we find, once and for all, the reason for the necessity of war. Frederick the Great said that the dream of perpetual peace is a phantom which every man casts off when force is marching against him; and he also said that it is impossible to imagine an international balance of power which can last.

It is, however, precisely within the field of war that the triumph of human reason reveals itself most clearly. All noble nations have felt that the unfettering of physical strength in war needs to be regulated by definite laws, and as a result, international rules of warfare have been elaborated on the basis of reciprocity. It is within the sphere of the rules of warfare, which fools regard as barbarous, that we meet with the greatest triumph of the science of international law. In modern times we are seldom confronted with barbarous violations of these rules. The especially fine thing about international law is the unmistakable fact that these rules show constant progress and that through a *universalis consensus* alone a series of principles of international law has been so firmly established as to warrant us in saying that they stand as securely as any principle in the private law of

INTRODUCTION lxxxix

any state. . . . In the course of the centuries, international law has reached such a degree of understanding of justice that its formal side may at least be regarded as fully secured. The publicity of our modern political life is contributing much to that end. . . . But the whole character of international life has become so public that any gross violation of international law will immediately arouse great indignation in all civilized countries.[1]

All international rights are guaranteed by international treaties. It is clear that in many respects these international treaties must differ from the contracts entered into under private law. They differ in the first place in that they can be concluded only upon a basis of loyalty and faith, because there is no judge who can compel their observance. . . . Hence, the Athenians understood the matter correctly when they contracted their international agreements only for a limited time. Christian peoples think otherwise; they conclude their treaties for all time. For all time, however, means for as long as the relations of power between the two states do not absolutely change. This we must emphasize and every sober-minded state must realize its soundness; for then treaties will be more secure, and every state will take care not to enter into treaties which can be readily denounced. . . .

. . . The life of nations is counted by centuries, so that a prescription period could enter into it only after an infinitely long period. Frederick the Great was absolutely justified in laying claim to the four Silesian duchies for his state, although treaties which secured them to his house were more than two hundred years old.[2]

When a war has actually begun, the uppermost principle of justice by which that war is conducted must be directed to the creation of a new international status of law such as will express the real relation of power between the contending parties, and which must then be recognized by both. It is right, therefore, to wage war in the most effective manner, because its goal, which is peace, will be more quickly reached. Therefore, we must endeavor to land our thrust in the heart of the enemy. The sharpest weapons, except when they cause needless suffering to the wounded, are in such cases absolutely permissible; nothing in all this can be changed by the declamations of philanthropists in regard to explosive shells landing in the powder chamber of wooden battleships. Such weapons as shall not be allowed have been decided upon by agreement of the states. At Russia's behest,

[1] Treitschke, *Politik*, vol. 2, pp. 553-555.
[2] *Ibid.*, pp. 556-558.

explosive bullets for small arms may not be used. It is permissible to take advantage of all weak points shown by the enemy. A state is allowed to use the conspirator and agitator of its enemy for its own purposes. . . .

Nor can the belligerent state be denied the right to use all its troops for fighting purposes no matter whether they be barbarians or civilized men. In this matter one must be unbiased in order to guard against prejudices against any nation. The Germans raised a great hue and cry against the French because, in the last war, they set the Turcos against a civilized European people. Such things may indeed happen amid the passions of war; science, however, must remain calm and sober and declare that this was in no way contrary to international law. For it remains ever true that the state engaged in war, is justified and bound to throw all of its physical resources and all of its available troops into the battle. How is it possible to draw the line in a matter of this kind? Where, for instance, would Russia, which has so many attractive races within its boundaries, draw the line in this matter? The physical strength of a state may and must be used to its full extent in war, but in accordance with the chivalrous usages which have been established as the result of much experience in war. It is true that the claim of the French that they march at the head of civilization was put in a curious light through the use of such troops. This leads to a long list of complaints because demands are made upon a state which it cannot possibly comply with. In the national wars of the present day every honest subject is a spy. Therefore, the expulsion of 80,000 Germans from France in 1870 was not contrary to international law. But the French laid themselves open to criticism in this matter because they went about it with some brutality. . . .[1]

Even although the force exerted by the enemy is purely military, still, private property should be respected to the widest extent whenever it is possible to distinguish between civilian property and property belonging to the enemy enrolled in the army. Requisitions are permitted; it is customary to give receipts in exchange; it devolves, of course, upon the defeated party to see to it that these receipts are subsequently redeemed. Destruction of private property as such, of which the devastation of the Palatinate by Melac, is such a fearful example, and the burning of villages from mere wantonness, now regarded by all civilized states as crimes against international

---

[1] Treitschke, *Politik*, vol. 2, pp. 564-565.

law. Private property may be injured only to the extent in which this is unavoidably necessary for the successful issue of the war. But international law becomes mere clap-trap when we mean to apply these principles to barbarous peoples. A negro tribe must be punished by the burning of its villages; without this one would get nowhere with such people. It is not owing to humaneness nor to a higher regard for law, but to shameful weakness, that the German empire is not now acting in accordance with these principles.[1]

It is self-evident that every state is not merely entitled to wage war, but to declare itself neutral in the wars of others, in so far as material conditions permit of a declaration of neutrality. If a state is not in position to uphold its neutrality, then it is mere mockery to speak of its neutrality. Neutrality needs defenders as much as do the respective belligerent states. Every armed soldier who crosses the frontier must be disarmed by the neutral state; if the latter is unable to do so, belligerent states are under certain circumstances justified in no longer recognizing the neutrality of the state, even if it let the armed enemy enter a single village.[2]

(1) *Kriegsbrauch im Landkriege* (1902)[3]

A vigorously prosecuted war can be directed not merely against the fighting force of the enemy state and its fortified places, but such a war should and must seek to destroy the total spiritual, material, and auxiliary resources of the state. Humanitarian claims, such as the sparing of life and property, can only be considered in so far as the nature and the purpose of the war permit.

Therefore, if the "reason for war" permits every belligerent state to use all means which make it possible to realize the object of the war, still, practice has taught that it is to one's own interest, on the one hand, to restrict the use of certain means of war, and, on the other hand, to renounce the use of others altogether. . . .[4]

But as the trend of thought of the past century was dominated by humanitarian considerations which frequently degenerated into sentimentality and unmanly emotionalism, attempts were not wanting to influence the development of the usages of war in a manner

---

[1] Treitschke, *Politik*, vol. 2, pp. 568-569.
[2] *Ibid.*, p. 572.
[3] *Kriegsbrauch im Landkriege* (Kriegsgeschichtliche Einzelschriften. Herausgegeben vom Grossen Generalstabe. Heft 31. Berlin, 1902). J. H. Morgan has translated and edited this book under the title *The War Book of the Great General Staff of the German Army* (New York, 1915), pp. 1-2.
[4] *Kriegsbrauch im Landkriege*, pp. 1-2.

not at all compatible with the nature of war and its ultimate object. . . .¹

A deep insight into the history of war will guard an officer against exaggerated humanitarian considerations; it will teach him that war cannot be waged without recourse to certain rigors; rather, that the only true humanity frequently lies in their ruthless application.. . . .¹

Every means of war, without which the object of the war cannot be attained, may be resorted to; on the other hand, every act of violence and of destruction not required for the realization of the object of the war is to be condemned.²

From these generally valid and fundamental principles it follows that wide limits are left to the subjective freedom and will of the commander.²

(m) *Friedrich von Bernhardi* (1849-)³

Whoever desires to direct the policy of a great state must have a perfectly clear idea of the aims which he pursues. . . .⁴

It is especially important in the times in which we are living that the German people should understand clearly the aims which they are pursuing and the tasks which they propose to themselves; for the German people stand undoubtedly at a turning point in their history. "World power or ruin" is the decisive question which calls for an answer. In the equivocal position in which we are now placed, that is to say, between the status of a manifold restricted European Continental power and the status of a World Power entitled and capable of securing everywhere to Germanism its justified place, we cannot persist for much longer. "This thing must be decided," Frederick the Great would say; for there is no standstill in political evolution. . . . In the midst of all the fine-sounding words of statesmen and the Utopian speeches of the apostles of peace, and in spite of the phantom-fetters by which European diplomacy endeavors to shackle the stupendous forces operating in the life of the nations, "I already hear God's advancing steps, tearing them asunder amid great calamity." ⁵

---

¹ *Kriegsbrauch im Landkriege*, p. 3.
² *Ibid.*, p. 9.
³ *Unsere Zukunft, ein Mahnwort an das deutsche Volk* (Stuttgart and Berlin; 1912), which appeared the year after his larger work, *Deutschland und der nächste Krieg*, had been published. The later book can be considered as an abridgment of the earlier, and the author's matured views are there stated with greater clearness, force, precision, and positiveness.
⁴ Bernhardi, *Unsere Zukunft*, p. 1.   ⁵ *Ibid.*, p. 3.

INTRODUCTION xciii

The German people must take thought of themselves and of their power; they must acquire that self-confidence which corresponds to this power, so that as a whole they may have the courage to strive for an enlarged circle of action and for a greater future such as the foremost minds of the nation have already contemplated. The mirrored image of its real greatness must be held up before the German nation so that it may thereby recognize the necessity of a further development and strengthen its will for the deed.[1]

Sure of our strength and of the value of our civilization, we Germans must, therefore, by all means strive to secure the political power which corresponds to our actual importance and to which we are entitled. It is certain that in this striving we shall meet with powerful opposition. On the other hand, it ought to be clear to us that if we are not staking our everything in order that we may become a real and very influential World Power, we will not be able to maintain our present position in the world. If our political power declines because we dare not assert it by acts or by deeds, it will not be long then before our economic importance will retrogress, and as in former times, the excess of our population will strengthen foreign powers, and as a result of our political decline, our intellectual power will also lose its freshness and its expansive force. It is only upon the enlarged stage of world politics that we will be able to solve our highest intellectual and moral tasks; as an exclusively European Continental power and as a Colonial power by the grace of England, we would sink back into that position of utter insignificance which we occupied before 1866. "World power or ruin" is the watchword forced upon us by the evolution of history. There is no alternative.[2]

The general aim of Germany's cultural and political tasks has been firmly established. Whoever recognizes the importance of Germanism in the field of human activities, an importance to which, in accordance with its achievements in the past, it is entitled in the future, will readily understand that Germanism must expand into a world power, in order to procure for the German people the necessary space for expansion and to secure to Germanism and to the German intellect that influence in the world to which they are entitled. That is our watchword, and as the Star of Bethlehem once pointed out to the Wise Men of the East the Way to the desired goal, even so shall this watchword bear a light before us on the way to a great and influential future.

[1] Bernhardi, *Unsere Zukunft*, p. 7. [2] *Ibid.*, pp. 25-26.

This goal cannot, however, be reached all at once. It must be won through self-sacrificing and self-denying labor.[1]

The task . . . consists in fostering, in accordance with their relative value, all the elements which are necessary and useful for the progress of the whole nation, and at the same time, within these limits, to secure for the individual the greatest possible degree of cultural possessions and of personal freedom. "Every expansion of the activities of the state," said Heinrich von Treitschke, "is a blessing and is reasonable as long as it stimulates the independent action of free and reasonable men; it is an evil if it stifles and stunts the independent action of free men."

In many quarters the view is held that this ideal can be realized only in the organized republic, because only under such an organization the individual can freely develop, and because the equality of all individuals finds actual expression, while in every form of monarchy there is a tendency towards servility. As against this view it should be observed that the republic ever leads to the rule of the majority, to the oppression of the minority, and that it lacks the power which might restrain the abuse of influential personalities over the ignorant masses, and further, that servility may luxuriate under a republican as well as under any other form of government. In monarchies, on the contrary, there is an independent power, a power essentially impartial, which stands above the strivings of the party, which recognizes the highest of the minority and is able to assert the will of the state with greater logic and with greater unity than the ever changing and vacillating majorities of a republic. History teaches that democracy is ever in danger of degenerating into demagogy; that the power of the state is controlled by the greedy and incalculable instincts of the masses and thus leads to moral and political collapse, while in a constitutionally restricted monarchy the power of the state is able to combat these destructive elements without the danger of such power being abused either by an individual or by a class.

In opposition to the radical political efforts of our day, it becomes, therefore, one of the most important cultural tasks of the German people to strengthen the monarchical idea, and to bring it to general acceptance. If we were to repudiate this idea, which has such a firm historical foundation among us, which we have inherited and of the correctness of which we are convinced, then in view of the individualistic character of the German people, we would, in all

---

[1] Bernhardi, *Unsere Zukunft*, p. 27.

probability, sink into complete anarchy and perish as a civilized nation. No nation more than our own needs a more coherent and closer unity in order to organize the opposing powers under one will.

This short survey of our cultural tasks shows that they can be solved only by great spiritual effort, such as from time immemorial has been the special attribute of the German people. German science must therefore remain conscious of its whole duty and contribute, with ever renewed energy, to the solution of the great world questions and scientifically to establish the moral duties of the people. At the same time, it must endeavor, with all means, to expand the mastery of men over nature, and thus to advance our economic development; but in all this striving, it must not forget its highest task, which consists in ever laying new foundations for the strengthening and expanding of ideal aims and indefatigable effort. . . .

To accomplish this purpose, three powerful auxiliary means are available to the state: the school, the press, and universal military service.[1]

These thoughts bring us immediately to a consideration of Germany's tasks which lie exclusively within the sphere of foreign policy.

As we have already shown elsewhere, Germany occupies a very dangerous political position. On nearly every side we are surrounded by hostile states whose united populations exceed that of Germany and which oppose all efforts of our foreign policy with a determined hostility and constantly confront us with the choice either to fight or to renounce. It is, therefore, our first duty to make an end of this state of affairs; *we must regain our political freedom,* before we can act as a World Power, we must establish our continental position as a power upon foundations that are unshakable by extending our sphere of power in Europe itself. In saying this, I do not, of course, have in mind a policy of conquest; such a policy would be against the spirit of the times and contrary to our true advantage; for in Europe we could acquire only territories whose subjugated populations would ever meet us in a spirit of hostility. But it seems necessary, after all, to have a final reckoning with France, and it seems furthermore quite possible to enlarge the Triple Alliance into a central European Union of States whose component elements would retain their complete independence; thus we would not merely improve our military position in essential respects, but give as well a broader basis to our over-sea policy.

[1] Bernhardi, *Unsere Zukunft,* pp. 31-33.

This Union of States would have to join the Triple Alliance, and the latter itself broadened beyond the scope of action which it has hitherto maintained. Its purely defensive professions have been proven sufficient in order to do justice to the interests of the parties composing it. These professions must be extended into a defensive and offensive alliance in accordance with a very definite regulation of the interests which are to be regarded as common to all concerned.

Only when we shall have attained this goal and freed ourselves from the condition of constraint which now prevents us from taking independent action, only then can we think of attending to the second task which accrues to us by reason of historic conditions: *the extension of our colonial empire and the strengthening of our world position.*

If we would assure to Germanism the respect to which it is entitled, and if we would win for German intelligence, for German labor and German idealism, that influence to which they are entitled by their civilizing importance, *then we must secure a firm footing on this earth and everywhere create points of support for our civilizing labor.* . . .[1]

Finally, however, although late, we have recognized the importance of colonial activities for the civilization of a people; that colonization which preserves emigrants for their nationality and thereby creates new centers for the civilization of this people, has become a factor of immeasurable importance for the future of the world. It will depend on colonization to what extent every people will, through the white race, take part in the mastery of the world; and it is quite conceivable that a country without colonies will no longer be counted among the great Powers of Europe, however powerful it may otherwise be.

Thus, if only for the general interest of civilization, it is our duty to strive to enlarge our colonial possessions and thus, although not politically, yet nationally, to gather together all Germans scattered throughout the whole world, and to regard German civilization as the most necessary factor of human progress; it is, furthermore, an imperative necessity that we should fulfill this duty. By all means we must strive to acquire new land, because we must politically preserve for the German Empire the millions of Germans who will be born in the future, and even under foreign climes procure for them not only food and labor, but a German life as well.[2]

[1] Bernhardi, *Unsere Zukunft*, pp. 39-40.
[2] *Ibid.*, p. 42.

INTRODUCTION

"Security and enlargement of power"; in these two words we may summarize our international political tasks. In order to be able to judge of the manner by which the object thus outlined may be achieved, we must become acquainted with the means available to German statecraft for its work, and we must at the same time consider the obstacles which, in present world conditions, we have to overcome. Finally, we must clearly realize that the struggle for high purpose, that the striving for an enlarged activity, in short, that *war itself* is a means for the progress of civilization.

The intellectual and moral powers which in the end are most important, cannot thrive and grow in the undisturbed quiet of a secure peace; they thrive and grow in the storm and stress of a great stirring time, under the influence of an active self-confident policy which places great, common aims before the people, which challenges self-sacrifice and which is not afraid of danger when the future and ideals of a noble people are at stake. Such a policy is the best educator of the people to patriotism, to moral earnestness and great successes.[1]

In view of the fact that the general law of humanity, which, to be sure, can never be codified, stands higher than all agreements based on formal law, it follows that international agreements have only a conditional value, that is to say, they are valid only so long as the conditions will at least generally remain like those under which they were concluded. It cannot be demanded of any state that it stake its own existence for the sake of a formal legal obligation, if such state can better and more securely maintain its existence in any other way.

Now, when by the assertion of the question of right, an agreement between states cannot be reached, the statesman has actually nothing else left but to appeal to *might* and to endeavor to find out how much he can accomplish when he throws the power of the state into the balance. This may sound contradictory, in view of the numerous negotiations which apparently take place in peaceful fashion between the different states: it is true, nevertheless, and has always been recognized by all *true* statesmen. . . .[2]

It is clear, furthermore, that actually existing and *effective* power is always the decisive factor in all negotiations, that is, therefore, all-important for every state which desires to assert itself in international relations and to enlarge its sphere of influence, to

[1] Bernhardi, *Unsere Zukunft*, p. 43.
[2] *Ibid.*, pp. 50-51.

increase its effective means of power, that is to say, its army, its navy, and its finances. . . .

The statesman who should deny the relation of interdependence between the defensive power and policy, and who should not, although he does not say so, constantly rely upon the living forces of the state, could never reckon upon success, if he were to enter the lists with a more cautious opponent.[1]

If in diplomatic negotiations, in the course of which we show our reliance upon our armed strength, we do not succeed by peaceful means either in carrying our point or in adjourning the decision: if, for instance, in case of serious differences concerning a question of territory, we cannot obtain its neutralization or the preservation of the *status quo*, then we must go to war and defend our justified claims. The stronger our armed forces are, the greater is the probability that we shall be successful. Besides, the better our army and navy are organized, the more highly developed is the military, moral, and mental strength of the nation and the greater is the confidence in the political determination of Germany among her allies, the more likely will be Germany's victory.

War is the continuation of policy with other means; at the same time, it is the most effective, even although the most dangerous means of policy. It may even be asserted that the *possibility of war* as one of the extreme means, is a necessary quality implied in the idea of policy. It is impossible to imagine a foreign policy without the possibility, under certain circumstances, of an appeal to arms. Between states unable to come to a peaceful settlement of opposing interests, there is no other gauge than war, and only a clear idea of the disadvantageous consequences which may result from war, can induce a state to sacrifice a part of its most valuable interests to its opponent.

This view of the matter has, to be sure, not been accepted generally. Even in many of the leading circles the erroneous view is held that real political advantages can be obtained through negotiations only, that is to say, that one may persuade the opponent to sacrifice his own interests; and in numerous social strata there is a manifest striving to banish war altogether from international life and to replace it with international legal organizations and courts of arbitration. These people think that war is barbarism which causes untold misery to mankind; that war opposes right through violence and arouses the brutal instincts of man; that it is in contradiction

[1] Bernhardi, *Unsere Zukunft*, p. 53.

to the Christian law of love, and therefore, that it must be characterized as unworthy of a modern and progressive civilized state. . . .

We must deprive this propaganda of all its props. We must restore the moral justification and political importance of war in the minds of the public. Its high significance as the mightiest promoter of civilization must be properly and generally recognized. We must realize that economic and personal interests alone must never be the decisive factor; that moral possessions and not material possessions are the ones which it is truly worth while striving for, and that sacrifices and suffering in the interest of a great cause place man on a higher plane than luxury and the greedy snatching after sensuous objects; in short, that war for ideal purposes or for the self-assertion of a noble people should not be regarded as barbarism, but as the *highest expression of true civilization;* and as a political necessity in the interest of biological, social, and moral progress.[1]

A continuous struggle for possession, for power and mastery dominates the relations between states, and right is generally respected only in so far as it can be made to coincide with it. While within the state the social struggle is regulated by law and by the public authority, there is no similar power of any sort which might act in the same way with regard to the society of states: there is neither a law of humanity nor a central power which might settle, moderate, or promote the interests of the parties involved. Therefore, when irreconcilable questions of interest come into conflict, there is, in the last analysis, nothing left but war to remedy that which is wrong and to afford the conditions for existence of which the forces of a promising people are in need.

If men and states everywhere would act unselfishly, this necessary result could be prevented. That would, however, predicate the condition of things which can neither be expected nor hoped for, and thus, from this single point of view, we must recognize the inevitableness of war.

It may happen, of course, that biologically weak nations unite and together constitute a superior force, in order to conquer a nation of vitality; frequently they may be successful for a time. But in the long run—and in the history of the world we must count by long periods of time—the stronger vitality gains the upper hand, and while the united opponents decline through the abuse of their victory,

---

[1] Bernhardi, *Unsere Zukunft,* pp. 54-56.

INTRODUCTION

the strong nation acquires new forces after a temporary defeat, forces which will be its final victory even over numerical superiority. German history is an eloquent illustration of this truth.

The biological law of war is found in the fact that it is conducive to the progressive development of humanity; for it is clear that the forces which prove their superiority in war, namely and above all, the intellectual and moral forces which can thrive only among a people of great vitality are at the same time the forces which make progressive development of civilization possible. For the very reason that they bear in themselves the elements of progress, they lead to the victory which provides for the people of strong vitality an enlarged and more favorable possibility for life and an increased influence. Without war we should probably find that less worthy and degenerate races would overcome the healthy and vigorous elements which would lead to general retrogression. The creative power of war lies in the fact that it causes *selection*. While war and war alone affects this selection, it becomes a biological necessity, a regulator in the life of mankind such as cannot be dispensed with, because without it there would result an unhealthy species, and a development which would exclude every sort of progress of the species, and hence, every sort of real civilization.[1]

Thus, if for biological reasons, we are led to the conviction that war is a necessary element of progress, we reach the same conclusion if we look at it from the moral point of view: for war is not only a biological necessity, but under circumstances it is a moral necessity, and as such an indispensable means of civilization. . . .[2]

It cannot be denied that this ideal side of war has its counterpart in the blessings of peace; still, history teaches that an all too long period of peace, in particular when it is secured through the abandonment of ideal possessions, and thus dishonors the people in its own eyes, cannot be a blessing for mankind. All narrow-minded selfish impulses extend their range of activity; idealism is destroyed by material enjoyment to which the austerity and simplicity of morals succumb. Money acquires an all-mighty and unjustified power and the proper meed of respect is denied to men of sturdy character.

The more deeply we study history, the more clearly we realize that peace is indeed the normal and desirable state, that, however, as human forces are constituted here on earth, the sweep of a martial tempest is required from time to time, in order to purify the moral atmosphere. Political tensions may become so

[1] Bernhardi, *Unsere Zukunft*, pp. 59-60.   [2] *Ibid.*, p. 63.

great, the contending interests may become so manifold and involved that the Gordian knot of these difficulties can be cut with the sword only, for it alone is able to bring the real relations of power into the light and to relegate arrogance to its proper place.

Therefore, when power, understood in its higher sense, is put into question—the power to solve one's own problems of civilization and to live for one's own ideals—and when no accord can be effected to secure the highest possessions of a people, *war then becomes a moral duty!* . . .

In view of the compelling logic of these considerations, it seems most surprising that the peace movement could acquire so great an influence. This fact may be explained in part by this other fact that it has been supported by very important private interests which operate through huge moneyed capital. . . .

A clear illustration of this may be found in the contrast between the views of the United States of North America and Germany with special reference to the question of peace, which views control public opinion in the two countries respectively.

In glorious battles, the United States has conquered its independence and unity; it has, as a result, acquired a heritage of glory, self-confidence and spirit of liberty which has given its impress to the nation, for a measurable space of time. At present, the Union has many competitors, but no enemies. Its relations with England are to some extent secured by the community of language, which is often but falsely interpreted as a community of race; even the present existing differences of interests with Japan—even if some day war were to break out between them—cannot seriously endanger the vital interests of the powerful republic. For a measurable space of time, America need not fear over-population; in the North and in the South of the United States there are wide expanses of territory to which, in case of need, the surplus population may be diverted without detriment to the American spirit. The wealth of the natural resources of the country which make it independent of foreign countries, and the spirit of enterprise of the people, on a large scale, secure to the country the most favorable conditions for peaceful competition. At the same time, the struggle with nature, which has not yet been subjected and mastered everywhere, offers an opportunity to steel the national muscles to undertake great and difficult tasks.

Under these circumstances it is quite natural that the people of that country should, in general, regard the peace movement with sympathy, for peace can only bring them advantages, while war might, to all appearances, impede the development of the country and disturb the security of the money market.

Look at Germany and see how different its position is! Since the collapse of its ancient splendor, the German people has had to defend itself against hostile forces. Through difficult wars it has wrested from the Slavs its infertile territories in the East, and to-day the Slavonic flood surges against its frontier with increased hostility. In the West and in the South, the German people had to defend itself against the Romanic peoples and through struggles extending over centuries it has had to defend its political independence without having been able to disarm the fanatical hostility of the French. The most recent political and economic rise of Germany has at last made England also our bitter enemy, for England is afraid to lose her mastery of the sea, and the supremacy of her trade. In all parts of the earth she meets us in hostile fashion and opposes our colonial expansion which for us is a vital question.

When we consider all these conditions it will be readily understood why the idea of universal peace has many adherents in Germany but that it meets with but little success among the masses of the patriotic and of the educated people. History has taught us that a state situated as ours is can assert itself only with sword in hand. . . .[1]

If we regard every war as a breach of right, and if we regard the absolute predominance of right not only as the highest expression of civilization, but also as the necessary foundation of the true welfare of the state, we cannot but conclude that the differences arising between states should be settled through arbitration, by looking upon these differences as resulting from different conceptions of that which is right.

This idea is extremely one-sided, for in the disagreements between great states we are concerned in no way, as we have seen already, with questions of right only, but especially with questions of power which formal law can never adjudicate. Still, there is much that is good in this idea, and this we cannot deny when we are considering a question of right. For this reason, arbitration treaties have been entered into between numerous states dealing with purely legal questions. When it is sought, however, to extend the scope of such treaties, to include in them the settlement of questions of power and thus to attribute to them a validity extending to all questions—as

[1] Bernhardi, *Unsere Zukunft*, pp. 65-68.

has been most recently the case with the United States—it has ever appeared that very definite restrictions have been laid upon the importance of international arbitration proceedings.[1]

A general law of humanity is therefore as impossible as is a general understanding of right. Individual questions and others of only secondary importance may indeed be regulated by international legal rules; all legal questions arising in the life of all nations cannot be sought in written provisions. It will never be possible to establish by law, how far the will to power is or is not justified. Even if this were attempted, and even if an all-encompassing international law were written, no self-respecting people would sacrifice to such a law its *own* conception of that which is right without surrendering its own ideals, without submitting to an injustice which violates its own conception of right and without dishonoring itself. . . .

Thus, the international court of arbitration lacks a generally recognized *legal* and *material* basis for its decisions, and I almost believe that even the second question with regard to the power which is to enforce its decisions, must be answered in a manner unfavorable to the champions of universal courts of arbitration.

In America, in 1908, the then Secretary of State, Elihu Root, expressed the opinion that the High Court of International Justice established by the Second Hague Conference could actually, *in virtue of the pressure exercised by public opinion,* reach final and unobjectionable decisions; and I believe that the present leaders of the American Peace Movement share this view. I think, however, that the conception of the uniformity of international views and its compelling force is greatly overestimated.

In reality, public opinion cannot be the same throughout the world, for the very reason that the conceptions of right in the different nations differ one from the other, and there would be nothing else to do in order to carry out the will of the court of arbitration, in case one of the parties would not submit, except to have recourse to war which it is precisely intended to prevent. In that case, who would wage the necessary war? We believe that on the sole question of solving this difficulty the idea of a universal court of arbitration will fall. Only in a universal state, as in the ancient Roman empire, could one imagine an arbitral court for the settlement of disputes between the individual component elements. But it will hardly be possible ever to establish such a universal state. To be

[1] Bernhardi, *Unsere Zukunft,* pp. 69-70.

sure, the idea of a world organization of the English speaking peoples has been frequently considered, and in England this aim is being openly pursued. I believe, however, that the world would not long put up with such a yoke, and at all events, I am quite certain that we Germans would never submit to it.

As long, therefore, as we live in the system of states as at present organized, the Imperial German Chancellor was right when declaring in a speech which he delivered on March 30, 1911, that arbitral treaties between states would have to be limited to clearly defined questions of right—even as I have stated in this present discussion—and that, on the other hand, a general arbitral treaty between two states can in no manner guarantee enduring peace between them. In matters touching upon the vital interests of the two states, it would lose all of its effect.

It should finally be observed, that even the practical consequences of an accepted arbitral decision can never take the place of a victory won by arms, not even of the state in whose interest the decision might be rendered. . . .

General treaties of arbitration could not but be especially dangerous to an upward-striving people which, like the German people, has not yet reached the height of its political and national development, and which is compelled to enlarge its power in order to do justice to its cultural tasks. . . .[1]

War will always remain a forcible means of policy which, under any circumstances, imposes great sacrifices upon the one resorting to it, and appears, therefore, only justifiable when the question at issue concerns the highest vital interests of really civilized peoples. It is, therefore, undoubtedly the duty of mankind to confine the political use of war to such cases, and as far as possible to eliminate all such causes of war as have nothing whatever to do with the great interests of mankind. Whoever resolves upon war takes a great responsibility upon himself; we must, therefore, consider more in detail the question as to the practical political aims which may justify the resort to arms.

It is exceedingly difficult to answer this question in a generally acceptable way. It seems to me, however, that it may be to some extent satisfactorily answered if we consider the nature of the task of the state. . . .

If it is a fact, as we have attempted to show in our discussion, that the task of the state consists in promoting the highest intellec-

[1] Bernhardi, *Unsere Zukunft*, pp. 71-74.

tual and moral development of its citizens and to contribute to the education of mankind, then the personal actions of the state must of necessity be subject to moral laws, and war must be justified on moral grounds. But, of course, we must not allow ourselves to be misled in this matter, that is to say, we must not apply the conception of individual morality to that of the state. The morality of the state must rather grow out of its own special nature; the moral judgment of the state must be sought in the nature and in the object of the existence of the state itself, even as the morality of the individual has its roots in its personal existence and in its social duties.

But the essence of the state is *power* because when in virtue of an increasing political power it is able, in its competition with the rest of the peoples, to do justice to its highest cultural tasks and to offer to its citizens ever wider and more advantageous possibilities of existence and of development. . . .

To sacrifice its own interests to those of a foreign state, no matter under what pretext, is, therefore, always an immoral act, because it is contrary to self-assertion which is the foremost task of the state. Weakness is, however, the most reprehensible and most contemptible political sin. It is, as Treitschke has expressed it, the sin against the Holy Ghost of policy. Equally immoral it is if policy is not directed to increase the power of the state which is needed as the necessary basis for the further cultural development of the people.[1]

Therefore, we see clearly, that for us Germans it is not only practically expedient but morally necessary to carry on an honest but at the same time strong, determined policy of power, a policy which looks not only to the welfare of the present, but above all to the organization of our national future; that arbitral courts in important political questions only impede our progressive development; finally that we have the right and the duty to take up arms when irreconcilable differences arise in our international relations and when we realize that the neighboring states intend to prevent and to repress our political development which is historically and biologically necessary.[2]

We must make the best of things as they are. The tension between the two states (England and Germany) will continue until the dispute has been settled either by resort to arms or until one of the two states voluntarily yields its point of view.

As a yielding to the demands and claims of England would be

[1] Bernhardi, *Unsere Zukunft*, pp. 74-75.
[2] *Ibid.*, pp. 77-78.

for us the same as a complete sacrifice of our political and national future, we must therefore resolve to view that other possibility and see if England will either extend her hand to us to effect an understanding, or if she will compel us to defend our best national claims with arms in hand.

Under these circumstances there still remains the possibility of a limited understanding with England, an understanding which would not render a final battle impossible, but which might put it off for a little while, if in doing so, we thought it might be of advantage to us. It is worth the trouble to study this possibility more in detail, because many of our people count upon such an understanding. I believe that in this expectation we shall be likewise miserably disappointed.[1]

We need not, therefore, give up the attempt to bring about such an understanding upon an acceptable basis, but we must draw a sharp line beyond which we shall make no concessions, and at the same time we must prepare with the utmost energy for the more probable result: that the sought for understanding will not be realized.

Such a result, however, means war, not only war with England, but with the United Powers of the Triple Entente. In view of the present world state of affairs it is our imperative duty to create the most favorable conditions possible for that struggle.[2]

To neglect the defensive power and thus undermine the defensive force of a people is the greatest crime that can be committed. The school of arms is the true iron-springs for character, and the defensive power based upon a healthy defensive force offers at all times to the state the only security and the only guarantee of a favorable political, social, and cultural development, which, as we well know, are all interdependent. The moral, the intellectual, and physical defensive power is at the same time the truest measure of civilization; it finds its living expression in actual defensive power. When the latter is neglected, or when it loses respect among the people, the organism of the nation sickens and gives rise to ominous agitations; on the other hand, a superior and properly used defensive power always guarantees political success, which in turn results in a moral economic and cultural progress.

The most recent history clearly shows this to be the truth.[3]

In view of this recognition, it is the imperative duty of every upwards-striving state to inquire ever and anon whether or not

[1] Bernhardi, *Unsere Zukunft*, pp. 100-101.
[2] *Ibid.*, p. 102.
[3] *Ibid.*, p. 103.

sufficient attention has been given to the improvement of the defensive force, whether or not the military organization responds to the demands of the political state of affairs, and whether or not the defensive force is sufficient to put the totality of the people on a military basis in such manner that the people will come to regard the benefits of military training as a high attribute. This self-examination becomes particularly necessary in times when great world-historic decisions are felt and recognized by everyone as impending.[1]

Today the German Empire finds itself in this position. It must be clear even to the most short-sighted—as has already been shown in another part of this discussion—that in the present conditions of world affairs Germany is confronted by the question as to whether she will seek and secure equal rights and privileges with the great world powers, England, Russia, and the United States, or whether in the matter of the European balance of power she will permit herself to be shoved to the level of a second-rate state and at the same time lose gradually her economic position as a great power.

We must not allow ourselves to be deceived by the constantly reëmphasized love of peace, or by the official agreement of the various cabinets! These diplomatic measures are, after all, only a cloak under which every state hides its own interests, and this cloak will be thrown off as soon as the favorable opportunity affords of the realization of the individual aims of the respective states. Power is the only regulator of policy, and every state would commit a crime against itself if at the favorable moment it did not make use of its power. We must take account of this and of everything else if in the last analysis we are not to be deceived and pay with our blood for our illusion.[2]

When we come to study the political history of the states, we soon reach the conclusion that the greatest successes have everywhere been obtained where an active policy with sharply defined aims and purposes has uninterruptedly endeavored to organize and utilize the state of world's affairs for its own advantage, and in all of its enterprises has relied only upon the actually existing means of power and recognized no other law than the law of its own advantage. On the other hand, when success has been expected from an inactive and waiting policy with the uncertain prospect that possibly some advantage might be snatched, or when the conduct of the state was even

[1] Bernhardi, *Unsere Zukunft*, p. 105.
[2] *Ibid.*, p. 111.

influenced by the sentimental peace dreams of its statesmen, the national policy was, as a rule, without beneficial results if it did not actually lead to ruin.

That this is so, and that it will ever remain so is predicated by the nature of things.[1]

Foreign policy is a struggle between opposing interests, and whoever does not retain the initiative in this struggle, will soon lose his favorable position and find himself surrounded by the pack of his enemies. . . .

I have already shown on the whole the aims for which we must strive. We are no longer to consider the means by which these aims may be attained. Let us, therefore, once more summarize the leading ideas which should guide our foreign policy:

Security of our position as a power on the European Continent can be attained only, provided we succeed in breaking the Triple Entente, and in reducing France, which cannot, once and for all, be pursuaded to coöperate with us, to that position which she deserves.

Our political power can be enlarged by gathering in a central European union all the middle European states which still occupy an independent position, a union which must not be concluded in a one-sided manner only for the purpose of defense, but a union for defense and offense which must be able actually to look after the manifold interests of its members.

This object can, in all probability, be realized only after a victorious war which shall finally strengthen the confidence in German power and make it impossible for its opponent to thwart our aims by force.

Enlargement of our colonial possessions and acquisition of colonies fit for settlements.

Within this field much can perhaps be accomplished by peaceful means. But we must not conceal from ourselves the fact that England will undoubtedly oppose all colonial acquisition that might actually increase our power, and prevent us by all means, to acquire coaling stations and supporting points for our fleet abroad. Colonies fit for settlement cannot be secured without military action against other states.

Whithersoever we turn our eyes we find that the road to the peaceful realization of our aims is barred and that we are confronted by the alternative of either giving up our plans or of preparing ourselves for the necessity of obtaining our objects by the sword. An

---

[1] Bernhardi, *Unsere Zukunft*, p. 132.

understanding with England by reason of which she would have to recognize the justice and necessity of our efforts and obligate herself to support us in our political efforts, would indeed essentially diminish the necessity of military complications. But, as we have already shown, we cannot reckon with such an understanding. England's hostility toward us is rather founded upon our entire political system and we will merely harm our most essential interests if we chase after the phantom of such an understanding or even if we make sacrifices in order to bring this mirage within our reach.

Even as Bismarck himself clearly and finally recognized that a further successful development of Prussia and of Germany was possible only after the rivalry between Austria and Prussia had been finally settled, even so must every unprejudiced man have now been convinced that Germany's further development as a world power is possible only when the rivalry with England shall have been settled finally; and even as a cordial alliance between Germany and Austria had become possible only after Austria's defeat in the war of 1899, so we shall come to the settlement with England which is desirable from every point of view, only after we shall some day have crossed swords with her. As long as our foreign policy does not make this its leading thought, it will, in my judgment, be forced to it without accomplishing much success.

It is evident that we need not acknowledge publicly this as our view of world conditions, nor openly submit our real political aims to our opponents; we may indeed earnestly endeavor to realize our aims by peaceful means and to win our opponents over to our viewpoint without resort to war. We must not, however, permit of our taking a single step which might be in conflict with our ultimate aims, and we must indefatigably keep before our eyes our *real task*, that is to say we must prepare politically and militarily for the apparently unavoidable struggle and to make sure of our ultimate success. . . .[1]

A farsighted policy is in such a case a command of self-preservation and political wisdom. Great danger lurks in a waiting policy. The truth of this is clearly shown by the history of our past. . . .

. . . Let us be on our guard not to wait again until our allies are defeated and we are placed before the choice of either fighting alone or to enter war under the most unfavorable conditions. Not only the army and the fleet, but our foreign policy also must be ready for immediate action.

[1] Bernhardi, *Unsere Zukunft*, pp. 133-135.

Our foreign policy must be restlessly active and bring about the most favorable conditions for the approaching struggle. Although, in order to attain special aims, our foreign policy may for the time being coöperate with the other great powers, still it must always bear in mind that the agreement with the powers of the Triple Entente can, in its nature, be only provisional and confined to definite objects; that the continuance of the agreement is guaranteed by nothing except paper which bears signatures; therefore, our foreign policy must be resolved to interfere by force of arms, whenever our interests are seriously endangered: for the responsibility of bringing about a necessary war under favorable conditions is much smaller than the responsibility of making an unfortunate war inevitable for the sake of momentary advantages or from lack of decision. . . .[1]

The foregoing pages were written before a decision had been reached in Turkey. . . .

For a long time, the Turkish Empire has been in the process of disintegration; still it was absolutely in the interests of the Triple Alliance to delay the absolute expulsion of the Turks from Europe until the great European War, which will decide the fate of the middle European states, shall have been fought.

The Triple Alliance will now have to wage this war under far less favorable conditions.

Before Turkey's defeat by the River Ergene, the Triple Alliance, in case of a European War, could count upon coöperation, on its side, by Turkey and Roumania. . . . Today all this has changed and a state of affairs has been created which bears the greatest dangers for Germany and her allies.

If Austria recognizes the enlargement of the Balkan states in the hope of securing in them an authoritative influence, she will clash with Russia, which is pursuing the same object. . . . Serbia at least will ever be hostile to Austria as long as several million Serbs are under Austrian rule who strive for a reunion with their compatriots; and, furthermore, as long as the Serbian state strives to secure an outlet on the Adriatic Sea, and she will never cease to work to that end. . . .

Roumania also will in all probability cease to be a possible future auxiliary power of the Triple Alliance. For the present she still sides, it is true, with the middle-European group of states, in order to secure through the latter an enlarged territory to the detriment

[1] Bernhardi, *Unsere Zukunft*, pp. 141-142.

of Bulgaria. It seems, however, more than doubtful whether she will be able to continue in this attitude. Wedged in between the mighty Russia and a considerably enlarged Bulgaria, Roumania will no longer be able to continue an independent policy, but in all probability will either completely fall under the influence of Russia or join the Balkan union. In either case she can hope for nothing more from the Triple Alliance, and forced by necessity, she will more or less side with our enemies. . . .[1]

Because of all these conditions the danger of a general war has been increased. The strained relations alone which exist between Austria and Serbia may possibly lead to such a war. But, even if that struggle may for the moment be settled, the Austro-Serbian contentions will continue, and it can scarcely be thought that the powers of the Triple Entente will not exploit the advantageous position in which they now find themselves, supported and urged thereto by public opinion, and attempt to force their orders upon Germany. It would be but the logical and natural consequence of their combined policy. There is still hope, of course, that it might be possible to use the opposing interests of Russia and England, arising from the Balkan question, in such a manner that coöperation against Germany on the part of these two powers might be prevented. Such a solution is, however, not probable. For this reason a far-sighted and cautious policy must take into account the possibility of a military conflict. Up to the present time France and Russia have not considered the present moment quite favorable for waging war. The unexpected Balkan events have totally altered their position also. Under these circumstances, it behooves those who conduct our foreign policy to watch out.

All the weak-spirited adherents of a "small policy," who ever and anon attempt to depress the justified claims of our people, who warn us to be moderate in our aims, who do not wish to know anything about a real world policy, and wish to see Germany persist in the narrow sphere of action of a Continental power, these adherents will, under the momentary circumstances, certainly assert themselves in order to prove that Germany has no sort of vital interests to look after in the Balkans and to warn against every attempt to any energetic action. Do not desire anything! Do not strive for anything! And above all, do not risk anything! These represent the watchword of those Philistine politicians who wish for peace above all things, even if the greatness and future of our Fatherland must be sacrificed

[1] Bernhardi, *Unsere Zukunft*, pp. 147-150.

for it. They will certainly not fail to point emphatically to the dangers of a war against superior opponents and demand that the Government should through "moderate" conduct avoid the war, no matter what the circumstances, instead of preparing for it by energetic action. . . .

Our enemies would even deprive us of our position of power which we have won through two victorious wars, and the world-wide trade, which increases our national wealth from year to year. Even as they would not that Frederick the Great should have "Silesia" nor the "hundred millions in his treasury," even so would they now pull us down and in its germ stifle our world-importance. . . .

Our claim to world importance may certainly lead to a war similar to the Seven Years' War; but we shall be as victorious in that war as Prussia's heroic king was in the Seven Years' War. That is my absolute and joyous confidence. . . .

Our future lies in our own hands.

The weak-spirited will discuss the financial question and complain that we cannot afford to spend the money necessary to wage such a war. I believe that in case of need we can provide the necessary money through a domestic loan. . . .

It seems absolutely criminal, in the tremendously wealthy Germany, to talk of financial difficulties when the future of the state and of the nation is at stake.

Germany does not lack money for the purpose of asserting its position; but we must have the courage to will great things and the active force to attain great things.

Every one of us must do a man's work; all true Germans must, as one, and willing to sacrifice, gather around the Emperor, and be ready at all times, with treasure and blood, to serve the honor, the greatness, and the future of the German people: through battle to victory![1]

(n) *Theobald von Bethmann-Hollweg* (1856-)

We are now in a state of necessity, and necessity knows no law. Our troops have occupied Luxembourg and perhaps are already on Belgian soil. Gentlemen, that is contrary to the dictates of international law. It is true that the French government has declared at Brussels that France is willing to respect the neutrality of Bel-

---

[1] Von Bernhardi, *Unsere Zukunft*, pp. 151-154.

gium, as long as her opponent respects it. We knew, however, that France stood ready for invasion. France could wait, but we could not wait. A French movement upon our flank upon the Lower Rhine might have been disastrous. So we were compelled to override the just protest of the Luxembourg and Belgian governments. The wrong —I speak openly—that we are committing we will endeavor to make good as soon as our military goal has been reached. Anybody who is threatened as we are threatened, and is fighting for his highest possessions, can only have one thought—how he is to hack his way through. . . .[1]

I found the Chancellor very agitated. His Excellency at once began an harangue which lasted for about twenty minutes. He said that the step taken by His Majesty's government was terrible to a degree; just for a word—"neutrality," a word which in war time had so often been disregarded—just for a scrap of paper Great Britain was going to make war on a kindred nation who desired nothing better than to be friends with her. . . .[2]

---

[1] Speech of the Imperial German Chancellor in the Reichstag, August 4, 1914. (London *Times*, August 11, 1914).

At the session of the Reichstag on August 27, 1915, the Imperial German Chancellor is reported to have said:

"On the part of Germany no attempt has ever been made to justify the German invasion of Belgium through subsequent allegations of guilty conduct on the part of the Belgian Government." (*Norddeutsche Allgemeine Zeitung*, August 28, 1915, p. 1.)

[2] *The British Blue Book* (No. 1), d. No. 160; *Diplomatic Documents Relating to the Outbreak of the European War*, vol. 2, p. 1007.

I was received this morning [August 4] at 9 o'clock by the Minister for Foreign Affairs. He said to me: "We have been obliged by absolute necessity to address to your Government the request of which you are aware. . . . It is only with the utmost anguish (*la mort dans l'âme*) that the Emperor and the Government have seen themselves obliged to come to this decision. For me it is the most painful one that I have ever had to make. . . . Germany has nothing with which to reproach Belgium, whose attitude has always been correct." . . .

On August 5 . . . I was received by the Under Secretary of State. Herr Zimmermann expressed to me, with much emotion, his profound regrets for the cause of my departure. . . . He sought no pretext to excuse the violation of our neutrality. He did not invoke the supposed French plan . . . of passing through Belgium in order to attack Germany on the lower Rhine. . . . [To all remonstrances he] simply replied that the Department for Foreign Affairs was powerless. Since the order for mobilization had been issued . . . all power now belonged to the military authorities. It was they who had considered the invasion of Belgium to be an indispensable operation of war. . . . (Reports of Baron Beyens, Belgian Minister at Berlin, to the Belgian Foreign Minister, *Belgian Grey Book* (No. 2), docs. 25, 51, 52; *Diplomatic Documents Relating to the Outbreak of the European War*, part 1, pp. 448, 474-477.)

(o) *William II, German Emperor and King of Prussia* (1859-)

Here it was that the Great Elector, by his own right, created himself the sovereign Duke in Prussia; here his son set the king's crown upon his head; and the sovereign house of Brandenburg thus became one of the European powers. . . . And here my grandfather, again, by his own right, set the Prussian crown upon his head, once more distinctly emphasizing the fact that it was accorded him by the will of God alone and not by parliament or by any assemblage of the people or by popular vote, and that he thus looked upon himself as the chosen instrument of Heaven and as such performed his duties as regent and sovereign. . . .

Looking upon myself as the instrument of the Lord, without regard for daily opinions and intentions, I go my way. . . .[1]

---

[1] Speech at Königsberg, August 25, 1910; Gauss, *The German Emperor as shown in his Public Utterances* (New York, 1915), pp. 280-284.

On other occasions the Emperor William has expressed the theory of divine right in pithy and telling phrases, such as "You Germans have only one will, and that is My will; there is only one law, and that is My law." "*Sic volo, sic jubeo.*" "Only one master in this country. That is I, and who opposes Me I shall crush to pieces." (See Barker's *Foundations of Germany*, London, 1916, p. 120.)

What William II meant by his statement that he would crush anyone standing in his way is evidenced by the treatment of Belgium.

In 1914 he said in his letter of August 14, to the President of the United States, that it was necessary for strategic reasons to invade Belgium. (Post.)

In 1910, as the guest of the King and Queen of Belgium he said, in an address delivered on October 27th at the Royal Palace in Brussels:

"It is with friendliest sympathy that I and all Germany follow the astounding results which have accrued to the untiring energy of the Belgian people in all departments of trade and industry, the crowning display of which we have seen in the brilliantly successful World Exposition of this year. Belgian commerce embraces the whole circle of the earth, and it is in the peaceful work of culture that Germans and Belgians everywhere meet. Their cultivation of the more spiritual arts fills us with similar wonder when we behold to what a conspicuous place the poets and artists of Belgium have attained. May the trustful and friendly feelings, to which in recent times the relations of our governments bore such pleasing evidence, be ever more closely preserved! From your Majesty's reign may happiness and blessing stream forth upon your house and upon your people! It is with this wish, which comes from the very depths of my heart, that I propose long life to your Majesties, the King and Queen of the Belgians!" (Gauss, *The German Emperor as shown in his Public Utterances*, pp. 291-292.)

4. DECLARATIONS OF A STATE OF WAR.[1]

1914

July	28	Austria	vs.	Serbia
August	1	Germany	vs.	Russia
August	3	Germany	vs.	France
August	3	France	vs.	Germany
August	4	Germany	vs.	Belgium
August	4	Great Britain	vs.	Germany
August	6	Austria	vs.	Russia
August	6	Serbia	vs.	Germany
August	8	Montenegro	vs.	Austria
August	9	Montenegro	vs.	Germany
August	9	Austria	vs.	Montenegro
August	13	Great Britain	vs.	Austria
August	13	France	vs.	Austria
August	23	Japan	vs.	Germany
August	27	Austria	vs.	Japan [2]
August	28	Austria	vs.	Belgium
November	3	Russia	vs.	Turkey
November	5	France	vs.	Turkey
November	5	Great Britain	vs.	Turkey
November	23	Turkey	vs.	Allies
November	23	Portugal	vs.	Germany [3]
December	2	Serbia	vs.	Turkey

1915

May	19	Portugal	vs.	Germany [4]
May	24	Italy	vs.	Austria
May	24	San Marino	vs.	Austria
August	21	Italy	vs.	Turkey
October	14	Bulgaria	vs.	Serbia
October	15	Great Britain	vs.	Bulgaria
October	16	Serbia	vs.	Bulgaria
October	16	France	vs.	Bulgaria
October	19	Russia	vs.	Bulgaria
October	19	Italy	vs.	Bulgaria

1916

March	9	Germany	vs.	Portugal
August	27	Roumania	vs.	Austria [5]
August	28	Italy	vs.	Germany
August	29	Turkey	vs.	Roumania
September	14	Germany	vs.	Roumania
November	28	Greece (Provisional Government)	vs.	Bulgaria
November	28	Greece (Provisional Government)	vs.	Germany

[1] The following list is, with two exceptions, identical with that published on December 11, 1917, in the *Official Bulletin* issued by the Committee on Public Information. In the first place, the declaration of Serbia against Germany appears to have been made August 6, instead of August 9, 1914, as stated by the *Bulletin*. In the second place, that of Japan against Germany appears to have been made August 23, 1914, instead of August 23, 1917, as stated by the *Bulletin*.

[2] On August 27, 1914, the Austro-Hungarian Ambassador to the United States notified the Department of State that Austria-Hungary had severed diplomatic relations with Japan and that the Austrian cruiser *Queen Elizabeth* had been ordered to join the German fleet in the Far East. On this information, the Department of State issued a neutrality proclamation, dated August 27, 1914. Neither Government has issued a declaration of war.

[3] Resolution passed authorizing military intervention as ally of England. *Official Bulletin*, Dec. 11, 1917.

[4] Military aid granted. *Official Bulletin*, Dec. 11, 1917.

[5] Allies of Austria also consider it a declaration. *Official Bulletin*, Dec. 11, 1917.

4. DECLARATIONS OF A STATE OF WAR (*Cont.*).

1917

April	6	United States	vs.	Germany
April	7	Cuba	vs.	Germany
April	7	Panama	vs.	Germany
July	2	Greece (Government of Alexander)	vs.	Bulgaria
July	2	Greece (Government of Alexander)	vs.	Germany
July	22	Siam	vs.	Austria
July	22	Siam	vs.	Germany
August	4	Liberia	vs.	Germany
August	14	China	vs.	Austria
August	14	China	vs.	Germany
October	26	Brazil	vs.	Germany
December	7	United States	vs.	Austria

A SURVEY OF INTERNATIONAL RELATIONS BETWEEN THE UNITED STATES AND GERMANY

CHAPTER I

GENESIS OF THE WAR OF 1914

While the purpose of the present volume is not to dwell upon the causes of the European War, but to state and consider the reasons which led the United States, on April 6, 1917, to declare the existence of a state of war with the Imperial German Government, it is nevertheless desirable to chronicle, by way of introduction, the events immediately preceding the declaration of war by Germany against Russia on August 1, 1914, and to sketch briefly the course of events since Prussia started out to weld the German states into an empire under its leadership, and since this empire, an enlarged Prussia,[1] started out to dominate the world, of which the United States is a part.

For generations it had been the desire and the longing of the German-speaking peoples, split up into hundreds of insignificant states and petty principalities, to be united into a large and powerful nation which would administer to their comforts at home and make them respected abroad. The Holy Roman Empire, which it has been wittily said was neither Holy nor Roman, was dissolved in 1806 as a consequence of the Napoleonic Wars, and upon the reorganization of Europe in 1814-15 at the Congress of Vienna the German

---

[1] When, one day, Bismarck observed to William I that the Empire would not give its consent in the matter of a certain political decision, the latter, in a moment of indignation, replied: "What, the Empire! the Empire, as you know, is merely an extended Prussia." This expresses the thing trooper fashion, but it is true. (Treitschke, *Politik*, vol. 1, p. 40.)

Prussia was not swallowed up in Germany. This expression, which is met with even in our time, denotes the exact opposite of the palpable fact: Prussia extended its own institutions over the rest of Germany. (*Ibid.*, vol. 2, p. 339.)

While the Federal States, as far as possible, must seek to prevent inequality between the members, yet, the German Empire rests upon this very inequality. That is to say, there is within the Empire one leading state which has federatively annexed and subordinated the other states to itself. What would become of Germany, if the Prussian State should cease to be? The German Empire, in such a case, could not continue to exist at all. From this results a truth unpleasant to most people, yet not at all offensive to non-Prussian people, to the effect, that within this German Empire, Prussia alone of the former German States has preserved its sovereignty. Prussia alone has remained a sovereign state. Prussia has not lost the right of arms; nor need Prussia permit other states to curtail its sovereign rights. The German Emperor is also the King of Prussia; he is the military leader of the nation, and we are indulging in unavailing hairsplitting when we imagine cases in which the German Emperor and the King of Prussia might come into conflict with one another. (*Ibid.*, pp. 343-344.)

States were loosely confederated under the leadership of Austria. The presence in the Confederation of Austria, composed in large part of foreign peoples, was disagreeable to the advocates of a union of the German States as such, and especially so to Prussia because it aspired to a leadership which was inconsistent with the presidency of the Confederation held by Austria.

In 1848 the overthrow of Louis Philippe led to revolutionary outbreaks in Germany and elsewhere, and representatives of the German people meeting in Frankfort sought to create an empire, from which Austria was to be excluded, and offered the crown to Frederick William IV, then King of Prussia. The offer was rejected. The reason given for the refusal was that Frederick William might have accepted the crown had it been freely offered to him by the German princes, but that he would never stoop "to pick up a crown out of the gutter."

In 1858, Frederick William, whose conduct had been erratic for years, was recognized as insane and his brother, Prince William, became Prince Regent. Upon the death of Frederick William in 1861 without children, Prince William became William I of Prussia, and later German Emperor. A year later Bismarck became Prime Minister, and in less than a decade thereafter the German Confederation was dissolved, Austria was excluded from the circle of German States, and the States, united in theory into a German empire, were in fact merged into an enlarged Prussia.

It had long been the ambition of Prussia to assume the leadership of the German States, and from the time of Frederick the Great the possibility of such leadership was evident. What Frederick began Bismarck finished, and the policy of Prussia, controlled and carried to a successful conclusion by Bismarck, was to put an end to the rivalry of Austria by crushing and excluding it from the circle of German States, in order that Prussia might be, in fact and in theory, the leader of the new Germany.

To accomplish this purpose two wars of the first water were "necessary," one with Austria, the other with France; and the statesmanship of Bismarck was equal to each occasion.

Denmark was to be the first victim on the altar of German nationalism.

For present purposes it is sufficient to say that the Duchies of Schleswig-Holstein, although separate, were closely united under a common Duke; that the northern part of Schleswig was wholly Danish, the southern slightly so; that Holstein was wholly German and that, while the King of Denmark was Duke of both, Holstein formed a part of the German Confederation, just as Hanover under an English king formed a part of the Holy Roman Empire and of its successor, the German Confederation. The Danes, very unwisely as it happened, attempted to stamp out the German element in Schleswig, and, contrary to the Treaty of London of 1852,[1] by which the Powers had settled the affairs of the Duchies, practically annexed Schleswig, leaving Holstein a part of the Confederation. As this body refused to intervene in the affairs of Schleswig, because the Duchy was beyond its sphere of influence, Bismarck turned to Austria to maintain the sanctity of a treaty to which both were parties. Austria consented, and an ultimatum was, on January 16, 1864, dispatched to Denmark, ordering a withdrawal within the space of two days of the Constitution practically annexing Schleswig. In vain the Danish Minister informed the self-constituted mandatories of the Powers that the Danish Parliament was not then in session and that it was impossible to comply with their demands within the time set. Upon the expiration of the limit of two days, or forty-eight hours, Prussia and Austria (which seem to have a fondness for this time-limit in their relations with small states) fell upon the gallant but misguided little country and dispossessed it of the Duchies of Schleswig-Holstein, one of which was placed under the control of Austria, the other under the control of Prussia, in order that a quarrel might be picked and a pretext be at hand for a war against Austria. This disposition of the Duchies was in the teeth of the Treaty of London.[2]

A distinguished English historian, the late Mr. C. A. Fyffe, says, in his *History of Modern Europe,* that:

> From this time the history of Germany is the history of the profound and audacious statecraft and of the overmastering will

[1] To the Treaty of London of May 8, 1852, Great Britain, Austria, France, Prussia, Russia, Sweden, and Norway, on the one hand, and Denmark, on the other, were parties. By the first article the succession to the Duchies, in default of the royal male line of Denmark, devolved upon Prince Christian of Schleswig-Holstein-Sonderbourg-Glücksbourg. By the second article the Powers were to consider the question of subsequent descent should Prince Christian have no heirs by his marriage with his then wife. By the third article the relations of the Duchies of Holstein and Lauenburg to Denmark, on the one hand, and to the Confederation, on the other, were not to be affected by the present treaty. For the text of this treaty see *British and Foreign State Papers*, vol. 41, p. 13.

[2] By the Treaty of Vienna of October 30, 1864, between Austria and Prussia, on the one hand, and Denmark, on the other, it was provided in the third article that "His Majesty the King of Denmark renounces all his rights over the Duchies of Schleswig, Holstein, and Lauenburg in favor of their Majesties the King of Prussia and the Emperor of Austria, engaging to recognize the dispositions which their said Majesties shall make with reference to those Duchies." (*Ibid.*, vol. 54, p. 522.)

of Bismarck; the Nation, except through its valour on the battlefield, ceases to influence the shaping of its own fortunes. What the German people desired in 1864 was that Schleswig-Holstein should be attached, under a ruler of its own, to the German Federation as it then existed; what Bismarck intended was that Schleswig-Holstein, itself incorporated more or less directly with Prussia, should be made the means of the destruction of the existing Federal system and of the expulsion of Austria from Germany.[1]

In later passages of his history, Mr. Fyffe says:

That Prussia should have united its forces with Austria in order to win for the Schleswig-Holsteiners the power of governing themselves as they pleased, must have seemed to Bismarck a supposition in the highest degree preposterous. He had taken up the cause of the Duchies not in the interest of the inhabitants but in the interest of Germany; and by Germany he understood Germany centered at Berlin and ruled by the House of Hohenzollern. . . . That Austria would not without compensation permit the Duchies thus to fall directly or indirectly under Prussian sway was, of course, well known to Bismarck; but so far was this from causing him any hesitation in his policy, that from the first he had discerned in the Schleswig-Holstein question a favorable pretext for the war which was to drive Austria out of Germany . . .[2]

An agreement was patched up at Gastein by which, pending an ultimate settlement, the government of the two provinces was divided between their masters, Austria taking the administration of Holstein, Prussia that of Schleswig, while the little district of Lauenburg on the south was made over to King William in full sovereignty.[3] An actual conflict between the representatives of the two rival Governments at their joint headquarters in Schleswig-Holstein was thus averted; peace was made possible at least for some months longer; and the interval was granted

---

[1] C. A. Fyffe, *A History of Modern Europe* (1889), vol. 3, pp. 346-347.
[2] *Ibid.*, p. 356.
[3] A convention was concluded between Austria and Prussia at Gastein on August 14, 1865. Article 1 is as follows:

The Exercise of the Rights acquired in common by the High Contracting Parties, in virtue of Article III of the Vienna Treaty of Peace of 30th October, 1864, shall, without prejudice to the continuance of those rights of both Powers to the whole of both Duchies, pass to His Majesty the Emperor of Austria as regards the Duchy of Holstein, and to His Majesty the King of Prussia as regards the Duchy of Schleswig.

Article 9 reads:

His Majesty the Emperor of Austria cedes to His Majesty the King of Prussia the Rights acquired in the aforementioned Vienna Treaty of Peace with respect to the Duchy of Lauenburg; . . . (*British and Foreign State Papers*, vol. 56, p. 1026.)

to Bismarck which was still required for the education of his Sovereign in the policy of blood and iron, and for the completion of his own arrangements with the enemies of Austria outside Germany.[1]

The quarrel came as Bismarck had planned it; his understanding with Russia in the Polish insurrection of 1863 made that Power his debtor; the ingratitude of Austria to Russia for the aid that saved Hungary in 1850, manifested by its unsympathetic attitude in the Crimean War, not only astonished the world but deprived Austria of help from Russia in the impending war with Prussia. Vague assurances of "compensation" to Louis Napoleon kept France neutral. Austria, therefore, stood alone; the war with Austria, after proper preparation of the ground, broke out in 1866, and the crowning victory of Sadowa accomplished the Prussian purpose.

Immediately after the peace with Austria, the North German Confederation was formed, composed of the northern States and of Prussia, swelled by the annexation of Hanover, the Duchy of Nassau, a part of Hesse, and the free city of Frankfort. An understanding was reached with the southern States by which they were to join Prussia in the event of a war with France—for a war with France lay, as Bismarck said, in the logic of events, and just as the war with Austria resulted in the acquisition of the northern States, so the war with France was to result in the acquisition of the southern States. That is to say, the war with France was not to be the initiation as in the case of Austria, but was to be the completion of German national unity under the leadership of the King of Prussia, and, that there might be no doubt about the leadership, the States were not to be formed into a confederation but into an empire, whose crown was to be held by the King of Prussia as such.[2]

[1] Fyffe's *History of Modern Europe*, vol. 3, pp. 358-359.
[2] The material portions of the treaty of peace between Austria and Prussia concluded at Prague on August 23, 1866, are:

Art. 2. For the purpose of carrying out Article VI of the Preliminaries of Peace concluded at Nikolsburg on the 26th July, 1866, and as His Majesty the Emperor of the French officially declared through his accredited Ambassador to His Majesty the King of Prussia, on the 29th July, 1866, " qu'en ce qui concerne le Gouvernement de l'Empereur, la Vénétie est acquise à l'Italie pour lui être remise à la Paix "—His Majesty the Emperor of Austria also accedes on his part to that Declaration and gives his consent to the Union of the Lombardo-Venetian Kingdom with the Kingdom of Italy, without any other burdensome condition than the liquidation of those Debts which, being charged on the Territories ceded, are to be recognized in accordance with the precedent of the Treaty of Zurich.

Art. 4. His Majesty the Emperor of Austria acknowledges the dissolution of the Germanic Confederation as hitherto constituted, and gives his consent to a new organization of Germany without the participation

But Prussian policy required that Austria should be a henchman, not an enemy, and, in pursuance of this policy, Bismarck did not saddle Austria with an impossible indemnity or impose humiliating conditions upon it. Austria was destined to become an ally, a friend, a satellite. In speaking of the policy to be pursued toward Austria, Bismarck says, in his autobiography:

> With a view to our future relations with Austria, I was very careful to avoid, as far as possible, cause for grievous memories, if this could be brought about without prejudice to our German policy. . . . A political reason lay back of this consideration; I was more inclined to avoid than to bring about a triumphal entry into Vienna in the Napoleonic style. In situations such as ours was at that time, it is a political precept, after a victory not to inquire how much one can squeeze out of one's opponent, but aim only to secure what is politically necessary.[1]

The reason for this seeming mercy on the part of Bismarck was due to his belief, as he wrote many years later in his autobiography, "that in the logic of history," which he himself was to make, "a war with France would succeed that with Austria."[2] Or as he expressed it at the time in an interview with our own Carl Schurz in 1868:

> Sound statesmanship required that the Austrian Empire, the existence of which was necessary for Europe, should not be

of the Imperial Austrian State. His Majesty likewise promises to recognize the more restricted Federal relations which His Majesty the King of Prussia will establish to the north of the line of the Main; and he declares his concurrence in the formation of an Association of the German States situated to the south of that line, whose national connexion with the North German Confederation is reserved for further arrangement between the parties, and which will have an independent international existence.

Art. 5. His Majesty the Emperor of Austria transfers to His Majesty the King of Prussia all the rights which he acquired by the Vienna Treaty of Peace of 30th October, 1864, over the Duchies of Holstein and Schleswig, with the condition that the populations of the Northern Districts of Schleswig shall be ceded to Denmark if, by a free vote, they express a wish to be united to Denmark.

Art. 6. . . . On the other hand, His Majesty the Emperor of Austria promises to recognize the new arrangements that will be made by His Majesty the King of Prussia in North Germany, including the Territorial alterations. (*British and Foreign State Papers*, vol. 56, p. 1050.)

It is of interest to note in this connection that the "free vote" to determine the ultimate destiny of Schleswig never took place, as Prussia insisted that it was a stipulation of a treaty between itself and Austria, giving no rights to third parties, and by the treaty between the two countries of October 11, 1878, the provision of this treaty regarding Schleswig was abrogated by Prussia, that is to say the German Empire, and Austria-Hungary. (*Ibid.*, vol. 69, p. 773.)

[1] Bismarck, *Gedanken und Erinnerungen*, p. 391.
[2] *Ibid.*

The difference in the effect of the shortened text of the Ems telegram as compared with that produced by the original was not the result of stronger words but the result of the form, which made it appear that this announcement was decisive, while the text as drafted by Abeken [the King's secretary] would only have appeared as a fragment of still pending negotiations which were to be continued at Berlin.[1]

Bismarck's purpose in publishing the telegram in "abbreviated" form is also stated in his autobiography as follows:

After I had read the condensed text to my two guests, Moltke remarked: "In this form, it has a different ring; it sounded before like a parley; now it sounds like a flourish in answer to a challenge." I went into details: "If in execution of His Majesty's order I forthwith communicate this text, which contains no alterations in and no addition to the telegram, not only to the newspapers, but as well by telegraph, to all our embassies, it will be known in Paris before midnight, and there, not only on account of its contents, but also because of the manner of its distribution, it will have the effect of a red rag upon a Gallic bull. We must fight if we do not want to appear in the rôle of the vanquished without a battle. Success depends essentially upon the impressions which the origin of the war produces upon us and others; it is important that we should be the party attacked, and the Gallic conceit and excitableness

I should authorize him to telegraph at once that I obligated myself for all future time never again to give my consent, in case the Hohenzollerns should renew their candidature. At last, I refused somewhat emphatically, by telling him that I had neither the right nor power to enter *à tout jamais* upon engagements of this kind. I replied, of course, that I had received no news as yet, and as he received earlier information about Paris and Madrid than myself, he could readily see that, once more, my Government had no hand in the matter." His Majesty has since received a communication from the Prince. Having told Count Benedetti that he was expecting news from the Prince, His Majesty, with reference to the above request and upon the proposition of Count Eulenburg and myself, had decided not to receive Count Benedetti again, but only to have him informed through an Adjutant: that His Majesty had received confirmatory news from the Prince, news that Benedetti had already received from Paris, and had nothing further to communicate to the Ambassador." (Bismarck, *Gedanken und Erinnerungen*, p. 437.)

The telegram as reduced by Bismarck " by striking out words, but without adding or altering " is as follows:

After the news of the renunciation of the hereditary Prince of Hohenzollern had been officially communicated to the Imperial French Government by the Royal Spanish Government, the French Ambassador at Ems further demanded of His Majesty the King to be authorized to telegraph to Paris that His Majesty the King obligated himself for all future time, never again to give his consent in case the Hohenzollerns should renew their candidature. His Majesty, the King, thereupon declined again to receive the French Ambassador and had him informed through the Adjutant on duty that His Majesty had nothing further to communicate to the Ambassador. (*Ibid.*, pp. 439-440.)

[1] *Ibid.*, p. 440.

what Bismarck wanted—war.[1] The victory lay with France, but the false step taken by Napoleon and his advisers, of requiring from the Prussian King a promise that he would not allow the candidacy to be renewed at some subsequent time, gave Bismarck the chance to snatch victory from defeat, which he did by the simple but not wholly reputable device of "concentrating" or "abbreviating" a telegram.

The announcement that the Prince of Hohenzollern had renounced his candidacy in order to avoid a war with France was so disappointing to Bismarck that his first idea was to retire from the service.[2] For the purpose of communicating this intention, he invited Moltke, Chief of the Prussian General Staff, and Roon, the Minister of War, to dine. During the course of the dinner Bismarck was handed the telegram sent by the King's secretary from Ems informing him of the demand of the French Ambassador upon the King of Prussia, that he should bind himself for all future time not to consent to the renewal of the candidacy of the Hohenzollerns for the crown of Spain, of the refusal of the King to undertake such an engagement, and of his decision not to receive the French Ambassador again but to communicate with him through an *aide-de-camp*. The telegram left it to Bismarck whether the French demand and its rejection should be communicated to the Prussian Ambassadors and to the press. After a consideration of the advantages of war and the expression of the belief that it could only be avoided at the cost of Prussia's honor, Bismarck states in his autobiography that he made use of the royal authorization to publish the contents of the telegram, and, in the presence of his guests, reduced it by striking out words, but without additions or alterations.[3] The difference between the abbreviated and the original text is thus stated by Bismarck himself:

[1] In his *Gedanken und Erinnerungen* (pp. 428, *et seq.*), Bismarck disclaims the authorship of the plan to place a Hohenzollern upon the throne of Spain, although that plan would have played into his hands and, irrespective of its authorship, he used it to bring about a war with France and to merge the German States into an enlarged Prussia. "From the political point of view I was rather indifferent to the entire question. Prince Anton, more than myself, was inclined to carry it peacefully to the desired goal. The memoirs of His Majesty, the King of Roumania, are not very exact as regards certain details of the ministerial coöperation in the matter." (*Ibid.*, p. 430.) His Majesty, the King of Roumania, a Hohenzollern himself and brother of the candidate, was of a different opinion, ascribing to Bismarck the candidacy of a Hohenzollern Prince for the vacant throne of Spain. (*Aus dem Leben König Karls von Rumänien, Aufzeichnungen eines Augenzeugen* [Stuttgart, 1897], vol. 2, pp. 62, 72, 93.) (See post, pp. 323-324.)

[2] *Ibid.*, pp. 434-435.

[3] The Ems telegram is thus given by Bismarck himself in his autobiography:

His Majesty writes me: "Count Benedetti joined me on the promenade and requested me in a last endeavor, and in a most urgent manner, that

foundation of the German Empire and the downfall of Napoleon were the results. No prediction was ever more shrewdly made and more accurately and amply fulfilled.[1]

It was indeed a marvelous prediction, but one which Bismarck could safely make, as to the time which he himself was to choose and as to the results which he had already predetermined. He was, as he said, ready. The pretext, as distinct from the cause, of the war, was found in the offer of the crown of Spain to a prince of the Hohenzollern-Sigmaringen line. The Spanish people had rid themselves of Queen Isabella and were looking around for a king. They hit upon Prince Leopold of this line, who was willing, although apparently not overanxious, to accept the crown, but Napoleon III, already tottering and fearful, was unwilling to be wedged in, as it were, between two Prussian rulers. As the result of Napoleon's protest, King William of Prussia, as the head of the Hohenzollern house, approved the refusal of the crown by his kinsman in order to avoid

---

[1] It is interesting to an American reader to learn that Carl Schurz, who found fortune and fame in the New World, refused to desert it for place and position in the Fatherland, as appears from the following quotation from his interview with Bismarck:

Throughout our conversation Bismarck repeatedly expressed his pleasure at the friendly relations existing between him and the German Liberals, some of whom had been prominent in the revolutionary troubles of 1848. He mentioned several of my old friends, Bucher, Kapp, and others, who, having returned to Germany, felt themselves quite at home under the new conditions, and had found the way open to public positions and activities of distinction and influence, in harmony with their principles. As he repeated this, or something like it, in a manner apt to command my attention, I might have taken it as a suggestion inviting me to do likewise. But I thought it best not to say anything in response. I simply dropped a casual remark in some proper connection that my activities in the United States were highly congenial to me and that, moreover, I was attached to the American Republic by a sense of gratitude for the distinctions which it had so generously bestowed upon me. (*Reminiscences of Carl Schurz*, vol. 3, p. 279.)

It is of more than passing interest to quote a further passage from the interview dealing with the question which must be uppermost in the minds of our people today. In reply to Bismarck's inquiry "whether the singular stories he had been told about the state of discipline existing in our armies in the Civil War were true," the distinguished American statesman, who had been a Major General and corps commander in the Civil War, thus answered:

I had to admit that that state of discipline would in many respects have shocked a thoroughbred Prussian officer, and I told him some anecdotes of outbreaks of the spirit of equality which the American is apt to carry into all relations of life, and of the occasional familiarities between the soldier and the officer which would spring from that spirit. Such anecdotes amused him immensely, but I suppose his Prussian pride inwardly revolted when I expressed the opinion that in spite of all this the American soldier would not only fight well, but would, in a prolonged conflict with any European army, although at first put at a disadvantage by more thorough drill and discipline, after some experience prove superior to all of them. (*Ibid.*, p. 278.)

reduced to a mere wreck; that it should be made a friend, and, as a friend, not too powerless; and what Prussia had gone to war for, was the leadership in Germany, and that this leadership in Germany would not have been fortified, but rather weakened, by the acquisition from Austria of populations which would not have fitted into the Prussian scheme. Besides, the Chancellor thought that, the success of the Prussians having been so decisive, it was wise to avoid further sacrifices and risks.[1]

The wisdom of this policy was seen in 1870 when Austria, then converted into the dual monarchy of Austria-Hungary, did not join France in the Franco-Prussian War as Napoleon III had anticipated.

The next victim was to be France.

Just as Bismarck had planned a war against Austria and had made his arrangements in advance, so he planned a war against France and made his arrangements in advance, saying: "I regarded it as certain that war with France would . . . necessarily have to be waged on the road to our further national development;" and "I had no doubt that a Franco-German war would have to be waged before the complete organization of Germany could be realized."[2]

Bismarck's purpose in the war with Austria was, as has been said, to exclude it from the circle of German States and to put Prussia in its place, or as Bismarck himself put it:

> Our task was the establishment or preparation for the establishment of a German national unity under the leadership of the King of Prussia.[3]

In an interview in 1868 with Carl Schurz, the distinguished American statesman, Bismarck adverted to the war with Austria, then two years behind him, and to the war with France, two years off, saying:

> My calculation is that the crisis will come in about two years. We have to be ready, of course, and we are. We shall win, and the result will be just the contrary of what Napoleon aims at—the total unification of Germany outside of Austria, and probably Napoleon's downfall.[4]

On this Mr. Schurz comments:

> This was said in January, 1868. The war between France and Prussia and her allies broke out in July, 1870, and the

[1] *Reminiscences of Carl Schurz* (New York; McClure, 1907-1908, 3 vols.), vol. 3, p. 271.
[2] Bismarck, *Gedanken und Erinnerungen*, p. 404.
[3] *Ibid.*, p. 399.
[4] *Reminiscenses of Carl Schurz*, vol. 3, p. 274.

will make us the party attacked if through a *European-wide publicity* we announce, so far as we can do so without the speaking-tube of the Reichstag, that we fearlessly meet the public threats of France.[1]

The effect produced upon Moltke was the effect produced upon the German people.

As in the case of the Austrian War, steps were taken to prevent interference. Russia was friendly because of Prussia's Polish policy and because Alexander's life was saved from a Polish assassin in Paris in 1867, and the favors of the past were added to in the present by the advice to break the Treaty of Paris excluding Russian men-of-war from the Black Sea. The friendly treatment of Austria in the treaty of peace and in the interval made it difficult for Austria-Hungary to attack, although it is well known that Francis Joseph had agreed to join Napoleon after the first campaign, as did also Italy, bound to Napoleon rather than to France for its unification. The Queen of England was friendly—her daughter had married the Crown Prince of Prussia—and after the war broke out Bismarck published Napoleon's project to annex Belgium made to Bismarck and which that astute statesman had had put in writing. England's neutrality was assured, its sympathy and the sympathy of Europe gained.

The Franco-Prussian War, so craftily planned in advance and so cleverly executed, resulted in the unification of the German States under the Prussian Crown, and on January 18, 1871, the King of Prussia was proclaimed German Emperor in the Palace of Versailles.[2]

In view of the Zimmermann letter, which will be presently discussed, proposing a union of Germany, Mexico, and Japan against the United States and the partition of American territory as the price of coöperation, it is interesting to note the careful preparation preceding a Prussian attack. In a passage previously quoted from Carl Schurz, recounting an interview which he had with Bismarck in 1868, two years before the Franco-Prussian War, Bismarck is reported by that upright and conscientious man of affairs as saying,

[1] Bismarck, *Gedanken und Erinnerungen*, p. 440.
[2] Just as in 1848, when the King of Prussia, who was offered a crown, was unwilling to pick it out of the gutter, so in 1870 his successor was unwilling to receive it from human hands. Thus Bismarck says that King William "cared at that time still more for the power and greatness of Prussia than for the constitutional union of Germany. He was free from any ambitious calculation with regard to Germany; in 1870 he even compared contemptuously the imperial title with that of 'Drum-Major' . . . So far as dynastic feeling was concerned, he felt more flattered in exercising the said power simply as the born King of Prussia, and not as the emperor established in virtue of a constitution." (*Ibid.*, p. 409.)

"We have to be ready, of course, and we are." The full significance of this preparation would be lost upon the reader who contents himself with the surface of things; for Prussian preparation involves not merely a competent staff, a marvelous army and the means of supporting it in the field, but the country to be attacked, overrun and mastered by a happy and unsuspected coöperation of the invisible army, sent in advance of the war, with the invincible army crossing the frontier upon its outbreak.

If the spy is not a Prussian creation, it is nevertheless in Prussia and Prussianized Germany that he has approved himself and come into his own and to honor. "I have one cook and a hundred spies," the great Frederick was wont to say, and it was no less a person than William, King of Prussia and first German Emperor, who said, "One must not confine oneself to giving money to spies. One must also know how to show them honor when they deserve it."

The preparations for the two wars which unified Germany were planned and carried into effect by Bismarck's understudy, one Stieber by name, the King of Sleuth-hounds, to use the title given him by Bismarck himself.[1] Shortly after the acquisition of the Duchies in 1864 to the summer of the war with Austria in 1866, Stieber was in Bohemia posting "landmarks," as he called his spies, on the line of march from Berlin to Prague and Sadowa, "disguised, now as a photographer, now as a basket-maker, or as a travelling peddler of plastercasts, or of religious or pornographic objects. And for two long years (from April, 1864, to May, 1866), he lived in a traveling cart, going to and fro and observing cities and villages, studying the mental attitude of these vast territories which he dotted with spies, and where, but a short time afterwards, the drama of Sadowa was to unfold itself."[2]

Without going into details—for it is only the method that is of interest in this connection—it will suffice to say that "at each halting-place of the army, the houses where the Staff and General Officers, together with their suites, were to be lodged, were marked with a sign. A 'peasant,'—a spy,—in a blouse and wearing wooden shoes, who had preceded the invading army . . . pointed out to the commander of the post the location of these houses, and gave to him the most detailed information in regard to the strength and the posi-

---

[1] Where not inclosed in quotation marks this portion of the text is paraphrased from Paul Lanoir's volume, entitled *L'Espionnage Allemand en France* (Paris; Cocuaud & Cie., 1908), translated and published in English under the title of *The German Spy System in France* (London; Mills & Boone, 1910). This is the work of a specialist based upon the writings of Stieber and his associates.

[2] Lanoir, *L'Espionnage Allemand en France*, p. 40.

tion of the enemy's armies, and with regard to the attitude of the people and the local resources in forage, meats, and vegetables."[1] Von Moltke, so chary of speech that Bismarck said of him that he could keep silent in seven languages, was so deeply impressed by these arrangements, the nature, extent, and precision of the information, that he actually said to Bismarck, "Whether it was young Stieber"—he was then forty-eight years old—"or anybody else who had charge of this important service: what he did was well done, well done, well done."[2]

So much for Austria; now as to the preparation for the war with France.

In the first place, it was necessary for Bismarck to come to an understanding with his neighbors in order to be free to use Prussia's resources against the next victim. The merciful treatment of Austria was not generosity but calculation. The treatment of Russia smacked of craft as well as of calculation. It was natural that Prussia should view with sympathy the repression of the Polish uprising of 1863, as the interests of the partitioners of Poland were identical in Warsaw and Posen, and upon community of interests understandings securely rest. But the Polish agreements concerned the past, and Bismarck was thinking now of the future and of France. In 1867 an International Exposition was held at Paris and Napoleon III made of it a brilliant affair. The Czar Alexander was to grace the occasion by his presence and Bismarck saw to it that King William of Prussia and the Emperor of All the Russias reached Paris together, so that Napoleon could be watched and, by overtures to Alexander, checkmated—because in autocracies the whims of the monarchs make and unmake nations. Stieber, the King of the Sleuth-hounds, accompanied the Prussian party and, on crossing the French frontier, he received an urgent message from his Parisian agent to see him immediately on reaching Paris. He did so and learned that on the morrow, June 6th, the Czar was to be assassinated by a young Pole while attending the Grand Review at Longchamps. Stieber at once laid the matter before Bismarck, whereupon the following colloquy took place:

> "It would be a cause for universal mourning if so noble and kind a prince as His Majesty Alexander II should fall by the stroke of a vulgar assassin. I hope you, Stieber, will do all that is necessary to prevent such a misfortune."
>
> "I have, of course, been very careful not to put the assassin under arrest; but I have given orders to one of my best agents to follow him step by step and not to leave him."

[1] Lanoir, *L'Espionnage Allemand en France*, p. 43. [2] *Ibid.*, p. 44.

"Well done; if by chance the French police do not arrest him betimes, there will most certainly be near him, at the propitious moment, one of your agents, who, without doing anything to prevent the shooting, will take hold of the arm of the assassin and deflect its mortal shot."

"I give you my word that things will take this course."[1]

And in his memoirs, Stieber relates the following observation of Bismarck:

"Thus, while the crime will be averted, the attempt will remain. Have you, my dear Stieber, thought of the political consequences of such an event? Realizing that the French police were not able to protect him, Czar Alexander will leave France with the most unfavorable impression."

"I know the Emperor! If things take the course described, there are many projects which will never be realized, and the 'charmer' (Napoleon III) will get nothing for all his amiability and projects of alliance."

"Your Excellency, I have been thinking about all this since yesterday."

"And if the author of the attempt were to escape the extreme penalty, and if a jury of simple-minded *bourgeois*, weeping like weak souls over the plea of the counsel for the defense in their sympathy for the fate of wretched Poland, should fail to condemn the assassin to death, this would cause a treble excitement in St. Petersburg, and there would be a deep and lasting estrangement between France and Russia . . ., and as for myself I should have one less trouble to worry about."

"Yes, for us Germans, this attempt is something providential."

"By having the assassin arrested, the French police might claim the honor of the discovery of the plot; they would receive the congratulations and thanks for their activity and solicitude."

"In such a case, Alexander would consider himself under obligations to France, and as for ourselves, we would have to be on the alert at St. Petersburg and doubly so at Paris."

. . . .

"May I ask who is the assassin?"

"A Pole . . . quite young: from twenty to twenty-two years old."

"A child . . . and a Pole," Bismarck remarked with a smile! "A Parisian jury will never condemn him to death; it would be contrary to all Mr. Prud'homme's middle-class sympathies . . ."

"It would be decidedly unfortunate if this boy were prevented from letting off his pistol."[2]

---

[1] Lanoir, *L'Espionnage Allemand en France*, pp. 59-60.   [2] *Ibid.*, pp. 60-62.

The shot was fired and guided as planned. The young Pole when apprehended calmly said, "I wished to avenge Poland, my beloved country. There is no use in questioning me: I have no accomplice, and I alone take the responsibility for my deliberate act."[1] The jury found extenuating circumstances, and the neutrality of Russia was fixed beyond doubt by Bismarck's scheme, which will be mentioned later, to take advantage of the war of 1870 to break the provisions of the Treaty of Paris forbidding Russia to keep men-of-war in the Black Sea.

Bismarck's most immediate preoccupation was to repeat the triumph of Bohemia on a larger—it could not be a more efficient—scale in France. Therefore, on June 14, 1867, on the day of his return to Berlin after the Paris outing, Bismarck bethought him of Stieber, and sending for that worthy, he said:

> "The liberty of action conferred upon you last year will not be interfered with; and as for your funds, I wonder if they are sufficient, or do you wish an increase, and if so how much?"
>
> "Your Excellency," answered Stieber, "no increase is necessary; what I have is sufficient. Within eighteen months the routes of invasion will be ready."[2]

And they were.

Without lingering over details, one incident will show the reader the perfection of the system and enable him to appreciate the importance of its results. Some thirty thousand spies were scattered along the line of march. Versailles swarmed with secret agents. Appropriate quarters were set apart for the Prussian invaders and headquarters secured for the invisible army at 3 Boulevard du Roi. The incident, based upon the account of Stieber and his principal lieutenants, is thus related:

> In January, 1871, Jules Favre was designated to negotiate with Bismarck for the surrender of Paris.
>
> As soon as this fact became known, Bismarck said to Stieber: "Favre is a man whom we must not lose sight of for a single instant. I rely upon you, Stieber."
>
> "You need have no fear," the latter coolly replied.
>
> Now, when Jules Favre—who knew well Versailles—disembarked at the Sèvres bridge, he got into an old carriage requisitioned and driven by one of Stieber's lieutenants:
>
> And do you know to what place Jules Favre was conducted by the coachman of the German police?

[1] Lanoir, *L'Espionnage Allemand en France*, p. 65. [2] *Ibid.*, pp. 69-70.

To No. 3 of the Boulevard du Roi, the headquarters of the German secret police . . .

And it was there that he lived throughout his first sojourn in Versailles, when he was negotiating the conditions of the surrender of the place.

Kaltenbach, the lieutenant of police who directed the German commissariat service established on the ground floor of the hotel, came to Jules Favre and said:

"The greatest honor for a good Frenchman like myself, a native of Versailles"—Kaltenbach refers to himself in these terms—"is to give shelter to an illustrious Frenchman like you (Favre)."

At No. 3, Boulevard du Roi, Jules Favre slept on the second floor in the very bed of the spy Kaltenbach, and the latter, immediately upon Favre's arrival . . . introduced Stieber to him as a servant to be trusted and upon whom he could depend with the utmost confidence.

And it was indeed Stieber himself who searched the trunk and the pockets of Jules Favre and who, wearing a white apron, brought him a cup of coffee every morning.[1]

The reader is now prepared to appreciate the following passage at arms recounted by the King of the Sleuth-hounds in his memoirs:

At the beginning of the campaign when on our way from Faulquemont I was invited to dine with the chief (Bismarck) and his staff of officials of the ministry of foreign affairs.

We were established in a small peasant's hut. After dinner and while he himself was preparing coffee for the entire company, Bismarck gave utterance to this prophecy which was to be realized six months afterwards: "It is quite decided that we shall not return either Alsace or Lorraine to France."

An officer of the great staff having remarked: "Our army is invincible," I arose in a fury and answered: "Say rather *our armies.*"

The chief of police explained his thought in the following way:

"The fighting army of which *you* are the chief remains *behind* you. Now, many months since, *my army* has been occupying the positions which it reached in silence, and where, without a single rifle, it is noiselessly accomplishing a task whose real danger and importance I wish you not to misjudge."[2]

In view of these passages we can understand the activity of German partisans in the United States in the days when we were neutral and when Germany, through its Ambassador, was professing friendship for the country to which he was accredited. We

---

[1] Lanoir, *L'Espionnage Allemand en France*, pp. 179-181.   [2] *Ibid.*, p. 73.

could not, indeed, see the invisible army, like a mole working in the dark and shunning the light; but we felt its presence, a presence made clearer and brought home to the most confiding by the Zimmermann letter, proving beyond peradventure that preparations had been made and that the stage was set for the foreign allies.

The past was glorious, the future must be safe. Bismarck was satisfied with the triumphs of 1866 and of 1870. Having united Germany, he wished to consolidate its power. He therefore labored to keep his neighbors on the west, east, and south busied and apart. This was his policy, and it was successful in large measure.

The problem which confronted the Imperial German Government after the war of 1870 was so to weaken France as to make an attack from the west seem impracticable or futile. The indemnity of five billion francs with which France was saddled and the loss of the provinces of Alsace and Lorraine in part were thought to have accomplished the desired result. Bismarck believed that France would profit by any favorable occasion to recover the lost provinces of Alsace and Lorraine, and he therefore sought to prevent an alliance between Russia and France which would expose the new Germany to an attack from both sides in case of a war with France. He felt that the Emperor of All the Russias would be less likely to consort with a republic, and the arch-monarchist therefore supported the cause of republican government in France. The modification of the Treaty of Paris, by which Russia was permitted to become the mistress of the Black Sea,[1] with the hope of Constantinople and the Dardanelles looming large in the near future and a preponderating influence in the Balkans, if not an annexation of the territory, seemed to secure the eastern frontier. Italy was under obligations to Prussia because, as the result of coöperation with Prussia in its war with Austria, it had received the province of Venetia and thus rounded out its ambitions to the north; although the failure to negotiate a satisfactory boundary between Austria and Italy displeased Italian statesmen, and the failure to secure the Dalmatian provinces across the Adriatic, in which Italian was spoken and whose people were apparently Italian at heart, carried within it the seeds of war.

---

[1] It was therefore a favor of fate that the situation offered a possibility of doing Russia a service. . . . With regard to the politically unreasonable, and therefore in the long run impossible, stipulations which limited the independence of Russia's Black Sea coasts. . . . Herein we had a means of fostering our relations with Russia.

With reluctance, Prince Gortschakow accepted the initiative with which I had sounded him in this direction. (Bismarck, *Gedanken und Erinnerungen*, pp. 452-453.)

Austria-Hungary, excluded from Germany and without chance of developing to the north or the west, was to be given a field of exploitation to the south through the Balkan peninsula to the Ægean, until such time as "the logic of events," as Bismarck would say, should force the Imperial German Government to supplant Austria.

To make assurance doubly sure, France was permitted, if not encouraged, to build up a colonial empire in Africa and in Asia, so as to withdraw attention from the Rhine and to occupy the minds of the statesmen and the resources of the people with the problems arising out of colonial expansion to such a degree that an attack upon Germany through Alsace-Lorraine for their recovery would be less likely. Russia was also to be encouraged to extend its empire towards and over western Asia, thus making of the Muscovite an Oriental. As a still further assurance, dissension was to be sown between France and Italy by allowing France to seize African territory, namely Tunis, which Italy coveted, in order that the Teuton might slip in, as it were, between the two branches of the Latin inheritance. England was to be embroiled with Russia because of Russian expansion in Asia, thus keeping those two countries facing each other in the outposts of empire so as not to trouble Prussia in its problem of absorbing the German peoples, as Prussia had already absorbed the German States.

Such was the purpose and such seems to have been the plan, and success outwardly crowned the policy of the Iron Chancellor. France was, by the Preliminary Treaty of Peace, signed at Versailles, February 26, 1871, and later embodied in the Treaty of Frankfort of May 10, 1871, allowed three years in which to pay the huge indemnity of approximately a billion dollars, during which time it was to be garrisoned by Prussia. The patriotism of the French peasants enabled France to pay off the indemnity and thus to free its territory from German soldiers before the appointed time. The snake had been scotched, it had not been killed. Therefore, in 1875, France was to be forced into a war which would, as Bismarck said, "finish it off." But French statesmen were unwilling to be driven into a contest in which their defeat was inevitable. They parried the blow, and the year 1875, full of German provocation, passed, and the Republic was enabled to emerge, as it were, from the ashes of empire.

Matters apparently did not move so rapidly in Russia as it had been anticipated. The Black Sea was indeed Russian, but Constantinople and the Balkans lay in the hands of the Turk. The Balkan countries were restless and the Turkish methods of oppression, culminating in massacres of Christians and the perpetration of unspeakable barbarities in Bulgaria, gave Russia a cause or pretext for intervention. The result was the Russo-Turkish War of 1877-78, of which Austria-Hungary and the Imperial German Government were interested spectators. It may be, as Bismarck said, that the Balkan States were "not worth the bones of a Pomeranian grenadier,"[1] but it was Prussian policy to rely in the first instance upon diplomacy and to keep the grenadier for use if diplomacy failed. The story of the Russo-Turkish War is quickly told. After heroic resistance—for they have always been physically brave—the Turks were beaten and the Russian army was on its way to Constantinople, which lay seemingly within its grasp. The Treaty of San Stefano of March 3, 1878, was concluded between victor and victim, but it was then supposed to be against the interests of Great Britain to have Russia installed at Constantinople, and the Imperial German Government began its career as arbiter of the destinies of Europe. A Congress met at Berlin, under Bismarck's presidency, to settle the terms of peace between Russia and Turkey and to adjust the Eastern Question. The result was, as far as necessary for present purposes, that Russia neither annexed nor established a protectorate over the Balkan peoples. Roumania, Servia, and Montenegro were recognized as independent.[2] Bulgaria was made an autonomous state, recognizing the suzerainty of the Turk.[3] The provinces of Bosnia and Herzegovina, Serb in race and Turkish in ownership, were handed over to the indefinite occupation of Austria-Hungary, and the province to the south, Novi-Bazar, was to be garrisoned by Austria-Hungary.[4]

[1] Speech in the Reichstag of December 6, 1876.
[2] By Article XLIII of the Treaty of Berlin of July 13, 1878, "The High Contracting Parties recognize the independence of Roumania. . . ." By Article XXXIV "The High Contracting Parties recognize the independence of the Principality of Servia, . . ." By Article XXVI "The independence of Montenegro is recognized by the Sublime Porte and by all those of the High Contracting Parties who had not hitherto admitted it." (*British and Foreign State Papers*, vol. 69, pp. 749-767.)
[3] By Article I of the treaty "Bulgaria is constituted an autonomous and tributary Principality under the Suzerainty of His Imperial Majesty the Sultan; it will have a Christian government and a national militia." (*Ibid.*)
[4] Article XXV of the treaty is as follows:

The Provinces of Bosnia and Herzegovina shall be occupied and administered by Austria-Hungary. The Government of Austria-Hungary, not desiring to undertake the administration of the Sanjak of Novi-Bazar, . . . the Ottoman administration will continue to exercise its functions there. Nevertheless, in order to assure the maintenance of the new political state of affairs, as well as freedom and security of communications, Austria-Hungary reserves the right of keeping garrisons and having military and commercial roads in the whole of this part of the ancient Vilayet of

The first great step had been taken. It has always been statecraft to divide in order to conquer. Roumania, Servia, and Montenegro were separated from Turkey and a wedge thrust in between them which might one day be pushed to the Ægean. In the meantime, the House of Hohenzollern held the crown of Roumania, Servia was to be brought into dependence upon Austria-Hungary, and Bulgaria was supplied with a German princeling. Thirty years later Austria-Hungary severed the slender thread uniting Bosnia and Herzegovina to the Ottoman Empire by annexing the territories,[1] and the German Prince of the House of Coburg, likewise breaking the bond to Turkey, assumed the title of Czar of Bulgaria.[2] Just as

> Bosnia. To this end the Governments of Austria-Hungary and Turkey reserve to themselves to come to an understanding on the details. (*British and Foreign State Papers*, vol. 69, pp. 749-767.)

By the subsequent agreement of April 21, 1879, between Austria-Hungary and Turkey, Austria exercised the right under the treaty to garrison certain localities in Novi-Bazar. (*Ibid.*, vol. 71, p. 1134.)

[1] On October 3, 1908, Austria-Hungary denounced Article XXV of the Treaty of Berlin according to it the rights of administrator in Bosnia and Herzegovina. The material portion of this denunciation is as follows:

> Bosnia and Herzegovina have arrived today—thanks to the assiduous work of the Austro-Hungarian administration—at a high degree of material and intellectual culture; accordingly the moment appears to have come to crown the work undertaken, by granting to these provinces the benefits of an autonomous and constitutional system of government, which is ardently desired by the entire population. The Imperial and Royal Government ought, however, in order to realize these generous intentions, to regulate in a precise fashion the situation of these two provinces and to provide an effective guarantee against the dangers which would be able to menace the stability of the system established in 1878. The Cabinet of Vienna accordingly finds itself under the imperious necessity of freeing itself from the reserves contained in the Convention of Constantinople, and of recovering, with regard to Bosnia and Herzegovina, its complete liberty of action.

At the same time Austria-Hungary withdrew its garrisons from Novi-Bazar, stating that "the Cabinet of Vienna is pleased to hope that the Ottoman Government will succeed, without other support, in maintaining order in the Sanjak and in fulfilling alone in these countries the task which there rested upon it, up till now, through the coöperation of the two Governments." (*Revue Générale de Droit International Public*, xv, Doc. 35-36.)

[2] TIRNOVO, October 5, 1908.

I have the honor of informing you that today, Monday, September 22 (October 5), His Highness the Prince, my August Sovereign, guided by the irrevocable desire of the people of all Bulgaria to remove the obstacles which have until the present retarded its regular development, and to put an end to the causes which have produced, with the neighboring Empire, relations of a nature to constantly disturb the peace and tranquillity of the Balkans, has proclaimed Bulgaria of the north and of the south an independent monarchy.

By this act His Royal Highness and his Government, in realizing the unanimous desire of the people, are animated by the sole desire of seeing Bulgaria come into the family of independent States, so as to devote itself wholly to peaceful prosperity.

The Government of His Majesty the King of Bulgaria is pleased to hope that your high Government will appreciate these legitimate desires of the people of Bulgaria and give to the Royal Bulgarian Government support and approval

Russia outwardly abrogated a provision of the Congress of Paris and assumed the control of the Black Sea, contrary to its provisions, Austria-Hungary outwardly abrogated the Treaty of the Congress of Berlin by annexing Bosnia and Herzegovina, as did Bulgaria by proclaiming its independence. Just as in 1871 Great Britain insisted upon a conference of the Powers parties to the Treaty of Paris in order to regularize what had been done by Russia and to prevent the recurrence of a like incident in the future, so in 1908 Great Britain proposed a conference of the Powers, parties to the Congress of Berlin and its treaty, to regularize the action of Austria-Hungary and Bulgaria, to adjust the Balkan situation, and to prevent a recurrence of this sort of thing in the future. In 1871 the conference was held because Germany was then only the first among equals and it suited Germany's purpose to meet in conference with the signatories of the Treaty of Paris. It was not held in 1908 because Germany had by this time become the arbiter of Europe and it did not suit the German purpose to meet in conference with the signatories of the Treaty of Berlin. In 1871 Bismarck affected surprise at the action of Russia and coöperated with Great Britain.[1] In 1908 Germany expressed indignation that the action of Austria-Hungary and of Bulgaria should be questioned by the signatories of the Treaty of Berlin; and the German Emperor roundly stated that, in case of an attack upon Austria-Hungary, he would appear "in shining armor" by the side of his imperial ally.

In 1912 the first Balkan war broke out, in which Bulgaria, Servia, Montenegro, and Greece were allied against the Turk, not only to redress grievances but in effect to round out their territories. The Turk was quickly and badly beaten, but the allies fell out about the division of the spoils, Servia, Montenegro, and Greece being unwilling to renounce the fruits of victory in behalf of Bulgaria, which

of this act of the people. (Minister for Foreign Affairs to American Minister Knowles, *Foreign Relations of the U. S.*, 1908, p. 57.)

See the protocol concluded between Bulgaria and Turkey for the settlement of railway, religious, and financial questions, and for the recognition of Bulgarian independence, signed at Constantinople, April 6/19, 1909. (*British and Foreign State Papers*, vol. 102, p. 375.)

[1] In a conversation with Lord Odo Russell, British Ambassador at Berlin, Bismarck stated "That the Russian Circular of the 19th October (denouncing the clauses in question) had taken him by surprise. That while he had always held that the Treaty of 1856 pressed with undue severity upon Russia, he entirely disapproved of the manner adopted and the time selected by the Russian Government to force the revision of the Treaty." (Reported by Lord Russell in a dispatch of November 22, 1870, to Lord Granville, and published in the *Parliamentary Papers* of 1871, Cd. 245.) See in this connection the passage already quoted from Bismarck's *Gedanken und Erinnerungen, supra*, p. 17.

claimed the lion's share.¹ Bulgaria refused to accept less than its demands, and the conference of the Powers at London failed to adjust the difficulties. Bulgaria appealed to the sword and was quickly and badly beaten by its former allies, Servia, Montenegro, and Greece, to which Roumania was added. The result was a new division of the spoils, by which Turkey obtained part of the territory which would otherwise have gone to Bulgaria and which Turkey had occupied in the meantime, and by which Bulgaria renounced under compulsion part of the territory it claimed to Servia and to Greece and part of the territory which it owned and which Roumania coveted.² Germany and Austria-Hungary consented to these readjustments; but Germany, Austria-Hungary, and Italy refused to allow Servia an outlet or, as it is called, a window on the Adriatic, and the Triple Alliance likewise refused to allow Servia an outlet on the Ægean. Why? Because the time was about ripe for the wedge to be driven through the Balkans and to have its keen edge cut through to the Persian Gulf, separating the Old World into two parts, with a line of communication from the Kiel Canal to the Persian Gulf, through Berlin, Vienna, and Bagdad. If Germany had come late to the banquet, it nevertheless arrived in time for dessert.

It is natural that peoples which have dreamed of being united under a government of their own, which would enable them to secure the respect abroad which they felt to be their due, the comforts at home of which they were deprived, and the development corresponding to a magnificent and dominating past, should, upon the realization of their prayers and of their hopes, yield to the enthusiasm of the moment and give to imagination greater play than peoples which have passed through the intoxication of power and have been sobered by its responsibility. As the founder of international law says in his immortal three books on the *Right of War and Peace*, "they take this course, as I conceive, with the purpose with which, when things have been twisted one way, we bend them the other, in order to make them straight. But this attempt to drive things too far, is often so far from succeeding, that it does harm."³

It was also natural that the new Germany should set its heart

---

¹ For the text of the treaty of May 15/30, 1913, between the victorious allies on the one hand and Turkey on the other, see Martens, *Nouveau Recueil*, 3me série, tome viii, pp. 16-19.

² For the text of the treaty between Roumania, Greece, Montenegro, Servia, and Bulgaria, signed at Bucharest July 28/August 10, 1913, see Martens, *Nouveau Recueil*, 3me série, tome viii, pp. 61-74.

³ Grotius, *De Jure Belli ac Pacis* (1625); accompanied by an abridged translation by W. Whewell, Cambridge, 1853; 3 vols., vol. 1, p. 9.

upon a development of its resources at least comparable to that which had taken place in other countries, that it should desire to reach the seas just as other countries have followed the river to its mouth— for the Rhine seems no less important to the new Germany than the Mississippi was to the early Republic. But between Germany and the North Sea lay Belgium, Holland, and Denmark, the Scheldt reaching the sea through Belgium and Holland, the Rhine at Rotterdam. To the east lay Russia, and, though Russia may yield for the moment, it does not withdraw.

If the greater Germany at home seemed blocked alike in the West and the East, might not a greater Germany in foreign parts be possible? Great Britain, Spain, and Portugal had colonized in the past, and distant provinces, indeed empires, bore testimony to their prowess; and in the very hour of Germany's unification territories were annexed. But the desirable portions of the world's surface were already preëmpted, and if Germany looked to the Western World the Monroe Doctrine stood in the way. If it turned toward Africa only the tropics or undesirable lands were open. The immense movement for colonial expansion with which Germany was agitated in the eighties only resulted in the acquisition of inferior territories in which the white man might dominate but in which he was unwilling to dwell.

There was, however, one highway to the future.

The wedge thrust through Europe, dividing the Old World, as it were, into two parts, was a project attractive from its very vastness, and the rewards were as boundless as the horizon. And there was something in the dream to impress the imagination, even although the longing for power and "the wealth of Ormus and of Ind" might have been a sufficient incentive; for the region in which the Kaiser sought concessions was, if tradition be correct, the very cradle of the human race and the origin of empire. It was likewise the garden of the early world, and what man had once done the German could do again. A concession, patience, industry, water, and out of the ruins of the past the empire of the future would be reared and the desert would again blossom as the rose. The Hohenzollern was not to be inferior to the Babylonian, the Assyrian, the Mede, and the Persian. Pan-Hellenism was not superior to pan-Germanism; nor Athens to—Berlin.

But although diplomacy worked like a mole in the dark, the line of steel from Kiel to Bagdad betrayed like a ridge its progress. Germany's neighbors were not blind, and little by little they grouped as their interests dictated. The acquisition of Tunis by France in 1881 alienated Italy and apparently cemented the alliance between Italy and the Teutonic Powers.[1] The acquisition by France of Morocco in 1911 was disagreeable to Germany and whetted the Italian appetite, only satisfied for the time being by the annexation of Tripoli in 1912 at the expense of the Turk.[2]

The way was thus cleared for the coöperation of France and Italy. Then, too, events had taken place to the east of the German Empire which distressed it and menaced the success of its projects. It was well enough to form an alliance with Russia, but it was a different matter to form an alliance with Austria-Hungary to protect it against a Russian attack. Either could have been maintained, but not both. The treaty with Russia was secret, as were the exact terms of the Triple Alliance, but secrets cannot always be hid. The mole inevitably comes to the surface. The terms of the Russian alliance became known. It was not renewed, and Russia and France, the neighbor

---

[1] The Triple Alliance which I first sought to conclude after the peace of Frankfort, and about which I had already in September, 1870, from Meaux, sounded Vienna and St. Petersburg, was an alliance of the three emperors with the additional idea that monarchical Italy might join it. It was designed for the struggle which I feared was confronting us as between the two European tendencies which Napoleon called Republican and Cossack, and which, according to our present ideas, I should characterize on the one hand as the system of organization on a monarchical basis, and on the other hand as the social republic to the level of which the anti-monarchical evolution would sink gradually or by leaps. . . . Since 1871 I have sought for the immediate assurance against those struggles in the alliance of the three Emperors, and in the endeavor to secure a firm support in that alliance for the monarchical principle in Italy. (Bismarck, *Gedanken und Erinnerungen*, pp. 569-570.)

It is our task to keep our two imperial neighbors at peace. We shall certainly be able to assure the future of the fourth great dynasty in Italy to the same extent that we shall succeed in maintaining agreement between the three imperial states, and in either curbing the ambition of our two eastern neighbors or in satisfying that ambition by a reciprocal understanding. Both are for us indispensable not only in the matter of the European balance of power, we cannot get along without either of them without endangering our own position, but the maintenance of an element of monarchical organization in Vienna and St. Petersburg, and in Rome on the basis of the latter two, is for us in Germany a task which coincides with the maintenance of our own political organization. (*Ibid.*, p. 589.)

Italy became a party to the Triple Alliance in 1882.

[2] See the treaty of peace between Italy and Turkey, concluded at Lausanne, October 18, 1912. Article 2 of this treaty reads as follows:

The two Governments pledge themselves respectively to give immediately after the signature of the present Treaty orders for the recall of their officers, their troops, as well as of their civil functionaries,—the Ottoman Government from the Tripolitana and Cyrenaica, and the Italian Government from the islands which it occupied in the Ægean Sea.

The effective evacuation of the aforesaid islands by the Italian officers, troops, and civil functionaries will take place immediately after the evacuation of the Tripolitana and Cyrenaica by the Ottoman officers, troops, and civil functionaries. (Martens, *Nouveau Recueil*, 3me série, tome vii, p. 7.)

on the east and the neighbor on the west, gradually drifted into an accord in case of war with Germany.

In 1901 Queen Victoria died and her son, Edward VII, unlike the mother, believing that the interests of his country required an understanding with France and Russia, set about removing the obstacles in the way of coöperation. He succeeded, and the Triple Alliance [1] found itself faced by the Triple Entente, with Italy out-

[1] The treaty of alliance between Germany and Austria, concluded at Vienna on October 7, 1879, became the Triple Alliance by the adherence of Italy thereto in May, 1882. The material portion of the treaty between Germany and Austria is as follows:

Art. I. Should, contrary to their hope, and against the loyal desire of the two High Contracting Parties, one of the two Empires be attacked by Russia, the High Contracting Parties are bound to come to the assistance one of the other with the whole war strength of their Empires, and accordingly only to conclude peace together and upon mutual agreement.

II. Should one of the High Contracting Parties be attacked by another Power, the other High Contracting Party binds itself hereby, not only not to support the aggressor against its high ally, but to observe at least a benevolent neutral attitude towards its fellow Contracting Party.

Should, however, in such a case the attacking Power be supported by Russia, either by an active coöperation or by military measures which constitute a menace to the Party attacked, then the obligation stipulated in Article I of this Treaty, for mutual assistance with the whole fighting force becomes equally operative, and the conduct of the war by the two High Contracting Parties shall in this case also be in common until the conclusion of a common peace.

III. This Treaty shall, in conformity with its peaceful character, and to avoid any misinterpretations, be kept secret by the two High Contracting Parties, and only be communicated to a third Power upon a joint understanding between the two Parties, and according to the terms of a special Agreement.

The two High Contracting Parties venture to hope after the sentiments expressed by the Emperor Alexander at the meeting at Alexandrowo, that the armaments of Russia will not in reality prove to be menacing to them, and have on that account no reason for making a communication; should, however, this hope, contrary to their expectation, prove to be erroneous, the two High Contracting Parties would consider it their loyal obligation to let the Emperor Alexander know, at least confidentially, that they must consider an attack on either of them as directed against both. (*British and Foreign State Papers*, vol. 73, p. 270.)

The official text of the Triple Alliance has not been published, with the exception of Articles 1, 3, 4, and 7, which appear in the correspondence between Austria-Hungary and Italy issued by the Austro-Hungarian Government. These articles are as follows:

1. The High Contracting Parties mutually promise peace and friendship, and shall not enter into any alliance or engagement directed against any one of their respective States.

They bind themselves to proceed to negotiations on such political and economic questions of a general nature as may arise; and, moreover, promise their mutual support within the scope of their own interests.

3. If one or two of the High Contracting Parties should be attacked without direct provocation on their part, and be engaged in war with two or several Great Powers not signatory to this Treaty, the *casus foederis* shall apply simultaneously to all the High Contracting Parties.

4. In the event that a Great Power not signatory to this Treaty should menace the safety of the States of one of the High Contracting Parties, and

wardly a member of the Alliance but at heart allied with the Entente.[1] The stage was set and the curtain rose on the 1st day of August, 1914.

There was, however, a prologue to the play, as there will be an epilogue, which must perforce be left to posterity.

On the 28th of June, 1914, one Gabrilo Princip, a subject of Bosnia, and of Servian race, shot and killed in the city of Serajevo, in the province of Bosnia, Archduke Francis Ferdinand, heir to the Austro-Hungarian throne, and the Duchess of Hohenberg, his morganatic wife. The Austro-Hungarian Government investigated the assassination, declared it to be due to the propaganda for a larger Servia, and that the outrage was perpetrated either with the knowledge of the Servian authorities or with the connivance and coöperation of Servian officials.

> that the menaced party should be forced to make war on that Power, the two others bind themselves to observe toward their ally a benevolent neutrality. Each one of them in that case reserves to herself the right to participate in the war, if she should consider it appropriate to make common cause with her ally. (*Austro-Hungarian Red Book* [No. 2], Appendix Nos. 14-16; *Diplomatic Documents Relating to the Outbreak of the European War*, p. 346.)
>
> 7. Austria-Hungary and Italy, being desirous solely that the territorial *status quo* in the near East be maintained as much as possible, pledge themselves to exert their influence to prevent all territorial modification which may prove detrimental to one or the other of the Powers signatory to this Treaty. To that end they shall communicate to one another all such information as may be suitable for their mutual enlightenment, concerning their own dispositions as well as those of other Powers. Should, however, the *status quo* in the regions of the Balkans, or of the Turkish coasts and islands in the Adriatic and Ægean Seas in the course of events become impossible; and should Austria-Hungary or Italy be placed under the necessity, either by the action of a third Power or otherwise, to modify that *status quo* by a temporary or permanent occupation on their part, such occupation shall take place only after a previous agreement has been made between the two Powers, based on the principle of reciprocal compensation for all advantages, territorial or otherwise, which either of them may obtain beyond the present *status quo*, a compensation which shall satisfy the legitimate interests and aspirations of both parties. (*Ibid.*, Appendix No. 1, pp. 335-336.)

[1] The documents relating to the Triple Entente are as follows:
   Agreement between Great Britain and France respecting Egypt and Morocco (London), April 8, 1904. (*British and Foreign State Papers*, vol. 97, p. 39.)
   Secret Articles.
   Agreement between Great Britain and France respecting Newfoundland and Senegambia (London), April 8, 1904. (*Ibid.*, p. 31.)
   Agreement between Great Britain and Russia respecting China (St. Petersburg), April 16/28, 1899. (*Ibid.*, vol. 91, p. 91.)
   Agreement between Great Britain and Russia respecting Persia, Afghanistan, and Thibet (St. Petersburg), August 31, 1907. (*Ibid.*, vol. 100, p. 555.)
   Question of Armed Coöperation between Great Britain and France, 1907-14. (*Ibid.*, vols. 100-106.)
   Agreement between Great Britain, France, and Russia respecting the war (London), September 5, 1914. (Great Britain, *Treaty Series No. 1*, 1915.)

On the 23d day of July, 1914, a lengthy memorandum containing ten demands was handed by the Austro-Hungarian Minister in Belgrade to the Servian Minister of Foreign Affairs, with the statement that an acceptance of and compliance with these demands should be notified to the Austro-Hungarian Minister within forty-eight hours. The demands were such as to be unthinkable between large and powerful nations; they were inconsistent with independence and only possible in the intercourse of a large with a small state, and then only when the larger state does not believe in the equality of nations.[1] The action of Austria-Hungary was with the knowledge and approval of the Imperial German Government.[2]

The gravity of the ultimatum was at once seen by the European statesmen, and, without entering into details, it is sufficient to say that an unsuccessful effort was made by Austria-Hungary, supported by its ally "in shining armor," to localize the Servian dispute, thus making of it an Austro-Servian question instead of a matter of European concern, as the Eastern Question has been in times past; that attempts were made by Russia, France, Great Britain, and Italy to persuade Austria-Hungary to extend the time [3] beyond the forty-eight hours of the ultimatum; to continue negotiations with Servia and to submit the matter to arbitration, mediation, or conference.[4]

Pressure was likewise brought upon Servia by Russia, France, and Great Britain to cause it to present such a conciliatory reply as would permit of negotiation and peaceful settlement.[5]

All too dangerously near the expiration of the forty-eight hours, Servia presented a reply which accepted, as it seemed to disinterested persons at the time, some eight of the ten demands, partially accepted another, and offered to submit the last to arbitration. An extension of time had been refused and negotiations discontinued. The reply was held by Austria-Hungary to be unsatisfactory; within a half-hour of its delivery the Austro-Hungarian Minister was with-

[1] For detailed references to diplomatic correspondence preceding the war see notes, pp. 36-42.

[2] The Imperial and Royal Government apprised Germany of these views and asked for our opinion. Whole-heartedly we were able to agree with our ally's view of the situation, and assure her that any action considered necessary to end the movement in Servia directed against the very existence of the Monarchy, would meet with our approval. . . .

We therefore granted Austria a completely free hand in her action towards Servia; we did not participate in her preparations. (Memorial laid before the Imperial Diet on August 3, 1914; *German White Book*, 1 Mem.; *Diplomatic Documents Relating to the Outbreak of the European War*, pp. 772-773.)

[3] See note 2 at end of chapter, p. 37.
[4] See note 3 at end of chapter, p. 39.
[5] See note 4 at end of chapter, p. 41.

drawn from Belgrade according to previous arrangements; and, on July 28, the Austro-Hungarian Government issued a formal declaration of war against Servia.[1] "So when the Thebans had offered to the Lacedaemonians all that they could in justice require, and they were yet for pushing matters further, Aristides said, that the good cause passed then from the party of the latter to that of the former."[2]

Russia had served notice that it could not remain indifferent to the Austro-Servian dispute, and on August 1, 1914, the Imperial German Government declared war against it on the ground that the mobilization of the Russian Army was an attack upon Germany,[3] although Russia insisted that the army was mobilized solely on the Austro-Hungarian frontier,[4] and offered to submit the entire dispute to arbitration.[5]

Germany declared itself to be in a state of war with France on the 3d of August, alleging that a French aeroplane had flown across and had dropped bombs on German territory, thus violating the neutrality of the German Empire—a charge denied by France which, to prevent a border incident, had withdrawn its troops ten kilometers from the German frontier.[6]

Great Britain had stated to Russia and to France that public opinion would not allow it to be involved in a war over Servia,[7] although events proved that public opinion would allow Great Britain to go to war over the violation of Belgian neutrality. In order to prevent the occurrence of this lamentable event, Great

[1] According to the instructions which I have meanwhile received, we shall leave Belgrade by train at 6:30 o'clock if diplomatic relations are broken off. (Austro-Hungarian Minister to Servia to Austro-Hungarian Minister of Foreign Affairs, dated Belgrade, July 25, 1914; *Austro-Hungarion Red Book* (No. 1), doc. No. 22; *Diplomatic Documents Relating to the Outbreak of the European War*, p. 76.)

The reply of the Royal Servian Government to our demands of the 23d instant being inadequate, I have broken off diplomatic relations with Servia and have left Belgrade with the staff of the legation.

The reply was handed to me at 5:58 p.m. (Austro-Hungarian Minister to Servia to Austro-Hungarian Minister of Foreign Affairs, dated Semlin, July 25, 1914; *ibid.*, doc. No. 24, p. 77.)

For the text of the declaration of war by Austria-Hungary against Servia, see *ibid.*, doc. No. 37, p. 99.

[2] Grotius, *De Jure Belli ac Pacis*, lib. 2, chap. 1; English translation of 1738, p. 142.

[3] *German White Book*, doc. No. 25; *Diplomatic Documents Relating to Outbreak of the European War*, pp. 812-813.

[4] *Russian Orange Book*, doc. No. 77; *ibid.*, pp. 1378-1380; *German White Book*, doc. No. 13; *ibid.*, p. 805.

[5] *Russian Orange Book*, doc. No. 67; *ibid.*, p. 1373.

[6] *French Yellow Book*, doc. No. 136; *ibid.*, p. 687.

[7] "I do not consider that public opinion here would or ought to sanction our going to war over a Servian quarrel. If, however, war does take place, the development of other issues may draw us into it, and I am therefore anxious to prevent it." British Secretary for Foreign Affairs to British Ambassador at St. Petersburg, July 25, 1914. (*British Blue Book*, doc. No. 24; *ibid.*, p. 895.)

Britain asked France to state that it would observe the neutrality of Belgium, to which it was a party, to which request France promptly replied in the affirmative. Great Britain likewise asked Germany if it would observe the neutrality of Belgium, to which it was also a party, and failed to receive an affirmative reply.[1] German troops having forcibly entered Belgium, Great Britain declared war upon Germany on August 4th.

Italy, a member of the Triple Alliance, first refused to line up alongside of its allies, stating that the war declared against Servia was aggressive, not defensive; that its obligation under the Triple Alliance only extended to a defensive war—a statement which it had made a year before to Austria-Hungary when that Power requested Italian coöperation in the war which Austria-Hungary then apparently contemplated against Servia,[2] months before the Serajevo incident, which, to many disinterested observers at the time, seemed a pretext rather than a cause. Italy later denounced the Triple Alliance and entered the war on the side of the Entente Allies.

The bands of steel from Kiel to the Persian Gulf were apparently to be laid peaceably if possible, by force if need be, and as the next step in the great adventure Servia should either be annexed to Austria or be made subservient to Austria and the ally in shining armor.

What were the Austrian demands and what were the Servian replies? Were these demands in whole or in part justiciable, in the sense that they could be referred to a court and settled by the recognized principles of justice, or were they such as might be arbitrated because Austria-Hungary and Servia were parties to the peaceful settlement convention of the First Hague Peace Conference of 1899, advocating if not prescribing a resort to arbitration in judicial questions? And it may be said in passing that the Austro-Hungarian delegation to the Second Hague Peace Conference came to that body in favor of a treaty of arbitration, and, upon its motion, a clause was annexed to the peaceful settlement convention, declaring it to be desirable that, in disputes of a legal nature, and especially those involving the interpretation or application of international

---

[1] *British Blue Book*, No. 1, doc. No. 114; *Diplomatic Documents Relating to the Outbreak of the European War*, p. 976.

    In the present case the dispute between Austria and Servia was not one in which we felt called upon to take a hand . . . our idea had always been to avoid being drawn into a war over a Balkan question. If Germany became involved and France became involved, we had not made up our minds what we should do. . . . We were free from engagements, and we should have to decide what British interests required us to do. (British Secretary for Foreign Affairs to British Ambassador at Paris, July 29, 1914 [*British Blue Book*, doc. No. 87; *ibid.*, p. 949.])

[2] See note 5 at end of chapter, p. 42.

conventions, resort should be had to arbitration. Servia had requested arbitration of the differences between the two countries; Russia had suggested arbitration, and Great Britain, France, and Italy arbitration, mediation, or conference.

It is difficult, with the best of intentions, to summarize complicated statements in which we are deeply interested without allowing the personal equation to appear and to color the summary. To avoid this and to allow each Nation to speak for itself without the intervention of third parties, the Austro-Hungarian demands and the Servian replies are here reproduced in full, and placed side by side in parallel columns:

Austro-Hungarian Note of July 23, 1914.

In order to give a solemn character to this undertaking the Royal Servian Government shall publish on the front page of its "journal officiel" of the 13th (26th) July the following declaration:

"The Royal Government of Servia condemns the propaganda directed against Austria-Hungary, of which the final aim is to detach from the Austro-Hungarian Monarchy territories belonging to it, and it sincerely deplores the fatal consequences of these criminal proceedings.

"The Royal Government regrets that Servian officers and functionaries have participated in the above-mentioned propaganda and thus compromised the good neighborly relations to which the Royal Government was solemnly pledged by its declaration of the 31st of March, 1909.

"The Royal Government, which disapproves and repudiates all idea of interfering or attempting to interfere with the destinies of

Reply of Servian Government of July 25, 1914.

Falling in, therefore, with the desire of the Imperial and Royal Government, they [the Royal Serbian Government] are prepared to hand over for trial any Serbian subject, without regard to his situation or rank, of whose complicity in the crime of Serajevo proofs are forthcoming, and more especially they undertake to cause to be published on the first page of the "journal officiel," on the date of the 13th (26th) July, the following declaration:

"The Royal Government of Serbia condemn all propaganda which may be directed against Austria-Hungary, that is to say, all such tendencies as aim at ultimately detaching from the Austro-Hungarian Monarchy territories which form part thereof, and they sincerely deplore the baneful consequences of these criminal movements. The Royal Government regret that, according to the communication from the Imperial and Royal Government, certain Serbian officers and

the inhabitants of any part whatsoever of Austria-Hungary, considers it its duty formally to warn officers and functionaries, and the whole population of the Kingdom, that henceforward it will proceed with the utmost rigour against persons who may be guilty of such machinations, which it will use all its efforts to prevent and suppress."

This declaration shall simultaneously be communicated to the royal army as an order of the day by His Majesty the King, and published in the official bulletin of the army.

The Royal Servian Government further undertakes:

1. To suppress any publication which incites to hatred and contempt of the Austro-Hungarian Monarchy and the general tendency of which is directed against its territorial integrity;

officials should have taken part in the above-mentioned propaganda, and thus compromised the good neighborly relations to which the Royal Serbian Government was solemnly engaged by the declaration of the 18th (31st) March, 1909, which declaration disapproves and repudiates all idea or attempt at interference with the destiny of the inhabitants of any part whatsoever of Austria-Hungary, and they consider it their duty formally to warn the officers, officials, and entire population of the Kingdom that henceforth they will take the most rigorous steps against all such persons as are guilty of such acts, to prevent and to repress which they will use their utmost endeavor."

This declaration will be brought to the knowledge of the Royal Army in an order of the day, in the name of His Majesty the King, by his Royal Highness the Crown Prince Alexander, and will be published in the next official army bulletin.

The Royal Government further undertake:

1. To introduce at the first regular convocation of the Skuptchina[1] a provision into the press law providing for the most severe punishment of incitement to hatred or contempt of the Austro-Hungarian Monarchy, and for taking action against any publi-

[1] The Serbian Parliament.

cation the general tendency of which is directed against the territorial integrity of Austria-Hungary. The Government engage at the approaching revision of the Constitution to cause an amendment to be introduced into Article 22 of the Constitution of such a nature that such publication may be confiscated, a proceeding at present impossible under the categorical terms of Article 22 of the Constitution.

2. To dissolve immediately the society called Narodna Odbrana, to confiscate all its means of propaganda, and to proceed in the same manner against all other societies and their branches in Servia which engage in propaganda against the Austro-Hungarian Monarchy. The Royal Government shall take the necessary measures to prevent the societies dissolved from continuing their activity under another name and form;

2. The Government possesses no proof, nor does the note of the Imperial and Royal Government furnish them with any, that the "Narodna Odbrana" and other similar societies have committed up to the present any criminal act of this nature through the proceedings of any of their members. Nevertheless, the Royal Government will accept the demand of the Imperial and Royal Government and will dissolve the "Narodna Odbrana" society and every other society which may be directing its efforts against Austria-Hungary.

3. To eliminate without delay from public instruction in Servia, both as regards the teaching body and the methods of instruction, everything that serves, or might serve, to foment the propaganda against Austria-Hungary;

3. The Royal Serbian Government undertake to remove without delay from their public educational establishments in Serbia all that serves or could serve to foment propaganda against Austria-Hungary, whenever the Imperial and Royal Government furnish them with facts and proofs of this propaganda.

4. To remove from the military service, and from the administration in general, all officers and functionaries guilty of propaganda against the Austro-Hungarian Monarchy whose names and deed the Austro-Hungarian Government reserves the right of communicating to the Royal Government;

5. To accept the coöperation in Servia of representatives of the Austro-Hungarian Government in the suppression of the subversive movement directed against the territorial integrity of the Monarchy;

6. To take judicial proceedings against accomplices in the plot of the 28th of June who are on Servian territory. Delegates of the Austro-Hungarian Government will take part in the investigation relating thereto;

4. The Royal Government also agree to remove from military service all such persons as the judicial inquiry may have proved to be guilty of acts directed against the integrity of the territory of the Austro-Hungarian Monarchy, and they expect the Imperial and Royal Government to communicate to them at a later date the names and the acts of these officers and officials for the purposes of the proceedings which are to be taken against them.

5. The Royal Government must confess that they do not clearly grasp the meaning or the scope of the demand made by the Imperial and Royal Government that Serbia shall undertake to accept the collaboration of the organs of the Imperial and Royal Government upon their territory, but they declare that they will admit such collaboration as agrees with the principle of international law, with criminal procedure, and with good neighborly relations.

6. It goes without saying that the Royal Government consider it their duty to open an inquiry against all such persons as are, or eventually may be, implicated in the plot of the 15th (28th) June, and who happen to be within the territory of the kingdom. As regards the participation in this inquiry of Austro-Hungarian agents or authorities

appointed for this purpose by the Imperial and Royal Government, the Royal Government cannot accept such an arrangement, as it would be a violation of the Constitution and of the law of criminal procedure; nevertheless in concrete cases communications as to the results of the investigation in question might be given to the Austro-Hungarian agents.

7. To proceed without delay to the arrest of Major Voja Tankositch and of the individual named Milan Ciganovitch, a Servian State employee, who have been compromised by the results of the preliminary investigation at Serajevo;

7. The Royal Government proceeded, on the very evening of the delivery of the note, to arrest Commandant Voislav Tankositch. As regards Milan Ciganovitch, who is a subject of the Austro-Hungarian Monarchy and who up to the 15th (28th) June was employed (on probation) by the directorate of railways, it has not yet been possible to arrest him.

The Austro-Hungarian Government are requested to be so good as to supply as soon as possible, in the customary form, the presumptive evidence of guilt, as well as the eventual proofs of guilt which have been collected up to the present, at the inquiry at Serajevo, for the purposes of the latter inquiry.

8. To prevent by effective measures the participation of the Servian authorities in the illicit traffic in arms and explosives across the frontier; to dismiss and punish severely the officials of the frontier service at Schabatz

8. The Serbian Government will reinforce and extend the measures which have been taken for preventing the illicit traffic of arms and explosives across the frontier. It goes without saying that they will immediately order

and Loznica who have been guilty of having assisted the perpetrators of the Serajevo crime by facilitating their passage across the frontier;

9. To furnish the Imperial and Royal Government with explanations regarding the unjustifiable utterances of high Servian officials, both in Servia and abroad, who, notwithstanding their official positions, did not hesitate after the crime of the 28th of June to give utterance, in published interviews, to expressions of hostility to the Austro-Hungarian Government; and finally,

10. To notify the Imperial and Royal Government without delay of the execution of the measures comprised under the preceding heads.

The Austro-Hungarian Government awaits the reply of the Royal Government at the latest by 6 o'clock on Saturday evening, the 25th of July.[1]

an inquiry and will severely punish the frontier officials on the Schabatz-Loznica line who have failed in their duty and allowed the authors of the crime of Serajevo to pass.

9. The Royal Government will gladly give explanations of the remarks made by their officials, whether in Serbia or abroad, in interviews after the crime, and which, according to the statement of the Imperial and Royal Government, were hostile towards the Monarchy, as soon as the Imperial and Royal Government have communicated to them the passages in question in these remarks, and as soon as they have shown that the remarks were actually made by the said officials, although the Royal Government will itself take steps to collect evidence and proofs.

10. The Royal Government will inform the Imperial and Royal Government of the execution of the measures comprised under the above heads, in so far as this has not already been done by the present note, as soon as each measure has been ordered and carried out.

"If the Imperial and Royal Government are not satisfied with this reply, the Serbian Government, considering that it is not to the common interest to precipitate

---

[1] *Austro-Hungarian Red Book*, No. 1, doc. No. 7; *Diplomatic Documents Relating to the Outbreak of the European War*, pp. 16-17.

the solution of this question, are ready, as always, to accept a pacific understanding, either by referring this question to the decision of the International Tribunal of The Hague, or to the Great Powers which took part in the drawing up of the declaration made by the Serbian Government on the 18th (31st) March, 1909."[1]

A distinguished American statesman, of large experience in foreign affairs, declared at the time, that the Austro-Hungarian note was purposely couched in such terms as rendered a satisfactory reply impossible, that the intent of Austria-Hungary could only be to prevent such a reply, and that if Servia had, in an effort to avert the war, accepted the Austro-Hungarian terms, it would have ceased to be an independent nation. Whether this is so or not, whether the assassination of the Austro-Hungarian heir was cause or pretext, whether Austria-Hungary had ulterior purposes seeking the subjection of Servia to its will and the will of its more powerful ally, are questions for the future to determine. The fact is that Austria-Hungary declared war on Servia on the 28th day of July, that the Imperial German Government declared war against Russia on the 1st of August, that the Imperial German Government declared war against France on the 3d of August, that Great Britain declared war against Germany on the 4th of August, and that other nations, for various reasons, have from time to time become parties to the conflict.

[1] *Serbian Blue Book*, doc. No. 39; *Diplomatic Documents Relating to the Outbreak of the European War*, pp. 1473-1476.

Note 1.—Documents showing the localization of the Austro-Serbian dispute are to be found in *Diplomatic Documents Relating to the European War*, at the pages noted.

"We cannot allow our demands, which, as a matter of fact, do not contain anything unusual in the intercourse between States which ought to be living in peace and friendship, to become the object of negotiations and compromises; and, with due regard to our economic interests, we cannot accept a political method which would enable Servia to prolong the crisis at her pleasure." (*Austro-Hungarian Red Book*, No. 1, doc. No. 9; *ibid.*, p. 21.)

See also for further statements of the Austrian attitude documents No. 10 (p. 22), No. 11 (p. 23), No. 14 (p. 24), No. 20 (p. 75), No. 26 (p. 81), No. 32 (p. 87), No. 44 (p. 106), No. 47 (p. 108), No. 48 (p. 110); *British Blue Book*, No. 1, docs. No. 5 (p. 879), No. 48 (p. 918), No. 118 (p. 979).

The Russian attitude that the dispute was a European, not an Austro-Hungarian or Servian one, and that it could not therefore be localized, is briefly recorded in the following telegram from the Imperial German Ambassador, dated St. Petersburg, July 24, to the Imperial German Chancellor:

> The Minister [Sazanof] indulged in immoderate accusations against Austria-Hungary and he was very much agitated. He declared most positively that Russia could not under any circumstances permit of the Servo-Austrian difficulty being settled between the two parties concerned. (*The German White Book*, doc. No. 4, p. 802.)

The following statement in the dispatch from the British Ambassador, dated Vienna, July 27, 1914, to the British Secretary of State, relating the substance of an interview of the Russian Ambassador with the Austro-Hungarian Under-Secretary of State, is illuminating:

> "He told him that, having just come back from St. Petersburg, he was well acquainted with the views of the Russian Government and the state of Russian public opinion. He could assure him that if actual war broke out with Servia it would be impossible to localize it, for Russia was not prepared to give away again, as she had done on previous occasions, and especially during the annexation crisis of 1909." (*British Blue Book*, No. 1, doc. No. 56, p. 928.)

For further statements of the Russian attitude, see *Austro-Hungarian Red Book* (No. 1), docs. Nos. 15 and 16 (p. 26); *The Belgian Grey Book*, No. 2, doc. No. 7 (p. 428); *The British Blue Book*, No. 1, docs. No. 6 (p. 880), No. 7 (p. 882), No. 94 (p. 958), No. 95 (p. 959); *The French Yellow Book*, docs. No. 18 (p. 564), No. 52 (p. 605); *The German White Book* (p. 771); *The Russian Orange Book*, No. 1, docs. Nos. 9 and 10 (p. 1339).

For British attitude that it was not directly interested in the merits of the dispute, but in its international aspect in so far as it concerned the peace of Europe, see *Austro-Hungarian Red Book*, No. 1, doc. No. 41 (p. 103); *British Blue Book*, No. 1, docs. No. 5 (p. 879), No. 24 (p. 895), No. 25 (p. 896), No. 48 (p. 918), No. 87 (p. 948), No. 91 (p. 953), Nos. 115 and 116 (p. 977); *French Yellow Book*, docs. No. 19 (p. 565), No. 36 (p. 588), No. 66 (p. 617); *Russian Orange Book*, No. 1, doc. No. 20 (p. 1348).

The German attitude in support of localization is briefly and impressively stated in the following telegram dated at Paris, July 24, 1914, from the Austro-Hungarian Ambassador to the Austro-Hungarian Minister of Foreign Affairs:

> "Baron Schoen, following out his instructions, will declare today that our dispute with Servia is regarded by the Berlin Cabinet as an affair concerning solely Austria-Hungary and Servia.
>
> "In connection with this information, he will make it understood that, should a third Power try to intervene, Germany, true to the obligations of her Alliance, would be found on our side." (*Austro-Hungarian Red Book*, No. 1, doc. No. 12, p. 24.)

For further references to Germany's attitude, see *Austro-Hungarian Red Book*, No. 1, docs. No. 16 (p. 26), No. 45 (p. 107); *Belgian Grey Book*, No. 2, doc. No. 10 (p. 432); *British Blue Book*, No. 1, docs. No. 2 (p. 864), No. 9 (p. 883), No. 46 (p. 916), Nos. 81, 82, and 83 (p. 945); *French Yellow Book*, docs. No. 27 (p. 579), No. 30 (p. 582), No. 37 (p. 589), No. 56 (p. 607), No. 57 (p. 609); *German White Book*, Mem. 1 (p. 771), docs. No. 1 (p. 798), No. 15 (p. 806), No. 30 (p. 815); *Russian Orange Book*, No. 1, docs. Nos. 7 and 8 (p. 1338), No. 18 (p. 1347), No. 36 (p. 1470).

Note 2.—Request for extension of the time-limit in Austro-Hungarian demands. On July 24, 1914, the Russian Minister of Foreign Affairs sent the following telegram to the Russian Chargé d'Affaires at Vienna:

> Please convey the following message to the Austro-Hungarian Minister for Foreign Affairs:
>
> "The Communication made by the Austro-Hungarian Government to the Powers the day after the presentation of the ultimatum at Belgrade affords to the Powers a period which is quite insufficient to enable them

to take any steps which might help to smooth away the difficulties that have arisen.

"In order to prevent the consequences, incalculable and equally fatal to all the Powers, which may result from the course of action followed by the Austro-Hungarian Government, it seems to us to be above all essential that the period allowed for the Servian reply should be extended. Austria-Hungary, having declared herself to be disposed to inform the Powers of the facts elicited by the inquiry upon which the Imperial and Royal Government base their accusations, should equally allow them sufficient time to study those facts.

"In this case, if the Powers were convinced that certain of the Austrian demands were well-founded, they would be in a position to offer corresponding advice to the Servian Government.

"A refusal to prolong the term of the ultimatum would render nugatory the step taken by the Austro-Hungarian Government in regard to the Powers, and would be in contradiction to the very bases of international relations.

"Communicated to London, Rome, Paris, Belgrade." (*Russian Orange Book*, No. 1, doc. No. 4, p. 1335-1336.)

On that date the Russian Minister of Foreign Affairs sent the following telegram to the Russian Representatives at London, Berlin, Rome, and Paris:

With reference to my telegram of today to Kudacheff [Russian Chargé d'Affaires in Vienna] we trust that the Government to which you are accredited will share the Russian point of view and will at once intrust their Representative at Vienna to hold similar language.

Communicated to Belgrade. (*Ibid.*, No. 5, p. 1336.)

Under date of July 25, 1914, Russian Chargé d'Affaires at Vienna telegraphed Russian Minister of Foreign Affairs: "I have just heard from Macchio that the Austro-Hungarian Government refuse our proposal to extend the time-limit of the note." (*Ibid.*, No. 12, p. 1340.)

For further statements of the Russian attitude on this matter see *Austro-Hungarian Red Book*, No. 1, doc. No. 21 (p. 75); *British Blue Book*, No. 1, docs. No. 13 (p. 887), No. 40 (p. 912); *French Yellow Book*, docs. No. 38 (p. 590), Nos. 42 and 43 (p. 593), No. 45 (p. 595); *Russian Orange Book*, No. 1, doc. No. 11 (p. 1340).

The Austro-Hungarian attitude towards the Russian proposal is thus stated by the Austro-Hungarian Minister for Foreign Affairs:

"The Russian Chargé d'Affaires has informed me by telegraph that his Government has urgently instructed him to demand an extension of the time-limit in the ultimatum to Servia. I request you to reply to him in my behalf, that we cannot consent to an extension of the time-limit. You will please add that, even after the breaking off of diplomatic relations, Servia will be in a position to bring about an amicable settlement by an unconditional acceptance of our demands. In such case, however, we would be compelled to demand from Servia an indemnification for all costs and damages caused to us by our military measures." (*Austro-Hungarian Red Book*, No. 1, doc. No. 20, p. 75.)

"As to the explanations given by the Russian Government in substantiation of its request, they appear to be based upon an erroneous conception of the premises. Our note to the Powers was by no means meant as an invitation to them to inform us of their views on this matter, but simply to convey information as a matter of international courtesy." (*Ibid.*, doc. No. 21, p. 76.)

Further statements of the Austro-Hungarian attitude are *Austro-Hungarian Red Book*, No. 1, docs. No. 9 (p. 21), No. 26 (p. 81); *Russian Orange Book*, No. 1, doc. No. 12 (p. 1340).

The British attitude towards the Russian proposal is stated within the compass of a line, when, under date of July 25, the British Secretary of State for Foreign Affairs instructed the British Ambassador at Vienna that "You may support in general terms the step taken by your Russian colleague." (*British Blue Book*, No. 1, doc. No. 26, p. 897.)

For further statements of the British attitude on the phase of the question see *Austro-Hungarian Red Book*, No. 1, doc. No. 10 (p. 22); *British Blue Book*, No. 1, docs. No. 3 (p. 864), No. 5 (p. 879), No. 6 (p. 880), No. 11 (p. 885); *French Yellow Book*, docs. No. 40 (p. 591), No. 41 (p. 592); *Russian Orange Book*, No. 1, doc. No. 16 (p. 1346).

The French attitude towards the Russian proposal is thus stated by the Russian Chargé d'Affaires in a telegram dated July 25, 1914:

"I have received your telegram of the 11th (24th) July respecting the extension of the time-limit of the Austrian ultimatum, and I have made the communication in accordance with your instructions. The French Representative at Vienna has been furnished with similar instructions." (*Russian Orange Book*, No. 1, doc. No. 15, p. 1345.)

For further expressions of the French attitude on this question see *French Yellow Book*, docs. No. 25 (p. 576), No. 31 (p. 584), No. 46 (p. 595), No. 75 (p. 624), No. 139 (p. 689).

The German attitude towards the Russian proposal is contained in the following quotations:

"Prince Lichnowsky [German Ambassador in London] said that Austria might be expected to move when the time-limit expired unless Servia could give unconditional acceptance of Austrian demands *in toto*." (Telegram from British Secretary of State to British Chargé d'Affaires at Berlin, *British Blue Book*, No. 1, doc. No. 11, pp. 885-886.)

"Secretary of State [Germany] said that he did not know what Austria-Hungary had ready on the spot, but he admitted quite freely that Austro-Hungarian Government wished to give the Servians a lesson, and that they meant to take military action. He also admitted that Servian Government could not swallow certain of the Austro-Hungarian demands." (Telegram from British Chargé d'Affaires at Berlin to the British Secretary of State, *ibid.*, doc. No. 18, pp. 891-892.)

For further statements as to the German attitude see *Russian Orange Book*, No. 1, doc. No. 14 (p. 1345); *British Blue Book*, No. 1, doc. No. 11 (p. 885); *French Yellow Book*, doc. No. 41 (p. 592).

The Italian attitude towards the Russian proposal is contained in the following dispatch, dated July 25, 1914, from the French Ambassador at Rome to the Acting Minister for Foreign Affairs:

"The Russian Ambassador has carried out at the Consulta the *démarche* which M. Sazanof requested the representatives of Russia at Paris, Berlin, Rome, and Bucharest to undertake, the object of which was to induce these various Cabinets to take action similar to that of Russia at Vienna, with a view of obtaining an extension of the time-limit imposed on Servia.

"In the absence of the Marquis di San Giuliano, M. Salandra and M. di Martino replied that they would put themselves into communication with the Minister for Foreign Affairs, but that his reply could not reach them until towards 6 o'clock, that is to say, too late to take any step at Vienna." (*French Yellow Book*, doc. No. 44, p. 594.)

Note 3.—The following is a list of the various proposals emanating from or meeting with the approval of Great Britain, France, Italy, and Russia for the peaceful settlement of the Austro-Servian dispute:

MEDIATION PROPOSALS.

British proposal that Servian reply be considered by Austria as basis for discussion. *Austro-Hungarian Red Book*, No. 1, docs. No. 38 (p. 99), No. 41 (p. 103), No. 43 (p. 105), No. 44 (p. 106); *British Blue Book* No. 1, docs. No. 27 (p. 898), No. 34 (p. 902), No. 46 (p. 916), No. 58 (p. 930), No. 63 (p. 932), No. 76 (p. 940), No. 86 (p. 948); *French Yellow Book*, doc. No. 92 (p 650); *Russian Orange Book*, No. 1, doc. No. 55 (p. 1366).

———. Austrian attitude. *Austro-Hungarian Red Book*, No. 1, docs. No. 29 (p. 85), No. 39 (p. 101), No. 44 (p. 106); *British Blue Book*, No. 1, docs. No. 61 (p. 931), No. 62 (p. 931), No. 75 (p. 939); *French*

Yellow Book, doc. No. 83 (p. 644); *German White Book*, Mem. 1 (p. 771).

————. German attitude. *British Blue Book*, No. 1, doc. No. 34 (p. 902); *French Yellow Book*, doc. No. 83 (p. 644); *German White Book*, Mem. 1 (p. 771).

British proposal for mediation by France, Germany, Great Britain, and Italy. *Belgian Grey Book*, No. 1, doc. No. 6 (p. 363); *British Blue Book*, No. 1, docs. No. 10 (p. 884), No. 11 (p. 885), No. 24 (p. 895), No. 25 (p. 896), No. 37 (p. 903), No. 111 (p. 974); *French Yellow Book*, docs. No. 32 (p. 585), No. 34 (p. 586), No. 36 (p. 588), No. 41 (p. 592), No. 69 (p. 619), No. 71 (p. 620); *German White Book*, Mem. 5 (p. 821), doc. No. 30 (p. 815); *Russian Orange Book*, No. 1, doc. No. 22 (p. 1349).

————. Austrian attitude. *Austro-Hungarian Red Book*, No. 1, Intro. (p. 3); *British Blue Book*, No. 1, docs. No. 61 (p. 931), No. 62 (p. 931); *French Yellow Book*, doc. No. 83 (p. 644); *German White Book*, doc. No. 18 (p. 807); *Russian Orange Book*, No. 1, doc. No. 73 (p. 1375).

————. French attitude. *British Blue Book*, No. 1, docs. No. 42 (p. 913), No. 51 (p. 922), No. 52 (p. 924); *French Yellow Book*, docs. No. 34 (p. 586), No. 70 (p. 619), No. 76 (p. 638), No. 79 (p. 641), No. 81 (p. 643); *Russian Orange Book*, No. 1, docs. No. 28 (p. 1351), No. 39 (p. 1357), No. 55 (p. 1366).

————. German attitude. *British Blue Book*, No. 1, docs. No. 18 (p. 891), No. 25 (p. 896), No. 46 (p. 916), No. 84 (p. 946), No. 94 (p. 958), No. 121 (p. 982); *French Yellow Book*, docs. No. 67 (p. 618), No. 77 (p. 639); *German White Book*, docs. No. 14 (p. 805), No. 15 (p. 806); *Russian Orange Book*, No. 1, docs. No. 34 (p. 1354), No. 39 (p. 1357).

————. Italian attitude. *Belgian Grey Book*, No. 2, doc. No. 6 (p. 426); *British Blue Book*, No. 1, doc. No. 78 (p. 941); *French Yellow Book*, docs. No. 71 (p. 620), No. 97 (p. 656).

————. Russian attitude. *Belgian Grey Book*, No. 2, doc. No. 17 (p. 440); *British Blue Book*, No. 1, doc. No. 78 (p. 941); *French Yellow Book*, docs. No. 85 (p. 646), No. 86 (p. 647); *Russian Orange Book*, No. 1, doc. No. 48 (p. 1362).

British proposal for conference of four Powers at London, and suspension of military operations. *British Blue Book*, No. 1, docs. No. 36 (p. 902), No. 42 (p. 913), No. 67 (p. 934); *French Yellow Book*, doc. No. 68 (p. 618).

————. Austrian attitude. *Austro-Hungarian Red Book*, No. 1, docs. No. 38 (p. 99), No. 41 (p. 103); *British Blue Book*, No. 1, doc. No. 62 (p. 931); *German White Book*, Mem. 1 (p. 771).

————. French attitude. *British Blue Book*, No. 1, docs. No. 40 (p. 912), No. 42 (p. 913), No. 51 (p. 922), No. 52 (p. 924); *French Yellow Book*, doc. No. 61 (p. 612).

————. German attitude. *Austro-Hungarian Red Book*, No. 1, doc. No. 35 (p. 98); *British Blue Book*, No. 1, docs. No. 43 (p. 914), No. 67 (p. 934), No. 71 (p. 936), No. 84 (p. 946), No. 121 (p. 982); *French Yellow Book*, docs. No. 73 (p. 622), No. 74 (p. 622), No. 78 (p. 640), No. 81 (p. 643), No. 92 (p. 650); *German White Book*, Mem. 1 (p. 771), doc. No. 17 (p. 806).

————. Italian attitude and suggestions. *British Blue Book*, No. 1, docs. No. 35 (p. 902), No. 49 (p. 920), No. 57 (p. 929), No. 64 (p. 933), No. 78 (p. 941), No. 80 (p. 944), No. 92 (p. 953), No. 106 (p. 971); *French Yellow Book*, docs. No. 71 (p. 620), No. 84 (p. 645).

————. Russian attitude. *Belgian Grey Book*, No. 2, doc. No. 17 (p. 440); *British Blue Book*, No. 1, docs. No. 40 (p. 912), No. 53 (p. 925), No. 55 (p. 927), No. 78 (p. 941), No. 93 (p. 954); *French Yellow Book*, docs. No. 68 (p. 618), No. 91 (p. 650); *Russian Orange Book*, No. 1, doc. No. 69 (p. 1374).

British-Russian proposal for submission to mediating Powers of Servia's satisfaction to Austria after occupation of Belgrade. *British Blue Book*,

No. 1, docs. No. 76 (p. 940), No. 88 (p. 949), No. 103 (p. 965), No. 104 (p. 966), No. 111 (p. 974), No. 131 (p. 988), No. 135 (pp. 991, 1023); *German White Book* (p. 821); *Russian Orange Book*, No. 1, doc. No. 71 (p. 1375).

———. Austrian attitude. *Austro-Hungarian Red Book*, No. 1, Intro. (p. 3), doc. No. 51 (p. 112); *British Blue Book*, No. 1, docs. No. 131 (p. 988), No. 135 (p. 991); *French Yellow Book*, docs. No. 93 (p. 652), No. 107 (p. 664), No. 112 (p. 669).

———. German attitude. *British Blue Book*, No. 1, docs. No. 98 (p. 961), No. 100 (p. 963), No. 112 (p. 975), No. 121 (pp. 982, 1023); *German White Book* (p. 821).

———. Russian attitude and modifications. *British Blue Book*, No. 1, docs. No. 88 (p. 949), No. 97 (p. 960), No. 99 (p. 962), No. 120 (p. 981), No. 132 (p. 989), No. 139 (p. 994); *French Yellow Book*, docs. No. 103 (p. 660), No. 113 (p. 670); *Russian Orange Book*, No. 1, docs. No. 60 (p. 1369), No. 64 (p. 1371), No. 67 (p. 1373).

Germany asked for formula of mediation. *British Blue Book*, No. 1, docs. No. 60 (p. 931), No. 68 (p. 935), No. 80 (p. 944), No. 84 (p. 946), No. 88 (p. 949), No. 92 (p. 953), No. 100 (p. 963), No. 107 (p. 972), No. 111 (p. 974); *French Yellow Book*, docs. No. 74 (p. 622), No. 81 (p. 643), No. 98 (p. 656), No. 108 (p. 665); *Russian Orange Book*, No. 1, doc. No. 54 (p. 1366).

Powers agree to accept any mediation proposals made by Austria and Germany which will preserve peace. *British Blue Book*, No. 1, docs. No. 78 (p. 941), No. 84 (p. 946), No. 111 (p. 974); *French Yellow Book*, doc. No. 86 (p. 647); *Russian Orange Book*, No. 1, doc. No. 64 (p. 1371).

Russian proposal for simultaneous direct negotiations and discussions by the four Powers. *Austro-Hungarian Red Book*, No. 1, doc. No. 56 (p. 115); *British Blue Book*, No. 1, doc. No. 133 (p. 989); *French Yellow Book*, doc. No. 103 (p. 660); *Russian Orange Book*, No. 1, docs. No. 49 (p. 1362), No. 63 (p. 1371).

Russian proposal for reference to The Hague. *German White Book*, doc. No. 22 (p. 810).

Suspension of mediation proposals pending direct negotiations between Austria and Russia. *British Blue Book*, No. 1, docs. No. 53 (p. 925), No. 55 (p. 927), No. 67 (p. 934), No. 68 (p. 935); *French Yellow Book*, docs. No. 80 (p. 641), No. 104 (p. 661); *Russian Orange Book*, No. 1, docs. No. 31 (p. 1353), No. 32 (p. 1353).

———. Renewal of mediation proposals. *British Blue Book*, No. 1, docs. No. 78 (p. 941), No. 93 (p. 954), No. 106 (p. 971); *French Yellow Book*, docs. No. 91 (p. 650), No. 97 (p. 656); *Russian Orange Book*, No. 1, doc. No. 50 (p. 1363).

Note 4.—Advice given by France, Great Britain, and Russia to the Servian Government so to reply to Austro-Hungarian note as to preserve peace.

The French attitude is thus recorded by the Austro-Hungarian Ambassador in the following telegram to France, dated Paris, July 24, 1914, to the Austro-Hungarian Minister for Foreign Affairs:

"The Servian Minister here has been advised that his Government should yield on all points as much as possible, yet with the restriction: 'As long as her rights of sovereignty were not touched.'" (*Austro-Hungarian Red Book*, No. 1, doc. No. 13, p. 24.)

For further references to French advice see *British Blue Book*, No. 1, doc. No. 16 (p. 889); *French Yellow Book*, docs. No. 26 (p. 578), No. 34 (p. 586); *Serbian Blue Book*, docs. No. 10 (p. 1446), No. 13 (p. 1448).

The attitude of Great Britain is expressed in the telegram, dated Nish, July 28, 1914, from the British Chargé d'Affaires at Belgrade to the British Secretary of State for Foreign Affairs, as follows:

"I have urged on the Servian Government the greatest moderation pending efforts being made towards a peaceful solution." (*British Blue Book*, No. 1, doc. No. 65, p. 934.)

For further references to British counsels of moderation, see *British Blue Book*, No. 1, docs. No. 12 (p. 886), No. 22 (p. 894), No. 30 (p. 899).

The attitude of the Russian Government is unmistakably put in the following telegram of the Czar, dated July 14/27, 1914:

"When your Royal Highness applied to me at a time of especial stress, you were not mistaken in the sentiments which I entertain for you, or in my cordial sympathy with the Servian people.

"The existing situation is engaging my most serious attention, and my Government are using their utmost endeavour to smooth away the present difficulties. I have no doubt that your Highness and the Royal Servian Government wish to render that task easy by neglecting no step which might lead to a settlement, and thus both prevent the horrors of a new war and safeguard the dignity of Servia.

"So long as the slightest hope exists of avoiding bloodshed, all our efforts must be directed to that end; but if in spite of our earnest wish we are not successful, your Highness may rest assured that Russia will in no case disinterest herself in the fate of Servia." (*Russian Orange Book*, No. 1, doc. No. 40, p. 1357.)

For further statements of the Russian advice to Servia urging a conciliatory reply to the Austro-Hungarian ultimatum, see *British Blue Book*, No. 1, docs. No. 22 (p. 894), No. 45 (p. 916), No. 56 (p. 928), No. 94 (p. 958); *Russian Orange Book*, No. 1, docs. No. 42 (p. 1359), No. 56 (p. 1367), No. 57 (p. 1368).

Note 5.—Signor Giolitti, formerly Prime Minister of Italy, said in the course of debate in the Italian Chamber of Deputies, on December 5, 1914: "Therefore, inasmuch as I hold it necessary that Italy's loyal observance of international treaties shall be considered as being above any possibility of dispute—(*Hear, hear*)—I feel it my duty to recall a precedent, which proves that the interpretation placed by the Government on the Treaty of the Triple Alliance is the correct interpretation, and was admitted as correct in identical circumstances by the Allied Powers.

"During the Balkan War, on the 9th of August, 1913, about a year before the present war broke out, during my absence from Rome, I received from my hon. colleague, Signor di San Guiliano, the following telegram:

"'Austria has communicated to us and to Germany her intention of taking action against Serbia, and defines such action as defensive, hoping to bring into operation the *casus foederis* of the Triple Alliance, which, on the contrary, I believe to be inapplicable. (*Sensation.*)

"'I am endeavoring to arrange for a combined effort with Germany to prevent such action on the part of Austria, but it may become necessary to state clearly that we do not consider such action, if it should be taken, as defensive, and that, therefore, we do not consider that the *casus foederis* arises.

"'Please telegraph me at Rome if you approve.'

"I replied:

"'If Austria intervenes against Serbia it is clear that a *casus foederis* cannot be established. It is a step which she is taking on her own account, since there is no question of defence, inasmuch as no one is thinking of attacking her. It is necessary that a declaration to this effect should be made to Austria in the most formal manner, and we must hope for action on the part of Germany to dissuade Austria from this most perilous adventure.' (*Hear, hear.*)

"This course was taken, and our interpretation was upheld and recognized as proper, since our action in no way disturbed our relations with the two Allied Powers. The declaration of neutrality made by the present Government conforms therefore in all respects to the precedents of Italian policy, and conforms also to an interpretation of the Treaty of Alliance which has been already accepted by the Allies.

"I wish to recall this, because I think it right that in the eyes of all Europe it should appear that Italy has remained completely loyal to the observance of her pledges." (*Serbian Blue Book*, Appendix, pp. 1489-1490.)

CHAPTER II

THE NEUTRALITY OF THE UNITED STATES

On August 4, 1914, the President by proclamation declared the United States to be neutral in the war between Austria-Hungary and Servia, Germany and Russia, Germany and France—for although Belgium had been invaded and its neutrality therefore violated by the Imperial German Government on the morning of the 4th of August, and although Great Britain had declared war against the Imperial German Government on the 4th, the first proclamations of neutrality issued by the United States in the European war were in response to formal declarations known to have been made before the 5th day of August. As all subsequent proclamations were similar if not identical, it will only be necessary to consider and to analyze the first of the series issued because of Germany's declaration of war on the first day of August, 1914, against Russia in order to appreciate and to understand the conception of neutrality obtaining in the United States.

In what may be considered the preamble to this proclamation, President Wilson declares that "the laws and treaties of the United States, without interfering with the free expression of opinion and sympathy, or with the commercial manufacture or sale of arms or munitions of war,[1] nevertheless impose upon all persons who may be within their territory and jurisdiction the duty of an impartial neutrality during the existence of the contest"; and in the passage immediately following he declares it to be the duty of a neutral government "not to permit or suffer the making of its waters subservient to the purposes of war."

After these general statements the President proceeds to state in summary form the laws and treaties and the principles of international law which all persons residing within the United States are bound to obey in order to preserve neutrality.

The provisions of the Penal Code of the United States approved March 4, 1909, declaring certain acts to be unneutral and forbidding them under severe penalties, are thus stated in the proclamation:

---

[1] See *Convention V, The Hague*, 1907, Art. 7; *Convention XIII, The Hague*, 1907, Arts. 6 and 7; *The Hague Conventions and Declarations*, p. 134.

1. Accepting and exercising a commission to serve either of the said belligerents by land or by sea against the other belligerent.

2. Enlisting or entering into the service of either of the said belligerents as a soldier, or as a marine, or seaman on board of any vessel of war, letter of marque, or privateer.

3. Hiring or retaining another person to enlist or enter himself in the service of either of the said belligerents as a soldier, or as a marine, or seaman on board of any vessel of war, letter of marque, or privateer.

4. Hiring another person to go beyond the limits or jurisdiction of the United States with intent to be enlisted as aforesaid.

5. Hiring another person to go beyond the limits of the United States with intent to be entered into service as aforesaid.

6. Retaining another person to go beyond the limits of the United States with intent to be enlisted as aforesaid.

7. Retaining another person to go beyond the limits of the United States with intent to be entered into service as aforesaid. . . .

8. Fitting out and arming, or attempting to fit out and arm, or procuring to be fitted out and armed, or knowingly being concerned in the furnishing, fitting out, or arming of any ship or vessel with intent that such ship or vessel shall be employed in the service of either of the said belligerents.

9. Issuing or delivering a commission within the territory or jurisdiction of the United States for any ship or vessel to the intent that she may be employed as aforesaid.

10. Increasing or augmenting, or procuring to be increased or augmented, or knowingly being concerned in increasing or augmenting, the force of any ship of war, cruiser, or other armed vessel, which at the time of her arrival within the United States was a ship of war, cruiser, or armed vessel in the service of either of the said belligerents, or belonging to the subjects of either, by adding to the number of guns of such vessels, or by changing those on board of her for guns of a larger calibre, or by the addition thereto of any equipment solely applicable to war.

11. Beginning or setting on foot or providing or preparing the means for any military expedition or enterprise to be carried on from the territory or jurisdiction of the United States against the territories or dominions of either of the said belligerents.[1]

These are, in concise form, the neutrality statutes of the United States, which had been found necessary in Washington's administration and in that of his immediate successor to preserve the neutral rights of the United States against violation by belligerents, and to secure the observance of the neutral duties of the United States in

[1] Official text, *American Journal of International Law*, Special Supplement, July, 1915, p. 195; *Statutes at Large*, vol. 35, part 1, p. 1088.

and to prevent the commission of any unneutral act in the United States or by the United States, but also to have his countrymen refrain from the expression of unneutral thought or of unneutral opinion. America was to be neutral in thought as well as in deed. Thus, on the 19th of August, 1914, President Wilson made an appeal to his fellow countrymen, couched in the following language:

> I suppose that every thoughtful man in America has asked himself, during these last troubled weeks, what influence the European War may exert upon the United States, and I take the liberty of addressing a few words to you in order to point out that it is entirely within our own choice what its effects upon us will be and to urge very earnestly upon you the sort of speech and conduct which will best safeguard the Nation against distress and disaster.
>
> The effect of the war upon the United States will depend upon what American citizens say and do. Every man who really loves America will act and speak in the true spirit of neutrality, which is the spirit of impartiality and fairness and friendliness to all concerned. The spirit of the Nation in this critical matter will be determined largely by what individuals and society and those gathered in public meetings do and say, upon what newspapers and magazines contain, upon what ministers utter in their pulpits, and men proclaim as their opinions on the street.
>
> The people of the United States are drawn from many nations, and chiefly from the nations now at war. It is natural and inevitable that there should be the utmost variety of sympathy and desire among them with regard to the issues and circumstances of the conflict. Some will wish one nation, others another, to succeed in the momentous struggle. It will be easy to excite passion and difficult to allay it. Those responsible for exciting it will assume a heavy responsibility, responsibility for no less a thing than that the people of the United States, whose love of their country and whose loyalty to its Government should unite them as Americans all, bound in honor and affection to think first of her and her interests, may be divided in camps of hostile opinion, hot against each other, involved in the war itself in impulse and opinion if not in action.
>
> Such divisions among us would be fatal to our peace of mind and might seriously stand in the way of the proper performance of our duty as the one great nation at peace, the one people holding itself ready to play a part of impartial mediation and speak the counsels of peace and accommodation, not as a partisan, but as a friend.
>
> I venture, therefore, my fellow countrymen, to speak a solemn word of warning to you against that deepest, most subtle, most essential breach of neutrality which may spring out of partisanship, out of passionately taking sides. The United States must

dent further declared in his proclamation (8) that the statutes and treaties of the United States and the law of nations required that no persons within the jurisdiction of the United States should directly or indirectly take part in the war, but that they should remain at peace with all of the belligerents and maintain strict and impartial neutrality; (9) and he enjoined the citizens of the United States and all persons within the jurisdiction thereof to observe the laws, to commit no acts contrary to the provisions of the statutes or treaties or in violation of the law of nations. He also warned citizen and foreigner alike that (10) while a full and free expression of sympathy, in public and private, with the belligerents was not forbidden by the laws of the United States, military forces in aid of a belligerent could not lawfully be set on foot and organized within the United States; (11) that all persons residing within the United States might lawfully manufacture and sell within the United States "arms and munitions of war, and other articles ordinarily known as 'contraband of war,'" but that (12) they cannot carry such articles upon the high seas for the use or service of a belligerent; (13) that the transportation of soldiers and officers of a belligerent upon the high seas is forbidden; (14) that the attempt to break any blockade which might be lawfully established and maintained during the war was subject to the risk of capture and confiscation by the law of nations; (15) and the proclamation closed with the statement that citizens of the United States and others claiming its protection disobeyed the statutes and treaties of the United States and the law of nations at their peril, and that they could not expect the protection of the Government of the United States against the consequences of their misconduct.

It should be said, however, in this connection, that President Wilson was not satisfied with this formal expression of neutrality on behalf of the United States, which would have more than complied with international law and practice, as thus stated by the *Kriegsbrauch im Landkriege:*

> It is here assumed that neutrality is not to be regarded as synonymous with indifference and impartiality with regard to the belligerent parties and the continuance of the war. As to the expression "partisanship," neutral States can only be expected to observe international courtesies; as long as these are observed, there is no reason to interfere.[1]

President Wilson not only wished to avoid participation in the war

[1] *Kriegsbrauch im Landkriege* (Berlin, 1902), p. 69.

tion that the neutral conduct of the United States was the conduct which the United States had itself prescribed more than a century before this war, which it had followed during a century and more after its promulgation, and which had become the accepted standard of neutrality in the world at large.

In the balance of the proclamation the President called attention to certain provisions of International Law sanctioned by the practice of nations in order to render neutrality effective. Thus he declared (1) the presence of armed vessels of belligerents within the territorial jurisdiction of the United States for purposes of hostile operations or as posts of observation, or to note the entry and departure of merchant vessels of a belligerent, as "unfriendly and offensive, and in violation of that neutrality which it is the determination of this government to observe."[1] (2) He warned the belligerents that their vessels of war should not make use of any port, harbor, roadstead, or waters subject to the jurisdiction of the United States from which a vessel of its enemy had departed until twenty-four hours after the departure of such vessel beyond American jurisdiction; (3) that any belligerent warship within or entering American jurisdiction should leave within twenty-four hours after entrance, except in case of stress of weather or need of provisions, supplies, and repairs;[2] (4) that in these exceptional cases the belligerent vessel should put to sea as soon as possible after the twenty-four hours and that the vessel should not be permitted to take on supplies beyond those required for immediate use; (5) that a war vessel permitted to remain in American jurisdiction to make repairs should depart within twenty-four hours after the completion of such repairs unless vessels of an opposing belligerent had sailed from the same port within that period, in which case the war vessel would be detained in order that it might leave twenty-four hours after the departure of the other vessel;[3] (6) that no belligerent war vessel within American jurisdiction should take on supplies other than provisions, except such as were necessary for the subsistence of the crew, and no more coal than that required to carry the vessel to the nearest port of its own country; and (7) that, without special permission, a vessel once supplied with coal should not receive a further amount within three months from the date thereof within the jurisdiction of the United States, unless the vessel had in the meantime entered a port of the home country. The Presi-

[1] *The Hague Convention of 1907 Concerning the Rights and Duties of Neutral Powers in Naval Warfare*, Art. 16; *The Hague Conventions and Declarations of 1899 and 1907*, pp. 213 214.
[2] *Ibid.*, Art. 14.
[3] *Ibid.*, Art. 19.

behalf of belligerents. Reissued with slight modifications in 1818 and incorporated in the Statutes at Large in 1874, they reappear as a section of the so-called Penal Code of the United States in 1909 with but trifling changes of phraseology.

From these statutes and their history the reader will understand that the United States, young as it is, has had practical experience with neutrality. It was the first country to feel the need of a code of municipal law dealing with the question of neutrality, and it was the first country to draft such a code. By its conduct as a neutral in the wars of the French Revolution in Washington's administration, it laid the basis of the modern law of neutrality. The late Mr. Hall, who cannot be classed as an undiscriminating friend of the United States, as even a casual examination of his treatise on international law will show, felt justified, or rather was forced to state in the edition published a hundred years after the event that "the policy of the United States in 1793 constitutes an epoch in the development of the usages of neutrality. There can be no doubt that it was intended and believed to give effect to the obligations then incumbent upon neutrals. But it represented by far the most advanced existing opinions as to what those obligations were; and in some points it even went further than authoritative international custom has up to the present time advanced. In the main however it is identical with the standard of conduct which is now adopted by the community of nations."[1]

The neutrality therefore which the United States proclaimed in 1914 was not a neutrality born of the moment. It was the neutrality given to the world by Washington and his conscientious advisers in 1793, with such additions as subsequent experience has suggested. It was the goal of neutrality in 1793, it was the standard of neutrality in 1914. It was not devised to favor one belligerent at the expense of the other, nor was it devised to benefit one neutral nation at the expense of another. It was the neutrality which recognized belligerent duties as well as neutral rights, and which, by apt laws, sought to prevent assaults upon neutral rights and to compel the performance of neutral duties.

It is important to bear these things in mind in considering the relations between the Imperial German Government and the United States when Germany was a belligerent as respects Europe and the United States was a neutral as respects Germany, in order that it may appear clear and beyond the possibility of successful contradic-

[1] Hall's *International Law*, 4th ed. (Oxford, 1895), sec. 213, p. 616.

be neutral in fact as well as in name during these days that are to try men's souls. We must be impartial in thought as well as in action, must put a curb upon our sentiments as well as upon every transaction that might be construed as a preference of one party to the struggle before another.

My thought is of America. I am speaking, I feel sure, the earnest wish and purpose of every thoughtful American that this great country of ours, which is, of course, the first in our thoughts and in our hearts, should show herself in this time of peculiar trial a Nation fit beyond others to exhibit the fine poise of undisturbed judgment, the dignity of self-control, the efficiency of dispassionate action; a Nation that neither sits in judgment upon others nor is disturbed in her own counsels and which keeps herself fit and free to do what is honest and disinterested and truly serviceable for the peace of the world.

Shall we not resolve to put upon ourselves the restraints which will bring to our people the happiness and the great and lasting influence for peace we covet for them?[1]

It is the experience of a neutral Government that questions taxing its neutrality almost to the breaking point arise in the early part of the contest; that neutral Nations take their positions shortly after the outbreak of the war if they have not been able to do so upon its declaration; that belligerents, claiming rights which to them may seem essential or convenient in the beginning of the conflict, either conform their actions to the protests of the neutrals or, weighing these protests in the balance and testing them by their sense of convenience, make up their minds to risk the consequences, to continue the conduct which has been the source of criticism, and to formulate a policy over protest which they are pleased to consider essential to their success. The neutral is obliged to consider very carefully the questions when and as they arise. It cannot delay, because if a violation of neutrality is permitted, liability attaches and the enemy of the belligerent is sure to make its rights known and to impress neutrals with their duties. If an act committed by the belligerent is not in itself a violation of neutrality, it may nevertheless be fraught with disagreeable consequences, it may be preliminary to unneutral conduct, and the neutral is therefore obliged to take action to prevent such contingencies. It must be just as between the belligerents. It must be prompt. It must be firm. If it yields, it opens the door to opportunity; if it is feeble, it is drawn into the war.

The situation, therefore, of the neutral, especially at the outbreak

[1] Official text, *American Journal of International Law,* Special Supplement, July, 1915, pp. 199-200.

of a war, is one of embarrassment for the present and anxiety for the future. It is ordinarily unprepared, and it cannot well foresee the conduct of the belligerent laboring under excitement, perhaps smarting under defeat. The problems which present themselves either seem to be or they are new. In any event, they are unfamiliar. In the course of a few months, however, the questions that arise begin to look familiar, and within a twelvemonth repetition takes the place of novelty.

By way of further introduction it should be stated that many of Germany's complaints of discrimination between the treatment it received and that meted out to Great Britain arose in large part from natural geographical conditions which were recognized as existing long before the present unfortunate war, and some illustrations of them may be cited from the proceedings of the Second Hague Peace Conference, when apparently none of the delegates expected war.

Take, for example, the subject of mines. It was strenuously maintained by Great Britain, upon humanitarian grounds, that the laying of mines should be forbidden. It was insisted on the contrary by Germany that mines were appropriate weapons. It was generally felt that mines were a defense for countries without large navies, and as Great Britain had a large navy it was intimated that self-interest rather than humanitarian reasons prompted it to object to the use of mines by Nations with smaller navies.

Again, the question of the destruction of neutral prizes was bitterly contested. Great Britain insisted that neutral prizes should not be destroyed, that they should be released if they could not be brought into a home port for adjudication. It was felt that Great Britain, with colonies scattered throughout the world, could easily take neutral prizes into port, whereas countries without colonies could not conveniently do so, and that therefore the destruction of such prizes was permissible. It was impossible to reach an agreement upon this subject, permitting destruction, although the Powers assembled at the Naval Conference of London in 1909 were able to compromise their differences of opinion. Perhaps this subject is best treated by the distinguished Russian publicist, the late M. de Martens, who says in his work on international law that the geographical situation of Russia made it necessary to destroy neutral prizes, but admitted that this measure would "undoubtedly cause a universal criticism of his country."[1]

Then further, Great Britain insisted that the captor should not be

[1] Martens, *Traité de droit international*, 1887; tome iii, p. 295.

allowed to take his prize into a neutral country, whereas the States without colonial possessions stood for the right to do so, and felt that the attitude of Great Britain was due solely to its geographical situation and that its protests were dictated by self-interest.

And finally, there was much difference of opinion concerning the supplies of coal to be furnished in neutral ports to belligerent vessels of war, Great Britain maintaining that coal up to the peace standard might indeed be allowed once in three months, but only in sufficient quantity to take the vessel to its nearest home port. The countries without the vast territorial possessions of Great Britain felt that such a position would inure to the advantage of Great Britain, and that a belligerent, such as Russia in its war with Japan, might properly have its ships coaled in different ports on the way to the scene of conflict without violating neutrality.

These views were oftener felt than expressed, or were discussed privately by the delegates, as public expression would seem to impugn the good faith of Nations. It is apparent, without argument and without impugning the good faith of any country, that its views would be colored by its material interests. It is, however, too much to ask that neutral Nations should take note of these differences of condition and modify their laws and practices in such a way as to overcome them. They are either natural advantages, or they are the result of fortunate development, and what can reasonably be asked of a neutral Nation is that it forbid the commission of acts which are unneutral in themselves, whether their application may work or seem to work a hardship in a particular case. Otherwise there would be no general or universal standard of conduct, for the neutral would be obliged to weigh special conditions, and treat the belligerents differently, so as to overcome these differences. The result of this would be that the neutral would subject itself to unlimited criticism, and would in the long run satisfy no country, not even itself. The United States, for example, might hold one view as to the proprieties of the case; another neutral might have a different view, and so on, with the result that there would be inextricable confusion instead of a general law or standard of conduct to be known in advance. It is a familiar axiom that law is no respecter of persons.

We do not need to consider for present purposes the relations of the United States with the other belligerents, and particularly with Germany's enemies, because a Nation protests the violation of its rights to the Nation charged with their violation. Other Nations are either not familiar or are pleased not to be familiar with these matters, and a Nation against which a protest has been lodged refuses to allow the Nation making this protest to inquire into its conduct with other Nations, and by so doing to pose as *censor morum*. In law the transaction with another country is considered to be *res inter alios acta,* or, to take the illustration from the broad domain of arbitration, Nations specifically reserve from the special agreement to arbitrate all questions affecting the interests of third parties.

In the course of the present war this principle was insisted upon by the United States and called to the attention of the Imperial German Government and Great Britain in appropriate cases. Thus, in a telegram dated April 12, 1915, the American Ambassador to London was instructed to "say to [the] British Government, in replying to its statement regarding release [of the] steamer *Wico,* that this Government considers that any seizure of American cargoes which might be made by the German authorities would be a matter which should be adjusted between the Government of the United States and the German Government, and further say that the Government of the United States does not perceive that any such action on the part of the German authorities could afford justification for seizures of American cargoes by the British authorities."[1] Within a fortnight of this date—to be accurate, on April 21, 1915—the United States had occasion to call this familiar principle to the attention of the Imperial German Ambassador to the United States. Thus, Mr. Bryan, Secretary of State, said in a note to the German Ambassador:

> I shall take the liberty, therefore, of regarding Your Excellency's references to the course pursued by the Government of the United States with regard to interferences with trade from this country, such as the Government of Great Britain have attempted, as intended merely to illustrate more fully the situation to which you desire to call our attention and not as an invitation to discuss that course. Your Excellency's long experience in international affairs will have suggested to you that the relations of the two Governments with one another cannot wisely be made a subject of discussion with a third Government, which cannot be fully informed as to the facts and which cannot be fully cognizant of the reasons for the course pursued.[2]

And it may be of interest to note in passing that when the United States referred to the conduct of Great Britain as inconsistent with

---

[1] Official text, *American Journal of International Law*, Special Supplement, July, 1915, pp. 346-347.
[2] *Ibid.*, p. 127.

the Declaration of Paris, of which Great Britain is a signatory, that Government replied in kind, saying, in a formal memorandum, that it was not necessary "to discuss the extent to which the second rule of the Declaration of Paris is affected by these measures, or whether it could be held to apply at all as between Great Britain and the United States" because the United States was not and is not now a party to the Declaration of Paris.[1]

[1] Official text, *American Journal of International Law*, Special Supplement, July, 1915, p. 161.

CHAPTER III

GERMAN CHARGES OF UNNEUTRAL CONDUCT

We can therefore consider the relations between the Imperial German Government and the United States, as the Nations themselves considered them, as an interesting and important chapter, with references betimes to the actions of others, but then solely by way of illustration.

We do not need to search the archives of the Department of State and to foot up the incidents or charges of unneutral conduct in the relations of the Imperial German Government and the United States, with which this chapter primarily deals, because Senator William J. Stone, Chairman of the Committee on Foreign Relations of the United States Senate, in the following letter to the Secretary of State, dated January 8, 1915, grouped and stated the grievances of the Imperial German Government and of its sympathizers into twenty categories:

DEAR MR. SECRETARY: As you are aware, frequent complaints or charges are made in one form or another through the press that this Government has shown partiality to Great Britain, France, and Russia as against Germany and Austria during the present war between those Powers; in addition to which I have received numerous letters to the same effect from sympathizers with Germany and Austria. The various grounds of these complaints may be summarized and stated in the following form:

1. Freedom of communication by submarine cables, but censorship of wireless messages.
2. Submission to censorship of mails and in some cases to the repeated destruction of American letters found on neutral vessels.
3. The search of American vessels for German and Austrian subjects—
    (a) On the high seas.
    (b) In territorial waters of a belligerent.
4. Submission without protest to English violations of the rules regarding absolute and conditional contraband, as laid down—

        (a) In The Hague Conventions.
        (b) In international law.
        (c) In the Declaration of London.
5. Submission without protest to inclusion of copper in the list of absolute contraband.
6. Submission without protest to interference with American trade to neutral countries—
        (a) In conditional contraband.
        (b) In absolute contraband.
7. Submission without protest to interruption of trade in conditional contraband consigned to private persons in Germany and Austria, thereby supporting the policy of Great Britain to cut off all supplies from Germany and Austria.
8. Submission to British interruption of trade in petroleum, rubber, leather, wool, etc.
9. No interference with the sale to Great Britain and her Allies of arms, ammunition, horses, uniforms, and other munitions of war, although such sales prolong the war.
10. No suppression of sale of dumdum bullets to Great Britain.
11. British warships are permitted to lie off American ports and intercept neutral vessels.
12. Submission without protest to disregard by Great Britain and her allies of—
        (a) American naturalization certificates.
        (b) American passports.
13. Change of policy in regard to loans to belligerents—
        (a) General loans.
        (b) Credit loans.
14. Submission to arrest of native-born Americans on neutral vessels and in British ports and their imprisonment.
15. Indifference to confinement of noncombatants in detention camps in England and France.
16. Failure to prevent transshipment of British troops and war material across the territory of the United States.
17. Treatment and final internment of German steamship *Geier* and the collier *Locksun* at Honolulu.
18. Unfairness to Germany in rules relative to coaling of warships in Panama Canal Zone.
19. Failure to protest against the modifications of the declaration of London by the British Government.
20. General unfriendly attitude of Government toward Germany and Austria.

If you deem it not incompatible with the public interest I would be obliged if you would furnish me with whatever information your department may have touching these various points of complaint, or request the counselor of the State Department to send me the information, with any suggestions you or he may deem advisable to make with respect to either the legal or political aspects of the subject. So far as informed I see no reason why all the matter I am requesting to be furnished should not be made public, to the end that the true situation may be known and misapprehensions quieted.[1]

To this letter, Mr. Bryan, then Secretary of State, sent a comprehensive, full, and detailed reply under date of January 24, 1917, which will be considered in connection with the discussion of the complaints contained in Senator Stone's letter.

[1] Official text, *American Journal of International Law*, Special Supplement, July, 1915, pp. 253-255; Senate doc. 716, 63d Cong., 3d sess.

CHAPTER IV

CENSORSHIP OF COMMUNICATIONS

Section 1. Cable and Wireless

The first point made by Senator Stone concerns the freedom of communication by submarine cables versus censored communication by wireless. In the matter of cables, the United States decided that no messages should be sent in cipher and that plain messages should be submitted to the censorship of the authorities in order to see whether, in their opinion, the message was or was not unneutral. In the case of wireless telegraphy the station at Tuckerton, N. J., under German ownership, was closed, the station at Sayville was taken in charge by the Navy and only messages were transmitted which the censor approved. This regulation, fair in itself and applied to all the belligerents, bore more heavily upon Germany than it did upon its enemies, because Great Britain had cables of its own from Canada and did not need to rely upon the United States, whereas Germany had no direct cable to the United States, and, after the cable was cut between the Canary Islands, had no indirect communication. Recognizing, however, that a diplomat accredited to the United States should have the right of rapid communication with his Government, the Imperial German Embassy was allowed to use freely and for official purposes the station at Sayville. Absolute neutrality was maintained by reason of the fact that all cables were uncensored, whereas all wireless news was censored; that is to say, there was no discrimination made in favor of messages sent by cable by any of the belligerents, nor was there any allegation that one country was treated differently from the other in the matter of news by wireless. Nor was there any objection apparently made because communications by cable were treated in one way, and communications by wireless in another way. The alleged discrimination existed in the fact that Great Britain preferred the use of the cable which was open to it, whereas Germany had to rely upon the wireless. Cable communications with Germany were severed, a proper belligerent act under international law, so that Germany could not use the cable for the transmission of news.[1] This was no doubt a serious interruption to the transmission of German news, because by the cable, to the use of which Germany was not admitted, Great Britain transmitted news uncensored, whereas the only source of communication open to Germany was by wireless, which, however, was subject to censorship. This was a misfortune for which the United States was in no wise to blame. It has the right to censor communications by wireless; it has exercised this right; and all Nations using wireless are treated alike. If it were alleged that British communications by wireless were uncensored, while those transmitted by Germany were censored, there would then be a direct and positive discrimination. If it be said that the same result is reached, in fact though not in theory, because Great Britain could use the uncensored medium of communication, whereas Germany could not, and was therefore forced to use the censored means of communication, the discrimination does not exist.

The action of the United States in these matters was in conformity with the Convention respecting the rights and duties of neutral Powers and persons in case of war on land, signed at The Hague October 18, 1907, which was ratified by Germany and the United States on November 27, 1909.[2] The provisions in question were:

> Belligerents are likewise forbidden to—
> (a) Erect on the territory of a neutral Power a wireless telegraphy station or other apparatus for the purpose of communicating with belligerent forces on land or sea;
> (b) Use any installation of this kind established by them before the war on the territory of a neutral Power for purely military purposes, and which has not been opened for the service of public messages. (Art. 3.)[3]

According to Article 8 of this Convention:

> A neutral Power is not called upon to forbid or restrict the use on behalf of the belligerents of telegraph or telephone cables

[1] It is to be observed that Germany has cut cables running to British possessions, so that the right claimed by Great Britain has been exercised by Germany. (Senate doc. 716, 63d Cong., 3d sess., p. 1.)

[2] The question may be overlooked whether this Convention is ratified by all the belligerents to the present war, because the United States was not acting as a belligerent, but as a neutral, and properly regarded the terms of the Convention as binding upon it, as they are meant to apply and do only apply to a neutral country. (*The Hague Conventions and Declarations of 1899 and 1907*, p. 139.)

[3] *Ibid.*, pp. 133-134.

or of wireless telegraphy apparatus belonging to it or to companies or private individuals.[1]

But if a neutral Power should consider it expedient to forbid or to restrict the belligerent use of the telegraph or of the telephone or of wireless telegraph, Article 9 provided that every measure of restriction or of prohibition should "be impartially applied by it to both belligerents."

Mr. Bryan's letter contains, however, the following additional justification of the attitude assumed and maintained by the United States.

> A more important reason, however, at least from the point of view of a neutral Government, is that messages sent out from a wireless station in neutral territory may be received by belligerent warships on the high seas. If these messages, whether plain or in cipher, direct the movements of warships or convey to them information as to the location of an enemy's public or private vessels, the neutral territory becomes a base of naval operations, to permit which would be essentially unneutral.
>
> As a wireless message can be received by all stations and vessels within a given radius, every message in cipher, whatever its intended destination, must be censored; otherwise military information may be sent to warships off the coast of a neutral. It is manifest that a submarine cable is incapable of becoming a means of direct communication with a warship on the high seas. Hence its use cannot, as a rule, make neutral territory a base for the direction of naval operations.[2]

Section 2. Mail

At the time of Senator Stone's letter to the Department of State, the question of the censorship of mails upon the high seas did not seem to have arisen, and the discussion of the subject at that time was academic rather than concrete. The Secretary of State said, however, that both Germany and Great Britain had censored private letters falling into their hands, that this practice was justified, and that "the unquestioned right to adopt a measure of this sort makes objection to it inadvisable."

The question, however, arose in acute form in the course of 1916

[1] *The Hague Conventions and Declarations of 1899 and 1907*, p. 134.
[2] Official text, *American Journal of International Law*, Special Supplement, July, 1915, pp. 255-256.

from the repeated interference by Great Britain and France with the mails. It should be said, in the first place, that there was little difficulty in reaching an agreement on what may be called the commercial phase of the matter, that is to say, that the parcel post should be considered as merchandise and that belligerents could properly exercise the right of visit and search as in the case of other merchandise. The case might be considered closer or open to doubt in the transmission of articles of commerce in sealed packages at the rates of letter postage, and the Allies insisted that the first class mails were used in this way to transmit samples of such a nature and to such an extent as to become a mere matter of commercial export. The United States was unwilling to yield to the representations of the Allies, and set itself like flint against any and every attempt to censor any letters upon a neutral vessel on the high seas or when such vessel was brought against its will into an allied port, there to be more easily examined, or when the vessel had voluntarily touched at an allied port in the course of its voyage. It admitted, however, the right of the allied Governments to censor mail matter of this class which came within the allied jurisdiction in ordinary course.

This attitude was firmly and persistently taken and maintained by Secretary Lansing. Thus, in a telegram dated January 4, 1916, to the American Ambassador to Great Britain, he stated that some 734 bags of parcel mail had been removed by British customs authorities from the Danish steamer *Oscar II* en route from the United States to Norway, Sweden, and Denmark; that fifty-eight bags of parcel mail had been removed from the Swedish steamer *Stockholm* en route from Gothenburg to New York; that 5,000 packages of American merchandise had been seized by British authorities on the Danish steamer *The United States* on her last voyage to this country; that 597 bags of parcel mail had been removed by the British customs authorities from the steamer *Frederick VIII* when in port at Kirkwall destined for Norway, Sweden, and Denmark. On these facts Secretary Lansing stated in the concise and crisp language of a telegram that the "Department [is] inclined to regard parcel post articles as subject to same treatment as articles sent as express or freight in respect to belligerent search, seizure, and condemnation. On the other hand, parcel post articles are entitled to the usual exemptions of neutral trade, and the protests of the Government of the United States in regard to what constitutes the unlawful bringing in of ships for search in port, the illegality of so-called blockade by Great Britain, and the improper assumption of jurisdiction of vessels and cargoes apply to commerce using parcel post service for the transmission of commodities."[1]

Secretary Lansing next noted that, on December 23, 1915, British authorities had removed all mails from the Dutch steamer *New Amsterdam* on its voyage from the United States to Holland, including therein sealed mails and presumably American diplomatic and consular pouches; that on December 20th the British authorities at the Downs had removed from the Dutch vessel *Noorder Dyke* and still held American mail on its way from the United States to Rotterdam; and he further mentioned that mails had likewise been removed from the Dutch steamers *Rotterdam* and *Noordam*. Upon this state of facts Secretary Lansing said:

> The Department cannot admit the right of British authorities to seize neutral vessels plying directly between American and neutral European ports without touching at British ports, to bring them into port, and, while there, to remove or censor mails carried by them. Modern practice generally recognizes that mails are not to be censored, confiscated, or destroyed on high seas, even when carried by belligerent mail ships. To attain [the] same end by bringing such mail ships within British jurisdiction for purposes of search and then subjecting them to local regulations allowing censorship of mails cannot be justified on the ground of national jurisdiction. In cases where neutral mail ships merely touch at British ports, the Department believes that British authorities have no international right to remove the sealed mails or to censor them on board ship. Mails on such ships never rightfully come into the custody of the British mail service, and that service is entirely without responsibility for their transit or safety.[2]

Secretary Lansing thereupon called attention to the consequences of such pretensions and actions on the part of British, and, in later communications, on the part of allied, authorities:

> As a result of British action, strong feeling is being aroused in this country on account of the loss of valuable letters, money orders and drafts, and foreign banks are refusing to cash American drafts, owing to the absence of any security that the drafts will travel safely in the mails. Moreover, the detention of diplomatic and consular mail is an aggravating circumstance in a practice which is generally regarded in this country as vexa-

[1] Official text, *American Journal of International Law*, Special Supplement, October, 1916, p. 404.
[2] *Ibid.*, p. 405.

tiously inquisitorial and without compensating military advantage to Great Britain.[1]

Secretary Lansing rightly regarded the matter as one of very great importance going to the root of neutral rights, and he directed the American Ambassador to lay it before the British authorities "in a formal and vigorous protest and press for a discontinuance of these unwarranted interferences with inviolable mails."

Great Britain and France gladly accepted Secretary Lansing's concession in the matter of parcel post, but they insisted, because of the alleged misconduct of Germany, in examining and censoring mail falling within Mr. Lansing's inhibited categories. The allied view, to which they adhered during the entire period of American neutrality, is thus stated in summary form in a memorandum transmitted on April 3, 1916, by the French Ambassador to the United States in behalf of the allied Powers.

> 1. That from the standpoint of their right of visitation and eventual arrest and seizure, merchandise shipped in post parcels needs not and shall not be treated otherwise than merchandise shipped in any other manner.
> 2. That the inviolability of postal correspondence stipulated by the Eleventh Convention of The Hague of 1907 does not in any way affect the right of the allied Governments to visit and, if occasion arise, arrest and seize merchandise hidden in the wrappers, envelopes, or letters contained in the mail bags.
> 3. That true to their engagements and respectful of genuine "correspondence," the allied Governments will continue, for the present, to refrain on the high seas from seizing and confiscating such correspondence, letters, or despatches, and will insure their speediest possible transmission as soon as the sincerity of their character shall have been ascertained.[2]

In a note to the British Ambassador at Washington, dated March 24, 1916, Secretary Lansing set forth at length and in detail the American position, which on this point never varied. From this important document the following passages are taken:

> It is noted with satisfaction that the British and French Governments do not claim, and, in the opinion of this Government, properly do not claim, that their so-called "blockade" measures are sufficient grounds upon which to base a right to interfere with all classes of mail matter in transit to or from

[1] Official text, *American Journal of International Law*, Special Supplement, October, 1916, p. 405.
[2] *Ibid.*, p. 410.

the central powers. On the contrary, their contention appears to be that, as "genuine correspondence" is under conventional stipulation "inviolable," mail matter of other classes is subject to detention and examination. While the Government of the United States agrees that "genuine correspondence" mail is inviolable, it does not admit that belligerents may search other private sea-borne mails for any other purpose than to discover whether they contain articles of enemy ownership carried on belligerent vessels or articles of contraband transmitted under sealed cover as letter mail, though they may intercept at sea all mails coming out of and going into ports of the enemy's coasts which are effectively blockaded. The Governments of the United States, Great Britain, and France, however, appear to be in substantial agreement as to principle. The method of applying the principle is the chief cause of difference.

Though giving assurances that they consider "genuine correspondence" to be "inviolable," and that they will, "true to their engagements," refrain "on the high seas" from seizing and confiscating such correspondence, the allied Governments proceed to deprive neutral Governments of the benefits of these assurances by seizing and confiscating mail from vessels in port instead of at sea. They compel neutral ships without just cause to enter their own ports or they induce shipping lines, through some form of duress, to send their mail ships *via* British ports, or they detain all vessels merely calling at British ports, thus acquiring by force or unjustifiable means an illegal jurisdiction. Acting upon this enforced jurisdiction, the authorities remove all mails, genuine correspondence as well as post parcels, take them to London, where every piece, even though of neutral origin and destination, is opened and critically examined to determine the "sincerity of their character," in accordance with the interpretation given that undefined phrase by the British and French censors. Finally the expurgated remainder is forwarded, frequently after irreparable delay, to its destination. Ships are detained *en route* to or from the United States or to or from other neutral countries, and mails are held and delayed for several days and, in some cases, for weeks and even months, even though not routed to ports of North Europe *via* British ports. This has been the procedure which has been practiced since the announcement of February 15, 1916. To some extent the same practice was followed before that date, calling forth the protest of this Government on January 4, 1916. But to that protest the memorandum under acknowledgment makes no reference and is entirely unresponsive. The Government of the United States must again insist with emphasis that the British and French Governments do not obtain rightful jurisdiction of ships by forcing or inducing them to visit their ports for the purpose of seizing their mails, or thereby obtain greater belligerent rights as to such ships than they could exercise on the high seas; for there is, in the opinion of the Government of the United States, no legal distinction between the seizure of mails at sea, which is announced as abandoned, and their seizure from vessels voluntarily or involuntarily in port. The British and French practice amounts to an unwarranted limitation on the use by neutrals of the world's highway for the transmission of correspondence. The practice actually followed by the allied Powers must be said to justify the conclusion, therefore, that the announcement of February 15th was merely notice that one illegal practice had been abandoned to make place for the development of another more onerous and vexatious in character.[1]

It should be said in this connection, before leaving this phase of the subject, that, although the allied Powers stated themselves as driven to the censorship of mails by Germany's illegal conduct of the war, they were nevertheless unable to cite a single instance in which Germany had tampered with the mails other than those passing through its territorial jurisdiction. It is safe to assume, therefore, that Germany did not censor mails. Indeed, in the case of the French steamer *Floride*, sunk early in 1915, the Postmaster General stated that "the German auxiliary cruiser *Prinz Eitel Friedrich* delivered to the postmaster at Newport News, Va., on March 12, 144 mail bags for places in South America which had been transshipped from the French steamer *Floride* to the said cruiser before it sank the steamer. The despatches, which appeared to be intact, were sent to the New York office, whence they were forwarded to destination in the same condition and at the first opportunity."[2] It is true that mail matter on board ships sunk by German vessels was lost, but it appears to be beyond controversy that, although mails went down and were lost with the vessels carrying them, the German authorities neither set nor followed the example of the Allies in the censorship of mails. And it should be further noted in this connection that the proposition to free mail from censorship upon the high seas adopted by the Second Hague Peace Conference was upon the motion of the Imperial German delegation,[3] that it was

---

[1] Official text, *American Journal of International Law*, Special Supplement, October, 1916, pp. 413-414.

[2] *Ibid.*, p. 410.

[3] On introducing the German proposal, Dr. Kriege said, on behalf of the Imperial German Government:

Il y a encore une autre question qui se rattache à celle de la contrebande et au sujet de laquelle la Délégation allemande a déposé une proposition spéciale. Il s'agit de la protection de la correspondance postale en temps de guerre maritime. Nous pensons qu'il y aurait avantage à établir le principe que la correspondance postale expédiée par mer est inviolable.

Les relations postales ont, à notre époque, une telle importance, il y a

supported by Great Britain and France, signed by the representatives of these countries, and ratified by Great Britain on November 27, 1909, and by France on October 7, 1910. The articles in question to be found in The Hague Convention restricting the right of capture in naval war are thus worded:

The postal correspondence of neutrals or belligerents, whatever its official or private character may be, found on the high seas on board a neutral or enemy ship, is inviolable. If the ship is detained, the correspondence is forwarded by the captor with the least possible delay.

The provisions of the preceding paragraph do not apply, in case of violation of blockade, to correspondence destined for or proceeding from a blockaded port. (*Article* 1.)

The inviolability of postal correspondence does not exempt a neutral mail ship from the laws and customs of maritime war as to neutral merchant ships in general. The ship, however, may not be searched except when absolutely necessary, and then only with as much consideration and expedition as possible. (*Article* 2.) [1]

tant d'intérêts, commerciaux et autres, basés sur le service régulier de la correspondance, qu'il est grandement désirable de la mettre à l'abri des perturbations qui pourraient être causées par la guerre maritime. De l'autre coté, il n'est guère probable que les belligérants, qui disposent pour la transmission de leurs dépêches des voies de la télégraphie et de la radiotélégraphie, aient recours au trafic ordinaire des postes en vue des communications officielles qui se rapportent aux opérations militaires. Le profit à retirer pour les belligérants du contrôle du service postal, n'est donc point en rapport avec les préjudices que l'exercice de ce contrôle entraîne pour le commerce légitime.

Le moyen le plus efficace pour atteindre au but, consisterait à exonérer de tout contrôle les navires qui font le service postal régulier. Cependant, cela ne paraît guère possible. Il faudrait se borner à édicter que les belligérants doivent tenir compte de leur caractère special et s'abstenir autant que possible, d'exercer sur eux le droit de visite. Mais l'inviolabilité devrait être absolue à l'égard de la correspondance même, quelle que fût la nationalité du navire qui la porte. Les belligérants n'auraient pas le droit, en cas de saisie d'un paquebot-poste, de desceller, dans un but de contrôle, les sacs qui contiennent les lettres, et ils seraient tenus de prendre les mesures nécessaires pour assurer leur prompte remise à destination. (*Deuxième Conférence de la Paix*, 1907, tome iii, pp. 860-861.)

[1] *The Hague Conventions and Declarations of 1899 and 1907*, pp. 182-183.

CHAPTER V

UNLAWFUL SEIZURE OF PERSONS UPON THE HIGH SEAS

Section 1. Searching of American Vessels for German and Austrian Subjects on the High Seas and in Territorial Waters of a Belligerent

Secretary Bryan's reply on this matter is very brief and to the point. It states the facts of two leading cases which had then occurred, to which a few other instances might be added, and it lays down the law admirably and within the compass of a couple of paragraphs. This portion of the letter is therefore quoted in full:

> So far as this Government has been informed, no American vessels on the high seas, with two exceptions, have been detained or searched by belligerent warships for German and Austrian subjects. One of the exceptions to which reference is made is now the subject of a rigid investigation, and vigorous representations have been made to the offending Government. The other exception, where certain German passengers were made to sign a promise not to take part in the war, has been brought to the attention of the offending Government with a declaration that such procedure, if true, is an unwarranted exercise of jurisdiction over American vessels in which this Government will not acquiesce.
>
> An American private vessel entering voluntarily the territorial waters of a belligerent becomes subject to its municipal laws, as do the persons on board the vessel.
>
> There have appeared in certain publications the assertion that failure to protest in these cases is an abandonment of the principle for which the United States went to war in 1812. If the failure to protest were true, which it is not, the principle involved is entirely different from the one appealed to against unjustifiable impressment of Americans in the British Navy in time of peace.[1]

The cases to which reference is made are those of August Piepen-

---

[1] Official text, *American Journal of International Law*, Special Supplement, July, 1915, pp. 256-257.

brink and *The Metapan,* and the facts in each case will be given, with a reference to the law on the subject.

One August Piepenbrink was serving as steward on board the American ship *Windber,* from which he was removed by the French cruiser *Condé* when both vessels were upon the high seas, taken to Kingston in the island of Jamaica and imprisoned by the British authorities as a German subject and therefore an enemy of the Allies. It appears from the evidence in the case that Piepenbrink was in fact a German subject, for although he had declared his intention to become an American citizen, he had not divested himself of German nationality by taking out his final papers, that is to say, by becoming an American citizen according to the laws of the United States. We do not need to speculate as to his status, because he was born in Hanover after its absorption by Prussia in 1866, and the so-called Bancroft Treaty of 1868 with the North German Confederation, of which Prussia then formed a part, specifically declares that "the declaration of the intention to become a citizen of one or the other country has not for either party the effect of naturalization."[1] Piepenbrink, therefore, was not a citizen of the United States. He had no right to claim the protection of the United States, and it was for the United States to determine whether and to what degree it should use its good offices in his behalf.

There was, however, in this case a very real ground for protest, irrespective of nationality or citizenship, namely, the fact that Piepenbrink was a member of the crew of an American ship; the right of the United States to protest would have been the same had he been a passenger instead of a member of the crew, and the American ship *Windber,* within the jurisdiction of the United States or upon the high seas, was subject to the exclusive jurisdiction of the United States. A neutral merchantman may be, in time of war, visited and searched by the belligerent in order to see whether it is or is not performing its neutral duties, but no person, whether member of the crew or passenger, can legally be removed from the vessel without a violation of the law of Nations or without a general or special treaty granting the alleged right.

The United States thought otherwise in 1861, or rather Captain Wilkes of *The San Jacinto* was of a contrary opinion, and the Government of the United States sought to justify his act in stopping and removing from the steamer *Trent,* a British and, therefore, a

[1] *Treaties, Conventions, etc., between the United States of America and other powers,* 1776-1900 [compiled by Wm. M. Malloy (Senate d. 357, 61st Cong., 2d sess.); Washington, 1910, 2 vols.], vol. 2, p. 1299.

neutral merchant vessel, on its voyage from Havana to St. Thomas (then belonging to Denmark) *en route* to England, Messrs. Mason and Slidell, commissioners of the Confederacy to Europe for the purpose of securing the recognition of and support for the Southern States. They were civilians; they were not embodied in the military forces of the Confederacy. Secretary of State Seward endeavored to assimilate them with contraband, and on that theory Captain Wilkes might have been justified in stopping the vessel, bringing it into port, and, by judicial procedure, securing the possession of the Confederate emissaries. However, Secretary Seward's subtlety yielded to President Lincoln's judgment and sense of expediency, and Messrs. Mason and Slidell were handed over to the British authorities with an appropriate expression of regret.

Secretary Seward's contention may or may not have been correct, but the United States could only lawfully remove Messrs. Mason and Slidell from a neutral vessel upon the high seas under a rule of law allowing this to be done. There was no such rule then and there is none now. There was a suggestion of such a rule in Article 47 of the Declaration of London, providing that persons embodied in the armed forces of the enemy could be removed from a vessel; but Piepenbrink was not embodied in the armed forces of Germany, and France could not claim the benefit of this article, because the Declaration of London was only an attempt at a treaty, and was not ratified by any nation. But even if the Declaration of London could have been appealed to, it would not have supported the contention, because this right was interpreted by the Nations in conference to apply solely to persons embodied in the military forces of the enemy and not to reservists. That is to say, it was limited to persons actually in the army or navy, not to those owing a duty to serve in the army or navy.

It is not necessary to pursue this phase of the subject further, because the three parties to this transaction are on record against it: first, Great Britain's protest in the matter of *The Trent;* second, France's protest likewise in the matter of *The Trent;* third, the surrender of Messrs. Mason and Slidell by the United States in consequence of these protests, and, above and beyond all, the protest which in 1812 resulted in the war of the United States against Great Britain, due in large measure to the removal from American vessels of persons claimed to be citizens of the United States. Nations live long and they should have long memories.

In his telegram of March 2, 1915, to the American Ambassador at London, protesting against Piepenbrink's seizure and requesting that he be delivered to the American authorities, Secretary Bryan quoted with approval Lord Russell's comment on the *Trent* case as follows:

> If the real terminus of the voyage be *bona fide* in a neutral territory, no English, nor, indeed, as Her Majesty's Government believe, any American, authority can be found which has ever given countenance to the doctrine that either men or despatches can be subject, during such a voyage, and on board such a neutral vessel, to belligerent capture as contraband of war.[1]

And in a telegram of the same date to the American Ambassador to Paris on the same subject, Secretary Bryan quoted with deadly effect the following passage from the French protest of December 3, 1861, to the United States, protesting against the violation of neutral right by the removal of Messrs. Mason and Slidell from a neutral vessel:

> The destination of *The Trent* was not a point belonging to one of the belligerents. She was carrying her cargo and her passengers to a neutral country, and, moreover, she had taken them on in a neutral port. If it were admissible that under such conditions the neutral flag did not completely cover the persons and merchandise which it was transporting, its immunity would not longer be anything but an empty word; at any time the commerce and navigation of third Powers would have to suffer from their harmless or even indirect relations with one or the other of the belligerents; the latter would no longer be entitled merely to require entire impartiality of a neutral and to forbid him from interfering in any way in the hostilities, but they would place upon his freedom of commerce and navigation restrictions the lawfulness of which modern international law has refused to admit.[2]

In the face of these protests Great Britain and France were powerless, but they did not yield gracefully to the inevitable. On April 3, 1915, the British Secretary of State for Foreign Affairs informed the American Ambassador to London that "His Majesty's Government, in common with the French Government, have decided to liberate this man as a friendly act, while reserving the question of principle involved." And on the 15th of the same month the French Minister of Foreign Affairs made an identical statement to the American Ambassador at Paris.

[1] Official text, *American Journal of International Law*, Special Supplement, July, 1915, p. 355.
[2] *Ibid.*, pp. 355-356.

The other case to which reference is made in Secretary Bryan's letter is that of *The Metapan,* an American steamer owned by the Metapan Steamship Company, a subsidiary branch of the United Fruit Company. *The Metapan* was boarded on October 4, 1914, by the French cruiser *Condé,* and passengers of German nationality, traveling from New York by way of Colon to Barranquila, were forced to sign an agreement "not to take up arms in the present European War or until exchanged, under threat of being forcibly taken from the ship as prisoners of war." There are some cases, Lord Mansfield was accustomed to say, so clear that they can only be obscured by argument, and this would seem to be one of them. The captain of *The Condé* did not seem to be better informed of the rights and duties of Nations under a reasonable system of international law than was Captain Wilkes of *The San Jacinto.* The act of both was illegal, the act of both was condemned, and the act of both stands condemned by the practice of Nations.

Within a month of Secretary Bryan's reply to Senator Stone—to be specific, on February 18th—the British cruiser *Laurentic* stopped the American steamship *China* on the high seas some ten miles from the coast of China, and, over the captain's protest, removed twenty-eight Germans, eight Austrians, and two Turks, taking them to Hongkong, where they were detained as prisoners of war. The United States protested against this action of the British man-of-war, inasmuch as none of the persons taken off *The China* were incorporated in the armed forces of Great Britain's enemies. Had they been so, they might probably have been taken off; but, as they were not embodied in the armed forces, they could not lawfully be removed, and the United States regarded the action of Great Britain "as an unwarranted invasion of the sovereignty of American vessels on the high seas." The United States further stated that the action of the British Government was in violation of Lord Russell's contention in the *Trent* case, and that it was surprised "at this exercise of belligerent power on the high seas so far removed from the zone of hostile operations." The American Ambassador was therefore directed by Mr. Lansing to lay the case before Great Britain, and "to insist vigorously that, if facts are as reported, orders be given for the immediate release of the persons taken from *The China.*"[1]

The British Government replied in a long, carefully prepared note, distinguishing the case of *The China* from that of *The Trent,* inasmuch

[1] Official text, *American Journal of International Law,* Special Supplement, October, 1916, p. 427.

as the persons removed from *The China* were reservists and therefore liable to military duty—although they were not incorporated in the armed forces of the enemy;—that they were actually engaged in the service of the enemy, in that they were plotting in neutral territory to collect arms and ammunition to organize expeditions against British India; and that, if they were not apprehended, they would continue their operations against Great Britain in other neutral territory.

In the case of *The Trent*, Messrs. Mason and Slidell were civilian passengers, proceeding to Europe on a diplomatic mission, at a time when "the suggestion that the functions of a diplomatic representative should include the organizing of outrages upon the soil of the neutral country to which he was accredited was unheard of, and the removal of the gentlemen in question could only be justified on the ground that their representative character was sufficient to bring them within the classes of persons whose removal from a neutral vessel was justifiable."[1] Without pausing to question the novel function with which Great Britain credited or debited the diplomatic agents of the enemy—which would be difficult, in view of the disclosures of German activity in the United States, at a time when it was neutral—the balance of the passage dealing with this phase of the question is quoted:

> The distinction between such persons and German agents whose object is to make use of the shelter of a neutral country in order to foment risings in British territory, to fit out ships for the purpose of preying on British commerce, and to organize outrages in the neutral country itself is obvious.[2]

The British Secretary of State, however, did not let the matter rest here, saying:

> I do not think it will be disputed that persons of this description must be placed within the category of individuals who may, without any infraction of the sovereignty of a neutral State be removed from a neutral vessel on the high seas. The object of their journey was to find another neutral asylum in which they might continue their operations against the interests of this country. The acts which they desired to perform upon the soil of the United States were such as possibly to compromise the neutrality of that country or to constitute an offense against its criminal laws. They were in effect persons whose past actions

[1] Official text, *American Journal of International Law*, Special Supplement, October, 1916, p. 432.
[2] *Ibid.*

and future intentions deprived them of any protection from the neutral flag under which they were sailing.[1]

Apparently, the disclaimer on the part of the British Government to overhaul indiscriminately and to justify specifically an act which might be considered an invasion of American sovereignty, coupled with the knowledge of the activity of German agents in the United States and elsewhere, led the authorities at Washington to overlook the technical violation of a right which was being used as the cover of a wrong, for there is no further correspondence on the case.

Section 2. Arrest of Americans on Neutral Vessels

In Senator Stone's letter there is a charge of "submission to arrest of native-born Americans on neutral vessels and in British ports and their imprisonment." This grievance differs from the one just considered in that native-born Americans are alleged to have been removed from neutral vessels on the high seas and in British ports and to have been imprisoned, whereas the charge under discussion relates to the removal of German and Austrian subjects from American vessels upon the high seas and in the territorial waters of the belligerent. It does not seem advisable to go over ground which has already been traversed and to descant further upon the unlawfulness of overhauling neutral vessels upon the high seas and removing therefrom any person, American or foreigner. The case is somewhat different, however, when a vessel forsakes the high seas and enters the territorial waters of a country, for if it does so voluntarily it subjects itself to the jurisdiction of that country. As a consequence, an American on board such a vessel can be arrested if he has violated the law of that jurisdiction, for merchant vessels are, under the law of Nations, subject to the jurisdiction of the port in which they happen to be. The action of Great Britain or of any foreign country under such circumstances would mean nothing more nor less than the arrest of an American citizen who happened to be sojourning or passing through Great Britain, and the rightfulness or wrongfulness of the act would be tested by the guilt or innocence of the American citizen according to British law.

In view of this state of affairs it does not seem necessary to add to the following statement on this subject contained in Secretary Bryan's letter:

[1] Official text, *American Journal of International Law*, Special Supplement, October, 1916, pp. 431-432.

The general charge as to the arrest of American-born citizens on board neutral vessels and in British ports, the ignoring of their passports, and their confinement in jails requires evidence to support it. That there have been cases of injustice of this sort is unquestionably true, but Americans in Germany have suffered in this way as Americans have in Great Britain. This Government has considered that the majority of these cases resulted from overzealousness on the part of subordinate officials in both countries. Every case which has been brought to the attention of the Department of State has been promptly investigated and, if the facts warranted, a demand for release has been made.[1]

[1] Official text, *American Journal of International Law*, Special Supplement, July, 1915, pp. 263-264.

CHAPTER VI

RESTRAINTS ON COMMERCE

Section 1. Contraband

Five headings of Senator Stone's letter and of Secretary Bryan's reply are so interrelated that they can be treated as phases of a single question, namely, American acquiescence in British interference with American trade. The headings, however, are interesting in themselves, and as they state the nature and limit the scope of the discussion they are quoted in their original order:

> 4. Submission without protest to British violations of the rules regarding absolute and conditional contraband as laid down in The Hague Conventions, the Declaration of London, and international law.
> 5. Acquiescence without protest to the inclusion of copper and other articles in the British lists of absolute contraband.
> 6. Submission without protest to interference with American trade to neutral countries in conditional and absolute contraband.
> 7. Submission without protest to interruption of trade in conditional contraband consigned to private persons in Germany and Austria, thereby supporting the policy of Great Britain to cut off all supplies from Germany and Austria.
> 8. Submission to British interference with trade in petroleum, rubber, leather, wool, etc.[1]

In regard to the charge contained in this group of headings, it should be said at once and without reservation that, although The Hague Conventions have been repeatedly invoked in the matter of contraband, they do not directly or indirectly regulate, touch, or concern this subject. And yet it should be mentioned in this connection that the delegates to the Second Hague Peace Conference attempted to do so and that a committee of the Conference considered contraband and agreed upon lists of absolute contraband which, although not adopted, nevertheless were submitted to the London

[1] Official text, *American Journal of International Law*, Special Supplement, July, 1915, pp. 257-258.

Naval Conference, adopted by that body of experts and included in Articles 21 and 22 of its Declaration; and that the London Conference also agreed upon a list of conditional contraband and a free list, that is to say, a list of articles which should not be considered either as absolute or as conditional contraband. But the Declaration of London was not ratified, and, in the absence of an international agreement negotiated at The Hague, at London, or elsewhere, we are thrown back upon the general principles of international law as evidenced by the practice of Nations.

In considering the subject of contraband we are met on the very threshold with a great difficulty which inheres in the thing itself, because, it cannot be too often pointed out, there is, in the absence of a general agreement upon the subject, no standard other than that of the individual interests of the belligerents by which to test the propriety of their actions. The belligerents have interests of their own which they look after with tender care and anxious solicitude. The neutrals also have interests of their own which determine their policy and which point their protests. The result, if result be reached, is a compromise based upon the balance of convenience or inconvenience, in reaching which the belligerents are ordinarily unmindful of their contentions when neutral, and the neutrals apparently are unmindful of their claims when belligerent and apparently blind to the fact that they may again be belligerents.

There is a general feeling that belligerents may properly prevent neutral supplies from reaching the enemy, but when we go beyond this we enter the realm of confusion and contradiction. Delivery to the enemy may mean delivery to the actual military forces or to the Government to which they belong, and there is a general agreement that belligerents may prevent this by intercepting the articles on the way. But if we probe beneath the surface we find that if the articles of commerce can only be used by military and naval forces it may be presumed that destination to the enemy country is tantamount to destination to the army or to the governmental authorities. There is a vast multitude of objects which may be used by the army and navy if they come into their possession and which might be used by the people generally if they did not fall into the hands of the armed forces. A belligerent possessing sea power will naturally seek to enlarge this list of commodities of doubtful use by insisting that, in fact if not in theory, they will find their way to the armed forces of the enemy, and will therefore use its maritime supremacy to seize them before they reach their point of destination. An enemy which imports its foodstuffs, or a large portion of its foodstuffs, in times of peace, and which necessarily relies upon the outer world for the enlarged supplies required by war, will find the markets of the world open in theory but closed in fact by its enemy if it possesses mastery of the seas. Such a belligerent is likely to use its naval forces to blockade the enemy country so that goods may neither go in nor come out, and, regarding a voyage to the enemy as continuous although through neutral territory, prevent articles of contraband from reaching the enemy country through neutral channels.

There is a general agreement that, in the absence of blockade, neutrals may trade with the enemy in articles which are meant for peaceable use in the sense that they cannot be used for war. But there is a great divergence of opinion as to these articles, for although, as raw material, they may be innocent, nevertheless they may be objects from which the means and instrumentalities of war are manufactured.

It is therefore fair to take it as admitted that the belligerent has the right to capture certain articles destined to his enemy. The method of exercising the right and the articles which may properly be seized are the subject of controversy. The United States conceded during the present war that when belligerent it had determined for itself the lists of contraband, that such lists were inconsistent with its views and policy when neutral, and that the right which it then claimed and exercised could not properly be denied to others now.

It was largely because of this divergence of view and diversity of practice that the United States proposed to the belligerents that they accept during the war the Declaration of London. If they had been willing to do so there would then have been a list of absolute contraband, which each belligerent might have enlarged according to a prescribed method; a list of conditional contraband, which might in the same way have been increased by a specified method; and a list of free goods, which could not be varied by any of the belligerents during the war. In this way the lists would have been known in advance; the belligerents, while able to vary the lists of the first two categories, would nevertheless have been required to make their arrangements in accordance with the lists and the method prescribed; and neutrals could have made their plans for the future with at least some assurance of certainty.

Germany and its Allies were willing to accept the Declaration of London in its entirety; Great Britain and its Allies were unwilling to do so; and as the Declaration required to be accepted as a whole, if accepted at all, the proposal of the United States was therefore rejected and withdrawn. It is fair to state in this connection that, while Germany and its Allies may be applauded for their willingness to accept the Declaration, Great Britain and its Allies are not subject to criticism because they were unwilling to do so. In the absence of an engagement each was a free agent, and until ratified the Declaration of London was not a binding agreement.

It has been thought advisable to make these observations before taking up the subject of contraband, as without understanding the exact nature of the situation the reader is likely to be confused by the divergent attitude of the belligerent claiming that the enemy is wrong and the attitude of the United States admitting, and quite properly, that neither was right.

Section 2. Copper

On May 23, 1862, there was issued by the Secretary of the Treasury of the United States a circular containing a very large and imposing list of contraband, and collectors of customs were directed before giving clearances to require bonds with sufficient sureties against the reshipment of the prohibited articles from their port of destination to the Southern armies. This paragraph, in which copper figures, is so important that it is quoted in full:

> You will be especially careful upon application for clearances to require bonds, with sufficient sureties, conditioned for fulfilling faithfully all the conditions imposed by law or departmental regulations, from shippers of the following articles to the ports opened, or to any other ports from which they may easily be, and are probably intended to be, reshipped in aid of the existing insurrection, namely: liquors of all kinds other than ardent spirits, coals, iron, lead, copper, tin, brass, telegraphic instruments, wire, porous cups, platina, sulphuric acid, zinc, and all other telegraphic materials, marine engines, screw propellers, paddle-wheels, cylinders, cranks, shafts, boilers, tubes for boilers, fire-bars, and every article or other component part of an engine or boiler, or any article whatever which is, can or may become applicable for the manufacture of marine machinery, or for the armor of vessels.[1]

By the President's Proclamation of April 29, 1865, issued when the Civil War had practically ended, the list of contraband was

[1] *Foreign Relations of the United States*, 1862, p. 425.

specifically declared to include "arms, ammunition, all articles from which ammunition is manufactured, gray uniforms and cloth, locomotives, cars, railroad iron, and machinery for operating railroads, telegraph wires, insulators, and instruments for operating telegraphic lines."[1] In the subsequent Proclamations of June 13 and of June 24, 1865, the expression "all articles from which ammunition is manufactured" is to be found.[2]

At the end of the Boxer troubles in China, when the intervening Powers were imposing conditions upon that unfortunate country, the question arose and was considered of permitting or of preventing the manufacture of certain articles by Chinese firms lest munitions of war should be made, fall into unsafe hands, and furnish the Powers with the cause or pretext of intervention to put down domestic outbreaks affecting foreigners and, therefore, foreign countries. It was necessary to enumerate the articles entering into the composition of munitions. On this point Secretary of State Hay, speaking for the United States, said in a telegram of March 19, 1901, to Mr. Rockhill, then American Commissioner and representing American interests:

> The materials principally employed in the manufacture of arms and ammunition are reported by the War Department to be as follows: Brass, copper, tin, niter, lead, charcoal, guncotton, sulphur, alcohol, nitroglycerine, sulphuric acid, nitric acid, picric acid, mercuric fulminate, raw cotton; steel tubes and hoops, forged and oil tempered.[3]

It will be noted that copper appears in this list; and before leaving this subject, it should be said that in the first treaty with Great Britain dealing with contraband of war, namely, the Jay Treaty of 1794, copper sheets are enumerated in Article 18 thereof as contraband, and, in a decision of Lord Stowell on a like clause in a Swedish treaty, he considered the copper sheets as absolute contraband.[4] The reason undoubtedly was that in those days sheet copper was particularly useful for the bottoms of vessels. If now copper is a necessary ingredient of munitions, it seems to be reasonable to consider it contraband because of that fact, even although it may be used also for peaceful purposes. Sheet copper could also be used for a peaceful purpose. Bearing in mind the doctrine of continuous voyage, to be

---

[1] *British and Foreign State Papers*, vol. 56, p. 191.
[2] *Ibid.*, pp. 194, 197.
[3] *Foreign Relations of the United States*, 1901, Appendix, p. 365; Moore, *International Law Digest*, vol. 7, p. 666.
[4] *The Charlotte*, 5 C. Robinson, p. 275.

presently discussed, applicable alike to absolute and conditional contraband, it would make very little difference in the ultimate result whether copper is to be considered as absolute or as conditional contraband.

Section 3. Trade With Neutral Countries

The United States, when belligerent, has insisted upon the ultimate destination in determining the question of contraband. We have captured goods shipped to a neutral port before they reached such port upon a well-grounded belief or upon suspicion that they were intended to be reshipped from the interposed neutral port to the enemy country or to the forces of the enemy, and such captures have been judicially sustained and the goods confiscated. Again, we have not accepted the principle that delivery to specific consignees in a neutral port settled the question of ultimate destination. We have claimed and exercised the right to determine from the circumstances whether the ostensible was the real destination. We have also held that the shipment "to order" of articles of contraband to a neutral port, from which, as a matter of fact, cargoes had been transshipped to the enemy, is in itself sufficient evidence that the cargo is really destined to the enemy, instead of to the neutral port of delivery. We have even held that a cargo of contraband shipped from one neutral port to another will be presumed to be meant for the enemy if it can be transported to the enemy by land conveyance. The cases which establish these points are *The Springbok*[1] and *The Peterhoff*.[2] It is thus seen that the doctrine which appears to bear harshly upon neutrals at the present time is not a concession to one or the other belligerent, but was the common understanding and settled policy of the United States when it was a belligerent.

With this record before us of belligerent pretensions when we were belligerent and of neutral rights when we were neutral, it becomes us to examine this subject in a chastened spirit and with an open mind, for we cannot well deny to belligerents the rights which we asserted and enforced when we ourselves were at war, unless these claims have been renounced by general agreement; and we cannot, with even a modest regard for consistency, claim rights for neutrals which as belligerents we refused to allow countries then neutral, unless neutrals have since acquired by general agreement greater

[1] 5 Wallace, p. 1.   [2] *Ibid.*, p. 28.

rights than we were willing to concede and actually did concede to them in the Civil War. Yet, notwithstanding our record, the United States has insisted that Great Britain, in the exercise of an acknowledged belligerent right, has so extended the list of absolute contraband as to include all articles which that Government did not care to have Germany receive, and that Great Britain has included in the list of conditional contraband all articles which, by an inadvertence or an oversight, were not included in the list of absolute contraband; so that, by means of blockade and by the application of the doctrine of continuous voyage to blockade and to contraband, conditional as well as absolute, Great Britain has closed to neutrals all avenues of trade to or from Germany in all articles of commerce by virtue of its control of the seas.

Let us look somewhat into the law on this matter as laid down by the Supreme Court of the United States, which justifies some of the American practices while rejecting others, and which justifies to a certain extent belligerent pretensions advanced in the course of the present war.

The first case to be considered is that of *The Peterhoff*, decided by the Supreme Court in 1866, after the end of the Civil War. *The Peterhoff* was a British, therefore a neutral, vessel, ostensibly on a voyage from London to the mouth of the Rio Grande with a cargo documented for Matamoras, a Mexican, and therefore a neutral port on the Mexican bank of the river, opposite the port of Brownsville on the American side of the Rio Grande, then in the possession of the Confederate forces. On April 19, 1862, President Lincoln issued a proclamation, duly notified to foreign Governments, to "blockade the whole coast from the Chesapeake Bay to the Rio Grande" and expressed the intention of making the blockade effective "by posting a competent force so as to prevent the entrance or the exit of vessels." The port of Brownsville was not mentioned in this proclamation, although in that of February 18, 1864, relaxing the blockade, it was recited as a matter of fact that Brownsville had been blockaded. Between these two dates, to quote the language of the reporter in the statement of the case, "*The Peterhoff*, a British built and registered merchant screw-propeller, drawing sixteen feet of water, . . . set sail from London upon a voyage documented by manifest, shipping list, clearance, and other papers for the port of Matamoras." Still further, according to the statement of the case in the official report, "the bills of lading, of which there were a large number, all stipulated for the delivery of the goods shipped 'off the

Rio Grande, Gulf of Mexico, *for Matamoras'*; adding, that they were to be taken from alongside the ship, providing lighters can cross the bar." It should further be said, as a large part of the cargo was undoubtedly contraband, that Mexico was at the time of this voyage at war with France because of the attempt on the part of the then Emperor of the French to seat and to maintain upon the throne of Mexico, created for this purpose, a prince of the House of Austria.

The nature and extent of the cargo and the circumstances under which *The Peterhoff* was captured are thus stated in the official report of the case:

> The cargo of *The Peterhoff*, valued at $650,000, was a miscellaneous cargo, and was shipped by different shippers, all British subjects except one, Redgate, hereafter described. *A part of it was owned by the owner of the vessel.*
>
> Of its numerous packages, a certain number contained articles useful for military and naval purposes in time of war. Among them, as specially to be noted, were thirty-six cases of artillery harness in sets for four horses, with two riding-saddles attached to each set. *The owner of this artillery harness owned also a portion of the non-military part of the cargo.* There were 14,450 pairs of "Blucher" or army boots; also "artillery boots"; 5,580 pairs of "Government regulation gray blankets"; 95 casks of horseshoes of a large size, suitable for cavalry service; and 52,000 horseshoe nails.
>
> There were also considerable amounts of iron, steel, shovels, spades, blacksmiths' bellows and anvils, nails, leather; and also an assorted lot of drugs; 1,000 pounds of calomel, large amounts of morphine, 265 pounds of chloroform, and 2,640 ounces of quinine. There were also large varieties of ordinary goods.
>
> Owing to the blockade of the whole Southern coast, drugs, and especially quinine, were greatly needed in the Southern States.[1]

Next, as to the circumstances of capture:

> *The Peterhoff* never reached the Rio Grande. She was captured by the United States vessel of war *Vanderbilt* on suspicion of intent to run the blockade and of having contraband on board. When captured she was in the Caribbean Sea south of Cuba, and in a course to the Rio Grande, through the Gulf of Mexico; having some days previously been boarded, but not captured, by another Federal cruiser, *The Alabama.*[2]

Finally, as to the status of Matamoras:

---

[1] 5 Wallace, pp. 31-32. The passages in italics are so marked in the official report.

[2] *Ibid.*, pp. 32-33.

During the rebellion, Matamoras, previously an unimportant place, became suddenly a port of immense trade; a vast portion of this new trade having been, as was matter of common assertion and belief, carried on through Brownsville, between merchants of neutral nations and the Southern States. And it was stated at the bar that the Federal Government had, for reasons of public policy, even granted several clearances from New York to Matamoras during the rebellion, though only on security being given that no supplies should be furnished to persons in rebellion.[1]

It was earnestly contended in argument that the vessel and cargo were destined to the blockaded coast. Mr. Chief Justice Chase, who had been Secretary of the Treasury during the war and who had himself issued the Treasury circular previously quoted, after stating that the case was very thoroughly argued and that it had been attentively considered, gave the circumstances as found and then disposed of this part of the case in the following manner:

> The evidence in the record satisfies us that the voyage of *The Peterhoff* was not simulated. She was in the proper course of a voyage from London to Matamoras. Her manifest, shipping list, clearance, and other custom-house papers, all show an intended voyage from the one port to the other. And the preparatory testimony fully corroborates the documentary evidence.
>
> Nor have we been able to find anything in the record which fairly warrants a belief that the cargo had any other direct destination. All the bills of lading show shipments to be delivered off the mouth of the Rio Grande, into lighters, for Matamoras. And this was in the usual course of trade. Matamoras lies on the Rio Grande forty miles above its mouth; and *The Peterhoff's* draught of water would not allow her to enter the river. She could complete her voyage, therefore, in no other way than by the delivery of her cargo into lighters for conveyance to the port of destination. It is true that, by these lighters, some of the cargo might be conveyed directly to the blockaded coast; but there is no evidence which warrants us in saying that such conveyance was intended by the master or the shippers.
>
> We dismiss, therefore, from consideration, the claim, suggested rather than urged in behalf of the government, that the ship and cargo, both or either, were destined for the blockaded coast.[2]

On appeal it had been maintained in argument, to quote the language of the learned Chief Justice:

> (1) That trade with Matamoras, at the time of the capture,

---

[1] 5 Wallace, p. 32.   [2] *Ibid.*, pp. 49-50.

was made unlawful by the blockade of the mouth of the Rio Grande; and if not, then (2) that the ulterior destination of the cargo was Texas and the other States in rebellion, and that this ulterior destination was in breach of the blockade.[1]

The first question, therefore, before the Court was whether the mouth of the Rio Grande was blockaded, which involved the further question whether the United States could in law blockade neutral territory, because the Rio Grande is the dividing line between the United States and Mexico and part of the Rio Grande is subject to Mexican jurisdiction. After a careful consideration of this phase of the subject, the Supreme Court came to the conclusion that the mouth of the Rio Grande was not blockaded, and the Chief Justice, speaking for the Court, said that "we are not aware of any instance in which a belligerent has attempted to blockade the mouth of a river or harbor occupied on one side by neutrals, or in which such a blockade has been recognized as valid by any court administering the law of nations."[2] The Court, therefore, had no hesitation in holding "that the mouth of the Rio Grande was not included in the blockade of the ports of the rebel States, and that neutral commerce with Matamoras, except in contraband, was entirely free."[3]

The Court then passed to the consideration of the next question, which, as stated by the Chief Justice, was "whether an ulterior destination to the rebel region, which we now assume as proved, affected the cargo of *The Peterhoff* with liability to condemnation."[3] It is evident that the question of blockade can be eliminated from the case, inasmuch as the Mexican portion of the Rio Grande could not be blockaded and the Court found that the vessel and cargo were destined to the Mexican port of Matamoras. It was contended that the consequences of ulterior destination to a belligerent country by inland conveyance from a neutral port were the same as they would have been under a blockade of Matamoras. On this point the Court had no doubt, as the contention had been advanced in argument and had been rejected by Sir William Scott in the cases of *The Stert* (4 C. Robinson, p. 65), and of *The Ocean* (3 C. Robinson, p. 297), decided in 1801. As these questions are involved in the attempt of Great Britain to prevent neutral commerce finding its way through Holland or other neutral countries to Germany, it is advisable to quote the judgment of the Supreme Court on this point:

During the blockade of Holland in 1799, goods belonging to

[1] 5 Wallace, p. 50.   [2] *Ibid.*, p. 52.   [3] *Ibid.*, p. 54.

Prussian subjects were shipped from Edam, near Amsterdam, by inland navigation to Emden, in Hanover, for transshipment to London. Prussia and Hanover were neutral. The goods were captured on the voyage from Emden, and the cause (*The Stert*, 4 C. Robinson, p. 65) came before the British Court of Admiralty in 1801. It was held that the blockade did not affect the trade of Holland carried on with neutrals by means of inland navigation. "It was," said Sir William Scott, "a mere maritime blockade effected by force operating only at sea." He admitted that such trade would defeat, partially at least, the object of the blockade, namely, to cripple the trade of Holland, but observed, "If that is the consequence, all that can be said is that it is an unavoidable consequence. It must be imputed to the nature of the thing which will not admit a remedy of this species. The court cannot on that ground take upon itself to say that a legal blockade exists where no actual blockade can be applied. . . . It must be presumed that this was foreseen by the blockading state, which, nevertheless, thought proper to impose it to the extent to which it was practicable."

The same principle governed the decision in the case of *The Ocean* (3 C. Robinson, p. 297), made also in 1801. At the time of her voyage Amsterdam was blockaded, but the blockade had not been extended to the other ports of Holland. Her cargo consisted partly or wholly of goods ordered by American merchants from Amsterdam, and sent thence by inland conveyance to Rotterdam, and there shipped to America. It was held that the conveyance from Amsterdam to Rotterdam, being inland, was not affected by the blockade, and the goods, which had been captured, were restored.[1]

On another point, also involved in the present practice of Great Britain, the Supreme Court said, by the mouth of its Chief Justice:

> These were cases of trade from a blockaded to a neutral country, by means of inland navigation, to a neutral port or a port not blockaded. The same principle was applied to trade from a neutral to a blockaded country by inland conveyance from the neutral port of primary destination to the blockaded port of ulterior destination in the case of *The Jonge Pieter* (4 Robinson, p. 79), adjudged in 1801. Goods belonging to neutrals going from London to Emden, with ulterior destination by land or an interior canal navigation to Amsterdam, were held not liable to seizure for violation of the blockade of that port. The particular goods in that instance were condemned upon evidence that they did not in fact belong to neutrals, but to British merchants, engaged in unlawful trade with the enemy; but the principle just stated was explicitly affirmed.

[1] 5 Wallace, pp. 54-55.

> These cases fully recognize the lawfulness of neutral trade to or from a blockaded country by inland navigation or transportation. They assert principles without disregard of which it is impossible to hold that inland trade from Matamoras, in Mexico, to Brownsville or Galveston, in Texas, or from Brownsville or Galveston to Matamoras, was affected by the blockade of the Texan coast.
>
> And the general doctrines of international law lead irresistibly to the same conclusion. We know of but two exceptions to the rule of free trade by neutrals with belligerents: the first is that there must be no violation of blockade or siege; and the second, that there must be no conveyance of contraband to either belligerent.[1]

And the Court concluded its judgment on this part of the case by holding "that trade, between London and Matamoras, even with intent to supply, from Matamoras, goods to Texas, violated no blockade, and cannot be declared unlawful." [2]

The question next arises whether articles declared by a belligerent to be contraband can legally be seized if they are in fact destined to a port of the enemy although a neutral port is interposed and they are deposited at this neutral port in order to be conveyed by water or by land to the enemy. In other words, is the voyage in fact continuous in law? That a voyage, under such circumstances, can be regarded as continuous and therefore considered as a voyage from a neutral to an enemy port, notwithstanding the interposition of a neutral port or territory, was squarely held in the case of *The Bermuda*, in which Mr. Chief Justice Chase, speaking for the Supreme Court, said:

> It makes no difference whether the destination to the rebel port was ulterior or direct; nor could the question of destination be affected by transshipment at Nassau, if transshipment was intended, for that could not break the continuity of transportation of the cargo.
>
> The interposition of a neutral port between neutral departure and belligerent destination has always been a favorite resort of contraband carriers and blockade-runners. But it never avails them when the ultimate destination is ascertained. A transportation from one point to another remains continuous, so long as intent remains unchanged, no matter what stoppages or transshipments intervene.
>
> This was distinctly declared by this court in 1855 (*Jecker v. Montgomery*, 18 Howard, p. 114) in reference to American shipments to Mexican ports during the war of this country with

---

[1] 5 Wallace, pp. 55-56.   [2] *Ibid.*, p. 57.

Mexico, as follows: "Attempts have been made to evade the rule of public law by the interposition of a neutral port between the shipment from the belligerent port and the ultimate destination in the enemy's country; but in all such cases the goods have been condemned as having been taken in a course of commerce rendering them liable to confiscation."

The same principle is equally applicable to the conveyance of contraband to belligerents; and the vessel which, with the consent of the owner, is so employed in the first stage of a continuous transportation, is equally liable to capture and confiscation with the vessel which is employed in the last, if the employment is such as to make either so liable.[1]

Taking up the application of the doctrine of continuous voyage to the cargo, the learned Chief Justice, upon the authority of British precedent, held that it was well established. Within the compass of a paragraph he traces the doctrine which, like so much of the American law, is of British origin. Thus:

> At first Sir William Scott held that the landing and warehousing of the goods and the payment of the duties on importation was a sufficient test of the termination of the original voyage; and that a subsequent exportation of them to a belligerent port was lawful (*The Polly*, 2 C. Robinson, p. 369). But in a later case, in an elaborate judgment, Sir William Grant (*The William*, 5 C. Robinson, p. 395; 1 Kent's *Commentaries*, p. 84, note) reviewed all the cases, and established the rule, which has never been shaken, that even the landing of goods and payment of duties does not interrupt the continuity of the voyage of the cargo, unless there be an honest intention to bring them into the common stock of the country. If there be an intention, either formed at the time of original shipment, or afterwards, to send the goods forward to an unlawful destination, the continuity of the voyage will not be broken, as to the cargo, by any transactions at the intermediate port.[1]

Fortified by these decisions the Chief Justice thus concluded, in a passage which is a classic in American jurisprudence:

> There seems to be no reason why this reasonable and settled doctrine should not be applied to each ship where several are engaged successively in one transaction, namely, the conveyance of a contraband cargo to a belligerent. The question of liability must depend on the good or bad faith of the owners of the ships. If a part of the voyage is lawful, and the owners of the ship conveying the cargo in that part are ignorant of the ulterior

[1] 3 Wallace, pp. 553-554.

destination, and do not hire their ship with a view to it, the ship cannot be liable; but if the ulterior destination is the known inducement to the partial voyage, and the ship is engaged in the latter with a view to the former, then whatever liability may attach to the final voyage, must attach to the earlier, undertaken with the same cargo and in continuity of its conveyance. Successive voyages, connected by a common plan and a common object, form a plural unit. They are links of the same chain, each identical in description with every other, and each essential to the continuous whole. The ships are planks of the same bridge, all of the same kind, and all necessary to the convenient passage of persons and property from one end to the other.[1]

We are now in a position to consider a shipment of contraband to Matamoras when vessel and cargo were destined to and actually delivered at Matamoras, but when the nature of the cargo and the nearness and convenience of Matamoras to Confederate territory suggested that the cargo was meant to be transported from Matamoras to Brownsville, a port in enemy territory. On reaching his conclusion, Mr. Chief Justice Chase, speaking for the Court, used the following language:

> Trade with a neutral port in immediate proximity to the territory of one belligerent, is certainly very inconvenient to the other. Such trade, with unrestricted inland commerce between such a port and the enemy's territory, impairs undoubtedly and very seriously impairs the value of a blockade of the enemy's coast. But in cases such as that now in judgment, we administer the public law of nations, and are not at liberty to inquire what is for the particular advantage or disadvantage of our own or another country. We must follow the lights of reason and the lessons of the masters of international jurisprudence. . . . we think it a fair conclusion from the whole evidence that the cargo was to be disposed of in Mexico or Texas as might be found most convenient and profitable to the owners and consignees, who were either at Matamoras or on board the ship.[2]

After saying that "destination in this case becomes specially important only in connection with the question of contraband," the learned Chief Justice puts and answers the question "Was any portion of the cargo of *The Peterhoff* contraband?" And, as in the case of *The Bermuda*, the language of the Chief Justice on this point, in accordance with the language of the founder of international law, is a classic passage in American jurisprudence:

[1] 3 Wallace, pp. 554-555. [2] 5 Wallace, pp. 57-58.

The classification of goods as contraband or not contraband has much perplexed text writers and jurists. A strictly accurate and satisfactory classification is perhaps impracticable; but that which is best supported by American and English decisions may be said to divide all merchandise into three classes. Of these classes, the first consists of articles manufactured and primarily and ordinarily used for military purposes in time of war; the second, of articles which may be and are used for purposes of war or peace, according to circumstances; and the third, of articles exclusively used for peaceful purposes (Lawrence's Wheaton, pp. 772-776, note; the *Commercen*, 1 Wheaton, p. 382; Dana's Wheaton, p. 629, note; Parsons' *Maritime Law*, pp. 93-94). Merchandise of the first class, destined to a belligerent country or places occupied by the army or navy of a belligerent, is always contraband; merchandise of the second class is contraband only when actually destined to the military or naval use of a belligerent; while merchandise of the third class is not contraband at all, though liable to seizure and condemnation for violation of blockade or siege.[1]

The Chief Justice then proceeds to examine the cargo of *The Peterhoff*, saying that a considerable portion thereof was of the third class, that is to say, innocent, and need not be further referred to because, in the opinion of the Supreme Court and in the opinion also of publicists, innocent articles are not and should not be treated as contraband. Another portion was of the second class, that is to say, useful for war or peace, and only could be treated as contraband if actually destined to the military forces. A final portion was, in the opinion of the Court, of the first class, or, as Mr. Chief Justice Chase said, "if of the second kind, destined directly to the rebel military service." This portion of the cargo was therefore condemned. The language of the Court on this point is:

> This portion of the cargo consisted of the cases of artillery harness, and of articles described in the invoices as "men's army bluchers," "artillery boots," and "government regulation gray blankets." These goods come fairly under the description of goods primarily and ordinarily used for military purposes in time of war. They make part of the necessary equipment of an army.[2]

The Chief Justice, however, was very careful to point out that even absolute contraband could not be captured if it were really intended for sale in Matamoras. Thus:

[1] 5 Wallace, p. 58.   [2] *Ibid.*, pp. 58-59.

> It is true that even these goods, if really intended for sale in the market of Matamoras, would be free of liability; for contraband may be transported by neutrals to a neutral port, if intended to make part of its general stock in trade.[1]

After laying down this rule of law, the Chief Justice stated that the circumstances convinced the Court, in the absence of direct testimony, that this portion was really meant for Brownsville. Thus:

> But there is nothing in the case which tends to convince us that such was their real destination, while all the circumstances indicate that these articles, at least, were destined for the use of the rebel forces then occupying Brownsville, and other places in the vicinity.[1]

And in a final passage to be quoted, the Chief Justice, speaking in behalf of the Court, used language as applicable to the present as it was applicable to the Civil War. Thus:

> And contraband merchandise is subject to a different rule in respect to ulterior destination than that which applies to merchandise not contraband. The latter is liable to capture only when a violation of blockade is intended; the former when destined to the hostile country, or to the actual military or naval use of the enemy, whether blockaded or not. The trade of neutrals with belligerents in articles not contraband is absolutely free unless interrupted by blockade; the conveyance by neutrals to belligerents of contraband articles is always unlawful, and such articles may always be seized during transit by sea. Hence, while articles, not contraband, might be sent to Matamoras and beyond to the rebel region, where the communications were not interrupted by blockade, articles of a contraband character, destined in fact to a State in rebellion, or for the use of the rebel military forces, were liable to capture though primarily destined to Matamoras.[1]

The case of *The Springbok,* to which reference has already been made, rendered it difficult if not impossible for the United States to protest the seizures of articles destined to a neutral port and consigned "to order" instead of being sent to specific consignees residing in the neutral port. After having "looked into all the evidence" and after having approved the rule of ultimate destination laid down in *The Bermuda,* the Court stated the facts of the case, sufficiently for present purposes, in the following passage from the opinion of Mr. Chief Justice Chase:

[1] 5 Wallace, p. 59.

> We think that *The Springbok* fairly comes within this rule. Her papers were regular, and they all showed that the voyage on which she was captured was from London to Nassau, both neutral ports within the definitions of neutrality furnished by the international law. The papers, too, were all genuine, and there was no concealment of any of them and no spoliation. Her owners were neutrals, and do not appear to have had any interest in the cargo; and there is no sufficient proof that they had any knowledge of its alleged unlawful destination.[1]

Yet, notwithstanding the facts as set forth by the Chief Justice, the Court inferred the ultimate destination, apparently because of the consignment to order instead of to specifically named consignees. Thus:

> We are next to ascertain the real destination of the cargo. . . . If the real intention of the owners was that the cargo should be landed at Nassau and incorporated by real sale into the common stock of the island, it must be restored, notwithstanding this misconduct.[2]

The Court then proceeds to ask and to answer the question, "What, then, was this real intention?" Thus:

> That some other destination than Nassau was intended may be inferred, from the fact that the consignment, shown by the bills of lading and the manifest, was to order or assigns. Under the circumstances of this trade, already mentioned, such a consignment must be taken as a negation that any sale had been made to any one at Nassau. It must also be taken as a negation that any such sale was intended to be made there; for had such sale been intended, it is most likely that the goods would have been consigned for that purpose to some established house named in the bills of lading.[3]

Notwithstanding these cases and the claims of the United States when belligerent, the Department of State insisted that Great Britain should conform its actions strictly to the requirements of "international law," although it was not in a position to assume an attitude inconsistent with the decisions of the Supreme Court. The Government even went so far as to protest seizures of cotton, because at that time Great Britain had not added cotton to its list of contraband, although in Secretary Hay's statement, previously quoted, cotton was included among the materials from which ammunition is made, and in the Treasury circular, likewise already quoted, materials entering into the manufacture of ammunition were declared contraband.

[1] 5 Wallace, p. 21.   [2] *Ibid.*, p. 25.   [3] *Ibid.*, pp. 25-26.

Great Britain was, however, much embarrassed in the matter of cotton, because, in the Russo-Japanese War, Russia had placed cotton upon the contraband list. Great Britain protested and, owing to the protest of Great Britain, Russia removed it from the list of contraband. And it may be said in passing that the person, then a Secretary of Embassy, who delivered the protest of the British Government on that occasion, is the present British Ambassador to the United States. Great Britain, therefore, made arrangements with the producers of cotton in the United States, purchasing their cotton and guaranteeing them against loss. Later, on August 23, 1915, Great Britain very properly placed cotton upon the contraband list, as it entered into the manufacture of explosives, and the Imperial German Government has since likewise placed cotton upon its lists of absolute contraband.[1]

Section 4. Trade With Germany

Leaving out of consideration the additions to the lists of absolute and conditional contraband, admittedly within the power of every Government to make, although it may abuse its right,—and, in the opinion of its enemy and of the neutral, every belligerent does abuse the right—the question of destination, of importance in conditional contraband, becomes doubly important because of the German contention that Great Britain was attempting to starve the non-combatant population of Germany by forbidding the entrance of foodstuffs to Germany, on the plea that upon entrance they would be seized by the German authorities and devoted to the use of the armed forces instead of the civilian population.

That a nation has a right to starve its enemy by means of a blockade is admitted by the law and practice of nations; that it may do so by intercepting foodstuffs destined to the enemy was the contention and practice of Great Britain. Within the limits of consent evidenced by the law and practice of Nations this is so; beyond this it was illegal, both as to Great Britain's enemy and neutrals. On January 25, 1915, a decree was passed by the Imperial German Federal Council, of which Article 45, in the opinion of the British Government, made "all grain and flour imported into Germany" after the 31st of January "deliverable only to certain organizations under direct Government control or to municipal authorities."[2]

[1] *Reichsgesetzblatt*, July 22, 1916.
[2] Official text, *American Journal of International Law*, Special Supplement, July, 1915, p. 174.

The Wilhelmina, an American ship carrying a cargo of wheat and bran destined to Germany, was seized by the British authorities. Admitting that foodstuffs were conditional contraband, delivery to German authorities would be delivery to the German Government as distinguished from delivery to the civilian population, and hence would subject the cargo to seizure and confiscation. The British Government said in its note of February 19, 1915, that the destination to Hamburg was one of the reasons causing the seizure of *The Wilhelmina.* The German Government specifically informed the United States, as appears from Secretary Bryan's note to Great Britain, dated February 15, 1915, that "a part of the order of the German Federal Council relating to food products has now been rescinded," and gave a formal assurance "that all goods imported into Germany from the United States directly or indirectly, which belong to the class of relative contraband, such as foodstuffs, will not be used by the German army or navy or by Government authorities, but will be left to the free consumption of the German civilian population, excluding all Government purveyors."[1]

This interpretation and this reply took the wind out of the British sails. There were, however, other reasons, among which were the bombardment of the "open towns" of Yarmouth, Scarborough, and Whitby, and the seizure by German cruisers of neutral vessels destined to English ports carrying cargoes declared by Germany to be conditional contraband, a practice which could only be justified, according to Great Britain, if "the cargo could have been proved to be destined for the British Government or armed forces and if a presumption to this effect had been established owing to Dublin or Belfast being considered a fortified place or a base for the armed forces."[2] The British Government admitted that foodstuffs were only liable to capture if destined to the enemy forces or Government, according to the general principle that the civil populations of the countries at war "are not to be exposed to the treatment rightly reserved for combatants," which distinction, as the British Government maintained, "has to all intents and purposes been swept away by the novel doctrines proclaimed and acted upon by the German Government." After calling attention to the fact that British merchant vessels had been torpedoed at sight "without any attempt being made to give warning to the crew or any opportunity being given to save their lives," that "a torpedo has been fired against a British hos-

[1] Official text, *American Journal of International Law,* Special Supplement, July, 1915, p. 175.
[2] *Ibid.,* pp. 176-177.

pital ship in daylight,"[1] and that neutral ships would, in the future, be treated by Germany the same as British merchant ships, the British Government made the following statement:

> Faced with this situation, His Majesty's Government consider it would be altogether unreasonable that Great Britain and her allies should be expected to remain indefinitely bound, to their grave detriment, by rules and principles of which they recognize the justice if impartially observed as between belligerents, but which are at the present moment openly set at defiance by their enemy.
>
> If, therefore, His Majesty's Government should hereafter feel constrained to declare foodstuffs absolute contraband, or to take other measures for interfering with German trade, by way of reprisals, they confidently expect that such action will not be challenged on the part of neutral states by appeals to laws and usages of war whose validity rests on their forming an integral part of that system of international doctrine which as a whole their enemy frankly boasts the liberty and intention to disregard, so long as such neutral states cannot compel the German Government to abandon methods of warfare which have not in recent history been regarded as having the sanction of either law or humanity.[2]

Acting upon this reservation of a right, Great Britain, on March 15, 1915, issued an Order in Council subjecting to seizure and detention, if not to confiscation, all commodities destined to a neutral country which might be transshipped to Germany, unless the vessel carrying such commodities touched at a British port and received a permit to land its cargo at its neutral destination, and subjecting to seizure and detention, if not confiscation, all commodities exported to the outer world through a neutral country contiguous to Germany, unless Great Britain should be minded to allow the vessel and cargo to pass, notwithstanding the provisions of the Declaration of Paris, to which Great Britain and Prussia were parties, that "the neutral flag covers enemy's goods, with the exception of contraband of war," and that "neutral goods, with the exception of contraband of war, are not liable to capture under enemy's flag."

In the note of the Imperial German Secretary of State, dated March 1, 1915, in reply to Secretary Bryan's proposal to assure the delivery of foodstuffs to the noncombatant populations of the countries at war, it was said that "The German Government would, there-

[1] Official text, *American Journal of International Law*, Special Supplement, July, 1915, pp. 177-178.
[2] *Ibid.*, p. 178.

fore, be willing to make the declarations of the nature provided in the American note so that the use of the imported food and foodstuffs solely by the noncombatant population would be guaranteed."[1] This acceptance, however, was not absolute, as Germany wished raw materials to be subjected to the same treatment, the Imperial German note saying on this point that:

> To that end the enemy Governments would have to permit the free entry into Germany of the raw material mentioned in the free list of the Declaration of London and to treat materials included in the list of conditional contraband according to the same principles as food and foodstuffs.[1]

Great Britain refused, because of the alleged illegal conduct of Germany, to accept the American propositions. In a note of April 4, 1915, the Imperial German Ambassador to Washington recounted the illegal acts of Great Britain and used them as a justification for acts of the Imperial German Government inconsistent with the law of nations, as hitherto understood and practiced, and in no uncertain terms made the United States a party to the illegal conduct of Great Britain because the United States as a neutral did not compel Great Britain to mend its ways.

In connection with the seizure of *The Wilhelmina*, the Imperial German Government showed itself solicitous of the right of the American shipper, when the cargo was destined to Germany—although the destruction of 668 neutral vessels other than those of the United States from the outbreak of the war on August 1, 1914, to April 1, 1917, discloses the consideration neutrals received at the hands of the German submarine when it was not in the interest of the Imperial Government to allow the neutral vessel to go its way unmolested. Thus:

> The various British Orders in Council have one-sidedly modified the generally recognized principles of international law in a way which arbitrarily stops the commerce of neutral nations with Germany. Even before the last British Order in Council, the shipment of conditional contraband, especially food supplies, to Germany was practically impossible. Prior to the protest sent by the American to the British Government on December 28 last, such a shipment did not actually take place in a single case. Even after this protest the Imperial Embassy knows of only a single case in which an American shipper has ventured

[1] Official text, *American Journal of International Law*, Special Supplement, July, 1915, p. 100.

to make such a shipment for the purpose of legitimate sale to Germany. Both ship and cargo were immediately seized by the English and are being held in an English port under the pretext of an order of the German Federal Council (Bundesrat) regarding the grain trade, although this resolution of the Federal Council relates exclusively to grain and flour, and not to other foodstuffs, besides making an express exception with respect to imported foodstuffs, and although the German Government gave the American Government an assurance, and proposed a special organization whereby the exclusive consumption by the civilian population is absolutely guaranteed.

Under the circumstances the seizure of the American ship was inadmissible according to recognized principles of international law. Nevertheless the United States Government has not to date secured the release of the ship and cargo, and has not, after a duration of the war of eight months, succeeded in protecting its lawful trade with Germany.

Such a long delay, especially in matters of food supply, is equivalent to an entire denial.

The Imperial Embassy must therefore assume that the United States Government acquiesces in the violations of international law by Great Britain.[1]

By way of comment upon this remarkable statement it may be said that, under international law and the practice of Nations, the United States does not owe a duty to Germany to supply it with food, and that the United States not only protested against the seizure of *The Wilhelmina*, but that the British Government honored the American protest and settled the case to its satisfaction. Thus, in a note of April 8, 1915, within three days of the note of the Imperial German Ambassador, the British Government said:

His Majesty's Government share the desire of the United States Government for an immediate settlement of the case of *The Wilhelmina*. This American ship laden with foodstuffs left New York for Hamburg on January 22nd. She called at Falmouth of her own accord on February 9th and her cargo was detained as prize on February 11th. The writ instituting prize court proceedings was issued on February 27th, and claimed that the cargo should be condemned as contraband of war. No proceedings were taken or even threatened against the ship herself, and in the ordinary course the cargo would have been unloaded when seized so that the ship would be free to leave. The owners of the cargo, however, have throughout objected to the discharge of the cargo and it is because of this objection that the ship is still at Falmouth with the cargo on board.

[1] Official text, *American Journal of International Law*, Special Supplement, July, 1915, pp. 125-126.

His Majesty's Government have formally undertaken that even should the condemnation of the cargo as contraband be secured in the prize court they would none the less compensate the owners for any loss sustained in consequence of the ship having been stopped and proceedings taken against the cargo.[1]

To prevent British interference with neutral trade with the civilian population of neutral countries, Germany was, in Secretary Bryan's note of February 20, 1915, urged to agree that "all importations of food or foodstuffs from the United States (and from such other neutral countries as may ask it) into Germany shall be consigned to agencies to be designated by the United States Government"[2] and to be delivered by these American agencies to retail dealers bearing licenses from the Imperial German Government, with the assurance that the commodities thus imported should not be "diverted to the use of the armed forces of Germany"; and Great Britain was to agree not to place food and foodstuffs upon the list of absolute contraband and not to interfere with the importation of food and foodstuffs to Germany consigned, as above stated, to American agencies and delivered to retail dealers in Germany under the formal assurance of the Imperial Government that the commodities thus imported should not be diverted to the use of the armed forces of Germany. The belligerent Governments failed to agree, and each country having adopted retaliatory measures because of the alleged misconduct of the other, continued their measures of retaliation and of reprisal at the expense of the neutral.

Section 5. Summary

Without entering into details, which would be necessary in order to indicate and to justify the protests of the United States against actions of Great Britain contrary to international law in respect to neutral trade and commerce, it is sufficient for present purposes to state that any and every interference on the part of Great Britain with neutral commerce to belligerents in violation of the rights of neutrals under international law has been the subject of vigorous, consistent, and continuous protest on the part of the United States. Thus, the United States has objected to the continuous addition of articles to the lists of absolute contraband and to the lists

[1] Official text, *American Journal of International Law*, Special Supplement, July, 1915, pp. 178-179.
[2] *Ibid.*, p. 98.

of conditional contraband. It has protested against the alleged blockade of Germany by Great Britain, holding that such blockade is by means unknown to international law and therefore cannot be recognized. The United States has also protested against all attempts on the part of Great Britain either to blockade neutral territory or, by indirection, to obtain the advantages that would accrue from the blockade of neutral ports of access if it were possible under international law. The United States has insisted from the beginning of the war that it was free to trade with neutral ports in all commodities, that the doctrine of continuous voyage does not apply to innocent articles, that the doctrine of contraband cannot be made to apply to goods leaving Germany for a neutral port; that under the Declaration of Paris, to which Great Britain was a party, the neutral flag covered enemy goods—that is to say, German goods transported in a neutral vessel were free from seizure; and the United States specifically reserved in all these cases its rights under international law to be made the basis of claims to be presented to the British Government if, in the judgment of the United States, this course should be desirable or necessary.

A full, impartial, and careful study of the diplomatic correspondence of the United States with the Imperial German Government and with Great Britain justifies, it is believed, Secretary Bryan's statement in his note dated April 21, 1915, to the German Ambassador, that "this Government has at no time and in no manner yielded any one of its rights as a neutral to any of the present belligerents."[1] The United States insisted upon the observance of its rights and protested against any violation of them by any and every belligerent. The contention of the Imperial German Government that the failure of the United States as a neutral to compel Germany's enemy to renounce illegal practices taxed the United States with acquiescence in them is wide of the mark, unless a neutral is obliged to maintain its neutral right by force of arms upon an allegation by a belligerent that its neutral right has been violated by its enemy. There is a familiar maxim of the common law which is not without application, *Cessante ratione legis cessat et ipsa lex.*

[1] Official text, *American Journal of International Law*, Special Supplement, July, 1915, p. 128.

CHAPTER VII

SALE OF MUNITIONS OF WAR

A further grievance, and a very serious one if it could be substantiated, is the ninth charge mentioned in Senator Stone's letter to Secretary Bryan, which reads as follows:

> No interference with the sale to Great Britain and her allies of arms, ammunition, horses, uniforms, and other munitions of war, although such sales prolong the conflict.[1]

The question really is not whether sales of the commodities mentioned prolong the conflict, but whether, under the law of Nations as at present understood and practiced, such sales are legal. It is believed that there is a confusion in the popular mind between transactions to which the Government may not be a party and transactions to which the subjects or citizens of a neutral Government may be parties. It would be wrong for a Government, as such, to sell munitions of war to any belligerent or to all belligerents, but under existing international law it may be and it is legal for the subjects and citizens of a country to do what their Governments could not do, namely, to sell munitions to belligerent Governments. The time may come when citizens will be prohibited from doing what their Governments cannot lawfully do, but that time has not yet arrived, and until it does transactions of this kind will be legal. It is simply a matter of commerce, a matter of trade; and recognizing that it is trade of a kind to enable the belligerents receiving munitions to continue the war, the belligerent's enemy is given the right to intercept the articles and, without paying for them unless there is a treaty to that effect, to destroy them or to use them against the enemy for which they were intended.

The distinction is drawn between innocent articles which have no effect upon the war and articles of contraband which affect the war. In the one case they may not be seized, in the second case they may be; and international law puts it in the hand of the belligerent to

[1] Official text, *American Journal of International Law*, Special Supplement, July, 1915, p. 254.

protect itself by seizing the articles in question instead of imposing a duty upon the neutral to prevent their exportation. It is therefore not the fault of the neutral if the belligerent does not avail itself of the right given by international law to capture and confiscate the articles. It is the duty of the belligerent to do so; it is his fault if he fails to do so.

In the present case it is proper to remark that Germany's complaint would seem to be due to the fact that British control of the seas enabled Great Britain and its Allies to receive munitions of war from the United States, which would be impossible if Germany controlled the seas. It is a fact that Prussian subjects sold large quantities of ammunition to Russia during the Crimean War, and, since the establishment of the Empire, German subjects have supplied indifferently all belligerents who have needed munitions and have had the money to buy them; and, as admirably pointed out by Secretary Lansing, subjects of Germany and of its ally, Austria-Hungary, sold munitions of war to Great Britain in its war with the Boer Republics, notwithstanding the fact that the Boers had neither ships nor seacoast and could neither buy the commodities nor import them if bought. It is only fair to state, however, in this connection, that the *Kriegsbrauch im Landkriege,* issued in 1902, after the sales in question had been made, recognized the right of subjects to supply belligerents with munitions, but nevertheless condemns sales if they be in large quantities. Thus:

> (b) The furnishing of contraband of war, in small quantities, on the part of subjects of a neutral State to one of the belligerents is, so far as it bears the character of a peaceable private business transaction and not that of an intentional aid to the war, not a violation of neutrality. No Government can be expected to prevent it in isolated and trivial cases, since it would impose on the States concerned quite disproportionate exertions, and on their citizens countless sacrifices of money and time. He who supplies a belligerent with contraband does so on his own responsibility and peril, and exposes himself to the risk of Prize.
>
> (c) On the other hand, the furnishing of war supplies on a large scale is an altogether different matter; undoubtedly this represents actual service to a belligerent, and in most cases, warlike coöperation as well. Therefore, if a neutral State wishes to evidence its full impartiality in the war, it must do its utmost to prevent the furnishing of such supplies. The instructions to the customs authorities must be so clearly and so precisely set forth that, on the one hand, they declare the will of the Government to oppose with all available might such business trans-

actions, but on the other hand, they do not arbitrarily restrict and cripple the entire domestic trade.¹

But perhaps it is not unfair to observe that Germany is the land of munitions, that preparation for war is a cardinal Prussian doctrine, and that, overstocked with munitions, its enemies would fall an easy prey if there were a rule of law preventing them from buying munitions of war in the market open to all. At least a distinguished English publicist, writing in 1870 as an outspoken friend of Prussia in its war with France, so held, and the language of Goldwin Smith, directed against the French autocrat of 1870, is applicable to the Prussian autocrat of today. Thus, in a letter dated November 15, 1870, to Max Müller, then Professor of Sanscrit in Oxford University, complaining against a sale of munitions by American merchants to France, Goldwin Smith used this pointed, weighty, and appropriate language:

> It is simply the American view of International Law, and, I venture to think, the right view.
>
> It would be too much to expect that, whenever any two nations chose to disturb the peace of the world, all the other nations should be required to prohibit lawful trading, and to turn their Governments into detectives armed, as they must be for such a purpose, with arbitrary powers. You cannot draw any real distinction between arms and other things needed by belligerents. One belligerent needs rifles, another saddlery, a third cloth for uniforms, a fourth biscuit, a fifth copper or iron.
>
> There is a special reason for not prohibiting the purchase of arms. If this were done a great advantage would be given, against the interests of civilization, to Powers which, during peace, employed their revenues in arming themselves for war instead of endowing professors. A moral and civilized Power, which had been benefiting humanity, would be assailed by some French Empire which had been collecting *chassepots,* and when it went to provide itself with the means of defense International Law would shut up the gunshop.²

Substitute for the *chassepot* the Krupp gun, and the language is wonderfully apt and impressive.

Secretary Lansing, in his reply to the Austrian protest against the manufacture and sale of munitions to one belligerent, stated Mr. Goldwin Smith's reasoning in different language, and added rea-

¹ *Kriegsbrauch im Landkriege,* pp. 71-72.
² A selection from *Goldwin Smith's Correspondence,* collected by Arnold Haultain (London, 1913), p. 35.

sons of his own in support of the manufacture and sale of munitions, which make a strong appeal to the civilian as distinguished from the militarist. Before, however, quoting Secretary Lansing on this point, it will be of interest to quote an earlier passage of Mr. Lansing's note, as showing the difference between practice and precept. Thus:

> In this connection it is pertinent to direct the attention of the Imperial and Royal Government to the fact that Austria-Hungary and Germany, particularly the latter, have during the years preceding the present European war produced a great surplus of arms and ammunition, which they sold throughout the world and especially to belligerents. Never during that period did either of them suggest or apply the principle now advocated by the Imperial and Royal Government.
>
> During the Boer War between Great Britain and the South African Republics the patrol of the coasts of neighboring neutral countries by British naval vessels prevented arms and ammunitions reaching the Transvaal or the Orange Free State. The allied Republics were in a situation almost identical in that respect with that in which Austria-Hungary and Germany find themselves at the present time. Yet, in spite of the commercial isolation of one belligerent, Germany sold to Great Britain, the other belligerent, hundreds of thousands of kilos of explosives, gunpowder, cartridges, shot, and weapons; and it is known that Austria-Hungary also sold similar munitions to the same purchaser, though in smaller quantities. While, as compared with the present war, the quantities sold were small (a table of the sales is appended), the principle of neutrality involved was the same. If at that time Austria-Hungary and her present ally had refused to sell arms and ammunition to Great Britain on the ground that to do so would violate the spirit of strict neutrality, the Imperial and Royal Government might with greater consistency and greater force urge its present contention.
>
> It might be further pointed out that during the Crimean War large quantities of arms and military stores were furnished to Russia by Prussian manufacturers; that during the recent war between Turkey and Italy, as this Government is advised, arms and ammunition were furnished to the Ottoman Government by Germany; and that during the Balkan wars the belligerents were supplied with munitions by both Austria-Hungary and Germany. While these latter cases are not analogous, as is the case of the South African War, to the situation of Austria-Hungary and Germany in the present war, they nevertheless clearly indicate the long-established practice of the two Empires in the matter of trade in war supplies.[1]

[1] Official text, *American Journal of International Law*, Special Supplement, July, 1915, pp. 167-168.

But to return to the matter in hand. Secretary Lansing, in a passage of his note above quoted, thus confirms and supplements Mr. Goldwin Smith's reasoning:

> But, in addition to the question of principle, there is a practical and substantial reason why the Government of the United States has from the foundation of the Republic to the present time advocated and practiced unrestricted trade in arms and military supplies. It has never been the policy of this country to maintain in time of peace a large military establishment or stores of arms and ammunition sufficient to repel invasion by a well equipped and powerful enemy. It has desired to remain at peace with all nations and to avoid any appearance of menacing such peace by the threat of its armies and navies. In consequence of this standing policy the United States would, in the event of attack by a foreign Power, be at the outset of the war seriously, if not fatally, embarrassed by the lack of arms and ammunition and by the means to produce them in sufficient quantities to supply the requirements of national defense. The United States has always depended upon the right and power to purchase arms and ammunition from neutral nations in case of foreign attack. This right, which it claims for itself, it cannot deny to others.
>
> A nation whose principle and policy it is to rely upon international obligations and international justice to preserve its political and territorial integrity might become the prey of an aggressive nation whose policy and practice it is to increase its military strength during times of peace with the design of conquest, unless the nation attacked can, after war had been declared, go into the markets of the world and purchase the means to defend itself against the aggressor.
>
> The general adoption by the nations of the world of the theory that neutral powers ought to prohibit the sale of arms and ammunition to belligerents would compel every nation to have in readiness at all times sufficient munitions of war to meet any emergency which might arise and to erect and maintain establishments for the manufacture of arms and ammunition sufficient to supply the needs of its military and naval forces throughout the progress of a war. Manifestly the application of this theory would result in every nation becoming an armed camp, ready to resist aggression and tempted to employ force in asserting its rights rather than appeal to reason and justice for the settlement of international disputes.
>
> Perceiving, as it does, that the adoption of the principle that it is the duty of a neutral to prohibit the sale of arms and ammunition to a belligerent during the progress of a war would inevitably give the advantage to the belligerent which had encouraged the manufacture of munitions in time of peace and which had laid in vast stores of arms and ammunition in antici-

pation of war, the Government of the United States is convinced that the adoption of the theory would force militarism on the world and work against that universal peace which is the desire and purpose of all nations which exalt justice and righteousness in their relations with one another.[1]

But this grievance, if such it can properly be called, is far from new. As far as the United States was concerned, the question first arose during the wars of the French Revolution, when France complained of the sale of munitions to Great Britain, then its enemy, insisting that the sale, because it benefited Great Britain, was illegal, whereas the illegality in all probability would not have been noted and branded as such if the sale, and therefore the benefit, had been to France. In the interest of fairness it is only proper to remark that the people of the North were much put out with Great Britain during the Civil War because subjects of that country supplied the Confederate States with arms and ammunition. And no doubt in the future complaints of a similar kind will be made; but, if Secretary Lansing's views are just, it is believed that the world will be unwilling to renounce the means of self-defense at the behest of a nation making of war a business and of peace a preparation for war.

It is feared, however, that the above discussion does not adequately state the contentions of Germany and of Austria-Hungary. Both these Governments admit that it is lawful for citizens of the United States to manufacture and to sell arms to belligerents, but that the situation is changed if in fact sales can only be made to one belligerent instead of to all belligerents, and that the creation of factories during war for the express purpose of furnishing supplies which can, in the nature of things, only be sold to one belligerent, is a violation of the spirit of neutrality if it is not a breach of the letter of the law. Thus, in a memorandum of the Imperial German Embassy dated April 4, 1915, the German Ambassador calls attention to the difference between this war and previous wars, stating that, in times past, arms and ammunition might be obtained from many countries, whereas in the present case the United States was the only neutral Power in which arms and ammunition could be made and supplied to the belligerents. The German Ambassador felt justified because of this to contend that:

> The conception of neutrality is thereby given a new purport, independently of the formal question of hitherto existing law. In contradiction thereto, the United States is building up a

[1] Official text, *American Journal of International Law*, Special Supplement, July, 1915, pp. 168-169.

powerful arms industry in the broadest sense, the existing plants not only being worked but enlarged by all available means, and new ones built. The international conventions for the protection of the rights of neutral nations doubtless sprang from the necessity of protecting the existing industries of neutral nations as far as possible from injury in their business. But it can in no event be in accordance with the spirit of true neutrality if, under the protection of such international stipulations, an entirely new industry is created in a neutral state, such as is the development of the arms industry in the United States, the business whereof, under the present conditions, can benefit only the belligerent powers.[1]

It is believed that this contention is without foundation. If it is right to make and to sell arms in ordinary course of trade, it is difficult to see how and why it is wrong to increase the output; and if, because of a market, the business flourishes to such an extent as to become a branch of industry or an industry, the merchants are to be charged with unlawful conduct merely because they are successful. We should not make success the test of right or wrong, and if it is right to do a thing, success in doing it cannot properly be considered a crime.

Statements of this kind are ingenious; they are not, however, convincing, for if the arms and ammunition made in the United States did not reach Germany's enemies there might be, to use a phrase of national law, *damnum absque injuria*, and Germany would suffer no injury from exports of arms and ammunition, however large they might be, destined to its enemies, if German cruisers operating on the surface, or if German submarines, plying their calling below the surface, could intercept the arms and ammunition and prevent them from falling into the hands of their enemies. The control of the seas enabled Great Britain to secure and its allies to supply themselves with arms and ammunition manufactured in foreign parts. The inability to control the seas has deprived Germany and its allies of neutral markets. This is Germany's misfortune, it is not the neutral's fault, and no amount of casuistry can change this fact, for fact it is, and justify a grievance grounded on a misinterpretation of existing law.

There was, however, another answer to the contentions of the Imperial German Government that the United States should either sell to both or sell to neither; that if in fact munitions could only be exported to Great Britain and its allies because of British control

[1] Official text, *American Journal of International Law*, Special Supplement, July, 1915, p. 126.

of the seas, the United States should equalize matters by forbidding the export of munitions. The answer was made by Secretary Bryan in the following passage from a note to the Imperial German Ambassador to the United States:

> In the third place, I note with sincere regret that, in discussing the sale and exportation of arms by citizens of the United States to the enemies of Germany, Your Excellency seems to be under the impression that it was within the choice of the Government of the United States, notwithstanding its professed neutrality and its diligent efforts to maintain it in other particulars, to inhibit this trade, and that its failure to do so manifested an unfair attitude toward Germany. This Government holds, as I believe Your Excellency is aware, and as it is constrained to hold in view of the present indisputable doctrines of accepted international law, that any change in its own laws of neutrality during the progress of a war which would affect unequally the relations of the United States with the nations at war would be an unjustifiable departure from the principle of strict neutrality by which it has consistently sought to direct its actions, and I respectfully submit that none of the circumstances urged in Your Excellency's memorandum alters the principle involved. The placing of an embargo on the trade in arms at the present time would constitute such a change and be a direct violation of the neutrality of the United States. It will, I feel assured, be clear to Your Excellency that, holding this view and considering itself in honor bound by it, it is out of the question for this Government to consider such a course.[1]

Unable to persuade the executive or legislative departments of the Government to put an embargo upon the export of munitions, one Pearson, a native of the Transvaal, attempted on two occasions to secure an injunction—in a Federal court in 1902 against the export of horses and mules by the British during the Boer War, alleging that by such export his property in the Transvaal was being irreparably injured and the war prolonged and that the export of contraband under such conditions was contrary to neutral conduct; and, in 1915, having become a citizen of the United States, he endeavored to have a court of Wisconsin enjoin the export of munitions to Great Britain, alleging that, by their export, property which he held in Germany was being irreparably injured, and the war itself prolonged, contrary to sound neutrality.[2]

---

[1] Official text, *American Journal of International Law*, Special Supplement, July, 1915, pp. 128-129.
[2] The first case is entitled Pearson *v.* Parsons, *et al.*, 108 *Federal Reporter*,

CHAPTER VIII

MISCELLANEOUS COMPLAINTS

Section 1. Sale of Dumdum Bullets

This grievance, like so many others without foundation, nevertheless deserves consideration because a specific complaint was made by the Imperial German Ambassador in a note dated December 5, 1914, to the Department of State, calling attention to "fresh violations of the Geneva Convention as well as of Section II, Article 23e of The Hague Convention of July 28, 1899, by the British Government. The violation of those Conventions consists in the use of dumdum bullets."[1] After calling attention to "soft-nosed cartridges," which

---

p. 491. The second, Pearson *v*. Allis-Chalmers Company, decided by the circuit court of Milwaukee County, State of Wisconsin, May 29, 1915, is to be found in the October, 1917, number of the *American Journal of International Law*. This second case discusses the treaty of May 1, 1828, between the United States and Prussia, the writings of publicists, and the practice of nations. A brief extract is quoted from Judge Turner's opinion:

> Counsel for the plaintiff readily conceded upon the argument that unless there is actionable wrong done or threatened by the defendant, no action in equity exists. War, today, is recognized by all nations as a legal act, when it is declared and conducted according to the rules of international law. When nations of the earth are ready to condemn war and accept the decision of an international court in lieu thereof, then the principle here urged by the plaintiff will become one of the governing rules of man, and anyone thereafter engaged in committing or furthering a state of war will be doing an act prohibited by the law of nations. It, therefore, follows that citizens of a neutral government who have the right to trade with a belligerent and furnish arms and munitions of war, cannot be said to be engaged in doing an unlawful and immoral act in view of the well recognized fact that for so many years such conduct has been recognized and permitted by treaty as well settled principles of international law. It is the convention of nations that makes international law, and not the wishes or decisions of the courts. The courts have the duty of construing the rules as laid down by the nations in their conventions, out of which arise the principles governing them in their relations with each other; but the courts cannot, in the face of the well settled principles of international law as here indicated, hold or conclude that the doing by a citizen of an act which the executive branch of the government recognizes in the light of the law of nations to be legal and lawful, is an unlawful and immoral act of such a character as to give rise to that species of actionable wrong without which the jurisdiction of a court of equity cannot attach.

[1] *MSS. Opinions, Joint State and Navy Neutrality Board.*

the Ambassador states were used by the British, the note continues to specify charges against American firms, which can best be stated in the Ambassador's own words. Thus:

> 2. It has come to the knowledge of the German Government that the British Government has ordered from the Winchester Repeating Arms Company 20,000 "Riot Guns," Model 1897, and 50,000,000 "Buckshot Cartridges" for the same. The buckshot cartridge contains nine shots.
> The use of those arms and munitions has not yet become known to civilized warfare.
> 3. The Union Metallic Cartridge Company of Bridgeport, Conn., on October 20th took out through Frank O. Hoagland the inclosed patent for the manufacture of a "Mushroom Bullet."
> According to information the accuracy of which is not to be doubted 8,000,000 of those cartridges have been delivered to Canada since October of this year by the Union Metallic Cartridge Company for the armament of the English army. Cartridges made by that process, although cut through, cannot be distinguished, for their external appearance, from the regular full jacketed cartridges. The soldiers in whose hands this kind of ammunition is placed by the British Government are not in position to know that they are firing dumdum bullets.
> Whether the use of the mushroom bullet is contrary to the law of nations is open to discussion.[1]

In a later portion of this note the Ambassador said:

> Even though there should be no intention to use the ammunition described under 2 and 3 on the theatre of war in Europe, although it may be inferred from the magnitude of the order, it is very plain that the intention is to use them in the English colonies against the Boers, Hindoos, Turks, and Egyptians.
> Even against this method of warfare which sets every rule of international law at defiance the Imperial Government raises its protest.
> It cannot be within the spirit of the neutrality repeatedly declared by the Government of the United States that the American industry supply the fighting forces of the Allies with arms and ammunition the use of which is contrary to international law and constitutes a violation of the above cited Conventions to which the United States is a signatory party.[2]

---

[1] *MSS. Opinions, Joint State and Navy Neutrality Board.*

[2] This note is very characteristic of belligerent correspondence. It assumes, but does not prove, a certain action on the part of the enemy or of a neutral country. It then states in general terms that such action is contrary to international law, sometimes referring to a convention or a principle of international law, without, however, quoting the text.

The Ambassador was requested by the Department of State to substantiate his charges in so far as the United States was concerned, a request with which he did not comply. The firms implicated were asked by the Department to explain their conduct, which they did, with the result that, instead of 8,000,000 cartridges manufactured and sold by the Union Metallic Cartridge Company, a little over 117,000 were manufactured, and 109,000 sold. This company stated that they were manufactured for sporting purposes and that the cartridges could not be used in the military rifles of any foreign Power; that, from the detailed list of persons to whom the cartridges were sold, some 960 cartridges went to British North America and some 100 to British East Africa. In regard to the orders, the reply from the Winchester Repeating Arms Company was equally categorical, assuring the Department of State, in reply to a request for information, that it had not received an order for such guns or cartridges or for the sale of such material from or to the British Government or from any other Government engaged in the war.[1] This information was communicated to the German Ambassador with a statement that, if he could furnish evidence that American firms were manufacturing and selling to the belligerents, to be used in the war, cartridges in violation of The Hague Conventions, the President would, as Secretary Bryan's note stated, "use his influence to prevent, so far as possible, sales of such ammunition to the Powers engaged in the European War without regard to whether it is the duty of this Government, upon legal or conventional grounds, to take such action." Notwithstanding the fact that the substance of the Ambassador's note had been given to the press, Secretary Bryan was able to conclude this part of his reply with the statement that "The Department has received no other complaints of alleged sales of dumdum bullets by American citizens to belligerent Governments."[1]

So much for the fact; now as to the law. A careful examination fails to identify the Geneva Convention or any provision thereof which, as the Imperial German Ambassador states, was violated by the use of dumdum bullets. The bullets referred to as soft-nosed cartridges, dumdum cartridges, and mushroom bullets, are of one general character, and can be generally described as expanding bullets, to use a conventional expression. In 1899 a declaration in the following language was adopted by the First Hague Peace Conference:

[1] Letter of the Secretary of State to the Chairman of the Senate Committee on Foreign Relations, January 20, 1915; Senate doc. No. 716, 63d Cong., 3d sess.; official text, *American Journal of International Law*, Special Supplement, July, 1915, p. 261.

The contracting Parties agree to abstain from the use of bullets which expand or flatten easily in the human body, such as bullets with a hard envelope which does not entirely cover the core or is pierced with incisions.

Portugal, Great Britain, and the United States did not sign this declaration, although, in the course of the Second Hague Peace Conference, Portugal adhered to it on August 29th and Great Britain on August 30, 1907.[1] The United States has not adhered, not because it was opposed to the principle, but because it then believed and still believes that the language was too specific, forbidding the use of this kind of a bullet, whereas the language should have been general, forbidding the use of any kind of a bullet producing unnecessary suffering. The United States, therefore, not having signed, ratified, or adhered to the declaration, is not bound by its terms, and as a matter of law, the German Ambassador would have had no ground to complain even if the fact had been as he alleged.

Finally, the German Ambassador refers to Article 23e of The Hague Conventions of 1899 and 1907 respecting the laws and customs of war on land. The text of the land warfare convention of 1899 has been ratified by all the belligerents; the revised text of 1907 has been signed but not ratified by Bulgaria, Italy, Montenegro, Servia, and Turkey; but as this particular article is the same in each Convention it may be considered for present purposes as accepted without reservation by all of the belligerents. The United States is also a signatory and a ratifying Power.

Article 23 reads:

Besides the prohibitions provided by special Conventions, it is especially prohibited— . . .
(e) To employ arms, projectiles, or material of a nature to cause superfluous injury.

The question arises whether this prohibition is in substance, though not in form, the same as the prohibition contained in the declaration. Without arguing the matter, it would appear that it is not the same because the American delegation would have excluded it from the ratification of the original and the revised convention, as the United States bitterly opposed the declaration in 1899 and renewed its opposition in 1907. But this does not settle the matter,

[1] *The Hague Conventions and Declarations of* 1899 *and* 1907, pp. 231, 232.

because, if the cartridges referred to by the German Ambassador as dumdum bullets cause superfluous injury, to quote the language of Article 23e, it follows that the United States should prohibit the manufacture, the sale, and the exportation of such bullets to belligerents and that, if it did not do so, it would render itself liable under the Convention. In the absence of further protest on the part of the German Ambassador, whose record during the war was largely one of protest, it is to be presumed that the elements were lacking to render protest in this matter effective; otherwise, he would not have dropped it.

SECTION 2. HOVERING OF BRITISH WARSHIPS OFF AMERICAN PORTS

The question involved in this heading is one of peculiar difficulty, because the undoubted exercise of the right to navigate freely the high seas permits a belligerent vessel to approach the line separating the high seas from the territorial waters of a neutral country, and while it may not legally commit a hostile action or exercise any act of sovereignty within the territorial waters of another country, it may nevertheless lawfully exercise all the rights of sovereignty upon the high seas. Legally it may exercise these rights just beyond the three-mile line; equitably, it should not. Within the three-mile limit the neutral is protected by international law; beyond the three-mile limit it can only appeal to comity. The situation is not unlike that of a country mobilizing its troops in the immediate vicinity of the line separating it from its neighbor. Legally this is proper; as a matter of fact it is regarded as highly inconvenient, and we know from the experience of this war, as pointed out in the correspondence dealing with this question, that mobilization within the territory of one of the belligerents was regarded by another of the belligerents as such an unfriendly act, indeed a menace, as to cause this latter country to declare a state of war against that country mobilizing its troops within its own territory but dangerously near its neighbor's frontier. Thus, Secretary Lansing said, in his note of April 26, 1916, to the British Ambassador in regard to this very matter:

> Further reasons, if necessary, may be adduced to oppose the British practice. In time of peace the mobilization of an army, particularly if near the frontier, has often been regarded as a ground for serious offense and been made the subject of protest by the Government of a neighboring country. In the present war it has been the ground for a declaration of war and the beginning of hostilities. Upon the same principle the constant

and menacing presence of cruisers on the high seas near the ports of a neutral country may be regarded according to the canons of international courtesy as a just ground for offense, although it may be strictly legal.[1]

In approaching this question it may be said that the President's proclamation of neutrality in the war between Germany and Great Britain, issued on the 6th of August, 1914, warned the belligerents "that any frequenting and use of the waters within the territorial jurisdiction of the United States by the armed vessels of a belligerent, whether public ships or privateers, for the purpose of preparing for hostile operations, or as posts of observation upon the ships of war or privateers or merchant vessels of a belligerent lying within or being about to enter the jurisdiction of the United States, must be regarded as unfriendly and offensive, and in violation of that neutrality which it is the determination of this Government to observe."[2]

This clause is to be found in all the proclamations of neutrality issued by the President of the United States during the present war, and is likewise to be found in the proclamation issued by President Grant on the 22d day of August, 1870, in the war between France and the North German Confederation and its allies. The present proclamation, therefore, followed precedent which had stood the test of the previous war to which Prussia was a party.

But the policy of the United States in this regard is much older and dates from the very early days of the Republic. Thus Mr. Madison, Secretary of State, writing under date of February 3, 1807, to Messrs. Monroe and Pinkney, who were then in London endeavoring to negotiate a treaty with Great Britain, used the following language:

> In no case is the temptation or the facility greater to ships of war for annoying our commerce, than in their hovering on our coasts and about our harbors; nor is the national sensibility in any case more justly or more highly excited than by such insults.[3]

And in a later note to Messrs. Monroe and Pinkney, dated May 20, 1807, Secretary Madison said in reference to the same matter:

> It is much regretted that a provision could not be obtained against the practice of British cruisers, in hovering and taking

[1] Official text, *American Journal of International Law*, Special Supplement, October, 1916, p. 385.
[2] *Ibid.*, July, 1915, p. 196.
[3] *American State Papers, Foreign Relations*, vol. 3, p. 155.

stations for the purpose of surprising the trade going in and out of our harbors; a practice which the British Government felt to be so injurious to the dignity and rights of that Nation, at periods when it was neutral.[1]

But in this as in many other matters, the views of Nations vary as they are belligerent or neutral. Great Britain objected to the practice when it was neutral, it followed the practice when belligerent; and during the present war it has sought to justify this practice to which the United States has strenuously objected, although the United States when belligerent followed the practice in the Civil War which Mr. Madison condemned and which Secretary Lansing has likewise condemned during that part of the present war in which we were neutral. Nevertheless, the practice is offensive, and although the conduct of American cruisers during the Civil War was subject to criticism, as was properly pointed out by Great Britain in its replies to Secretary Lansing's protest, Mr. Lansing was justified in calling the subject to the attention of the British Government and requesting that the practice should cease. It is possible, indeed, to distinguish the cases, as pointed out by Secretary Lansing, inasmuch as the instances to which Great Britain referred took place in waters adjacent to the United States, in which the war was actively prosecuted, whereas in the present war British men-of-war hovering off our coasts have, as it were, brought the war to our very doors, from which we were then separated by the waters of the ocean.

Within the first month of the war Mr. Lansing, then Counselor, called the attention of the British Government to the fact that the presence of British cruisers in near proximity to the harbor of New York, where the commerce of that port converges, caused a very bad impression, and that the continuance of this policy might be construed as an unfriendly act requiring official action. In the last days of the year Mr. Lansing further stated that two British men-of-war lay habitually from three to six miles southeast of Ambrose Channel Light. Mr. Lansing, however, paraphrasing the language of his previous note, felt justified in warning the British Ambassador of the fact that, in the past, the Government had taken a very strong stand against the hovering of foreign warships in the vicinity of our great ports, and that the continuance of the practice would assuredly require action on the part of the Government.

The matter came to an issue in the case of *The Vinland*, a Danish vessel proceeding in ballast from New York to Norfolk in the month

[1] *American State Papers, Foreign Relations*, vol. 3, p. 170.

of November, 1915, in order to load a cargo of coal for South America. *The Vinland* kept within the three-mile limit, and its master asserted that he was found by a British cruiser within American territorial waters and ordered to stop. The British Ambassador was immediately notified of this complaint and in his reply of December 1, 1915,[1] he said that "the British ships of war employed in the Atlantic have strict orders against the violation of American territorial waters" and in a later note, dated December 11, 1915,[2] he specifically stated, as the result of an official report from his Government, that "the cruiser was never within four and a half miles of the shore, nor within one mile of *The Vinland*" and that "the cruiser was generally about three or four miles off *The Vinland.*"

On this state of affairs the two Governments argued the question. In his note of December 16, 1915,[3] Secretary Lansing, referring to previous correspondence, called the Ambassador's "attention to the annoyance which His Majesty's cruisers, lying off the principal commercial ports of the United States and stopping and searching vessels immediately beyond American waters, have given to shipping both overseas and coastwise, and to the seriousness with which the Government of the United States regarded the hovering of belligerent warships about American coasts and ports." He further informed the Ambassador that "this Government has always regarded the practice of belligerent cruisers patrolling American coasts in close proximity to the territorial waters of the United States and making the neighborhood a station for their observations as inconsistent with the treatment to be expected from the naval vessels of a friendly Power in time of war, and has maintained that the consequent menace of such proceedings to the freedom of American commerce is vexatious and uncourteous to the United States." He concluded the note with the earnest request that "instructions be issued to His Majesty's ships to desist from a practice which this Government is convinced has been maintained for long periods at a time and which is peculiarly disagreeable to it and to American traders concerned."

Following the usual delay of diplomacy, the British Ambassador replied to this note on March 20, 1916,[4] but the British Government seems to have been busied in the meantime with American precedents, with which the reply bristles. In the first place, the Ambassa-

[1] Official text, *American Journal of International Law*, Special Supplement, October, 1916, p. 375.
[2] *Ibid.*, p. 376.   [3] *Ibid.*, pp. 376-377.   [4] *Ibid.*, pp. 379-381.

dor calls attention to the fact that no charge was made that the British cruisers entered the territorial waters of the United States, but that, on the contrary, an exception was taken "to proceedings of these vessels when navigating admittedly on the high seas." And this objection, he said, appeared "to rest upon a claim to distinguish between different parts of the high seas, a claim which causes surprise to His Majesty's Government who are unaware of the existence of any rules or principles of international law which render belligerent operations, which are legitimate in one part of the high seas, illegitimate in another." On this point the Ambassador was well advised, but whether there is or is not a distinction between parts of the high seas, hovering always is and always will be offensive to neutrals. With this by way of introduction the Ambassador states that "the rights asserted in this respect by the United States Government in previous wars will no doubt be conceded by the United States Government as well founded when exercised by others," and in this connection he refers to the conduct of Admiral Wilkes, whose fame as an Arctic explorer seems destined to be overshadowed by his misconduct in the case of *The Trent*. For that officer, while denying that he entered British ports in the West Indies to lie in wait for Southern vessels, nevertheless asserted that his vessels "maintained a system of cruising outside of the neutral waters of Bermuda in excess of his rights as a belligerent." This was an admission on the part of Wilkes and it became an admission on the part of the Government of the United States when, on January 15, 1863, Secretary of State Seward transmitted it to the British Legation in Washington in refutation of the charges of illegal conduct against Wilkes.

With this precedent in his favor, the British Ambassador called attention to the large number of ships in American ports and the necessity of taking such position on the high seas as to capture such vessels if they should put out to sea. And he concluded by asserting that, while his Government could not abandon any of its rights "so far as they are in accordance with international law and the practice of the United States Government," Great Britain would nevertheless try to exercise such rights in such a way as to inconvenience neutrals as little as possible.

On April 26, 1916,[1] Secretary Lansing answered the Ambassador's note in what appears to be the last of the series on this subject which

[1] Official text, *American Journal of International Law*, Special Supplement, October, 1916, pp. 383-386.

has been given to the press. At the very beginning of his note the Secretary of State was very careful to point out that the United States did not claim that British vessels cruising beyond the three-mile limit were not "within their strict legal rights under international law," and he pointed out that the objection of the United States to this practice was based "not upon the illegality of such action but upon the irritation which it naturally caused to a neutral country." He thus distinguished present British from past American practice, saying:

> The circumstances in those cases, however, were very different from the present, and the practice complained of far less offensive. The cruising, against which Great Britain protested, was done in the vicinity of small islands near the American coast which, after the blockade of the southern ports had been established, were used as rendezvous for vessels notoriously engaged in running the blockade. In the present case British cruisers are patrolling off the great ports of this country from which trade routes diverge to all parts of the world, particularly to Great Britain and her allies.[1]

In reply to the Ambassador's contention that British warships were stationed in proximity to ports in which German vessels were laid up, the Secretary informed the Ambassador that "a considerable number of American naval vessels have been constantly engaged since the war opened—and, I think Your Excellency will admit, successfully engaged—in preventing the use of American ports as bases of naval operations. . . . In fact, Your Excellency has not called the possibility of the escape of supply ships to my attention since March, 1915."[2] Secretary Lansing then concluded his careful and discriminating note, saying:

> I have shown, I believe, that this Government's contention is supported not only by ample precedents extending through American and British relations since the early years of the Republic and by the analogy in the mobilization of armed forces near an international boundary, but also by the lack of a sufficient excuse for such an objectionable practice as I have had the unpleasant duty of bringing to Your Excellency's attention. I trust, therefore, that your Government will be willing to recognize my Government's contention to the extent of instructing His Majesty's cruisers to withdraw from the vicinity of the territorial waters of the United States and remain at such dis-

---

[1] Official text, *American Journal of International Law*, Special Supplement, October, 1916, p. 384.
[2] *Ibid.*, p. 385.

tances from American harbors and coasts as to avoid the annoying and inquisitorial methods which have compelled this Government to complain formally to Your Excellency's Government.[1]

It should be stated, before passing from this phase of the subject, that the Government of the United States, when it was a belligerent and when it was therefore against its interests, recognized the impropriety of lying off neutral ports in order to capture the vessels of its enemy. Secretary Seward informed Lord Lyons, the British Minister, under date of July 29, 1863, that the Secretary of the Navy had issued instructions that "it was not proper to make a convenience in any manner of neutral territory for the purpose of exercising the belligerent right of search or capture. A capture of a neutral vessel made after standing off and on a neutral harbor, or mouth of a river, or lying in wait within it for the purpose, although actually made beyond the neutral jurisdiction, would not be recognized as valid, and the right of search cannot properly be exercised when it is known previously that, whatever the event of the search, the capture would not be lawful."[2]

It is believed that, notwithstanding embarrassing precedents, the United States is not open to the objection that British warships were permitted without protest to lie off American ports and to intercept neutral vessels.

Section 3. Disregard of American Citizenship Papers and Passports

In the early part of the war there were charges and counter-charges of the violation of American passports, and the arrest by British authorities of any person bearing an American passport was promptly called to the attention of the American Government. The Department of State said, over Mr. Bryan's signature, that "American citizenship papers have been disregarded in a comparatively few instances by Great Britain, but the same is true of all the belligerents. Bearers of American passports have been arrested in all the countries at war. In every case of an apparent illegal arrest the United States Government has entered vigorous protests

---

[1] Official text, *American Journal of International Law*, Special Supplement, October, 1916, pp. 385-386.

[2] Mr. Seward, Secretary of State, to Lord Lyons, British Minister, July 29, 1863. *Manuscript Notes to Great Britain*, vol. 10, p. 175. Quoted from Moore, *International Law Digest*, vol. 7, p. 935.

with request for release. The Department does not know of any cases, except one or two which are still under investigation, in which naturalized Germans have not been released upon representations by this Government. There have, however, come to the Department's notice authentic cases in which American passports have been fraudulently obtained and used by certain German subjects."[1]

Even at this early date it was clear that American passports were being systematically misused by German authorities, and ugly rumors were afloat that passports were fraudulently prepared by or with the connivance of German authorities in the United States. Mr. Bryan felt justified in saying, within the first six months of the war, that "The Department of Justice has recently apprehended at least four persons of German nationality who, it is alleged, obtained American passports under pretense of being American citizens and for the purpose of returning to Germany without molestation by her enemies during the voyage." Indeed, he continued, in language which subsequent events have unfortunately more than justified, "There are indications that a systematic plan has been devised to obtain American passports through fraud for the purpose of securing safe passage for German officers and reservists desiring to return to Germany."[1]

It is not necessary to dwell upon this phase of the subject to show how vigilant and how vigorous the Government was in protesting the arrest of bearers of American passports, as the Department has solemnly assured the American public and foreign Nations by the publication of this note that this is so. In view of judicial proceedings which were begun in American courts, taxing German subjects with fraudulently procuring and manufacturing passports in the United States in furtherance of German interests during the war, and the implication of officials of the German Embassy in such fraudulent transactions, the conviction of persons indicted who had coöperated with and worked under the orders of officials of the Imperial German Embassy, and the dismissal of the German naval and military attachés for complicity in such transactions, and others even more reprehensible, it does not seem to be necessary to descant upon this subject at the instance of charges preferred by German officials or German sympathizers in the United States.

[1] Official text, *American Journal of International Law*, Special Supplement, July, 1915, p. 262.

SECTION 4. CHANGE OF POLICY IN REGARD TO LOANS TO BELLIGERENTS

Shortly after the outbreak of the war it was decided by the Government, at the instance of Secretary Bryan, to discountenance and if possible to prevent loans made by American citizens to belligerent Governments. It is, of course, forbidden by international law for countries as such to lend money to belligerents, for such an act is equivalent to participation in hostilities. International law allows the citizens or subjects of neutral countries to sell supplies and to lend moneys to the belligerents, which would be improper in their Governments, drawing a clean-cut distinction between the action of the Government on the one hand and the act of the individual on the other. For some time past, however, there has been considerable discussion as to the advisability of permitting citizens or subjects of neutral countries to lend money to foreign Governments engaged in war, apparently on the theory that the act itself is unneutral, as, where one's treasure is, one's heart is likewise supposed to be, and a lender of money to a country is naturally desirous that that country be successful and may be inclined to do more than pray for its success. It is alleged that loans, in addition to being unneutral, tend to prolong the war—for is not money called the sinews of war?—just as, in the same way, arms and ammunition furnished to the belligerents are said to prolong war. This may indeed be so, but if so, Secretary Lansing's defense of the manufacture, the sale, and the export of arms and ammunition by neutral subjects or citizens to belligerent countries is applicable to each transaction, and a failure to allow a country which had followed the ways of peace to borrow money on the outbreak of war with which to procure the means of defense, would be to enable the country, which had in times of peace hoarded its wealth and realized upon its credit and which was armed to the teeth, to crush its opponent before it had the opportunity of preparing itself to meet the blow.

As previously stated, upon the outbreak of the war the United States frowned upon the attempts of foreign Governments to place loans in the United States, and informed prospective lenders of money that they need not expect the protection of their Government in the event of trouble with belligerents. The following notice was given out by the Department of State to the press:

> Inquiry having been made as to the attitude of this Government in case American bankers were asked to make loans to

foreign Governments during the war in Europe, the following announcement is made:

> There is no reason why loans should not be made to the Governments of neutral nations, but in the judgment of this Government loans by American bankers to any foreign nation which are at war is inconsistent with the true spirit of neutrality.[1]

An attempt was made to distinguish between loans to belligerent Governments, on the one hand, and sales of contraband on the other, but Secretary Lansing's statement in the Austrian note is to be preferred. It is better to admit frankly and without reservation that the policy in regard to loans to belligerents was changed in order to bring the policy of American citizens into harmony with international law as it then existed and as it now exists. The money market of the United States has been open to any belligerent since this change of policy. Germany has been free to avail itself of it as Great Britain and France were free. Moneys have been raised in the United States and sent to each of these countries, and German, French, and English loans have been floated in the United States.

Section 5. Indifference to Confinement of Noncombatants in Detention Camps in England and France

It is dangerous as well as bad form for a neutral country to meddle in what is peculiarly regarded as the business of belligerents. It is, in the first place, difficult to determine in any given case whether a person is a combatant or a noncombatant, and it is somewhat presuming on the part of a neutral to attempt to determine for the belligerents the treatment to be accorded to noncombatants in camps in which belligerents have determined to detain them. The fact, therefore, that a neutral nation does not intervene in such matters may properly be attributed to other motives than those of indifference. And yet, notwithstanding the delicacy of the subject, the United States did, as a matter of fact, endeavor to investigate conditions in such camps, with the results stated by Secretary Bryan in the following passage of his letter to Senator Stone:

> As to the detention of noncombatants confined in concentration camps, all the belligerents, with perhaps the exception of Servia and Russia, have made similar complaints and those for whom this Government is acting have asked investigations, which representatives of this Government have made impartially. Their

[1] Statement to the press, Dept. of State, August 16, 1914.

reports have shown that the treatment of prisoners is generally as good as possible under the conditions in all countries, and that there is no more reason to say that they are mistreated in one country than in another country or that this Government has manifested an indifference in the matter. As this Department's efforts at investigations seemed to develop bitterness between the countries, the Department on November 20 sent a circular instruction to its representatives not to undertake further investigation of concentration camps.

But at the special request of the German Government that Mr. Jackson, former American Minister at Bucharest, now attached to the American Embassy at Berlin, make an investigation of the prison camps in England, in addition to the investigations already made, the Department has consented to dispatch Mr. Jackson on this special mission.[1]

SECTION 6. FAILURE TO PREVENT TRANSSHIPMENT OF BRITISH TROOPS AND WAR MATERIAL ACROSS THE TERRITORY OF THE UNITED STATES

There can be no doubt that an attempt to send British troops or war material through the United States would be an interference on the part of British authorities with American sovereignty, and, as far as Great Britain's enemies were concerned, permission to British authorities so to do would be regarded, and properly, as a violation of neutrality. These principles are so well recognized that it seems a waste of time and space to quote them. The Convention respecting the rights and duties of neutral Powers and persons in war on land, adopted by the Second Hague Peace Conference on October 18, 1907, and ratified by most of the Powers, including Germany and the United States,[2] provides (Article 1) that the territory of neutral Powers is inviolable and the second article provides that belligerents are forbidden to move troops or convoys of either munitions of war or supplies across the territory of a neutral Power. And in the fifth article a neutral Power is likewise forbidden to allow any of the acts referred to in Article 2 to take place within its territory.

---

[1] Official text, *American Journal of International Law*, Special Supplement, July, 1915, p. 264.

[2] This Convention, which was not ratified by Great Britain, contains the clause that no belligerents are bound by it unless all the belligerents are contracting parties. But in the matter of neutrality, the Convention is declaratory, not amendatory, of the law of Nations, and for this reason its provisions may be referred to in this connection. *The Hague Conventions and Declarations of 1899 and 1907*, pp. 133-139.

On the matter of the passage of troops, Mr. Bryan thus speaks in his letter:

> The Department has had no specific case of the passage of convoys of troops across American territory brought to its notice. There have been rumors to this effect, but no actual facts have been presented. The transshipment of reservists of all belligerents who have requested the privilege has been permitted on condition that they travel as individuals and not as organized, uniformed, or armed bodies. The German Embassy has advised the Department that it would not be likely to avail itself of the privilege, but Germany's ally, Austria-Hungary, did so.[1]

In regard to the shipment of war material through American territory, Secretary Bryan's note states that the question was only raised once by the Canadian Government to be denied by the United States.[2]

It should be said in this connection that the United States has been so solicitous to maintain its neutrality that it requested the British Government not to send by rail across the State of Maine Canadian sick and wounded returning from the war, on the ground that, although individuals might freely cross our territory, detachments stood in a different category, and this although the sick and wounded for whom permission was asked had been discharged because of unfitness for further service.

SECTION 7. INTERNMENT OF GERMAN STEAMSHIP "GEIER" AND THE COLLIER "LOCKSUN" AT HONOLULU

On October 15, 1914, the German gunboat *Geier* arrived in Honolulu, and its captain requested permission to take on coal, claiming a port in Southwest Africa as its nearest home port, and to make necessary repairs, which it was estimated would require a week to

---

[1] Official text, *American Journal of International Law*, Special Supplement, July, 1915, p. 264.
[2] The Collector of Customs of Juneau, Alaska, telegraphed the Treasury Department on August 31, 1914, "May shipment of war ammunition and equipment belonging to Canadian Government pass in transit through Alaska from Dawson to Vancouver?" and the Customs Division of the Treasury Department, in explanation of this request, stated that "The only way in which merchandise of any kind can pass, or does pass, between Canada and Dawson, or other points in British Yukon, is in transit across American territory under the customs regulations under which the merchandise is sealed." To this request and under these circumstances the United States answered in the negative. *MSS. Opinions, Joint State and Navy Neutrality Board.*

complete. Under the President's proclamation and in accordance with international law, men-of-war were to be allowed to enter and to remain in American jurisdiction for the period of twenty-four hours, to take on supplies necessary for immediate use, to load a sufficient quantity of coal to enable the vessel to reach the nearest home port, to remain for a longer period than twenty-four hours to make necessary repairs, and not to receive further supplies without special permission within three months unless the war vessel had, in the interval, entered a port of the Government to which it belongs.

The Hague Convention of October 18, 1907, concerning the Rights and Duties of Neutral Powers in Naval War, is declaratory of international law and of international practice in these matters, and its provisions are therefore quoted irrespective of the clause that it is only binding in case all the belligerents are contracting parties:

> Article 9. A neutral Power must apply impartially to the two belligerents the conditions, restrictions, or prohibitions made by it in regard to the admission into its ports, roadsteads, or territorial waters, of belligerent war-ships or of their prizes.
>
> Nevertheless, a neutral Power may forbid a belligerent vessel which has failed to conform to the orders and regulations made by it, or which has violated neutrality, to enter its ports or roadsteads.
>
> Article 14. A belligerent war-ship may not prolong its stay in a neutral port beyond the permissible time except on account of damage or stress of weather. It must depart as soon as the cause of the delay is at an end.
>
> Article 17. In neutral ports and roadsteads belligerent warships may only carry out such repairs as are absolutely necessary to render them seaworthy, and may not add in any manner whatsoever to their fighting force. The local authorities of the neutral Power shall decide what repairs are necessary, and these must be carried out with the least possible delay.
>
> Article 18. Belligerent war-ships may not make use of neutral ports, roadsteads, or territorial waters for replenishing or increasing their supplies of war material or their armament, or for completing their crews.
>
> Article 19. Belligerent war-ships may only revictual in neutral ports or roadsteads to bring up their supplies to the peace standard.
>
> Similarly these vessels may only ship sufficient fuel to enable them to reach the nearest port in their own country. They may,

on the other hand, fill up their bunkers built to carry fuel, when in neutral countries which have adopted this method of determining the amount of fuel to be supplied.

If, in accordance with the law of the neutral Power, the ships are not supplied with coal within twenty-four hours of their arrival, the permissible duration of their stay is extended by twenty-four hours.

Article 20. Belligerent war-ships which have shipped fuel in a port belonging to a neutral power may not within the succeeding three months replenish their supply in a port of the same power.[1]

It is, of course, for the neutral to determine the quantity of supplies which a belligerent vessel enjoying the hospitality of its port shall receive and the nature and extent of the repairs which it may make under the supervision of the local authorities, and the amount of fuel, whether it be coal or oil, which the vessel may take on. Otherwise the neutral port might be used as a base of hostile operations and, because of its sojourn in neutral waters, the belligerent vessel of war might quit neutral waters in order to engage in hostile operations. In the case of *The Geier* the time was extended from one week to three weeks and the third day of November was fixed either for the departure or internment of the vessel. The presence of a Japanese cruiser off Honolulu decided the matter. *The Geier's* captain asked to be interned and the United States interned the vessel. As internment is a modern and indeed, it may be said, an American practice, and as some important questions were raised in connection with *The Geier* and its crew after internment, it may be well to enlarge somewhat upon this subject.

The leading case of this kind is that of *The Lena,* a Russian transport or auxiliary cruiser, which entered the harbor of San Francisco September 11, 1904, during the war between Japan and Russia. Later the Japanese Minister was instructed by his Government to call the attention of the United States to the arrival of the vessel and to say, as he did two days later, "that the Imperial Government expect that appropriate measures regarding the matter will be taken by the United States Government without delay."[2] On the same day the Russian Ambassador informed the Department of State that the condition of the boilers of the vessel and other damages would not permit it to continue its voyage, and expressed the opinion that

[1] *The Hague Conventions and Declarations of 1899 and 1907,* pp. 211 *et seq.*
[2] *Foreign Relations of the United States,* 1904, p. 428.

"*The Lena* will receive from the authorities of San Francisco, and in conformity with the prescriptions of international law to which a vessel in her condition is entitled, all aid compatible with the neutrality proclaimed by the Federal Government."[1] The Russian Ambassador was informed on the 14th that:

> The President feels constrained to reach an immediate solution of the question whether *The Lena* shall be repaired immediately so as to put to sea or be disarmed and laid up until the close of the war. If repaired, only such bare repairs can be allowed as may be necessary for seaworthiness and for taking her back to nearest home port, and even such repairs can be permitted only on condition that they do not prove to be too expensive. . . . Inspection made by United States officers at San Francisco discloses that the repairs asked for include complete outfit of new boilers and reconstruction of engines, consuming at least four or five months, or according to the captain's estimate eight months, and amounting to renovation of the vessel. This cannot be allowed with due regard to neutrality.[2]

The American authorities refused to consent to a delay, and there was really no alternative, as the captain of *The Lena* stated in writing that the ship, being unseaworthy, must disarm, and asked to be allowed to make the needed repairs. Thereupon, on the 15th, the Department of State telegraphed the Russian Ambassador that:

> The President has this afternoon issued an order directing that the Russian armed transport *Lena*, now at San Francisco, be taken in custody by the naval authorities of the United States and disarmed, under the following conditions:
>
> First. Vessel to be taken to Mare Island Navy-Yard and there disarmed by removal of small guns, breechblocks of large guns, small arms, ammunition and ordnance stores, and such other dismantlement as may be prescribed by the commandant of the navy-yard.
>
> Second. Written guarantee that *Lena* shall not leave San Francisco until peace shall have been concluded. Officers and crew to be paroled, not to leave San Francisco until some other understanding as to their disposal may be reached between this Government and both belligerents.
>
> Third. After disarmament, vessel may be removed to private dock for such reasonable repairs as will make her seaworthy and preserve her in good condition during detention, or be so repaired at the navy-yard, should the Russian commander so elect. While

---

[1] *Foreign Relations of the United States*, 1904, p. 785.
[2] *Ibid.*, pp. 785-786.

at private dock the commandant of the navy-yard at Mare Island shall have custody of the ship, and the repairs shall be overseen by an engineer officer to be detailed by commandant of navy-yard.

Fourth. The cost of repairs, of private docking, and of maintenance of the ship and her officers and crew while in custody to be borne by the Russian Government, but the berthing at Mare Island and the custody and surveillance of the vessel to be borne by the United States.

Fifth. When repaired, if peace shall not then have been concluded, the vessel to be taken back to Mare Island and there held in custody until the end of the war.[1]

This action of the United States has commended itself to the world at large, to such an extent, indeed, that at the Second Hague Peace Conference of 1907 it was embodied in the following language as Article 24 of the Convention concerning the rights and duties of neutral Powers in naval war:

If, notwithstanding the notification of the neutral Power, a belligerent ship of war does not leave a port where it is not entitled to remain, the neutral Power is entitled to take such measures as it considers necessary to render the ship incapable of taking the sea during the war, and the commanding officer of the ship must facilitate the execution of such measures.

When a belligerent ship is detained by a neutral Power, the officers and crew are likewise detained.

The officers and crew thus detained may be left in the ship or kept either on another vessel or on land, and may be subjected to the measures of restriction which it may appear necessary to impose upon them. A sufficient number of men for looking after the vessel must, however, be always left on board.

The officers may be left at liberty on giving their word not to quit the neutral territory without permission.[2]

In the case of *The Geier* the question arose as to whether the officers and crew should be considered as individuals, and thus allowed a very large degree of personal freedom, or whether they should be considered as members of an armed force and to be treated as a unit. The Government very properly decided that, while not prisoners, they were nevertheless to be treated as an organized force of a belligerent permitted to remain by courtesy but subject to the supervision and control of the American authorities.

A further question arose in the matter of coal to be supplied to

[1] *Foreign Relations of the United States*, 1904, p. 787.
[2] *The Hague Conventions and Declarations of 1899 and 1907*, p. 214.

the vessel, as it appeared that it could not obtain from private sources the coal needed for its daily needs. The question was unusual and delicate, inasmuch as it would, under ordinary circumstances, be an unneutral act on the part of the United States to supply belligerents with contraband of war. But the circumstances of this case were extraordinary. *The Geier* was, to be sure, the property of the Imperial German Government, but it was interned within American jurisdiction during the continuance of war and was therefore in the custody of the United States. As an act of courtesy *The Geier* was therefore furnished by the Government from its own supplies with the amount of coal necessary for its daily needs.

Finally, the question presented itself as to whether the crew of *The Geier* should receive parcels free from custom duties. If prisoners of war, they would be so entitled under Article 16 of The Hague Convention of 1907 concerning the Laws and Customs of War. The question was indeed novel, as stated by the Imperial German Ambassador, and after careful consideration of this question Secretary Lansing, on July 27, 1915, delivered to the German Ambassador the following memorandum, which settles the status of interned persons in a neutral country in so far as such a status, which is of interest to the society of Nations, can be determined by one country:

> The Department of State acknowledges the receipt of the memorandum of the Imperial German Embassy, dated July 8, 1915, in which, with reference to previous correspondence, concerning import duties levied on certain of the articles sent by mail to the German war vessel *Geier,* inquiry is made as to the attitude of the Treasury Department in the matter.
>
> In reply the Department of State informs the Imperial German Embassy that a letter has been received from the Secretary of the Treasury on the subject, from which it appears that his Department knows of no statute or treaty under which articles so addressed would be exempt from duty, and that it has issued no regulations in this relation.
>
> The Secretary of the Treasury points out that Article 16, chapter 2, of section 1 of The Hague Convention respecting the Laws and Customs of War on Land (36 Stat., p. 2277) provides that presents and relief in kind for prisoners of war must be admitted free of all import or other duties; and that the Attorney-General of the United States held, in the case of interned Mexican soldiers, that they were not prisoners of war within the meaning of the said Convention. The Treasury Department holds to that opinion. Therefore, as the status of the officers and members of the crew of *The Geier* in this respect is the same as that of the Mexican soldiers referred to, the action of the customs officers

at Honolulu in examining packages and assessing duty thereon is correct.[1]

In connection with *The Geier* a question was raised as to the treatment to be accorded to *The Locksun,* which appears to have met and to have coaled *The Geier* upon the high seas and to have followed it into Honolulu. *The Locksun* was a German vessel. If it were a merchant vessel it would have been able to enter Honolulu, to take on cargo, and to withdraw at its pleasure. If, on the contrary, it was to be treated as a man-of-war, it could only properly enjoy the limited hospitality of the port. The facts were that *The Locksun* had coaled *The Geier* upon the high seas and that it was therefore not to be looked upon as a merchant vessel in the ordinary sense of the word, nor as a vessel of war, irrespective of its connection with *The Geier.* The question of its nature and of its treatment was carefully considered by the Department of State, and it was held to be a tender to *The Geier* in accordance with the Geneva award in the case of *The Alabama,* which, in so far as it is material, reads as follows:

> And so far as relates to the vessels called *The Tuscaloosa* (tender to *The Alabama*), *The Clarence, The Tacony,* and *The Archer* (tenders to *The Florida*), the tribunal is unanimously of opinion that such tenders or auxiliary vessels, being properly regarded as accessories, must necessarily follow the lot of their principals, and be submitted to the same decision which applies to them respectively.[2]

The action taken and the reason for such action in the case of *The Locksun* are thus stated in the following passage from the note of Mr. Lansing, when Counselor of the Department of State, to the German Ambassador, dated November 16, 1914:

> In reply to your note of the 11th instant, inquiring on which rule or regulation the internment of the German ship *Locksun* is based, I would advise you that *The Locksun* has been interned on the principle that she has been acting as a tender to the German warship *Geier,* as the facts set forth in my note of the 7th instant substantiate. If, under the circumstances, *The Locksun* has been in fact a tender to *The Geier,* the question involved does not relate to the amount of coal which either *The Locksun* or *The Geier* has taken on within three months, but rather relates to the association and coöperation of the two vessels in

[1] *MSS. Opinions, Joint State and Navy Neutrality Board.*
[2] Official text, *American Journal of International Law,* Special Supplement, July, 1915, p. 251.

belligerent operations. *The Locksun,* having been shown to have taken the part of a supply ship for *The Geier,* is, in the opinion of this Government, stamped with the belligerent character of that vessel, and has really become a part of her equipment. In this situation it is difficult to understand on what basis it would have been possible to distinguish between the two vessels, so as to intern the one and not the other. This Government, therefore, has taken what appears to it to be the only reasonable course, under the circumstances, and directed that both vessels be interned.[1]

The doctrine thus laid down in a case involving Germany was, upon the request of the German Ambassador, applied to Great Britain. Thus, in a note of December 21, 1914, addressed to Mr. Lansing as Counselor, the German Ambassador stated that "the British S.S. *Mallina* and *Tremeadow,* who served as tenders to British cruisers, now demand to be allowed to coal in Panama and to leave for Australia, alleging that they have ceased to be tenders of British warships." On this statement of facts the Ambassador called Mr. Lansing's attention to the fact that, "as far as can be seen from here, their case, in the principal points, is identical with the case of the German steamship *Locksun.*" On the 23d of the same month Mr. Lansing as Counselor wrote as follows to the German Ambassador:

In reply to your note of the 21st instant, with reference to the British S.S. *Mallina* and *Tremeadow,* which you state have served as tenders to British cruisers, and are demanding coal in the Panama Canal Zone, I would advise you that these vessels have been considered by the Canal authorities as coming under Rule 2 of the President's proclamation of November 13 last in relation to the neutrality of the Panama Canal Zone, which accords to transports or fleet auxiliaries the same treatment as that given to belligerent vessels of war.[2]

SECTION 8. COALING OF WARSHIPS IN PANAMA CANAL ZONE

The proclamation of neutrality issued by the President stated the principles whose observance the United States would require from belligerents during the course of the war and the treatment which the United States would, in accordance with the law of Nations, accord to belligerents in appropriate cases. It was recognized that

[1] Official text, *American Journal of International Law,* Special Supplement, July, 1915, pp. 247-248.
[2] *Ibid.,* p. 209.

the Panama Canal Zone, although subject to the jurisdiction of the United States, required very special regulation in order that its neutrality might not be compromised and that it might not, by becoming a base of hostile operations, suffer, because of its geographical position, by the acts or operations of the belligerents. It was also recognized that the Republic of Panama was deeply interested in the regulations concerning neutrality which the United States might draft and promulgate concerning the use of the Canal during the war, and because of this fact a protocol was concluded by Mr. Lansing, then Counselor and Acting Secretary of State, with the Panama Minister to the United States. On October 10, 1914, after reciting the close association of the interests of their respective Governments and that the neutral obligations of both Governments as neutrals might be maintained during the war, the two Governments agreed upon the following article:

> That hospitality extended in the waters of the Republic of Panama to a belligerent vessel of war or a vessel belligerent or neutral, whether armed or not, which is employed by a belligerent power as a transport or fleet auxiliary or in any other way for the direct purpose of prosecuting or aiding hostilities, whether by land or sea, shall serve to deprive such vessel of like hospitality in the Panama Canal Zone for a period of three months, and *vice versa*.[1]

Without an understanding of this kind a belligerent war vessel could enjoy the hospitality of the Canal Zone and immediately thereafter the hospitality of Panama, and the Zone as well as the Republic would be liable to be used as a base of hostile operations.

It was charged that this regulation operated to the advantage of Great Britain and to the disadvantage of Germany. Secretary Bryan's letter of January 20, 1915, puts the question on its proper basis as one of geography, which the United States could not control. Thus Mr. Bryan said:

> By proclamation of November 13, 1914, certain special restrictions were placed on the coaling of warships or their tenders or colliers in the Canal Zone. These regulations were framed through the collaboration of the State, Navy, and War Departments and without the slightest reference to favoritism to the belligerents. Before these regulations were proclaimed, war vessels could procure coal of the Panama Railway in the zone

[1] Official text, *American Journal of International Law*, Special Supplement, July, 1915, p. 201.

ports, but no belligerent vessels are known to have done so. Under the proclamation fuel may be taken on by belligerent warships only with the consent of the canal authorities and in such amounts as will enable them to reach the nearest accessible neutral port; and the amount so taken on shall be deducted from the amount procurable in United States ports within three months thereafter. Now, it is charged the United States has shown partiality because Great Britain and not Germany happens to have colonies in the near vicinity where British ships may coal, while Germany has no such coaling facilities. Thus, it is intimated the United States should balance the inequalities of geographical position by refusing to allow any warships of belligerents to coal in the canal until the war is over. As no German warship has sought to obtain coal in the Canal Zone the charge of discrimination rests upon a possibility which during several months of warfare has failed to materialize.[1]

SECTION 9. FAILURE TO PROTEST AGAINST THE MODIFICATION OF THE DECLARATION OF LONDON BY THE BRITISH GOVERNMENT

Owing to the geographical situation of the United States it would only be indirectly or incidentally affected by breaches of neutrality in land warfare, whereas it was likely to be directly affected in its neutral rights in maritime warfare and to be called upon to maintain its rights as a neutral over belligerent vessels within its jurisdiction, to perform its duties as a neutral toward belligerent vessels and property within its jurisdiction, and to compel obedience to the laws of neutrality by its citizens and all other persons residing within its jurisdiction.

It was foreseen that difficulties would arise, as they had arisen when only two nations were at war, and that they would be many and complicated, given the number of belligerents and the extent of belligerent operations. The United States felt that it would be highly desirable if the belligerents would agree upon a definite statement of maritime warfare. The United States expressed its willingness to be a party to such a statement for the purpose and during the continuance of the war, and suggested the Declaration of London, which was drafted by ten leading nations in conference at London during the winter of 1908-09—which had been advised and consented to by the Senate of the United States, and which the Government was willing to promulgate, not because it liked, much less approved, all the provisions of this document, but for the sake of

[1] Official text, *American Journal of International Law*, Special Supplement, July, 1915, p. 265-266.

uniformity. Therefore, the Government of the United States, on August 6, 1914, proposed to the belligerents that they should, for the purposes of the war and during its continuance, accept and apply the principles of the Declaration of London. Great Britain and its allies were willing to do so with certain specified modifications; Germany and Austria-Hungary were willing to accept the Declaration as it was if their enemies accepted it in its entirety, as by Article 65 thereof the Declaration was to be accepted as a whole, not accepted in those parts which were favorable and rejected in those parts which were unfavorable. As Great Britain, on August 22, 1914, and subsequently its allies, refused to comply with the requirements of Article 65, the United States withdrew its proposals on October 22, 1914, leaving the operations of the belligerents to be conducted and to be tested by the law of Nations as derived from the usage and practice of Nations.[1] Mr. Lansing's note withdrawing, on behalf of the United States, the suggestion, is so short and states in such clear and precise terms the policy to be followed and which actually was pursued by the United States, that it is here quoted in full:

> Inasmuch as the British Government consider that the conditions of the present European conflict make it impossible for them to accept without modification the Declaration of London, you are requested to inform His Majesty's Government that in the circumstances the Government of the United States feels obliged to withdraw its suggestion that the Declaration of London be adopted as a temporary code of naval warfare to be observed by belligerents and neutrals during the present war; that therefore this Government will insist that the rights and duties of the United States and its citizens in the present war be defined by the existing rules of international law and the treaties of the United States irrespective of the provisions of the Declaration of London; and that this Government reserves to itself the right to enter a protest or demand in each case in which those rights and duties so defined are violated or their free exercise interfered with by the authorities of His Britannic Majesty's Government.[2]

Subsequently Great Britain, as the result of its experience, be-

[1] Secretary of State to Ambassador Page, Washington, August 6, 1914; official text, *American Journal of International Law*, Special Supplement, July, 1915, p. 1; British Minister for Foreign Affairs to Ambassador Page, London, August 22, 1914, *ibid.*, p. 3; Chargé Wilson to the Secretary of State, St. Petersburg, August 27, 1914, *ibid.*, p. 5; Ambassador Herrick to the Secretary of State, Paris, September 3, 1914, *ibid.*, p. 6; Ambassador Gerard to the Secretary of State, Berlin, August 22, 1914, *ibid.*, p. 2.

[2] Proposal to adopt Declaration of London withdrawn by the United States on October 22, 1914, *ibid.*, p. 7.

came convinced that other provisions of the Declaration were unacceptable as opposed to its interests, and from time to time excluded them, explaining that it did not issue the Declaration of London as such, but as a statement of certain principles of law which it was prepared to accept. It would, however, have been better if Great Britain had rejected the Declaration of London at the outset, adopting at the same time such of its articles, separate and distinct from the Declaration, as it intended to observe. In this way the Declaration would not have had any validity as such, confusion would have been avoided, and the opportunity would have been denied to Germany of charging Great Britain with the violation of the Declaration, which it had a right to repudiate, and of taxing the United States with remissness in not protesting against these violations.

Secretary Bryan was therefore justified in saying on this point:

> As this Government is not now interested in the adoption of the Declaration of London by the belligerents, the modifications by the belligerents in that code of naval warfare are of no concern to it except as they adversely affect the rights of the United States and those of its citizens as defined by international law.[1]

And he was further justified by the diplomatic correspondence of the United States during the period of its neutrality in the statement that "In so far as those rights have been infringed, the Department has made every effort to obtain redress for the losses sustained."[1]

Section 10. General Unfriendly Attitude of United States Toward Germany and Austria

It is impossible to read the correspondence between the United States and Germany without being impressed by its uniformly kind and courteous tone, and without noting the stress laid upon the friendship to which appeal is constantly made, and which the American Government at that time apparently thought existed between Prussianized Germany and the United States. The reader experiences a shock, on turning from the German to the British correspondence, to note the

---

[1] Official text, *American Journal of International Law*, Special Supplement, July, 1915, p. 266.

cold and unyielding terms in which American rights concerning only property were insisted upon. It would seem as if the American Government feared a rupture with the Imperial German Government, that it examined each and every question as it arose from the standpoint of its possible effects upon relations with Germany and its people, and that the President and his advisers had determined that no act on the part of the United States, that no unguarded word or expression in correspondence with Germany, should give the Imperial Government a pretext, much less a cause, to turn against the United States if it should seem to stand in the way of the realization of the purpose upon whose realization the German Government had bent its energies and upon which the German people had set their heart.

It is difficult to know just how to handle a grievance or a complaint of this kind, and it is difficult to see how a charge of this nature can be met and overcome if it has not already been disposed of. Friendship is at best a relative term, and the United States was not in a position to choose its attitude, for it is a Government of laws. The President and his advisers are the creatures and the servants of law, and more especially of international law, which, by the Constitution of the United States and by the decisions of the Supreme Court, is and is declared to be a part of the law of the United States. The President and his advisers were bound to yield implicit obedience to international law; international law prescribed the neutrality and the duties laid upon neutrals; and international law, therefore, determined the conduct of the President and his advisers. In the conception of law there is neither friendship nor enmity, and the impartiality which any belligerent can ask is only the impartiality which flows from compliance with the law. The President and his advisers might have done less, they could not have done more to show their neutrality, for the neutrality which the President impressed upon his fellow countrymen was not merely the neutrality of the *Kriegsbrauch im Landkriege,* which simply requires compliance with international courtesies; it was not merely the neutrality of action, it was the neutrality of thought and of expression. Secretary Bryan was speaking in the fullness of knowledge when he regarded the categorical replies to the specific complaints set out in his letter as a sufficient answer to the charge of unfriendliness to Germany and Austria-Hungary; and in the last paragraph but one of his letter he stated the cause of the apparent difference in the treatment of Germany and Great Britain, a cause which was not of his making and which neither the President nor the United States could alter. Thus he said:

> If any American citizens, partisans of Germany and Austria-Hungary, feel that this administration is acting in a way injurious to the cause of those countries, this feeling results from the fact that on the high seas the German and Austro-Hungarian naval power is thus far inferior to the British. It is the business of a belligerent operating on the high seas, not the duty of a neutral, to prevent contraband from reaching an enemy. Those in this country who sympathize with Germany and Austria-Hungary appear to assume that some obligation rests upon this Government in the performance of its neutral duty to prevent all trade in contraband, and thus to equalize the difference due to the relative naval strength of the belligerents. No such obligation exists; it would be an unneutral act, an act of partiality on the part of this Government to adopt such a policy if the Executive had the power to do so. If Germany and Austria-Hungary can not import contraband from this country, it is not, because of that fact, the duty of the United States to close its markets to the allies. The markets of this country are cpen upon equal terms to all the world, to every nation, belligerent or neutral.[1]

Section 11. Summary

The charges contained in Senator Stone's letter of January 8, 1915, and specifically answered by Secretary Bryan in his reply of January 20th to Senator Stone, have been enumerated and discussed in very considerable detail because, as far as known, Senator Stone's letter contained all the grievances both of the Imperial German Government and its sympathizers in the United States, and Secretary Bryan's reply justified the conduct of the United States on the eve of the announcement by Germany of its intention to use the submarine against Great Britain, even although by its use neutrals should suffer as well as its enemy. The war entered upon a new phase, and it is because of the injuries to American life and property resulting from the conduct, or rather misconduct, of the submarine which brought about that state of war declared by the Congress and President of the United States to exist on the 6th day of April, 1917, between the United States and the Imperial German Government. There were, indeed, grave assaults upon American

---

[1] Official text, *American Journal of International Law*, Special Supplement, July, 1915, pp. 266-267.

sovereignty within the United States and attacks upon American rights beyond the United States by other agencies than that of the submarine, but in comparison they were as aggravations. They added, it might be said, insult to injury; they were not of themselves, and they would not have been of themselves, a cause of war, although, even without the menace of the submarine, they would have created resentment and embittered the relations of the two countries. They will only be referred to as occasion requires and mentioned in passing, for the direct and impelling cause of the war arose through the use of the submarine, and its abuse.

CHAPTER IX

SUBMARINE WARFARE

In a note dated February 6, 1915, from the German Ambassador to the Secretary of State occurs the following paragraph:

> It is known to the Imperial Government that Great Britain is on the point of shipping to France large forces of troops and quantities of implements of war. Germany will oppose this shipment with every war means at its command.[1]

What steps the Imperial German Government meant to take are stated in the proclamation of the 4th of February, 1915, in which it declared the waters surrounding Great Britain and Ireland to be comprised within the seat of war and that neutral vessels entering such waters did so at their peril. The text of the proclamation as transmitted by the American Ambassador is thus worded:

> 1. The waters surrounding Great Britain and Ireland including the whole English Channel are hereby declared to be war zone. On and after the 18th of February, 1915, every enemy merchant ship found in the said war zone will be destroyed without its being always possible to avert the dangers threatening the crews and passengers on that account.
> 2. Even neutral ships are exposed to danger in the war zone as in view of the misuse of neutral flags ordered on January 31 by the British Government and of the accidents of naval war, it cannot always be avoided to strike even neutral ships in attacks that are directed at enemy ships.
> 3. Northward navigation around the Shetland Islands, in the eastern waters of the North Sea and in a strip of not less than 30 miles width along the Netherlands coast, is in no danger.[2]

The proclamation was accompanied by a memorandum setting forth the misconduct of Great Britain as the justification for the declaration of the war zone.

Before taking up the provisions of the memorandum—a revela-

---

[1] *Papers Relating to Maritime Danger Zones*, p. 22.
[2] Official text, *American Journal of International Law*, Special Supplement, July, 1915, pp. 83-84.

tion of national psychology—it is to be observed that, according to the proclamation, enemy merchant ships are to be destroyed without the necessity of saving the crew and passengers, and that neutral ships may be treated as enemy ships without saving the crew and passengers, for the twofold reason that British vessels had been ordered to use neutral flags, and that neutral vessels might be accidentally sunk because of a failure to visit and search them. In the memorandum accompanying the proclamation the illegal acts of the British Government are set forth in considerable detail, which may be thus summarized: That, (1) although Great Britain had ordered its naval forces to be guided by the Declaration of London, nevertheless the Declaration has been repudiated in its essential points; (2) the British Government has obliterated the distinction between absolute and conditional contraband and has placed upon the list of contraband articles which are not such under the Declaration of London or under the generally acknowledged rules of international law; (3) the British Government has violated the provision of the Declaration of Paris that the neutral flag covers enemy property; (4) the British Government has removed German subjects from neutral ships and made them prisoners of war and that such action was not justified by the provisions of the Declaration of London which Great Britain had acknowledged; (5) the British Government has declared the North Sea in its whole extent to be a seat of war, thus establishing a blockade of neutral coasts and ports contrary to the elementary principles of generally accepted international law. The memorandum declares that the purpose of these measures is to reduce Germany to famine by "intercepting legitimate neutral commerce by methods contrary to international law."[1]

By way of comment, it may be said in this connection that, even supposing every British measure complained of to be illegal, it appears that the act was the act of Great Britain, that it was not the act of the neutral Powers and that they were in no way responsible for it. The necessity of charging the neutrals as *participes criminis* evidently appealed to the Imperial German authorities, for in the succeeding paragraph they are blamed for not having prevented Great Britain from doing what Germany itself and by force of arms did not and apparently could not prevent Great Britain from doing. The language of this part of the memorandum should be quoted, as a

[1] Official text, *American Journal of International Law*, Special Supplement, July, 1915, pp. 84-85.

paraphrase might seem to be unjust to Germany. Thus, the memorandum said:

> The neutral powers have in the main acquiesced in the measures of the British Government; in particular they have not been successful in securing the release by the British Government of the German subjects and German merchandise illegally taken from their vessels. To a certain extent they have even contributed toward the execution of the measures adopted by England in defiance of the principle of the freedom of the seas by prohibiting the export and transit of goods destined for peaceable purposes in Germany, thus evidently yielding to pressure by England. The German Government have in vain called the attention of the neutral powers to the fact that Germany must seriously question whether it can any longer adhere to the stipulations of the Declaration of London, hitherto strictly observed by it, in case England continues to adhere to its practice, and the neutral powers persist in looking with indulgence upon all these violations of neutrality to the detriment of Germany. Great Britain invokes the vital interests of the British Empire which are at stake in justification of its violations of the law of nations, and the neutral powers appear to be satisfied with theoretical protests, thus actually admitting the vital interests of a belligerent as a sufficient excuse for methods of waging war of whatever description.[1]

It is not necessary to indulge in comment upon these statements. It is sufficient to say that, as far as the United States is concerned, it protested and has continued to protest against every action of Great Britain which it considered to be illegal, and that it was for the United States, not for Germany, to determine whether the United States should go to war if its peaceful protests were unsuccessful. In the next place, it is for the neutral Nation possessing sovereignty to decide for itself whether it would or would not export goods destined for Germany or for any other country, and that it was obviously a matter of indifference to neutrals whether Germany adhered to the Declaration of London or repudiated it, as long as Germany's conduct was in accordance with the principles of generally accepted international law. And finally, it would seem that if the invocation of vital interests could not be a justification of British actions contrary to the elementary principles of generally accepted international law, of which Germany complained, the invocation of vital interests on behalf of Germany would not be a justification of the violation of

[1] Official text, *American Journal of International Law*, Special Supplement, July, 1915, p. 85.

the principles of generally accepted international law by which the conduct of belligerents was to be tested. Nevertheless, Germany proceeded to do what it condemned in Great Britain, saying in the opening lines of the next paragraph:

> The time has come for Germany also to invoke such vital interests. It therefore finds itself under the necessity, to its regret, of taking military measures against England in retaliation of the practice followed by England. Just as England declared the whole North Sea between Scotland and Norway to be comprised within the seat of war, so does Germany now declare the waters surrounding Great Britain and Ireland, including the whole English Channel, to be comprised within the seat of war, and will prevent by all the military means at its disposal all navigation by the enemy in those waters.[1]

For the reasons stated, neutrals were warned not to place their persons or property upon enemy vessels entering the proscribed area, and neutrals were furthermore advised to recommend their vessels to keep away from such area. Thus:

> To this end it will endeavor to destroy, after February 18 next, any merchant vessels of the enemy which present themselves at the seat of war above indicated, although it may not always be possible to avert the dangers which may menace persons and merchandise. Neutral powers are accordingly forewarned not to continue to entrust their crews, passengers, or merchandise to such vessels. Their attention is furthermore called to the fact that it is of urgency to recommend to their own vessels to steer clear of these waters.[2]

This was rather questionable language from a Power confessedly acting in behalf of the freedom of the seas. Accordingly, it was tempered by the statement that German naval officers would refrain from destroying neutral vessels which were recognizable as such; but the fear was expressed that the misuse of the neutral flag ordered by Great Britain would endanger neutral vessels within the area, although it is difficult to see how this would be liable to happen if the commander of the submarine exercised the right of visit and search which, as regards a neutral, is not merely a right but a duty. Thus the memorandum continued:

> It is true that the German Navy has received instructions to abstain from all violence against neutral vessels recognizable as

[1] Official text, *American Journal of International Law*, Special Supplement, July, 1915, p. 85.
[2] *Ibid.*

such; but in view of the hazards of war, and of the misuse of the neutral flag ordered by the British Government, it will not always be possible to prevent a neutral vessel from becoming the victim of an attack intended to be directed against a vessel of the enemy.[1]

The reference to the misuse of the neutral flag need not impress the well-informed reader, because, however repulsive the use may be of a neutral flag by a belligerent, the law of Nations permits it. The German Prize ordinance of August 3, 1914, allows its men-of-war to fly the neutral flag, and the United States when at war has likewise done so. In any event, the United States did not authorize Great Britain to use the American flag or consent to such use, but protested vigorously against it. The threat against neutrals was, therefore, as far as the United States was concerned, groundless and was in effect the punishment of a neutral for the act of a belligerent against which that neutral had protested but which it was apparently unwilling to go to war in order to prevent. The German act was admittedly an act of retaliation, which might be justified if its effects were confined to the enemy giving cause for the retaliation, but which was certainly not permissible against neutrals and will not, it is believed, be permissible until the distinction between guilt and innocence is destroyed.

The real justification for Germany's declaration of unrestricted submarine warfare was that it was necessary to its vital interests; but as the Imperial German Government had objected to those acts against which it was retaliating, alleged by Great Britain to be necessary to its vital interests, the German action was without justification, unless two wrongs should make a right.

The proclamation of the Imperial Government declaring the waters surrounding Great Britain and Ireland, including the whole of the English Channel, as comprising the seat of war, did not pass unnoticed by the United States, for it was in the nature of a challenge of neutral rights. Therefore in an instruction of Secretary Bryan dated February 10, 1915, to the American Ambassador to Berlin, the United States requested the German Government "to consider before action is taken the critical situation in respect of the relations between this country and Germany which might arise were the German naval forces, in carrying out the policy foreshadowed in the Admiralty's proclamation, to destroy any mer-

---

[1] Official text, *American Journal of International Law*, Special Supplement, July, 1915, p. 85.

chant vessel of the United States or cause the death of American citizens."[1] As was natural and to be expected, the note dealt with the rights of neutrals upon the high seas and the treatment which they should receive at the hands of belligerents, laying down broadly and correctly the principle that the right of a belligerent in the absence of blockade is limited to visit and search, and that by visit and search, not by the display of a flag, the neutral character of the vessel is to be determined as well as the quantity and quality of its cargo. Thus:

> It is of course not necessary to remind the German Government that the sole right of a belligerent in dealing with neutral vessels on the high seas is limited to visit and search, unless a blockade is proclaimed and effectively maintained, which this Government does not understand to be proposed in this case. To declare or exercise a right to attack and destroy any vessel entering a prescribed area of the high seas without first certainly determining its belligerent nationality and the contraband character of its cargo would be an act so unprecedented in naval warfare that this Government is reluctant to believe that the Imperial Government of Germany in this case contemplates it as possible. The suspicion that enemy ships are using neutral flags improperly can create no just presumption that all ships traversing a prescribed area are subject to the same suspicion. It is to determine exactly such questions that this Government understands the right of visit and search to have been recognized.[2]

After stating that "the Government of the United States is open to none of the criticisms for unneutral action to which the German Government believe the Governments of certain of other neutral Nations have laid themselves open," that the "Government of the United States has not consented to or acquiesced in any measures which may have been taken by the other belligerent nations in the present war which operate to restrain neutral trade," and that this Government had "on the contrary, taken in all such matters a position which warrants it in holding those governments responsible in the proper way for any untoward effects upon American shipping which the accepted principles of international law do not justify," the Secretary of State firmly stated that the destruction of American life or property upon the high seas within the proscribed area and under the circumstances and conditions set forth in the German

[1] Official text, *American Journal of International Law*, Special Supplement, July, 1915, p. 86.
[2] *Ibid.*, pp. 86-87.

proclamation would be regarded as an unfriendly act, and that the United States would be constrained to hold the Imperial German Government to a "strict accountability" for any act committed by it not in accord with the generally accepted principles of international law. Thus:

> If the commanders of German vessels of war should act upon the presumption that the flag of the United States was not being used in good faith and should destroy on the high seas an American vessel or the lives of American citizens, it would be difficult for the Government of the United States to view the act in any other light than as an indefensible violation of neutral rights which it would be very hard indeed to reconcile with the friendly relations now so happily subsisting between the two Governments.
>
> If such a deplorable situation should arise, the Imperial German Government can readily appreciate that the Government of the United States would be constrained to hold the Imperial German Government to a strict accountability for such acts of their naval authorities and to take any steps it might be necessary to take to safeguard American lives and property and to secure to American citizens the full enjoyment of their acknowledged rights on the high seas.[1]

In conclusion the Government of the United States requested an assurance of the Imperial German Government that American citizens and their vessels would not be molested by the naval forces of Germany "otherwise than by visit and search, though their vessels may be traversing the sea area delimited in the proclamation of the German Admiralty."[2] And in order that the good faith of the United States might be beyond question, and that the plea of the misuse of the neutral flag should be withdrawn, the note terminated with the statement that representations had been made to Great Britain "in respect to the unwarranted use of the American flag for the protection of British ships."[2]

The Imperial German Government was equally prompt in its reply to Secretary Bryan's instruction of February 10th, which appears to have been delivered to the German Foreign Office on the 12th of the month, and on the 16th the Imperial Secretary for Foreign Affairs replied at length and in detail to the contentions of the American Government, showing by the promptness and fullness of discussion that the use of the submarine was not what might be called the result of a sudden inspiration, but rather of measured, cold

[1] Official text, *American Journal of International Law*, Special Supplement, July, 1915, p. 87.
[2] *Ibid.*, p. 88.

and determined calculation, weighing in advance as in a balance the advantages which would accrue from this method of warfare and the disadvantages which the Imperial Government evidently believed would be limited to diplomatic protests.

Omitting the introductory portion of the note which aptly referred to the good will and friendship which prompted the American communication, Secretary von Jagow hastened to assure the United States that the action of his Government was "in no wise directed against the legitimate trade and navigation of neutral states" and that it merely represented "an act of self-defense which Germany's vital interests force her to take against England's methods of conducting maritime war in defiance of international law, which no protest on the part of neutrals has availed to bring into accordance with the legal status generally recognized before the outbreak of hostilities."[1] We here have as reasons advanced: the vital interests of Germany, as decided by Germany, forced Germany to commit an act of self-defense, likewise determined by Germany, to put a stop to the unlawful actions of Great Britain which it was the duty of the neutrals to prevent, and as these neutrals had not complied with their duty Germany was free to take any course of action calculated in its opinion to keep British action within the bounds of law.

The Imperial Secretary of State then proceeds to state anew his country's cause; and in his very first sentence he makes an admission, the nature and importance of which he did not apparently recognize, because, armed with this statement, the neutral does not need to argue the question of illegality, saying that "Up to now Germany has scrupulously observed the existing provisions of international law relative to maritime war,"—leaving it to be understood that henceforth the Imperial German Government forsakes the beaten track of precedent to embark on unknown and troubled seas. The Imperial Secretary next denounces Great Britain's unlawful interference with Germany's peaceable trade with neutral countries, and in so doing makes a second admission that the United States in its note dated December 28, 1914, "has dealt with this point very aptly if not very exhaustively on the ground of the experiences of months," thus freeing the United States from the imputation of condoning British conduct, considered by both countries as unwarranted by the generally accepted principles of international law.

In the next paragraph the Imperial Secretary summarizes the

[1] Official text, *American Journal of International Law*, Special Supplement, July, 1915, p. 90.

British acts as intended "to deliver up to death by famine a peaceful civilian population, a procedure contrary to the law of war and every dictate of humanity." In view of the fact that the law of Nations which was universally recognized before the outbreak of the war in 1914, permitted a belligerent to blockade the ports of its enemy and to starve its enemy into submission if possible, and in view also of the fact that the policy of Germany was intended to starve out the island kingdom of Great Britain by sinking on sight enemy or neutral vessels found traversing those waters, it would seem that the statement of the German Secretary in this matter is neither convincing nor felicitous.

After a further reference to the lack of success which had crowned the efforts of the United States in its protests, the German Government considered itself obliged "to point out very particularly and with the greatest emphasis, that a trade in arms exists between American manufacturers and Germany's enemies which is estimated at many hundred million marks." The Imperial Secretary admitted that it was the right of the citizens or subjects of a neutral Nation to indulge in this trade, but added that it had the right, "although unfortunately not exercised, to stop trade in contraband, especially the trade in arms, with Germany's enemies."[1] But if the citizens of a neutral country had the right to trade with one belligerent, they also had the right to do so with another belligerent, and the request to place an embargo upon the commerce of American citizens with England was in effect a justification of a refusal of neutral Powers to trade with Germany should they so decide.

These various statements of the note have been analyzed by way of introduction to the policy which Germany had determined upon and which it stated and attempted to justify in the following brief but weighty paragraphs:

> In view of this situation the German Government see themselves compelled, after six months of patience and watchful waiting, to meet England's murderous method of conducting maritime war with drastic counter measures. If England invokes the powers of famine as an ally in its struggles against Germany with the intention of leaving a civilized people the alternative of perishing in misery or submitting to the yoke of England's political and commercial will, the German Government are today determined to take up the gauntlet and to appeal to the same grim ally. They rely on the neutrals who have

[1] Official text, *American Journal of International Law*, Special Supplement, July, 1915, p. 92.

hitherto tacitly or under protest submitted to the consequences, detrimental to themselves, of England's war of famine to display not less tolerance toward Germany, even if the German measures constitute new forms of maritime war, as has hitherto been the case with the English measures.

In addition to this, the German Government are determined to suppress with all the means at their disposal the supply of war material to England and her allies and assume at the same time that it is a matter of course that the neutral Governments which have hitherto undertaken no action against the trade in arms with Germany's enemies do not intend to oppose the forcible suppression of this trade by Germany.[1]

As a means to accomplish this end, clearly and unmistakably expressed, at the expense of neutrals if success should require it, the Imperial German Government thus, within a single sentence and without circumlocution, sealed up, as far as was within its power, every avenue of approach to and from Great Britain: "Proceeding from these points of view the German Admiralty has declared the zone prescribed by it the seat of war; it will obstruct this area of maritime war by mines wherever possible and also endeavor to destroy the merchant vessels of the enemy in any other way."[2]

It is true that, in the above announcement, enemy ships alone are mentioned, but it is well known that mines are no respecters of persons or of property, and immediately thereafter the Imperial Secretary stated that, if it were necessary to destroy neutral shipping in order to effect Germany's purpose, neutral shipping would be destroyed. Thus, after disclaiming the intention to destroy "neutral lives and neutral property," he states that his Government "cannot be blind to the fact that dangers arise through the action to be carried out against England which menace without discrimination all trade within the area of maritime war." And the Imperial German Secretary plainly, curtly, indeed bluntly, informs neutrals that "the safest way of doing this is to stay away from the area of maritime war."

Lest, however, the full meaning and import of this statement might pass unnoticed, Herr von Jagow makes the meaning of his Government clear even to the uninitiated in such matters, saying:

> Neutral ships entering the closed waters in spite of this announcement, given so far in advance, and which seriously impairs the accomplishment of the military purpose against

[1] Official text, *American Journal of International Law*, Special Supplement, July, 1915, p. 92.
[2] *Ibid.*, pp. 92-93.

England, bear their own responsibility for any unfortunate accidents. The German Government on their side expressly decline all responsibility for such accidents and their consequences.[1]

The great Mirabeau is reported to have said that war was Prussia's favorite industry.[2] It has been so often said, that no authority is needed for it, that Prussia has made its enemies pay for its wars. The Imperial German Secretary announced the further development in this form of industry by shifting the burden of the industry upon neutrals and carrying it on at their expense.

The Imperial Secretary, after this frank statement of the intentions of his Government, discusses the measures which could be taken in order either to cause neutral merchantmen to be recognized as such or to restrict the cargoes they should carry in order to render their voyages to and from Great Britain through the forbidden area harmless as far as Germany's interests are concerned, and the Secretary expressed a willingness to give "the most earnest consideration to any measure that might be calculated to assure the safety of legitimate shipping of neutrals within the seat of war."[3] He admitted, however, that two circumstances militated against an agreement: first, the misuse of the neutral flag by English merchant vessels; second, the trade in contraband, especially war materials, by neutral vessels. After discussing the misuse of the neutral flag by British merchantmen and stating that the British Government had recommended the use of such flags, the Secretary added that any agreement which might be reached would be defeated if British merchant vessels were permitted to use neutral flags and thus escape detection. The Secretary welcomed the fact that the American Government had made representations to Great Britain concerning the use of the American flag and he gave expression to the expectation "that this action would cause England to respect the American flag in future," and, to quote his exact language, "in this expectation the commanders of the German submarines have been instructed, as was already stated in the note of the fourth instant, to abstain from violence to American merchant vessels when they are recognizable as such."[4]

[1] Official text, *American Journal of International Law*, Special Supplement, July, 1915, p. 93.
[2] Mirabeau's expression is usually paraphrased in the form reproduced in the text. He actually said: "I shall consider finally the military system of this country given over wholly to war, a kind of industry truly Prussian and hitherto one of the most solid bases of the power to which the House of Brandenburg has raised itself." (Mirabeau, *De la Monarchie Prussienne, sous Frédéric le Grand*, 1788, tome I, Introduction, unpaged.)
[3] Official text, *American Journal of International Law*, Special Supplement, July, 1915, p. 94.
[4] *Ibid.*

The meaning of this is tolerably clear. American vessels, clearly recognized as such without the formalities of visit and search, were not to be destroyed, but this concession was based upon the expectation that the American protest to Great Britain against the use of the American flag by British merchantmen would be successful. Otherwise, this concession was likely to be withdrawn. It might happen, however, that an American vessel would be mistaken for a British merchantman, even although Great Britain had renounced the use of the American flag, and, recognizing the possibility of this, the Imperial Secretary proceeded to point out "the safest manner" to avoid the mistake of an American for a hostile vessel. This "safest manner" was for the United States to convoy its ships carrying peaceable cargoes navigating the seas surrounding Great Britain. This would obviate the necessity of visiting and searching the merchant vessel, as the word of the commander of the convoy would be taken as to the nationality of the vessel; but the German Government meant something more than establishing the nationality. The ships convoyed were to be those carrying peaceable cargoes, and, if only those ships were to be spared, Germany must naturally decide for itself the question of the peaceable cargo. In order that there might be no misunderstanding on this point, Germany stated it as a condition "that only such ships should be convoyed as carry no merchandise which would have to be considered as contraband according to the interpretation applied by England against Germany," that is to say, no vessel carrying any article declared by Great Britain to be contraband would be entitled to safety. The Secretary stated the willingness of his Government to enter into negotiations concerning the matter of convoy; but, in the meantime, the American Government was recommended to warn its ships to abstain from British waters, at any rate until the flag question was settled.

The "safest manner" to avoid sinking neutral merchantmen was to follow the law of Nations, which, in this matter, requires belligerent war vessels to visit and to search the merchantman in order to ascertain its nationality and the nature and extent of its cargo. As the use of neutral flags is permitted, the flag is not a safe guide as to nationality, a fact pointed out many years ago by Secretary of State Cass in 1860 before the outbreak of the Civil War. The prize ordinance issued by Germany on the 3d of August, 1914, permits its vessels of war to use neutral flags, and, so far as known, no nation prevents its merchantmen from saving themselves at the expense of a bit of bunting.

Without stopping to argue the question, which will be considered later, it should be stated that the German note points out the reason why visit and search would not be the "safest manner" to the German submarine, although it is recognized by international law to be the "safest manner" to the merchantman. Thus, the Imperial German Secretary says: "Moreover, the British Government have armed English merchant vessels and instructed them to resist by force the German submarines. In these circumstances it is very difficult for the German submarines to recognize neutral merchant vessels as such, for even a search will not be possible in the majority of cases, since the attacks to be anticipated in the case of a disguised English ship would expose the commanders conducting the search and the boat itself to the danger of destruction."[1] It is to be observed that in this note the Imperial Secretary refers to the fact that *The Lusitania* had recently raised the American flag in order to escape its enemy and, as coming events are said to cast their shadow before, *The Lusitania* was soon to suffer at the hands of the submarine for the misuse of the American flag, by virtue of which it either did or tried to escape destruction.

Four days later, that is to say, on the 20th of February, 1915, the Government of the United States earnestly besought both Great Britain and Germany to come to an agreement upon the conduct of maritime warfare, and an identic note concerning this matter was sent to the two Governments. In doing so, Secretary Bryan was careful to point out that the United States, in addressing the belligerents, did not assume the right to dictate, but that, as a friend of each and in the common interests of humanity, it ventured to suggest a basis of agreement which, if accepted, would be a blessing to the world. The suggestions were of three kinds. The first related to an agreement of Germany and Great Britain, the second to an agreement of Germany, the third to an agreement of Great Britain. This part of the note is as follows:

> Germany and Great Britain to agree:
> 1. That neither will sow any floating mines, whether upon the high seas or in territorial waters; that neither will plant on the high seas anchored mines except within cannon range of harbors for defensive purposes only; and that all mines shall bear the stamp of the Government planting them and be so constructed as to become harmless if separated from their moorings.
> 2. That neither will use submarines to attack merchant ves-

[1] Official text, *American Journal of International Law*, Special Supplement, July, 1915, p. 94.

sels of any nationality except to enforce the right of visit and search.

3. That each will require their respective merchant vessels not to use neutral flags for the purpose of *disguise or ruse de guerre.*

Germany to agree:

That all importations of food or foodstuffs from the United States and (from such other neutral countries as may ask it) into Germany shall be consigned to agencies to be designated by the United States Government; that these American agencies shall have entire charge and control without interference on the part of the German Government, of the receipt and distribution of such importations, and shall distribute them solely to retail dealers bearing licenses from the German Government entitling them to receive and furnish such food and foodstuffs to noncombatants only; that any violation of the terms of the retailers' licenses shall work a forfeiture of their rights to receive such food and foodstuffs for this purpose; and that such food and foodstuffs will not be requisitioned by the German Government for any purpose whatsoever or be diverted to the use of the armed forces of Germany.

Great Britain to agree:

That food and foodstuffs will not be placed upon the absolute contraband list and that shipments of such commodities will not be interfered with or detained by British authorities if consigned to agencies designated by the United States Government in Germany for the receipt and distribution of such cargoes to licensed German retailers for distribution solely to the noncombatant population.[1]

It is sufficient for present purposes to say that the attempt of the United States to bring about an agreement by a *modus vivendi* between Germany and Great Britain was unsuccessful.[2]

Section 1. The "Lusitania"

On the 7th of May, 1915, *The Lusitania* was sunk by a German submarine off the coast of Ireland. The vessel was on its voyage from New York and, in addition to cargo, it carried 1,153 passengers. Of this number 783 lost their lives, and among these were over a hundred American citizens, men, women, and children. *The Lusitania* was torpedoed without warning at 2:30 o'clock in the afternoon

[1] Official text, *American Journal of International Law*, Special Supplement, July, 1915, pp. 98-99.
[2] Ambassador Gerard to the Secretary of State, Berlin, March 1, 1915, *ibid.*, p. 99; Ambassador W. H. Page to the Secretary of State, London, March 15, 1915, *ibid.*, p. 106.

and no attempt was made by the submarine to remove the passengers from the torpedoed vessel or to rescue them from the water after the liner had sunk. This was not the first passenger steamer which had been sunk by the Germans since the submarine campaign was announced in February and relentlessly and indiscriminately prosecuted. In a note of Secretary Bryan to the American Ambassador at Berlin dated May 13, 1915, he stated:

> The sinking of the British passenger steamer *Falaba* by a German submarine on March 28, through which Leon C. Thrasher, an American citizen, was drowned; the attack on April 28 on the American vessel *Cushing* by a German aeroplane; the torpedoing on May 1 of the American vessel *Gulflight* by a German submarine, as a result of which two or more American citizens met their death; and, finally, the torpedoing and sinking of the steamship *Lusitania*, constitute a series of events which the Government of the United States has observed with growing concern, distress, and amazement.[1]

The sinking of *The Lusitania* was therefore not an isolated act, but it was one of a series, and, unfortunately, as events proved, it was but one of a continuing series. It stood out, however, and it still stands out as the chief among the many victims of the submarine, just as in a later period the torpedoing of *The Sussex* stands out among the many victims of the submarine. The sinking of *The Lusitania* amazed and dazed the American people. The sinking of *The Sussex* convinced them that there would be a break between the two countries unless there were a radical change in submarine warfare. Each incident was the occasion for an elaborate and a frank interchange of views, resulting in a statement and a promise, which would have maintained peace between the two countries had the promises not been broken. Each of these two instances will be considered in detail. First, as to *The Lusitania*.

The Imperial German Government evidently meant *The Lusitania* to be a test case. It had apparently formed an intention in advance to destroy this vessel, either because of its use of a neutral flag on two occasions in order to elude the submarine or because the destruction of a huge liner plying between New York and Liverpool would call the attention of the United States to the gravity of the situation and force the issue. It is common knowledge that persons intending to travel on *The Lusitania* were in some cases warned by anonymous

[1] Official text, *American Journal of International Law*, Special Supplement, July, 1915, p. 130.

telegrams not to take passage upon the ship, and the following notice appeared in the American press shortly before the sailing of *The Lusitania* purporting to come from the Imperial German Embassy, warning American citizens not to take passage on the liner.

NOTICE!

TRAVELERS intending to embark on the Atlantic voyage are reminded that a state of war exists between Germany and her allies and Great Britain and her allies; that the zone of war includes the waters adjacent to the British Isles; that, in accordance with formal notice given by the Imperial German Government, vessels flying the flag of Great Britain, or of any of her allies, are liable to destruction in those waters and that travelers sailing in the war zone on ships of Great Britain or her allies do so at their own risk.

IMPERIAL GERMAN EMBASSY
Washington, D. C., April 22, 1915.[1]

This is an astounding document to issue from an Embassy, and its issuance has never been denied or repudiated. It can only be paralleled by Citizen Genêt's appeal from the President of the United States to the American people in behalf of what he was pleased to call, during the early days of the French Revolution, the rights of his countrymen against Presidential usurpation. It would have been proper to ask the Imperial German Ambassador to deny its authenticity or the Imperial German Government to disavow the act, and in case of a refusal to do one or the other, to hand the Ambassador his passports. Instead of that, Secretary Bryan thus referred to this phase of the incident:

> There was recently published in the newspapers of the United States, I regret to inform the Imperial German Government, a formal warning purporting to come from the Imperial German Embassy at Washington, addressed to the people of the United States, and stating, in effect, that any citizen of the United States who exercised his right of free travel upon the seas would do so at his peril if his journey should take him within the zone of waters within which the Imperial German Navy was using submarines against the commerce of Great Britain and France, notwithstanding the respectful but very earnest protest of his Government, the Government of the United States. I do not refer to this for the purpose of calling the attention of the Imperial German Government at this time to the surprising irregularity of a communication from the Imperial German Embassy at Washington addressed to the people of the United States through the

[1] *The New York Times*, May 1, 1915, adv., p. 19.

newspapers, but only for the purpose of pointing out that no warning that an unlawful and inhumane act will be committed can possibly be accepted as an excuse or palliation for that act or as an abatement of the responsibility for its commission.[1]

Secretary Bryan in *The Lusitania* note recalled to the attention of the Imperial German Government the statements he had previously made, that he could not accept the proclamation of a war zone as "an abbreviation of the rights of American shipmasters or of American citizens bound on lawful errands as passengers on merchant ships of belligerent nationality," and that the United States intended to hold the Imperial German Government "to a strict accountability for any infringement of those rights, intentional or incidental." Secretary Bryan further stated, on behalf of the United States Government, that Germany should, in the conduct of naval warfare, admit and act upon the principle that the lives of noncombatants, whether they be enemy or neutral, "cannot lawfully or rightfully be put in jeopardy by the capture or destruction of an unarmed merchantman" and that the Imperial German Government should, "as all other nations do," recognize "the obligation to take the usual precaution of visit and search to ascertain whether a suspected merchantman is in fact of belligerent nationality or is in fact carrying contraband of war under a neutral flag"; that, if the submarine could not comply with the requirements of international law as hitherto understood and accepted in the premises, the use of such an instrumentality could not be permitted; and the United States made it very clear in this note that it was impossible to conform the actions of the submarine to the requirements of international law, and that therefore the submarine was an outlaw in the domain of law. Thus:

> The Government of the United States, therefore, desires to call the attention of the Imperial German Government with the utmost earnestness to the fact that the objection to their present method of attack against the trade of their enemies lies in the practical impossibility of employing submarines in the destruction of commerce without disregarding those rules of fairness, reason, justice, and humanity which all modern opinion regards as imperative. It is practically impossible for the officers of a submarine to visit a merchantman at sea and examine her papers and cargo. It is practically impossible for them to make a prize of her; and, if they cannot put a prize crew on board

[1] Official text, *American Journal of International Law*, Special Supplement, July, 1915, p. 132.

of her, they cannot sink her without leaving her crew and all on board of her to the mercy of the sea in her small boats.[1]

After a statement of the right of American citizens to send their ships and to intrust their persons upon enemy ships upon the high seas and within the war zone without jeopardy to their lives, and after making it easy for the Imperial German Government to disavow the act of the submarine on the ground of failure to recognize the noncontraband character of its cargo, Secretary Bryan stated on behalf of his Government that:

> It confidently expects, therefore, that the Imperial German Government will disavow the acts of which the Government of the United States complains, that they will make reparation so far as reparation is possible for injuries which are without measure, and that they will take immediate steps to prevent the recurrence of anything so obviously subversive of the principles of warfare for which the Imperial German Government have in the past so wisely and so firmly contended.[2]

He made it clear that the United States did not rely wholly upon principles of international law, but that its rights in the premises were based upon the Treaty of 1828 between the United States and the Kingdom of Prussia, although he did not stop to specify its provisions. He also called attention to the fact that expressions of regret "satisfy international obligations, if no loss of life results," but that they cannot recall the dead or justify their sacrifice. He also stated it to be the intention of the United States to perform "its sacred duty of maintaining the rights of the United States and its citizens and of safeguarding their free exercise and enjoyment"; and he did so in the gentlest of terms under the greatest of provocations. Notwithstanding the fate of Belgium before his eyes and the lawlessness of the submarine, he recalled "the humane and enlightened attitude hitherto assumed by the Imperial German Government in matters of international right and particularly with regard to the freedom of the seas." Further, "having learned to recognize the German views and the German influence in the field of international obligation as always engaged upon the side of justice and humanity; and having understood the instructions of the Imperial German Government to its naval commanders to be upon the same plane of humane action prescribed by the naval codes of other

[1] Official text, *American Journal of International Law*, Special Supplement, July, 1915, p. 131.
[2] *Ibid.*, pp. 132-133.

Nations, the Government of the United States was loath to believe—it cannot now bring itself to believe—that these acts, so absolutely contrary to the rules, the practices, and the spirit of modern warfare, could have the countenance or sanction of that great Government."[1]

A note of this kind, in its assertion of American rights, courteous and friendly in their statement, required either an acknowledgment or a repudiation of those rights and a justification of the conduct of the Imperial German Government alleged to be in violation not merely of rights but of elementary principles of humanity; but the Imperial Government did not appreciate the gravity of the situation.

In the course of the correspondence dealing with this question, which fully stated its views, the Imperial German Secretary referred to the friendly manner in which the American Government had presented its case, and declared that, if American vessels had come to grief "through the German submarine war during the past few months by mistake," this was "traceable to the misuse of flags by the British Government in connection with careless or suspicious actions on the part of captains of the vessels." After this somewhat labored and wholly infelicitous introduction, and a belated expression of regret, he replied to the American assurance that *The Lusitania* was an unarmed merchant vessel and should be treated as such, by stating that *The Lusitania* was built with Government funds as an auxiliary cruiser, and that it was carried on the lists of the British Admiralty as such; that, like all the more valuable English merchant vessels, it was provided with guns and ammunition and other weapons, and that, upon leaving New York, it "had guns on board which were mounted under decks and masked." According, therefore, to the German contention, *The Lusitania* was not an ordinary merchant vessel and was not entitled to be treated as such because, if not actually employed as an auxiliary cruiser, it nevertheless could be taken over by the British Government and employed as such, and that in any event it was armed during this voyage and could not therefore be considered as an unarmed vessel.

A particular reference was made to the fact that the British Government had directed the use of neutral flags and markings, and, when so disguised, "to attack submarines by ramming them." It is important to note this statement, because the Imperial Secretary

[1] Official text, *American Journal of International Law*, Special Supplement, July, 1915, p. 130.

gives it as the reason for the failure on the part of the German commanders to observe the generally recognized principles of international law, saying expressly, "the German commanders are consequently no longer in a position to observe the rules of capture otherwise usual and with which they invariably complied before this." Here is an admission that the action of the German commanders was not in accordance with international law, and, if justifiable at all, it could only be upon the ground of retaliation for the unlawful acts of its enemy and only if confined to the enemy and not extended to innocent and unoffending neutrals.

Finally, the Imperial Secretary asserted that *The Lusitania*, as on earlier occasions, "had Canadian troops and munitions on board, including not less than 5,400 cases of ammunition." *The Lusitania*, therefore, was not merely to be considered as a possible auxiliary, but as an armed merchant vessel using a neutral flag as a *ruse de guerre* under instructions to carry on warfare by attacking submarines, and as a transport because carrying a cargo of contraband and Canadian troops.

Instead, therefore, of a repudiation of the instructions to the German naval officers and a disavowal of the act as unauthorized, Herr von Jagow expressly justified both the instructions and the act on the ground that "The Imperial German Government believes that it acts in just self-defense when it seeks to protect the lives of its soldiers by destroying ammunition destined for the enemy with the means of war at its command."[1]

Without directly charging that the American passengers had made the trip in order to protect *The Lusitania* from destruction, the Imperial Secretary states that the company "deliberately tried to use the lives of American citizens as protection for the ammunition carried,"[2] and that the company "violated the clear provisions of

[1] Official text, *American Journal of International Law*, Special Supplement, July, 1915, pp. 133-135.
[2] If Great Britain had "deliberately tried to use the lives of American citizens as protection for the ammunition carried," it would have had authority of no mean order for its action. Thus, the *Kriegsbrauch im Landkriege* (pp. 49-50) says:

> The German army command instituted a new application of the "hostage-right" in the war of 1870-1871 by compelling prominent citizens of French towns and villages to ride on the locomotives of trains, in order to safeguard the railroad communications which were threatened by the people. Peaceful inhabitants thus, without any fault on their part, were placed in serious danger. Authorities outside of Germany regarded this measure as contrary to international law, and as unjustified with regard to the nationals of the enemy country. As against this unfavorable judgment, attention must be called to the fact that, while Germany also regarded it as rigorous and cruel, the means was resorted to only after explanations

American laws which expressly prohibit, and provide punishment for, the carrying of passengers on ships which have explosives on board."[1] We are thus prepared for the conclusion, which the Imperial Secretary does not leave us to draw but which he himself states, that "the company thereby wantonly caused the death of so many passengers."[1]

On the 9th of June Mr. Lansing, who had succeeded Mr. Bryan as Secretary of State, sent a note to the American Ambassador to Berlin, directing him to deliver it "textually" to the German Minister of Foreign Affairs. This note was intended to be and it was a clean-cut and authoritative statement of the views of the American Government on the questions involved in the sinking of *The Lusitania*. In the first place, Secretary Lansing summarizes and states the charges of the German Government, in order that his reply may be responsive to those charges. Thus:

> It is stated in the note that *The Lusitania* was undoubtedly equipped with masked guns, supplied with trained gunners and special ammunition, transporting troops from Canada, carrying a cargo not permitted under the laws of the United States to a vessel also carrying passengers, and serving, in virtual effect, as an auxiliary to the naval forces of Great Britain.[2]

These, Secretary Lansing says, are questions of fact, concerning which he was in a position to supply the Imperial German Government with official information. If true, he admitted that the United States would be taxed with duties in the premises. For example, he said:

> It was its duty to see to it that *The Lusitania* was not armed for offensive action, that she was not serving as a transport, that she did not carry a cargo prohibited by the statutes of the United States, and that, if in fact she was a naval vessel of Great Britain, she should not receive clearance as a merchantman.[2]

After admitting the duty incumbent upon the United States, he stated that "it performed that duty and enforced its statutes with

and instructions given to the population had proved ineffective, and because it was the only measure which promised, in the particular circumstances, to be successful with regard to an undoubtedly unjustified, nay, criminal conduct of a fanatical population. Herein lies its justification, under the rules of war, but even more in the fact that the measure met with full success, and that wherever prominent persons thus accompanied trains, whether owing to the increased watchfulness of the communities or to the immediate effect upon the people, the security of traffic was restored.

[1] Official text, *American Journal of International Law*, Special Supplement, July, 1915, p. 136.
[2] *Ibid.*, p. 139.

scrupulous vigilance through its regularly constituted officials," and that he was able "to assure the Imperial German Government that it has been misinformed."[1]

The importance of this statement is fundamental, because these very facts were advanced by the Imperial German Government in justification of the sinking of *The Lusitania*, and if the alleged facts were found to be nonexistent the special justification of the German Government fell with the facts. Secretary Lansing, assuming responsibility on behalf of his Government for the nonexistence of the facts as alleged, therefore eliminated them from discussion and devoted his attention to the principles of law which should govern *The Lusitania* case in the absence of special facts and circumstances. Thus he said:

> Whatever be the other facts regarding *The Lusitania*, the principal fact is that a great steamer, primarily and chiefly a conveyance for passengers, and carrying more than a thousand souls who had no part or lot in the conduct of the war, was torpedoed and sunk without so much as a challenge or a warning, and that men, women, and children were sent to their death in circumstances unparalleled in modern warfare. The fact that more than one hundred American citizens were among those who perished made it the duty of the Government of the United States to speak of these things and once more, with solemn emphasis, to call the attention of the Imperial German Government to the grave responsibility which the Government of the United States conceives that it has incurred in this tragic occurrence, and to the indisputable principle upon which that responsibility rests.[2]

Secretary Lansing conceived and therefore stated that:

> The Government of the United States is contending for something much greater than mere rights of property or privileges of commerce.[2]

He did not, however, leave the Imperial German Government in doubt as to the principles involved, saying:

> It is contending for nothing less high and sacred than the rights of humanity, which every Government honors itself in respecting and which no Government is justified in resigning on behalf of those under its care and authority.[2]

---

[1] Official text, *American Journal of International Law*, Special Supplement, July, 1915, p. 139.

Gustav Stahl, a German reservist, made an affidavit in the premises regarding the armament of *The Lusitania*, which affidavit was forwarded to the Department of State by Ambassador von Bernstorff. Stahl later admitted that the affidavit was false, pleaded guilty to an indictment charging perjury, and was sentenced to the penitentiary. (H. R. Report No. 1, 65th Cong., 1st session; *Congressional Record*, vol. 55, No. 4, p. 193.)

[2] *Ibid.*, p. 140.

He then proceeded to state the rule of law by which the German commander should have guided his conduct. Thus:

> Only her actual resistance to capture or refusal to stop when ordered to do so for the purpose of visit could have afforded the commander of the submarine any justification for so much as putting the lives of those on board the ship in jeopardy.[1]

In the preceding portion of the note he had called attention to the contentions of the German Government in the sinking of *The Falaba,* and as the principles which he laid down in that matter were in his mind and within the knowledge of the Imperial German Secretary when he read this statement concerning *The Lusitania,* they are here quoted, in order that the reader may be in the position of the Secretaries of State of the respective Governments. Thus:

> With regard to the sinking of the steamer *Falaba,* by which an American citizen lost his life, the Government of the United States is surprised to find the Imperial German Government contending that an effort on the part of a merchantman to escape capture and secure assistance alters the obligation of the officer seeking to make the capture in respect of the safety of the lives of those on board the merchantman, although the vessel has ceased her attempt to escape when torpedoed. These are not new circumstances. They have been in the minds of statesmen and of international jurists throughout the development of naval warfare, and the Government of the United States does not understand that they have ever been held to alter the principles of humanity upon which it has insisted. Nothing but actual forcible resistance or continued efforts to escape by flight when ordered to stop for the purpose of visit on the part of the merchantman has ever been held to forfeit the lives of her passengers or crew.[2]

With these principles before his eyes the reader will understand the full meaning and importance of the following passage of the note immediately succeeding the passage already quoted concerning *The Lusitania:*

> This principle the Government of the United States understands the explicit instructions issued on August 3, 1914, by the Imperial German Admiralty to its commanders at sea to have recognized and embodied, as do the naval codes of all other nations, and upon it every traveler and seaman had a right to depend. It is upon this principle of humanity as well as upon the law founded upon this principle that the United States must stand.[1]

[1] Official text, *American Journal of International Law,* Special Supplement, July, 1915, p. 140.
[2] *Ibid.,* p. 139.

In conclusion, Secretary Lansing called attention to the note of the 15th of May, and reaffirmed the principles there stated, repudiated the binding effect of a proclamation, to which the United States did not consent, to abbreviate the rights of American citizens upon the high seas, and voiced the expectation of the United States that Germany would modify submarine warfare in such a way as to conform to these principles, which were not merely the principles and practice of the United States, but the principles and practice of Nations, because they were the prescribed practice of humanity. Thus:

> The Government of the United States cannot admit that the proclamation of a war zone from which neutral ships have been warned to keep away may be made to operate as in any degree an abbreviation of the rights either of American shipmasters or of American citizens bound on lawful errands as passengers on merchant ships of belligerent nationality. It does not understand the Imperial German Government to question those rights. It understands it, also, to accept as established beyond question the principle that the lives of noncombatants cannot lawfully or rightfully be put in jeopardy by the capture or destruction of an unresisting merchantman, and to recognize the obligation to take sufficient precaution to ascertain whether a suspected merchantman is in fact of belligerent nationality or is in fact carrying contraband of war under a neutral flag. The Government of the United States therefore deems it reasonable to expect that the Imperial German Government will adopt the measures necessary to put these principles into practice in respect of the safeguarding of American lives and American ships, and asks for assurances that this will be done.[1]

On July 8, 1915,[2] a month lacking two days after the receipt of Secretary Lansing's note, the Imperial German Secretary transmitted the reply of his Government, observing with satisfaction "how earnestly the Government of the United States is concerned in seeing the principles of humanity realized in the present war," and receiving with gratitude the statements contained in the American note of May 15, 1915, that Germany "had always permitted itself to be governed by the principles of progress and humanity in dealing with the law of maritime war," and expressing the hope that, after the war and perhaps earlier, it may be possible to "regulate the law of maritime war in a manner guaranteeing the freedom of the seas." The Imperial German Secretary then proceeded to a justification of the destruction of *The Lusitania*.

[1] Official text, *American Journal of International Law*, Special Supplement, July, 1915, p. 141.
[2] *Ibid.*, p. 149.

He began by denouncing British action as contrary to the generally recognized principles of maritime warfare, and then made the usual statement that Germany has, as an act of self-defense, been forced to submarine warfare. To quote his exact language:

> While our enemies thus loudly and openly have proclaimed war without mercy until our utter destruction, we are conducting war in self-defense for our national existence and for the sake of peace of assured permanency. We have been obliged to adopt submarine warfare to meet the declared intentions of our enemies and the method of warfare adopted by them in contravention of international law.[1]

This is the usual cry of distress of the belligerent which finds itself at the mercy of its enemy, and its constant repetition would suggest that neutrals are somewhat hard of hearing. During the Civil War Secretary Seward sought to enlist the sympathies of Great Britain by informing Her Majesty's Government that the war in which his country was then engaged was a war of liberty and therefore deserving of the sympathy of Great Britain and that, as it was a war of existence, the United States felt that Great Britain, appreciating this fact, would be a mild and sympathetic judge of its breaches of the law. The shortest way, however, as the United States found, to obtain the sympathy and the respect of neutral countries is for the belligerent to conform its actions to the requirements of law.

The principal grievance mentioned is that "Germany's adversaries . . . have aimed from the very beginning . . . at the destruction not so much of the armed forces as the life of the German nation, repudiating in so doing all the rules of international law and disregarding all the rights of neutrals."[2] To show that this was no new thing for Great Britain, he adroitly cited the following illustration from recent history, knowing that it would not be lost upon the American public which sympathized with the Boers in their heroic struggle against Great Britain: "Just as was the case with the Boers, the German people is now to be given the choice of perishing from starvation, with its women and children, or of relinquishing its independence."[3] It was perhaps not to be expected that the Imperial German Secretary should say in this connection that Germany supplied Great Britain with the arms and ammunition which ended the Boers, but such is the fact, as already pointed out.

---
[1] Official text, *American Journal of International Law*, Special Supplement, July, 1915, p. 151.
[2] *Ibid.*, p. 150.   [3] *Ibid.*, p. 151.

The first illustration of British disregard of all the rules of international law and of all the rights of neutrals was the declaration of November 3, 1914, of the North Sea as a war area; the second was by "planting poorly anchored mines"; the third was the stoppage and capture of vessels, making "passage extremely dangerous and difficult for neutral shipping, so that it is actually blockading neutral coasts and ports contrary to all international law." Admitting that each of the actions specified was wrong, this does not condone a wrong on Germany's part. Thus, in the Imperial Secretary's actual, measured language and mature judgment, "Germany was driven to submarine war on trade."

He was, however, apparently worried by the consequences which might flow from the injury to neutral life and property in unrestricted submarine warfare, and crediting his Government with the desire and the effort "in principle to protect neutral life and property from damage as much as possible"—consistent, he might have added, with the success of the undertaking—"the German Government," he continues, "recognized unreservedly in its memorandum of February 4th that the interests of neutrals might suffer from submarine warfare."

We now come to the one reason which, in the opinion of the Imperial Secretary, speaking in the name and in behalf of the Imperial German Government, justifies submarine warfare and any kind of warfare calculated to crown the German arms with success:

> However, the American Government will also understand and appreciate that in the fight for existence which has been forced upon Germany by its adversaries and announced by them, it is the sacred duty of the Imperial Government to do all within its power to protect and to save the lives of German subjects. If the Imperial Government were derelict in these, its duties, it would be guilty before God and history of the violation of those principles of the highest humanity which are the foundation of every national existence.[1]

If Germany can do this, Great Britain may also do it, as well as the United States, in its war with Germany, and we would find ourselves in that state of nature described by Hobbes, in which there would exist, "no arts, no letters, no society; and which is worst of all, continual fear and danger of violent death, and the life of man solitary, poor, nasty, brutish, and short."[2] This quotation from

[1] Official text, *American Journal of International Law*, Special Supplement, July, 1915, p. 151.
[2] Hobbes' *Leviathan* (London, 1887), chap. 13, p. 64.

Hobbes is aptly borne out by the case of *The Lusitania,* to which the Imperial Secretary now, and for the first time in his note, devotes his attention, justifying the act of his Government by blaming its adversary, unconsciously no doubt following Lord Mansfield's humorous advice, "No case, abuse plaintiff's attorney." "The case of *The Lusitania,*" he says, "shows with horrible clearness to what jeopardizing of human lives the manner of conducting war employed by our adversaries leads," declaring that, by the order to British merchantmen to arm themselves and to ram submarines "and the promise of rewards therefor," neutrals traveling upon merchantmen had been exposed "in an increasing degree" to all the dangers of war. And to show what is meant by the dangers of war, the Secretary next says, and it is his language which is quoted, that "if the commander of the German submarine which destroyed *The Lusitania* had caused the crew and travelers to put out in boats before firing the torpedo this would have meant the sure destruction of his own vessel." Unconsciously, in the succeeding passage, he points out the value of experience, not merely in the laboratory, but in the science of warfare upon the high seas, saying that "after the experiences in the sinking of much smaller and less seaworthy vessels, it was to be expected that a mighty ship like *The Lusitania* would remain above water long enough, even after the torpedoing, to permit the passengers to enter the ship's boats." Here is an admission that Germany had been sinking "much smaller and less seaworthy vessels," and apparently the German submarine commander had the right to expect better workmanship at the hands of British shipwrights. But as this was the largest ship which the Germans had sunk, the commander of the submarine should not perhaps be condemned for the vulnerability of his target, especially as there was another reason. "Circumstances of a very peculiar kind," to quote the Secretary, "especially the presence on board of large quantities of highly explosive materials, defeated this expectation." It may be said in passing, that the presence of these explosives has not been proven, but however that may be, the Secretary advanced a conclusive reasoning, saying:

> In addition, it may be pointed out that if *The Lusitania* had been spared thousands of cases of ammunition would have been sent to Germany's enemies and thereby thousands of German mothers and children robbed of their supporters.[1]

[1] Official text, *American Journal of International Law,* Special Supplement, July, 1915, p. 152.

Again it should be said in this connection that it has not been proven that thousands of cases of ammunition formed a part of the cargo of *The Lusitania*, but it is admitted that hundreds of passengers did, and that of these some hundred American men, women, and children lost their lives that German mothers and children might not be robbed of their supporters.

It is to be borne in mind, in considering this case, that the German Government in its various notes holds itself out as imbued with the spirit of friendship for the American people and as desirous "to do all it can during the present war also to prevent the jeopardizing of the lives of American citizens." Because of this the Secretary, in behalf of his country, thereupon states that:

> The Imperial Government therefore repeats the assurances that American ships will not be hindered in the prosecution of legitimate shipping, and the lives of American citizens on neutral vessels shall not be placed in jeopardy.[1]

But it is to be observed that this assurance is limited to legitimate shipping, as to which the views of Germany and of the United States might be opposed, and only "the lives of American citizens on neutral vessels" are not to be placed in jeopardy. The vessel is to be engaged in legitimate shipping and it is to be neutral. Otherwise, the lives of American citizens might, under this concession, be placed in jeopardy.

In the next paragraph the concession is further restricted to passenger ships, and the carriage of contraband is apparently excluded from "the prosecution of legitimate shipping." Thus:

> In order to exclude any unforeseen dangers to American passenger steamers, made possible in view of the conduct of maritime war on the part of Germany's adversaries, the German submarines will be instructed to permit the free and safe passage of such passenger steamers when made recognizable by special markings and notified a reasonable time in advance. The Imperial Government, however, confidently hopes that the American Government will assume the guarantee that these vessels have no contraband on board. The details of the arrangements for the unhampered passage of these vessels would have to be agreed upon by the naval authorities of both sides.[1]

As indicating the nature and extent of the desire to spare American citizens engaged in the prosecution of legitimate shipping, the

[1] Official text, *American Journal of International Law*, Special Supplement, July, 1915, p. 152.

Imperial Secretary makes two propositions which, lest they be misunderstood or unintentionally modified in a paraphrase, are quoted in his own language:

> In order to furnish adequate facilities for travel across the Atlantic Ocean for American citizens, the German Government submits for consideration a proposal to increase the number of available steamers by installing in the passenger service a reasonable number of neutral steamers, the exact number to be agreed upon, under the American flag under the same conditions as the American steamers above mentioned.
>
> The Imperial Government believes that it can assume that in this manner adequate facilities for travel across the Atlantic Ocean can be afforded American citizens. There would therefore appear to be no compelling necessity for American citizens to travel to Europe in time of war on ships carrying an enemy flag. In particular the Imperial Government is unable to admit that American citizens can protect an enemy ship through the mere fact of their presence on board. Germany merely followed England's example when it declared part of the high seas an area of war. Consequently accidents suffered by neutrals on enemy ships in this area of war cannot well be judged differently from accidents to which neutrals are at all times exposed at the seat of war on land when they betake themselves into dangerous localities in spite of previous warning.[1]

By way of comment upon this concession it may be said that if Americans possess a right to use belligerent merchantmen for travel or for trade, a right which the Supreme Court of the United States has solemnly declared to exist, in a case of *The Nereide,* later to be considered, it is for the American citizen possessing the right to determine whether he will use it or not, not the person illegally opposing the use of this right. In the next place it may be observed that the comparison between land and naval warfare is not well drawn, because land is occupied and can be controlled by the occupant stepping into the shoes, as it were, and assuming the functions of its owner, whereas the high seas cannot be occupied to the exclusion of any one nation, because no nation can lawfully exercise exclusive jurisdiction upon the high seas, which are the patrimony of the nations, open to all nations, and in which all nations have equal rights of which they cannot be deprived without their own consent. In this connection it is only necessary to declare that the United States has not consented to be deprived of its rights upon the high seas, either by Great Britain

---

[1] Official text, *American Journal of International Law,* Special Supplement, July, 1915, pp. 152-153.

or its allies or by Germany and its allies, or by all of them put together.

The second proposition is thus worded:

> If, however, it should not be possible for the American Government to acquire an adequate number of neutral passenger steamers, the Imperial Government is prepared to interpose no objections to the placing under the American flag by the American Government of four enemy passenger steamers for the passenger traffic between America and England. The assurances of "free and safe" passage for American passenger steamers would then be extended to apply under the identical pre-conditions to these formerly hostile passenger ships.[1]

This concession but adds insult to injury.

The note of the Imperial German Government of July 8, 1915, was duly received by the Department of State, and it was considered so important that the reply of Secretary Lansing was cabled instead of being sent through the mails. The very first sentence of this note states that the Government of the United States finds the German reply to be very unsatisfactory, because it failed "to meet the real differences between the two Governments," indicated "no way in which the accepted principles of law and humanity may be applied in the grave matter in controversy," but proposed, on the contrary, "arrangements for a partial suspension of those principles which virtually set them aside."[2]

By way of summary, the note states the acceptance by the Imperial German Government of the principle that "the high seas are free, that the character and cargo of a merchantman must first be ascertained before she can be lawfully seized or destroyed, and that the lives of noncombatants may in no case be put in jeopardy unless the vessel resists or seeks to escape after being summoned to submit to examination."[2] Secretary Lansing evidently took the Imperial Government at its word that each of its acts was in retaliation for alleged illegal acts of Great Britain, and he therefore declared them to be illegal in the sense that they were not legal, "for a belligerent act of retaliation," he said, "is *per se* an act beyond the law, and the defense of an act as retaliatory is an admission that it is illegal."[2]

In coming to the conclusion that the German Government accepted the American contentions on the matter in hand, Sec-

[1] Official text, *American Journal of International Law*, Special Supplement, July, 1915, p. 153.
[2] *Ibid.*, p. 155.

retary Lansing relied not merely upon the formal statements contained in the correspondence, but upon the following statement made to the American Ambassador on May 9, 1915, by the German Foreign Office, which, taken in conjunction with the more elaborate documents, seems to justify Mr. Lansing's conclusions:

> First. Imperial German Government has naturally no intention of causing to be attacked by submarines or air craft such neutral ships of commerce in the zone of naval warfare, more definitely described in the notice of the German Admiralty staff of February 4 last, as have been guilty of no hostile act; on the contrary, the most definite instructions have repeatedly been issued to German war vessels to avoid attacks on such ships under all circumstances. Even when such ships have contraband of war on board, they are dealt with by submarines solely according to the rules of international law applying to prize warfare.
>
> Two. Should a neutral ship, nevertheless, come to harm through German submarines or air craft on account of an unfortunate (* * *)[1] in the above-mentioned zone of naval warfare, the German Government will unreservedly recognize its responsibility therefor. In such a case it will express its regrets and afford damages without first instituting a prize court action.
>
> Three. It is the custom of the German Government as soon as the sinking of a neutral ship in the above-mentioned zone of naval warfare is ascribed to German war vessels to institute an immediate investigation into the cause. . . . In case the German Government, contrary to the viewpoint of the neutral government, is not convinced by the result of the investigation, the German Government has already on several occasions declared itself ready to allow the question to be decided by an international investigation commission according to chapter three of The Hague Convention of October 18, 1907, for the peaceful solution of international disputes.[2]

It is to be observed, in the first place, that this statement deals only with neutral shipments, not with the contention of the United States that its citizens have the right to travel upon belligerent merchant ships without having their lives put in jeopardy by the destruction of the vessel without warning and without putting into a place of safety passengers and crew. It will be noted in the second place that this statement of the Foreign Office, satisfactory in some respects, is a misapprehension of the point of view of the neutral, who wants his rights, not compensation for their violation

---

[1] In the official text " * * * " with footnote " apparent omission."
[2] Official text, *American Journal of International Law*, Special Supplement, October, 1916, pp. 161-162.

and loss because of injury. The German view is that the submarine can do anything making for success and that the payment of dollars rights the wrong.

But to return to the cable of July 21, 1915. After expressing satisfaction at the acceptance of the American contentions, Secretary Lansing insists, on behalf of the United States, that acceptance of the principle is not enough, for the principle accepted must be observed in practice. Thus, he says:

> The Government of the United States is, however, keenly disappointed to find that the Imperial German Government regards itself as in large degree exempt from the obligation to observe these principles, even where neutral vessels are concerned, by what it believes the policy and practice of the Government of Great Britain to be in the present war with regard to neutral commerce.[1]

He next proceeds to state that the action of a third Government is to be discussed by the United States with that Government and not with Germany, and that its disputes with that third Government are to be arranged by the United States directly with that Government, not by, with, or through the Imperial German Government. Thus:

> The Imperial German Government will readily understand that the Government of the United States cannot discuss the policy of the Government of Great Britain with regard to neutral trade except with that Government itself, and that it must regard the conduct of other belligerent governments as irrelevant to any discussion with the Imperial German Government of what this Government regards as grave and unjustifiable violations of the rights of American citizens by German naval commanders. Illegal and inhuman acts, however justifiable they may be thought to be against an enemy who is believed to have acted in contravention of law and humanity, are manifestly indefensible when they deprive neutrals of their acknowledged rights, particularly when they violate the right to life itself. If a belligerent cannot retaliate against an enemy without injuring the lives of neutrals, as well as their property, humanity, as well as justice and a due regard for the dignity of neutral powers, should dictate that the practice be discontinued. If persisted in it would in such circumstances constitute an unpardonable offense against the sovereignty of the neutral nation affected.[1]

[1] Official text, *American Journal of International Law*, Special Supplement, July, 1915, p. 156.

After admitting that the conditions of the present war are extraordinary and that changed conditions naturally bring new methods into being, he insists that those methods must conform to principle, not principle to those methods. Thus:

> The rights of neutrals in time of war are based upon principle, not upon expediency, and the principles are immutable. It is the duty and obligation of belligerents to find a way to adapt the new circumstances to them.[1]

In regard to the German proposal to set aside a certain number of ships which it would respect, apparently leaving itself free to destroy all others, Secretary Lansing repudiates this in the following measured language:

> The Government of the United States, while not indifferent to the friendly spirit in which it is made, cannot accept the suggestion of the Imperial German Government that certain vessels be designated and agreed upon which shall be free on the seas now illegally proscribed. The very agreement would, by implication, subject other vessels to illegal attack and would be a curtailment and therefore an abandonment of the principles for which this Government contends and which in times of calmer counsels every nation would concede as of course.[2]

After saying that the Government of the United States will continue to contend for that freedom, from whatever quarter violated, without compromise and at any cost, Secretary Lansing concludes his note with the very solemn warning, always portending grave consequences between great Nations, that:

> Friendship itself prompts it to say to the Imperial Government that repetition by the commanders of German naval vessels of acts in contravention of those rights must be regarded by the Government of the United States, when they affect American citizens, as deliberately unfriendly.[2]

Section 2. The "Arabic"

Before taking up the case of *The Sussex*, brief mention should be made of *The Arabic*, a steamer of the White Star Line, which was torpedoed without warning at 9 o'clock on the morning of August 15, 1915. It sank in eleven minutes. At the time it was torpedoed it

---
[1] Official text, *American Journal of International Law*, Special Supplement, July, 1915, p. 156.
[2] *Ibid.*, p. 157.

had on board 181 passengers, among them 25 Americans. No attempt was made by the submarine to put passengers or crew in a place of safety, and 44 lives were lost, including therein three Americans. The Imperial German Government apparently appreciated the seriousness of this incident, as in a note of September 1, 1915, its Ambassador to the United States informed Secretary Lansing that the following passage occurred in the last note which he had received from his Government concerning the *Lusitania* case:

> Liners will not be sunk by our submarines without warning and without safety of the lives of noncombatants, provided that the liners do not try to escape or offer resistance.[1]

Although, in a note of September 4th,[2] the German Ambassador repeated the contention of his Government that "American citizens who travel on such vessels do so on their own responsibility and incur the greatest risk," the representations of the American Government in case of *The Arabic* caused the Imperial German Government to state to its Ambassador, on October 5, 1915,[3] that "the orders issued by His Majesty the Emperor to the commanders of the German submarines—of which I notified you on a previous occasion—have been made so stringent that the recurrence of incidents similar to the *Arabic* case is considered out of the question." The Ambassador, after referring to the belief of the German commander that the liner intended to ram the submarine, added that "the attack of the submarine, therefore, was undertaken against the instructions issued to the commander. The Imperial Government regrets and disavows this act and has notified Commander Schneider accordingly." He ended the note with an offer, made on behalf of his Government, to pay an indemnity for the American lives lost on *The Arabic*. On October 6, 1915, Secretary Lansing, in an acknowledgment to the German Ambassador, expressed satisfaction with the foregoing assurances of the German Government and stated his readiness to negotiate regarding the amount of the indemnity.

Section 3. The "Sussex"

In the face of these assurances and in disregard of the apparent accord between the two Governments, the British passenger steamer

---

[1] Official text, *American Journal of International Law*, Special Supplement, October, 1916, p. 166.
[2] *Ibid.*, p. 167.
[3] *Ibid.*, p. 172.

Sussex, plying between an English and a French port and having American passengers on board, was torpedoed on March 24, 1916, without the formalities of visit and search, without warning, and without an attempt made to save the lives of passengers and crew or to put them in a place of safety. The question involved something more than the destruction of a passenger vessel and the loss of American lives. It involved the good faith of the Imperial German Government and the degree to which the United States could rely upon the solemn pledge of that Government given after negotiations extending over a period of more than a year. The facts of the case, as stated by Secretary Lansing in his cable of April 18, 1916,[1] after careful investigation by the United States, were as follows:

> On the 24th of March, 1916, at about 2:50 o'clock in the afternoon, the unarmed steamer *Sussex,* with 325 or more passengers on board, among whom were a number of American citizens, was torpedoed while crossing from Folkestone to Dieppe. *The Sussex* had never been armed; was a vessel known to be habitually used only for the conveyance of passengers across the English Channel; and was not following the route taken by troop ships or supply ships. About eighty of her passengers, noncombatants of all ages and sexes, including citizens of the United States, were killed or injured.[2]

Recognizing the peculiar gravity of the case and that the United States must stand upon the issue raised, Secretary Lansing thus stated the care with which the United States had ascertained the facts involved:

> A careful, detailed, and scrupulously impartial investigation by naval and military officers of the United States has conclusively established the fact that *The Sussex* was torpedoed without warning or summons to surrender and that the torpedo by which she was struck was of German manufacture.[2]

After observing that the Government of the United States had given careful consideration to the Imperial German note of April 10, 1916, in which that Government denied that *The Sussex* was destroyed by a German submarine, introducing, in support of this statement, "a sketch of the vessel attacked" made by the German commander, and in which the Imperial German Government proposed that the facts be ascertained by a mixed committee of investigation pursuant

---

[1] Official text, *American Journal of International Law,* Special Supplement, October, 1916, pp. 186-190.   [2] *Ibid.,* p. 187.

to the third title of The Hague Convention of October 18, 1907, for the pacific settlement of international disputes, Secretary Lansing added that "the Imperial Government has failed to appreciate the gravity of the situation which has resulted, not alone from the attack on *The Sussex*, but from the whole method and character of submarine warfare as disclosed by the unrestrained practice of the commanders of German undersea craft during the past twelvemonth and more in the indiscriminate destruction of merchant vessels of all sorts, nationalities, and destinations."

Secretary Lansing was willing to concede that, if the case were an isolated one, although "so tragical as to make it stand forth as one of the most terrible examples of the inhumanity of submarine warfare as the commanders of German vessels are conducting it," the "ends of justice might be satisfied by imposing upon him [the commander] an adequate punishment, coupled with a formal disavowal of the act and payment of a suitable indemnity by the Imperial Government." But, under present circumstances, the destruction of *The Sussex* could only be looked upon as one of a series and as evidence "of the deliberate method and spirit of indiscriminate destruction of merchant vessels of all sorts, nationalities, and destinations." Secretary Lansing referred to the attitude of the United States upon the announcement of the submarine campaign in 1915, when "it took the position that such a policy could not be pursued without constant gross and palpable violations of the accepted law of nations, particularly if submarine craft were to be employed as its instruments, inasmuch as the rules prescribed by that law, rules founded on the principles of humanity and established for the protection of the lives of noncombatants at sea, could not in the nature of the case be observed by such vessels."

Notwithstanding the requirements of the law of Nations in these matters, based upon the principles of humanity and having "the express assent of all civilized nations," the Imperial Government, to quote Secretary Lansing's exact words, "persisted in carrying out the policy announced, expressing the hope that the dangers involved, at any rate to neutral vessels, would be reduced to a minimum by the instructions which it had issued to the commanders of its submarines, and assuring the Government of the United States that it would take every possible precaution both to respect the rights of neutrals and to safeguard the lives of noncombatants." But, in spite of these promises and the protest of the United States, the submarine warfare continued, suggesting that the "Imperial Government has found it impracticable to put any such restraints upon them as it had hoped and promised to put.''

After calling attention to the fact that in February, 1916, the German Government declared that it would treat armed merchantmen as vessels of war and that by so doing it pledged itself by implication ''to give warning to vessels which were not armed and to accord security of life to their passengers and crews,'' and, after stating that commanders of German submarines ''had recklessly ignored'' even this limitation, Secretary Lansing used the following spirited but just language:

> Vessels of neutral ownership, even vessels of neutral ownership bound from neutral port to neutral port, have been destroyed along with vessels of belligerent ownership in constantly increasing numbers. Sometimes the merchantmen attacked have been warned and summoned to surrender before being fired on or torpedoed; sometimes their passengers and crews have been vouchsafed the poor security of being allowed to take to the ship's boats before the ship was sent to the bottom. But again and again no warning has been given, no escape even to the ship's boats allowed to those on board. Great liners like *The Lusitania* and *Arabic* and mere passenger boats like *The Sussex* have been attacked without a moment's warning, often before they have even become aware that they were in the presence of an armed ship of the enemy, and the lives of noncombatants, passengers, and crew have been destroyed wholesale and in a manner which the Government of the United States cannot but regard as wanton and without the slightest color of justification. No limit of any kind has in fact been set to their indiscriminate pursuit and destruction of merchantmen of all kinds and nationalities within the waters which the Imperial Government has chosen to designate as lying within the seat of war. The roll of Americans who have lost their lives upon ships thus attacked and destroyed has grown month by month until the ominous toll has mounted into the hundreds.[1]

After mentioning that the American Government has been very patient, that it has allowed itself ''to be guided by sentiments of very genuine friendship for the people and Government of Germany,'' and that ''it has made every allowance for unprecedented conditions and has been willing to wait until the facts became unmistakable and were susceptible of only one interpretation,'' Secretary Lansing asserted, on behalf of the United States, that ''it now owes

[1] Official text, *American Journal of International Law*, Special Supplement, October, 1916, pp. 189-190.

it to a just regard for its own rights to say to the Imperial Government that that time has come. It has become painfully evident to it that the position which it took at the very outset is inevitable, namely, the use of submarines for the destruction of an enemy's commerce, is, of necessity, because of the very character of the vessels employed and the very methods of attack which their employment of course involves, utterly incompatible with the principles of humanity, the long-established and incontrovertible rights of neutrals, and the sacred immunities of noncombatants."[1] And Secretary Lansing, still speaking for the United States "in behalf of humanity and the rights of neutral nations," solemnly stated that "unless the Imperial Government should now immediately declare and effect an abandonment of its present methods of submarine warfare against passenger and freight-carrying vessels, the Government of the United States can have no choice but to sever diplomatic relations with the German Empire altogether."[1]

On May 4, 1916,[2] the Imperial German Secretary of State for Foreign Affairs handed the American Ambassador a formal reply and assurance, and, recognizing the gravity of the case and the possibility of misunderstanding of its terms and a misconception of the purposes of the German Government, the text of the reply was in English as well as German.

At the very outset of his note the Imperial Secretary emphatically repudiates Secretary Lansing's assertion "that this incident is to be considered as one instance for the deliberate method of indiscriminate destruction of vessels of all sorts, nationalities, and destinations by German submarine commanders." He stated again that commanders of German submarines had been ordered "to conduct submarine warfare in accordance with the general principles of visit and search and destruction of merchant vessels as recognized by international law." He admitted, however, that the Imperial Government had made an exception, which he was bold enough to call the "sole exception," in the case of "enemy trade carried on enemy freight ships that are encountered in the war zone surrounding Great Britain," and that "with regard to these no assurances have ever been given to the Government of the United States." He stated that "the German Government cannot admit any doubt that these orders have been given and are executed in good faith," although he conceded that "errors have actually occurred"; and

[1] Official text, *American Journal of International Law*, Special Supplement, October, 1916, p. 190.
[2] *Ibid.*, pp. 195-199.

he asserted once again, and in what would seem to be unmistakable terms, as the German Government has repeatedly declared, that "it cannot dispense with the use of the submarine weapon in the conduct of warfare against enemy trade."

A considerable portion of the note is taken up with the denunciation of Great Britain, which, according to the Imperial German Secretary, "ignoring all the accepted rules of international law, has extended this terrible war to the lives and property of noncombatants, having no regard whatever for the interests and rights of the neutrals and noncombatants that through this method of warfare have been severely injured," and that "in self-defense against the illegal conduct of British warfare, while fighting a bitter struggle for her national existence, Germany had to resort to the hard but effective weapon of submarine warfare."[1]

Again, the claim is advanced that Germany is resolved "to use the submarine weapon in strict conformity with the rules of international law as recognized before the outbreak of the war, if Great Britain were likewise ready to adapt her conduct of warfare to these rules," thus again admitting the unlawful conduct of the submarine and again justifying its use by what it denounced as the unlawful conduct of Great Britain. After mentioning that the United States has failed in its attempts to cause Great Britain to adhere to international law and stating that "the German people knows that the Government of the United States has the power to confine this war to the armed forces of the belligerent countries in the interest of humanity," the Imperial Secretary insists in language which may be quoted, but upon which it is very difficult to comment, that "the German people is under the impression that the Government of the United States, while demanding that Germany, struggling for her existence, shall restrain the use of an effective weapon, and while making the compliance with these demands a condition for the maintenance of relations with Germany, confines itself to protests against the illegal methods adopted by Germany's enemies." However, the German Government, wishing to preserve peace between the two nations and "to confine the operations of war for the rest of its duration to the fighting forces of the belligerents" and to insure "the freedom of the seas," notifies the Government of the United States that the German naval forces have received the following orders: "In accordance with the general principles of visit and search and destruction

---

[1] Official text, *American Journal of International Law*, Special Supplement, October, 1916, p. 197.

of merchant vessels recognized by international law, such vessels, both within and without the area declared as naval war zone, shall not be sunk without warning and without saving human lives, unless these ships attempt to escape or offer resistance."[1]

This the Imperial Secretary regarded as a concession, and apparently he wished it to be considered as such, because, in the paragraph of his note immediately following it, he says:

> But neutrals cannot expect that Germany, forced to fight for her existence, shall, for the sake of neutral interest, restrict the use of an effective weapon if her enemy is permitted to continue to apply at will methods of warfare violating the rules of international law. Such a demand would be incompatible with the character of neutrality, and the German Government is convinced that the Government of the United States does not think of making such a demand, knowing that the Government of the United States has repeatedly declared that it is determined to restore the principle of the freedom of the seas, from whatever quarter it is violated.[2]

Finally, the German Secretary stated that "should the steps taken by the Government of the United States not attain the object it desires—to have the laws of humanity followed by all belligerent nations,—the German Government would then be facing a new situation in which it must reserve to itself complete liberty of decision."[3]

Instead of commenting upon the contentions of the German Government contained in this note, it will perhaps be best to quote, likewise without comment, Secretary Lansing's note in reply, dated May 8, 1916,[4] indicating the agreement which was supposed to have been reached between the two Governments:

> The note of the Imperial German Government under date of May 4, 1916, has received careful consideration by the Government of the United States. It is especially noted, as indicating the purpose of the Imperial Government as to the future, that it "is prepared to do its utmost to confine the operations of the war for the rest of its duration to the fighting forces of the belligerents," and that it is determined to impose upon all its commanders at sea the limitations of the recognized rules of international law upon which the Government of the United States has insisted. Throughout the months which have elapsed since the Imperial Government announced, on February 4, 1915, its submarine policy, now happily abandoned, the Government of the United States has been constantly guided and restrained by

[1] Official text, *American Journal of International Law*, Special Supplement, October, 1916, p. 198.
[2] *Ibid.*, pp. 198-199. [3] *Ibid.*, p. 199. [4] *Ibid.*, pp. 199-200.

motives of friendship in its patient efforts to bring to an amicable settlement the critical questions arising from that policy. Accepting the Imperial Government's declaration of its abandonment of the policy which has so seriously menaced the good relations between the two countries, the Government of the United States will rely upon a scrupulous execution henceforth of the now altered policy of the Imperial Government, such as will remove the principal danger to an interruption of the good relations existing between the United States and Germany.

The Government of the United States feels it necessary to state that it takes it for granted that the Imperial German Government does not intend to imply that the maintenance of its newly announced policy is in any way contingent upon the course or result of diplomatic negotiations between the Government of the United States and any other belligerent Government, notwithstanding the fact that certain passages in the Imperial Government's note of the 4th instant might appear to be susceptible of that construction. In order, however, to avoid any possible misunderstanding, the Government of the United States notifies the Imperial Government that it cannot for a moment entertain, much less discuss, a suggestion that respect by German naval authorities for the rights of citizens of the United States upon the high seas should in any way or in the slightest degree be made contingent upon the conduct of any other Government affecting the rights of neutrals and noncombatants. Responsibility in such matters is single, not joint; absolute, not relative.[1]

To this note and to Secretary Lansing's statement that the United States did not accept the concession of the German Government conditioned upon the success of any negotiations with Great Britain, no reply has ever been received.[2]

[1] Official text, *American Journal of International Law*, Special Supplement, October, 1916, pp. 199-200.
[2] See statement to this effect in Secretary Lansing's note of February 3, 1917, to the German Ambassador, handing him his passports. *MSS. Department of State.*

CHAPTER X

REPRISALS, RETALIATION, NECESSITY

Section 1. Reprisals

Even a casual consideration of the correspondence between the Imperial German Government and the United States and the British Government and the United States will have shown each belligerent justifying a certain line of conduct because of an illegal act of the enemy which must be met and overcome. If the enemy committed the act as alleged, then necessity, vital interests, or self-defense required the belligerent—Germany, Great Britain, or France—to resort to appropriate measures in order to counteract it.

Let us take, by way of illustration, the matter of mines. Germany scattered mines, according to its notice to neutrals, on August 7, 1914. Great Britain alleged that Germany was using mines improperly; this Germany denied. Great Britain alleged that Germany was scattering mines indiscriminately and improperly, using neutral vessels for this purpose; this Germany denied. Great Britain intimated that if Germany continued its unlawful use of mines, Great Britain might be obliged to resort to like measures, and in due course of time mines were scattered by Great Britain in the North Sea, which was declared a military area. Germany denounced this action on the part of Great Britain and declared the British Isles to be a war zone, with the result that, each alleging the misconduct of the other as justification for its various measures, the neutral was ground as it were between the upper and the nether millstone.

After giving the reasons for a law of the sea and stating the modest results accomplished in the direction of law, the President said in his address of April 2, 1917, to the Congress:

> This minimum of right the German Government has swept aside under the plea of retaliation and necessity and because it had no weapons which it could use at sea except these which it is impossible to employ as it is employing them without throwing to the winds all scruples of humanity or of respect for the understandings that were supposed to underlie the intercourse of

the world. I am not now thinking of the loss of property involved, immense and serious as that is, but only of the wanton and wholesale destruction of the lives of noncombatants, men, women, and children, engaged in pursuits which have always, even in the darkest periods of modern history, been deemed innocent and legitimate. Property can be paid for; the lives of peaceful and innocent people cannot be. The present German submarine warfare against commerce is a warfare against mankind.[1]

In the matter of reprisals, akin to if not identical with retaliation, perhaps the clearest statement to be found in the correspondence between the United States and the Imperial German Government is contained in a memorandum of the German Embassy, handed to Secretary Lansing on March 8, 1916, which enumerates in some detail the illegal acts of its arch enemy, Great Britain, which "compelled" the Imperial Government to resort to reprisals. After performing this not uncongenial task, the memorandum states that:

> Protests from neutrals were of no avail, and from that time on the freedom of neutral commerce with Germany was practically destroyed. Under these circumstances Germany was compelled to resort, in February, 1915, to reprisals in order to fight her opponents' measures, which were absolutely contrary to international law.[2]

Admitting that the law and the practice of nations allowed reprisals, and that Germany was justified in using the submarine against its enemy if its actions were confined to the enemy and did not injure or destroy indiscriminately the neutral, the resort to reprisals is an extreme right, depending as it does upon the will of one nation acting in passion with the danger ever present that the will of all, as expressed in the law of nations, will be overridden. But there are bounds to reprisals, which, if not illegal, are extra legal, and the bounds are thus admirably stated in conformity with the law and practice of nations by the distinguished German jurist, Ferdinand Perels, for many years adviser to the German Admiralty:

> From time immemorial, even down to the modern era, the manner of waging war, has, in all respects, been barbarous. Every means serviceable for realizing the object of the war, was looked upon as proper. The old maxim, "*etiam hasti fides servanda,*" was not always observed. Even although discipline, as a rule, was exercised in an extraordinarily rigid way, still, in

---

[1] H. R. doc. No. 1, 65th Cong., 1st sess.
[2] Official text, *American Journal of International Law*, Special Supplement, October, 1916, p. 179.

the land of the enemy, and as so frequently happened, during the Thirty Years' War, for instance, murder, incendiarism, pillage, rape, and atrocities of all sorts were the order of the day even in one's own land.

Ever since the law of nations has regarded war as a legal status, attempts have been made to settle the bounds commanded by humanity and by honor, to limit, thereby, the horrors of war to what is strictly necessary, and to permit a violation thereof only in case of reprisals. But, even measures of this sort, made necessary for the realization and security of the objects of war, must conform to the customs of war as they have been formed during the latter decades; and it is only upon the basis of such restriction that the military commander is authorized to resort to the use of those means, imposed upon him by his duty, to execute his task and his orders as quickly and as completely as possible, and at the same time to provide for the security and for the maintenance of his troops.

In regard to the laws and customs of land warfare, the Convention of July 29, 1899, adopted by The Hague Peace Conference contains, in so far as the special conditions of maritime warfare do not permit of departures therefrom, a number of provisions which are to be equally observed in hostilities between maritime powers, because they represent the general rules of warfare as developed from the concept of the modern law of nations, and also because it is not always possible, in all hostile situations, strictly to distinguish between warfare on land and warfare on sea.

Three declarations have resulted from the said convention, and concern:

1. Inhibition of throwing bombs and explosives from airships or in new ways similar thereto;
2. Inhibition of the use of bombs containing asphyxiating or poisonous gases;
3. Inhibition of the use of projectiles which will readily flatten or expand in the human body.

Opinions differ as regards the admissibility of the exercise of reprisals. Even although disregard of the customs of war by one party may justify the opponent in violating the accepted usages of war, nay, under circumstances, in resorting to extraordinary measures, still, the fundamental principles of humanity should be observed at all times. Satisfaction and vengeance to be had only by harsh measures will not always be renounced. But, even in such cases, barbarity and unrestrained arbitrariness passing the bounds of necessity must be condemned.[1]

Just as in the first edition of his work published in 1881, Professor Perels began the last paragraph by quoting, in justification

[1] Perels, *Das Internationale Öffentliche Seerecht der Gegenwart*, 2d edition, revised, 1903, pp. 179-180.

of his views, Article 27 of the *Instructions to American Armies in the Field:* "A reckless enemy often leaves to his opponent no other means of securing himself against the repetition of barbarous outrage," so he closes the corresponding paragraph of the edition of 1903 with the quotation, in justification of his views, of Article 8 of *Naval War Code* of the United States: "In the event of an enemy failing to observe the laws and usages of war, if the offender is beyond reach, resort may be had to reprisals, if such action should be considered a necessity, but due regard must always be had to the duties of humanity."[1]

And also in the first edition of his work Professor Perels invoked the authority of Bluntschli, who, as is well known, relied upon the distinguished American publicist of German origin, Francis Lieber, the author of the American *Instructions* which Perels had quoted. The passage from Bluntschli to which Perels referred reads as follows in English:

> In case the enemy disregards the bounds of the accepted custom of war or resorts to agencies of war which are against international law, reprisals may then be resorted to. Still, in the practice of reprisals, the fundamental laws of humanity must not be violated.

Upon this article Bluntschli thus comments:

> Cf. § 499 above, and Articles of War of the United States, 27, 28. The barbarity of the enemy does not justify barbarity on the part of the opponent. When savages torture enemy prisoners to death, civilized troops may *at most, on the ground of reprisals, kill* the enemy savages, but not *torture them.* The enemy passion of hatred and of revenge attempts to palliate its misdeeds by appealing to the *right of reprisals.* The elaboration of a more humane law of nations demands, therefore, a restriction of this law of necessity to the really necessary. It is more honorable, to resort to this law as little as possible.[2]

Other publicists might be cited, but President Wilson can well afford to rest his case upon the authority of Perels and of Bluntschli.

---

[1] Perels, *Das Internationale Öffentliche Seerecht der Gegenwart*, 2d edition, revised, 1903, pp. 179-180.
[2] Bluntschli, *Das Moderne Völkerrecht der Civilisirten Staaten als Rechtsbuch dargestellt*, 3d edition, 1878, sec. 567, p. 319.

Section 2. Retaliation

In the matter of retaliation, it may be said that the correspondence between the United States and the belligerents fairly teems with it.

> In retaliation of the regulations adopted by England and her allies, deviating from the London declaration of maritime law of February 26, 1909, I [the Kaiser himself is speaking] approve of the following amendments of the prize ordinance of September 30, 1909.[1]
>
> * * * * * * *
>
> It is impossible [said the British Secretary of State for Foreign Affairs] for one belligerent to depart from rules and precedents and for the other to remain bound by them.[2]

And again, after saying that "the German declaration [of blockade of the British Isles by the submarines] substitutes indiscriminate destruction for regulated capture," the British Ambassador states on behalf of his country and indeed of the Allies:

> Her opponents are therefore driven to frame retaliatory measures in order in their turn to prevent commodities of any kind from reaching or leaving Germany.[3]

But while the belligerents are, as it were, tarred with the same stick, the Allies recognize the limitation of retaliation and confine it within its legitimate sphere, declaring (and although international law has suffered somewhat in the process, they have lived up to their declaration) that:

> These measures will, however, be enforced by the British and French Governments without risk to neutral ships or to neutral or noncombatant life and in strict observance of the dictates of humanity.[3]

Without indulging in further quotations from the belligerents invoking the right to commit reprisals and to take retaliatory measures, it is advisable to state the attitude of the United States towards the claims and actions of the belligerents, which is, it is believed, in this phase of the subject the attitude of international law.

In the first place, Secretary Bryan makes clear the extent to which

---

[1] Official text, *American Journal of International Law*, Special Supplement, July, 1915, p. 43.
[2] *Ibid.*, p. 83.   [3] *Ibid.*, p. 102.

the United States would be disposed to consider retaliation legitimate. Thus:

> The Government of the United States notes that in the Order in Council His Majesty's Government give as their reason for entering upon a course of action, which they are aware is without precedent in modern warfare, the necessity they conceive themselves to have been placed under to retaliate upon their enemies for measures of a similar nature which the latter have announced it their intention to adopt and which they have to some extent adopted; but the Government of the United States, recalling the principles upon which His Majesty's Government have hitherto been scrupulous to act, interprets this as merely a reason for certain extraordinary activities on the part of His Majesty's naval forces and not as an excuse for or prelude to any unlawful action. If the course pursued by the present enemies of Great Britain should prove to be in fact tainted by illegality and disregard of the principles of war sanctioned by enlightened nations, it cannot be supposed, and this Government does not for a moment suppose, that His Majesty's Government would wish the same taint to attach to their own actions or would cite such illegal acts as in any sense or degree a justification for similar practices on their part in so far as they affect neutral rights.[1]

That is to say, extraordinary activity was to be expected and the inconvenience occasioned by it endured, provided it was not "an excuse for or prelude to any unlawful action."

When, however, the narrow and somewhat flexible line separating right from wrong was crossed, the United States did not merely explain. It protested. Thus:

> The Government of the United States has been apprised that the Imperial German Government considered themselves to be obliged by the extraordinary circumstances of the present war and the measures adopted by their adversaries in seeking to cut Germany off from all commerce, to adopt methods of retaliation which go much beyond the ordinary methods of warfare at sea, in the proclamation of a war zone from which they have warned neutral ships to keep away. This Government has already taken occasion to inform the Imperial German Government that it cannot admit the adoption of such measures or such a warning of danger to operate as in any degree an abbreviation of the rights of American shipmasters or of American citizens bound on lawful errands as passengers on merchant ships of belligerent

[1] Secretary of State to American Ambassador to Germany, May 13, 1915; official text, *American Journal of International Law*, Special Supplement, July, 1915, p. 119-120.

nationality; and that it must hold the Imperial German Government to a strict accountability for any infringement of those rights, intentional or incidental. It does not understand the Imperial German Government to question those rights. It assumes, on the contrary, that the Imperial Government accept, as of course, the rule that the lives of noncombatants, whether they be of neutral citizenship or citizens of one of the nations at war, cannot lawfully or rightfully be put in jeopardy by the capture or destruction of an unarmed merchantman, and recognize also, as all other nations do, the obligation to take the usual precaution of visit and search to ascertain whether a suspected merchantman is in fact of belligerent nationality or is in fact carrying contraband of war under a neutral flag.[1]

Finally, Secretary Lansing, speaking for his Government, and, it is believed, for all governments, whether neutral or belligerent, thus laid down the line of conduct which alone can be tolerated if neutrals are not to be made parties to the war or to suffer without protest its consequences. Thus:

> Illegal and inhuman acts, however justifiable they may be thought to be against an enemy who is believed to have acted in contravention of law and humanity, are manifestly indefensible when they deprive neutrals of their acknowledged rights, particularly when they violate the right to life itself. If a belligerent cannot retaliate against an enemy without injuring the lives of neutrals, as well as their property, humanity, as well as justice and a due regard for the dignity of neutral powers, should dictate that the practice be discontinued. If persisted in it would in such circumstances constitute an unpardonable offense against the sovereignty of the neutral nation affected.[2]

* * * * * * *

> The United States, therefore, cannot submit to the curtailment of its neutral rights by these measures, which are admittedly retaliatory, and therefore illegal, in conception and in nature, and intended to punish the enemies of Great Britain for alleged illegalities on their part. The United States might not be in a position to object to them, if its interests and the interests of all neutrals were unaffected by them, but, being affected, it cannot with complacence suffer further subordination of its rights and interests to the plea that the exceptional geographic positions of the enemies of Great Britain require or justify oppressive and illegal practices.[3]

[1] Secretary of State to American Ambassador to Germany, May 13, 1915; official text, *American Journal of International Law*, Special Supplement, July, 1915, pp. 130-131.

[2] Secretary of State to American Ambassador to Germany, July 21, 1915; *ibid.*, p. 156.

[3] Secretary of State to American Ambassador to England, October 21, 1915; official text, *American Journal of International Law*, Special Supplement, October, 1916, p. 88.

184 A SURVEY OF INTERNATIONAL RELATIONS

If the matter rested here, it might be questioned whether retaliation finds a place in a scheme of law, but certainly retaliation involving injury to neutral right is a very different thing from retaliation which affects solely the enemy. But the matter does not rest here, for, on February 16, 1916, the Imperial German Government solemnly stated to the United States that:

> Germany has limited her submarine warfare because of her long-standing friendship with the United States, and because by the sinking of *The Lusitania*, which caused the death of citizens of the United States, the German retaliation affected neutrals, which was not the intention, as retaliation should be confined to enemy subjects.[1]

Section 3. Necessity

In the matter of necessity, priority may be claimed for Germany, for as early as the 4th of August, 1914, the Imperial German Chancellor von Bethmann-Hollweg made the following announcement in the Reichstag applying the doctrine to the invasion of Luxemburg and Belgium, not only in violation of international law but of solemn treaties to which Germany was a party:

> We are now in a state of necessity, and necessity knows no law. Our troops have occupied Luxemburg and perhaps are already on Belgian soil. Gentlemen, that is contrary to the dictates of international law. It is true that the French Government has declared at Brussels that France is willing to respect the neutrality of Belgium, as long as her opponent respects it. We knew, however, that France stood ready for invasion. France could wait, but we could not wait. A French movement upon our flank upon the Lower Rhine might have been disastrous. So we were compelled to override the just protest of the Luxemburg and Belgian Governments. The wrong—I speak openly—that we are committing we will endeavor to make good as soon as our military goal has been reached. Anybody who is threatened as we are threatened, and is fighting for his highest possessions, can only have one thought—how he is to hack his way through.[2]

It will be observed that in this passage the Imperial Chancellor frankly admitted that the invasion of Belgium was contrary to the dictates of international law; that, in invading Belgium, Germany committed a wrong, which, however, his Government would endeavor to right when it had achieved its purpose.

[1] MSS., Department of State.
[2] *London Times*, August 11, 1914.

The Chancellor was correctly advised and stood upon firm ground when he informed the Reichstag that international law condemned the action of the government, and no statement concerning international law made by a German authority in the past three years has met with such universal approval as that the invasion of Belgium was contrary to international law. It was contrary not merely to international law, by virtue whereof a nation has a right to be neutral, but it was contrary to express stipulations of treaties to which Germany was a party, creating an independent Belgium and guaranteeing its neutrality.

First, as to the right of a nation to remain neutral and the duty of a belligerent to respect its neutrality.

It is not necessary to refer to treatises on international law to establish the right and the duty, because the Chancellor had at hand the *Kriegsbrauch im Landkriege,* published for the guidance of officers and soldiers in the conduct of land warfare. This remarkable manual states that:

> 1. The territory of neutral states is unavailable for any of the belligerents, while the war lasts. When war has been declared, the government of the neutral state must prevent individuals of either belligerent party from marching through it; . . .
> 2. If the neutral state is contiguous to the territory where the war is taking place, its government must see to it that a sufficiently strong force be on its frontier to prevent its crossing by portions of the belligerent armies with the object of marching through. . . .[1]

It will be observed that a neutral state may not allow the forces of the belligerents to enter its territory and that if they do they are to be regarded as trespassers. The *Kriegsbrauch im Landkriege,* however, modifies the strictness of this provision by the following concession, in the interest of humanity:

> 4. The neutral state may grant right of passage or transport of wounded or sick through its territory without violating its neutrality thereby; it must, however, see to it that such hospital trains do not carry either war personnel or war material, except such as is necessary for the care of the sick.[2]

This concession, however, is not to be allowed to prisoners of war.

[1] *Kriegsbrauch im Landkriege,* p. 69.
[2] *Ibid.,* p. 73.

> 5. The passage or transport of prisoners of war through neutral territory is, on the other hand, not to be granted, since this would be open favoring of him who was in a position to take prisoners of war in great numbers, while his railroads, water highways, and other means of transport are left at his disposal for actual war purposes.[1]

In the comment with which the *Kriegsbrauch im Landkriege* is supplied the following flagrant cases of the violation of neutrality are cited:

> The passage of French troops through Prussian territory in October, 1805, was a disregard of Prussian neutrality.—When the Swiss Government permitted the Allies to march through its territory in the year 1814, it thereby renounced the rights of a neutral State.—In the Franco-Prussian War the Prussian Government complained of the behavior of Luxemburg in not stopping a passage *en masse* of fugitive French soldiers after the fall of Metz through the territory of the Grand Duchy.[2]

After having enumerated and illustrated the "most important duties of neutral states so far as land warfare is concerned," the *Kriegsbrauch im Landkriege* proceeds to lay down the punishment incurred by a neutral State which violates its neutrality. Thus:

> If they are disregarded by the neutral State itself, then it has to give satisfaction or compensation to the belligerent who is prejudiced thereby. This case may also occur if the Government of the neutral State, with the best intentions to abstain from proceedings which violate neutrality, has, through domestic or foreign reasons, not the power to make its intentions good.[1]

The maintenance of neutrality is considered to be so important, and the principle just formulated so fundamental, that the *Kriegsbrauch im Landkriege* deems it necessary in this connection to cite an example lest the meaning of the text be not sufficiently clear. Thus:

> If, for example, one of the two belligerents by main force marches through the territory of a neutral State and this State is not in a position to put an end to this violation of its neutrality, then the other belligerent has the right to engage the enemy on the hitherto neutral territory.[1]

After this accurate statement of some of the duties of neutral States, the *Kriegsbrauch im Landkriege* next recognizes that duties involve corresponding rights, such as:

[1] *Kriegsbrauch im Landkriege*, p. 73.
[2] *Ibid.*, p. 69.

1. For the neutral State the status of peace times still continues, even in its relation with the belligerents.

2. The belligerent States have to respect the inviolability of the neutral and the undisturbed exercise of its sovereignty in its home affairs, to abstain from any attack upon the same, even if the necessity of war should make such an attack desirable. Neutral States, therefore, possess also the right of asylum for single members or nationals of the belligerent Powers, so far as no favor to one or other of them is thereby implied. Even the reception of a smaller or larger detachment of troops which is fleeing from pursuit does not give the pursuer the right to continue his pursuit across the frontier of the neutral territory. It is the business of the neutral State to prevent troops crossing over in order to reassemble in the chosen asylum, to re-form, and there to prepare for a new attack.

3. If the territory of a neutral State is trespassed upon by one of the belligerent parties for the purpose of battle, then this State has the right to proceed against this violation of its territory with all the means in its power and to disarm the trespassers. If the trespass has been committed on the orders of the Army Command, then the State concerned is bound to give satisfaction and compensation; if it has been committed on their own responsibility, then the individual offenders can be punished as criminals. If the violation of the neutral territory is due to ignorance of its frontiers and not to evil intention, then the neutral State can demand the immediate removal of the wrong, and can insist on necessary measures being taken to prevent a repetition of such disregard.

4. Every neutral State can, so long as it itself keeps faith and loyalty, demand that the same respect shall be paid to it as in time of peace. It is entitled to the presumption that it will observe strict neutrality and will not make use of any declarations or other transactions as a cloak for an injustice against one belligerent in favor of the other, or will use them indifferently for both. This is particularly important in regard to passes, commissions, and credentials.

6. Neutral States may continue to maintain diplomatic intercourse with the belligerent Powers undisturbed, so far as military measures do not raise obstacles in the way of it.[1]

Four of the neutral rights corresponding to neutral duties have been quoted in full, and the reader's attention is particularly called to the duty imposed upon belligerent Powers to abstain from any attack upon neutral territory, "even if," to quote the exact language of the *Kriegsbrauch im Landkriege*, "the necessity of war should make such an attack desirable." The reader has no doubt observed that, in the section devoted to neutral duties, no illustration is given

[1] *Kriegsbrauch im Landkriege*, pp. 72-75.

of the violation of neutrality by Prussia, although Prussia is shown as a sufferer in 1805 at the hands of the French, and Switzerland, when neutralized, is criticised as renouncing the rights of a neutral State because it allowed the allied armies to march through its territory in the year 1814 to reach France. Luxemburg, likewise a neutralized State, was blamed for its failure to observe a strict neutrality in the Franco-Prussian War. The war of 1914 supplies a Belgian precedent necessarily lacking in the edition of 1902. There are three neutralized States of Europe—Switzerland, Luxemburg, and Belgium—and in some future edition of the *Kriegsbrauch im Landkriege* Belgium's name may appear and be apportioned its blame for the violation of neutrality in 1914.

So much for the accuracy of the Chancellor's statement in so far as it is based upon the unwritten or customary law of Nations. Next, as to the provisions of treaties creating an independent Belgium and guaranteeing its neutrality.

On April 19, 1839, Great Britain, Austria, France, Prussia, and Russia, on the one part, and the Netherlands, on the other, concluded a treaty, of which the seventh article is thus worded:

> Belgium within the limits specified in Articles I, II, and IV shall form an Independent and perpetually Neutral State. It shall be bound to observe such Neutrality towards all other States.[1]

Lest there may be some doubt as to the meaning of the contracting parties, although their meaning would seem to be tolerably clear from the portion of their handiwork already quoted, it is to be noted that, in the first article of the treaty, "His Majesty the King of the Netherlands, Grand Duke of Luxemburg, engages to cause to be immediately converted into a treaty with His Majesty the King of the Belgians, the articles annexed to the present act, and agreed upon by common consent, under the auspices of the courts of Great Britain, Austria, France, Prussia, and Russia."[1] Article 7 is one of these articles.

But this is not all. By Article 2 of the treaty of the same date, concluded by the five great Powers and thus called the Quintuple Treaty, "Her Majesty the Queen of the United Kingdom of Great Britain and Ireland, His Majesty the Emperor of Austria, King of Hungary and Bohemia, His Majesty the King of the French, His Majesty the King of Prussia, and His Majesty the Emperor of All

[1] *British and Foreign State Papers*, vol. 27, p. 994.

the Russias, declare that the articles mentioned in the preceding article, are considered as having the same force and validity as if they were textually inserted in the present act, and that they are thus placed under the guarantee of their said Majesties."[1] Article 7 was one of these articles.

But this is not all. Their Dutch and their Belgian Majesties concluded on the same day the treaty, which they were obliged to do to the satisfaction of the other Majesties.

But this is not all. His Majesty the King of Prussia and His Majesty the Emperor of Austria, King of Hungary and Bohemia, caused themselves to be authorized by the Diet of the German States to approve on their behalf the treaty of April 19, 1839, including Article 7, so that not only Prussia and Austria but every German political entity approved this treaty. It would seem, therefore, as if it should bind the Imperial German Empire, composed of Prussia and of the German-speaking states ratifying this treaty.

In 1870, the war with France, "which lay in the logic of history," broke out and Great Britain, fearing that the treaty of April 19, 1839, might be violated by Prussia and the North German Confederation (of which it formed a part), on the one hand, and by France, on the other, concluded a treaty with Prussia on the 9th of August[2] and two days later[3] a similar one with France, in which the contracting parties expressed themselves as "desirous at the present time of recording in a solemn act their fixed determination to maintain the independence and neutrality of Belgium, as provided in Article VII of the treaty signed at London on the 19th April, 1839, between Belgium and the Netherlands, which article was declared by the Quintuple Treaty of 1839 to be considered as having the same force and value as if textually inserted in the said Quintuple Treaty"; and because of this desire "their said Majesties have determined to conclude between themselves a separate treaty, which, without impairing or invalidating the conditions of the said Quintuple Treaty, shall be subsidiary and accessory to it."[4] Therefore, Great Britain

---

[1] *British and Foreign State Papers*, vol. 27, p. 991.
[2] *Ibid.*, vol. 60, p. 13.
[3] *Ibid.*, p. 10.
[4] Article I of the treaty between Great Britain and Prussia reads:

His Majesty the King of Prussia having declared that notwithstanding the hostilities in which the North German Confederation is engaged with France, it is his fixed determination to respect the neutrality of Belgium, so long as the same shall be respected by France, Her Majesty the Queen of the United Kingdom of Great Britain and Ireland on her part declares that, if during the said hostilities the armies of France should violate that neutrality, she will be prepared to coöperate with His Prussian Majesty

and Prussia—for, fortunately, it is not necessary to consider France in this connection, although a like treaty was concluded between Great Britain and France—agreed, in the event of the violation of Belgium's neutrality, to employ their land and naval forces to secure "then and thereafter, the independence and neutrality of Belgium." The agreement was to run for the period of twelve months after the conclusion of the treaty of peace between the then belligerents, "and on the expiration of that time the independence and neutrality of Belgium will, so far as the High Contracting Parties are respectively concerned, continue to rest as heretofore on Article I of the Quintuple Treaty of the 19th April, 1839."

It appears, therefore, that, upon the expiration of the twelve months for which the treaty was concluded, Germany—for Prussia had by this time become Germany—and Great Britain reverted to the Quintuple Treaty which they had expressly recognized in 1870 as binding their future conduct. Belgium, it would seem, was justified in considering its independence and its neutrality assured, for the treaty concluded by Holland and Belgium on April 19, 1839, was guaranteed by the five great Powers of Europe on the same day, and this treaty was solemnly recognized in 1870 and declared to be binding upon Great Britain and Germany, then easily the first Powers of Europe.

But this was not all. In the year of 1871, when Great Britain,

> for the defence of the same in such manner as may be mutually agreed upon, employing for that purpose her naval and military forces to insure its observance, and to maintain, in conjunction with His Prussian Majesty, then and thereafter, the independence and neutrality of Belgium.
>
> It is clearly understood that Her Majesty the Queen of the United Kingdom of Great Britain and Ireland does not engage herself by this Treaty to take part in any of the general operations of the war now carried on between the North German Confederation and France, beyond the limits of Belgium, as defined in the Treaty between Belgium and the Netherlands of 19th April, 1839.
>
> Article II reads:
>
> His Majesty the King of Prussia agrees on his part, in the event provided for in the foregoing Article, to coöperate with Her Majesty the Queen of the United Kingdom of Great Britain and Ireland, employing his naval and military forces for the purpose aforesaid; and, the case arising, to concert with Her Majesty the measures which shall be taken, separately or in common, to secure the neutrality and independence of Belgium.
>
> Article III reads:
>
> This Treaty shall be binding on the High Contracting Parties during the continuance of the present war between the North German Confederation and France, and for twelve months after the ratification of any Treaty of Peace concluded between those Parties; and on the expiration of that time the independence and neutrality of Belgium will, so far as the High Contracting Parties are respectively concerned, continue to rest as heretofore on Article I of the Quintuple Treaty of the 19th April, 1839. (*British and Foreign State Papers*, vol. 60, pp. 13-17.)

Germany, and France—for France was likewise a party to the treaty—were remitted to the Treaty of 1839, the Protocol of London, signed January 17, 1871, to which France adhered on March 13, 1871, gave to international agreements a force and effect and a guarantee which they had not hitherto possessed, by providing that they could not be changed without the consent of the contracting parties amicably had.[1] And the exceptional and favored position of Belgium, caused by these treaties, was referred to by the distinguished Belgian statesman, the late Monsieur Beernaert, in an address at the First Hague Peace Conference of 1899.[2]

But still this was not all. In 1911, in 1913, and on July 31, 1914, four days before the neutrality of Belgium was violated by German troops, the Belgian Government was privately and publicly assured of the binding effect of the treaty of April 19, 1839, and of Germany's intention to observe its provisions. Thus, Monsieur Davignon, the Belgian Minister for Foreign Affairs, writing under date of July 31, 1914, to the Belgian Ministers at Berlin, London, and Paris, records a conversation of the Secretary-General of the Ministry of Foreign Affairs, who asked the German Minister (Herr von Bülow) "if he knew of the conversation which he had had with his predecessor, Herr von Flotow, and of the reply which the Imperial Chancellor had instructed the latter to give."[3] The circumstances relating to each of the three incidents are thus related by Monsieur Davignon in the note under consideration:

> In the course of the controversy which arose in 1911 as a consequence of the Dutch scheme for the fortification of Flushing, certain newspapers had maintained that in the case of a Franco-German war Belgian neutrality would be violated by Germany.

[1] The Plenipotentiaries of the North German Confederation, Austria-Hungary, (France), Great Britain, Italy, Russia, and Turkey, assembled today in conference, recognize that it is an essential principle of the law of nations that no Power can liberate itself from the engagements of a treaty, nor modify the stipulations thereof, except as the result of the consent of the contracting parties, by means of an amicable understanding. (*British and Foreign State Papers*, vol. 61, pp. 1198-99.)

[2] As to Belgium you know its situation is special. It is neutral and its neutrality is guaranteed by the great Powers, and particularly by our powerful neighbors. We therefore cannot be invaded, and how could the Belgian Government submit for the approval of our legislature a convention based on the assumption that the great States will fail in their engagements regarding us, a convention that could sanction in advance acts that could only be an indisputable abuse of force? (*Conférence Internationale de la Paix;* La Haye, 18 mai-20 juillet, 1899; nouvelle édition; La Haye, M. Nyhoff, 1907; part 3, p. 89.)

[3] *Belgian Grey Book* (No. 1), doc. No. 12; *Diplomatic Documents Relating to the Outbreak of the European War*, p. 366.

The Department of Foreign Affairs had suggested that a declaration in the German Parliament during a debate on foreign affairs would serve to calm public opinion, and to dispel the mistrust which was so regrettable from the point of view of the relations between the two countries.

Herr von Bethmann-Hollweg replied that he had fully appreciated the feelings which had inspired our representations. He declared that Germany had no intention of violating Belgian neutrality, but he considered that in making a public declaration Germany would weaken her military position in regard to France, who, secured on the northern side, would concentrate all her energies on the east.

Baron van der Elst, continuing, said that he perfectly understood the objections raised by Herr von Bethmann-Hollweg to the proposed public declaration, and he recalled the fact that since then, in 1913, Herr von Jagow had made reassuring declarations to the Budget Commission of the Reichstag respecting the maintenance of Belgian neutrality.

Herr von Bülow replied that he knew of the conversation with Herr von Flotow, and that he was certain that the sentiments expressed at that time had not changed.[1]

On August 1, 1914, Count de Lalaing, Belgian Minister at London, informed Monsieur Davignon that "Great Britain has asked

---

[1] *Belgian Grey Book* (No. 1), doc. No. 12; *Diplomatic Documents Relating to the Outbreak of the European War*, p. 367.

For the completeness of the record, the inclosure contained in Monsieur Davignon's instruction is here reproduced, consisting of a note dated May 2, 1913, from Baron Beyens, Belgian Minister to Berlin, to Monsieur Davignon, Belgian Minister for Foreign Affairs:

I have the honour to bring to your notice the declaration respecting Belgian neutrality, as published in the semi-official *Norddeutsche Allgemeine Zeitung*, made by the Secretary of State and the Minister of War, at the meeting of the Budget Committee of the Reichstag on April 29th:—

"A member of the Social Democrat Party said: 'The approach of a war between Germany and France is viewed with apprehension in Belgium, for it is feared that Germany will not respect the neutrality of Belgium.'

"Herr von Jagow, Secretary of State, replied: 'Belgian neutrality is provided for by International Conventions and Germany is determined to respect those Conventions.'

"This declaration did not satisfy another member of the Social Democrat Party. Herr von Jagow said that he had nothing to add to the clear statement he had made respecting the relations between Germany and Belgium.

"In answer to fresh inquiries by a member of the Social Democrat Party, Herr von Heeringen, the Minister of War, replied: 'Belgium plays no part in the causes which justify the proposed reorganization of the German military system. That proposal is based on the situation in the East. Germany will not lose sight of the fact that the neutrality of Belgium is guaranteed by international treaty.'

"A member of the Progressive Party having once again spoken of Belgium, Herr von Jagow repeated that this declaration in regard to Belgium was sufficiently clear." (*Diplomatic Documents Relating to the Outbreak of the European War*, pp. 367-368.)

France and Germany separately if they intend to respect Belgian territory in the event of its not being violated by their adversary. Germany's reply is awaited. France has replied in the affirmative."[1]

On August 4, 1914, the British Secretary for Foreign Affairs informed the British Ambassador at Berlin that:

> The German Government have delivered to the Belgian Government a note proposing friendly neutrality entailing free passage through Belgian territory, and promising to maintain the independence and integrity of the kingdom and its possessions at the conclusion of peace, threatening in case of refusal to treat Belgium as an enemy. An answer was requested within twelve hours.
> We also understand that Belgium has categorically refused this as a flagrant violation of the law of nations.
> His Majesty's Government are bound to protest against this violation of a treaty to which Germany is a party in common with themselves, and must request an assurance that the demand made upon Belgium will not be proceeded with and that her neutrality will be respected by Germany. You should ask for an immediate reply.[2]

In compliance with this direction, the British Ambassador to Berlin "called," to quote his report, "upon the Secretary of State that afternoon and inquired, in the name of His Majesty's Government, whether the Imperial Government would refrain from violating Belgian neutrality. Herr von Jagow at once replied that he was very sorry to say that his answer must be 'No,' as, in consequence of the German troops having crossed the frontier that morning, Belgian neutrality had already been violated."[3]

The break between the two Governments had come, for the British demand was an ultimatum and the failure to comply with it was war. Later in the day the British Ambassador waited upon the Chancellor, who had just returned from the Reichstag, where he had justified the invasion of Belgium on the plea of necessity. Of the interview the British Ambassador gives the following account:

> I found the Chancellor very agitated. His Excellency at once began a harangue, which lasted for about twenty minutes. He said that the step taken by His Majesty's Government was terrible to a degree; just for a word—"neutrality," a word which in war time had so often been disregarded—just for a

[1] *Diplomatic Documents Relating to the Outbreak of the European War,* p. 368.
[2] *The British Blue Book* (No. 1), doc. No. 153; *ibid.,* pp. 1002-1003.
[3] *Diplomatic Documents Relating to the Outbreak of the European War,* doc. No. 160, p. 1006.

scrap of paper Great Britain was going to make war on a kindred nation who desired nothing better than to be friends with her.[1]

In vino veritas, and in moments of excitement the truth escapes. Yet this truth about Belgium was expressed ten days later, on a very solemn occasion, by Kaiser William himself in a letter in his own handwriting, delivered to the American Ambassador for transmission to the President of the United States, in which the King of Prussia and German Emperor, referring to his proposition to Sir Edward Grey to leave France alone if Great Britain forced it to remain neutral, said:

> Instead he declared England had to defend Belgian neutrality, which had to be violated by Germany on strategical grounds, news having been received that France was already preparing to enter Belgium and the King of the Belgians having refused my petition for a free passage under guarantee of his country's freedom.[2]

Ernst Moritz Arndt, the poet of the War of Liberation and of German unity, and the protagonist of Pan-Germanism, foresaw and predicted the future with a ruthless and brutal frankness that makes the blood curdle of those who really believe that little states and little peoples should have some little place in the sun. In 1834, after Belgium had broken away from Holland, but before its independence was definitely recognized and its international position as a neutralized state fixed under the guarantee of the German-speaking peoples, Arndt wrote:

> Belgium, the granary and armory, is predestined to be the battlefield in the struggle for the Meuse and the Rhine. I ask any General or Statesman who has seriously considered the problems of war and politics, whether Belgium can remain neutral in a European war—that is to say, can be respected as neutral any longer than may appear expedient to the Power which feels itself possessed of the best advantages for attack.[3]

This question Arndt's countrymen have answered, for did not Bismarck say, in the course of negotiations with Italy in 1887, that

---

[1] *Diplomatic Documents Relating to the Outbreak of the European War,* doc. No. 160, p. 1007.
[2] *United States Official Bulletin Issued by the Committee on Public Information,* August 14, 1917, p. 4.
[3] Arndt, *Schriften für und an seine lieben Deutschen* (Leipzig, 1845), vol. 3, p. 178.

a treaty is "a scrap of paper,"[1] or, more euphemistically but not less certainly expressed in his autobiography, that "International policy is a fluid element which, under certain conditions, will solidify, but, on a change of atmosphere, reverts to its original diffuse condition."[2]

But to return to Arndt. Knowing the England of his day and divining the Germany of the future, he instinctively felt that the island kingdom stood in the way of a greater Germany. Therefore, whether in the teeth of a treaty or not, England and Germany were to meet in the Low Countries:

> On the fields of Belgium Germany and England will of necessity be everlastingly at war for the possession of the Rhine and the supremacy of the Channel.[3]

The plea of necessity, discarded by the *Kriegsbrauch im Landkriege*, proclaimed by the Chancellor in terms which Arndt would have approved, has had its day in courts of municipal law and has been found wanting; and we have with our own eyes seen, as through a glass darkly, the consequences which would follow if the plea of necessity, banished from private law, should find a refuge in the public law between nations.

In the case of *Regina v. Dudley*, decided by an English court of justice in 1884, some shipwrecked sailors, "subject to terrible temptation and to sufferings which might break down the bodily power of the strongest man and try the conscience of the best," to quote the language of the case, "put to death a weak and unoffending boy upon the chance of preserving their own lives by feeding upon his flesh and blood after he was killed." They were later picked up by a

---

[1] During the last days of March (1887), when a dispatch announced that Mr. Depretis was in conference with Messrs. Crispi and Zanardelli, in order to persuade them to enter into the ministry, Count Herbert von Bismarck told Count de Launay that "his father was amazed when he realized that a reconstruction of the cabinet was being effected in the interest of the radical Left." According to the judgment of the German Chancellor, this was a step toward a Republic! When the news reached Berlin that Mr. Depretis, president of the Council, assumed at the same time the portfolio of Foreign Affairs, Prince Bismarck was profoundly disturbed. The German Ambassador at Rome, and the Italian Ambassador at Berlin, tried in their dispatches, but in vain, to convince him that the successor to Count de Robilant would conform faithfully to the Treaty: "Treaties," answered the Prince, "are scraps of paper (sic). All depends upon the manner of turning them to account. Even an excellent weapon, in inexperienced hands, may cause more damage than good." (Chiala, *Pagine di storia contemporanea*, 1897, t. 3, pp. 497-498.)

[2] Bismarck, *Gedanken und Erinnerungen*, pp. 596-597.

[3] Arndt, *Schriften für und an seine lieben Deutschen*, vol. 3, p. 164.

passing vessel, brought to England, indicted for the murder of the boy, and convicted, and the conviction was affirmed on appeal. In delivering the unanimous opinion of the Court sentencing the prisoners convicted of murder, Lord Chief Justice Coleridge entered into a very careful and elaborate examination of the only plea advanced in behalf of the prisoners:

> Now it is admitted that the deliberate killing of this unoffending and unresisting boy was clearly murder, unless the killing can be justified by some well-recognized excuse admitted by the law. It is further admitted that there was in this case no such excuse, unless the killing was justified by what has been called necessity. But the temptation to the act which existed here was not what the law has ever called necessity. Nor is this to be regretted. Though law and morality are not the same, and though many things may be immoral which are not necessarily illegal, yet the absolute divorce of law from morality would be of fatal consequence, and such divorce would follow if the temptation to murder in this case were to be held by law an absolute defense of it.[1]

After rejecting the plea of necessity, Lord Chief Justice Coleridge thus points out the consequences of the admission of the plea of necessity:

> It is not needful to point out the awful danger of admitting the principle which has been contended for. Who is to be the judge of this sort of necessity? By what measure is the comparative value of lives to be measured? Is it to be strength, or intellect, or what? It is plain that the principle leaves to him who is to profit by it to determine the necessity which will justify him in deliberately taking another's life to save his own. In this case the weakest, the youngest, the most unresisting was chosen. Was it more necessary to kill him than one of the grown men? The answer must be, No.
>
> "So spake the Fiend; and with necessity,
>   The tyrant's plea, excused his devilish deeds."[1]

[1] 15 Cox Criminal Cases, 624, 14 Queens Bench 273; Beale, *Selection of Cases on Criminal Law* (Cambridge, Mass., 1894), pp. 362-363.

CHAPTER XI

BELLIGERENT USE OF NEUTRAL FLAG

The German correspondence bristles with denunciation of the use of false flags. Just when false flags were used in the present war it would be hard to say. The misuse of the neutral flag became the subject of discussion because of the use of the American flag by the steamer *Lusitania* in an inward or outward passage, or both, to protect itself, in so far as the flag was a means of protection, against the German submarine. The Imperial German Government called this incident to the attention of the United States in support of the charge that the British Government had directed its merchant marine to use neutral flags in order to disguise its merchantmen from the submarine. It would seem, however, that the flag was of no great importance, inasmuch as commanders of the German submarines, acting under instructions to refrain from attacking neutral vessels, were apparently unable to distinguish the flag until the fatal shot had been fired.

But, however small and insignificant the flag may appear to the commander, it looms large in the correspondence. It may be premised, before looking into the matter, that the flag which a vessel flies is not the proof of its nationality, for behind the flag is the right to fly it, and not even the right to fly it settles the question of nationality. The flag may be a rule of thumb, but the practice of Nations prescribes visit and search of the vessel to determine its character irrespective of the flag which the vessel claims the right to fly. The correct doctrine, it is believed, was thus stated by Secretary of State Cass, writing in 1860 to the American Minister to England:

> In the despatch of Lord John Russell, I perceive he refers to the American flag as if it were contended that that national ensign afforded protection to the vessel bearing it. I beg you to assure his lordship that this country advances no such pretension. The immunity of a vessel upon the ocean depends upon her national character, to be ascertained, if contested, by her papers, and, if need be, by other circumstances, but not by the flag under which she sails. If a foreign cruiser boards a vessel with American colors, and she proves not to belong to this coun-

try, we have no right to complain of her examination or capture; but if the papers justify an assumption of the flag, and she is actually an American vessel, then a trespass has been committed by such cruiser, for which the government to which it belongs is responsible; and the act itself will be more or less condemnable as the circumstances leading to it are of a character to justify suspicion or to repel it, and as the conduct of the boarding party is more or less offensive or injurious.[1]

The United States naval war code, issued by the Navy Department (General Orders 551) on June 27, 1900, forbade the use of false colors in Article 7:

> The use of false colors in war is forbidden, and when summoning a vessel to lie to, or before firing a gun in action, the national colors should be displayed by vessels of the United States.[2]

This prohibition was an attempt to subject naval operations to the same rule which obtains in land warfare, where the use of false colors has been absolutely prohibited.[3] The question was reconsidered by American naval officers at the Naval War College in 1903 and they reported that:

> The use of "false colors" is evidently subject to much difference of opinion (see Perels, *Seerecht der Gegenwart*, p. 182). No scheme of such use has been proposed which seems satisfactory, and it is difficult to see how honorable warfare can be conducted upon such a basis as is implied in the use of false colors. Undoubtedly, the rule prohibiting the use of false colors in war should be made with definite provisions in regard to legitimate ruses in maritime warfare.[4]

In view of the fact that international practice permitted the use of the foreign flag, and that the United States would be at a disadvantage if they should renounce the employment of an admitted *ruse de guerre*, the officers were of the opinion "that this rule should be stricken from the code pending some international agreement upon the use of false colors."

[1] Mr. Cass, Secretary of State, to Mr. Dallas, Minister to England, October 27, 1860, H. Ex. doc. 7, 36th Cong., 2d sess., p. 505; quoted from Moore, *International Law Digest*, vol. 2, p. 893.
[2] *Naval War College, International Law Discussions*, 1903, p. 37.
[3] *Instructions, United States Army, 1863*, art. 65; *Declaration of Brussels*, art. 13; *Hague Convention Respecting the Laws and Customs of War on Land*, art. 23.
[4] *Naval War College, International Law Discussions*, 1903, p. 41.

As a consequence of the criticism of this and of other provisions of the Naval Code, the Secretary of the Navy revoked the code by General Orders 150, dated February 4, 1904. It is to be borne in mind that this conclusion was reached exactly a decade before the outbreak of the present war, and that there has been no international agreement on the subject during the interval.

It will be observed that the American officers referred to Perels' *Das Internationale Offentliche Seerecht der Gegenwart,* a second edition of which appeared in 1903. This is a standard work, the revised edition of which appeared eleven years before the outbreak of the European War, and it is peculiarly deserving of consideration because of the fact that its author, a sound international lawyer, was for many years adviser to the German Admiralty. On this subject he says:

> The use of a false national flag in naval warfare is not to be regarded as forbidden in all circumstances. At the latest, with the opening of the military action in the narrow sense, that is to say, with the opening of battle or with the execution of the right of visit, the proper national flag is to be hoisted, and during the action, if at night, the flag is to be made recognizable by a lantern placed above it.[1]

This distinguished author recognizes the right of vessels of war to display a foreign flag in order the more conveniently to pursue the enemy and to lure it to destruction, but, in accordance with universally recognized practice on this subject, a shot should not be fired nor battle engaged without flying the national colors.

It is difficult to see how the enemy is to be deprived of the right to fly a foreign flag to escape attack when its opponent is permitted the employment of a foreign flag to make attack, and it is difficult to see how a naval commander, whose honor is supposed to be infinitely superior to that of a master of a merchantman, is to be permitted to fly a foreign flag to steal upon his enemy and the master is to be deprived of the right to escape by the use of false colors from a naval commander, himself approaching, it may be, under false colors. A further passage should be quoted from Perels which should have made it appear to the German authorities very difficult indeed for the United States to object to the use of a foreign flag. Thus:

> During the Spanish-American War of 1898 the people of Spain were greatly aroused by the fact that, on May 22, two American warships, flying the Spanish flag, had put into Guan-

[1] Perels, *Das Internationale Öffentliche Seerecht der Gegenwart,* p. 182.

tanamo Bay on the north coast of Cuba. After the matter had been discussed in the Spanish Senate the Spanish cabinet issued a circular note to the neutral Powers protesting against the use of false flags.[1]

Dr. Georg Schramm published a year before the war an elaborate work entitled *Das Prisenrecht in Seiner Neuesten Gestalt*, and this work, like that of Perels, is entitled to very great respect because of the fact that its author succeeded Perels as adviser to the German Admiralty. The younger thus confirms the statement of his elder and illustrious predecessor:

> According to the laws of war the regular warships are entitled to resort to war ruses, such for instance as the flying of a false national flag.[2]

After quoting with approval the passage already quoted in the text he thus continues:

> Accordingly, even regular warships may conceal their true character from the neutral merchant ships as long as they deem this necessary, and under certain circumstances they are entitled to disclose themselves as enemy warships only when they have reached the immediate vicinity of the neutral merchant ships they are to stop and search.[2]

In accordance with the views of Perels, legal adviser to the Admiralty when the German Prize Ordinance was drafted in 1909, and in accordance with the view of Schramm, adviser to the Admiralty when the ordinance was issued on August 3, 1914, Article 82 of the German Prize Ordinance provides: "During a pursuit the war ensign need not be displayed, and the use of any merchant flag is permitted."[3]

It would seem that it should have been as difficult for the Imperial German Government to protest to the United States against the use of a foreign flag as it was for the United States to insist that Great Britain should prevent its merchant vessels from flying a foreign flag in order to avoid certain destruction and sudden death at the hands of the submarine. Nevertheless, the Imperial Govern-

---

[1] Perels, *Das Internationale Öffentliche Seerecht der Gegenwart*, p. 183.
[2] Schramm, *Das Prisenrecht in Seiner Neuesten Gestalt*, Berlin, 1913, p. 294.
[3] Germany, "Prisenordnung," *Reichsgesetzblatt*, 1915, pp. 275, 301, 314, 315; *ibid.*, 1915, p. 193; Prize Code of the German Empire as in force July 1, 1915. Translated and edited by Chas. H. Huberich and Richard King (New York; Baker, Voorhis & Co., 1915), pp. 50, 51.

ment protested, and, because of the use of foreign flags, justified the resort to submarine warfare; and the United States, notwithstanding its use of foreign flags in times past and the repeal of the code forbidding the use of foreign flags, protested vigorously against the use of the American flag by British merchantmen. Consistency was sacrificed on the one hand to military necessity, and on the other to the desire to placate an enemy which had not as yet discarded the mask of friendship.

On the 10th of February, 1915, the United States, reserving "for future consideration the legality and propriety of the deceptive use of the flag of a neutral power in any case for the purpose of avoiding capture,"[1] pointed out to the British Government the serious consequences which might "result to American vessels and American citizens if this practice is continued."[1] The United States accepted it as true, for the purposes of this discussion, that the captain of *The Lusitania* had raised the American flag pursuant to orders from his Government, and while admitting that an occasional use might be justified, nevertheless insisted that frequent use degenerating into a practice was without justification. Thus:

> The occasional use of the flag of a neutral or an enemy under the stress of immediate pursuit and to deceive an approaching enemy, which appears by the press reports to be represented as the precedent and justification used to support this action, seems to this Government a very different thing from an explicit sanction by a belligerent government for its merchant ships generally to fly the flag of a neutral power within certain portions of the high seas which are presumed to be frequented with hostile warships. The formal declaration of such a policy of general misuse of a neutral's flag jeopardizes the vessels of the neutral visiting those waters in a peculiar degree by raising the presumption that they are of belligerent nationality regardless of the flag which they may carry.[2]

The reason for the protest is placed beyond doubt by the following paragraph of the note:

> In view of the announced purpose of the German Admiralty to engage in active naval operations in certain delimited sea areas adjacent to the coasts of Great Britain and Ireland, the Government of the United States would view with anxious solici-

[1] Official text, *American Journal of International Law*, Special Supplement, July, 1915, p. 88.
[2] *Ibid.*, p. 89.

> tude any general use of the flag of the United States by British vessels traversing those waters. A policy such as the one which His Majesty's Government is said to intend to adopt, would, if the declaration of the German Admiralty is put in force, it seems clear, afford no protection to British vessels, while it would be a serious and constant menace to the lives and vessels of American citizens.[1]

The United States therefore trusted that Great Britain would restrain its vessels from the use of the American flag within the area declared by Germany to be a war zone, and indeed went so far as to say that the refusal to do so "would even seem to impose upon the Government of Great Britain a measure of responsibility for the loss of American lives and vessels in case of an attack by a German naval force."[1]

In a communication of February 16, 1915, from the German Secretary for Foreign Affairs, the Imperial German Government stated that the British Admiralty "recommends English merchant vessels to use neutral flags and has in the meantime been confirmed by a statement of the British Foreign Office which refers to the municipal law of England and characterizes such action as quite unobjectionable."[2]

On February 19, 1915, in reply to the American note, the British Secretary of State for Foreign Affairs put the matter in its true light and made some observations which could not have been palatable to the American Government. In the first place, the note thus refers to *The Lusitania*, showing that the use of the American flag was not by direction of the British authorities but at the request of American passengers traveling upon that vessel:

> It was understood that the German Government had announced their intention of sinking British merchant vessels at sight by torpedoes without giving any opportunity of making any provision for saving the lives of noncombatant crews and passengers. It was in consequence of this threat that *The Lusitania* raised the United States flag on her inward voyage and on her subsequent outward voyage. A request was made by the United States passengers who were embarking on board her that the United States flag should be hoisted presumably to insure their safety. Meanwhile the memorandum from Your Excellency had been received. His Majesty's Government did not give any advice to the company as to how to meet this request and it is

[1] Official text, *American Journal of International Law*, Special Supplement, July, 1915, p. 89.
[2] *Ibid.*, p. 94.

understood that *The Lusitania* left Liverpool under the British flag.[1]

As to the British law on the subject, he said:

> The British merchant shipping act makes it clear that the use of the British flag by foreign merchant vessels is permitted in time of war for the purpose of escaping capture. It is believed that in the case of some other nations there is a similar recognition of the same practice with regard to their flags and that none have forbidden it. It would therefore be unreasonable to expect His Majesty's Government to pass legislation forbidding the use of foreign flags by British merchant vessels to avoid capture by the enemy. Now that the German Government have announced their intention to sink merchant vessels at sight with their noncombatant crews, cargoes, and papers, a proceeding hitherto regarded by the opinion of the world not as war, but as piracy, it is felt that the United States Government could not fairly ask the British Government to order British merchant vessels to forego the means—always hitherto permitted—of escaping not only capture but the much worse fate of sinking and destruction. Great Britain has always when neutral accorded to the vessels of other States at war liberty to use the British flag as a means of protection against capture, and instances are on record when United States vessels availed themselves of this facility during the American Civil War. It would be contrary to fair expectation if now when the conditions are reversed the United States and neutral nations were to grudge to British ships liberty to take similar action. The British Government have no intention of advising their merchant shipping to use foreign flags as general practice or to resort to them otherwise than for escaping capture or destruction.[2]

The British legislation to which reference was made by Germany appears to be contained in Article 69 of the Merchant Shipping Act passed in 1894, which punishes the use of the British flag by a vessel not entitled to fly it "unless the assumption has been made for the purpose of escaping capture by an enemy or by a foreign ship of war in the exercise of some belligerent right."

The British Secretary of State maintained that no damage would accrue to neutrals and no advantage would be lost to the belligerent by the use of neutral flags if visit and search, as recognized and required by international law, were followed by its enemy. Thus:

[1] Official text, *American Journal of International Law*, Special Supplement, July, 1915, p. 96.
[2] *Ibid.*, pp. 96-97.

If that obligation is fulfilled, hoisting a neutral flag on board a British vessel cannot possibly endanger neutral shipping and the British Government hold that if loss to neutrals is caused by disregard of this obligation it is upon the enemy vessel disregarding it and upon the Government giving orders that it should be disregarded that the sole responsibility for injury to neutrals ought to rest.[1]

As further indicating the desire of the United States to remove from Germany any pretext for unrestricted submarine warfare, the United States proposed in its note of February 20, 1915, that Germany and Great Britain should require "their respective merchant vessels not to use neutral flags for the purpose of disguise or *ruse de guerre*."[2] This proposition was part of a general scheme to avert the horrors of submarine warfare which has already been discussed and which, it will be recalled, was unacceptable to both of these countries.

[1] Official text, *American Journal of International Law*, Special Supplement, July, 1915, p. 97.
[2] *Ibid.*, p. 98.

CHAPTER XII

MINES, WAR ZONES, AND BLOCKADE

It is an admitted right of a belligerent, deeply imbedded in the practice of Nations, for which authority need not be quoted, to blockade the ports and the coasts of the enemy provided that a proclamation of blockade be made, that the fact of the blockade be notified to neutral Governments or that neutral Governments to be taxed with its provisions have notice of the blockade, that the blockading force be employed within the vicinity of the coast of the blockaded ports, either to prevent vessels from entering and from leaving the blockaded region or making the entry and departure of such vessels dangerous, that the blockade be applied impartially to all nations and not relaxed in the case of any one or more; and provided further and always, that neutral countries be not directly or indirectly blockaded by a belligerent. Blockade applies solely to trade entering or departing from belligerent territory. Trade seeking to enter the territory of the enemy through a neutral country is subject to confiscation if it be contraband and seized in accordance with the methods in such cases made and provided. Just as communication may be closed by investment on land, so communication may be shut off by blockade by water, and indeed a port may be at one and the same time invested by land and blockaded by sea. The purpose in each case is the same: to starve the enemy into submission. Famine is a weapon, used alike in land and naval warfare, for it is the experience of mankind, recognized by nations and therefore incorporated in the law of nations, that an army never fights upon an empty stomach. To deprive the army of sustenance is therefore legitimate; and to starve the civilian population in order that by such starvation the army shall surrender (as in the case of Lee's surrender at Appomattox) is the endeavor of every belligerent, commended by the victor and denounced by the victim.

It may be said, before taking up the matter of the war zone, that the United States labored with Great Britain to prevent the scattering of mines to which Germany had already resorted and which was the cause alleged by Great Britain for making a war zone of the

North Sea; and before further proceeding it should be mentioned that the United States, on February 19, 1917, before the outbreak of war with Germany and while it was still hoped that war might be averted, in a formal note to the British Ambassador, called attention to the Department's memorandum of August 13, 1914, and the subsequent correspondence between Great Britain and the United States, and then squarely and unequivocally protested against the action of Great Britain in the following language:

> As the question of appropriating certain portions of the high seas for military operations, to the exclusion of the use of the hostile area as a common highway of commerce, has not become a settled principle of international law assented to by the family of nations, it will be recognized that the Government of the United States must, and hereby does, for the protection of American interests, reserve generally all of its rights in the premises, including the right not only to question the validity of these measures, but to present demands and claims in relation to any American interests which may be unlawfully affected, directly or indirectly, by virtue of the enforcement of these measures.[1]

First, as to the matter of mines. On August 7, 1914, that is to say, three days after the outbreak of war between Germany and Great Britain, the American Ambassador to Berlin reported that "he is informed by the German Foreign Office that German ports are strewn with mines," and the Foreign Office requested "that timely warning be given shippers against navigating in ports which foreign forces might use as bases." On the 11th of August the British Embassy informed the Department of State that "The Germans are scattering contact mines indiscriminately about the North Sea in the open sea without regard to the consequences to merchantmen" and that "in view of the methods adopted by Germany the British Admiralty must hold themselves fully at liberty to adopt similar measures in self-defense which must inevitably increase the dangers to navigation in the North Sea. But, before doing so, they think it right to issue this warning in order that merchant ships under neutral flags trading with North Sea ports should be turned back before entering the area of such exceptional danger."[2]

In reply to this memorandum the Department of State, on the

---

[1] United States, Department of State, *Papers Relating to Maritime Danger Zones, etc.* (April 4, 1917), pp. 33-34.
[2] *Ibid.*, p. 6.

13th of August, used language which foreshadows the issue raised by the United States of the freedom of the seas. Thus:

> The Secretary of State is loath to believe that a signatory to that Convention [Hague Convention of 1907 relative to the Laying of Automatic Submarine Contact Mines] would willfully disregard its treaty obligation, which was manifestly made in the interest of neutral shipping.
>
> All restrictions upon the rights of neutrals upon the high seas, the common highway of nations, during the progress of a war, are permitted in the interests of the belligerents, who are bound in return to prevent their hostile operations from increasing the hazard of neutral ships in the open sea so far as the exigencies of the war permit.[1]

After this statement of the principle, the memorandum made a personal appeal to the British Government, which seems greatly to have impressed it. Thus, the memorandum continues and concludes:

> If an enemy of His Majesty's Government has, as asserted, endangered neutral commerce by an act in violation of The Hague Convention, which cannot be justified on the ground of military necessity, the Secretary of State perceives no reason for His Majesty's Government adopting a similar course, which would add further dangers to the peaceful navigation of the high seas by vessels of neutral powers.
>
> The Secretary of State, therefore, expresses the earnest and confident hope that His Majesty's Government may not feel compelled to resort, as a defensive measure, to a method of naval warfare which would appear to be contrary to the terms of The Hague Convention and impose upon the ships and lives of neutrals a needless menace when peaceably navigating the high seas.[1]

In a memorandum of August 19th, the British Embassy took notice in the following terms of the hope expressed by the United States that Great Britain would not resort to the laying of mines, saying on this point:

> His Majesty's Government share the reluctance of the Secretary of State to see the practice extended and the danger to neutral shipping increased. At the same time His Majesty's Chargé d'Affaires is instructed to point out that if Great Britain refrains from adopting the methods of Germany the result is that Germany receives impunity unless the neutral Powers can

[1] United States, Department of State, *Papers Relating to Maritime Danger Zones, etc.* (April 4, 1917), p. 7.

find some means of making Germany feel that she cannot continue to preserve all facilities for receiving trade and supplies through neutral shipping while impeding British commerce by means the use of which by Great Britain is deprecated by the United States Government.[1]

In a memorandum of the 23d of August the British Embassy pointed out the danger of traveling in the North Sea and called the attention of neutral shipping to "the vital importance of touching at British ports before entering the North Sea in order to ascertain according to the latest information the routes and channels which the Admiralty are keeping swept and along which these dangers to neutrals and merchantmen are reduced as far as possible."[2] The memorandum closes with the following statement:

> The Admiralty, while reserving to themselves the utmost liberty of retaliatory action against this new form of warfare, announce that they have not so far laid any mines during the present war and that they are endeavouring to keep the sea routes open for peaceful commerce.[2]

On September 10, 1914, the German Ambassador notified the Secretary of State that "the assertions from England that the North Sea has been infested with mines by Germany are wrong"; that "neutral vessels bound for German ports in the North Sea must steer by day for a point ten nautical miles N.W. off Helgoland"; and that pilots were there to be found "in readiness to pilot the ships into port."[3]

On September 26, 1914, the British Government delivered a carefully prepared memorandum regarding the laying of mines by Germany, which it declared to be in violation of The Hague Convention relating to the laying of submarine contact mines. It should be said, however, that Article 7 of this Convention contains the clause that its provisions only apply if all of the belligerents are contracting parties, and that Servia, with which Germany was at war, was not a contracting party. Nevertheless, it is fair to invoke the provisions of this Convention as stating the convictions of the Powers in a time of profound peace as to the conduct which should be pursued if they should be at war, and it is perhaps proper to remark in this connection that Servia, the only non-contracting Power then at war,

---

[1] United States, Department of State, *Papers Relating to Maritime Danger Zones, etc.* (April 4, 1917), p. 8.
[2] Ibid., p. 9.
[3] Ibid., p. 10.

was, like Switzerland and Bolivia, an inland country without an outlet to the sea. It was felt at the Second Conference that the sowing of mines interfered seriously with the freedom of the seas, and the learned reporter of the Commission, Mr. Georges Streit, then professor of international law at the University of Athens, and later Greek Minister to Vienna and Minister of Foreign Affairs of his country, said in his report to the Conference on the matter of mines, that "even apart from any written stipulation, it can never fail to be present in the minds of all that the principle of the liberty of the seas, with the obligations which it implies on behalf of those who make use of this way of communication open to the Nations, is the indisputable prerogative of the human race."[1] The preamble to the Convention declares the contracting Powers as "inspired by the principle of the freedom of sea routes, the common highway of all Nations," and as "seeing that, although the existing position of affairs makes it impossible to forbid the employment of automatic submarine contact mines, it is nevertheless desirable to restrict and regulate their employment in order to mitigate the severity of war and to insure, as far as possible, to peaceful navigation the security to which it is entitled, despite the existence of war." After this declaration of the principles by which the delegates were guided, the Convention itself thus reads:

Article 1. It is forbidden—
1. To lay unanchored automatic contact mines, except when they are so constructed as to become harmless one hour at most after the person who laid them ceases to control them;
2. To lay anchored automatic contact mines which do not become harmless as soon as they have broken loose from their moorings;
3. To use torpedoes which do not become harmless when they have missed their mark.

Article 2. It is forbidden to lay automatic contact mines off the coast and ports of the enemy, with the sole object of intercepting commercial shipping.

Article 3. When anchored automatic contact mines are employed, every possible precaution must be taken for the security of peaceful shipping.

The belligerents undertake to do their utmost to render these mines harmless within a limited time, and, should they cease to be under surveillance, to notify the danger zones as soon as

[1] *Deuxième Conférence de la Paix, Actes et Documents*, tome i, p. 289; *Reports to The Hague Conferences of 1899 and 1907* (1917), p. 650.

military exigencies permit, by a notice addressed to ship owners, which must also be communicated to the Governments through the diplomatic channel.[1]

There was perhaps no subject more hotly debated at the Second Hague Peace Conference than that of mines and the debate became the occasion of an exchange of personalities between the British and German delegates. Great Britain wished to prevent the use of mines and invoked in its behalf the freedom of the seas and the principles of humanity. Baron Marschall von Bieberstein said on behalf of Germany:

> We do not intend, if I may use an expression employed by the British delegate, "to sow mines in profusion on every sea." . . . We do not hold the opinion that everything which is not expressly forbidden is permitted.[2]

In the course of the Conference the Baron Marschall further stated that:

> A belligerent who lays mines assumes a very heavy responsibility toward neutrals and peaceful shipping. . . . No one will resort to such means unless for military reasons of an absolutely urgent character. But military acts are not governed solely by principles of international law. There are other factors: conscience, good sense, and the sentiment of duty imposed by principles of humanity will be the surest guides for the conduct of sailors, and will constitute the most effective guarantee against abuses. The officers of the German Navy, I emphatically affirm, will always fulfil, in the strictest fashion, the duties which emanate from the unwritten law of humanity and civilisation.[3]

On October 2, 1914, the British Government decided to lay mines, alleging that this was necessary on military grounds to counteract "the German policy of mine laying combined with their submarine activities." In a telegram of this date, Sir Edward Grey said that:

> His Majesty's Government have therefore authorized a minelaying policy in certain areas and a system of minefields has been established and is being developed upon a considerable scale. In order to reduce risks to noncombatants the Admiralty announce that it is dangerous henceforward for ships to cross area between Latitude 51 degrees 15 minutes north and 51 degrees.

[1] *The Hague Conventions and Declarations of 1899 and 1907*, pp. 151-152.
[2] United States, Department of State, *Papers Relating to Maritime Danger Zones, etc.* (April 4, 1917), p. 11.
[3] *Ibid.*, p. 12.

40 minutes north and Longitude 1 degree 35 minutes east and 3 degrees east. In this connection it must be remembered that the southern limit of the German minefield is latitude 52 degrees north. Although these limits are assigned to the danger area it must not be supposed that navigation is safe in any part of the southern waters of the North Sea. Instructions have been issued to His Majesty's ships to warn east-going vessels of the presence of this new minefield.[1]

On November 3, 1914, alleging still further activity on the part of the Germans in the matter of mines, the British Government gave notice that "the whole of the North Sea must be considered a military area. Within this area merchant shipping of all kinds, traders of all countries, fishing craft, and all other vessels will be exposed to the gravest dangers from mines which it has been necessary to lay and from warships searching vigilantly by night and day for suspicious craft."[2] It should be said in connection with this notice that the British Government advised all neutral shipping destined to or from Norway, the Baltic, Denmark, and Holland to enter the English Channel by the Straits of Dover, where they would be given sailing instructions which, if followed, "would pass them safely so far as Great Britain is concerned."

On November 7th Germany delivered a memorandum to the American Ambassador to be transmitted to the United States, in reply to the protest of the British Government against the laying of German mines. In the opening paragraphs of this memorandum Germany calls attention to the fact that the mine Convention was not applicable, but that Germany nevertheless had held itself bound by its provisions. It does not deny that it has laid mines, but claims that they were laid in accordance with the provisions of the Convention, that neutral trade routes had not been blocked, that no German mines had been laid in a trade route from the high seas to a neutral port, and that it gave notice to the neutral Powers. The German reply, however, has two paragraphs in the nature of an admission. Thus:

> 3. The British protest maintains further that in numerous cases German mines were found adrift without having become harmless. The anchoring of mines by Germany has been carried out with all possible precaution. If some have drifted from their moorings in consequence of currents or storms their number is certainly much smaller than that of mines laid by England,

[1] United States, Department of State, *Papers Relating to Maritime Danger Zones, etc.* (April 4, 1917), p. 12.
[2] *Ibid.*, p. 15.

which have drifted ashore on the Belgian and Dutch coasts and have caused damage there through their undiminished explosive power.

4. The obligation of keeping mines under surveillance which the British Government complains has been violated can naturally be enjoined upon a belligerent only as long as he retains command over that part of the seat of war where he has laid mines in a manner permitted by international law. As a rule therefore this obligation will apply only to defensive mines, but not to offensive mines. When a belligerent has properly laid offensive mines and has duly notified their laying he is relieved of all further responsibility.[1]

The German proclamation of February 4, 1915, declared "the waters surrounding Great Britain and Ireland including the whole English Channel . . . to be war zone."[2] The proclamation, to go into effect on February 18, 1915, was to apply primarily to British ships, public or private, found within the proscribed zone, and to neutral ships, their passengers, crews, and cargoes, unless they could be distinguished from enemy ships by the submarine, which was declared to be the means of rendering this proclamation effective. This is a blockade in effect, although the proclamation does not specifically term it a blockade.

Hitherto portions of a coast have been blockaded. The largest blockade rendered effective appears to have been the blockade of the coast of the Confederate States, extending from Delaware to Mexico, a distance of some 2,200 miles. To render this blockade effective, surface ships, the known and tried agencies, were used. It was not effective to begin with; it became more and more effective with time and it ended by bottling up the Confederacy. The blockade of the United Kingdom of Great Britain and Ireland was to be made effective by a new weapon, the submarine.

It was anticipated that the submarine would cause damage to neutrals, a fact pointed out in the proclamation of February 4, 1915, and admitted to have been the case in the memorandum received by the Department of State March 8, 1916, after a very considerable experience with the new weapon. The memorandum stated:

> The use of the submarine naturally necessitated a restriction of the free movements of neutrals and constituted a danger for them which Germany intended to ward off by a special warning

[1] United States, Department of State, *Papers Relating to Maritime Danger Zones, etc.* (April 4, 1917), p. 17.
[2] Official text, *American Journal of International Law*, Special Supplement, July, 1915, p. 83.

avowed object of preventing commodities of all kinds, including food for the civil population, from reaching or leaving the British Isles or northern France.

Her opponents are therefore driven to frame retaliatory measures in order in their turn to prevent commodities of any kind from reaching or leaving Germany. These measures will, however, be enforced by the British and French Governments without risk to neutral ships or to neutral or noncombatant life and in strict observance of the dictates of humanity.[1]

Admitting, for the purposes of argument, the right of a belligerent to devise and to put into effect measures by way of retaliation or reprisal in so far as they concern merely the enemy, it cannot be admitted and it was not admitted by the United States that a belligerent could indulge in retaliation and reprisals which wounded the neutral over the shoulder of the enemy.

[1] Official text, *American Journal of International Law*, Special Supplement, July, 1915, p. 102.

CHAPTER XIII

STATUS OF MERCHANT VESSELS

Section 1. The Right of Merchant Vessels to Arm

The contention has been repeatedly advanced in the course of the present war that the presence of armament on board a belligerent merchantman, and in a lesser degree upon a neutral merchantman, deprives the vessel of the right to be treated as an ordinary merchant vessel; that the presence of an armament, although for defensive purposes, changes the rule of law and renders the vessel liable to destruction as an enemy cruiser, without warning, visit, and search, and without removing the officers, crew, and passengers, and if possible their effects, from the vessel before destruction. It has been further contended that it is the duty of a belligerent merchant vessel to submit to the visit and search of an enemy cruiser, that it has neither the right to defend itself aggressively nor by flight. This contention finds no justification in practice if we have in mind vessels hitherto employed in maritime warfare. It has also been contended that a neutral merchantman with armament is not to be considered as an ordinary merchantman because it is in a position to resist visit and search, and that if it can it probably will, with resultant danger to the belligerent vessel. But it may also be said that this danger has not heretofore deprived vessels of the kind hitherto employed in maritime warfare from complying with the requirements of visit and search. Each of these classes of vessels will be considered in turn.

It would be easy to show that in times past merchantmen were in the habit of carrying arms for their defense upon the high seas and that the mere presence of arms on board did not convert the vessel carrying them into a privateer, that is, into a vessel owned by private persons and authorized by a Government to engage in hostilities for private gain. Indeed, it has been held and affirmed, after great consideration, by the Supreme Court of the United States in the case of *The Nereide,* confirmed on appeal in the case of *The Atlanta,* that a belligerent vessel was entitled to arm in its own defense and ordinarily did so; that it was not only entitled as of right to resist, but that it was its duty to resist capture at the hands of its enemy; that, being its right to resist, it forfeited nothing of its right by its unsuccessful resistance; that if its resistance were overcome, it would be treated as a capture of an ordinary merchant vessel which had not resisted; that a neutral could intrust his person and his property to such a vessel and that neither he nor his property was affected by the resistance of the vessel, unless he took part in such resistance. This opinion was not the view of a scholarly publicist, but of a judge upon the bench; it was not merely the view of one judge, but of a majority of the Court, and the judgment of the Court and the opinion justifying it bear the name of Marshall and the impress of his intellectual supremacy.

The opinion of Chief Justice Marshall in this case was not incidental to the judgment of the Court. It was involved in the judgment; indeed, it was the judgment.

> A belligerent has a perfect right to arm in his own defense; and a neutral has a perfect right to transport his goods in a belligerent vessel. These rights do not interfere with each other. The neutral has no control over the belligerent right to arm—ought he to be accountable for the exercise of it? By placing neutral property in a belligerent ship, that property, according to the positive rules of law, does not cease to be neutral. Why should it be changed, by the exercise of a belligerent right, universally acknowledged, and in common use when the rule was laid down, and over which the neutral had no control?[1]

The Chief Justice, who had been Secretary of State and left the Foreign Office for the bench, was of course aware that the belligerent would object to the arming of the merchant vessels of the enemy, as the presence of armament would make them more difficult to capture, and indeed might enable them to elude capture altogether. Considering this question, Chief Justice Marshall said:

> The belligerent answers, that by arming, his rights are impaired. By placing his goods under the guns of an enemy, the neutral has taken part with the enemy, and assumed the hostile character. Previous to that examination which the Court has been able to make of the reasoning by which this proposition is sustained, one remark will be made, which applies to a great part of it. The argument which, taken in its fair sense, would prove that it is unlawful to deposit goods for transportation in the

[1] 9 Cranch, pp. 426-427.

vessel of an enemy, generally, however imposing its form, must be unsound, because it is in contradiction to acknowledged law.[1]

In the next portion of his judgment—for these are successive steps in the reasoning by which Chief Justice Marshall reached his conclusion—the Chief Justice considered the contention which has been so frequently advanced in the present war, that the belligerent right of visit and search will be impaired. On this point he said:

> It is said, that by depositing goods on board an armed belligerent, the right of search may be impaired; perhaps, defeated. What is this right of search? Is it a substantive and independent right, wantonly, and in the pride of power, to vex and harass neutral commerce, because there is a capacity to do so? or to indulge the idle and mischievous curiosity of looking into neutral trade? or the assumption of a right to control it? If it be such a substantive and independent right, it would be better that cargoes should be inspected in port, before the sailing of the vessel, or that belligerent licenses should be procured. But this is not its character. Belligerents have a full and perfect right to capture enemy goods, and articles going to their enemy which are contraband of war. To the exercise of that right, the right of search is essential. It is a mean justified by the end. It has been truly denominated a right growing out of, and ancillary to the greater right of capture. Where this greater right may be legally exercised, without search, the right of search can never arise or come into question.
>
> But it is said, that the exercise of this right may be prevented by the inability of the party claiming it, to capture the belligerent carrier of neutral property. And what injury results from this circumstance? If the property be neutral, what mischief is done, by its escaping a search? In so doing, there is no sin, even as against the belligerent, if it can be effected by lawful means. The neutral cannot justify the use of force or fraud, but if, by means, lawful in themselves, he can escape this vexatious procedure, he may certainly employ them.
>
> To the argument, that by placing his goods in the vessel of an armed enemy, he connects himself with that enemy, and assumes the hostile character; it is answered, that no such connection exists. The object of the neutral is the transportation of his goods. His connection with the vessel which transports them is the same, whether that vessel be armed or unarmed. The act of arming is not his—it is the act of a party who has a right so to do. He meddles not with the armament, nor with the war. Whether his goods were on board or not, the vessel would be armed and would sail. His goods do not contribute

[1] 9 Cranch, pp. 426-427.

to the armament, further than the freight he pays, and freight he would pay, were the vessel unarmed. It is difficult to perceive in this argument anything which does not also apply to an unarmed vessel. In both instances, it is the right and the duty of the carrier to avoid capture, and to prevent a search. There is no difference, except in the degree of capacity to carry this duty into effect. The argument would operate against the rule which permits the neutral merchant to employ a belligerent vessel, without imparting to his goods the belligerent character.

The argument respecting resistance stands on the same ground with that which respects arming. Both are lawful. Neither of them is chargeable to the goods or their owner, where he has taken no part in it. They are incidents to the character of the vessel; and may always occur where the carrier is belligerent.[1]

After having disposed of these arguments, the Chief Justice next asks and answers a very pertinent question:

> If the neutral character of the goods is forfeited by the resistance of the belligerent vessel, why is not the neutral character of the passengers forfeited by the same cause? The master and crew are prisoners of war, why are not those passengers who did not engage in the conflict, also prisoners? That they are not, would seem to the Court to afford a strong argument in favor of the goods. The law would operate in the same manner on both.[2]

In a previous portion of Chief Justice Marshall's opinion, which it is difficult not to quote in full, but which is so material that it must at least be quoted in part, that great, just, and upright man, deciding as he was against the contentions of his country, said:

> In point of fact, it is believed, that a belligerent merchant vessel rarely sails unarmed, so that this exception from the rule would be greater than the rule itself. At all events, the number of those who are armed, and who sail under convoy, is too great, not to have attracted the attention of writers on public law; and this exception to their broad general rule, if it existed, would certainly be found in some of their works. It would be strange, if a rule laid down, with a view to war, in such broad terms as to have universal application, should be so construed, as to exclude from its operation almost every case for which it purports to provide, and yet that not a *dictum* should be found in the books, pointing to such construction. The antiquity of the rule is certainly not unworthy of consideration. It is to be

[1] 9 Cranch, pp. 427-428.   [2] *Ibid.*, pp. 429.

traced back to the time when almost every merchantman was in a condition for self-defense, and the implements of war were so light and so cheap, that scarcely any would sail without them.[1]

It is to be observed that, in the course of Chief Justice Marshall's elaborate opinion, that profound jurist states it to be the fact and the custom that merchant ships armed, and that, if this were the custom of the Nations, it would follow that it is a principle of international law unless it has been renounced, and that it remains a custom for those Nations which have been unwilling to renounce it. This principle and its consequences could not be better stated than by the great Chief Justice himself in the case of *The Antelope* (10 Wheaton 66), in which he held that, while the slave trade might be made piracy by international law, it was not piracy by the law of Nations, and that therefore a Nation which had not renounced the right could continue its exercise. In the course of his opinion he spoke of fundamentals, and as the slave trade was obnoxious to him, the language which he felt himself forced to use, being as much against his feelings as it was in conformity with the dictates of a sound judgment, has a double value:

> In this commerce thus sanctioned by universal assent, every nation had an equal right to engage. How is this right to be lost? Each may renounce it for its own people; but can this renunciation affect others?
>
> No principle of general law is more universally acknowledged, than the perfect equality of nations. Russia and Geneva have equal rights. It results from this equality, that no one can rightfully impose a rule on another. Each legislates for itself, but its legislation can operate on itself alone. A right, then, which is vested in all, by the consent of all, can be divested only by consent; and this trade, in which all have participated, must remain lawful to those who cannot be induced to relinquish it. As no nation can prescribe a rule for others, none can make a law of nations; and this traffic remains lawful to those whose governments have not forbidden it.[2]

It may perhaps be said with some show of truth that the provision of the Declaration of Paris of 1856 abolishing privateering is the international agreement which meets Marshall's requirements. But on the threshold it should be said, even if this were admitted, that it would not affect the right of the United States to engage in privateering, much less to arm its merchant vessels for offensive purposes, because the United States was not and is not now a party to

[1] 9 Cranch, p. 426.   [2] 10 Wheaton, p. 120.

the Declaration of Paris. Indeed, it may further be said that it specifically refused to assent to the convention relating to the conversion of merchant ships into warships adopted by the Second Hague Peace Conference in 1907, as this project was understood and stated to be the corollary of the Declaration.

A belligerent cannot maintain that a treaty to which the United States is not a party is binding upon it, and indeed, in the course of the diplomatic correspondence with Great Britain, that Government roundly informed the United States, which had invoked the benefit of the Declaration of Paris in another matter, that, not being a party to the agreement, it could not invoke the provisions of the Declaration or claim as of right any benefit from it. Let us, however, consider further this phase of the subject, as great stress has been laid upon it.

Privateering was abolished in 1856, not because merchant vessels should be unarmed and should not seek to defend themselves if attacked by the enemy, but because experience had shown beyond the possibility of successful contradiction that a captain of a merchantman could not be commissioned to take part in hostilities for his private gain and the gain of his associates, for much the same reason that today there is a tendency to deprive naval officers of the interest in the prize which by universal practice they have heretofore enjoyed. War has become a thing of the State. It is carried on by regularly organized forces on land recruited by the State, drilled, disciplined, subject and responsible to the State. It is carried out upon the high seas by men-of-war built and owned by the nation, manned by commissioned officers who, like the crew, are subject to military discipline and the orders of the State. But this does not mean that on land a noncombatant may not defend himself if attacked, although he may not attack unless complying with certain formalities; nor does it mean that a merchant vessel upon the high seas, subject to capture by international law, may not defend itself if attacked, using force to repel force, or eluding capture by flight. There is, and it is believed there always has been, a distinction between force used to ward off attack and force used aggressively, and although the line may seem difficult to draw at times, it nevertheless exists, and courts of justice are called upon to draw it as a matter of course. A simple illustration will make this clear. While a man may not attack, and while, if assaulted, he should withdraw if possible to save his life, nevertheless, to protect his life, he may use the force necessary to do so, even to the extent of taking the life of his assailant, *vi repellere vim.* The question is one of fact, though this principle may be said to be universally recognized, because a failure to do so would put a person at the mercy of any freebooter running amuck. This principle of law, however, must be strictly construed, otherwise we would doubtless have evil-minded persons compelling assault and justifying their action as taken in self-defense. The use of force by attack and the use of force to repel attack, are facts to be proved as such, and when proved the principle of law will automatically apply.

To return to the question of privateering, the United States was not and is not a party to the Declaration abolishing it, and the reason is very simple. The United States has, in season and out of season, stood for the immunity from capture of innocent private property of the enemy upon the high seas, meaning thereby property other than what is called contraband. The United States has on a number of occasions expressed its willingness to accept all the provisions of the Declaration of Paris, provided the signatory Powers should in their turn accept, in principle and in practice, the immunity of private property on the high seas. Because of the unwillingness of the leading Powers to do this, the United States reserves the right to commission its merchantmen as privateers for the protection of the property of its citizens. But in the one foreign war to which it has been a party since the Declaration of Paris was adopted, it adhered during the continuance of that war to the principles of the Declaration and did not commission privateers in the Civil or Spanish American Wars.

If we look a little closer at the matter, we see that the Declaration of Paris does not refer directly or indirectly to the question of arming a merchant ship, or to the right of a merchant ship to carry an armament for defensive purposes and to protect itself from capture. It is a familiar rule of construction that a statute in derogation of common law is to be strictly construed. The signatories of the Declaration of Paris renounced the right to commission in the future the officers and crew of a merchant vessel to prey upon the enemy for the benefit of the owners of the vessel, its officers, and its crew. That only was renounced, leaving untouched the right of the merchant ship to defend itself against attack by arms which it may carry for this purpose, but withdrawing from that vessel the exercise of belligerent rights associated with a war vessel, namely, the right to open and to commit hostilities against the enemy, the right to visit and search merchant ships of the enemy, the right to attack them and to capture them, and the right to visit and to search neutral ships which happened to be found upon the high seas.

It may be recalled that Prussia, on behalf of itself and of the North German Confederation, proposed during the war of 1870 with France to create a so-called volunteer fleet, to be composed of merchant vessels placed at the disposition of the Government. The crews were to be engaged by the owners of the merchantmen, to enter the Federal Navy during the continuance of the war, to wear uniforms, and to be subjected to military discipline. The officers, likewise enrolled by the owners, were to receive temporary commissions, and, as a reward for extraordinary service, the assurance was held out to them of retention in the navy. The vessels, "hired ships," as they are called in the decree, were to sail under the Federal flag, and were to "be armed by the Federal Royal Navy and fitted out for the service allotted to them." They were to "capture or destroy ships of the enemy," meaning by that term, French vessels of war, for which they were to receive compensation based upon a generous scale.[1]

It is commonly said that the Volunteer Navy was created because the Prussian fleet at that time was inferior to that of France, and

---

[1] Royal Prussian Decree of the 26th July, 1870, relative to the Constitution of a Voluntary Naval Force.

On your representation I have approved the formation of a voluntary naval force under the following form:
1. To issue a summons to all German seamen and shipowners to place themselves, and their forces and ships suitable thereto, at the service of the Fatherland, and under the following conditions:
(*a*) The vessels to be placed at the disposition of the service will be examined and taxed by a Commission composed of two naval officers and one naval contractor as to their capabilities for the intended purpose. In this case the owner receives one-tenth of the price taxed as deposit, whereupon he has to hire the necessary volunteer crews.
(*b*) Officers and crews enrolled in this way enter into the Federal navy for the continuance of the war, and wear its uniform and badge of rank, acknowledge its competency, and take oath to the Articles of War. The officers receive a patent of their rank, and the assurance that, in case of extraordinary service rendered, they can, at their request, be permanently established in the navy. Officers and men who are rendered, by this service, unfit to acquire a livelihood, without any fault on their side, receive a pension calculated at the standard of the Royal Federal Navy.
2. The hired ships sail under the Federal flag.
3. These will be armed by the Federal Royal Navy, and fitted out for the service allotted to them.
4. The ships destroyed in the service of their country will be paid for to their owners at the price taxed. If at the end of the war they can be restored to the owners uninjured, the sum paid as deposit is reckoned as hire.
5. A premium will be paid to such ships as capture or destroy ships of the enemy, according to the following standard: For an iron-plated frigate 50,000 thalers, an iron-plated corvette or ram 30,000 thalers, an iron-plated battery 20,000 thalers, a large screw-vessel 15,000 thalers, a screw-vessel 10,000 thalers. These premiums will be paid to the owners of the ships, to whom will be confided the distribution in proper proportions amongst the crew. . . .

(Signed) WILHELM.

(Franco-German War, No. 1 [1871], *Parliamentary Papers*, C-244, p. 20.)

that the Prussian Government had, for the same reason, proposed at the beginning of the war to exempt from capture unoffending private property of the enemy found at sea, in the hope that France, with a larger and more powerful navy, might do the same.[1] We are not, however, concerned with this phase of the subject, other than to say that France did not agree to spare Prussian commerce, and that in January, 1871, Prussia withdrew its decree to respect the immunity of private property as an act of reprisal due to the destruction by the French cruiser *Desaix* of Prussian cruisers upon the high seas, instead of taking them, as international law required, into a French port for adjudication.[2]

France promptly protested against the proposal of the volunteer navy as contrary to the Declaration of Paris, and addressed the British Government on the subject. Lord Granville, then Secretary of State for Foreign Affairs, acting upon the advice of the law officers of the Crown, declared himself unable to object to the proposal, as it did not seem to violate the Declaration of Paris.[3] And yet a little reflection must convince us that it was dangerously near the border line, for if war be a relation between State and State and is to be carried on by agencies of the State, not by private persons acting in their own behalf although with the approval of

---

[1] The following is the material portion of the decree of the North German Confederation concerning the immunity of private property from capture, issued July 18, 1870:

> French merchant vessels shall not be subject to be captured or seized as prizes of war by vessels of the Royal Navy of the Confederation. This rule does not of course apply to those vessels which would be subject to capture or seizure if they were neutral vessels. (*British and Foreign State Papers*, vol. 60, p. 923.)

[2] *Bundesgesetzbuch*, 1870, p. 485; *British and Foreign State Papers*, vol. 61, p. 986.

[3] They advise me that there are, in their opinion, substantial distinctions between the proposed naval volunteer force sanctioned by the Prussian Government, and the system of privateering, which, under the designation of "la course," the Declaration of Paris was intended to suppress.

The Law Officers say that, as far as they can judge, the vessels referred to in the Notification of the 24th of July, will be for all intents and purposes in the service of the Prussian Government, and the crews will be under the same discipline as the crews on board vessels belonging permanently to the Federal navy.

This being the case now, and as long as it continues to be so, the law officers consider that Her Majesty's Government cannot object to the decree of the Prussian Government as infringing the Declaration of Paris.

Her Majesty's Government will, however, with reference to the Prussian notification, call the attention of the Prussian Government to the Declaration of Paris, and will express their hope and belief that Prussia will take care to prevent by stringent instructions any breach of that Declaration. (Lord Granville to the Marquis de Lavalette, August 24, 1870.) (Franco-German War No. 1 [1871], *Parliamentary Papers*, C-244, p. 22.)

governmental authorities, it would seem that the distinction between the volunteer navy and the erstwhile privateer was somewhat nebulous.

In both cases the vessels were privately owned; in both they were manned by a crew engaged by the owners of the vessels, and commanded by officers engaged by the owners of the vessels, authorized, in the case of privateers, by letters of marque and reprisal, in the case of the volunteer fleet commissioned by the government, to wage aggressive warfare—in the case of the privateers against vessels of war and commerce, in the case of the volunteer navy solely against vessels of war. It is only fair to admit, however, that, although private vessels and manned by seafaring men instead of officers of the navy, both crew and officers of the volunteer fleet were subject to military discipline, and that the commission from the Government would have been no small guarantee against the abuse of its terms. Nevertheless, they were private, not public, vessels, and the motive was the destruction of public vessels of the enemy and private gain for themselves.

The right of merchant ships to carry arms, recognized before the Declaration of Paris, has been restated by the executive and judicial departments of the United States. Thus, in 1877, Hamilton Fish, a very careful and experienced Secretary of State, stated:

> I am not aware of any international prohibition or of any treaty provision which would prevent a vessel trading amid the groups of islands of the South Sea from carrying a couple of guns and arms for the proper and necessary protection of the vessel against violence on the part of lawless or partially civilized communities, or of the piratical crews which are represented to occasionally frequent those waters, providing always that the vessel carrying such guns and arms itself be on a lawful voyage and be engaged in none other than peaceful commerce, and that such guns and arms be intended and be used solely for the purpose of defense and of self-protection.[1]

In the case of *Cushing v. United States*,[2] decided in 1886, the Court of Claims had occasion to consider whether permission given by the statutes of the United States to carry arms for defensive purposes subjected them because of this fact to treatment as men-of-war. After considering the nature of offensive warfare, Mr. Justice Davis, speaking for the Court, said:

[1] Mr. Fish to Mr. Morrill, Feb. 8, 1877, 117 Dom. Let. 54; quoted from Moore's *International Law Digest*, vol. 2, p. 1070.
[2] 22 U. S., *Court of Claims Reports*, p. 1.

The statutes we have cited have no such object; they are not aggressive in their provisions or in the power they give, but entirely defensive, except in the instance of seizing armed vessels or retaking captured American vessels. The aim of the statute is defense of our merchantmen, not depredations upon the commerce of France, not compensation to the United States for losses already incurred, not security for demands heretofore made, but protection and safety in the future. It seems to us, therefore, that these acts lack the essential elements of statutes of reprisals.[1]

And on reconsideration the Court of Claims affirmed these views in the case of *Hooper, Admr., v. United States:*[2]

A privateer is an armed vessel belonging to one or more private individuals, licensed by Government to take prizes from an enemy; its authority in this regard must depend altogether upon the extent of the commission issued to it, and is qualified and limited by the laws under which the commission is issued. (*The Thomas Gibbons,* 8 Cranch, p. 421.)

The Hooper case is very interesting as showing the flagrant disregard of international law in the matter of capture. After describing the conditions obtaining at the end of the eighteenth century, Mr. Justice Davis stated that merchant vessels carried armament and he thus pointed out the distinction between armament for defense and for attack:

Judges "are not to shut their eyes to what is generally passing in the world" (*Blatchford Prize Cases,* p. 448), nor as to what has already taken place. In danger from native pirates, in danger from French privateers often as irresponsible (*Cushing's Administrator,* ante, p. 1), the mere possession of some armament by a merchantman is devoid of marked significance. It is improbable that any important venture was sent to sea without an effort on the part of the ship-owner to protect his property and that laden on his vessel; cannon enough or muskets enough he would put on board to give his crew a fair chance of escape from a small force. The statute, however, said that no armed merchantman should receive a clearance or permit, or be suffered to depart unless the owners and the master gave bond conditioned, among other things, that the vessel should not commit any depredation, outrage, unlawful assault, or unprovoked violence upon the high seas against the vessel of any nation in amity with the United States. (1 Stat. L., p. 573.) . . .

In our view of the case it is vital to note the distinction between armament for protection simply and armament for attack upon armed vessels or for attack upon captured American vessels

[1] 22 U. S., *Court of Claims Reports,* pp. 39-40.   [2] *Ibid.,* pp. 408, 428.

necessarily in charge of prize crews. A privateer is maintained for profit; the venture is most speculative in its nature, bringing large returns for great risk. Given the right to prey upon the mercantile marine, great armament is not necessary, as combat may be avoided by speed and quickness in manoeuvre. The privateering authorized by the acts of 1798 was of no such nature; not a prize could be taken without conflict, for only armed vessels, or vessels in charge of prize crews, could be seized; not a merchantman was allowed to be molested.[1]

That a vessel fitted with defensive armament in accordance with the statutes of the United States, to protect itself against unlawful aggression on the part of French vessels, was nevertheless a merchant vessel and as such subject to the exercise of the belligerent right of visit and search, is specifically stated in the case of *The Schooner Jane v. The United States*,[2] decided in 1901, on the ground that the statute of no nation could vary the rule of international law, and that by the law of nations visit and search was a belligerent right to which a vessel of the United States, then a neutral, was subjected.

But a decision of the Supreme Court of the United States of the year 1900 can be invoked, decided at a time when armament had not become a burning question. *The Panama* (176 U.S., p. 535), "a Spanish mail steamship," to quote the headnote of the case, was "on a voyage from New York to Havana, carrying a general cargo, passengers and mails, and having mounted on board two breech-loading Hontoria guns of nine centimetre bore, and one Maxim rapid-firing gun, and having also on board twenty Remington rifles and ten Mauser rifles, with ammunition for all the guns and rifles, and thirty or forty cutlasses." This armament had been placed on board the vessel a year before the outbreak of the war with Spain, "for her own defense," to quote again the headnote of the case, "as required by her owner's mail contract with the Spanish Government, which also provided that, in case of war, that government might take possession of the vessel with her equipment, increase her armament, and use her as a war vessel, and, in these and other provisions, contemplated her use for hostile purposes in time of war." Mr. Justice Gray, speaking for the Court, overruled the plea that a mail vessel was by international law exempt from capture, and he also overruled the plea of the government that the presence of armament subjected *The Panama* to capture, even although a mail steamer should be exempt. After having decided this question in the negative, Mr. Justice Gray

[1] 22 U.S., *Court of Claims Reports*, pp. 433-434.
[2] 37 U.S., *Court of Claims Reports*, p. 24.

thus stated the further question upon which the Court was obliged to render a judgment:

> The remaining question in the case is whether *The Panama* came within the class of vessels described in the fourth clause of the President's proclamation of April 26, 1898, as "Spanish merchant vessels," and not as "Spanish vessels having on board any officer in the military or naval service of the enemy, or any coal (except such as may be necessary for their voyage), or any other article prohibited or contraband of war, or any despatch of or to the Spanish Government."
>
> On the part of the claimant, it was argued that the arms which *The Panama* carried, under the requirements of her mail contract and for the protection of the mails, are not to be regarded as contraband or munitions of war, within the sense of this clause; that "contraband," as therein referred to, means contraband cargo, not contraband portion of the ship's permanent equipment; and that, if the furnishings of a ship could be regarded as contraband, every ship would have contraband on board.
>
> On the other hand, it was contended, in support of the condemnation, that the arms which *The Panama* carried, belonging to her owner, were contraband of war, and rendered her liable to capture; and that by reason of her being so armed, and of the provisions of her mail contract with the Spanish Government, requiring her armament, and recognizing the right of that Government, in case of a suspension of the mail service by war, to take possession of her for warlike purposes, she cannot be considered as a merchant vessel, within the meaning of the proclamation, but must be treated like any regular vessel of the Spanish Navy under similar circumstances.[1]

On the first part of this question Mr. Justice Gray thus said for the Court:

> The claimant much relied on a case decided in 1800 by the French Council of Prizes, in accordance with the opinion and report of Portalis, himself a high authority. (Wheaton, 8th ed., p. 460; De Boeck, sec. 81.) In the case referred to, an American vessel, carrying ten cannon of various sizes, together with muskets and munitions of war, had been captured by French frigates; and had been condemned by two inferior French tribunals, upon the ground that she was armed for war, and had no commission or authority from her own government. The claimants contended that their ship, being bound for India, was armed for her own defense, and that the munitions of war, the muskets and the cannon that composed her armament did not exceed what was usual in like cases for long voyages. Upon

[1] 176 U. S., *Reports*, p. 543.

this point, Portalis, acting as commissioner of the French Government, reported his conclusion on the question of armament as follows: "For my part, I do not think it is enough to have or to carry arms, to incur the reproach of being armed for war. Armament for war is of a purely offensive nature. It is established when there is no other object in the armament than that of attack, or, at least, when everything shows that such is the principal object of the enterprise; then a vessel is deemed enemy or pirate, if she has no commission or papers sufficient to remove all suspicion. But defense is a natural right, and means of defense are lawful in voyages at sea, as in all other dangerous occupations of life. A ship which had but a small crew, and a considerable cargo, was evidently intended for commerce, and not for war. The arms found on this ship were evidently intended, not for committing acts of rapine or hostility, but for preventing them; not for attack, but for self-defense. The pretext of being armed for war therefore appears to me to be unfounded." The Council of Prizes, upon consideration of the report of Portalis, adjudged that the capture of the vessel and her cargo was null and void, and ordered them to be restored, with damages. (*The Pégou*, or *Pigou*, 2 Pistoye et Duverdy, *Prises Maritimes*, p. 51; S. C. 2 Cranch, pp. 96-98, and note.)

But in that case the only question at issue was whether a neutral merchant vessel, carrying arms solely for her own defense, was liable to capture for want of a commission as a vessel of war or privateer. That the capture took place while there was no state of war between France and the United States is shown by her being treated, throughout the case, as a neutral vessel; if she had been enemy's property, she would have been lawful prize, even if she had a commission, or if she were unarmed. She was not enemy's property, nor in the enemy's possession, nor bound to a port of the enemy; nor had her owner made any contract with the enemy by which the enemy was, or would be, under any circumstances, entitled to take and use her, either for war, or for any other purpose.[1]

After saying that, "generally speaking, arms and ammunition are contraband of war," and invoking the authority of *The Peterhoff* (5 Wallace, p. 28), the learned justice thus continued:

Yet it must be admitted that arms and ammunition are not contraband of war, when taken and kept on board a merchant vessel as part of her equipment, and solely for her defense against "enemies, pirates, and assailing thieves," according to the ancient phrase still retained in policies of marine insurance.[2]

[1] U. S., *Court of Claims Reports*, pp. 543-545.
[2] *Ibid.*, pp. 545-546.

Section 2. Visit and Search

It is perhaps not too much to say that the question of visit and search, which was thought to have been as well settled as any principle of international law and recognized in the practice of Nations, has proved to be the most troublesome question with which neutrals have been confronted during the war, and that the failure to comply with the requirements of visit and search as hitherto understood and practiced has caused the United States to slip from its neutral moorings and to range itself with the Allies against the Imperial German Government. The cause of the trouble seems to be due to the fact that the new weapon, the submarine, which the Imperial German Government has introduced and upon which it has pinned its hopes of victory, is so frail in structure and so small in size that it cannot expose itself to the danger of attack from a merchant ship which a surface cruiser would overhaul, and it cannot take on board the passengers and crew of the merchant vessel, which it is unable to carry into port and which it therefore destroys. It is every-day experience that we must take the bad with the good, the loss with the profit, or, as this principle is expressed in Roman law and incorporated in every system of jurisprudence, *cujus est commodum, ejus est periculum*.

The question of visit and search has to be considered from two points of view, from the standpoint of the belligerent and from the standpoint of the neutral, or, expressed in other terms, when a belligerent and a neutral merchantman are involved. While a belligerent man-of-war possesses the right to overhaul any merchantman of any nationality irrespective of the flag it flies, its rights against enemy and neutral vessels are very different. It may capture and, under exceptional circumstances, destroy the one; it may detain and, through judicial procedure, condemn the other. Because of this it behooves the belligerent cruiser to determine whether the vessel is enemy or neutral, lest the undoubted right in the one case become an actionable wrong in the other.

To obviate mistake and the liability for its consequences, to confine belligerent operations to the enemy and not, by a policy of aggression, convert the neutral into an opponent, the law of Nations, common to all, and similar if not identical in practice, prescribes that the belligerent cruiser shall by visit and search ascertain the character of the vessel before it takes action. The right of visit and search is strictly a belligerent right. It does not exist in time of peace. Although no authority is needed on this point, the following statement from the opinion of Mr. Justice Story in *The Marianna Flora* (11 Wheaton 1), decided in 1826, is quoted:

> In considering these points, it is necessary to ascertain, what are the rights and duties of armed, and other ships, navigating the ocean, in time of peace. It is admitted, that the right of visitation and search does not, under such circumstances, belong to the public ships of any nation. This right is strictly a belligerent right, allowed by the general consent of nations, in time of war, and limited to those occasions. . . .
>
> Upon the ocean, then, in time of peace, all possess an entire equality. It is the common highway of all, appropriated to the use of all; and no one can vindicate to himself a superior or exclusive prerogative there. Every ship sails there with the unquestionable right of pursuing her own lawful business, without interruption; but whatever may be that business, she is bound to pursue it in such a manner as not to violate the rights of others. The general maxim in such cases is, *sic utere tuo, ut non alienum laedas*.[1]

In deciding this case Mr. Justice Story referred to and relied upon that of *Le Louis* (2 Dodson 210), decided in 1817, by Sir William Scott, later Lord Stowell, whose language is so pertinent that it may well serve as a conclusion to this general statement and as an introduction to the discussion which is to follow, as it lays down principles which were fundamental when uttered and which must remain fundamental and be respected if nations are ever to live in peace and harmony.

A French vessel, *Le Louis*, was taken upon the high seas by a British cruiser in time of peace pursuant to an act of Parliament condemning as piracy the slave trade, in which the French vessel was engaged. On the case as thus presented and on the question whether the right of visit and search existed under these circumstances in time of peace, his Lordship said:

> Upon the first question, whether the right of search exists in time of peace, I have to observe, that two principles of public law are generally recognized as fundamental. One is the perfect equality and entire independence of all distinct states. Relative magnitude creates no distinction of right; relative imbecility, whether permanent or casual, gives no additional right to the more powerful neighbor; and any advantage seized upon that ground is mere usurpation. This is the great foundation of

[1] 11 Wheaton, p. 42.

public law, which it mainly concerns the peace of mankind, both in their politic and private capacities, to preserve inviolate. The second is, that all nations being equal, all have an equal right to the uninterrupted use of the unappropriated parts of the ocean for their navigation. In places where no local authority exists, where the subjects of all states meet upon a footing of entire equality and independence, no one state, or any of its subjects, has a right to assume or exercise authority over the subjects of another. I can find no authority that gives the right of interruption to the navigation of states in amity upon the high seas, excepting that which the rights of war give to both belligerents against neutrals. This right, incommodious as its exercise may occasionally be to those who are subjected to it, has been fully established in the legal practice of nations, having for its foundation the necessities of self-defense, in preventing the enemy from being supplied with the instruments of war, and from having his means of annoyance augmented by the advantages of maritime commerce. Against the property of his enemy each belligerent has the extreme rights of war. Against that of neutrals, the friends of both, each has the right of visitation and search, and of pursuing an inquiry whether they are employed in the service of his enemy, the right being subject, in almost all cases of an inquiry wrongfully pursued, to a compensation in costs and damages.[1]

The nature and the extent of the right of the belligerent to visit and search the vessels of the neutral have been stated in terms which have become classic by Lord Stowell in his judgment in the case of *The Maria*,[2] decided in 1799, shortly after his advent to the bench. In this early judgment he apparently felt the necessity of declaring the principles by which he should be guided in cases of this kind. They were, in his opinion, three in number:

> 1st. That the right of visiting and searching merchant ships upon the high seas, whatever be the ships, whatever be the cargoes, whatever be the destinations, is an incontestable right of the lawfully commissioned cruisers of a belligerent nation. I say, be the ships, the cargoes, and the destinations what they may, because, till they are visited and searched, it does not appear what the ships, or the cargoes, or the destinations are; and it is for the purpose of ascertaining these points that the necessity of this right of visitation and search exists. This right is so clear in principle, that no man can deny it who admits the legality of maritime capture; because if you are not at liberty to ascertain by sufficient inquiry whether there is property that can legally be captured, it is impossible to capture. . . .

[1] 2 Dodson, p. 243. [2] 1 C. Robinson, p. 340.

2dly. That the authority of the sovereign of the neutral country being interposed in any manner of mere force cannot legally vary the rights of a lawfully commissioned belligerent cruiser. . . .

3dly. That the penalty for the violent contravention of this right is the confiscation of the property so withheld from visitation and search. For the proof of this I need only refer to Vattel, one of the most correct and certainly not the least indulgent of modern professors of public law.[1] . . .

Sir William Scott was very sure of the principles he was laying down and he was also sure of the exception he was about to mention, because he felt himself justified in debating, and proclaiming publicly:

But I stand with confidence upon all fair principles of reason,—upon the distinct authority of Vattel,—upon the Institutes of other great maritime countries, as well as those of our own country,—when I venture to lay it down, that by the law of nations, as now understood, a deliberate and continued resistance to search, on the part of a neutral vessel to a lawful cruiser, is followed by the legal consequence of confiscation.[2]

It is believed that no stronger statement is to be found in the books of the duty of the neutral to submit to visit and search, and it is also believed that no stronger statement is to be found in the books of the duty of the belligerent cruiser to visit and search the neutral vessel in order to determine whether it or its cargo is liable to seizure or confiscation. And while planting himself firmly upon all fair principles of reason, upon the authority of publicists and upon the practice of maritime Nations, he nevertheless felt it necessary to provide for the exceptional case justifying resistance against the unlawful acts of a belligerent in the matter of visit and search, raising the issue of self-preservation. Thus:

How stands it by the general law? I don't say that cases may not occur in which a ship may be authorized by the natural rights of self-preservation to defend itself against extreme violence threatened by a cruiser grossly abusing his commission; but where the utmost injury threatened is the being carried in for inquiry into the nearest port, subject to a full responsibility in costs and damages if this is done vexatiously and without just cause, a merchant vessel has not a right to say for itself, (and an armed vessel has not a right to say for it), "I will submit to no such inquiry, but I will take the law into my own hands by

[1] 1 C. Robinson, pp. 360-364.   [2] *Ibid.*, p. 369.

force." What is to be the issue, if each neutral vessel has a right to judge for itself in the first instance whether it is rightly detained, and to act upon that judgment to the extent of using force? Surely nothing but battle and bloodshed, as often as there is anything like an equality of force or an equality of spirit.[1]

This is no doubt true, and the neutral should not resist if it is not to pass upon in the matter of visit and search which it is inclined to consider unlawful. As Sir William Scott says, the inconvenience is that of being carried into the port of the captor with compensation in damages for the unlawful act; but if the captor is known to sink at sight and without warning, and even in the case of warning to cast officers and crew and passengers adrift to shift for themselves without taking them aboard, as was not done even by France when it was running amuck in the days of the Revolution, an exceptional case is clearly made out in the sense of Sir William Scott. Accepting this judgment in its full extent as correct in principle, and therefore correct in law, the right of the belligerent against the property of its enemy is the right of capture, and the right of visit and search is ancillary to that right. The right of the belligerent against neutrals is the right of self-defense in preventing the "enemy from being supplied with the instruments of war, and from having his means of annoyance augmented by the advantages of maritime commerce," and to the exercise of this right visit and search are an indispensable prerequisite, because without visit and search it cannot be determined whether the neutral vessel is engaged in a transaction which renders it obnoxious to the belligerent.

Section 3. Destruction of Prizes

On principle it is clear that, if the property of the enemy be liable to capture, a belligerent cruiser may seize an enemy merchantman and that by the fact of war the title passes from the enemy to the country of the captor; and it is immaterial to the private owner if he is thus deprived of his property whether it be used or destroyed by the belligerent. It is, however, a matter of importance to the individual captors who, by virtue of the laws of their country, are entitled to a share in the spoils, that the capture be valid, because otherwise they have no claim, and that the title, vested by capture in the sovereign, be divested by a court of the sovereign and passed

---

[1] 1 C. Robinson, p. 374.

to the captors, a prerequisite of which is that the vessel was an enemy vessel and therefore lawful prize. It is also material to a neutral who may claim an interest in the vessel or cargo that his rights in the premises be determined and safeguarded, which can best be done in a judicial proceeding according to the rules of law, in the quiet of the courtroom, instead of by a decision of the commander of the capturing vessel laboring under excitement and given offhand from the quarter-deck.

Therefore it has become a rule of the law of Nations and a practice of belligerents to pass enemy prizes before a court of justice for the benefit of the officers and crew making the capture and entitled to a share of the proceeds and for the benefit of neutrals whose rights may be involved. In exceptional cases, however, it is the practice of Nations to destroy an enemy prize. This is allowed when the prize cannot be brought into a port of the captor, or when such action would, in the judgment of the captor, seriously interfere with the military operations.

An authority or two is quoted on each of these points, although it may seem superfluous to do so because of their universal recognition.

In the leading case of *The Elsebe* (5 C. Robinson 173), decided in 1804, Sir William Scott was obliged to consider the interest of the Crown as distinct from the interest of the individual captors in the prize, and in the course of his observations that very learned and upright judge said:

> Prize is altogether a creature of the crown. No man has, or can have, any interest but what he takes as the mere gift of the crown. Beyond the extent of that gift, he has nothing. This is the principle of law on the subject, and founded on the wisest reasons. The right of making war and peace is exclusively in the crown. The acquisitions of war belong to the crown; and the disposal of these acquisitions may be of the utmost importance for the purposes both of war and peace. This is no peculiar doctrine of our constitution; it is universally received as a necessary principle of public jurisprudence, by all writers on the subject, *Bello parta cedunt reipublicae*. It is not to be supposed that this wise attribute of sovereignty is conferred without reason; it is given for the purpose assigned, that the power to whom it belongs to decide on peace or war may use it in the most beneficial manner for the purposes of both.[1]

Next as to the right of the belligerents to destroy the enemy prize, tempered by the interest of neutrals. Again the great authority of

---

[1] 5 C. Robinson, p. 181.

Sir William Scott is invoked. In the case of *The Felicity* (2 Dodson, p. 381), decided in 1819, the question was as to the right of the captor to destroy an American vessel captured during the war of 1812 between Great Britain and the United States.

The facts of the case are thus stated by his Lordship:

> This ship and cargo, American property, were destroyed by Captain Hope of his Majesty's ship *Endymion* on the 1st of January, 1814, being then in the prosecution of a voyage from Cadiz (where she had carried provisions) to Boston, where her owners resided. She had encountered a continuance of most tempestuous weather, and had suffered most severely under it, so as to make it more than doubtful whether she could possibly reach America. Under a strong sense of their danger, they had determined, upon a general council of the master and mariners, to make for the island of Bermuda, but were baffled by the opposition of a head-wind, and compelled to resume their course to America in their shattered condition; and under the unsettled and boisterous weather which belongs to that season of the year in such latitudes, she is met with by his Majesty's ship *Endymion*, Captain Hope, by whose orders she was destroyed, after her captain and crew, with their baggage, were removed on board *The Endymion*.[1]

His Lordship then considered the right of the captor to destroy the vessel under these circumstances. On this point he says:

> Taking this vessel and cargo to be merely American, the owners could have no right to complain of this act of hostility, for their property was liable to it, in the character it bore, at that period, of enemy's property. There was no doubt that *The Endymion* had a full right to inflict it, if any grave call of public service required it. Regularly a captor is bound by the law of his own country, conforming to the general law of nations, to bring in for adjudication, in order that it may be ascertained whether it be enemy's property; and that mistakes may not be committed by captors, in the eager pursuit of gain, by which injustice may be done to neutral subjects, and national quarrels produced with the foreign states to which they belong. Here is a clear American vessel and cargo, alleged by the claimants themselves to be such, and consequently the property of enemies at that time. They share no inconvenience by not being brought in for the condemnation, which must have followed if it were mere American property; and the captors fully justify themselves to the law of their own country, which prescribes the bringing in, by showing that the immediate service in which they were engaged, that of watching the enemy's ship of war,

[1] 2 Dodson, p. 385.

The President, with intent to encounter her, though of inferior force, would not permit them to part with any of their own crew to carry her into a British port. Under this collision of duties nothing was left but to destroy her, for they could not, consistently with their general duty to their own country, or indeed its express injunctions, permit enemy's property to sail away unmolested. If impossible to bring in, their next duty is to destroy enemy's property. Where doubtful whether enemy's property, and impossible to bring in, no such obligation arises, and the safe and proper course is to dismiss. Where it is neutral, the act of destruction cannot be justified to the neutral owner, by the gravest importance of such an act to the public service of the captor's own state; to the neutral it can only be justified, under any such circumstances, by a full restitution in value. These are rules so clear in principle and established in practice, that they require neither reasoning nor precedent to illustrate or support them.[1]

It will be observed that not only the captain and crew, but also the baggage were taken aboard *The Endymion* before the enemy prize was destroyed, although *The Endymion* was at that very moment "watching the enemy ship of war, *The President*, with intent to encounter her."

The action of France in the case of *The Ludwig*, captured during the war of 1870, is sometimes pressed into service in defense of the destruction of neutral prizes, which will be considered later, and the case is only referred to here as showing the generality of the rule that enemy prizes may only be destroyed if they cannot be brought into port for adjudication. It appeared that the French cruiser *Desaix* captured three German vessels, and because of the large number of prisoners on board the captain destroyed the vessels as he considered it unsafe to spare a prize crew in order to escort the vessels into port. A claim for restitution made by the owners of the captured vessels, disallowed in first instance, was likewise disallowed on appeal because it was held that "from the ship's papers and from the proceedings it appears that the vessels belonged to German subjects, thus making them good and valuable prize, that the destruction having been caused by *force majeure*, in order to maintain the safety of the captain's operations, there was no cause to restore the captured property; that in acting as they had done they had no doubt made use of a rigorous right but one provided for by the laws of war and recommended by the instructions they carried."[2]

[1] 2 Dodson, pp. 385-386.
[2] Barboux, *Jurisprudence du Conseil des Prises pendant la guerre de 1870-71*, pp. 153 *et seq.*

It is interesting to note in this connection that in the one war to which Prussia was a party before the outbreak of the war of 1914 the North German Confederation, of which Prussia was the dominant member, protested against the destruction of enemy prizes without bringing them into a French port, there to be passed upon by the court of the captor, and to such a degree was the Iron and imperturbable Chancellor aroused and annoyed by this violation of international law on the part of France that he considered it just ground for reprisals, revoking the decree of July 18, 1870, exempting unoffending French property from capture and confiscation. Thus, Count von Bismarck said:

> In the naval warfare the French have likewise scouted international law. The French war-steamer *Desaix* has destroyed, by burning or sinking on the high seas, three German merchantmen which it had captured, *The Ludwig*, *The Vorwärts*, and *The Charlotte*, instead of taking them to a French port and obtaining the sentence of a prize court. The German ships will therefore be directed to make reprisals on French ships.[1]

Whatever may be the right of a captor to destroy an enemy prize, it is and has long been the practice of Nations to bring the prize into port, and this is true to such a degree that the late Mr. Hall felt justified in saying and retaining in the fourth and last edition of his treatise on international law which he was permitted to revise, that:

> Perhaps the only occasions on which enemy's vessels have been systematically destroyed, apart from any serious difficulty in otherwise disposing of them, were during the American revolutionary war and that between Great Britain and the United States in 1812-14."[2]

The case of *The Felicity* shows that Great Britain justified the sinking of an enemy prize, saving, however, the captain, crew, and baggage, when, owing to adverse circumstances, the vessel could not be brought into port and passed before a prize court. The practice of the United States in that war shows that it not only permitted, but that it enjoined systematic destruction in the instructions issued to American commanders. In an article entitled *Why Semmes of the Alabama was not Tried*, written by John A. Bolles, Solicitor of the Navy, and

---

[1] Count Bismarck to Count Bernstorff (communicated to Earl Granville by Count Bernstorff, January 16), January 9, 1871, *British and Foreign State Papers*, vol. 61, p. 986-987.

[2] Hall's *International Law*, 4th ed., p. 475.

published in the *Atlantic Monthly* for July, 1872, that well-informed and fair-minded writer says that, although the earlier records are imperfect, it is a fact that "many vessels captured in the War of the Revolution were destroyed at sea."[1] Of the War of 1812 he thus speaks:

> Of the history and policy of the later period we have abundant proofs. Not less than seventy-four British merchantmen were captured, and destroyed as soon as captured, under express instructions from the Navy Department, and in pursuance of a deliberate purpose and plan, without any attempt or intent to send or bring them in as prizes for adjudication. The orders of the Department upon this subject are numerous, emphatic, and carefully prepared.[2]

Mr. Bolles cites some of these orders, which are not very pleasant reading to Americans of today, but which it is well to read and to ponder before embarking upon universal condemnation and criticism. Some of these orders are quoted from Mr. Bolles' article.

> The great object is the destruction of the commerce of the enemy, and the bringing into port the prisoners, in order to exchange against our unfortunate countrymen who may fall into his hands.[3]

It will be observed that this very first order cited by Mr. Bolles shows that the officers and crew were not to be sunk with the vessels, as they were to be brought into port in order to be exchanged for their countrymen in British captivity.

> You will, therefore, man no prize, unless the value, place of capture, and other favorable circumstances shall render safe arrival morally certain.
>
> You will not agree to the ransoming of any prize.
>
> Grant no cartel, nor liberate any prisoners, unless under circumstances of extreme and unavoidable necessity.
>
> You will, therefore, unless in some extraordinary cases that shall clearly warrant an exception, destroy all you capture; and by thus retaining your crew and continuing your cruise, your services may be enhanced tenfold.[3]

---

[1] The records of the Revolutionary War are fragmentary, yet they show that John Paul Jones, the first American sailor and with whom the taking of prizes was an ordinary occurrence, removed all persons on board before destroying a captured vessel. (See Gardner W. Allen, *A Naval History of the American Revolution*, 1913, 2 vols., vol. 1, pp. 121, 124.)

[2] *Atlantic Monthly*, vol. 30, p. 95.

[3] *Ibid.*, p. 96.

Your own sound judgment and observation will sufficiently demonstrate to you how extremely precarious and injurious is the attempt to send in a prize, unless taken very near a friendly port, and under the most favorable circumstances. . . . Policy, interest, and duty combine to dictate the destruction of all captures, with the above exceptions.

The commerce of the enemy is the most vulnerable point of the enemy we can attack, and its destruction the main object; and to this end all your efforts should be directed. Therefore, unless your prizes should be very valuable and near a friendly port, it will be imprudent and worse than useless to attempt to send them in; the chances of recapture are excessively great; the crew, the safety of the ship under your command, would be diminished and endangered, as well as your own fame and the national honor, by hazarding a battle after the reduction of your officers and crew by manning prizes. In every point of view, then, it will be proper to destroy what you capture, except valuable and compact articles, that may be transshipped. This system gives to one ship the force of many.

A single cruiser, if ever so successful, can man but a few prizes, and every prize is a serious diminution of her force; but a single cruiser, destroying every captured vessel, has the capacity of continuing, in full vigor, her destructive power, so long as her provisions and stores can be replenished, either from friendly ports or from the vessels captured. . . . Thus has a single cruiser, upon *the destructive plan,* the power, perhaps, of twenty acting upon pecuniary views alone; . . . and thus may the employment of our small force in some degree compensate for the great inequality [of our force] compared with that of the enemy.[1]

A careful examination has been made of the archives of the Government, without finding any evidence of the destruction of a neutral prize or of the loss of captain, crew, or passengers.

Another instance of the systematic destruction of enemy prizes on the allegation of necessity, likewise cited by the late Mr. Hall, who was accustomed to speak of his American cousins with candor if not with kindness, is furnished by the American Civil War, and the career of Captain Semmes of the Confederate Navy furnishes us the picture of the naval officer sitting as a prize judge upon his quarter-deck, dispensing justice under what must be considered as difficult and trying circumstances.

However, notwithstanding the most searching criticism of the actions of Captain Semmes, it appears that he did not destroy a

[1] *Atlantic Monthly,* vol. 30, p. 96.

single prize without first removing crew and passengers, and that when he could not accommodate the crew and passengers of the proposed victim he released it, as in the case of the valuable prize of *The Ariel*, "and sent her and her large number of her passengers on their way rejoicing." Indeed, this man of the seas, whom his countrymen of the North were accustomed to look upon as a pirate, even applied the same rule to the case of the warship. Thus, before destroying *The Hatteras*, a Federal war vessel, he stated that "every living being in it was safely conveyed to *The Alabama*." And the words with which he sought to justify his conduct have lost neither point nor application with the lapse of time. "We were making war," he said, "upon the enemy's commerce, not upon his unarmed seamen." After this offhand and blunt statement of the fundamental principle of naval warfare, he mentioned in passing the reason for it: "It gave me as much pleasure to treat these with humanity as it did to destroy his ships."

The captain, be it said to his honor, did not destroy neutral prizes, despite the greatest of temptations, and he has himself reported his prize decisions. As captain of *The Sumter* and *The Alabama* he had occasion to sit in judgment upon some seventy cases of prize. In a note to his *Cases on International Law* the late Freeman Snow quotes the following extracts from what may be called Semmes' *Admiralty Reports*. Many others might be added to the same effect, but it is believed that these are amply sufficient for present purposes. Thus, in the case of *The Lafayette*, Captain Semmes, sitting as prize judge, decided:

> Ship and cargo condemned. The cargo of this ship was condemned by me as enemy's property, notwithstanding there were depositions of the shippers that it had been purchased by them on neutral account. These *ex parte* statements are precisely such, as every unscrupulous merchant would prepare, to deceive his enemy and save his property from capture."[1]

After an extended consideration of the case, finding the presence of fraud and that the neutrality of the cargo was not established, Captain Semmes, sitting as prize judge, thus continued:

> 3d Phillimore, 599, to the effect, that "further proof" is always necessary where the master cannot swear to the ownership of the property (as in this case). And as I cannot send my prizes in for adjudication, I must of necessity condemn in all cases where "further proof" is necessary, since the granting

[1] Semmes, *Cruise of the Alabama*, vol. 1, p. 346; Snow, *Cases on International Law* (Boston, 1893), p. 520.

of "further proof" proceeds on the presumption that the neutrality of the cargo is not sufficiently established; and where the neutrality of the property does not fully appear from the ship's papers and the master's deposition, I had the right to act upon the presumption of enemy's property.[1]

Again, in the case of *The Express*, in which the ship and the cargo were condemned, Captain Semmes, sitting as prize judge, said:

> It must be admitted that this is a case in which, perhaps, a prize court would grant "further proof"; but as I cannot do this, and as a distinct neutral character is not impressed upon the property by former evidence, I must act under the presumption of law. See 3d Phill., p. 589.[2]

Captain Semmes' method did not pass unchallenged by neutrals, and Great Britain apparently was unable to reconcile his procedure with that of Lord Stowell, as appears from the following extract from the interview with the doughty captain taken from *The Cape Argus*:

> You English people won't be neighborly enough to let me bring my prizes into your ports and get them condemned, so that I am obliged to sit here a *court of myself*, try every case, and condemn the ships I take.[3]

So far the question of the destruction of neutral prizes has only been touched upon incidentally, as it was hitherto the purpose to show that an enemy merchantman was, by generally recognized principles of international law, entitled to a hearing in a court of justice, not in its own behalf but in behalf of the neutral. From this it would appear that if, as a general rule, an enemy prize should not be destroyed unless in exceptional circumstances, a neutral merchantman should not be the subject of destruction; because if the incidental interest of the neutral would cause an enemy ship to be saved and to be passed before the prize court, complete ownership by the neutral would entitle the vessel in all cases to be saved and to be passed before a prize court; or, if it should be impossible to bring the vessel into port, that it be released.

A very careful examination has been made of the practice of Nations, in the matter of the destruction of prizes, in connection with the practice of the United States when it not only permitted but enjoined destruction of enemy prizes, in order to determine if pos-

---

[1] Semmes, *Cruise of the Alabama*, vol. 1, p. 346; Snow, *Cases of International Law* (Boston, 1893), p. 520.
[2] *Ibid.*, p. 167; *ibid.*
[3] *Ibid.*, vol. 2, p. 358; *ibid.*

sible whether the command to destroy enemy prizes extended in practice to the destruction of neutral prizes. As a result of this examination it appears that the destruction of the neutral prize is a thing of our day, and that as a system it dates from the Russo-Japanese War. It is believed that there is neither a rule nor a principle of international law permitting the destruction of neutral prizes. The commander of a belligerent vessel destroying a neutral prize can indeed plead the command of his government, but his government is responsible to the neutral government for the destruction; because, in the absence of a rule or principle of international law permitting destruction, and in the absence of the consent of the neutral government to the act of destruction, there is no justification which can be established against it.

This statement may be made with the greater assurance because the question was long and hotly debated at the Second Hague Peace Conference of 1907, where the partisans of the destruction of neutral prizes sought and failed to obtain a recognition of the right to destroy neutral property under any circumstances and where they were unable, although requested, to produce an unequivocal authority other than the act of Russia in its war with Japan, which would justify the proposal which they had made. At the London Naval Conference an agreement was reached, after much debate, discussion, and misgiving, to permit the destruction of a neutral prize in specifically defined cases, stating, however, the preservation of neutral prize to be the rule, its destruction the exception. But as the Declaration of London was not ratified by the Powers, and never has been and is not now a compact of the Nations, even this guarded permission does not exist. Therefore, the Nations are thrown back upon international law as it existed before the Declaration of London and before the outbreak of the war. That law does not contain permission on the part of neutrals that their property upon the high seas, open to all and subject to the exclusive jurisdiction of none, may be destroyed, although some Nations have recently claimed the right to do so.

A reference should be made to a case arising in the Russo-Japanese War which made of the destruction of neutral prizes a burning question in more senses than one. *The Knight Commander* was a British ship, stopped by a Russian cruiser on July 23, 1904, on its voyage from New York to Yokohama and Kobe, that is to say, bound from a neutral to a belligerent port. The vessel was considered as engaged in carrying contraband, as its cargo consisted largely of railway material declared to be contraband by Russia.

The vessel was set on fire and destroyed by the Russian cruiser. The official reason given for this action was "the proximity of the enemy's port, the lack of coal on board the vessel to enable her to be taken into a Russian port and the impossibility of supplying her with coal from one of the Russian cruisers owing to the high seas running at the time." This action was in accordance with Article 21 of the Russian naval prize regulations, which reads:

> In exceptional cases, when the preservation of a captured vessel appears impossible on account of her bad condition or entire worthlessness, the danger of her recapture by the enemy, or the great distance or blockade of ports, or else on account of danger threatening the ship which has made the capture or the success of her operations, it is permissible for the Commander, on his own responsibility, to burn or sink the captured vessel, after he has taken off all persons on board, and as much of the cargo as possible, and arranged for the safety of the vessel's papers and any other objects which may be necessary for throwing light on the case at the inquiry to be instituted in accordance with the procedure in prize cases.[1]

It is to be observed from the official report of the case that the crew and papers were taken on board the cruiser before the vessel was destroyed. *The Knight Commander* was condemned by the Russian Prize Court at Vladivostok on August 16, 1904, and the sentence was affirmed on December 5, 1905, by the Court of Appeals of St. Petersburg, which held that it is "impossible to agree that the destruction of a neutral vessel was contrary to the principles of international law." The Russian Government has, so to speak, stood by its guns, and in 1908 declined to submit the case to arbitration.

The Knight Commander, while it is the leading, is not the only case, because, during the war with Japan, Russia sank, in addition, the following British vessels: *St. Kilda*, *Oldhamia*, *Ikhona*, and *Hipsang*, in all five; two German vessels, *The Thea* and *Tetartos;* and the Danish vessel *Princesse Marie*.[2] In each instance the crew were saved.

In the case of *The Felicity*, an enemy prize, Lord Stowell took occasion to consider, in passing, the case of the destruction of a neutral vessel, saying on this point:

> Where it is neutral, the act of destruction cannot be justified to the neutral owner, by the gravest importance of such an

---

[1] *Russian and Japanese Prize Cases* (edited by C. J. B. Hurst; London; Wyman & Sons, 1912-13), 2 vols., vol. 1, pp. 315-316.
[2] *Ibid.*, vol. 1, pp. 21, 96, 145, 166, 188, 226, 276.

act to the public service of the captor's own state; to the neutral it can only be justified, under any such circumstances, by a full restitution in value.[1]

His Lordship felt justified in thus concluding his remarks on this subject: "These are rules so clear in principle and established in practice, that they require neither reasoning nor precedent to illustrate or support them."[1] Lord Stowell's meaning seems to be that there is no right to destroy neutral prize; that if it should be destroyed the commission of the wrong would not create the right, but the absence of right would require full restitution. In the previous case of *The Acteon*,[2] decided in 1815, his Lordship was called upon to consider the action to be taken by the court because of the illegal destruction of that American vessel. On this phase of the subject he said:

> This question arises on the act of destruction of a valuable ship and cargo by one of his Majesty's cruisers. On the part of the claimants, restitution has been demanded, and there can be no doubt that they are entitled to receive it; . . .
>
> If the captor has been guilty of no wilful misconduct, but has acted from error and mistake only, the suffering party is still entitled to full compensation, provided, as I before observed, he has not, by any conduct of his own, contributed to the loss. (*The Felicity*, 2 Dod., p. 381.) The destruction of the property by the captor may have been a meritorious act towards his own government, but still the person to whom the property belongs must not be a sufferer. As to him, it is an injury for which he is entitled to redress from the party who has inflicted it upon him; and if the captor has, by the act of destruction, conferred a benefit on the public, he must look to the government for his indemnity. The loss must not be permitted to fall on the innocent sufferer.[3]

The case of *The Acteon* was carefully argued by Dr. Lushington, then at the bar, who many years later thus commented upon it from the bench:

> The act of destruction of the ship by Captain Capel was in itself illegal, even if the vessel was liable to condemnation; it could only be justified on the grounds of public policy, and for illegal acts done for such a reason responsibility must attach.[4]

---
[1] 2 Dodson, p. 387.
[2] *Ibid.*, p. 48.
[3] *Ibid.*, pp. 51-52.
[4] Spinks, p. 217; Roscoe, *Reports of Prize Cases* (London, 1905), vol. 2, pp. 473, 488.

As judge and as a worthy successor of Lord Stowell, Dr. Lushington felt called upon to express his views in a case of neutral prize arising in 1855 out of the Crimean War, and on the point in question he said:

> We must bear in mind the wide difference between the detention of a vessel under the colours of the enemy or under neutral flags.
>
> The destruction of a vessel under hostile colours is a matter of duty; the Court may condemn on proof which would be inadmissible or wholly irregular in the instance of a neutral vessel. It may be justifiable or even praiseworthy in the captors to destroy an enemy's vessel. Indeed, the bringing to adjudication at all of an enemy's vessel is not called for by any respect to the right of the enemy proprietor where there is no neutral property on board. But for totally different considerations, which I need not now enter upon, where a vessel under neutral colours is detained, she has the right to be brought to adjudication according to the regular course of proceeding in the Prize Court; and it is the very first duty of the captor to bring it in, if it be practicable.
>
> From the performance of this duty the captor can be exonerated only by showing that he was a *bonâ fide* possessor, and that it was impossible for him to discharge it. No excuse for him as to inconvenience or difficulty can be admitted as between captors and claimants. If the ship be lost, that fact alone is no answer; the captor must show a valid cause for the detention as well as the loss. If the ship be destroyed for reasons of policy alone, as to maintain a blockade or otherwise, the claimant is entitled to costs and damages. The general rule, therefore, is that if a ship under neutral colours be not brought to a competent Court for adjudication, the claimants are, as against the captor, entitled to costs and damages.

And further on in the course of his opinion he said:

> Indeed, if the captor doubt his power to bring a neutral vessel to adjudication, it is his duty, under ordinary circumstances, to release her.[1]

It would perhaps be too much to say that the destruction of neutral prize is, under international law and the practice of Nations, forbidden in all cases. It is, however, accurate to insist that it is not expressly authorized. It is further believed to be in accordance with the facts to maintain that, before the Russo-Japanese War, the classification of captured vessels into enemy and neutral prizes does not appear to have been made; that when prizes are spoken of enemy

---

[1] Roscoe, *Reports of Prize Cases*, vol. 2, p. 477.

prizes are meant if we are to judge by the practice of Nations, which had hitherto confined itself to the destruction of enemy prizes, and then only in exceptional cases for which they felt specific justification was necessary; and that, even during the Russo-Japanese War, when neutral prizes were destroyed by Russia—not under a claim that international law permitted it, be it said, but that it was not forbidden by international law—the officers and crew in every case during that war were saved from destruction. It is therefore well within the mark to say that, before the outbreak of the great war of 1914, there were no instances to be found in the books of the destruction of neutral prizes without first saving the officers and crew, including passengers, on the part of any Nation belonging to the society of civilized Nations and claiming the right to sink a neutral prize.

Section 4. Treatment of Armed Merchant Vessels in the Present War

From the attitude of the British Government in the matter of the Prussian Volunteer Navy, we would be prepared to expect that British authorities would not regard the carrying of guns for purely defensive purposes as a resort to privateering and that such action on their part would not be inconsistent with the Declaration of Paris abolishing the privateer. On March 26, 1913, the Right Hon. Winston Churchill, then First Lord of the Admiralty, proposed, as a means of protection, to place armament upon first-class British liners to repel the attacks of armed foreign merchant cruisers. To do this certain changes were made, at the expense of the owners, in the structure of the vessels to fit them for the carriage of guns, and the guns were loaned, the ammunition supplied, and the gun crews trained at the expense of the Government. The vessels thus fitted out were, in the contemplation of the Government, to continue as a part of the merchant marine. They were to defend themselves against, not to provoke, attack, and they were to be under their own officers, not under commissioned officers of the Government. The First Lord of the Admiralty justified this action on the ground that certain of the great Powers claimed the right to convert merchant vessels into armed cruisers not only in home ports but upon the high seas, if necessary or convenient, and that there was reason to believe that a considerable number of these vessels would be converted into armed ships. In this event, the food-carrying liners and vessels carrying raw materials found in the well-known trade routes "would be at the mercy of any foreign liner carrying one effective gun and a few rounds of ammunition" if the British vessels did not carry an armament to ward off attack. The First Lord of the Admiralty regretted the need of the measure he was advocating, saying that: "No one can pretend to view these measures without regret, or without hoping that the period of retrogression all over the world which has rendered them necessary, may be succeeded by days of broader international confidence and agreement, than those through which we are now passing."[1]

Early in August, 1914, it was announced that British vessels would enter American ports carrying a light armament and their Government asked to have them treated as merchantmen. Great Britain was anxious to learn the attitude of the United States "in view of the fact that a number of British armed merchantmen will now be visiting United States ports."

The reason for which these vessels were armed was not left to speculation, as in a memorandum from the British Embassy dated September 9, 1914, the British Government, notwithstanding Mr. Winston Churchill's announcement a year previously, justified the armament of merchant ships because of the illegal conduct of Germany. Thus, the memorandum says:

> The German Government have openly entered upon the policy of arming merchant ships as commerce destroyers and even claim the right to carry out the process of arming and equipping such merchant ships in neutral harbours or on the high seas.[2]

It is immaterial for present purposes to stop to consider whether this statement be true or not, as the question is one of retaliation, not one of right. Thus:

> It is in consequence of this that the British Admiralty have been compelled, in accordance with the practice followed in the great wars of history, to arm a certain number of British merchant ships for self-defence only.[2]

The British Embassy considered the action legal on its part, although it intimated that this action would not have been taken unless Germany had already armed merchant ships as commerce destroyers and had illegally converted them into cruisers in neutral ports and on the high seas. In the final paragraph of the memorandum from

[1] Official text, *American Journal of International Law*, Special Supplement, October, 1916, p. 320.
[2] *Ibid.*, July, 1915, p. 232.

which a quotation has already been made, the Embassy thus justifies the arming of merchant ships and points out the real distinction between a merchant ship, on the one hand, armed for purely defensive purposes, and an auxiliary cruiser, on the other, armed for aggressive purposes:

> A merchant vessel armed purely for self-defence is therefore entitled under international law to enjoy the status of a peaceful trading ship in neutral ports and His Majesty's Government do not ask for better treatment for British merchant ships in this respect than might be accorded to those of other Powers. They consider that only those merchant ships which are intended for use as cruisers should be treated as ships of war and that the question whether a particular ship carrying an armament is intended for offensive or defensive action must be decided by the simple criterion whether she is engaged in ordinary commerce and embarking cargo and passengers in the ordinary way. If so, there is no rule in international law that would justify such vessel even if armed being treated otherwise than as a peaceful trader.[1]

The Government of the United States was clear that a merchantman, frequenting American waters, subject to requisition by a belligerent Government and carrying an armament which could properly be considered offensive and which it was the purpose of the vessel to use offensively, could not be treated as an ordinary merchantman; but, on the other hand, it felt and stated that the presence of armament on board a merchant vessel of this kind for a purely defensive purpose did not convert such a merchantman into a man-of-war, and that such a merchantman could not be allowed the belligerent right of visit and search upon the high seas, which is a right exclusively belonging to the public armed vessels of a belligerent. It was therefore not satisfied with the mere fact that the armament was stated to be for defense, not for offense. It required and received a solemn assurance from the British Government that a British merchantman enjoying the hospitality of the United States and supplied with an armament declared to be defensive, should not, upon reaching the high seas, use that armament for offensive purposes and should not convert itself into a man-of-war acting under commission during the homeward voyage. On September 19, 1914, the Department of State issued a circular on the subject, of which the first three paragraphs are quoted as showing the attitude which the United States as a

[1] Official text, *American Journal of International Law*, Special Supplement, July, 1915, p. 233.

neutral took at the beginning of the war and maintained throughout the entire period of its neutrality:

> A. A merchant vessel of belligerent nationality may carry an armament and ammunition for the sole purpose of defense without acquiring the character of a ship of war.
>
> B. The presence of an armament and ammunition on board a merchant vessel creates a presumption that the armament is for offensive purposes, but the owners or agents may overcome this presumption by evidence showing that the vessel carries armament solely for defense.
>
> C. Evidence necessary to establish the fact that the armament is solely for defense and will not be used offensively, whether the armament be mounted or stowed below, must be presented in each case independently at an official investigation. The result of the investigation must show conclusively that the armament is not intended for, and will not be used in, offensive operations.
>
> Indications that the armament will not be used offensively are:
>
> 1. That the caliber of the guns carried does not exceed six inches.
> 2. That the guns and small arms carried are few in number.
> 3. That no guns are mounted on the forward part of the vessel.
> 4. That the quantity of ammunition carried is small.
> 5. That the vessel is manned by its usual crew, and the officers are the same as those on board before war was declared.
> 6. That the vessel intends to and actually does clear for a port lying in its usual trade route, or a port indicating its purpose to continue in the same trade in which it was engaged before war was declared.
> 7. That the vessel takes on board fuel and supplies sufficient only to carry it to its port of destination, or the same quantity substantially which it has been accustomed to take for a voyage before war was declared.
> 8. That the cargo of the vessel consists of articles of commerce unsuited for the use of a ship of war in operations against an enemy.
> 9. That the vessel carries passengers who are as a whole unfitted to enter the military or naval service of the belligerent whose flag the vessel flies, or of any of its allies, and particularly if the passenger list includes women and children.
> 10. That the speed of the ship is slow.[1]

It may perhaps be said, in this connection, that the principle applied in the case of a merchant ship carrying armament for defen-

[1] Official text, *American Journal of International Law*, Special Supplement, July, 1915, pp. 234-235.

sive purposes was precisely the principle applied by the United States on the later occasion to the case of the submarine *Deutschland*, which twice entered American jurisdiction, and was declared to be a merchantman because it was without the means of waging offensive war, contrary to the contentions of the Allied Governments.

This action on the part of the British Government, concurred in by the Department of State in its circular of September 19, 1914, did not pass without notice by and protest from the Imperial German Government. A memorandum dated October 13, 1914, was handed to the American Ambassador to Berlin, in which the German Foreign Office stated that the ruling of the United States was inconsistent with neutrality and that the arming of merchant vessels was for the purpose of resisting German cruisers, which was illegal, and that armed merchantmen, if admitted at all within neutral ports, should only be treated as men-of-war. As this very brief memorandum states, at the very beginning of the controversy, in clear, precise and unmistakable terms, the attitude which the Imperial German Government has maintained throughout the controversy, this portion of it is quoted in full:

> The equipment of British merchant vessels with artillery is for the purpose of making armed resistance against German cruisers. Resistance of this sort is contrary to international law, because in a military sense a merchant vessel is not permitted to defend itself against a war vessel. . . . If the Government of the United States considers that it fulfills its duty as a neutral nation by confining the admission of armed merchant ships to such ships as are equipped for defensive purposes only, it is pointed out that so far as determining the warlike character of a ship is concerned, the distinction between the defensive and offensive is irrelevant. The destination of a ship for use of any kind in war is conclusive, and restrictions as to the extent of armament afford no guarantee that ships armed for defensive purposes only will not be used for offensive purposes under certain circumstances.[1]

The United States was unable to accept this point of view, and in an instruction to the American Ambassador to Berlin, dated November 7, 1914, Acting Secretary of State Lansing replied at length justifying the contentions of the American Government. In the first place, he appealed to the practice of Nations and the opinion of publicists, saying:

[1] Official text, *American Journal of International Law*, Special Supplement, July, 1915, p. 238; *ibid.*, October, 1916, p. 321.

The practice of a majority of nations and the consensus of opinion by the leading authorities on international law, including many German writers, support the proposition that merchant vessels may arm for defense without losing their private character and that they may employ such armament against hostile attack without contravening the principles of international law.[1]

In the next place, he pointed out the attendant circumstances which would, in the opinion of the United States, raise a conclusive presumption that the armament was to be used solely for defensive purposes:

> This Government considers that in permitting a private vessel having a general cargo, a customary amount of fuel, an average crew, and passengers of both sexes on board, and carrying a small armament and a small amount of ammunition, to enjoy the hospitality of an American port as a merchant vessel, it is in no way violating its duty as a neutral.[1]

From the attitude of the Imperial German Government, Mr. Lansing was obliged to recognize that there might be a difference of opinion on this point, that the admission of vessels with defensive armament to the jurisdiction of the United States would give rise to complaint, and that, in the interest of friendly relations, it was the part of wisdom to prevent such questions from arising. He therefore informed the Imperial Government that:

> This Government, as soon as a case arose, while frankly admitting the right of a merchant vessel to carry a defensive armament, expressed its disapprobation of a practice which compelled it to pass upon a vessel's intended use, which opinion if proven subsequently to be erroneous might constitute a ground for a charge of unneutral conduct.[1]

Because of this action on the part of the United States he was able to inform the German Government that: "As a result of these representations no merchant vessels with armaments have visited the ports of the United States since the 10th of September."[1] He was further able to assure the German Government that: "In fact from the beginning of the European war but two armed private vessels have entered or cleared from ports of this country, and as to these vessels their character as merchant vessels was conclusively

---

[1] Official text, *American Journal of International Law*, Special Supplement, July, 1915, p. 239.

established."[1] In the last paragraph of the note, after directing the American Ambassador to bring these views to the notice of the German Government, he instructed the Ambassador to "express the hope that they will also prevent their merchant vessels from entering the ports of the United States carrying armaments even for defensive purposes though they may possess the right to do so by the rules of international law.[1]

It was one thing, however, to consider vessels with a defensive armament as merchant vessels and to treat them as such if they entered American jurisdiction; it was an entirely different matter to secure from Germany their recognition and treatment upon the high seas as merchant vessels, because, although all Nations admit that the high seas are a common highway to all, each endeavors to apply its own conception of international law to the wayfarer found on the highway. There would have been little or no difficulty but for the submarine. In his instruction to the American Ambassador dated May 13, 1915, concerning the destruction of *The Lusitania* without warning, and without an attempt to save the lives of passengers and crew, Secretary Bryan, speaking for the United States, said that:

> It assumes, on the contrary, that the Imperial Government accept, as of course, the rule that the lives of noncombatants, whether they be of neutral citizenship or citizens of one of the nations at war, cannot lawfully or rightfully be put in jeopardy by the capture or destruction of an unarmed merchantman, and recognize also, as all other nations do, the obligation to take the usual precaution of visit and search to ascertain whether a suspected merchantman is in fact of belligerent nationality or is in fact carrying contraband of war under a neutral flag.[2]

The note then went to the root of the matter, stating that the objection of the United States to the use of the submarine "lies in the practical impossibility of employing submarines in the destruction of commerce without disregarding those rules of fairness, reason, justice, and humanity which all modern opinion regards as imperative." Lest this statement should appear to be too general, Secretary Bryan pointed out specifically the reasons why, in the opinion of the Government of the United States, the submarine could not be considered as a legitimate agent of warfare. Thus:

> It is practically impossible for the officers of a submarine

[1] Official text, *American Journal of International Law*, Special Supplement, July, 1915, pp. 239-240.
[2] *Ibid.*, p. 131.

to visit a merchantman at sea and examine her papers and cargo. It is practically impossible for them to make a prize of her; and, if they cannot put a prize crew on board of her, they cannot sink her without leaving her crew and all on board of her to the mercy of the sea in her small boats. These facts it is understood the Imperial German Government frankly admit. We are informed that in the instances of which we have spoken time enough for even that poor measure of safety was not given, and in at least two of the cases cited not so much as a warning was received. Manifestly submarines cannot be used against merchantmen, as the last few weeks have shown, without an inevitable violation of many sacred principles of justice and humanity.[1]

In the reply of the German Secretary for Foreign Affairs dated May 28, 1915, it was asserted that *The Lusitania* was armed and that the British merchantmen not only sheltered themselves behind neutral flags and markings but that, when so disguised, they attacked German submarines "by ramming them"; that "high rewards have been offered by the British Government as a special incentive for the destruction of the submarines by merchant vessels, and such rewards have already been paid out."[2] In this reply the justification later so common is indicated that *The Lusitania* need not be visited and searched because carrying armament and because of the danger to the German submarine by "ramming."

In the note of the Imperial Secretary, dated June 1, 1915, the justification given for the attack on the American vessel *Gulflight* is more specific. The commander of the submarine thought, from the distance and attendant circumstances, that *The Gulflight*, accompanied by two small vessels, was an English vessel of such considerable value as to be convoyed. "Since such vessels," the note says, "are regularly armed, the submarine could not approach the steamer on the surface of the water without running the danger of destruction."[3] Again, it appears that the commander was unwilling to risk the safety of his little craft by approaching the steamer in order to determine whether it was or was not neutral. "The commander," the note runs, "could see no neutral markings on it of any kind—that is, distinctive marks painted on the freeboard, recognizable at a distance, such as are now usual on neutral ships in the English zone of naval warfare." The upshot was that the commander, without investigation, for the reasons advanced by his Government, came to the

[1] Official text, *American Journal of International Law*, Special Supplement, July, 1915, p. 131.
[2] *Ibid.*, p. 135.
[3] *Ibid.*, p. 137.

conclusion "that he had to deal with an English steamer and attacked submerged."[1] The torpedo, it seems, was discharged inconveniently near one of the ships which, to quote the note, "at once rapidly approached the point of firing."[1] By this action, to quote again the note, "the submarine was forced to go to a great depth to avoid being rammed,"[1] and this action on the part of the surface vessel apparently convinced the German commander that it was English.

We here have two justifications of the failure to visit and search the vessel, the danger to the submarine at the hands of an armed vessel, and the danger to the submarine because of the fear of ramming. A cruiser would have visited and searched and let the vessel go if it had been neutral; and a cruiser would have visited and searched a suspected vessel and, if found to be that of the enemy, would have taken aboard the officers and crew, as German surface vessels, notably *The Emden, The Karlsruhe, The Eitel Friedrich*, had done, before sinking it.

The note from which these extracts have been made, overlooked visit and search and only incidentally explained its absence. But the United States was not to be put off with disquisitions about armed vessels, the presence or absence of neutral markings—which in themselves were humiliating—and with the hardship involved in forcing the submarine to go to a great depth in order to avoid being rammed. The question was not one of method; it was one of principle, and the principle was the necessity of visit and search as a prerequisite to any action taken against a merchant vessel, whether of an enemy or of a neutral Power. Therefore, in the second *Lusitania* note of June 9, 1915, Secretary Lansing brought visit and search to the fore and insisted that the requirements of international law in that respect be complied with. In the first place, he dealt with *The Falaba*, a British passenger vessel which was sunk without regard to the safety of the lives of those on board, and on this point Mr. Lansing stated that:

> The Government of the United States is surprised to find the Imperial German Government contending that an effort on the part of a merchantman to escape capture and secure assistance alters the obligation of the officer seeking to make the capture in respect of the safety of the lives of those on board the merchantman, although the vessel has ceased her attempt to escape when torpedoed.[2]

[1] Official text, *American Journal of International Law*, Special Supplement, July, 1915, p. 137.
[2] *Ibid.*, p. 139.

According to the German theory of nonresistance on the part of a merchant vessel, an attempt to escape was a violation of international law and placed the vessel beyond the pale of protection. It is not, as has been shown, the theory or practice of Nations, a view correctly and concisely stated by Secretary Lansing in the following passage:

> Nothing but actual forcible resistance or continued efforts to escape by flight when ordered to stop for the purpose of visit on the part of the merchantman has ever been held to forfeit the lives of her passengers or crew.[1]

Taken in connection with the circumstances of the case, this statement is correct; but if standing alone it is open to misconception, because neither resistance nor flight forfeits life, although either one or the other gives the right to use force to overcome resistance or bring the flight to an end, in the course of which life, as a consequence of the use of force, may be lost. That this was the purpose which Secretary Lansing had in mind is shown by a later passage in the same note, in which he says:

> Only her actual resistance to capture or refusal to stop when ordered to do so for the purpose of visit could have afforded the commander of the submarine any justification for so much as putting the lives of those on board the ship in jeopardy.[2]

Germany's contention was clearly stated and carried a step further in the reply of the Imperial Secretary for Foreign Affairs on July 8, 1915, to Secretary Lansing's note of June 9th. The action of Great Britain in permitting its merchantmen to arm was clearly stated to be a violation of international law, the distinctions between merchantmen and vessels of war were declared to be thereby "obliterated," the rewards to ram submarines were again mentioned, and the danger to neutrals traveling upon English vessels was pointed out and illustrated by the fate of *The Lusitania*.

Now, the meaning of all this is very clear. The submarine, by reason and because of its frailty, was not able, as was a surface cruiser, to visit and search a merchant vessel and by visit and search to ascertain its nationality, its cargo, its destination. Therefore, the fact that English merchant vessels were armed for defense, that they endeavored to destroy the submarine whenever they located it either

[1] Official text, *American Journal of International Law*, Special Supplement, July, 1915, p. 139.
[2] *Ibid.*, p. 140.

by firing a gun or ramming it—actions which would be impossible or of no effect in the case of a surface vessel—are pleaded in justification of the omission to comply with the law and practice of Nations requiring visit and search in all such cases. And, because of its size, the submarine was to be freed from the requirement of putting the officers, crew, and passengers in a place of safety before destroying the merchant vessel, if destruction was to be permitted. A false analogy was stretched to the breaking point in order to keep American citizens from traveling upon British ships, armed or unarmed. Without directly denying to Americans the right to travel on a belligerent merchantman, the Imperial German Government denied that, in so doing, "American citizens can protect an enemy ship through the mere fact of their presence on board."[1] This is not and never was the contention of the United States. A merchant vessel, with or without the presence of Americans, was, in the opinion of the American Government, entitled to have its character determined by visit and search, and if it was permissible, in view of all the circumstances, to destroy it, that, whether Americans were present or not, officers, crew, and passengers should be removed and put in a place of safety, and their effects saved if possible, before the vessel was destroyed. The presence or absence, therefore, of Americans was immaterial from the American point of view, except that their presence and their death through the misconduct of German commanders made it the duty, as it would otherwise have been the right, to protest against the violation of international law in which all Nations have an equal interest.

But if American citizens came to grief it was their own fault, for "Germany merely followed England's example when it declared part of the high seas an area of war,"[1] and the false analogy which has already been mentioned, but which it is important to make clear, is contained in the following passage:

> Consequently accidents suffered by neutrals on enemy ships in this area of war cannot well be judged differently from accidents to which neutrals are at all times exposed at the seat of war on land when they betake themselves into dangerous localities in spite of previous warning.[1]

If the Imperial German Government is really a partisan of the freedom of the seas, it cannot maintain that it has a right in any part

[1] Official text, *American Journal of International Law*, Special Supplement, July, 1915, p. 153.

to the exclusion of other countries, and the question at issue is only obscured by suggesting an analogy between land and maritime warfare. In the former an army occupies territory to the exclusion of all other authority, and anyone coming within the range of occupation subjects himself to this authority and to the consequence of his presence; whereas, in the latter, the portion declared to be a war zone is not at the expense of the belligerent, and if occupied or if entrance is made dangerous or impossible it is not occupation at the expense of its enemy, for its enemy does not own the high seas, but it is occupation at the expense of other countries and it is a danger created and suffered at the expense of others. A person entering, with warning and without permission, occupied territory on land is a trespasser. He is not a trespasser on the high seas, which are as much his as they can be the property of anyone.

In any event, the United States protested, as has been pointed out, against making of the North Sea a military area, just as it did against the action of Germany in making of the waters surrounding Great Britain a war zone, and not having conceded the right of either, the warning was either null and void as against the United States or had only the effect which the United States cared to give it, derogating, as it did, from the freedom of the seas.

As has been frequently mentioned, it would have made no difference to a surface cruiser if merchant vessels had been armed and if they had attempted to ram the cruiser. In the first case, they would have invited destruction; in the second case, they would have run to destruction. As the Germans were unwilling to renounce the use of the submarine, which would have great difficulty in complying with the formalities of visit and search and which would probably have been unable to do so in the case of armed merchantmen, as the submarine could be rammed by a merchantman or destroyed by a single well-directed shot, it was hoped, nevertheless, that it might be possible to reach a compromise by the terms of which the Imperial German Government would conduct submarine warfare according to the requirements of international law in consideration of certain concessions on the part of the Allied Powers. Therefore, on January 18, 1916, Secretary Lansing sent an informal and confidential letter to the diplomatic agents of the Allied Powers in Washington, suggesting a possible basis for an agreement. Secretary Lansing stated frankly that he regarded "the present method of destroying merchant vessels without removing the persons on board to places of safety" as contrary to the principles of humanity which should control the actions of belligerents, and at the same time he denied with equal frankness that "a belligerent should be deprived of the proper use of submarines in the interruption of enemy commerce, since those instruments of war have proven their effectiveness in this particular branch of warfare on the high seas."[1] His comments were, as he said, predicated on the following propositions:

> 1. A noncombatant has a right to traverse the high seas in a merchant vessel entitled to fly a belligerent flag and to rely upon the observance of the rules of international law and principles of humanity if the vessel is approached by a naval vessel of another belligerent.
> 2. A merchant vessel of enemy nationality should not be attacked without being ordered to stop.
> 3. An enemy merchant vessel, when ordered to do so by a belligerent submarine, should immediately stop.
> 4. Such vessel should not be attacked after being ordered to stop unless it attempts to flee or to resist, and in case it ceases to flee or resist, the attack should discontinue.
> 5. In the event that it is impossible to place a prize crew on board of an enemy merchant vessel or convoy it into port, the vessel may be sunk, provided the crew and passengers have been removed to a place of safety.[2]

It was evident that the crux of the matter was that of armament on the one hand, and visit and search on the other. It was likewise evident that either the Allied Governments would have to give up what they considered the undoubted right of protecting themselves from attack of the enemy, or that Germany would have to renounce the use of the submarine. Secretary Lansing proposed that the Allies should, in the interest of saving human life, renounce a doubtful legal right which may be denied on account of new conditions, meaning by that the right of carrying armament. Secretary Lansing did not, of course, mean that in his opinion the right was doubtful, because as Counselor and as Secretary of State he had stood for the right to arm merchantmen and for their character as merchantmen when so armed, and he had also stood for the duty of visit and search, admitting the right of a merchant vessel to resist visit and search by the use of force or to elude it by flight. He meant that, because of Germany's denial of the right, it might be considered doubtful rather than that it was doubtful in itself. In supporting his compromise Secretary Lansing felt justified in saying:

[1] Official text, *American Journal of International Law*, Special Supplement, October, 1916, p. 310.
[2] *Ibid.*, p. 311.

> It would, therefore, appear to be a reasonable and reciprocally just arrangement if it could be agreed by the opposing belligerents that submarines should be caused to adhere strictly to the rules of international law in the matter of stopping and searching merchant vessels, determining their belligerent nationality, and removing the crews and passengers to places of safety before sinking the vessels as prizes of war, and that merchant vessels of belligerent nationality should be prohibited and prevented from carrying any armament whatsoever.[1]

By way of reënforcing the argument which he had made, he concluded:

> I should add that my Government is impressed with the reasonableness of the argument that a merchant vessel carrying an armament of any sort, in view of the character of submarine warfare and the defensive weakness of undersea craft, should be held to be an auxiliary cruiser and so treated by a neutral as well as by a belligerent Government, and is seriously considering instructing its officials accordingly.[2]

Secretary Lansing's proposal, conceived not in the interest of any belligerent but in the interest of human life, did not meet with the approval of the Allied Powers, at whose expense, apparently, the agreement could only be realized. Before, however, the reply of the Allied Powers (which was contained in an informal letter from the British Ambassador to Secretary Lansing, dated March 23, 1916) was received, Germany and Austria-Hungary simultaneously announced that orders had been given to treat "all merchant vessels armed with cannon as vessels of war." In the German memorandum of February 10, 1916, it is stated that:

> a merchantman assumes a warlike character by armament with guns, regardless of whether the guns are intended to serve for defense or attack. It considers any warlike activity of an enemy merchantman contrary to international law, although it accords consideration to the opposite view by treating the crew of such a vessel not as pirates but as belligerents.[3]

The memorandum of the Allied Powers was clear and firm on the right to arm merchant vessels, saying: "From a strictly legal standpoint it must be admitted that the arming of merchant vessels for

---

[1] Official text, *American Journal of International Law*, Special Supplement, October, 1916, p. 312.
[2] *Ibid.*, pp. 312-313.
[3] *Ibid.*, p. 316.

defense is their acknowledged right."[1] The memorandum then proceeded to state that a belligerent should not be asked to forego the lawful means for protection from the unlawful attack of the enemy without an assurance that the enemy would desist from its unlawful attacks in consideration of the renunciation of a lawful belligerent right, and the British Ambassador stated in the memorandum, concluding this portion of the subject, that:

> Great Britain is unable to agree that upon a non-guaranteed German promise, human life may be surrendered defenseless to the mercy of an enemy who, in circumstances of this kind as in many others, has shown himself to be both faithless and lawless.[2]

In regard to the proposal to consider armed merchantmen as auxiliary cruisers, the memorandum pointed out that: "Finally, if armed merchant vessels were to be treated as auxiliary cruisers they would possess the right of making prizes, and this would mean the revival of privateering."[3]

This matter has been dwelt upon somewhat at length in order to show the earnest and persistent desire of the United States, even at the sacrifice of consistency, to reach an agreement with the Powers by virtue of which the loss of human life might be avoided in submarine warfare, and in order that that warfare should be made to comply with the requirements of visit and search in the matter of armed merchantmen as well as in the matter of unarmed ships. The United States failed in its attempt to reach a compromise, and submarine warfare continued as before.

The statement of the Imperial German Government, dated February 10, 1916, that it would thereafter treat armed vessels as auxiliary cruisers and that it would sink them, their passengers and crew on sight, may have been given to the public to force the Allied Governments to reject Secretary Lansing's proposal of January 18, 1916, which would have placed a limitation or restraint upon the activity of the submarine by forcing it to care for its victims, which, it would seem, would have rendered impossible what the German government considered its legitimate operations. But it was not a new decision of the German Government, as the ruling had been made in the early days of the war (to be accurate, on October 13, 1914), and com-

---

[1] Official text, *American Journal of International Law*, Special Supplement, October, 1916, pp. 336-337.
[2] *Ibid.*, p. 337.
[3] *Ibid.*, p. 338.

municated to the diplomatic agents of the Powers accredited to Berlin.

The material portion of the memorandum of October 13, 1914, in which this ruling is contained, is as follows:

> The equipment of British merchant vessels with artillery is for the purpose of making armed resistance against German cruisers. Resistance of this sort is contrary to international law, because in a military sense a merchant vessel is not permitted to defend itself against a war vessel, an act of resistance giving the warship the right to send the merchant ship to the bottom with crew and passengers. It is a question whether or not ships thus armed would be admitted into ports of a neutral country at all. Such ships, in any event, should not receive any better treatment in neutral ports than a regular warship, and should be subject at least to the rules issued by neutral nations restricting the stay of a warship. If the Government of the United States considers that it fulfils its duty as a neutral nation by confining the admission of armed merchant ships to such ships as are equipped for defensive purposes only, it is pointed out that, so far as determining the warlike character of a ship is concerned, the distinction between the defensive and offensive is irrelevant. The destination of a ship for use of any kind in war is conclusive, and restrictions as to the extent of armament afford no guarantee that ships armed for defensive purposes only will not be used for offensive purposes under certain circumstances.[1]

As the result of negotiations throughout almost the entire period of its neutrality, the United States obtained now and then a recognition of the duty of a belligerent man-of-war to visit and search merchantmen. But this recognition was only in part and does not seem to have been a full compliance with the American request. In fairness to Germany, it should be said that it was in the nature of a concession, not a confession of a duty owing to the changed conditions of maritime warfare. As far as can be learned from the published documents, the nature and the extent of this recognition, and the right and the duty of its submarines to visit and to search merchantmen are stated by the Imperial German Government in the following passage from its note of May 4, 1916:

> The German submarine forces have had, in fact, orders to conduct submarine warfare in accordance with the general principles of visit and search and destruction of merchant vessels

---

[1] Official text, *American Journal of International Law*, Special Supplement, October, 1916, p. 321.

as recognized by international law, the sole exception being the conduct of warfare against the enemy trade carried on enemy freight ships that are encountered in the war zone surrounding Great Britain; with regard to these no assurances have ever been given to the Government of the United States; no such assurance was contained in the declaration of February 8, 1916.[1]

After expressing the hope that the diplomatic relations between the United States and the Imperial German Government would not be severed, as was more than intimated in Secretary Lansing's note in the *Sussex* case, dated April 18, 1916, to which the German note under consideration was a reply, the Imperial authorities, for the reasons stated, made what they were pleased to call a special concession for the balance of the war. Thus:

> The German Government, moreover, is prepared to do its utmost to confine the operations of war for the rest of its duration to the fighting forces of the belligerents, thereby also insuring the freedom of the seas, as principle upon which the German Government believes, now as before, to be in agreement with the Government of the United States.
> The German Government, guided by this idea, notifies the Government of the United States that the German naval forces have received the following orders: In accordance with the general principles of visit and search and destruction of merchant vessels recognized by international law, such vessels, both within and without the area declared as naval war zone, shall not be sunk without warning and without saving human lives, unless these ships attempt to escape or offer resistance.[2]

It is to be observed that, by the express terms of this concession, enemy freight ships encountered in the war zone surrounding Great Britain were not to have the benefit of the general principles of visit and search and destruction of merchant vessels as recognized by international law, that other merchant ships were to be treated in accordance with the general principles of visit and search and destruction of merchant vessels recognized by international law; that, however, the benefit of international law was to be denied them should they "attempt to escape or offer resistance"; and in a passage previously quoted this concession—regarded only as such by the German Government—was not to be enjoyed by neutrals "if her enemy is permitted to continue to apply at will methods of warfare

[1] Official text, *American Journal of International Law*, Special Supplement, October, 1916, p. 196.
[2] *Ibid.*, p. 198.

violating the rules of international law"; and that, finally, armed vessels (meaning by that term apparently any vessel armed with a gun sufficient to stop the submarine) were to be treated as auxiliary cruisers and sent to the bottom with crew and passengers.

This may seem but a small result of constant and persistent negotiation extending over a period of well-nigh two years, for it merely amounted to the statement that Germany would conduct its maritime operations hereafter in accordance with the generally recognized principles of international law, which Germany should have done from the beginning of the war. Yet it was very important to procure a pledge of this kind, because it was a recognition on the part of Germany that its actions had been contrary to international law, as this relieved the United States of the burden of proof in the future. The reservation of the right to continue its conduct contrary to the generally recognized principles of international law during the remainder of the war if the enemy did not mend its ways was a claim on the part of the German Government to do wrong, at the expense of the neutral, if its enemy did not do right. This concession, therefore, judged by the past, was ominous for the future, as was also the pledge to be bound by the general principles "recognized by international law," because Germany reserved to itself the interpretation of the general principles recognized by international law, and in each statement visit and search are coupled with destruction, thus placing, apparently, visit, search, and destruction upon an equality.

CHAPTER XIV

THE ACCEPTED RULES OF MARITIME WARFARE

Section 1. Views of German Publicists

The contentions of the Imperial German Government and of the United States in regard to the conduct of Germany's warfare upon the high seas have been laid before the reader in the form in which they are to be found in the official correspondence between the two Governments, without reference, or with very slight or incidental reference, to the views of publicists whose writings are, according to the decisions of the Supreme Court of the United States, to be taken as evidence of the law of Nations. It is proposed in this place, therefore, to consider the contentions of the two Governments in the light of the law of Nations as expounded by publicists, and for this purpose, in order that the German conception of international law may be adequately represented, only the writings of German publicists of repute will be considered. For if the conduct of the Imperial German Government is in accordance with the views of its accredited publicists published before the war, and indeed before this war could be supposed to have been in contemplation of the Government and, in any event, beyond the knowledge of the publicists, it must be conceded that, although the views of our Government may differ from those expressed and acted upon by Germany, there is authority of no mean order for our Imperial antagonist, and that its actions, however contrary to what we may be pleased to consider the dictates of humanity, cannot be regarded as in violation of international law as the German Government conceives it to be.

First, as to visit and search and the formalities required by the practice of Nations in the exercise of this belligerent right. The nature and extent of the right and the reason for its existence are admirably and fully stated by the distinguished Prussian publicist, August Wilhelm Heffter, a man of large learning, a lawyer by profession, a judge by position, and for many years professor of international law in the University of Berlin.

His treatise entitled *Das Europäische Völkerrecht der Gegenwart*, first published in 1844, has frequently been reprinted and, enriched with Geffcken's notes, it occupies the position in German literature which Dana's edition of Wheaton's *Elements of International Law* holds in the English-speaking world. Indeed, a no less competent authority than the broad-minded and liberal publicist Robert von Mohl considered it from the legal standpoint by far the best in any language.[1]

On the subject-matter in hand Heffter says:

> The means generally resorted to by the belligerents for the purpose of maintaining neutral commerce within the necessary or conventional limits, is called the right of visit. This right entitles the belligerents, either by national vessels, or by commissioned armed vessels, to stop other vessels which they encounter on the seas, to ascertain their nationality, to establish the nature of their cargo and their destination. . . .
>
> The right of search is granted in order that the belligerent may make good his title to certain rights with regard to the enemy and the neutral Nations. . . .
>
> The belligerent may exercise the right of visit:
> 1. Within his own territory;
> 2. Within the territory of his adversary, that is to say, within the enemy roadways, ports, and territorial waters, even including the rivers;
> 3. Lastly, upon the high seas.
>
> But the visit may not be operated within neutral waters, nor within those of the friendly Powers, without the latter's express or tacit consent.
>
> The merchantmen encountered within the above-mentioned areas and whose peaceful destination, dissociated from the operations of the war, is not established by evident and incontrovertible signs, are subject to the visit. The neutral warships are not subject to visit, provided their nationality is undisputed. It should, however, be observed that the flag does not necessarily guarantee their nationality. The belligerents may, on the contrary, stop upon the high seas any kind of transports whose harmlessness is not sufficiently established, both with regard to their cargo and their owner, and with regard to the port whence they came and to which they are destined.
>
> The visit has for its special purpose:
> 1. To ascertain the ownership of the vessel and of the cargo and to establish if the one or the other may not belong to the enemy;

---

[1] Holtzendorff's *Handbuch des Völkerrechts* (Berlin, 1885-1889, 4 vols.), **vol. 1**, p. 486.

2. To ascertain if enemy persons may not be on board of the vessel visited;
3. To establish that the vessel does not carry articles of contraband or of prohibited assistance to the enemy;
4. To prevent the vessel from communicating with blockaded localities.

In consequence, the visit must establish:
1. The nationality of the vessel;
2. The quality, the origin, and the destination of the cargo;
3. The nationality of the crew.[1]

After thus stating the general nature and extent of the right, the place where it may be exercised, its specific purposes and the facts to be established by visit and search, Heffter next indicates the agents of the belligerents by which the right may properly be exercised. Thus, on this point, he says:

The right of visit of neutral vessels is exclusively reserved to the commanders of naval and military forces, especially to the war vessels and to all others provided with commissions issued by the belligerent sovereign, including privateers, provided piracy has not been abolished.[2]

But experience has shown, to speak only of times past, that belligerents are a law unto themselves, and that unless a right granted them be regulated and carefully safeguarded, it is likely to be abused. Because of this the formalities to be observed in the execution of this right are no less important than the right itself, and they are as clear and definite, well understood and recognized as is the right. Therefore, in the next passage to be quoted Heffter mentions the formalities to be followed in boarding the vessel to be visited and searched, if need be, the documents to be examined proving the character of the vessel, its cargo, and the venture in which it is engaged. Thus:

The exercise of the right of visit has been regulated, especially by the Treaty of the Pyrenees,[3] whose dispositions upon this

---

[1] Heffter, *Das Europäische Völkerrecht der Gegenwart* (Berlin, 1888), 8th ed., pp. 372-374.
[2] *Ibid.*, p. 374.
[3] The Treaty of the Pyrenees, concluded between France and Spain in 1659, and which is properly called by Heffter the leading treaty on the subject, affirms and incorporates the law of Nations upon this subject, in its seventeenth article, which reads as follows:

Que s'ils estoient entrez dans les Rades, ou estoient rencontrez en pleine mer, par quelques Navires dudit Seigneur Roi Catholique, ou d'Armateurs particuliers ses Sujets, lesdits Navires d'Espagne, pour éviter

matter have become the European maritime law. These dispositions deal with: the warning to stop; the distance at which the cruiser is to remain; the sending of a limited number of men on board neutral vessels; the examination of the ship's papers. The warning is given by cannon shot fired from the cruiser to inform the vessel of the latter's intention to visit it. The vessel must obey the warning to stop and await the visit. If it does not comply, it exposes itself to being constrained by the use of force. The cruiser may send a boat to the vessel visited, and only two or three men may go on board.

The last formality of the visit, and the most important, is the examination of the ship's papers. The papers which may be examined and serve as proof, are as follows:

The passport and any other certificates establishing the origin of the vessel and of the cargo;

The bill of lading and the charter-party;

The register of the crew;

Lastly, the ship's log-book.[1]

Further details are added from a work of very great authority entitled *Das Moderne Völkerrecht der Civilisirten Staaten*,[2] which is universally considered to be the first adequate statement of international law in the form of a code. Its author, Johann Caspar Bluntschli, Swiss by birth, German by naturalization, and professor of international law in the University of Heidelberg, upheld the traditions of this seat of learning, if he could not be said to have enhanced its prestige,—for it must not be forgotten that the first chair of international law in the world was established in Heidelberg in 1661 and that its first professor was no less a person than Samuel von Pufendorf. Thus, Bluntschli says:

> tout desordre, n'approcheront pas de plus prés les François, que de la portée du canon, & pourront envoyer leur petite Barque ou Chaloupe au bord des Navires ou Barques Françoises, & faire entrer dedans deux ou trois hommes seulement à qui seront montrez les Passeports, par le Maistre ou Patron du Navire François, en la maniere cy-dessus specifiée, selon le Formulaire qui fera inferé à la fin de ce Traité; par lequel il puisse apparoître non seulement de sa charge, mais aussi du lieu de sa demeure & residence, & du nom tant du Maistre & Patron, que du Navire mesme; afin que par ces deux moyens on puisse connoître s'ils portent des Marchandises de Contre-bande, & qu'il apparoisse suffisamment, tant de la qualité du dit Navire, que de son Maistre & Patron: ausquels Passeports & Lettres de Mer, se devra donner entiere foi & creance. Et afin que l'on connoisse mieux leur validité, & qu'elles ne puissent en aucune maniere estre falsifiées & contrefaites, seront données certaines marques & contreseings de chaque costé des deux Seigneurs Rois. (*Corps universal diplomatique au droit des gens*, . . . par J. Dumont [La Haye, 1728, 8 vols.], vol. 6, part 2, p. 264.)

[1] Heffter, *Das Europäische Völkerrecht der Gegenwart*, 8th ed., pp. 374-375.
[2] *Das Moderne Völkerrecht der Civilisirten Staaten*, von J. C. Bluntschli (Nördlingen, 1878).

> The visit consists solely in the examination of the ship's papers.
>
> In case of serious suspicion, *search* of the vessel may be made, and the latter may be seized only in case it transports war contraband.
>
> The State whose vessels are charged with exercising the right of visit is responsible toward the neutral State for any acts of violence or of harshness committed in the course of the visit or of the search.[1]

The reasons for the rule and for the restrictions upon the exercise of the right are thus stated by Bluntschli in connection with the passage last quoted:

> This rule is the necessary corrective measure of the right of visit. The belligerent State which stops a neutral vessel on the high seas, engages always in an act of violation of the freedom and independence of the neutral territory of which such vessel is a floating part. The neutral State tolerates such violation because it deems it inevitable in time of war; but it does not permit such violation beyond certain limits. The crew proceeding to the visit must bear in mind that they are on foreign, neutral territory, and control the conduct of citizens of a friendly State over whom their Government has no right of sovereignty. The war vessel proceeding to the search must therefore take into account the relations of friendship which unite the States living at peace, and must refrain from any act of authority or of violence, so long as no evident guilt has been established.[1]

In order to round out this phase of the subject a further quotation will be made from Bluntschli's distinguished successor, August von Bulmerincq, in the chair of international law in the University of Heidelberg. Like Bluntschli, he was a foreigner by birth, being of Russian nationality, but by naturalization a German subject. He was a specialist in maritime law, indeed the recognized authority on prize law and procedure, and it will always redound to his credit that, through his initiative, a movement was started in behalf of an international prize court, culminating in the Second Hague Peace Conference, which adopted a convention for the creation of this much needed international tribunal upon the proposals of the German and British delegations. Bulmerincq thus separates into its constituent parts the right in question:

> The right to stop, visit, and search indicates the authority of warships of belligerent States to stop, to visit, and to search

[1] Bluntschli, *Das Moderne Völkerrecht der Civilisirten Staaten*, pp. 461-462.

foreign privately owned ships. The three rights are included under the term "right of search." But we must distinguish between the right of visit and the right of search; they correspond to the French *droit de visite* and *recherche* and to the English *right of visit* and *search*. The right of visit indicates, therefore, the international authority of authorized ships to visit private ships, while the right of search confers the right to search them. In treaties and in the instructions issued to the commanders of warships for their conduct in war time towards merchantmen, reference is made only to the right of visit; according to prize regulations, the right of search arises only after the visit has been effected.

After having spoken of the formalities to be observed in effecting the visit, Bulmerincq passes to a consideration of the conditions under which search may be made and seizure effected. On the question of search he says:

> If the ship's papers are not in proper order or if the visit which has taken place has given rise to a well-founded suspicion, then the officer who performed the visit is authorized to proceed with the search of the ship. The ship may not resist search; but should it nevertheless resist, then the search may be carried through by force.
>
> There exists, however, a well-founded suspicion:
> 1) When the ship stopped has not obeyed the order of the warship to stop;
> 2) When the ship stopped has resisted the visit of the holds with regard to which suspicion has arisen that they may hide ship's papers or contraband;
> 3) When duplicate, false, fraudulent, secret, insufficient, or no papers whatever are found on board;
> 4) When the papers have been cast overboard or been destroyed in any other manner, especially when such acts have been resorted to when the ship became aware of the approach of the warship;
> 5) When the ship stopped is sailing under a false flag.
>
> The persons to whom are committed the right of search are not authorized to open or break open any holds which might contain part of the cargo, nor are they authorized arbitrarily to search parts of the cargo which lie about loose on the ship. Rather, in the suspicious cases alluded to, the searching officer must cause the holds to be opened by the captain and have the loose part of the cargo examined with the coöperation of the captain.[1]

Second, as to the sinking of the prize and the saving of crew and

---

[1] *Das Völkerrecht oder das Internationale Recht* (1887), von August von Bulmerincq, p. 372.

passengers. On this point, Heffter, whose authority has already been invoked in the matter of visit and search, has little to say, indicating that in his opinion it was a custom, if a custom at all, more honored in the breach than in the observance. He compresses what he has to say on the subject within the limits of a sentence: "The destruction of the prize may not be effected except in cases of extreme necessity."[1]

It is to be observed that he does not differentiate between enemy and neutral prizes, and rightly so, because, when the first edition of his treatise appeared, the destruction of neutral prizes had not been considered. Indeed, the subject first received attention in the sessions of the Institute of International Law and, while that learned body permitted the destruction of enemy prizes, it rejected the destruction of neutral prizes after much consideration at the session of Heidelberg in 1887. In its International Regulations Concerning Prizes, adopted in 1882, the word enemy was omitted by mistake before vessel in Article 50 of the definitive text (*Annuaire*, vol. 6, p. 221), but the Institute at its Heidelberg session corrected the text by inserting the word "enemy" before vessel (*Annuaire*, vol. 9, pp. 200, 202), thus limiting destruction to enemy vessels. In the eighth edition of Heffter's masterly treatise, which appeared in 1888, its learned editor, Geffcken, like Heffter a member of the Institute of International Law, added the following note to Heffter's text, drawing the distinction between the destruction of enemy and neutral prizes, which had been called to the attention of publicists by the discussions of the Institute:

> Destruction of a neutral ship is admissible only in a case of extreme necessity, for the reason that the status of such a ship is different from that of a clearly enemy ship whose condemnation is certain. Such necessity may be assumed when the ship is no longer seaworthy, or when the captor is being pursued by a superior force by the enemy.

The learned commentator evidently thought that human life was of more importance than the ship, because, while he permitted the inanimate object to be destroyed, he refused to sanction the death of his fellow-beings, saying:

> In any case he must bring the crew of the ship in safety, carefully preserve its papers, and remains responsible to the

---

[1] Heffter, *Das Europäische Völkerrecht der Gegenwart*, p. 301.

owner for the destruction, if the prize court does not confirm the seizure.[1]

On the destruction of prizes and the exceptional circumstances justifying it, the late Ferdinand Perels, the distinguished authority on maritime law and for many years adviser to the Imperial German Admiralty, has this to say in a treatise entitled *Das Internationale Öffentliche Seerecht der Gegenwart,* the second edition of which was published in 1903:

> Destruction of the prize is authorized only in the most exceptional circumstances. It must be so, indeed, because of the absolute necessity of having to resort to a decision of a prize court to ascertaian the validity of the seizure. Such an act as, in general, any resort to force, can be legitimate only in case the prize cannot be taken to a place of safety without running serious danger, or in case the captor cannot preserve the prize without exposing his own vessel to serious danger. . . .
>
> Even if the prize has been destroyed, a judicial decision must confirm the validity of the capture; if the decision declares the seizure illegal the Government of the captor must then make full compensation to the party interested for the loss sustained, and it may not refer such party to the commander of the capturing vessel in order to secure such reparation; the responsibility of the officer is a domestic question which in no way concerns the owner of the vessel or of the cargo.
>
> If the prize is lost through a maritime accident, no damages are paid either for the vessel or the cargo, even although the capture is invalidated by a prize court.[2]

The destruction of neutral prizes had ceased to be academic from the outbreak a year later of the Russo-Japanese War, because of the fact that Russia claimed and exercised the right to destroy neutral prizes, but invariably saved the crew and passengers. As has been pointed out, the subject was discussed at the Second Hague Peace Conference, but no agreement could be forced through permitting or recognizing the destruction of a neutral prize. In the interval between the adjournment of this Conference and the London Naval Conference, where the destruction of a neutral prize was rejected in principle but admitted in exceptional cases and under prescribed conditions, Dr. Emanuel von Ullmann, professor of international law in the University of Munich, published the second edition of his treatise on international law, in which he thus deals with this question:

---

[1] Heffter, *Das Europäische Völkerrecht der Gegenwart,* p. 380, note 6.
[2] Perels, *Das Internationale Öffentliche Seerecht der Gegenwart,* pp. 298-299.

> Ships and cargoes which have been seized must, by the capturing warship, be taken to the nearest port of its State or of an ally for the purpose of securing decision from a prize court. If for any reason whatever a neutral prize cannot be taken to a prize court for action, then (as in the case of enemy private ships) the rule is that destruction of the prize may not follow. It is a matter of controversy as to whether destruction of a neutral prize is *exceptionally* permitted before the prize court has rendered a decision.[1]

After stating that "English practice holds that the neutral prize shall be released" and calling attention to the different practices of other countries, the learned author adds that "In such cases, however, the crew and if possible the cargo, as well as the ship's papers, must be taken to a place of safety." And in another portion of his treatise the same author says, in speaking of the destruction of war vessels that "humanitarian custom commands the rescuing of the shipwrecked in case of the sinking of the ship. . . ."

In the edition of his treatise on international law published in 1913, just one year before the outbreak of the European War, Dr. Franz von Liszt, professor of international law in the University of Berlin, admitted the right to destroy enemy merchantmen, but he hastened to add "in case of destruction care must be exercised for the safety of the persons on board and the preservation of the ship's papers."

In speaking of the destruction of neutral prizes, he says:

> In 1907, the question of the destruction of the neutral prize was the object of animated discussion. According to the Anglo-American proposition, such destruction was to be unreservedly forbidden; but no agreement was come to in this matter. The London Conference has opposed it on principle, but permitted it in case of necessity; namely, if in the attempt to take the captured ship to port, the warship might expose itself to danger, or jeopardize the success of the military operations in which it may at the time be engaged.[2]

Professor von Liszt, however, subordinates the destruction to the saving of human life, saying:

> Before destroying the neutral prize the persons on board must be put into a place of safety and the ship's papers and any other documentary proof must be put on board the warship.

---

[1] *Völkerrecht*, von Emanuel von Ullmann (Tübingen, 1908), pp. 534-535 (*Das Öffentliche Recht der Gegenwart*, vol. 3).

[2] *Das Völkerrecht*, von Franz von Liszt (Berlin, 1913), p. 342.

The statements of von Liszt are based upon the provisions of the Declaration of London regarding the destruction of neutral prizes. Admitting that the Declaration was not binding because not ratified, it nevertheless fairly represented at the time the views of the ten Governments—Germany, Austria-Hungary, France, Great Britain, Italy, Japan, Netherlands, Russia, Spain, United States— taking part in the Conference, and a compromise of opposing views in the interest of all; and, bearing in mind the fact mentioned in the German diplomatic correspondence that the document was declaratory, not amendatory, of the law of Nations, although the preliminary provisions only state that "the rules contained in the following chapters correspond in substance with the generally recognized principles of international law," the Declaration of London is worthy of careful consideration in the matter of neutral prizes. Its provisions, in so far as they relate to the matter in hand, are:

> Article 48. A neutral vessel which has been captured may not be destroyed by the captor; she must be taken into such port as is proper for the determination there of all questions concerning the validity of the prize.
> Article 49. As an exception, a neutral vessel which has been captured by a belligerent warship, and which would be liable to condemnation, may be destroyed if the observance of Article 48 would involve danger to the safety of the warship or to the success of the operations in which she is engaged at the time.
> Article 50. Before the vessel is destroyed all persons on board must be placed in safety, and all the ship's papers and other documents which the parties interested consider relevant for the purpose of deciding on the validity of the capture must be taken on board the warship.

Third, as to resistance of neutral and of enemy merchantmen to capture. On this point only one German authority need be quoted, together with a statement of the views of the Institute of International Law. The German work, to which reference is made, is entitled *Das Seekriegsrecht* (Stuttgart, 1915), by Dr. Hans Wehberg, a young but very distinguished and rising German publicist, then in the judicial service of his country in Düsseldorf, now serving it in the field "somewhere in France."

On the question of resistance of neutral and of enemy merchantmen to visit and search, he says, and his views are quoted on this subject at very great length:

> It has already been emphasized that resistance of neutral merchant ships against search is inadmissible, because the bellig-

erents are entitled to the right of search. On the other hand, enemy merchant ships not excepted from the prize law may resist capture by force. We are here dealing with an act of hostility, and not with the exercise of a repressive right.

It is true that requisitions, etc., may be exacted in warfare on land and that resistance thereto is not admissible. But, in such case, conditions are essentially different. It is quite certain that originally there existed no "right" of requisition, and whenever requisitions were exacted, they represented acts of force against which the population had a right to defend itself. In modern times, however, the States have recognized a "right" to make requisitions in warfare on land. The necessary consequence was that private persons were enjoined not to resist by force when requisitions were made. The idea that only organized troops may resort to force has been fully recognized with regard to warfare on land. This result was quite natural in view of the fact that requisitions were made not in order to injure the enemy, but merely to provide for the needs of the army of occupation.

It is, however, erroneous to say that, because in warfare on land armed resistance may not be resorted to by peaceful persons, this must therefore equally apply to naval warfare. If this were so, it would be equally true to say that private property being inviolable in warfare on land, the same idea should apply to naval warfare; but we have repeatedly emphasized the indefensibility of this idea. Such conclusions lose sight of the fact that the peculiar nature of the scene of maritime operations introduces a sharp distinction between land and maritime warfare. It was possible to recognize in warfare on land a "right" to make requisitions because in such case the seizure of private property was not the primary purpose of the act, and consequently, the interests of private persons could be given proper consideration. The ancient, unrestricted right to seize enemy property on land, the primary object of which was to do all possible harm to the country, developed into a real "right" because bounds were thus set to the former unlimited right, and this was made possible only by recognizing a limited "right." In maritime warfare, however, the belligerents aim to destroy maritime commerce as far as possible. To grant to the adversary a "right to capture property" would be to issue to him a license without at the same time requiring from him an equivalent consideration. It is evident, therefore, that no conclusions, applicable to maritime warfare, can be derived from principles which have been generally applied in warfare on land.

The idea that "armed resistance may be offered only on the part of organized troops" is in a general way just as erroneous as the assertion that war is only a legal relation between States from which the peaceful population is excluded. It must be remembered that the States have never yet recognized this principle unreservedly. They have established principles only for certain situations which most frequently arise in time of war. The idea that war is being waged only between organized troops may be admitted unreservedly with regard to warfare on land. The same idea must be held to be true with regard to operations between the maritime forces. In all other respects, however, and in most recent times during which the modern principles of warfare have asserted themselves, the States have never discussed the problem of armed resistance on the part of enemy merchant ships; and though some theorists and ideologists have insisted upon the absolute application of that principle to all imaginable cases, this question, which has its very peculiar aspects, cannot be decided in the same way. The men who hastily called for the acceptance of general principles have had no idea whatever of the difference between naval warfare and warfare on land, and, in consequence, have recommended basic principles which are most unreasonable.

Resistance of enemy merchant ships to capture would be then inadmissible only in case a rule against this had found common recognition. But in truth, no single example can be produced from international precedents in which the States have held resistance as illegal. Rather, in the celebrated decision of Lord Stowell in the case of *The Catharina Elizabeth*,[1] resistance was declared permissible, and Article 10 of the American Naval War Code takes the same viewpoint. Also by far the greater number of authors and the Institute of International Law share this view.

Also, *de lege ferenda*, the prevailing view is to be advocated. Should great merchant ships worth millions allow themselves to be taken by small ships only because the latter comply with the requirements of a so-called warship? Is it not more chivalrous to have the power of arms rather than a (pretended) rule of international law, on paper, decide the matter? It must be remembered that in the earliest stages of privateering the merchant ships fought valiantly against the privateers, and many a one, seriously damaged, had to return to its base. This condition of affairs finally led to a stronger military control over the privateers and care was taken that only strongly equipped ships were employed to capture enemy merchant ships. In time the privateers were so stoutly armed that enemy merchant ships surrendered voluntarily in ever increasing numbers. With the advent of the modern auxiliary cruisers the possibility has been offered merchant ships successfully to escape capture through armed resistance. For what reason then should auxiliary cruisers which have replaced the ancient privateers be forbidden to engage in acts which privateers had undoubtedly been permitted to engage in before? We know nothing at all as to whether or not enemy merchantmen were not formerly permitted to defend

[1] 5 Robinson, p. 206.

themselves against warships. Whosoever declares that resistance against warships is forbidden, must prove that the States have declared unanimously against resistance to warships as contrasted with privateers. If this were so, resistance against auxiliary cruisers would of course be forbidden, because the latter, as contrasted with privateers, are warships. The fact that practice does not supply us with decisions in regard to the right of defense against warships clearly indicates that the States regarded such an act as permissible. Are we to believe that such cases did not occur or that a stout merchant ship invariably surrendered to a small warship? In addition to all this it should be stated that, when accurately interpreted, the prize law confers upon enemy merchant ships authority to defend themselves against any and all attacks on the part of the warships.

An enemy merchant ship is therefore entitled to defend itself against an enemy attack; it is even entitled to this right with regard to the matter of visit. For the visit constitutes the first act of capture. The merchant ship which has been attacked may even seize the warship which it has overcome. This situation which corresponds with the prevailing right is nevertheless subject to serious misgivings in so far as the seizure of the attacked merchant ship is concerned, and this for the reason that the lines of separation between attack and defense can be easily infringed.[1]

The Institute of International Law, to which Dr. Wehberg refers, met at Oxford in the first week of August, 1913, exactly one year before the outbreak of the European War. The sessions were largely attended and publicists representing eighteen different countries were present. The session was almost exclusively devoted to the consideration of the proposed manual of the laws of maritime warfare. The draft of the manual was carefully considered and adopted as modified by fifty-three of the fifty-four members present, one not voting because he had not taken part in the previous proceedings.

For present purposes it is only necessary to call attention to Article 12 of the manual as adopted, which reads as follows:

> Article 12. *Privateering, private vessels, public vessels not warships.* Privateering is forbidden.
> Apart from the conditions laid down in Articles 3 and following, neither public nor private vessels, nor their personnel, may commit acts of hostility against the enemy.
> Both may, however, use force to defend themselves against the attack of an enemy vessel.[2]

[1] *Das Seekriegsrecht*, von Hans Wehberg (Stuttgart, 1915), pp. 282-286 (*Handbuch des Völkerrechts*, vol. 4, parts 1 and 2).
[2] *Resolutions of the Institute of International Law* (New York, Oxford Press 1916), p. 177.

It will be observed that by this article public vessels (other than men-of-war) and merchantmen may not commit acts of hostility against the enemy; that is to say, not being commissioned as war vessels, they cannot engage in aggressive or offensive warfare. But, if attacked, they may, nevertheless, by the third paragraph of the article, defend themselves against the enemy. When this article was up for consideration, Dr. Triepel, professor of international law in the University of Berlin, moved that its third paragraph be suppressed, stating that "a merchantman never has the right of self-defense, even in case the attack directed against it is unlawful. The vessel is not entitled to sit in judgment upon this point." Dr. Niemeyer, professor of international law in the University of Kiel, observed that the right of self-defense against an act of force was self-evident and, like his colleague, he proposed the suppression of the third paragraph, but for the very different reason that "to insert a disposition of this kind would be equivalent to conceding that a contrary opinion was possible."

Lord Reay, who had been a member of the British delegation to the Second Hague Peace Conference, called attention to the importance of the article, stating that the lawfulness of the permission given by the Admiralty to certain large steamers to carry on board four cannon had been contested even by well-informed persons. The text of the third paragraph of Article 12 (originally 13) would, he stated, remove all doubt on this point. He therefore asked the Institute to proclaim for merchantmen under the given conditions the right of legitimate defense. The Institute thus had before it not merely a question of the right in the abstract but a case in the concrete, namely, the right of British merchantmen to use arms placed upon them for defense against attack. Dr. Triepel's motion was put to a vote and lost. Another attempt to amend the article was likewise defeated and, as the official report of the proceedings says:

> Article 13, which was proposed by the Commission, was voted by the Institute by a large majority.

and, as previously stated, the manual, containing this very article, was adopted without a dissenting vote.[1]

After the Oxford session of the Institute of International Law, Professor Oppenheim, who had taken part in the discussions, published an article showing that enemy ships have the right to defend

[1] *Annuaire de l'Institut de Droit International*, 1913, pp. 515-521, 600-609.

themselves against attack.¹ Dr. Triepel, who, it will be remembered, had moved in the Oxford session that merchant ships should be denied the right to defend themselves against attack, published a reply to Professor Oppenheim in which he said:

> He is right. The literature is upon his side. Not only in the English and the Anglo-American works on international law and especially on maritime law, but also in the French, Belgian, Italian, and Swedish science the right of self-defense as far as I can see is generally acknowledged. Only in very isolated cases a doubt is ventured. The majority of the later German writers maintain silence on the question. In the older writers, the English doctrine is followed.²

It is not necessary to comment upon the views of the German publicists. The extracts quoted speak for themselves. The views of the Institute of International Law, although it is not an official body, are accepted often as of greater weight than the actions of Government, whose motives are sometimes questioned; and it is common knowledge that the labors of the Institute supplied The Hague Peace Conferences with the materials which its delegates put in the form of international conventions. Indeed, a great statesman of our day has gone so far as to say that, without the preliminary work of the Institute, the work of the Conferences would have been impossible.

And, finally, the views of ten Governments in the matter of the destruction of neutral prizes should not be overlooked, requiring passengers and crew to be saved, even although the declaration itself was not ratified, because, if the provisions of the Declaration of London were not wholly declaratory of the law of Nations, they nevertheless represented the rules of conduct which the great maritime Powers, in time of peace, professed themselves willing to apply in time of war.

But, we do not need to test the conduct of the Imperial German Government by the views expressed by its most distinguished publicists, for, after all, the views of publicists are binding only in so far as they state the law and practice of Nations, and they are only evidence of this law and of this practice.

[1] Oppenheim, "*Die Stellung der feindlichen Kauffahrteischiffe im Seekrieg*," *Zeitschrift für Völkerrecht*, vol. 8, pp. 154-159.
[2] Triepel, "*Der Widerstand feindlicher Handelsschiffe gegen die Aufbringung*," *Zeitschrift für Völkerrecht*, vol. 8, pp. 378-406.

Section 2. The German Prize Ordinance [1]

We do not need to speculate as to the general principles of visit and search and destruction of merchant vessels as recognized by international law before the outbreak of the war, as these were authoritatively stated in the rules and regulations of the different nations, and by no nation more clearly, positively, and unmistakably than by Germany in its prize ordinance, approved September 30, 1909, in time of peace, and promulgated on August 3, 1914, in time of war. Under the caption "Object of stoppage and search" and "Manner of exercising the right," the German Prize Code says in Article 4:

> The object of the stoppage and search of a merchant vessel is to determine:
> a) the nationality of the vessel;
> b) whether she has contraband on board;
> c) whether she is assisting the enemy in an unneutral manner;
> d) whether she is guilty of a breach of blockade.
>
> The stoppage and search shall take place only if the commander deems that it will be successful. All acts shall be done in such manner—even against the enemy—as to be compatible with the honor of the German Empire, and with such regard towards neutrals as may be in conformity with the law of Nations and the interests of Germany.

Under the caption "Determination of national character of vessel," the Prize Code provides, in Article 11, that "the enemy or neutral character of a vessel is determined by the flag which she is entitled to fly." After explaining that the flag which a vessel is entitled to fly is usually set forth in an official document which every merchant vessel must have on board, Article 11 stipulates that: "If the nationality of a vessel cannot be determined beyond question, more especially if the official document required by the flag law of the particular state is lacking, the vessel is to be treated as an enemy vessel." Under the caption "Resistance to search or capture," the Prize Code says in Article 16 that: "A neutral vessel is to be regarded as having an enemy character, if . . . (b) it resists by force the measures taken against it under the prize law. Force of arms may be employed against such vessel, until it ceases to resist. A mere attempt to escape is not to be regarded as a forcible resistance."

[1] "*Prisenordnung,*" *Reichsgesetzblatt*, September 30, 1909; April 15, 1911; August 3, 1914; March 26, 1915; *The Prize Code of the German Empire* as in force July 1, 1915 (translated and edited by Charles Henry Huberich and Richard King; New York; Baker, Voorhis & Co., 1915).

Part VI of the Prize Code is devoted to procedure in cases of stoppage, search, and capture of neutral vessels. It is provided that when a vessel under a neutral flag is stopped to be searched, this must be done with as little inconvenience as possible to the neutral ship. (Article 81.) The command to stop is given by means of signals, and the ensign or pennant is sooner or simultaneously displayed. "During a pursuit the war ensign need not be displayed and the use of any merchant flag is permitted." (Article 82.) If the vessel does not stop or offers resistance, force may be used to stop it. (Article 83.) When the vessel has stopped, a boarding party, consisting of an officer, a second officer, and a limited number of unarmed members of the crew, conveyed in an unarmed boat, is sent from the cruiser to the merchant vessel. (Article 84.) The commander can under no circumstances require the master to come on board the war vessel or to send a boat, members of the crew, the ship's papers, etc., to the latter. (Article 81.) If conditions of the weather make it impossible to launch a boat, the merchant vessel may be ordered to follow the warship until it is possible to carry out the search. (Article 85.) The method of conducting the search is prescribed in detail as follows: The officer, accompanied only by the second officer, goes on board and requests an inspection of the ship's papers. If the master refuses, the officer demands an inspection, and a further refusal is good ground for the capture of the vessel. (Article 86.) So far as possible, the identity and nationality of the vessel, as well as its home port, port of sailing, destination, and character and destination of its cargo, are determined from the ship's papers. (Article 87.) If the officer concludes from the investigation of the papers that the vessel is not subject to capture, he releases her, after making an entry of the visit and search in the ship's log. (Article 88.) The master is entitled to file with him written exceptions to the manner in which the visit took place. (Article 89.)

If, upon inspection of the ship's papers, the officer concludes that there are grounds to suspect the vessel, he proceeds to a search, which is carried out, according to Article 90, by "a more minute determination of the identity of the ship from the statements in her papers (alterations in external features, marks, shipping marks, name plates to be noted), and an investigation of the correctness and completeness of the statements in the ship's papers regarding the status of the vessel and cargo. The search involves an examination of the master, the crew (in case there are grounds for suspecting a transfer from one flag to another, and the law of the flag determines the national composition of the crew, there should be a comparison of the signatures of the crew and those on the muster roll), and passengers. No coercion by threats is to be used. The vessel and cargo are also to be examined. This latter takes place with the assistance of the boat's crew, which may, if necessary, be increased, and, unless the master refuses, in his presence. The master shall cause the opening of the seals and wrappings or state the best manner of opening the same. So far as possible injuries are to be avoided.''

If the search cannot be immediately accomplished, it may be deferred until a subsequent time at a suitable place. (Article 91.) If, as the result of the search, the officer concludes that the vessel is not subject to capture, the vessel and cargo must be carefully restored to their former condition and released, after proper entries in the ship's log. (Article 92.) If parts of the cargo only are subject to condemnation, the commander may either make a capture, seize the parts of the cargo in question, or release the vessel without further action, but he may not relinquish the right to seize against the payment of money. (Article 93.) If the commander believes the vessel subject to condemnation, he proceeds to a capture (Article 94), the method of which is prescribed in Article 95 as follows:

> The capture is effected by notice, of which a protocol is given to the master, placing the vessel in charge of a prize crew, and raising the war ensign. If at the outset it is impossible to place a prize crew on board, and together with the placing of such crew on board to raise the war ensign, the vessel is to be ordered to lower her flag, and to follow the course designated to her by the commander.
>
> The flying of the war ensign does not convert the vessel into a vessel of war.

A report of the capture is sent immediately to the Admiralty. (Article 96.) If, after capture, it appears from further evidence that the vessel was captured illegally, it is released immediately. (Article 97.) Demands for compensation, either after search without capture or upon release after capture, are adjusted, if possible, before the release of the vessel. (Articles 92 and 97.)

Part VIII of the Prize Code is devoted to the method of dealing with captured vessels and cargo seized. Article 113 deals with the destruction of prizes and is as follows:

Where a neutral vessel has been captured under the circumstances set forth in Article 39, for carrying contraband, or in Articles 77 and 78, for breach of blockade, or in Article 51, for rendering unneutral services, the commander may destroy the same, provided that:

    a) the vessel is subject to condemnation . . . and, in addition thereto,

    b) the bringing into port would subject the war vessel to danger, or be liable to impede the success of the operations in which it is at the time engaged. Among other circumstances, this may, *inter alia*, be assumed to be the case, if:

        a) the vessel, on account of its defective condition or by reason of deficiency of supplies, cannot be brought into port; or

        b) the vessel cannot follow the war vessel, and is therefore liable to recapture; or

        c) the proximity of the enemy forces gives ground for a fear of recapture; or

        d) the war vessel is not in a position to furnish an adequate prize crew.

Article 116 relates to the safety of persons on board and reads literally as follows:

Before proceeding to a destruction of the vessel, the safety of all persons on board, and, so far as possible, their effects, is to be provided for, and all ship's papers and other evidentiary material, which, according to the views of the persons at interest, is of value for the formulation of the judgment of the prize court, are to be taken over by the commander.

It will be observed that, in the provisions of the Prize Code which have been quoted, there is no reference to visit and search of merchant vessels of the enemy, and the articles which have been quoted apply expressly to neutral merchantmen. There are, however, several statements from which a neutral could presume, although apparently the German authorities have not drawn this conclusion, that merchant vessels of the enemy were entitled to the formalities of visit and search. Indeed, the very opening paragraph of the Prize Code is more than an intimation. This paragraph reads literally:

During a war the commanders of H. M. ships of war have the right to stop and search enemy and neutral merchant vessels, and to seize—and, in exceptional cases, to destroy—the same, together with the enemy and neutral goods found thereon.

In the second article it is stated that "public vessels of the enemy are confiscable under the laws of war, without further proceedings," which would seem to imply that private vessels are subject to further proceedings. It is, therefore, important to determine what are and what are not private vessels. This the next paragraph of the article proceeds to do and at the same time to lay down the ear-marks of public vessels.

> Public vessels comprise ships of war as well as ships used in the public service of and subject to the command of the state. Other ships, the property of the state, are placed in the same category.
> The necessary criteria of a ship of war are: the war ensign (usually in conjunction with the pennant), a commander appointed by the state, whose name appears in the list of officers of the navy, and a crew under naval discipline.

A proper construction of this would seem to be that, if a vessel did not meet these requirements it was not to be considered a public vessel, although it is only fair to add that it does not of necessity follow that all vessels not war vessels are to be considered as entitled to the privileges of merchantmen. However, some light appears to be thrown on the subject by the schedule annexed to the Prize Code, dated June 22, 1914, prepared apparently in contemplation of war. This schedule consists of two paragraphs, the first relating to offensive action of an armed ship, the second dealing with the resistance of an armed ship to measures taken against it and the treatment to be accorded it. Thus:

> 1. The exercise of the right of stoppage, search, and capture, as well as any attack made by an armed merchant vessel against a German or neutral merchant vessel is piracy. The crew is to be dealt with under the ordinance relating to extraordinary martial law.
> 2. If an armed enemy merchant vessel offers armed resistance against measures taken under the law of prize, such resistance is to be overcome with all means available. The enemy government bears all responsibility for any damages to the vessel, cargo, and passengers. The crew are to be taken as prisoners of war. The passengers are to be left to go free, unless it appears that they participated in the resistance. In the latter case they may be proceeded against under extraordinary martial law.

The wording of this schedule seems to make it clear that we are here dealing with "an armed merchant vessel" which has not been incorporated in the navy and which is not commanded by a naval officer, or with the crew subject to military discipline. Otherwise it would have the right of stoppage, search, and capture, which a merchant vessel would not possess. This interpretation seems to be confirmed by the second paragraph, because by its express terms "an armed merchant vessel" in the sense of the schedule appears to be one carrying "cargo and passengers," and it is well known that men-of-war carry neither cargo nor passengers. Again, the statement that "the crew are to be taken as prisoners of war" can only refer to a merchantman, because it would be unnecessary to state that the crew of a war vessel should be made prisoners of war notwithstanding resistance, whereas it might be doubted whether the crew of an armed merchant vessel which resisted would be treated as prisoners of war or, like passengers taking part in resistance, subjected to the extraordinary provisions of martial law.

However this may be, the American Government from the beginning to the end of its neutrality considered a merchant ship, armed for defensive purposes, and only using force as a defense against attack, as a merchantman and subject to the treatment of a merchantman, namely, to visit and search and the preservation of the lives of the officers, crew, and passengers. Although the United States did not concede the right to destroy neutral prizes, it had a right to expect, from the express provisions of the German Prize Ordinance of August 3, 1914, that, before resorting to this extreme measure, the merchantman should be subjected to visit and search in order that the neutral vessel should not by mistake be treated as an enemy vessel, and that, in any event, the lives of persons aboard, of one as well as the other, should be saved. This was expressly provided for in respect to neutral merchantmen and it was incidentally provided for in the case of armed enemy merchant vessels, because not even the most powerful and efficient of belligerents can make of the dead prisoners of war.

SECTION 3. THE PRUSSIAN-AMERICAN TREATIES

But whether the German publicists whose views have been invoked would condemn or justify the action of the Imperial German Government in its conduct upon the high seas, or whether the views of publicists of other nationalities would condemn or justify that action, is immaterial from the legal, although not from the moral, point of view, because the Imperial German Government was not a free agent or, to use a favorite German expression, did not have a free hand in these matters, as it was bound hand and foot, so to speak, by the provisions of treaties concluded long before the war, repeatedly recognized and invoked before the war, and indeed cited by the Imperial German Government itself during the course of the war as binding that Government and the United States.

The provisions of these treaties are not the result of a sudden inspiration, but of negotiation extending over many years, and they had stood the test of the wars of the French Revolution and of the Empire. The treaty of May 1, 1828, between Prussia and the United States, in force and applicable, in the opinion of both Governments, to the German Empire as well as to the United States, revived the twelfth article of the first treaty between the two countries of September 10, 1785, and articles thirteen to twenty-four of the second treaty of July 11, 1799, between them.

Article 12 of the treaty of 1785 reads as follows:

> If one of the contracting parties should be engaged in war with any other Power, the free intercourse and commerce of the subjects or citizens of the party remaining neuter with the belligerent Powers shall not be interrupted. On the contrary, in that case, as in full peace, the vessels of the neutral party may navigate freely to and from the ports and on the coasts of the belligerent parties, free vessels making free goods, insomuch that all things shall be adjudged free which shall be on board any vessel belonging to the neutral party, although such things belong to an enemy of the other; and the same freedom shall be extended to persons who shall be on board a free vessel, although they should be enemies to the other party, unless they be soldiers in actual service of such enemy.[1]

This article means, if it means anything, that the United States had the right of free intercourse and commerce with Germany's enemy or enemies to the same degree and under the same conditions as if war had not broken out and as if the world were at peace. The article does not stop here, but states that the principle of free ships, free goods, shall apply not merely to the vessel and to its cargo but to all persons on board, "although they should be enemies to the other party," with the very proper restriction, "unless they be soldiers in actual service of such enemy." And yet the Imperial German Government, in the teeth of this treaty, has prohibited all trade with Great Britain and has actually sunk American vessels attempt-

[1] Malloy's *Treaties, etc., between the United States and Other Powers*, vol. 2, p. 1481.

ing to trade with Great Britain, together with the neutral members of the crew and passengers on board.

It was not to be expected that there should be no restrictions placed upon intercourse with Prussia's enemy, even although the article under consideration seemed to imply that intercourse and commerce with the enemy should be free and untrammeled. Incidents would be sure to arise if the matter were left here. Therefore, Article 13 of the treaty of 1799, dealt with and specified the commerce which should be illegal in order, as the treaty said, to prevent "all the difficulties and misunderstandings that usually arise respecting merchandise of contraband." It therefore enumerated the articles that should be considered contraband by the two countries, stating them generally as "arms, ammunition, and military stores of every kind." In the same connection, indeed in the same sentence and without interruption, the treaty provided that "no such articles carried in the vessels, or by the subjects or citizens of one of the parties to the enemies of the other, shall be deemed contraband, so as to induce confiscation or condemnation and a loss of property to individuals."

It was likewise foreseen that the delivery of contraband to the enemy would prejudice the warlike operations of the belligerent party, but the treaty was to be satisfied, not by causing loss to the contracting party happening to be neutral, but by enabling the party belligerent to intercept and to purchase the contraband for its own use, thus supplying its needs at its own expense and depriving the enemy of the contraband without causing loss to the other contracting party. Thus Article 13 continues:

> Nevertheless, it shall be lawful to stop such vessels and articles, and to detain them for such length of time as the captors may think necessary to prevent the inconvenience or damage that might ensue from their proceeding, paying, however, a reasonable compensation for the loss such arrest shall occasion to the proprietors: And it shall further be allowed to use in the service of the captors the whole or any part of the military stores so detained, paying the owners the full value of the same, to be ascertained by the current price at the place of its destination.[1]

Foreseeing further that disputes were likely to occur as to the price to be paid for the articles thus detained and used, it was wisely provided that neither party was to determine the price, but that, as this would require negotiation and might result in disagree-

[1] Malloy, *Treaties between the United States and Other Powers*, vol. 2, p. 1481.

ment, the price at the place of delivery, however large it might be, was to be accepted by the parties and paid by the belligerent availing itself of the right to possess itself of the articles.

But this was not all. It was further foreseen that detaining the articles for a considerable period of time might throw a loss upon the neutral owner without a corresponding advantage to the belligerent, whose purpose was to prevent delivery to the enemy. Therefore the treaty contains a provision calculated to prevent the difficulties that were sure to arise unless the neutral party were permitted, by delivery to the belligerent, to escape the consequences of unlimited detention on the part of a belligerent. This provision runs as follows:

> But in the case supposed, of a vessel stopped for articles heretofore deemed contraband, if the master of the vessel stopped will deliver out the goods supposed to be of contraband nature, he shall be admitted to do it, and the vessel shall not in that case be carried into any port, nor further detained, but shall be allowed to proceed on her voyage.

It would seem to need no legal subtlety to condemn the action of the Imperial German Government in stopping in the South Atlantic waters the American schooner *Frye* on a voyage to Great Britain, carrying articles which the Imperial Government declared to be contraband and, instead of allowing the master to deliver out the articles and to proceed upon his voyage without delay, to sink the vessel.

It was likewise foreseen that difficulties were likely to arise regarding the identity of each other's vessels in the matter of visit and search when one of the contracting parties was at war with another party. Therefore "to insure to the vessels of the two contracting parties the advantage of being readily and certainly known in time of war," the two nations agreed by Article 14 that their vessels should carry certain sea-letters and documents, to wit: a passport, charter party, and a list of the ship's company. The meaning of this provision would seem to be clear, that a vessel provided with these papers was to be considered as an American vessel and as such entitled to the protection of the treaty.

To prevent all disorder and violence in cases of visit and search Article 15 stipulated that:

> When the vessel of the neutral party, sailing without convoy, shall be met by any vessel of war, public or private, of the other party, such vessel of war shall not approach within cannon-

shot of the said neutral vessel, nor send more than two or three men in their boat on board the same to examine her sea-letters or passports. And all persons belonging to any vessel of war, public or private, who shall molest or injure in any manner whatever, the people, the vessels, or effects of the other party, shall be responsible in their persons and property for damages and interest, sufficient security for which shall be given by all commanders of private armed vessels before they are commissioned.[1]

It is difficult to comment on the provisions of these articles without seeming to reflect upon the intelligence of the reader, as they either mean what they say or are a solemn mockery, unworthy of two great Nations. They mean and they were intended to mean that the belligerent had a right under international law and by the treaty to ascertain the character of the vessel claiming to be neutral, and, in so far as a vessel claiming to be American was concerned, the treaty provided the evidence to establish American character and the formalities of visit and search in order to ascertain the destination and nature of its cargo. It hardly needs to be called to the reader's attention that the action of German submarines has been opposed alike to the letter and the spirit of this treaty, and that, as far as the United States was concerned, the submarine has operated illegally because it has not allowed American vessels free intercourse and commerce with Germany's enemies, it has not "admitted" the vessel to proceed upon its voyage upon delivery out of the cargo when contraband, and it has not observed the formalities of visit and search prescribed by the two countries, binding the conduct as well as the conscience of each.

If it should be contended that the provisions of these treaties, acceptable in 1828, had become unacceptable in 1914 as tending to restrict the conduct of the party belligerent without a corresponding benefit to the neutral party, it should be said that, upon the eve of the outbreak of the war, as well as after its outbreak, the Imperial German Government itself insisted that the relations between the two countries were determined by the provisions of the Prussian treaties, which each country considered as binding Prussia when it became merged in the North German Confederation, as binding the North German Confederation of which Prussia became a part, and as still binding Prussia when the North German Confederation was dissolved and the German Empire was formed under the leadership of Prussia.

[1] Malloy, *Treaties between the United States and Other Powers*, vol. 2, p. 1482.

CHAPTER XV

RENEWAL OF SUBMARINE WARFARE

On January 31, 1917, more than a month after the President of the United States had tried to elicit from the belligerents a statement of the terms of peace which they would consider in order to furnish a basis of negotiations tending towards peace, and within a week of the address of the President to the Senate, in which he outlined the international conditions and the principles which, in his opinion, were requisite to a durable peace—that is to say, while the President of the United States was thinking of the means whereby peace might be brought about and maintained, not whereby war might be declared and prosecuted—a note was addressed by the German Ambassador to Secretary Lansing, stating that on and after the 1st day of February, 1917, submarine warfare would be prosecuted without distinction between neutral and enemy ships found within the proscribed areas, thus withdrawing from the United States the guarantees hitherto made, and especially the pledge of May 4, 1916.

This action was foreshadowed in the Zimmermann letter, dated January 19, 1917, addressed to the German Minister in Mexico, which was intercepted on its passage through the United States by American authorities. This letter indicates a determination already reached by Germany to prosecute submarine warfare even more ruthlessly than theretofore, notwithstanding its assurance to the United States and notwithstanding the possibility of rupture with the United States, although the Imperial German Government affected to believe that the United States might be kept a neutral. But in the event that the United States resented, as it did, the repudiation of Germany's promises and resorted to arms, an alliance was to be made in time of peace with Mexico, with which Germany was friendly, and with Japan, with which it was at war, for the partition of the United States.[1]

The German Ambassador's note of January 31, 1917, opens with language of friendly regard and commendation of the President's

[1] For a full consideration of the Zimmermann letter see *infra*, p. 309.

motives and expresses the regret of his country at the impossibility of realizing the President's lofty ideal because of the attitude of its enemies. These observations are evidently intended to show that a new situation has been "forced" upon the Imperial German Government which it must meet with vigor and effect, because the Ambassador, after this introduction, begins what may be regarded as the second part of his note:

> A new situation has thus been created which forces Germany to new decisions. Since two years and a half England is using her naval power for a criminal attempt to force Germany into submission by starvation. In brutal contempt of international law the group of Powers led by England does not only curtail the legitimate trade of their opponents but they also by ruthless pressure compel neutral countries either to altogether forego every trade not agreeable to the Entente Powers or to limit it according to their arbitrary decrees. The American Government knows the steps which have been taken to cause England and her allies to return to the rules of International Law and to respect the freedom of the seas. The English Government, however, insists upon continuing its war of starvation, which does not at all affect the military power of its opponents, but compels women and children, the sick and the aged to suffer, for their country, pains and privations which endanger the vitality of the nation. Thus British tyranny mercilessly increases the sufferings of the world, indifferent to the laws of humanity, indifferent to the protests of the Neutrals whom they severely harm, indifferent even to the silent longing for peace among England's own allies. Each day of the terrible struggle causes new destruction, new sufferings. Each day shortening the war will, on both sides, preserve the life of thousands of brave soldiers and be a benefit to mankind.[1]

It seems proper to repeat in this connection that international law allows a belligerent, both by land and sea, to starve its opponent into submission and that, if Great Britain did not have the right to starve its enemy into submission, Germany would not have the right to starve Great Britain into submission. The methods adopted by Great Britain to effect this right may be open to criticism and the methods employed by the Imperial German Government may likewise be open to criticism, without, however, affecting the right to starve the enemy by means recognized and allowed by the law of Nations. The impossibility of the German statement, however, for present purposes lies in the fact that the unrestricted warfare which

---

[1] Official text published by the Department of State.

the note and its inclosed memorandum announced is put upon the basis of retaliation for the illegal acts of Great Britain. Thus:

> The Imperial Government could not justify before its own conscience, before the German people, and before history the neglect of any means destined to bring about the end of the war. Like the President of the United States the Imperial Government had hoped to reach this goal by negotiations. After the attempts to come to an understanding with the Entente Powers have been answered by the latter with the announcement of an intensified continuation of the war, the Imperial Government—in order to serve the welfare of mankind in a higher sense and not to wrong its own people—is now compelled to continue the fight for existence, again forced upon it, with the full employment of all the weapons which are at its disposal.[1]

After these statements of a general nature, suggesting but not actually declaring an intention to resort to submarine warfare, unless it is conveyed by the expression "with the full employment of all the weapons at its disposal," the Ambassador concludes this remarkable communication with an expression of trust and of hope, which, with the *Sussex* correspondence in mind, should have seemed to him as unjustified as it certainly did appear unjustified to the President, the Secretary of State, and to the American people, "that the people and Government of the United States will understand the motives for this decision and its necessity," and "that the United States may view the new situation from the lofty heights of impartiality and assist, on their part, to prevent further misery and avoidable sacrifice of human life."[1]

The Ambassador then refers to "two memoranda regarding the details of the contemplated military measures at sea," which he inclosed, announcing unrestricted submarine warfare contrary to the assurances given to the American Government and in derogation of the principles stated in the communication transmitting them.

The first memorandum is a general announcement in the language of the Zimmermann note of "submarine warfare unrestricted" and the "employment of ruthless submarine warfare." The second prescribes the area in which "submarine warfare unrestricted" and the "employment of ruthless submarine warfare" will be prosecuted. The first memorandum is a restatement of the views of the Imperial

[1] Official text published by the Department of State.

German Government contained in its previous notes, and more especially in the note of the Ambassador accompanying the memorandum. It states that "Germany has so far not made unrestricted use of the weapon she possesses in her submarines"; that "Germany is unable further to forego the full use of her submarines"; that the United States, understanding the situation forced upon Germany by the brutal methods of warfare adopted by Germany's enemies and their determination to destroy the Central Powers, "will further realize that the now openly disclosed intentions of the Entente Allies give back to Germany the freedom of action which she reserved in her note addressed to the Government of the United States on May 4, 1916."

The reservation referred to was the freedom of action apparently to prosecute submarine warfare unrestricted and ruthless submarine warfare in case the United States did not secure from Great Britain the renunciation of the illegal practices copiously set forth in the various German notes to the United States. Contenting itself with this reference without a quotation of the pledge and of the reservation, the memorandum thus continues:

> Under these circumstances Germany will meet the illegal measures of her enemies by forcibly preventing after February 1, 1917, in a zone around Great Britain, France, Italy, and in the Eastern Mediterranean, all navigation, that of neutrals included, from and to England and from and to France, etc., etc. All ships met within that zone will be sunk.[1]

It will again be observed that this act is retaliation, and the final justification of it and the hope of concurrence in its provisions are thus stated in what is believed to be the final note on this question to the United States. It is therefore quoted in full:

> The Imperial Government is confident that this measure will result in a speedy termination of the war and in the restoration of peace which the Government of the United States has so much at heart. Like the Government of the United States, Germany and her allies had hoped to reach this goal by negotiations. Now that the war, through the fault of Germany's enemies, has to be continued, the Imperial Government feels sure that the Government of the United States will understand the necessity of adopting such measures as are destined to bring about a speedy end of the horrible and useless bloodshed. The

---

[1] Official text published by the Department of State.

Imperial Government hopes all the more for such an understanding of her position, as the neutrals have, under the pressure of the Entente Powers, suffered great losses, being forced by them either to give up their entire trade or to limit it according to conditions arbitrarily determined by Germany's enemies in violation of international law.[1]

[1] Official text published by the Department of State.

CHAPTER XVI

THE SEVERANCE OF DIPLOMATIC RELATIONS AND PROCLAMATION OF ARMED NEUTRALITY

On February 3, 1917, the President of the United States appeared before the Congress, in which is lodged the war-making power, and addressed its members upon the situation resulting from the proclamation of January 31, 1917, in which the Imperial German Government stated its intention to "begin submarine warfare unrestricted," and outlined what, in his opinion, the United States should do under the changed conditions. The President recalled the note of April 18, 1916, referring to the sinking of *The Sussex*, in which the United States declared that, unless the Imperial German Government should cease "its present methods of warfare against passenger and freight-carrying vessels," the United States would be obliged to sever all diplomatic relations with that Government. The German pledge of May 4, 1916, in reply to this warning on behalf of the United States, stated that "In accordance with the general principles of visit and search and destruction of merchant vessels recognized by international law, such vessels, both within and without the area declared as naval war zone, shall not be sunk without warning and without saving human lives, unless these ships attempt to escape or offer resistance."[1] The President next quoted the acceptance of this pledge, contained in the note of May 8, 1916, rejecting, however, the conditions attached to the German pledge that neutrals could not expect Germany to live up to her pledge "if her enemy is permitted to continue to apply at will methods of warfare violating the rules of international law." After mentioning that the German Government did not reply to the note of May 8th, and quoting the declaration of the 31st of January that all ships met within the zone will be sunk, the President informed the Congress that he had directed the Secretary of State "to announce to His Excellency the German Ambassador that all diplomatic relations between the United States and the German Empire are severed, and that the American Ambassador at Berlin

[1] Official text, *American Journal of International Law*, Special Supplement, October, 1916, p. 198.

will immediately be withdrawn; and, in accordance with this decision, to hand to His Excellency his passports."[1]

In thus severing diplomatic relations between the two countries the President did not, however, contemplate war, although its possibility was present to his mind. He apparently took this step in order to show the German Government that, without a change of policy on its part, the United States would resort to war in defense of its rights, although it preferred peace to war if in peace and through peace justice could be secured. He hoped against hope, as events showed, that, when brought face to face with the inevitable consequences of a refusal to comply with the requirements of international law, the German Government would, if not for the sake of humanity at least for the sake of that friendship which Germany had repeatedly proclaimed in its notes to the United States and in accordance with the treaties existing between the two countries, finally yield to justice what the United States would otherwise seek to obtain by force.

The Secretary of State complied with the directions of the President, handing passports to the Imperial German Ambassador and the personnel of the Imperial German Embassy and securing for them safe conducts in order that they might enjoy, as a concession from their enemies, that freedom of the seas which they were unwilling to grant to their fellows.

The Imperial German Government did not renounce "the employment of ruthless submarine warfare." American ships continued to be sunk, and, seeing no prospect of a change of heart on behalf of the Imperial German authorities, the President of the United States again addressed the Congress on February 26, 1917, and, after calling attention to the situation as he understood it, stated:

> Since it has unhappily proved impossible to safeguard our neutral rights by diplomatic means against the unwarranted infringements they are suffering at the hands of Germany, there may be no recourse but to *armed* neutrality, which we shall know how to maintain and for which there is abundant American precedent.[2]

---

[1] *Congressional Record*, vol. 54, p. 2550.
[2] *Ibid.*, p. 4273.

On March 12, 1917, that is to say, more than a month after the severing of diplomatic relations, Secretary Lansing sent the following statement to all the foreign missions for their information:

> In view of the announcement of the Imperial German Government on January 31, 1917, that all ships, those of neutrals included, met within

Here again there was no recourse to war, although the President had taken a further step in that direction. To the unwarranted infringements of the German Government upon the rights of the American people the United States was to interpose an armed neutrality. Arms are indeed mentioned, but they were to be used not to attack but to ward off an attack which Germany might or might not make. The President had spoken of interference with our neutral rights to the injury of American property and loss of American life, but the issue between the two countries had ceased to be one affecting American property or even American life. It had become, indeed, a larger issue, and, unwilling to leave the impression that he was unconscious of this, the President thus concluded his address:

> I have spoken of our commerce and of the legitimate errands of our people on the seas, but you will not be misled as to my main thought, the thought that lies beneath these phrases and gives them dignity and weight. It is not of material interests merely that we are thinking. It is, rather, of fundamental human rights, chief of all the right of life itself. I am thinking, not only of the rights of Americans to go and come about their proper business by way of the sea, but also of something much deeper, much more fundamental than that. I am thinking of those rights of humanity without which there is no civilization. My theme is of those great principles of compassion and of protection which mankind has sought to throw about human lives, the lives of noncombatants, the lives of men who are peacefully at work keeping the industrial processes of the world quick and vital, the lives of women and children and of those who supply the labor which ministers to their sustenance. We are speaking of no selfish material rights but of rights which our hearts support and whose foundation is that righteous passion for justice upon which all law, all structures alike of family, of state, and of mankind must rest, as upon the ultimate base of our existence and our liberty. I cannot imagine any man with American principles at his heart hesitating to defend these things.[1]

certain zones of the high seas, would be sunk without any precautions being taken for the safety of the persons on board, and without the exercise of visit and search, the Government of the United States has determined to place upon all American merchant vessels sailing through the barred areas an armed guard for the protection of the vessels and the lives of the persons on board. (Official documents published by Department of State.)

[1] *Congressional Record*, vol. 54, p. 4273.

CHAPTER XVII

THE DECLARATION OF WAR

On the 2d day of April, 1917, President Wilson appeared before the Congress of the United States and, after setting forth the lawless actions of the Imperial German Government and the impossibility of protecting the lives and property of his fellow countrymen engaged in pursuits which have always, "even in the darkest periods of modern history, been deemed innocent and legitimate," advised the Congress of the United States, in which body the power to declare war is vested by the Constitution, to declare the existence of a state of war between the Imperial German Government and the United States, saying:

> With a profound sense of the solemn and even tragical character of the step I am taking and of the grave responsibilities which it involves, but in unhesitating obedience to what I deem my constitutional duty, I advise that the Congress declare the recent course of the Imperial German Government to be in fact nothing less than war against the government and people of the United States; that it formally accept the status of belligerent which has thus been thrust upon it; and that it take immediate steps not only to put the country in a more thorough state of defense but also to exert all its power and employ all its resources to bring the Government of the German Empire to terms and end the war.[1]

On the 6th day of April, 1917, the Congress, after grave deliberation and with a full sense of the responsibility which it would thus assume, declared a state of war to exist between the Imperial German Government and the United States, in the following terms:

> Whereas the Imperial German Government has committed repeated acts of war against the Government and the people of the United States of America: Therefore be it
> *Resolved by the Senate and House of Representatives of the United States of America in Congress assembled,* That the state

[1] *Congressional Record*, vol. 55, No. 1, p. 3.

of war between the United States and the Imperial German Government which has thus been thrust upon the United States is hereby formally declared; and that the President be, and he is hereby, authorized and directed to employ the entire naval and military forces of the United States and the resources of the Government to carry on war against the Imperial German Government; and to bring the conflict to a successful termination all of the resources of the country are hereby pledged by the Congress of the United States.[1]

What were the reasons which caused the President of the United States to advise the Congress to declare the existence of a state of war between the Imperial German Government and the United States; what were the reasons which caused the Congress to act upon the advice of the President to declare the existence of a state of war between the two countries; and what are the consequences which the President, the Congress, and the people of the United States consider as likely to follow from this state of war and its effective prosecution? We do not need to speculate as to the reasons, for the President himself has stated them, and if he had not they would be sufficiently in evidence, as the actions of Germany since the first day of August, 1914, in so far as the United States is concerned, speak louder than words; and we do not need to indulge in prophecy in order to forecast the consequences of this declaration on behalf of the United States, for the President himself has stated, in clear and unmistakable terms, that the autocracy which made these acts possible should end with the war.

The first part of the President's address deals with the specific acts of the Imperial German Government as causes of the war. The second part deals with the motives and purposes of the United States in entering the war, for while the acts of the Imperial German Government would justify resistance on behalf of the United States, the President wished it clearly to be understood, and therefore he put it plainly, that the motive and purpose in entering the war which had been thrust upon the United States were not merely to secure redress for the loss of property, not even redress for the loss of human life, but to secure the repudiation of the Prussian conception of State and Government, which could force a people to commit such acts, and to secure some form of international organization calculated to guarantee peace among Nations through the administration of justice.

[1] *Congressional Record*, vol. 55, No. 4, p. 183; *Public Resolution No. 1*, 65th Cong., 1st sess.

As far as the United States is concerned, the cause of its war with the Imperial German Government is the submarine, for the disputes of a serious nature and of a kind calculated to produce war between the two Governments related to the conduct of the submarine, which, because Great Britain controlled the seas, was the only form of maritime warfare left to Germany; and Germany was apparently as unwilling to renounce maritime warfare as it was unwilling to allow its surface fleet to put to sea and to give battle to the British Navy. The United States did not object to the employment of the submarine. It recognized it as a vessel of war, possessed of all the rights of a vessel of war and subject to all the duties of a vessel of war. But the United States insisted from the beginning that the submarine should conform its actions to the rules of law to which vessels of war were subjected, and that, if it could not or would not conform its actions to such rules, it should not be used; for the law could not be changed to suit the submarine, which should itself be changed to meet the law if it could not, as then constructed, comply with the law as it then stood.

The Imperial German Government, on the contrary, insisted that, because of its frailty, the submarine could not comply with the laws and customs of war controlling the acts of surface vessels, that it could not comply with the formalities of visit and search, because, to do so, it would have to comport itself as a surface vessel, and as a surface vessel it would endanger its existence if it approached within gunshot of ordinary surface vessels. The Imperial German Government claimed for the submarine the right to operate under the surface to protect itself from attack, and, thus protected, to attack any vessel approaching it because, under the surface, it could not distinguish the vessel of the enemy from the vessel of a friendly Power. It claimed the right to attack the vessel within range without warning because, if it gave warning, it exposed itself to danger. Finally, it claimed the right to torpedo and thus destroy the vessel without first putting its passengers and crew in a place of safety because the submarine was too small to take them on board. The contention of the United States was that the rules of law controlling the principal should also control the conduct of the agent; the contention of the Imperial German Government was that the rules of law controlling the principal should be subordinated to the convenience of the agent.

If matters had rested here the question at issue between the two Governments would have been academic. But matters did not rest here, because the Imperial German Government put its conception of submarine warfare into practice, with the result, as the President informed the Congress in his address of the 2d of April, 1917, that "Vessels of every kind, whatever their flag, their character, their cargo, their destination, their errand, have been ruthlessly sent to the bottom without warning and without thought of help or mercy for those on board, the vessels of friendly neutrals along with those of belligerents. Even hospital ships and ships carrying relief to the sorely bereaved and stricken people of Belgium, though the latter were provided with safe conduct through the proscribed areas by the German Government itself and were distinguished by unmistakable marks of identity, have been sunk with the same reckless lack of compassion or of principle."[1]

In the report of the Committee on Foreign Affairs of the House of Representatives accompanying the text of the declaration of a state of war with the Imperial German Government, numerous instances are given justifying the President's indictment, and while these instances are but few of the many, they are given as a sample of the indiscriminate submarine warfare of the Imperial German Government.

After a brief reference to the diplomatic correspondence between the two Governments, in which Germany stated that instructions had been given "to abstain from all violence against neutral vessels recognizable as such" and that "it is very far indeed from the intention of the German Government . . . ever to destroy neutral lives and neutral property," the official report to which reference has been made continues:

> Nevertheless the German Government proceeded to carry out its plans of submarine warfare and torpedoed the British passenger steamer *Falaba* on March 27, 1915, when one American life was lost, attacked the American steamer *Cushing* April 28 by airship, and made submarine attacks upon the American tank steamer *Gulflight* May 1, the British passenger steamer *Lusitania* May 7, when 114 American lives were lost, and the American steamer *Nebraskan* on May 25, in all of which over 125 citizens of the United States lost their lives, not to mention hundreds of noncombatants who were lost and hundreds of Americans and noncombatants whose lives were put in jeopardy.
>
> The British mule boat *Armenian* was torpedoed on June 28, as a result of which twenty Americans are reported missing.[2]

---

[1] *Congressional Record*, vol. 55, No. 1, p. 2. [2] *Ibid.*, No. 4, p. 191.

After a further reference to the diplomatic correspondence, the official report thus proceeds:

> Subsequently the following vessels carrying American citizens were attacked by submarines:
> British liner *Orduna* July 9.
> Russian steamer *Leo* July 9.
> American steamer *Leelanaw* July 25.
> British passenger liner *Arabic* August 19.
> British mule ship *Nicosian* August 19.
> British steamer *Hesperian* September 4.
> In these attacks twenty-three Americans lost their lives, not to mention the large number whose lives were placed in jeopardy.[1]

After another reference to diplomatic correspondence, citing German promises, the official report goes on to say:

> Following this accumulative series of assurances, however, there seems to have been no abatement in the rigor of submarine warfare, for attacks were made in the Mediterranean upon the American steamer *Communipaw* on December 3, the American steamer *Petrolite* December 5, the Japanese liner *Yasaka Maru* December 21, and the passenger liner *Persia* December 30. In the sinking of *The Persia* out of a total of some 500 passengers and crew only 165 were saved. Among those lost was an American consul traveling to his post.[1]

After again referring to the correspondence between the two countries, continuing the assurance of the German Government, in the language of the report, "that neutral and enemy merchant vessels, passenger as well as freight ships, should not be destroyed except upon the passengers and crew being accorded safety," the official report thus chronicles the loss of life and property during the year 1916:

> On March 1, 1916, the unarmed French passenger steamer *Patria*, carrying a number of American citizens, was attacked without warning. On March 9 the Norwegian bark *Silius*, riding at anchor in Havre Rhodes, was torpedoed by an unseen submarine, and one of the seven Americans on board was injured. On March 16 the Dutch passenger steamer *Tubantia* was sunk in the North Sea by a torpedo. On March 16 the British steamer *Berwindale* was torpedoed without warning off Bantry Island with four Americans on board. On March 24 the British un-

[1] *Congressional Record*, vol. 55, No. 4, p. 192.

armed steamer *Englishman* was, after a chase, torpedoed and sunk by the submarine U-19, as a result of which one American on board perished. On March 24 the unarmed French cross-channel steamer *Sussex* was torpedoed without warning, several of the twenty-four American passengers being injured. On March 27 the unarmed British liner *Manchester Engineer* was sunk by an explosion without prior warning, with Americans on board, and on March 28 the British steamer *Eagle Point*, carrying a Hotchkiss gun, which she did not use, was chased, overtaken, and sunk by a torpedo after the persons on board had taken to the boats.[1]

And after a final reference to the correspondence between the two Governments, resulting in the assurance of May 4, 1916, that new orders had been issued to the German naval forces "in accordance with the general principles of visit and search and the destruction of merchant vessels recognized by international law," and quoting the withdrawal of this assurance contained in the German note of January 31, 1917, the report continues and concludes as follows this phase of the question:

> On February 3 [1917] one American ship was sunk, and since that date six American ships flying the American flag have been torpedoed, with a loss of about thirteen American citizens. In addition, fifty or more foreign vessels of both belligerent and neutral nationality with Americans on board have been torpedoed, in most cases without warning, with a consequent loss of several American citizens.[1]

The President's statement thus appears to be borne out by the facts.

But there is a further charge made by the President of even a more serious character, for in the address of the 2d of April he states that "hospital ships and ships carrying relief to the sorely bereaved and stricken people of Belgium" had been destroyed by German submarines, although these vessels were supposed to be protected by the promise of the Imperial German Government, evidenced by safe conducts. On this point the official report previously quoted says:

> When the Commission for Relief in Belgium began its work in October, 1914, it received from the German authorities, through the various Governments concerned, definite written assurances that ships engaged in carrying cargoes for the relief

[1] *Congressional Record*, vol. 55, No. 4, p. 192.

of the civil population of Belgium and northern France should be immune from attack. In order that there may be no room for attacks upon these ships through misunderstanding, each ship is given a safe conduct by the German diplomatic representative in the country from which it sails, and, in addition, bears conspicuously upon its sides markings which have been agreed upon with the German authorities; furthermore, similar markings are painted upon the decks of the ships in order that they may be readily recognizable by aeroplanes.

Upon the rupture of relations with Germany the commission was definitely assured by the German Government that its ships would be immune from attack by following certain prescribed courses and conforming to the arrangements previously made.

Despite these solemn assurances there have been several unwarranted attacks upon ships under charter to the commission.

On March 7 or 8 the Norwegian ship *Storstad*, carrying 10,000 tons of corn from Buenos Aires to Rotterdam for the commission, was sunk in broad daylight by a German submarine despite the conspicuous markings of the commission, which the submarine could not help observing. *The Storstad* was repeatedly shelled without warning and finally torpedoed.

On March 19 the steamships *Tunisie* and *Haelen*, under charter to the commission, proceeded to the United States under safe conducts and guarantees from the German minister at The Hague and bearing conspicuous marking of the commission, were attacked without warning by a German submarine outside the danger zone (56° 15′ north, 5° 32′ east). The ships were not sunk, but on the *Haelen* seven men were killed, including the first and third officers; a port boat was sunk; a hole was made in the port bunker above the water line; and the ships sustained sundry damages to decks and engines.[1]

In a later portion of the President's address he calls attention to the difficulty of maintaining peace with the Imperial German Government and enumerates a series of transactions within American jurisdiction comparable to the conduct of the submarine warfare upon the high seas. They are apparently not mentioned by the President as in themselves the cause of war but as a matter of aggravation. Thus he says:

> One of the things that has served to convince us that the Prussian autocracy was not and could never be our friend is that from the very outset of the present war it has filled our unsuspecting communities and even our offices of government with spies and set criminal intrigues everywhere afoot against our national unity of counsel, our peace within and without, our

[1] *Congressional Record*, vol. 55, No. 4, p. 193.

industries, and our commerce. Indeed, it is now evident that its spies were here even before the war began; and it is unhappily not a matter of conjecture but a fact proved in our courts of justice that the intrigues which have more than once come perilously near to disturbing the peace and dislocating the industries of the country have been carried on at the instigation, with the support, and even under the personal direction of official agents of the Imperial Government accredited to the Government of the United States. Even in checking these things and trying to extirpate them we have sought to put the most generous interpretation possible upon them because we knew that their source lay, not in any hostile feeling or purpose of the German people toward us (who were, no doubt, as ignorant of them as we ourselves were), but only in the selfish designs of a Government that did what it pleased and told its people nothing. But they have played their part in serving to convince us at last that that Government entertains no real friendship for us and means to act against our peace and security at its convenience. That it means to stir up enemies against us at our very doors the intercepted note to the German Minister at Mexico City is eloquent evidence.[1]

In the official report of the Committee on Foreign Affairs of the House of Representatives, there is an elaborate but far from complete enumeration of the acts of German officials and of German sympathizers in the domestic affairs of the United States. The few instances actually collected, which are to be taken as a sample of the many which are not chronicled, are twenty-one in number and are thus stated in the report in brief and summary form:

1. By direct instructions received from the foreign office in Berlin the German Embassy in this country furnished funds and issued orders to the Indian independence committee of the Indian Nationalist Party in the United States. These instructions were usually conveyed to the committee by the military information bureau in New York (Von Igel) or by the German consulates in New York and San Francisco.

Dr. Chakrabarty, recently arrested in New York City, received, all in all, according to his own admission, some $60,000 from Von Igel. He claims that the greater portion of this money was used for defraying the expenses of the Indian revolutionary propaganda in this country, and, as he says, for educational purposes. While this is in itself true, it is not all that was done by the revolutionists. They have sent representatives to the Far East to stir up trouble in India, and they have attempted to ship arms and ammunition to India. These expeditions have failed. The German Embassy also employed Ernest T. Euphrat

[1] *Congressional Record*, vol. 55, No. 1, p. 4.

to carry instructions and information between Berlin and Washington under an American passport.

2. Officers of interned German warships have violated their word of honor and escaped. In one instance the German consul at Richmond furnished the money to purchase a boat to enable six warrant officers of the steamer *Kronprinz Wilhelm* to escape after breaking their parole.

3. Under the supervision of Captain von Papen and Wolf von Igel, Hans von Wedell and, subsequently, Carl Ruroede maintained a regular office for the procurement of fraudulent passports for German reservists. These operations were directed and financed in part by Captain von Papen and Wolf von Igel. Indictments were returned, Carl Ruroede sentenced to the penitentiary, and a number of German officers fined. Von Wedell escaped and has apparently been drowned at sea. Von Wedell's operations were also known to high officials in Germany. When Von Wedell became suspicious that forgeries committed by him on a passport application had become known, he conferred with Captain von Papen and obtained money from him wherewith to make his escape.

4. James J. F. Archibald, under cover of an American passport and in the pay of the German Government through Ambassador Bernstorff, carried dispatches for Ambassador Dumba and otherwise engaged in unneutral activities.

5. Albert Sanders, Charles Wunnonberg, and others, German agents in this country, were engaged, among other activities, in sending spies to England, equipped with American passports, for the purpose of securing military information. Several such men have been sent. Sanders and Wunnonberg have plead guilty to indictments brought against them in New York City, as has George Voux Bacon, one of the men sent abroad by them.

6. American passports have been counterfeited and counterfeits found on German agents. Baron von Cupenberg, a German agent, when arrested abroad, bore a counterfeit of an American passport issued to Gustav C. Roeder; Irving Guy Ries received an American passport, went to Germany, where the police retained his passports for twenty-four hours. Later a German spy named Carl Paul Julius Hensel was arrested in London with a counterfeit of the Ries passport in his possession.

7. Prominent officials of the Hamburg-American Line, who, under the direction of Captain Boy-Ed, endeavored to provide German warships at sea with coal and other supplies in violation of the statutes of the United States, have been tried and convicted and sentenced to the penitentiary. Some twelve or more vessels were involved in this plan.

8. Under the direction of Captain Boy-Ed and the German consulate at San Francisco, and in violation of our law, the steamships *Sacramento* and *Mazatlan* carried supplies from San Francisco to German war vessels. The *Olsen* and *Mahoney*,

which were engaged in a similar enterprise, were detained. The money for these ventures was furnished by Captain Boy-Ed. Indictments have been returned in connection with these matters against a large number of persons.

9. Werner Horn, a lieutenant in the German reserve, was furnished funds by Captain Franz von Papen and sent, with dynamite, under orders to blow up the International Bridge at Vanceboro, Me. He was partially successful. He is now under indictment for the unlawful transportation of dynamite on passenger trains and is in jail awaiting trial following the dismissal of his appeal by the Supreme Court.

10. Captain von Papen furnished funds to Albert Kaltschmidt, of Detroit, who is involved in a plot to blow up a factory at Walkerville, Canada, and the armory at Windsor, Canada.

11. Robert Fay, Walter Scholtz, and Paul Daeche have been convicted and sentenced to the penitentiary and three others are under indictment for conspiracy to prepare bombs and attach them to allied ships leaving New York Harbor. Fay, who was the principal in this scheme, was a German soldier. He testified that he received finances from a German secret agent in Brussels, and told Von Papen of his plans, who advised him that his device was not practicable, but that he should go ahead with it, and if he could make it work he would consider it.

12. Under the direction of Captain von Papen and Wolf von Igel, Dr. Walter T. Scheele, Captain von Kleist, Captain Wolpert, of the Atlas Steamship Company, and Captain Rode, of the Hamburg-American Line, manufactured incendiary bombs and placed them on board allied vessels. The shells in which the chemicals were placed were made on board the steamship *Friedrich der Grosse*. Scheele was furnished $1,000 by Von Igel wherewith to become a fugitive from justice.

13. Captain Franz Rintelen, a reserve officer in the German Navy, came to this country secretly for the purpose of preventing the exportation of munitions of war to the allies and of getting to Germany needed supplies. He organized and financed Labor's National Peace Council in an effort to bring about an embargo on the shipment of munitions of war, tried to bring about strikes, etc.

14. Consul General Bopp, at San Francisco, Vice Consul General von Schaick, Baron George Wilhelm von Brincken (an employee of the consulate), Charles C. Crowley, and Mrs. Margaret W. Cornell (secret agents of the German consulate at San Francisco) have been convicted of conspiracy to send agents into Canada to blow up railroad tunnels and bridges, and to wreck vessels sailing from Pacific coast ports with war material for Russia and Japan.

15. Paul Koenig, head of the secret-service work of the Hamburg-American Line, by direction of his superior officers,

largely augmented his organization and under the direction of Von Papen, Boy-Ed, and Albert carried on secret work for the German Government. He secured and sent spies to Canada to gather information concerning the Welland Canal, the movements of Canadian troops to England, bribed an employee of a bank for information concerning shipments to the allies, sent spies to Europe on American passports to secure military information, and was involved with Captain von Papen in plans to place bombs on ships of the allies leaving New York Harbor, etc. Von Papen, Boy-Ed, and Albert had frequent conferences with Koenig in his office, at theirs, and at outside places. Koenig and certain of his associates are under indictment.

16. Captain von Papen, Captain Hans Tauscher, Wolf von Igel, and a number of German reservists organized an expedition to go into Canada, destroy the Welland Canal, and endeavor to terrorize Canadians in order to delay the sending of troops from Canada to Europe. Indictments have been returned against these persons. Wolf von Igel furnished Fritzen, one of the conspirators in this case, money on which to flee from New York City. Fritzen is now in jail in New York City.

17. With money furnished by official German representatives in this country, a cargo of arms and ammunition was purchased and shipped on board the schooner *Annie Larsen*. Through the activities of German official representatives in this country and other Germans a number of Indians were procured to form an expedition to go on the steamship *Maverick*, meet the *Annie Larsen*, take over her cargo, and endeavor to bring about a revolution in India. This plan involved the sending of a German officer to drill Indian recruits and the entire plan was managed and directed by Captain von Papen, Captain Hanz Tauscher, and other official German representatives in this country.

18. Gustav Stahl, a German reservist, made an affidavit which he admitted was false, regarding the armament of *The Lusitania*, which affidavit was forwarded to the State Department by Ambassador Bernstorff. He pleaded guilty to an indictment charging perjury, and was sentenced to the penitentiary. Koenig, herein mentioned, was active in securing this affidavit.

19. The German Embassy organized, directed, and financed the Hans Libeau Employment Agency, through which extended efforts were made to induce employees of manufacturers engaged in supplying various kinds of material to the allies to give up their positions in an effort to interfere with the output of such manufacturers. Von Papen indorsed this organization as a military measure, and it was hoped through its propaganda to cripple munition factories.

20. The German Government has assisted financially a number of newspapers in this country in return for pro-German propaganda.

21. Many facts have been secured indicating that Germans

have aided and encouraged financially and otherwise the activities of one or the other factions in Mexico, the purpose being to keep the United States occupied along its borders and to prevent the exportation of munitions of war to the allies; see, in this connection, the activities of Rintelen, Stallforth, Kopf, the German consul at Chihuahua, Krum-Hellen, Felix Somerfeld (Villa's representative at New York), Carl Heynen, Gustav Steinberg, and many others.[1]

It will be observed that these interferences with the domestic economy of the United States were at a time when this country was neutral, when the Imperial German Secretary of State for Foreign Affairs abounded in expressions of friendship and consideration, and when the Imperial German Ambassador enjoyed the hospitality of the country.

It is hard to believe that these things are so. But they are not all. On the 1st of March, 1917 (after the President's address of February 26th and before his address to the Congress on the 2d of April the American people were astounded, to speak only of our own country, by the publication, with Secretary of State Lansing's assurance as to its genuineness,[2] of an instruction of the Imperial German Secretary of State, Dr. Zimmermann, to the Imperial German Ambassador in Washington, Count von Bernstorff, directing him to transmit the text of the message which he had received to the German Minister in Mexico. The text of this note, which is so extraordinary as to

[1] *Congressional Record*, vol. 55, No. 4, pp. 192-193.
[2] In response to a resolution of the Senate, Secretary Lansing on March 1, 1917, informed the President, who transmitted the statement to the Senate, that "the Government is in possession of evidence which establishes the fact that the note referred to is authentic, and that it is in possession of the Government of the United States." Any remaining doubt as to the authenticity of the note was removed by the following statement of Dr. Zimmermann on March 29, 1917, in reply to a criticism directed against him by Hugo Haase, leader of the Socialist minority in the Reichstag:

> I wrote no letter to General Carranza. I was not so naïve. I merely addressed, by a route that appeared to me to be a safe one, instructions to our representative in Mexico. It is being investigated how these instructions fell into the hands of the American authorities. I instructed the Minister to Mexico, in the event of war with the United States, to propose a German alliance to Mexico, and simultaneously to suggest that Japan join the alliance. I declared expressly that, despite the submarine war, we hoped that America would maintain neutrality. . . .
> When I thought of this alliance with Mexico and Japan I allowed myself to be guided by the consideration that our brave troops already have to fight against a superior force of enemies, and my duty is, as far as possible, to keep further enemies away from them. . . . Thus, I considered it a patriotic duty to release those instructions, and I hold to the standpoint that I acted rightly. (Reuter dispatch from Amsterdam, *New York Times* "*Current History*," May, 1917, pp. 236-237.)

require no commentary, and may become as famous in the annals of diplomacy as the telegram of Ems, reads as follows:

BERLIN, January 19, 1917.

On the 1st of February we intend to begin submarine warfare unrestricted. In spite of this it is our intention to endeavor to keep neutral the United States of America.

If this attempt is not successful, we propose an alliance on the following basis with Mexico: That we shall make war together and together make peace. We shall give general financial support, and it is understood that Mexico is to reconquer the lost territory in New Mexico, Texas, and Arizona. The details are left to you for settlement.

You are instructed to inform the President of Mexico of the above in the greatest confidence as soon as it is certain there will be an outbreak of war with the United States, and suggest that the President of Mexico on his own initiative should communicate with Japan suggesting adherence at once to this plan; at the same time offer to mediate between Germany and Japan.

Please call to the attention of the President of Mexico that the employment of ruthless submarine warfare now promises to compel England to make peace in a few months.

(Signed) ZIMMERMANN.[1]

It was therefore under the eyes of Congress, as it was in the mind of the President and in the heart of the American people. Without it there were causes of war; with it there was slight chance that war could be avoided. It is doubtful whether it would have produced war if there had not been other and impelling reasons for the resort to arms. It is doubtful if it can properly be included among the causes of the war. Certainly it was not a distinct cause; it was the culmination of a series of unfriendly acts, and it showed the spirit and purpose with which those acts had been committed. It was rather a matter of aggravation, throwing fuel on the flames, than creating of itself a conflagration.

[1] *Congressional Record*, vol. 55, No. 4, p. 194.

CHAPTER XVIII

WHY NOT ARBITRATION?

SECTION 1. THE ORIGIN AND EXTENT OF THE MODERN PRACTICE OF ARBITRATION

It would be fair to ask why the United States did not arbitrate its difficulties with Germany, and although this question has not been raised or put in such a way as to become an issue between the two countries, it seems advisable to consider the attitude of Prussia and of the Imperial German Government to arbitration before the outbreak of the present war; for if it should appear that the Imperial Government was constantly and consistently opposed to arbitration, the proposal of arbitration made during the war would naturally be looked upon and considered from a different standpoint than if the attitude of the Imperial Government before the war had been favorable to this method of settling international disputes. Therefore, the question is material to the matter in hand and will be considered at some length.

While it would be too great a digression to stop to inquire why arbitration, which had disappeared from the memory of Nations, if we are to judge by their practice, was adopted by the English-speaking peoples in the midst of a world at war, it is nevertheless within the scope of this narrative to say in passing that the then Prime Minister of Great Britain, the younger Pitt, whose mind was open to suggestion, had had his attention drawn to arbitration,[1] and

---

[1] William Pulteney wrote to Pitt on September 14, 1786, "in terms that," as Mr. Rose properly says, "deserve to be remembered." Thus:

It is to be considered whether this is not a good opportunity to ingraft upon this treaty some arrangement that may effectually tend to prevent future wars, at least for a considerable time. Why may not two nations adopt, what individuals often adopt who have dealings that may lead to disputes, the measure of agreeing beforehand that in case any differences shall happen which they cannot settle amicably, the question shall be referred to arbitration? The matter in dispute is seldom of much real consequence, but the point of honour prevents either party from yielding, but if it is decided by third parties, each may be contented. The arbitrators should not be sovereign princes; but might not each nation name three judges, either of their own courts of law, or of any other country, out of whom the opposite nation should choose one, and these two hear the question and

had, some eight years before the treaty with the United States, proposed the limitation of armament to his powerful neighbor across the Channel;[1] that Jay had mastered the immortal treatise of Grotius on the law of Nations before he began to read law, that on graduating from Kings College (now Columbia University) he delivered an address on the blessings of peace; that as Secretary of State for Foreign Affairs he had, in 1785, proposed to the Congress of the Confederation the settlement of the boundary disputes with the mother country by a mixed commission, that as Acting Secretary of State in Washington's cabinet, before the return of Jefferson from France to assume the Secretaryship of State, he again proposed the arbitral settlement of the same disputes with Great Britain, and that Washington sent Jay's original proposal and report to the First Congress under the Constitution, with a statement that "it is desirable that all questions between this and any other nation be speedily and amicably settled." It should be said, in this connection, that Lord Liverpool was at this time Chancellor of the Duchy of Lancaster in Pitt's cabinet, that he was one of his familiars and had great influence with him, and that he was a professed partisan of arbitration. It was natural, therefore, that Pitt's ministry should agree to Jay's proposal to arbitrate the outstanding differences between the two countries, and that Great Britain and the United States should conclude at a later date the first treaty of disarmament of modern times,[2] when the first Lord Liverpool's son was Prime Minister.

> either determine it or name an umpire—the whole proceedings to be in writing? This would occasion the matter to be better discussed than is commonly done, and would give time for the parties to cool and most probably reconcile them to the decision, whatever it might be.
>
> It has frequently occurred to my mind that, if France and England understood each other, the world might be kept in peace from one end of the globe to the other. And why may they not understand each other? I allow that France is the most intriguing nation upon earth; that they are restless and faithless; but is it impossible to show them that every object of their intrigue may be better assured by good faith and a proper intelligence with us, and might we not arrange everything together now so as completely to satisfy both? (Pitt MSS., p. 169.)

Quoted from J. Holland Rose, *William Pitt and National Revival* (London, 1911), p. 340.

[1] On this point Mr. Rose says: "Pitt, we may note, had sought to take a first step towards the limitation of armaments, by suggesting that the two Powers should lessen their squadrons in the East Indies; but to this Vergennes, on 1st April, 1786, refused his assent." (Rose, *ibid.*, pp. 340-341.)

[2] The treaty referred to is the so-called Rush-Bagot agreement, concluded just a century ago (April 28-29, 1817), and whose terms have been faithfully kept, limiting the armament to be kept upon the Great Lakes. For the text of this very important and, we may yet hope, epoch-making document see Malloy, *Treaties, Conventions, etc., between the U. S. and Other Powers*, p. 628.

For the origin, nature, and history of the Rush-Bagot agreement see ex-Secre-

Without prolonging a digression which may perhaps be considered foreign to the present purpose, it is advisable to mention in passing that the treaty of 1794 between Great Britain and the United States, to which reference has been made, negotiated by John Jay, then Chief Justice of the United States but on special mission to Great Britain, and which is properly called the Jay Treaty, provided in Articles 5, 6, and 7 for a submission to mixed commissions of the outstanding difficulties between Great Britain and the United States; that the successful operation of the commission formed under Article 7 of this treaty convinced the two countries, and has convinced all other countries open to conviction, of the efficacy of arbitration as a method of settling not merely legal but equitable disputes between Nations; that from the meeting of this commission in 1798 Great Britain has arbitrated 98 disputes with foreign Nations; that the United States since the same date has arbitrated 76 disputes with foreign Nations; that, of the arbitrations of these two countries, 23 were between Great Britain and the United States; that, in the period from 1798 to 1904 there have been 241 instances of arbitration between all Nations; and that two Nations, namely, Great Britain and the United States, have been parties to more than two-thirds of them. If it be borne in mind that treaties of arbitration often submit categories of disputes embracing many cases (as in the case of the special treaty of arbitration between Mexico and the United States of 1868),[1] it is seen that the mere enumeration of the treaties gives no adequate idea of the number of individual cases actually decided under the treaties.[2]

To the contention, in the nature of a criticism, that nations only submit to arbitration insignificant disputes that would not be the cause of war if they were left unsettled, it may be answered that, when war does not break out, we cannot say with certainty that it might not have occurred, and that two disputes between Great Britain and the United States were of a kind to have produced war. It is indeed difficult to believe that the so-called *Alabama* disputes, arising out of the unneutral conduct of Great Britain during the Civil War, might not have caused war between Great Britain and the United

tary of State Foster's *Limitation of Armament on the Great Lakes*, republished, 1915, by the Carnegie Endowment for International Peace.

[1] Under this treaty, 2,015 cases were submitted. They were disposed of as follows: Cases decided, 1,983 (of which 1,662 were dismissed or disallowed); cases consolidated with other cases, 25; cases withdrawn, 7. (Moore, *International Arbitrations*, vol. 2, p. 1314.)

[2] These arbitration statistics are taken from Fried's *Handbuch der Friedensbewegung* (Vienna and Leipzig, 1905), pp. 104-105, 123-157.

States had the treaty of May 8, 1871, not submitted them to arbitration by the so-called Geneva Tribunal in 1872; and it is more than conceivable that the North Atlantic Fisheries dispute might have resulted in armed conflict if it had not been submitted to arbitration in 1909 and actually decided by a temporary tribunal of arbitration at The Hague in 1910. In any event, these two disputes would have produced a tense feeling between the two countries rendering war between them easier, even although the immediate cause might have been another question.

If the record of the Kingdom of Prussia be considered it will be seen that it has been chary of submitting a dispute with a foreign Nation to arbitration; that, in fact, it has submitted one case to arbitration and has acted as arbiter in 2 cases. And if the Imperial German Government be considered it will be seen that the enlarged Prussia has followed Prussian precedent and practice, improving upon it however, as it has resorted to arbitration in 13 cases and has acted as arbiter in 2 cases. It has been significantly cautious in submitting its disputes with foreign Nations to arbitration, and because of this unwillingness, it is to be said to its credit, German statesmen have scrupulously and honorably refrained from concluding treaties of arbitration.[1]

Section 2. German Attitude Towards Arbitration

It will be sufficient for present purposes to use by way of illustration the attitude of the Imperial German Government towards arbitration at the First and Second Hague Peace Conferences, the refusal of the Imperial Government to negotiate with the United States a treaty of General Arbitration upon the adjournment of the Second Conference, and in the year of the war of 1914, to conclude with the United States one of the series of treaties for the advancement of peace by agreeing to submit disputes of all kinds to the investigation and report of a Commission of Inquiry invested with the power of recommending but not of deciding.

The First Hague Peace Conference met on May 18, 1899, a delicate compliment to the Czar of Russia, who had proposed the Conference and whose birthday that day happened to be. It adjourned on the 29th day of July, 1899, adopting among other projects the Pacific Settlement Convention advocating, but not prescribing, arbitration, creating machinery for the constitution of temporary tribunals if the parties themselves did not create others, and recom-

[1] Fried, *Handbuch der Friedensbewegung*, 1905, pp. 104-105, 123-127.

mending a method of arbitral procedure if the countries in dispute did not themselves prefer some other method. These were indeed important results, but they were only obtained at the expense of a general treaty of arbitration, which the Imperial German Government opposed and made of its rejection the price of accepting the provisions concerning a tribunal of arbitration.

The Honorable Andrew D. White, American Ambassador to Germany and Chairman of the American Delegation to the First Hague Peace Conference, kept a diary of important occurrences from day to day, and he has many interesting things to say about the attitude of the Imperial German Delegation and of the state of mind of its Chairman, Count, later Prince, von Münster. Under date of May 24th, Mr. White said:

> Meeting Count Münster, who, after M. de Staal [President of the Conference], is very generally considered the most important personage here, we discussed the subject of arbitration. To my great regret, I found him entirely opposed to it, or, at least, entirely opposed to any well-developed plan. He did not say that he would oppose a moderate plan for voluntary arbitration, but he insisted that arbitration must be injurious to Germany; that Germany is prepared for war as no other country is or can be; that she can mobilize her army in ten days; and that neither France, Russia, nor any other power can do this. Arbitration, he said, would simply give rival powers time to put themselves in readiness, and would therefore be a great disadvantage to Germany.[1]

Under date of June 9, he wrote:

> It now appears that the German Emperor is determined to oppose the whole scheme of arbitration, and will have nothing to do with any plan for a regular tribunal, whether as given in the British or the American scheme. This news comes from various sources, and is confirmed by the fact that, in the subcommittee, one of the German delegates, Professor Zorn of Königsberg, who had become very earnest in behalf of arbitration, now says that he may not be able to vote for it. There are also signs that the German Emperor is influencing the minds of his allies—the sovereigns of Austria, Italy, Turkey, and Roumania—leading them to oppose it.[2]

But the Conference was set on arbitration to such a degree that Count Münster began to find himself in an uncomfortable position;

---

[1] *Autobiography of Andrew D. White* (New York, 1905, 2 vols.), vol. 2, p. 265.
[2] *Ibid.*, pp. 293-294.

for although he claimed that a proposal for a general treaty of arbitration was in the interest of Russia and France, as Germany was armed to the teeth and was prepared at a moment's notice to settle its disputes with either of these countries or with both of them by the time-honored appeal to the sword, he was nevertheless unwilling to expose his Imperial Master to the criticism which was making itself heard because of German opposition to arbitration. He was therefore more inclined to listen, indeed to court, advice, and on June 15th Mr. White, seeing this weakening of the line, had a long interview with his colleague, who had called to see him, which probably convinced him that, in the interest of Germany, his own attitude as well as that of his country should become more favorable to arbitration. Mr. White thus records the interview:

> He was very much in earnest, and declared especially against compulsory arbitration. To this I answered that the plan thus far adopted contemplated entirely voluntary arbitration, with the exception that an obligatory system was agreed upon as regards sundry petty matters in which arbitration would assist all the states concerned; and that if he disliked this latter feature, but would agree to the others, we would go with him in striking it out, though we should vastly prefer to retain it.
> He said, "Yes; you have already stricken out part of it in the interest of the United States," referring to the features concerning the Monroe Doctrine, the regulation of canals, rivers, etc.
> "Very true," I answered, "and if there are any special features which affect unfavorably German policy or interests, move to strike them out, and we will heartily support you.[1]

Count Münster was not to be won over by an offer of this kind. He was unfriendly to arbitration and he criticised the substitution of inexperienced persons such as "university professors and the like to carry on the machinery of the tribunal," but he was somewhat mollified when informed that the council was to be composed of the diplomats accredited at The Hague under the presidency of the Dutch Minister of Foreign Affairs. Mr. White urged the importance of coöperation, showing that a failure to do so would subject the Kaiser to criticism and obloquy, and the Russian Czar, whom the Count considered insincere, to universal commendation, and that, if he supported arbitration in addition to the publicity of the proceedings of the Conference, the honor of the Conference would be his and the German Emperor would "be looked upon as, after all,—the arbiter of Europe."

[1] *Autobiography of Andrew D. White*, vol. 2, pp. 301-302.

Mr. White also called his attention to the fact that by opposing arbitration he "not only put a club into the hands of Socialists, Anarchists, and all the other anti-social forces," but that he also alienated "the substantial middle class and the great body of religious people in all nations."

After having pursued this line of thought, Mr. White touched upon a difficulty which had found a lodgment in the mind of Count Münster's Imperial Master. Thus, to quote Mr. White's own words:

> I then took up an argument which, it is understood, has had much influence with the Emperor,—namely, that arbitration must be in derogation of his sovereignty,—and asked, "How can any such derogation be possible? Your sovereign would submit only such questions to the arbitration tribunal as he thought best; and, more than all that, you have already committed yourselves to the principle. You are aware that Bismarck submitted the question of the Caroline Islands for arbitration to the Pope, and the first Emperor William consented to act as arbiter between the United States and Great Britain in the matter of the American northwestern boundary. How could arbitration affect the true position of the sovereign?"[1]

As illustrating the advantage of arbitration Mr. White mentioned the variety of petty but troublesome questions between Germany and the United States, which the Reichstag in Berlin and the Congress in Washington would condemn if Foreign Offices of the two countries should compromise, but which could be got out of the way easily and quietly by arbitration to the advantage of both. "And," to quote Mr. White's language on the point, "this is just what would take place between Germany and other nations. A mass of vexatious questions would be settled by the tribunal, and the sovereign and his Government would thus be relieved from parliamentary chicanery based, not upon knowledge, but upon party tactics of personal grudges or inherited prejudices." The Count seemed impressed with these views, and Mr. White was encouraged to believe that he would advise the Imperial Government accordingly.

The crisis came by the 16th, under which date Mr. White made the following entry in his diary:

> This morning Count Münster called and seemed much excited by the fact that he had received a despatch from Berlin in which the German Government—which, of course, means the Emperor—had strongly and finally declared against everything like an

[1] *Autobiography of Andrew D. White*, vol. 2, p. 305.

arbitration tribunal. He was clearly disconcerted by this too liberal acceptance of his own earlier views, and said that he had sent to M. de Staal insisting that the meeting of the subcommittee on arbitration, which had been appointed for this day (Friday), should be adjourned on some pretext until next Monday; "for," said he, "if the session takes place today, Zorn *must* make the declaration in behalf of Germany which these new instructions order him to make, and that would be a misfortune."[1]

It need only be stated that Mr. White joined the Count in securing an adjournment, the consequence of which is thus related in Mr. White's own words:

> Later Count Münster told me that he had decided to send Professor Zorn to Berlin at once in order to lay the whole matter before the Foreign Office and induce the authorities to modify the instructions. I approved this course strongly, whereupon he suggested that I should do something to the same purpose, and this finally ended in the agreement that Holls should go with Zorn.[2]

The time had indeed come to act. The delegates at The Hague had begun to see and to feel that they must either bend or break. The instructions received from Wilhelmstrasse had to be changed and Dr. Zorn, technical delegate of Germany, and Dr. Holls, of the American delegation, were sent to Berlin to interview and to influence the authorities in behalf of concession and compromise. Mr. White, taking advantage of his personal friendship, furnished Dr. Holls with a letter of introduction and a personal letter to Von Bülow, then Imperial Secretary of State for Foreign Affairs, which restated the arguments already made and which must have had a large influence in persuading Germany to yield, because Mr. White wrote not merely as a personal friend and as a delegate to the Conference, whose labors he wished to have succeed, but as Ambassador of the United States accredited to the Imperial German Government, in which at that very moment Von Bülow, later Imperial German Chancellor, was Imperial Secretary of State for Foreign Affairs.

After a reference to their friendly relations and a further reference to Mr. White's friendly relations of twenty years' standing with Von Bülow's father, giving him the right to speak frankly as a friend and as man to man, Mr. White said:

[1] *Autobiography of Andrew D. White*, vol. 2, p. 308.
[2] *Ibid.*, pp. 308-309.

It is generally said here that Germany is opposed to the whole thing, that she is utterly hostile to anything like arbitration, and that she will do all in her power, either alone or through her allies, to thwart every feasible plan of providing for a tribunal which shall give some hope to the world of settling some of the many difficulties between nations otherwise than by bloodshed.

No rational man here expects all wars to be ended by anything done here; no one proposes to submit to any such tribunal questions involving the honor of any nation or the inviolability of its territory, or any of those things which nations feel instinctively must be reserved for their own decision. Nor does any thinking man here propose obligatory arbitration in any case, save, possibly, in sundry petty matters where such arbitration would be a help to the ordinary administration of all governments; and, even as to these, they can be left out of the scheme if your Government seriously desires it.

The great thing is that there be a provision made for easily calling together a court of arbitration which shall be seen of all nations, indicate a sincere desire to promote peace, and, in some measure, relieve the various peoples of the fear which so heavily oppresses them all—the dread of an outburst of war at any moment.[1]

After restating the arguments used in the interview with Count Münster which have been noted, and after calling attention to the fact that only voluntary arbitration was proposed, leaving the Emperor free to decide in each case the questions to be submitted or withheld from the tribunal, Mr. White thus continued:

As you are aware, what is seriously proposed here now, in the way of arbitration, is not a tribunal constantly in session, but a system under which each of the signatory powers shall be free to choose, for a limited time, from an international court, say two or more judges who can go to The Hague if their services are required, but to be paid only while actually in session here; such payment to be made by the litigating parties.

As to the machinery, the plan is that there shall be a dignified body composed of the diplomatic representatives of the various signatory powers, to sit at The Hague, presided over by the Netherlands minister of foreign affairs, and to select and to control such secretaries and officers as may be necessary for the ordinary conduct of affairs.

Such council would receive notice from powers having differences with each other which are willing to submit the questions between them to a court, and would then give notice to the judges

[1] *Autobiography of Andrew D. White*, vol. 2, pp. 309-310.

selected by the parties. The whole of the present plan, except some subordinate features of little account, which can easily be stricken out, is voluntary. There is nothing whatever obligatory about it. Every signatory power is free to resort to such a tribunal or not, as it may think best. Surely a concession like this may well be made to the deep and wide sentiment throughout the world in favor of some possible means of settling controversies between nations other than by bloodshed.[1]

Expressing the hope that he was not going beyond his province, Dr. White ended the letter with the statement that he had laid the above facts and considerations before him as man to man, "not only in the interest of good relations between Germany and the United States, but of interests common to all the great nations of the earth,—of their common interest in giving something like satisfaction to a desire so earnest and wide-spread as that which has been shown in all parts of the world for arbitration."

The result of the conferences of Messrs. Zorn and Holls, in which each appears to have played an honorable and an influential part, is stated by Mr. White in the following passage of his diary under date of June 23d:[2]

> But the great matter of the day was the news, which has not yet been made public, that Prince Hohenlohe, the German chancellor, has come out strongly for the arbitration tribunal, and has sent instructions here accordingly. This is a great gain, and seems to remove one of the worst stumbling-blocks. But we will have to pay for this removal, probably, by giving up section 10 of the present plan, which includes a system of obligatory arbitration in various minor matters,—a system which would be of use to the world in many ways.[3]

The Imperial German Government yielded and accepted the proposed tribunal, misnamed the Permanent Court of Arbitration at

---

[1] *Autobiography of Andrew D. White*, vol. 2, pp. 312-313.

[2] Under date of June 21, Dr. White wrote as to the effect of his letter and the combined activity of Count Münster, himself, and their agents:

> Early in the morning received a report from Holls, who arrived from Hamburg late last night. His talks with Bülow and Prince Hohenlohe had been most encouraging. Bülow has sent to the Emperor my long private letter to himself, earnestly urging the acceptance by Germany of our plan of arbitration. Prince Hohenlohe seems to have entered most cordially into our ideas, giving Holls a card which would admit him to the Emperor, and telegraphing a request that his Majesty see him. But the Emperor was still upon his yacht, at sea, and Holls could stay no longer. Bülow is trying to make an appointment for him to meet the Emperor at the close of the week. (*Ibid.*, p. 318.)

[3] *Ibid.*, p. 321.

The Hague. In accordance with Mr. White's premonition, the Imperial Government insisted that the general treaty of arbitration should be dropped as the price of concession, and it was so dropped.

The record of Germany at the Second Hague Peace Conference in 1907 is so well known that it only needs to be called to the reader's attention. As, however, it is material to the present purpose to show that the attitude of the Imperial Government at the Second Conference, although outwardly friendly, was nevertheless inwardly hostile to arbitration, some observations of a general nature will be in place.

Thus, in his address on the subject of arbitration delivered on July 23, 1907, His Excellency Baron Marschall von Bieberstein, then Ambassador to Turkey and formerly Secretary of State for Foreign Affairs of the Empire and destined to be Imperial Ambassador to Great Britain, said:

> At the time of the First Peace Conference the German delegate declared in the name of his Government that the experience had up to that time in the field of arbitration was not of a nature to permit it to obligate itself at that time in favor of obligatory arbitration.
>
> Eight years have elapsed since that declaration and experience in the field of arbitration has grown to considerable degree. The question has also been the object of deep and prolonged study on the part of the German Government. As a result of this examination and impressed by the happy results produced by arbitration, the Government is now favorable, in principle, to the idea of obligatory arbitration.[1]

Encouraged by this attitude on the part of the Imperial German Government, the Conference settled down to the preparation of a draft. But every proposal of the Conference to incorporate in it the concrete principle, accepted by Germany in the abstract, met with the outspoken opposition of the German delegation. Thus, when the draft of the treaty had been prepared and accepted in committee—over Germany's protest, be it said—and submitted for its approval to the First Commission dealing with arbitration, the Baron stated, according to the official report of the proceedings,

> that, while he was an advocate of compulsory arbitration and applauded the arbitration treaty recently concluded between Italy and Argentina, the project of the committee was unacceptable for the reasons which he stated later; that there were two

[1] *Deuxième Conférence Internationale de la Paix, Actes et Documents,* tome ii, p. 286.

systems for putting compulsory arbitration into practice which he characterized as the individual system and the universal system; that according to the former each nation reserves the individual freedom of choosing the parties with whom it is to agree, the cases are defined and specified, those subjects which seem susceptible of arbitration are chosen and the details are adapted to those subjects; that with regard to disputes concerning the interpretation of treaties, the nations which have concluded them are the ones which insert therein the stipulations to arbitrate which may be done between two nations, between several, and even between all the nations of the world when the treaty is of a universal character as in the case of the Postal Union. He then stated that he would uphold and defend two theses:

1. The conclusion of a treaty of compulsory arbitration is only possible by applying the individual system, whereas in the universal system the word "compulsory" will be but an honorary title the use of which will not cover the numberless defects of the legal obligation inherent in the system.

2. Progress toward the peaceful solution of international disputes can only be realized by means of individual treaties, while a universal treaty, with its necessarily vague, elastic and general terms, will tend rather to engender fresh discord than to furnish a solution of the original difficulty.[1]

Many of the reasons advanced by His Excellency are weighty and worthy of consideration, but they need not be set forth at length or even summarized, as they were either born of the moment or advanced for the express purpose of defeating a universal, while confessing faith in the individual treaty, and we are in a position to test the sincerity of this profession by the refusal of Germany, after the adjournment of the Conference, to enter into an individual treaty of arbitration with the United States. But, before leaving this subject and taking up Secretary Root's experience with Germany in the matter of arbitration, the impression which Baron Marschall von Bieberstein's utterances in conference made upon his colleagues should not pass unnoticed. For this purpose a brief passage of the reply made by the Honorable Joseph H. Choate, Chairman of the American delegation, on behalf of the United States, is quoted:

> I should like to say a few words in reply to the important discourse delivered by the First Delegate of Germany, with all the deference and regard to which he is justly entitled because of the mighty empire that he represents, as well as for his own great merits and his unfailing personal devotion to the con-

[1] *Deuxième Conférence Internationale de la Paix, Actes et Documents,* tome II, p. 50.

sideration of the important subjects that have arisen before the Conference. But with all this deference, it seems to me that either there are, in this Conference, two First Delegates of Germany or, if it be only the one whom we have learned to recognize and honor, he speaks with two different voices. Baron Marschall is an ardent admirer of the abstract principle of arbitration and even of obligatory arbitration between those whom he chooses to act with, but when it comes to putting this idea into concrete form and practical effect he appears as our most formidable adversary. He appears like one who worships a divine image in the sky, but when it touches the earth, it loses all charm for him. He sees as in a dream a celestial apparition which excites his ardent devotion, but when he wakes and finds her by his side he turns to the wall, and will have nothing to do with her.[1]

Upon the adjournment of the Conference, Secretary Root decided to take the Imperial German Government at its word and, as Baron Marschall von Bieberstein, speaking in its behalf, had declared himself in favor of individual treaties with Nations of its choice, Mr. Root proposed that Germany should conclude with the United States a treaty of the kind which France and Great Britain had signed October 14, 1903, and because of its general acceptance was then, as it is now, the model of a general treaty of arbitration. It was one of a series of which Mr. Root negotiated twenty-five during the year succeeding the adjournment of the Second Conference. It bound the nations, in case of a failure to reach an agreement through diplomatic channels, to arbitrate disputes of a legal nature relating to the interpretation of treaties existing between the contracting parties, with the restriction, however, that they did not affect the vital interests, independence, or honor of the contracting States and that they did not concern the interests of third parties. The Imperial German Government refused to conclude such a treaty, although Mr. Root urged the matter.

Again, in 1913 and in 1914, Secretary Bryan earnestly besought the Imperial German Government to negotiate a treaty by which the contracting parties pledged their faith to submit all disputes between them to a Commission of Inquiry, to be composed of five members, which Commission would have a year within which to examine and report upon any dispute submitted by the parties or by one or the other of them, during which period each party bound itself not to resort to force or a hostile action against the other.

The Imperial German Ambassador, as was the case with Baron

[1] *Deuxième Conférence Internationale de la Paix, Actes et Documents,* tome II, p. 72.

Marschall von Bieberstein, accepted in principle but refused to put the principle in concrete and binding form. Yet, this treaty would have been but one of thirty negotiated by Secretary Bryan in the course of 1913-14, and would have been similar to the treaties concluded with Great Britain and France after the outbreak of the war of 1914. The reason for this refusal seems to be that the Imperial German Government was as unwilling in 1914, as in 1899 and in 1907, to tie its hands by arbitration, and the language used by the Imperial Secretary of State in 1914 to the British Ambassador at Berlin strangely recalls the language of Count Münster to Ambassador White at The Hague.

In an interview of August 1, 1914, between Herr von Jagow, Imperial German Secretary of State, and Sir Edward Goschen, British Ambassador at Berlin, the latter communicated the substance of Sir Edward Grey's telegram of that date informing him of "the readiness of Austria to discuss with Russia and the readiness of Austria to accept a basis of mediation."[1]

According to the British Ambassador's report, Herr von Jagow said "that Austria's readiness to discuss was the result of German influence at Vienna, and, had not Russia mobilized against Germany, all would have been well. But Russia, by abstaining from answering Germany's demand that she should demobilize, had caused Germany to mobilize also. Russia had said that her mobilization did not necessarily imply war, and that she could perfectly well remain mobilized for months without making war. This was not the case with Germany. She had the speed and Russia had the numbers, and the safety of the German Empire forbade that Germany should allow Russia time to bring up masses of troops from all parts of her wide dominions."[2] And in the interview of August 4th, as reported by the British Ambassador, between the Imperial German Secretary of State and the Ambassador, the latter asked in the name of his Government whether "the Imperial Government would refrain from violating Belgian neutrality. Herr von Jagow at once replied that he was very sorry to say that his answer must be 'No,' as, in consequence of the German troops having crossed the frontier that morning, Belgian neutrality had been already violated. Herr von Jagow again went into the reasons why the Imperial Government had

---

[1] Sir Edward Grey to Sir Edward Goschen, British Ambassador at Berlin, *British Blue Book*, No. 1, d. No. 131; *Diplomatic Documents Relating to the Outbreak of the European War*, p. 988.

[2] Sir Edward Goschen, British Ambassador at Berlin, to Sir Edward Grey, *British Blue Book*, No. 1, d. No. 138; *ibid.*, p. 993.

been obliged to take this step, namely, that they had to advance into France by the quickest and easiest way, so as to be able to get well ahead with their operations and endeavor to strike some decisive blow as early as possible. It was a matter of life and death for them, as if they had gone by the more southern route they could not have hoped, in view of the paucity of roads and the strength of the fortresses, to have got through without formidable opposition entailing great loss of time. This loss of time would have meant time gained by the Russians for bringing up their troops to the German frontier. Rapidity of action was the great German asset, while that of Russia was an inexhaustible supply of troops."[1]

In a remarkable article entitled "Military Strategy v. Diplomacy," written by Mr. Munroe Smith, professor of jurisprudence in Columbia University in the City of New York and a doctor of jurisprudence of the University of Göttingen, thus comments upon the views of Count von Münster and Herr von Jagow and the practice of the Imperial German Government as stated by the latter in 1914:

> There is, however, a far broader aspect to the problem. Of all means which civilization has provided to avert war, negotiation is the most important. Direct negotiation may be and often is supplemented by the friendly offices of nations not immediately concerned and by offers of mediation; but these are but extensions of negotiation. Arbitration is a potent agency for the peaceful settlement of controversies, but arbitration cannot be set in motion without negotiation. For negotiation time is essential. In the interest of the peace of the world, therefore, it is of the highest importance that the political heads of every state should be ever on their guard against the attempts of their military advisers to convince them that immediate attack is necessary. It is usually declared to be a matter of life or death. To the nation primarily concerned it is almost always, in fact, only a matter of greater or less chance of initial success. To peace, however, it is always a matter of death.[2]

It is therefore a fact, which may indeed be explained but which cannot be controverted, that the Imperial German Government has stood aloof from arbitration, that it has rarely obligated itself to apply this form of settlement; that, in the two Hague Peace Conferences, its delegates opposed projects of arbitration with such energy

---

[1] Sir Edward Goschen, British Ambassador at Berlin, to Sir Edward Grey, August 8, 1914, *British Blue Book*, No. 1, d. No. 160; *Diplomatic Documents Relating to the Outbreak of the European War*, p. 1006.
[2] *Political Science Quarterly*, March, 1915, vol. 30, No. 1, pp. 81-82.

and vigor that they were able to check for the moment a movement which they could not wholly dam. But there are some things which physical power cannot accomplish, and opposition to arbitration as a form of peaceful settlement is as futile as opposition to the Pythagorean theorem, which Sydney Smith once wittily dared Lord Hawksbury, when leader of the Tory Majority in Parliament, to repeal by statute.

Section 3. The "Frye" Case

If the United States should be criticised, as a partisan of arbitration, and indeed as its sponsor in the modern world, for not offering to arbitrate its disputes with Germany, notwithstanding Germany's known repugnance to arbitration, it is proper to suggest that something more than an offer and an agreement to arbitrate are required. The given word must be kept, and it must be said with regret that the attitude of the Imperial German Government towards solemn international agreements during the present war, not to speak of the past, leaves something to be desired, and that, in plain terms, the United States would have had no assurance, after a violation of its pledged word by Germany on the plea of necessity in the international agreements concerning Luxemburg and Belgium, that the Imperial Government would keep its agreement to arbitrate, that it would refrain from the commission of the unlawful acts submitted to arbitration, until the question of right or wrong should be determined by the award of an arbitral tribunal, that it would execute the award of that tribunal after it had been rendered if the award were contrary to its contentions, and that it would not, pleading necessity or vital interests, self-preservation or self-defense, continue the conduct complained of until the close of the war, leaving the entire matter to be patched up by the payment of an indemnity to compensate American interests for the losses which they had incurred either because of Germany's refusal to abide by the award or because of its interpretation of the award in a way inconsistent with the interpretation put upon it by the United States. During the period of its neutrality, the United States intimated that it would not make a treaty of arbitration concerning the loss of life, for it was unwilling to arbitrate the right of a foreign Nation to put to death American citizens, although, if the United States had had a treaty of arbitration with the Imperial Government such as it has with Great Britain and France, which Germany was requested to negotiate but would not, or if it had had a treaty providing for a Commission of Inquiry similar to treaties of this kind with Great Britain and France, which Germany was urged to conclude but did not, the United States would have been forced to arbitrate Germany's contentions, or submit them to investigation and report at Germany's request unless the United States was prepared to consider solemn compacts as "scraps of paper."

But it is difficult to see, in view of the whole situation, how the United States could have been compelled, although it might have been justified, in submitting to arbitration or to a Commission of Inquiry at the request of the Imperial Government all of its outstanding differences without an existing agreement to do so; but it would assuredly not have been justified in so doing unless the Imperial Government would have agreed to stop, during the arbitral proceedings, its conduct whereof complaint was made. We know, however, that Germany was unwilling, even when the question of peace and war hung in the balance, to suspend its actions, although the United States expressed its willingness to consider Germany's proposals after the severing of diplomatic relations if, during the interval of negotiations, the actions complained of should be renounced.[1]

But we do not need to speculate as to what the attitude or conduct of Germany would have been in the case of an offer and an acceptance by one or the other country to submit to arbitration the disputes which had arisen out of the war, because we have in the sinking and in the arbitration of *The William P. Frye* a concrete case.

On January 27, 1915, *The William P. Frye,* a steel sailing vessel owned by American citizens, and navigating under the American flag, carrying a cargo of 186,950 bushels of wheat from the port of Seattle in the State of Washington to Queenstown, Falmouth, or Plymouth for orders, was encountered in the South Atlantic on the high seas by

---

[1] Under date of February 12, 1917, Secretary Lansing thus addressed Paul Ritter, Minister for Switzerland, who was in charge of the interests of Germany in the United States after the rupture of diplomatic relations:

> I am requested by the President to say to you, in acknowledging the memorandum which you were kind enough to send me on the 11th instant, that the Government of the United States would gladly discuss with the German Government any questions it might propose for discussion were it to withdraw its proclamation of the 31st of January, in which, suddenly and without previous intimation of any kind, it cancelled the assurances which it had given this Government on the 4th of May last, but that it does not feel that it can enter into any discussion with the German Government concerning the policy of submarine warfare against neutrals which it is now pursuing unless and until the German Government renews its assurances of the 4th of May and acts upon the assurance. (Official text published by the Department of State.)

the *Prinz Eitel Friedrich*, an auxiliary cruiser of the Imperial German Navy, which compelled the *Frye* to stop and sent on board an armed boarding party which took possession of the vessel. After an examination of the ship's papers, the commander of the cruiser directed that the cargo be thrown overboard, but subsequently decided to destroy the vessel, and on the following morning, by his order, the *Frye* was sunk. On April 3, 1915, the United States presented a claim for the value of the ship and the damages involved in its destruction, amounting to $228,059.54. No claim was made for the cargo, which before the destruction had apparently ceased to be American property. The Imperial German Government promptly replied on the following day, assuming liability for the claim.[1]

Without going into details, it is sufficient to state for present purposes that Article 13 of the treaty of 1799, revived by the treaty of 1828, provides that "in the case supposed of a vessel stopped for articles of contraband, if the master of the vessel stopped will deliver out the goods supposed to be of contraband nature, he shall be admitted to do it, and the vessel shall not in that case be carried into any port, nor further detained, but shall be allowed to proceed on her voyage."

The Imperial German Government maintained that, because of the provisions of the Declaration of London permitting the sinking of neutral prizes, it could sink the *Frye*, but because of the provisions of the treaty of 1799, carried over by the treaty of 1828, it would have to pay damages for the destruction of the vessel. The United States, on the other hand, maintained that the Declaration of London was not binding upon it, not having been ratified by any of the signatories, that therefore it was not international law, and that the obligation of the treaty allowing an American vessel to pursue its course upon an offer to deliver out its cargo, was not satisfied by a willingness to pay damages for the sinking of the vessel.

The German Government submitted the case to its prize court at Hamburg, which justified the sinking of the vessel on principles of international law, admitting however the validity of the Prussian Treaty, but it was unable to assess damages, because the interested parties failed to appear, or to submit the necessary data.[2] The Im-

---

[1] Official text, *American Journal of International Law*, Special Supplement, July, 1915, pp. 180-193.

[2] "The Court found by its judgment of the 10th instant (July 10, 1915) that the cargo of the American vessel, *William P. Frye*, was contraband, that the vessel could not be carried into port, and that the sinking was therefore justified; at the same time the Court expressly recognized the validity of the Prussian-American treaty stipulations severally mentioned for the relations

perial German Government therefore suggested, instead of diplomatic negotiations, that each Government designate an expert, that the two should jointly fix the amount of indemnity of the vessel and the amount of any American property that might have been destroyed with it, under reservation, that such payment would not constitute a satisfaction for the violation of American rights "but a duty or policy of this Government founded on the existing treaty stipulations." The Imperial Government further proposed that, if this method of settlement should prove unsatisfactory to the United States, it would submit the interpretation of the treaties to the tribunal at The Hague, pursuant to Article 38 of The Hague Convention for the pacific settlement of international disputes. The United States agreed on August 10, 1916, to the appointment of experts to determine the amount of the indemnity, and accepted the condition upon which it would be paid, provided that "the acceptance of such payment should likewise be understood to be without prejudice to the contention of the Government of the United States that the sinking of the *Frye* was without legal justification, and provided also that an arrangement can be agreed upon for the immediate submission to arbitration of the question of legal justification in so far as it involves the interpretation of existing treaty of stipulations."[1]

The facts were admitted. The liability of Germany to pay indemnity was likewise admitted. The amount in dispute was trifling and was as nothing to the real issue between the two Governments, namely, the right of Germany to sink American vessels in the teeth of the treaties with Prussia invoked by the United States.

In order to test the good faith of the German Government in this controversy and the good faith that might be expected in other matters, it is only necessary to consider somewhat in detail various phases of the *Frye* case.

As to the question of an umpire. The United States proposed that an umpire should be selected in order to pass upon the question of the indemnity if the experts should fail to agree, but this Germany rejected on the ground that "in the cases of the ascertainment of damages hitherto arranged between the German Government and a neutral Government from similar causes, the experts named by the

between the German Empire and America, so that the sinking of the ship and cargo, so far as American property, makes the German Empire liable for indemnity. The prize court was unable to fix the indemnity itself, since it had no data before it, failing the receipt of the necessary detail from the parties interested." (Official text, *American Journal of International Law*, Special Supplement, July, 1915, pp. 190-191.)

[1] *Ibid.*, p. 192.

two parties have always reached an agreement as to the amount of the damage without difficulty; should it not be possible, however, to reach an agreement on some point, it could probably be settled by diplomatic negotiation."[1] That is to say, Germany rejected the proposal of the United States that the nature and amount of the indemnity should be arranged through diplomatic channels, yet it proposed, after the delay of appointing experts, to resort to diplomatic channels, should the experts fail to agree. In reply to Germany's objection to an umpire, the United States waived the point, but insisted that "in agreeing to this arrangement it should be understood in advance that in case the amount of indemnity is not settled by the joint commission of experts or by diplomatic negotiation, the question will then be referred to an umpire if that is desired by the Government of the United States."[2]

To this note of October 12, 1915, Germany replied in a note of November 29, 1915, stating that "the consultation of an umpire would depend materially upon whether the differences of opinion between the two experts pertained to questions of principle or merely to the appraisement of certain articles. The consultation of an umpire could only be considered at all in the case of appraisements of this nature."[3]

As to the meeting place of the commission of experts. The United States, in its note of October 12, proposed "that its meetings should be held in the United States because . . . any evidence which the German Government may wish to have produced is more accessible and can more conveniently be examined there than elsewhere."

To this proposal Germany thus replied on November 29th:

> The German Government regrets that it cannot comply with the wish of the American Government to have the experts meet in Washington, since the expert nominated by it, Dr. Greve, of Bremen, director of the North German Lloyd, is unable to get away from here, and furthermore would be exposed to the danger of capture during a voyage to America in consequence of the conduct of maritime war by England contrary to international law. Should the American expert likewise be unable to get away, the two experts might perhaps get in touch with each other by correspondence.
>
> Should the American Government insist on its demands for

---

[1] German note of September 19, 1915; official text, *American Journal of International Law*, Special Supplement, October, 1916, p. 345.

[2] American note of October 12, 1915; official text, *American Journal of International Law*, Special Supplement, October, 1916, p. 347.

[3] *Ibid.*, p. 350.

the meeting of the experts at Washington or the early choice of an umpire, the only alternative would be to arrange the fixing of damages by diplomatic negotiation. In such an event the German Government begs to await the transmission of a statement of particulars of the various claims for damages accompanied by the necessary proofs.[1]

Here again the German Government, having rejected the settlement by diplomatic negotiation, reverts to this method after the interposition of delay.

As to arbitration. The United States agreed to Germany's request that the negotiations concerning the form of the agreement of arbitration be conducted in Berlin upon a draft to be submitted by Germany, but suggested that the arbitration should be by the summary procedure provided by the revised convention for the pacific settlement of international disputes, rejecting the oral in favor of written proceedings. To this Germany objected on the ground that "the summary procedure is naturally intended only for differences of opinion of inferior importance, whereas the German Government attaches very particular importance to the interpretation of the Prussian-American treaties which have existed for over 100 years."[2]

Finally, as to the American proposal for the conduct of naval operations pending the award. To this proposal the Imperial German Government stated in its note of September 19, 1915, that "it has issued orders to the German naval forces not to destroy American merchantmen which have loaded conditional contraband, even when the conditions of international law are present, but to permit them to continue their voyage unhindered if it is not possible to take them into port. On the other hand, it must reserve to itself the right to destroy vessels carrying absolute contraband wherever such destruction is permissible according to the provisions of the Declaration of London."[3]

In view of the statement repeatedly made in the course of this narrative, that the Declaration of London was not an international agreement and not binding between Germany and the United States, it is unnecessary to observe that it could not be invoked to supersede the treaty between Prussia and the United States. To this statement, Secretary Lansing thus replied in his note of October 12, 1915:

[1] Official text, *American Journal of International Law*, Special Supplement, October, 1916, p. 350.
[2] *Ibid.*, pp. 350-351.
[3] *Ibid.*, p. 346.

> Without admitting that the Declaration of London is in force, and on the understanding that the requirement in Article 50 of the Declaration that "before the vessel is destroyed all persons on board must be placed in safety" is not satisfied by merely giving them an opportunity to escape in lifeboats, the Government of the United States is willing, pending the arbitral award in this case, to accept the Declaration of London as the rule governing the conduct of the German Government in relation to the treatment of American vessels carrying cargoes of absolute contraband.[1]

And to this concession, for such it was, the Imperial German Government replied as follows on November 29, 1915:

> The German Government quite shares the view of the American Government that all possible care must be taken for the security of the crew and passengers of a vessel to be sunk. Consequently, the persons found on board of a vessel may not be ordered into her lifeboats except when the general conditions, that is to say, the weather, the condition of the sea, and the neighborhood of the coasts afford absolute certainty that the boats will reach the nearest port. For the rest the German Government begs to point out that in cases where German naval forces have sunk neutral vessels for carrying contraband, no loss of life has yet occurred.[2]

Here the *Frye* case apparently ended, for no further correspondence has been issued by either Government concerning it. The net result of it all seems to be that the rights and duties of the United States and of Germany in regard to this matter were defined by the treaty of 1828 between Prussia and the United States reviving Article 13 of the treaty of 1799; that notwithstanding the express provision of this treaty that a ship carrying material supposed to be contraband should continue on its voyage unmolested, upon an offer to deliver out the articles supposed to be contraband, the Imperial German Government claimed the right to destroy the vessel and to satisfy the treaty by the payment of damages; that the matter of damages was to be settled not through diplomatic channels but by a commission of two experts; that if the experts disagreed an umpire was to be appointed, provided he passed merely upon the question of assessment; that questions of principle should be adjusted through diplomatic channels; that the difference concerning the interpreta-

---

[1] Official text, *American Journal of International Law*, Special Supplement, October, 1916, p. 348.
[2] *Ibid.*, p. 351.

tion of the treaty between the two governments should be submitted to arbitration; that the discussion of the form of arbitration should take place in Berlin and that it should be according to Article 38 of the pacific settlement convention; and that, pending the award, a *modus vivendi* should be adopted which would prevent the recurrence of the incident according to a form of procedure consistent with the Declaration of London but inconsistent with the treaty between Prussia and the United States.

The state of mind in which the Imperial German Government approach the settlement of the *Frye* case may be judged by the fact that it refused the request of the American Ambassador, acting under instructions from the Department of State, to furnish a copy of the judgment delivered by the prize court at Hamburg in that case;[1] and the futility of an attempt to settle the disputes between the United States and Germany by arbitration is made apparent by the action of the Imperial German Government, which not only refused to furnish a copy of the decision of its prize court—which might have aided the United States in the presentation of its claim—but also to carry out the terms of a present agreement to arbitrate the case of *The William P. Frye*.

Instead of concluding from this case the extent to which the pledged word of the Imperial German Government can be accepted, some extracts from documents bearing upon a question previously discussed will be quoted.

In July, 1870, when it became known that the Prince of Hohenzollern had been offered and had accepted the throne of Spain, the French Chargé d'Affaires inquired of the Prussian Foreign Office, where he was told that the Prussian Government knew absolutely nothing about the matter (ignorait absolument cette affaire).

This statement was subsequently confirmed by a circular to the Prussian diplomatic agents containing the following assurance:

> The North-German Government declared that the matter had nothing to do with Prussia. . . . The Prussian Government has always considered and treated this affair as one in which Spain and the selected candidate are alone concerned, as the respect due to the rights and independence of the Spanish people naturally requires.[2]

The statement contained in this circular was further confirmed by

[1] MSS., Department of State.
[2] *British and Foreign State Papers*, vol. 60, pp. 796, 897, 907, 928. See letter of J. W. Headlam, *The Times* (London), August 3, 1917.

the King of Prussia himself, who said in a conversation to Benedetti, the French Ambassador:

> The negotiations opened on the subject had been pursued between the Spanish Government and the Prince Hohenzollern; the Prussian Government has not only been unconnected with them, it has been ignorant of them (Le gouvernement prussien n'y est pas seulement resté étranger, il les a ignorées). The King himself has avoided associating himself with them. . . . The King has been informed of the determination of the Prince; the King has (in this matter) neither called together nor consulted the Council of Ministers; the Prussian Government could not be interpellated on a matter which it has not known and with which it had no more to do than any other European Cabinet.[1]

In 1897 the King of Roumania, the brother of Prince Leopold of Hohenzollern, who had been offered and had refused the Spanish throne, gave the full details of the transaction, showing that the Prussian Government, instead of being ignorant of the candidacy, had proposed it, supported it, and forced it upon the Hohenzollern prince, and that the candidacy had been formally approved at a meeting of the Prussian Ministers specially called to consider the matter.

The following extracts from the memoirs of King Charles of Roumania, written in German and published in Germany in 1897, are quoted without comment:

> Count Bismarck is pleading with great warmth for the acceptance of the throne by the hereditary prince: in a memorial to King William he emphasizes the great importance, which the calling of the Prince of Hohenzollern to the Spanish throne would have for Germany; it would be of incalculable political value to have a friendly country in the rear of France.[2]

Prince Karl Anton and his son Leopold went to Berlin to confer with the authorities as to the candidacy of the young man and on March 20, 1870, that is, five days after the event, he thus wrote to his son Karl in Roumania, who was naturally interested in the fortunes of the family and of the younger brother:

> On the fifteenth there was a very important and interesting consultation here, under the presidency of the king, and at which the crown prince, both of us [Prince Karl Anton, the

---

[1] Benedetti, *Ma Mission en Prusse*, 2d ed. (1871), p. 331.
[2] *Aus dem Leben König Karls von Rumänien, Aufzeichnungen eines Augenzeugen* (Stuttgart, 1897, 2 vols.), vol. 2, p. 68.

father, and Leopold, the son], Bismarck, Roon, Moltke, Schleinitz, Thile, and Delbrück were present. The unanimous decision of these advisers was in favor of acceptance, as the patriotic duty of a Prussian.[1]

Count Bismarck has repeatedly and most decisively declared that the acceptance of the Spanish crown by one of the princes of Hohenzollern was a political necessity.[2]

[1] *Aus dem Leben König Karls von Rumänien, Aufzeichnungen eines Augenzeugen* (Stuttgart, 1897, 2 vols.), vol. 2, p. 72.
[2] *Ibid.*, p. 93.

CHAPTER XIX

THE FREEDOM OF THE SEAS

The President, in his address of April 2, 1917, stated that Germany was running amuck, and in view of this fact, which was only too true, the United States could not very well appear before posterity as the champion of the freedom of the seas if it stood aside and allowed the Imperial German Government to continue to run amuck on the high seas. As President Wilson had advocated the freedom of the seas when his country was neutral—and it is to be hoped that he will stand for it as steadfastly when his country is belligerent—and as the Imperial German Government has repeatedly proclaimed the freedom of the seas and has declared in the official correspondence with the United States that its actions are conceived and executed in behalf of the freedom of the seas, it becomes material to consider in what sense this phrase can be used to condemn and to sustain one and the same action.

It is well to define the term "high seas" in order that we may have a firm foundation upon which to build; otherwise, with the best of intentions, we are liable to fall into the confusion which we criticise in others; and it seems peculiarly appropriate, where interests are involved and passions aroused, to leave the atmosphere of the chancelleries and to take refuge in the cool and the calm of courts of justice. For this reason, a decision of a court of justice will be invoked.

The circumstances surrounding the case are interesting in themselves and calculated to show that the Court was obliged, by the very terms of the act giving it jurisdiction, to define the "high seas" in the sense in which that phrase is used in international law. The origin of the Court was peculiarly international. The United States alleged that Great Britain had been unneutral in the American Civil War, and that, because of Great Britain's failure to comply with the requirements of neutrality, especially in the matter of Confederate cruisers, built, fitted out, and equipped in Great Britain and permitted to make of British ports the base of hostile operations, the United States and its citizens had suffered damage. As the result of a bitter controversy, the questions involved were submitted to arbitration by a treaty between the two countries, concluded on May 8, 1871, and commonly called the Treaty of Washington.

The first article states in the portion material to the matter in hand that differences existed between the two Governments growing out of acts committed by various Confederate vessels, of which *The Alabama* was the chief; that the British Government in a "friendly spirit" expressed regret for the escape "under whatever circumstances" of *The Alabama* and other vessels from British ports and for the depredations committed by those vessels; that to adjust those differences and speedily to settle all claims growing out of acts committed by *The Alabama* and other vessels, generally known as the *Alabama* Claims, the United States and Great Britain agreed to refer such claims to a tribunal of arbitration composed of five arbitrators, one to be appointed by the United States, one by Great Britain, one by Italy, one by Switzerland, and one by Brazil. The second article provided that the arbitrators were to meet at Geneva, and, therefore, the tribunal and the award are known respectively as the Geneva Tribunal and the Geneva Award. The sixth article provided that the arbitrators should be governed by three rules generally known as the three rules of Washington,[1] "which are agreed upon by the high contracting parties as rules to be taken as applicable to the case, and by such principles of international law not inconsistent therewith as the arbitrators shall determine to have been applicable to the case."

Article 7 provided, among other things, that the tribunal should consider each of the cases separately in accordance with the three rules and the principles of international law not inconsistent with them, and that it should, if it found Great Britain at fault and if it thought

---

[1] The following is the text of the three rules of Washington:

A neutral Government is bound—
First, to use due diligence to prevent the fitting out, arming, or equipping, within its jurisdiction, of any vessel which it has reasonable ground to believe is intended to cruise or to carry on war against a Power with which it is at peace; and also to use like diligence to prevent the departure from its jurisdiction of any vessel intended to cruise or carry on war as above, such vessel having been specially adapted, in whole or in part, within such jurisdiction, to warlike use.

Secondly, not to permit or suffer either belligerent to make use of its ports or waters as the base of naval operations against the other, or for the purpose of the renewal or augmentation of military supplies or arms, or the recruitment of men.

Thirdly, to exercise due diligence in its own ports and waters, and, as to all persons within its jurisdiction, to prevent any violation of the foregoing obligations and duties. (Malloy, *Treaties, etc., between the United States and Foreign Powers*, vol. 1, p. 703.)

it proper, award a sum in gross to be paid by Great Britain to the United States for all the claims referred to it.

It is sufficient for present purposes to state that the tribunal met at Geneva in 1872, that it decided that in some respects the conduct of Great Britain was in conflict with the three rules of Washington or the principles of international law not inconsistent therewith and applicable to the case, and that "The tribunal," to quote the language of the award, "making use of the authority conferred upon it by Article VII [1] of the said treaty, by a majority of four voices to one awards to the United States a sum of $15,500,000 in gold as the indemnity to be paid by Great Britain to the United States, for the satisfaction of all the claims referred to the consideration of the tribunal, conformably to the provisions contained in Article VII of the aforesaid treaty." Great Britain paid and the United States accepted this award in full satisfaction of the claims submitted to arbitration and, assuming liability to satisfy the individual claimants out of this fund, created a so-called Alabama Court of Claims by an Act of Congress of June 23, 1874, to which the claimants were to present their claims, with the necessary proofs, in order that they might be judicially passed upon and determined, and the amounts found justly due them paid out of the fund.

An Alabama Court of Claims was created by Act of Congress of June 5, 1882, to consider two classes of the so-called Alabama claims, and in Section 5 of the act it is stated:

> That the first class shall be for claims directly resulting from damage done on the high seas by Confederate cruisers during the late rebellion, including vessels and cargoes attacked on the high seas, although the loss or damage occurred within four miles of the shore . . .[2]

It will be observed that each of these tribunals was of limited jurisdiction, and that the second Court of Alabama Claims was limited in its jurisdiction to "claims directly resulting from damage done upon the high seas." It was necessary, therefore, for the judges composing it to determine the sense in which the phrase "high seas" was used. The question, therefore, met the judges of the Court upon the threshold and they were forced to decide it before assuming jurisdiction of any claim; for if the damage did not occur upon the high seas, the judgment or award of the Court would be null and void and without effect.

[1] Malloy, *Treaties, etc., between the United States and Foreign Powers*, p. 703.
[2] 22 Statutes at Large, p. 98.

The case to which reference has been made is that of *Rich v. The United States,* decided in 1884 by the Second Court of Alabama Claims and is of importance as it discusses in principle, unembarrassed by legislative act or judicial decision, the meaning to be ascribed to the term "high seas" standing alone and without qualifying expression. To the English-speaking peoples it has the additional advantage of having been considered by counsel for government and counsel for claimants as a case of first impression, and it was argued and decided as such. Because of these two facts, and because also of its importance to the subject at hand, the opinion in this case, which is not so well known as it deserves to be, will be laid under requisition. The facts of the case were simple and are thus stated by Judge Harlan, who delivered the opinion of the Court:

> The claimants in this case represent that they were owners of one-fourth part of the American ship *John H. Jarvis,* and its cargo, captured May 16, 1861, on the high seas, near the mouth of the Mississippi river, by the Confederate cruiser *Music,* and pray judgment for the value of their said interest in the property so lost to them.[1]

On the question of the meaning to be given to the phrase "high seas" contained in the statute, and the reasons which led the Court to its conclusion as to the meaning of the phrase, Judge Harlan said, on behalf of the Court:

> The decision of the question thus raised must depend on the meaning which Congress intended should be given by the Court to the phrase or compound word "high-seas," as used in this statute.[2]

After stating that in admiralty law the statutes interpret the high seas as meaning "waters of the ocean from shore to shore to low-water mark," the learned judge thus continued his examination:

> On account of the imperfection of human language the meaning of words must be construed by the subject-matter to which they apply. "High seas" is not an exception. As used in literature, and by writers on elementary law, it does not always mean the waters of the ocean from shore to shore [as in the case of admiralty proceedings].
>
> It is a settled rule of interpretation, also, that words found

[1] *Opinions of the Court of Commissioners of Alabama Claims,* November, 1884. Compiled by J. F. Manning. (Boston, Smith and Porter, 1884), p. 48.
[2] *Ibid.,* p. 50.

in a statute should retain their usual meaning, if that is practicable, within the meaning of the act. It may therefore be proper to endeavor to ascertain the usual literal meaning of this term, composed as it is of two primary words—the descriptive adjective "high," and the substantive "seas."

"Sea," as originally used, meant a body of water smaller than the ocean, usually connected with the ocean, but sometimes a body of water entirely surrounded by land. But its meaning has gradually changed, as used by the English-speaking people, until, it has come to mean the ocean more frequently than a smaller inland body of water. And, in fact, the two words, "ocean" and "sea," or "seas," are used interchangeably as synonymous. "Sea," being the more modest word, is probably more frequently used in descriptive and narrative language, and "ocean" preferred when the heroic style of expression is adopted. Hence, "sea-shore" now usually means the ocean shore; "at sea" out on the ocean; "seaman," one who navigates the ocean as well as interior waters; so that "sea" or "seas," as now generally used, means the open waters of the ocean from shore to shore; therefore the term "high-seas" must mean, literally, the waters of the ocean in some different sense, indicated by the prefix "high," which was probably adopted as descriptive of the apparent elevation of its surface towards the horizon when looked at from the shore. And the term "high-seas" is so used in descriptive geography and narrative as meaning the sea at a distance from the shore, and interchangeable with the term "deep seas."[1]

After appealing to the lexicographer as to the meaning of the word "high" and finding it to mean "elevated from any starting point for measurement, as a line or surface," and coming to the conclusion that the "high seas," therefore, meant the sea from beyond a given line, the Court made the following application of the definition:

> For the purpose of defining the territorial jurisdiction of a nation, the starting point is one marine league, or about four statute English miles from the shore. Hence the words "high seas," when used with such reference, must mean the waters of the ocean exterior to such boundary; and the most casual examination of standard works on international law will furnish abundant proof that it is constantly so used in defining the rights and duties of neutrals and belligerents on the "high-seas" in contradistinction to their rights, duties, and privileges within a marine league of a neutral shore.[2]

The Court next appealed to the international lawyer, choosing for this purpose Chancellor Kent, and wisely, because he was not only a

[1] Manning, *Opinions, Court of Commissioners of Alabama Claims*, November, 1884, pp. 50-51.
[2] *Ibid.*, p. 51.

lawyer by profession and one of the glories of the American bench, but also the author of a brief survey of the law of Nations which competent authorities have been pleased to consider as the best in the language.[1] To the appeal Kent responded that "high seas" meant "the ocean without the boundary of any country; also the uninclosed waters of the ocean which are without the limits of the low-water mark." Armed with the authority of the lexicographer and of the international lawyer, the Court proceeded.

> And this double meaning appears to be in harmony with the more modern use of the term; that is to say, it means either the waters of the ocean from shore to shore, or the waters of the ocean bounded by a line drawn one marine league from the shore, that being the territorial jurisdictional boundary of a nation, depending on the subject-matter to which it is applied. In defining the jurisdiction of admiralty courts "high-seas" means the waters of the ocean from shore to shore at low-water mark. In defining the rights and duties and privileges of neutrals and belligerents "high-seas" means the ocean exterior to the league limit from the shore.[2]

After having reached this conclusion, based upon the nature of the thing and the views of Nations as drawn from their practice, the learned judge asked in what sense the Congress used the term "in the statute" and correctly answered the question just put by stating that

> that must be determined from a consideration of the language used and the subject-matter treated.

The Court first considered the subject which the legislature had in mind and on this point the judge said:

> The subject referred to is the destruction of American merchant ships and cargoes on the high-seas by Confederate cruisers.

[1] Thus Sir William Vernon Harcourt said in the Letters which that distinguished lawyer and statesman contributed under the pseudonym *Historicus* to the *London Times*:

> "The lectures of Chancellor Kent at the commencement of the Commentaries are a perfect specimen of judicial exposition. The 'Elements of International Law,' by Mr. Wheaton, slight as they are, nevertheless present, on the whole, next to that of Kent, the best general attempt which has yet been made at a discussion of these questions." And again: "Permit me, while I am warning your readers against false lights, to refer them to a guide who will never lead them astray—to the greatest jurist whom this age has produced—I mean the American Chancellor Kent. Of his writings it may safely be said that they are never wrong." (*Letters of Historicus on Some Questions of International Law;* London; Macmillan, 1863, p. 129.)

[2] Manning, *Opinions, Court of Commissioners of Alabama Claims*, November, 1881, pp. 51-52.

The so-called Confederate States had been recognized by the leading States of Europe as belligerents, which enabled their armed cruisers to make legal captures on the high-seas, but not within the jurisdictional waters of any neutral State. As to them the "high-seas" meant the waters of the ocean outside the marine league limit from the shore. Of course, captures thus made within the marine league of the shore at low-water mark of the other belligerents were equally lawful, and so would have been such captures made between low-water mark and high-water mark, or on the internal waters of the other belligerent, and, likewise in this case, enemies' property captured within the marine league of the shores and on the internal waters of the Confederate States. And as between the two belligerent captures made on land were equally lawful with captures made on the water. Therefore, the question of the terminal boundaries of the "high-seas," as intended by Congress in this act, cannot be settled by the question of the legality of the capture.[1]

Inasmuch as this line of approach was not decisive, the Court looked to the facts of the case and attendant circumstances. Thus:

> But the Court may derive some aid in this respect from the consideration of other facts and circumstances relating to the subject-matter. Within the marine league from a neutral shore the property of citizens of the United States was under the protection of the neutral government, and not legally subject to capture by the belligerent cruisers, and within the marine league of the shore of the United States and on its interior waters it was under the protection of the guns, shore batteries, harbor defenses, and land forces of the United States, and consequently less liable to capture by belligerent ships of the public enemy; and the entrance of merchant ships for the purpose of trade into the harbors and on the interior waters of the Confederate States had been prohibited by the United States before the sailing of any Confederate cruiser. Hence the presence of a merchant ship of the United States within the marine league of the Confederate coast was presumably illegal, being in defiance of the laws of its sovereign.
>
> From this condition of facts the conclusion may safely be drawn by the Court that Congress probably intended to distinguish between the class of sufferers whose property was destroyed within a marine league and also on the interior waters of the United States and of the Confederate States, to exclude them from the beneficial provisions of this statute, and to provide for them, if deemed advisable, by future legislation.[2]

[1] Manning, *Opinions, Court of Commissioners of Alabama Claims*, November, 1884, p. 53.
[2] *Ibid.*, pp. 53-54.

The learned judge then took up the language of the act, saying on this point:

> In this view of the language of the statute, "That the first class shall be for claims directly resulting from damage done on the high-seas by Confederate cruisers during the late rebellion, including vessels and cargoes attacked on the high-seas, although the loss or damage occurred within four miles of the shore," is clear and explicit—free from all ambiguity—nothing appearing as surplusage or as redundancy, and nothing in conflict with any other part of the statute. And in this view the enlarging clause, "including vessels and cargoes attacked on the high-seas, although the loss or damage occurred within four miles of the shore," does increase the scope of the beneficial provisions of the act, and is also in harmony with the preceding clause to which it is attached. And, moreover, can be equally applied on neutral as well as on belligerent shores.[1]

And, as the result of the consideration of the subject, subject-matter, facts, attendant circumstances, and the language of the statute,

> The Court therefore concludes that Congress intended to adopt, for the purposes of this act, as the exterior boundaries of the "high-seas," a line four miles seaward from the shore.[2]

In the case of *United States v. Rodgers* (150 U. S. 249), decided by the Supreme Court of the United States in 1893, the Court had occasion to consider whether large bodies of water other than the open

---

[1] Manning, *Opinions, Court of Commissioners of Alabama Claims*, November, 1884, p. 54.

In the case of *The Alleganean*, an American merchantman destroyed in the Chesapeake Bay on its voyage from Baltimore to London on October 22, 1862, by tenders from the Confederate cruiser *Patrick Henry*, manned by duly commissioned officers thereof, the same Court had occasion to reconsider the meaning of the "high seas" in international law, invoked by national or local statute. And on this point, Judge Draper, speaking for the Court, said:

> The term "high seas" as used by legislative bodies, the courts, and text-writers, has been construed to express a widely different meaning. As used to define the jurisdiction of admiralty courts, it is held to mean the waters of the ocean exterior to low-water mark. As used in international law, to fix the limits of the open ocean, upon which all peoples possess common rights, the "great highway of Nations," it has been held to mean only so much of the ocean as is exterior to a line running parallel with the shore, and some distance therefrom, commonly such distance as can be defended by artillery upon the shore, and, therefore, a cannon-shot or a marine league (three nautical or four statute miles). This court, after very able argument by learned counsel, and after much deliberation, has held that the term was used in the act of June 5, 1882, in the same sense in which it is employed by the international law writers. ([*Rich v. United States*], Moore's *International Arbitrations*, vol. 4, p. 4335.)

[2] Manning, *Opinions, Court of Commissioners of Alabama Claims*, November, 1884, p. 55.

ocean and the smaller bodies of water connecting them could be considered "high seas" in the sense of international law, and on this point, Mr. Justice Field, speaking for the Court, said:

> If there were no seas other than the ocean, the term "high seas" would be limited to the open, uninclosed waters of the ocean. But as there are other seas besides the ocean, there must be high seas other than those of the ocean. A large commerce is conducted on seas other than the ocean and the English seas, and it is equally necessary to distinguish between their open waters and their ports and havens, and to provide for offences on vessels navigating those waters and for collision between them. The term "high seas" does not, in either case, indicate any separate and distinct body of water; but only the open waters of the sea or ocean, as distinguished from ports and havens and waters within narrow headlands on the coast. This distinction was observed by Latin writers between the ports and havens of the Mediterranean and its open waters—the latter being termed the high seas.
> "Insula *portum*
> Efficit objectu laterum, quibus omnis ab *alto*
> Frangitur, inque sinus scindit sese unda reductos."[1]

After having considered the "high seas" as synonymous with the open uninclosed waters which we call the ocean, Mr. Justice Field proceeded to point out that large bodies of waters, such as the Baltic and the Black Sea, are, like the Mediterranean, to be considered "high seas." Thus, he said:

> In that sense the term may also be properly used in reference to the open waters of the Baltic and the Black Sea, both of which are inland seas, finding their way to the ocean by a narrow and distant channel. Indeed, wherever there are seas in fact, free to the navigation of all nations and people on their borders, their open waters outside of the portion "surrounded or inclosed between narrow headlands or promontories," on the coast, as stated by Mr. Justice Story, or "without the body of a county," as declared by Sir Matthew Hale, are properly characterized as high seas, by whatever name the bodies of water of which they are a part may be designated. Their names do not determine their character. There are, as said above, high seas on the Mediterranean, (meaning outside of the inclosed waters along its coast), upon which the principal commerce of the ancient world was conducted and its great naval battles fought. To hold that on such seas there are no high seas, within the true meaning of that term, that is, no open, uninclosed waters, free to the navigation of all nations and people on their borders, would be to place upon that term

[1] *The Æneid*, Lib. 1, v. 159-161; 150 U. S., pp. 254-255.

a narrow and contracted meaning. We prefer to use it in its true sense, as applicable to the open, uninclosed waters of all seas, than to adhere to the common meaning of the term two centuries ago, when it was generally limited to the open waters of the ocean and of seas surrounding Great Britain, the freedom of which was then the principal subject of discussion. If it be conceded, as we think it must be, that the open, uninclosed waters of the Mediterranean are high seas, that concession is a sufficient answer to the claim that the high seas always denote the open waters of the ocean.[1]

And the learned judge, likewise speaking for the Court, pointed out that "high" was used in the sense of "high" way, and that "high" way in that sense was synonymous with "public" way, and he thus concluded his opinion on this point:

> It is to be observed also that the term "high" in one of its significations is used to denote that which is common, open, and public. Thus every road or way or navigable river which is used freely by the public is a "high" way. So a large body of navigable water other than a river, which is of an extent beyond the measurement of one's unaided vision, and is open and unconfined, and not under the exclusive control of any one nation or people, but is the free highway of adjoining nations or people, must fall under the definition of "high seas" within the meaning of the statute. We may as appropriately designate the open, uninclosed waters of the lakes as the high seas of the lakes, as to designate similar waters of the ocean as the high seas of the ocean, or similar waters of the Mediterranean as the high seas of the Mediterranean.[2]

It has been thought advisable to pay more than passing attention to the extent and limitation of the "high seas" in order to gain a clear conception and understanding of the catch phrase "freedom of the seas," which, if it be not one and the same as "high seas" is nevertheless the consequence of the sense in which "high seas" is understood in theory and applied in practice; for if the high seas be a highway, open to all and closed to none, it necessarily follows that no nation can of right enjoy exclusive jurisdiction. Under these circumstances, there is a right of all and a special privilege of none, and the right of all to and upon the high seas is a right to use them in common. Since the days of Bynkershoek it has been recognized by common consent that each nation, and therefore all nations, can lawfully exercise special if not exclusive jurisdiction over the small

[1] 150 U. S., p. 255.   [2] Ibid., pp. 258-259.

portions of the high seas surrounding their territory to the extent of a marine league from low-water mark. Beyond this fringe of the seas, indifferently called the territorial waters or marine belt, the ocean is not subject to occupation, and because it is not subject to occupation it is not the property of any one Nation. Because the waters adjacent to the shore might be commanded from the shore for the space of a marine league, in 1702, Bynkershoek's dictum met with the approval of the Nations; and until the Nations have enlarged the marine belt its true extent is three marine miles, leaving out of consideration, as immaterial to the present purpose, the question of bays and inlets, regarding which there appears to be a tendency to recognize the jurisdiction of the State over those portions of the high seas extending into land and which approximate, but do not exceed, ten miles in width at the opening. Mr. Justice Field, in the passage quoted from his opinion in the case of *United States v. Rodgers*, refers to the attempts of Spain and of Portugal to ascribe to themselves a property in the ocean, and to the claims of Great Britain to the waters washing its shores and including vast portions of the seas and of the ocean itself beyond its shores. These pretensions have one by one dropped by the wayside and have left no traces in the waters in which armed forces sought to make them good.

An attempt has been made from time to time, and has been supported by writers of repute within the past few years, to apply to vessels navigating the high seas the dictum of Bynkershoek, thus investing them with jurisdiction over a radius of three marine miles or of cannon-shot over the waters whereon they ride. This attempt which would be entitled to serious consideration if a ship were to be taken literally instead of figuratively as a floating portion of the country whose flag it flies, is fatal to the freedom of the seas in time of peace and would be doubly and unbearably so in time of war. The contention, for it has never got beyond this stage, has always been unsuccessful and has hardly caused a ripple upon the surface. It was advanced by counsel in the leading case of *The Marianna Flora*, tried in the Supreme Court of the United States in 1826, and it was thus stated and rejected by Mr. Justice Story in delivering the opinion of the Court:

> It has been argued, that no ship has a right to approach another at sea; and that every ship has a right to draw round her a line of jurisdiction, within which no other is at liberty to intrude. In short, that she may appropriate so much of the ocean as she may deem necessary for her protection, and prevent any

nearer approach. This doctrine appears to us novel, and is not supported by any authority. It goes to establish upon the ocean a territorial jurisdiction, like that which is claimed by all nations, within cannon-shot of their shores, in virtue of their general sovereignty. But the latter right is founded upon the principle of sovereign and permanent appropriation, and has never been successfully asserted beyond it. Every vessel, undoubtedly, has the right to the use of so much of the ocean as she occupies, and as is essential to her own movements. Beyond this, no exclusive right has ever yet been recognized, and we see no reason for admitting its existence. Merchant ships are in the constant habit of approaching each other on the ocean, either to relieve their own distress, to procure information, or to ascertain the character of strangers; and, hitherto, there has never been supposed in such conduct any breach of the customary observances, or of the strictest principles of the law of nations. In respect to ships of war, sailing, as in the present case, under the authority of their government, to arrest pirates, and other public offenders, there is no reason why they may not approach any vessels descried at sea, for the purpose of ascertaining their real characters. Such a right seems indispensable for the fair and discreet exercise of their authority; and the use of it cannot be justly deemed indicative of any design to insult or injure those they approach, or to impede them in their lawful commerce. On the other hand, it is as clear, that no ship is, under such circumstances, bound to lie by, or wait the approach of any other ship. She is at full liberty to pursue her voyage, in her own way, and to use all necessary precautions to avoid any suspected sinister enterprise or hostile attack. She has a right to consult her own safety; but, at the same time, she must take care not to violate the rights of others. She may use any precautions dictated by the prudence or fears of her officers; either as to delay, or the progress of course of her voyage; but she is not at liberty to inflict injuries upon other innocent parties, simply because of conjectural dangers. These principles seem to us the natural result of the common duties and rights of nations, navigating the ocean in time of peace. Such a state of things carries with it very different obligations and responsibilities from those which belong to public war, and is not to be confounded with it.[1]

In speaking of war as an armed contest between States and not between the subjects or citizens thereof, it is usual to cite Rousseau,[2]

[1] 11 Wheaton 1, pp. 41-42.
[2] " War is not a relation between one man and another, but is a relation between one state and another, in which private individuals are enemies only by accident, not as men, nor even as citizens, but as soldiers; nor as members of the home country, but as its defenders. Finally, any state can have for enemies other states only, and not any member, in view of the fact that as between things of different natures, no true relation can be established." (*Contrat Social*, 1762, liv. i, ch. iv.)

who coined the phrase, and to quote the language of Portalis,[1] who introduced it into the practice of Nations. So in the case of the freedom of the seas, it is advisable to state the meaning of the phrase in the language of Grotius—whose tractate, if it did not first proclaim, nevertheless succeeded in introducing into the practice of Nations the freedom of the seas. It is also of importance to note in this connection that this little book, published in 1608, was not an academic exercise, but that it was the brief of a lawyer, written in a prize case growing out of the capture of certain Portuguese vessels in East Indian waters, claimed by Portugal, then united with Spain, to be subject to its jurisdiction under the award of Pope Alexander VI, thus closing those seas to Dutch traders, a contention which the brave little Republic of the Netherlands refused to admit, and whose most distinguished son, then on the eve of his marvelous career, rejected and tore into shreds.

In these days when our ears are vexed by the clash of arms and our eyes are blinded by passion and our judgment swayed by the conflicting claims of national interest and of international right, it is well to turn away from the contentions of belligerents and neutrals concerning the freedom of the seas and to consider the dispute regarding these things between Holland and Portugal, which, three hundred years ago, defined the freedom of the seas in the sense in which the law of Nations accepts and defines it today. It is also well to state the case fully and to see the doctrine grow, as it were, under our very eyes; for by so doing we shall understand that there is nothing new in the freedom of the seas except its violation, that the argument of Grotius which follows in its entirety and largely in his own words, has lost little of its timeliness, that is, is applicable to more than one of the belligerents in the days when the United States was neutral and that more than one Nation could justly say, *Nomine mutato de te, fabula narratur.*

In the address to the rulers and to the free and independent Na-

---

[1] On opening the French Prize Court on May 4, 1800, M. Portalis, as Commissioner of the Government, delivered an address in which he said:

> War is a relation of state to state, and not of individual to individual. Between two or more belligerent nations the private persons of whom those nations are composed are only enemies by accident; they are not so as men, they are not so as citizens, they are so only as soldiers. (Quoted from Hall's *International Law*, 4th ed., pp. 68-69.)

It is interesting to note that the doctrine proclaimed by Rousseau and prescribed by Portalis was applied in the case of *Le Hardy contre La Voltigeante*, decided in 1801. See Pistoye et Duverdy, *Traité des Prises Maritimes*, 1859, tome I, pp. 321, 322.

tions of Christendom, which serves as an introduction to the tractate, Grotius says:

> There is not one of you who does not openly proclaim that every man is entitled to manage and dispose of his own property; there is not one of you who does not insist that all citizens have equal and indiscriminate right to use rivers and public places; not one of you who does not defend with all his might the freedom of travel and of trade.[1]

Grotius next states that, while the King of the universe reserves to himself the final punishment, slow and unseen but nevertheless inevitable, yet he appoints to intervene in human affairs two judges "whom the luckiest of sinners does not escape, namely, Conscience, or the innate estimation of oneself, and Public Opinion, or the estimation of others."

After having thus laid down what he considers fundamental principles, he next puts the question, which he answers in the affirmative:

> If it be thought that the small society which we call a state cannot exist without the application of these principles (and certainly it cannot), why will not those same principles be necessary to uphold the social structure of the whole human race and to maintain the harmony thereof?[1]

"To this double tribunal," he says, speaking on behalf of his country, "we bring a new case," and he outlines, within the compass of a paragraph, the extent of the case:

> It is in very truth no petty case such as private citizens are wont to bring against their neighbors about dripping eaves or party walls; nor is it a case such as nations frequently bring against one another about boundary lines or the possession of a river or an island. No! It is a case which concerns practically the entire expanse of the high seas, the right of navigation, the freedom of trade![2]

The nature of the case he states in the formal questions which he thus puts to the tribunal of conscience and public opinion:

> Can the vast, the boundless sea be the appanage of one kingdom alone, and it not the greatest? Can any one nation have the right to prevent other nations, which so desire, from selling to one another, from bartering with one another, actually from communicating with one another?[2]

[1] *The Freedom of the Seas.* A dissertation by Hugo Grotius. Translated by Ralph Van Deman Magoffin (New York; Oxford Press, 1916), p. 3.
[2] *Ibid.*, p. 4.

After making his bow, as it were to the tribunal, he thus begins his argument in the opening words of the first chapter of his brief:

> My intention is to demonstrate briefly and clearly that the Dutch—that is to say, the subjects of the United Netherlands—have the right to sail to the East Indies, as they are now doing, and to engage in trade with the people there.[1]

After having framed his case, he thus indicates to the tribunal the evidence by which it is to be supported:

> I shall base my argument on the following most specific and unimpeachable axiom of the Law of Nations, called a primary rule or first principle, the spirit of which is self-evident and immutable, to wit: Every nation is free to travel to every other nation, and to trade with it.[1]

In the second chapter, which may be called his next point, Grotius maintains that the Portuguese have no right by title of discovery to sovereignty over the East Indies to which the Dutch make voyages. In support of this view he uses the following apt passage:

> The Portuguese are not sovereigns of those parts of the East Indies to which the Dutch sail, that is to say, Java, Ceylon, and many of the Moluccas. This I prove by the incontrovertible argument that no one is sovereign of a thing which he himself has never possessed, and which no one else has ever held in his name. These islands of which we speak, now have and always have had their own kings, their own government, their own laws, and their own legal systems. The inhabitants allow the Portuguese to trade with them, just as they allow other nations the same privilege.[2]

Grotius then proceeds to deny that the lands came under the jurisdiction of the Portuguese as a reward of discovery, and he also lays bare the claim which still rings in our ears of the superior rights which superior civilization or culture gives to those who profess its possession. He quotes Victoria, a wise and a great man and one of the founders of the law of Nations, to the effect that:

> The Spaniards have no more legal right over the East Indians because of their religion, than the East Indians would have had over the Spaniards if they had happened to be the first foreigners to come to Spain.[3]

[1] Grotius, *Freedom of the Seas*, p. 7.
[2] *Ibid.*, p. 11.
[3] *Ibid.*, p. 13.

And on the question of superior culture and civilization giving a superior right, Grotius proceeds:

> Such a pretext on its very face is an injustice. Plutarch said long ago that it was greed that furnished the pretext for conquering barbarous countries, and it is not unsuspected that greedy longing for the property of another often hid itself behind a pretext of civilizing barbarians. And now that well-known pretext of forcing nations into a higher state of civilization against their will, the pretext once seized by the Greeks and by Alexander the Great, is considered by all theologians, especially those of Spain, to be unjust and unholy.[1]

In the third place, Grotius maintains that the "Portuguese have no right of sovereignty over the East Indies by virtue of title based on the Papal Donation." On this point the mere statement, without the reasoning of Grotius, is sufficient for present purposes.

In the next place, he insists that the Portuguese have no right of sovereignty over the East Indies by title of war, concluding after an investigation that, as a matter of fact, "both possession and a title of possession are lacking" to the claim of the Portuguese.

At this point Grotius reaches the argument, to which the others previously advanced are in the nature of an introduction and which a modern reader might properly consider immaterial, especially after the elaborate argument in the fifth chapter, in which he contends that neither the "Indian Ocean nor the right of navigation thereon belongs to the Portuguese by title of occupation." And assuredly this portion of the tractate was not lost upon the conscience and public opinion to which he appealed, and it should not be lost upon the conscience and public opinion of the present day called again to sit in judgment upon the freedom of the seas.

> Now, in the legal phraseology of the Law of Nations, [he says] the sea is called indifferently the property of no one (*res nullius*), or a common possession (*res communis*), or public property (*res publica*).[2]

Without following the argument of Grotius, which is very elaborate and very detailed, it is sufficient for present purposes to state that he makes of occupation the source of title, whether it be title by the State or title by the individual, and occupation is therefore the test of public and of private property. Summing up a portion of his reasoning, he says:

[1] Grotius, *Freedom of the Seas*, p. 14.   [2] *Ibid.*, p. 22.

> Two conclusions may be drawn from what has thus far been said. The first is, that that which cannot be occupied, or which never has been occupied, cannot be the property of anyone, because all property has arisen from occupation. The second is, that all that which has been so constituted by nature that although serving some one person it still suffices for the common use of all other persons, is today and ought in perpetuity to remain in the same condition as when it was first created by nature.[1]

By way of illustration he appeals to an element whose use has not yet been regulated, but which must soon be the subject of international agreement:

> The air belongs to this class of things for two reasons. First, it is not susceptible of occupation; and second, its common use is destined for all men. For the same reasons the sea is common to all, because it is so limitless that it cannot become a possession of anyone, and because it is adapted for the use of all, whether we consider it from the point of view of navigation or of fisheries. . . .
> These things therefore are what the Romans call 'common' to all men by natural law, or as we have said, 'public' according to the law of nations; and indeed they call their use sometimes common, sometimes public.[2]

Although neither the air itself nor the sea can be occupied so as to become the property of anyone or of any nation, the fowls of the air and the fish of the sea may be seized and by seizure they may become the property of him who possesses them. On this distinction and its reason Grotius says:

> Nevertheless, although those things are with reason said to be *res nullius,* so far as private ownership is concerned, still they differ very much from those things which, though also *res nullius,* have not been marked out for common use, such for example as wild animals, fish, and birds. For if anyone seizes those things and assumes possession of them, they can become objects of private ownership, but the things in the former category by the consensus of opinion of all mankind are forever exempt from such private ownership on account of their susceptibility to universal use; and as they belong to all they cannot be taken away from all by any one person any more than what is mine can be taken away from me by you.[3]

As occupation is the test of property, private as well as public, Grotius considers that:

[1] Grotius, *Freedom of the Seas,* p. 27.   [2] *Ibid.,* pp. 28-29.   [3] *Ibid.,* p. 29.

> Whatever by occupation can become private property can also become public property, that is, the private property of a whole nation.[1]

He also holds that, by the application of this principle, a Nation could acquire the shore of the sea, although not the sea itself, for he says:

> The nature of the sea, however, differs from that of the shore, because the sea, except for a very restricted space, can neither easily be built upon, nor inclosed; if the contrary were true yet this could hardly happen without hindrance to the general use.[2] . . .
> Therefore the sea is one of those things which is not an article of merchandise, and which cannot become private property.[3]

After this line of argument, Grotius thus sums up what may be considered as the general conclusions which he has reached, and the only ones which are of a permanent as distinct from a temporary interest:

> It has therefore been demonstrated that neither a nation nor an individual can establish any right of private ownership over the sea itself (I except inlets of the sea), inasmuch as its occupation is not permissible either by nature or on grounds of public utility.[4] . . .
>
> The question at issue then is not one that concerns an INNER SEA, one which is surrounded on all sides by the land and at some places does not even exceed a river in breadth, although it is well known that the Roman jurists cited such an inner sea in their famous opinions condemning private avarice. No! the question at issue is the OUTER SEA, the OCEAN, that expanse of water which antiquity describes as the immense, the infinite, bounded only by the heavens, parent of all things; the ocean which the ancients believed was perpetually supplied with water not only by fountains, rivers, and seas, but by the clouds, and by the very stars of heaven themselves; the ocean which, although surrounding this earth, the home of the human race, with the ebb and flow of its tides, can be neither seized nor inclosed; nay, which rather possesses the earth than is by it possessed.[5] . . .
> Therefore the Portuguese have neither just reason nor respectable authority to support their position, for all those persons who assume that the sea can be subjected to the sovereignty of anyone assign it to him who holds in his power the nearest ports and the circumjacent shores. But in all that great extent of coast line

---

[1] Grotius, *Freedom of the Seas*, p. 30.
[2] *Ibid.*, p. 31. [3] *Ibid.*, p. 34. [4] *Ibid.*, pp. 36-37. [5] *Ibid.*, p. 37.

reaching to the East Indies the Portuguese have nothing which they can call their own except a few fortified posts.

And then even if a man were to have dominion over the sea, still he could not take away anything from its common use, just as the Roman people could not prevent anyone from doing on the shores of their dominions all those things which were permitted by the law of nations. And if it were possible to prohibit any of those things, say for example, fishing, for in a way it can be maintained that fish are exhaustible, still it would not be permissible to prohibit navigation, for the sea is not exhausted by that use.

The most conclusive argument on this question by far however is the one that we have already brought forward based on the opinions of eminent jurists, namely, that even over land which had been converted into private property either by states or individuals, unarmed and innocent passage is not justly to be denied to persons of any country, exactly as the right to drink from a river is not to be denied. The reason is clear, because, inasmuch as one and the same thing is susceptible by nature to different uses, the nations seem on the one hand to have apportioned among themselves that use which cannot be maintained conveniently apart from private ownership; but on the other hand to have reserved that use through the exercise of which the condition of the owner would not be impaired.[1]

In Chapter VI Grotius denies the right to navigation, just as he had previously denied the right of title to the sea, by virtue of Papal Donation. In Chapter VII he states that the Portuguese can have neither right to the sea nor to exclusive navigation by prescription or custom, and he argues this matter at very considerable length. For present purposes it may be said, in passing, that if title cannot be acquired by grant it cannot be acquired by prescription, which either presupposes a grant or has the effect of a grant, and if the high seas are incapable of occupation it is indifferent what the claim and title may be, whether by prescription or by custom, which also can be of a thing which might be granted.

In the eighth chapter Grotius states that, by the law of Nations, trade is free to all persons whatsoever. It would seem that this heading is a consequence of the foregoing observations, and Grotius himself says that the claim of the Portuguese to an exclusive right to trade with the East Indians is "refuted by practically all the same arguments which already have been brought forward." He nevertheless feels it necessary to repeat them briefly, but for present purposes it may be said that, upon the introduction of private ownership,

[1] Grotius, *Freedom of the Seas*, pp. 43-44.

"a change brought about by necessity," there straightway arose, "a method of exchange by which the lack of one person was supplemented by that of which another person had an oversupply"; that for the purpose of exchange shipping was necessary and that to deny the right of trade upon the high seas was to deny the right of exchange essential to the full enjoyment of property; and for other reasons, which are not material, as the matter to us seems to be an axiom which either does not or cannot need a justification. Grotius' conclusion, however, is well worth the quoting, irrespective of the reason upon which it is based:

> Therefore freedom of trade is based on a primitive right of nations which has a natural and permanent cause; and so that right cannot be destroyed, or at all events it may not be destroyed except by the consent of all nations.[1]

Passing over the observations of the brief which are the consequences of the principles laid down, Grotius contends in Chapter IX that trade with the East Indies does not belong to the Portuguese by title of occupation; in Chapter X, that trade with the East Indies does not belong to the Portuguese by virtue of title based on the Papal Donation; in Chapter XI, that trade with the East Indies does not belong to the Portuguese by title of prescription or custom; and in Chapter XII, that the Portuguese prohibition of trade has no foundation in equity, in which chapter, however, there is more than one passage worthy of quotation and which may well be pondered, as human nature is much the same today as it was in 1608, and as it was centuries before. Thus, Grotius says:

> Moreover, it is natural and conformable to the highest law as well as equity, that when a gain open to all is concerned every person prefers it for himself rather than for another, even if that other had already discovered it.[2]

But after this statement, which cannot be gainsaid, he puts the embarrassing question:

> Who would countenance an artisan who complained that another artisan was taking away his profits by the exercise of the same craft?[2]

And he answers this adroitly, if not directly, saying:

[1] Grotius, *Freedom of the Seas*, pp. 63-64.
[2] *Ibid.*, pp. 69-70.

> But the cause of the Dutch is the more reasonable, because their advantage in this matter is bound up with the advantage of the whole human race, an advantage which the Portuguese are trying to destroy.[1]

And on this point, which is really involved in the freedom of the seas, he thus proceeds, as is his wont, by question and answer:

> Indeed can anything more unjust be conceived than for the Spaniards to hold the entire world tributary, so that it is not permissible either to buy or to sell except at their good pleasure? In all states we heap odium upon grain speculators and even bring them to punishment; and in very truth there seems to be no other sort of business so disgraceful as that of forcing up prices in the grain market. That is not to be wondered at, for such speculators are doing an injury to nature, who, as Aristotle says, is fertile for all alike. Accordingly it ought not to be supposed that trade was invented for the benefit of a few, but in order that the lack of one would be counterbalanced by the oversupply of another, a fair return also being guaranteed to all who take upon themselves the work and the danger of transport.[1]

Again pursuing the method of question and answer, he writes:

> Is the same thing then which is considered grievous and pernicious in the smaller community of a State to be put up with at all in that great community of the human race? Shall the people of Spain, forsooth, assume a monopoly of all the world? Ambrose inveighs against those who interfere with the freedom of the sea; Augustine against those who obstruct the overland routes; and Gregory of Nazianzus against those who buy goods and hold them, and thus (as he eloquently says) make profits for themselves alone out of the helplessness and need of others. . . .
> Therefore the Portuguese may cry as loud and as long as they shall please: 'You are cutting down our profits!' The Dutch will answer: 'Nay! we are but looking out for our own interests! Are you angry because we share with you in the winds and the sea?'[1]

Therefore, in theory and in practice the high seas are not subject to the exclusive jurisdiction of any one Power. They are high or open seas, to distinguish them from the inland or closed seas which are subject to the jurisdiction of the country within whose territory they are situated, or to the jurisdiction of the countries bordering upon them. We are here dealing with a general truth and not with an

---

[1] Grotius, *Freedom of the Seas*, pp. 70-71.

academic question, for innumerable attempts have been made to subject the open seas to the exclusive control of countries feeling themselves powerful enough to make good by force the claim which right denied. But the attempt has failed and nothing remains of the claim except the right admitted by international law to exercise jurisdiction, which is far from exclusive, within the territorial waters, or rather so much of the waters washing the coast of any particular country as can be controlled by the cannon of land batteries. The vast bodies of water, with the possible exception of coastal waters, are the common highway of Nations, with equal rights to all and special privileges to none. And while a Nation retains its jurisdiction over its vessels upon the high seas, this jurisdiction does not extend to the waters which they navigate but only to the vessels themselves, their crews, their passengers, their cargoes.

The Imperial German Government cannot in the matter of the high seas rightfully impose its will upon the United States. The United States can only be deprived of its right to navigate the high seas by its own consent, and the United States has not consented.

The freedom of the seas is a phrase much in vogue during the present war, but those who use it most define it least. Yet it is to be pointed out that from the publication of the little tractate on the freedom of the seas at the beginning of the seventeenth century, the term has had a definite, known meaning, and the meaning attached to it by the youthful Grotius is the same as the definition and meaning attached to it by President Wilson, who is now engaged in preserving that system of law expounded by Grotius.

Now, the freedom of the seas proclaimed by Grotius and defended by the President means the right of every Nation to navigate the high seas without permission of or obstruction from any one Nation, and that no group of Nations has any exclusive right to the patrimony of all. Such is the rule and such is the practice of Nations in time of peace. In time of war belligerent Nations are, by the consent of all, permitted to give battle upon the high seas, to destroy the fighting forces of the enemy wherever found, to visit and to search neutral merchantmen in order to satisfy themselves that the vessels are engaged in a neutral, not in an unneutral or prohibited service. The freedom of the seas, although limited by war, is not abrogated by it, and in time of war the freedom of the seas obtains, means, and requires that neutral vessels may lawfully trade with the enemy unless its ports are closed by blockade declared and maintained in the form required by the law of Nations; that if the ports are not legally blockaded, neutral vessels may still carry their cargoes to enemy ports, subject to capture and confiscation of the cargoes if they fall within the category of contraband; and that neutral vessels may, by the law of Nations, trade with all neutral ports, unless the cargoes fall within the category of contraband and the neutral ports are interposed to conceal ultimate destination to the enemy. But, excepting men-of-war, which may be sunk without warning, neither merchant vessels of the enemy nor neutral vessels can lawfully be destroyed and sunk without first removing crew and passengers to places of safety and without taking possession of the ships' papers, in order that the validity of the action may be tested and decided by the prize courts of the captor's country, where, indeed, every presumption is in favor of the capture but where, nevertheless, the law of Nations regulating such a matter is presumed to be administered.

When the Imperial German Government proclaims the freedom of the seas in its correspondence with the United States, it means the liberation of Nations from the alleged unlawful interference of Great Britain with the rights of neutrals to trade with Great Britain's enemies; when Great Britain mentions the freedom of the seas in its correspondence with the United States, it means the alleged unlawful interference of Germany with the rights of neutrals to trade with Germany's enemies; and when the United States advocates the freedom of the seas in its correspondence with the Imperial German Government and Great Britain, it means the rights of neutrals to trade indifferently with both without interference from one or the other, according to the principles of international law generally recognized on the first day of August, 1914. Each of these three countries appeals to the freedom of the seas in the sense in which belligerents on the one hand and neutrals on the other understand that term. The rights of the many must prevail over the claims of the few and of the one; by reason, if possible, by force, if necessary.

In the thirteenth and last chapter of the *Mare Liberum,* Grotius declares that his countrymen must maintain their right of trade by peace, by treaty, or by war, saying:

> Wherefore since both law and equity demand that trade with the East Indies be as free to us as to anyone else, it follows that we are to maintain at all hazards that freedom which is ours by nature, either by coming to a peace agreement with the Spaniards, or by concluding a treaty, or by continuing the war. So far as

peace is concerned, it is well known that there are two kinds of peace, one made on terms of equality, the other on unequal terms. The Greeks call the former kind a compact between equals, the latter an enjoined truce; the former is meant for high souled men, the latter for servile spirits. Demosthenes in his speech on the liberty of the Rhodians says that it was necessary for those who wished to be free to keep away from treaties which were imposed upon them, because such treaties were almost the same as slavery. Such conditions are all those by which one party is lessened in its own right, according to the definition of Isocrates. For if, as Cicero says, wars must be undertaken in order that people may live in peace unharmed, it follows that peace must be called not a pact which entails slavery, but an undisturbed liberty, especially as peace and justice according to the opinion of many philosophers and theologians differ more in name than in fact, and as peace is a harmonious agreement based not on individual whim, but on well ordered regulations. . . .

But if we are driven into war by the injustice of our enemies, the justice of our cause ought to bring hope and confidence in a happy outcome. . . .

Therefore, if it be necessary, arise, O nation unconquered on the sea, and fight boldly, not only for your own liberty, but for that of the human race. "Nor let it fright thee that their fleet is winged, each ship, with an hundred oars. The sea whereon it sails will have none of it."[1]

So Hugo Grotius in 1608; so Woodrow Wilson in 1917.

[1] Grotius, *Freedom of the Seas*, pp. 72-73.

CONCLUSION

The President properly stated in his address of April 2d to the Congress that he was assuming a grave responsibility in recommending a declaration of the existence of a state of war against the Imperial German Government, for the day has long since passed, at least in democratic countries, where the head of a State, whether he be monarch or president, can go to war as the king went a-hunting. War may be an imperial, it is no longer a royal, sport, and it never has been and it never will be, it is to be hoped, a presidential one. War is ordinarily declared in a moment of excitement and reason is likely to be swayed by enthusiasm, but we cannot today in democracies justify a declaration of war unless the cause be just, and, however we may deceive ourselves, we cannot deceive posterity, which passes alike upon the acts of autocrat, constitutional monarch, president, and people. We must decide according to our knowledge of present conditions and according to these conditions our actions are to be judged in first instance; but the future must finally decide the question.

The President has stated the case of the United States against the Imperial German Government clearly and in detail. He has enumerated the special reasons which, in his opinion, would be a proper cause of armed action. He has searched his own heart and the conscience of the American people, that the motives and objects of the war may not only justify but require in the circumstances and conditions the declaration of a state of war. It is indeed a grave responsibility which the President assumed in recommending the war, which the Congress assumed in declaring its existence, and which the people of the United States assume in carrying it on.

We believe that the reasons given are causes, not pretexts, that the motives and purposes are sincere and sufficient; but on all these matters posterity has the final word. For whether we will or no, "Die Weltgeschichte ist das Weltgericht."[1]

JAMES BROWN SCOTT.

WASHINGTON, D. C.
September 16, 1917.

[1] "The history of the world is the world's court of judgment." From: Hegel's *Philosophy of Right*. Translated by S. W. Dyde (London, Geo. Bell & Sons, 1896), p. 341.

POST SCRIPTUM

POST SCRIPTUM

1. REPLY OF THE PRESIDENT OF THE UNITED STATES TO THE PEACE APPEAL OF THE POPE, AUGUST 27, 1917:

To His Holiness Benedictus XV, Pope:

In acknowledgment of the communication of Your Holiness to the belligerent peoples, dated August 1, 1917, the President of the United States requests me to transmit the following reply:

Every heart that has not been blinded and hardened by this terrible war must be touched by this moving appeal of His Holiness the Pope, must feel the dignity and force of the humane and generous motives which prompted it, and must fervently wish that we might take the path of peace he so persuasively points out. But it would be folly to take it if it does not in fact lead to the goal he proposes. Our response must be based upon the stern facts and upon nothing else. It is not a mere cessation of arms he desires; it is a stable and enduring peace. This agony must not be gone through with again, and it must be a matter of very sober judgment what will insure us against it.

His Holiness in substance proposes that we return to the *status quo ante bellum,* and that then there be a general condonation, disarmament, and a concert of nations based upon an acceptance of the principle of arbitration; that by a similar concert freedom of the seas be established; and that the territorial claims of France and Italy, the perplexing problems of the Balkan States, and the restitution of Poland be left to such conciliatory adjustments as may be possible in the new temper of such a peace, due regard being paid to the aspirations of the peoples whose political fortunes and affiliations will be involved.

It is manifest that no part of this program can be successfully carried out unless the restitution of the *status quo ante* furnishes a firm and satisfactory basis for it. The object of this war is to deliver the free peoples of the world from the menace and the actual power of a vast military establishment controlled by an irresponsible Government which, having secretly planned to dominate the world, proceeded to carry the plan out without regard either to the sacred obligations of treaty or the long-established practices and long-cherished principles of international action and honor; which chose its own time for the war; delivered its blow fiercely and suddenly; stopped at no barrier either of law or of mercy; swept a whole continent within the tide of blood—not the blood of soldiers only, but the blood of innocent women and children also and of the helpless poor; and now stands balked but not defeated, the enemy of four-fifths of the world. This power is not the German people. It is the ruthless master of the German people. It is no business of ours how that great people came under its control or submitted with temporary zest to the domination of its purpose; but it is our business to see to it that the history of the rest of the world is no longer left to its handling.

To deal with such a power by way of peace upon the plan proposed by His Holiness the Pope would, so far as we can see, involve a recuperation of its strength and a renewal of its policy; would make it necessary to create a permanent hostile combination of nations against the German people, who are its instruments; and would result in abandoning the new-born Russia to the intrigue, the manifold subtle interference, and the certain counter-revolution which would be attempted by all the malign influences to which the German Government has of late accustomed the world. Can peace be based upon a restitution of its power or upon any word of honor it could pledge in a treaty of settlement and accommodation?

Responsible statesmen must now everywhere see, if they never saw before, that no peace can rest securely upon political or economic restrictions meant to benefit some nations and cripple or embarrass others, upon vindictive action of any sort, or any kind of revenge or deliberate injury. The American people have suffered intolerable wrongs at the hands of the Imperial German Government, but they desire no reprisal upon the German people, who have themselves suffered all things in this war, which they did not choose. They believe that peace should rest upon the rights of peoples, not the rights of Governments—the rights of peoples great or small, weak or powerful—their equal right to freedom and security and self-government and to a participation upon fair terms in the economic opportunities of the world, the German people of course included if they will accept equality and not seek domination.

The test, therefore, of every plan of peace is this: Is it based upon the faith of all the peoples involved or merely upon the word of an ambitious and intriguing Government, on the one hand, and of a group of free peoples, on the other? This is a test which goes to the root of the matter; and it is the test which must be applied.

The purposes of the United States in this war are known to the whole world, to every people to whom the truth has been permitted to come. They do not need to be stated again. We seek no material advantage of any kind. We believe that the intolerable wrongs done in this war by the furious and brutal power of the Imperial German Government ought to be repaired, but not at the expense of the sovereignty of any people—rather a vindication of the sovereignty both of those that are weak and of those that are strong. Punitive damages, the dismemberment of empires, the establishment of selfish and exclusive economic leagues, we deem inexpedient and in the end worse than futile, no proper basis for a peace of any kind, least of all for an enduring peace. That must be based upon justice and fairness and the common rights of mankind.

We cannot take the word of the present rulers of Germany as a guarantee of anything that is to endure, unless explicitly supported by such conclusive evidence of the will and purpose of the German people themselves as the other peoples of the world would be justified in accepting. Without such guarantees treaties of settlement, agreements for disarmament, covenants to set up arbitration in the place of force, territorial adjustments, reconstitutions of small nations, if made with the German Government, no man, no nation could now depend on. We must await some new evidence of the purposes of the great peoples of the Central Powers. God grant it may be given soon and in a way to restore the confidence of all peoples everywhere in the faith of nations and the possibility of a covenanted peace.

ROBERT LANSING,
Secretary of State of the United States of America.[1]

---

[1] *Official Bulletin*, August 29, 1917.

2. ADDRESS OF THE PRESIDENT OF THE UNITED STATES DELIVERED AT A JOINT SESSION OF THE TWO HOUSES OF CONGRESS, DECEMBER 4, 1917:

GENTLEMEN OF THE CONGRESS:

Eight months have elapsed since I last had the honour of addressing you. They have been months crowded with events of immense and grave significance for us. I shall not undertake to retail or even to summarize those events. The practical particulars of the part we have played in them will be laid before you in the reports of the Executive Departments. I shall discuss only our present outlook upon these vast affairs, our present duties, and the immediate means of accomplishing the objects we shall hold always in view.

I shall not go back to debate the causes of the war. The intolerable wrongs done and planned against us by the sinister masters of Germany have long since become too grossly obvious and odious to every true American to need to be rehearsed. But I shall ask you to consider again and with a very grave scrutiny our objectives and the measures by which we mean to attain them; for the purpose of discussion here in this place is action, and our action must move straight towards definite ends. Our object is, of course, to win the war; and we shall not slacken or suffer ourselves to be diverted until it is won. But it is worth while asking and answering the question, When shall we consider the war won?

From one point of view it is not necessary to broach this fundamental matter. I do not doubt that the American people know what the war is about and what sort of an outcome they will regard as a realization of their purpose in it. As a nation we are united in spirit and intention. I pay little heed to those who tell me otherwise. I hear the voices of dissent,—who does not? I hear the criticism and the clamour of the noisily thoughtless and troublesome. I also see men here and there fling themselves in impotent disloyalty against the calm, indomitable power of the nation. I hear men debate peace who understand neither its nature nor the way in which we may attain it with uplifted eyes and unbroken spirits. But I know that none of these speaks for the nation. They do not touch the heart of anything. They may safely be left to strut their uneasy hour and be forgotten.

But from another point of view I believe that it is necessary to say plainly what we here at the seat of action consider the war to be for and what part we mean to play in the settlement of its searching issues. We are the spokesmen of the American people and they have a right to know whether their purpose is ours. They desire peace by the overcoming of evil, by the defeat once for all of the sinister forces that interrupt peace and render it impossible, and they wish to know how closely our thought runs with theirs and what action we propose. They are impatient with those who desire peace by any sort of compromise,—deeply and indignantly impatient,—but they will be equally impatient with us if we do not make it plain to them what our objectives are and what we are planning for in seeking to make conquest of peace by arms.

I believe that I speak for them when I say two things: First, that this intolerable Thing of which the masters of Germany have shown us the ugly face, this menace of combined intrigue and force which we now see so clearly as the German power, a Thing without conscience or honour or capacity for covenanted peace, must be crushed and, if it be not utterly brought to an end, at least shut out from the friendly intercourse of the nations; and, second, that when this Thing and its power are indeed defeated and the time comes that we can discuss peace,—when the German people have spokesmen whose word we can believe and when those spokesmen are ready in the name of their people to accept the common judgment of the nations as to what shall henceforth be the bases of law and of covenant for the life of the world,—we shall be willing and glad to pay the full price for peace, and pay it ungrudgingly. We know what that price will be. It will be full, impartial justice,—justice done at every point and to every nation that the final settlement must affect, our enemies as well as our friends.

You catch, with me, the voices of humanity that are in the air. They grow daily more audible, more articulate, more persuasive, and they come from the hearts of men everywhere. They insist that the war shall not end in vindictive action of any kind; that no nation or people shall be robbed or punished because the irresponsible rulers of a single country have themselves done deep and abominable wrong. It is this thought that has been expressed in the formula 'No annexations, no contributions, no punitive indemnities.' Just because this crude formula expresses the instinctive judgment as to right of plain men everywhere it has been made diligent use of by the masters of German intrigue to lead the people of Russia astray—and the people of every other country their agents could reach, in order that a premature peace might be brought about before autocracy has been taught its final and convincing lesson, and the people of the world put in control of their own destinies.

But the fact that a wrong use has been made of a just idea is no reason why a right use should not be made of it. It ought to be brought under the patronage of its real friends. Let it be said again that autocracy must first be shown the utter futility of its claims to power or leadership in the modern world. It is impossible to apply any standard of justice so long as such forces are unchecked and undefeated as the present masters of Germany command. Not until that has been done can Right be set up as arbiter and peace-maker among the nations. But when that has been done,—as, God willing, it assuredly will be,—we shall at last be free to do an unprecedented thing, and this is the time to avow our purpose to do it. We shall be free to base peace on generosity and justice, to the exclusion of all selfish claims to advantage even on the part of the victors.

Let there be no misunderstanding. Our present and immediate task is to win the war, and nothing shall turn us aside from it until it is accomplished. Every power and resource we possess, whether of men, of money, or of materials, is being devoted and will continue to be devoted to that purpose until it is achieved. Those who desire to bring peace about before that purpose is achieved I counsel to carry their advice elsewhere. We will not entertain it. We shall regard the war as won only when the German people say to us, through properly accredited representatives, that they are ready to agree to a settlement based upon justice and the reparation of the wrongs their rulers have done. They have done a wrong to Belgium which must be repaired. They have established a power over other lands and peoples than their own,—over the great Empire of Austria-Hungary, over hitherto free Balkan states, over Turkey, and within Asia,— which must be relinquished.

Germany's success by skill, by industry, by knowledge, by enterprise we did not grudge or oppose, but admired, rather. She had built up for herself a real empire of trade and influence, secured by the peace of the world. We were content to abide the rivalries of manufacture, science, and commerce that were involved for us in her success and stand or fall as we had or did not have the brains and the initiative to surpass her. But at the moment when she had conspicuously won her triumphs of peace she threw them away, to establish in their stead what the world will no longer permit to be established, military and political domination by arms, by which to oust where she could not excel the rivals she most feared and hated. The peace we make must remedy that wrong. It must deliver the once fair lands and happy peoples of Belgium and northern France from the Prussian conquest and the Prussian menace, but it must also deliver the peoples of Austria-Hungary, the peoples of the Balkans, and the peoples of Turkey, alike in Europe and in Asia, from the impudent and alien dominion of the Prussian military and commercial autocracy.

We owe it, however, to ourselves to say that we do not wish in any way to impair or to rearrange the Austro-Hungarian Empire. It is no affair of ours what they do with their own life, either industrially or politically. We do not purpose or desire to dictate to them in any way. We only desire to see that their affairs are left in their own hands, in all matters, great or small. We shall hope to secure for the peoples of the Balkan peninsula and for the people of the Turkish Empire the right and opportunity to make their own lives safe, their own fortunes secure against oppression or injustice and from the dictation of foreign courts or parties.

And our attitude and purpose with regard to Germany herself are of a like kind. We intend no wrong against the German Empire, no interference with her internal affairs. We should deem either the one or the other absolutely unjustifiable, absolutely contrary to the principles we have professed to live by and to hold most sacred throughout our life as a nation.

The people of Germany are being told by the men whom they now permit to deceive them and to act as their masters that they are fighting for the very life and existence of their Empire, a war of desperate self-defense against deliberate aggression. Nothing could be more grossly or wantonly false, and we must seek by the utmost openness and candour as to our real aims to convince them of its falseness. We are in fact fighting for their emancipation from fear, along with our own,—from the fear as well as from the fact of unjust attack by neighbours or rivals or schemers after world empire. No one is threatening the existence or the independence or the peaceful enterprise of the German Empire.

The worst that can happen to the detriment of the German people is this, that if they should still, after the war is over, continue to be obliged to live under ambitious and intriguing masters interested to disturb the peace of the world, men or classes of men whom the other peoples of the world could not trust, it might be impossible to admit them to the partnership of nations which must henceforth guarantee the world's peace. That partnership must be a partnership of peoples, not a mere partnership of governments. It might be impossible, also, in such untoward circumstances, to admit Germany to the free economic intercourse which must inevitably spring out of the other partnerships of a real peace. But there would be no aggression in that; and such a situation, inevitable because of distrust, would in the very nature of things sooner or later cure itself, by processes which would assuredly set in.

The wrongs, the very deep wrongs, committed in this war will have to be righted. That of course. But they cannot and must not be righted by the commission of similar wrongs against Germany and her allies. The world will not permit the commission of similar wrongs as a means of reparation and settlement. Statesmen must by this time have learned that the opinion of the world is everywhere wide awake and fully comprehends the issues involved. No representative of any self-governed nation will dare disregard it by attempting any such covenants of selfishness and compromise as were entered into at the Congress of Vienna. The thought of the plain people here and everywhere throughout the world, the people who enjoy no privilege and have very simple and unsophisticated standards of right and wrong, is the air all governments must henceforth breathe if they would live. It is in the full disclosing light of that thought that all policies must be conceived and executed in this midday hour of the world's life. German rulers have been able to upset the peace of the world only because the German people were not suffered under their tutelage to share the comradeship of the other peoples of the world either in thought or in purpose. They were allowed to have no opinion of their own which might be set up as a rule of conduct for those who exercised authority over them. But the congress that concludes this war will feel the full strength of the tides that run now in the hearts and consciences of free men everywhere. Its conclusions will run with those tides.

All these things have been true from the very beginning of this stupendous war; and I cannot help thinking that if they had been made plain at the very outset the sympathy and enthusiasm of the Russian people might have been once for all enlisted on the side of the Allies, suspicion and distrust swept away, and a real and lasting union of purpose effected. Had they believed these things at the very moment of their revolution and had they been confirmed in that belief since, the sad reverses which have recently marked the progress of their affairs towards an ordered and stable government of free men might have been avoided. The Russian people have been poisoned by the very same falsehoods that have kept the German people in the dark, and the poison has been administered by the very same hands. The only possible antidote is the truth. It cannot be uttered too plainly or too often.

From every point of view, therefore, it has seemed to be my duty to speak these declarations of purpose, to add these specific interpretations to what I took the liberty of saying to the Senate in January. Our entrance into the war has not altered our attitude towards the settlement that must come when it is over. When I said in January that the nations of the world were entitled not only to free pathways upon the sea but also to assured and unmolested access to those pathways I was thinking, and I am thinking now, not of the smaller and weaker nations alone, which need our countenance and support, but also of the great and powerful nations, and of our present enemies as well as our present associates in the war. I was thinking, and am thinking now, of Austria herself, among the rest, as well as of Serbia and of Poland. Justice and equality of rights can be had only at a great price. We are seeking permanent, not temporary, foundations for the peace of the world and must seek them candidly and fearlessly. As always, the right will prove to be the expedient.

What shall we do, then, to push this great war of freedom and justice to its righteous conclusion? We must clear away with a thorough hand all impediments to success and we must make every adjustment of law that will facilitate the full and free use of our whole capacity and force as a fighting unit.

One very embarrassing obstacle that stands in our way is that we are at war with Germany but not with her allies. I therefore very earnestly recommend that the Congress immediately declare the United States in a state of war with Austria-Hungary. Does it seem strange to you that this should be the conclusion of the argument I have just addressed to you? It is not. It is in fact the inevitable logic of what I have said. Austria-Hungary is for the time being not her own mistress but simply the vassal of the German Government. We must face the facts as they are and act upon them without sentiment in this stern business. The government of Austria-Hungary is not acting upon its own initiative or in response to the wishes and feelings of its own peoples but as the instrument of another nation. We must meet its force with our own and regard the Central Powers as but one. The war can be successfully conducted in no other way. The same logic would lead also to a declaration of war against

Turkey and Bulgaria. They also are the tools of Germany. But they are mere tools and do not yet stand in the direct path of our necessary action. We shall go wherever the necessities of this war carry us, but it seems to me that we should go only where immediate and practical considerations lead us and not heed any others.

The financial and military measures which must be adopted will suggest themselves as the war and its undertakings develop, but I will take the liberty of proposing to you certain other acts of legislation which seem to me to be needed for the support of the war and for the release of our whole force and energy.

It will be necessary to extend in certain particulars the legislation of the last session with regard to alien enemies; and also necessary, I believe, to create a very definite and particular control over the entrance and departure of all persons into and from the United States.

Legislation should be enacted defining as a criminal offense every willful violation of the presidential proclamations relating to alien enemies promulgated under section 4067 of the Revised Statutes and providing appropriate punishment; and women as well as men should be included under the terms of the acts placing restraints upon alien enemies. It is likely that as time goes on many alien enemies will be willing to be fed and housed at the expense of the Government in the detention camps and it would be the purpose of the legislation I have suggested to confine offenders among them in penitentiaries and other similar institutions where they could be made to work as other criminals do.

Recent experience has convinced me that the Congress must go further in authorizing the Government to set limits to prices. The law of supply and demand, I am sorry to say, has been replaced by the law of unrestrained selfishness. While we have eliminated profiteering in several branches of industry it still runs impudently rampant in others. The farmers, for example, complain with a great deal of justice that, while the regulation of food prices restricts their incomes, no restraints are placed upon the prices of most of the things they must themselves purchase; and similar inequities obtain on all sides.

It is imperatively necessary that the consideration of the full use of the water power of the country and also the consideration of the systematic and yet economical development of such of the natural resources of the country as are still under the control of the federal government should be immediately resumed and affirmatively and constructively dealt with at the earliest possible moment. The pressing need of such legislation is daily becoming more obvious.

The legislation proposed at the last session with regard to regulated combinations among our exporters, in order to provide for our foreign trade a more effective organization and method of coöperation, ought by all means to be completed at this session.

And I beg that the members of the House of Representatives will permit me to express the opinion that it will be impossible to deal in any but a very wasteful and extravagant fashion with the enormous appropriations of the public moneys which must continue to be made, if the war is to be properly sustained, unless the House will consent to return to its former practice of initiating and preparing all appropriation bills through a single committee, in order that responsibility may be centred, expenditures standardized and made uniform, and waste and duplication as much as possible avoided.

Additional legislation may also become necessary before the present Congress again adjourns in order to effect the most efficient coördination and operation of the railway and other transportation systems of the country; but to that I shall, if circumstances should demand, call the attention of the Congress upon another occasion.

If I have overlooked anything that ought to be done for the more effective conduct of the war, your own counsels will supply the omission. What I am perfectly clear about is that in the present session of the Congress our whole attention and energy should be concentrated on the vigorous, rapid, and successful prosecution of the great task of winning the war.

We can do this with all the greater zeal and enthusiasm because we know that for us this is a war of high principle, debased by no selfish ambition of conquest or spoliation; because we know, and all the world knows, that we have been forced into it to save the very institutions we live under from corruption and destruction. The purposes of the Central Powers strike straight at the very heart of everything we believe in; their methods of warfare outrage every principle of humanity and of knightly honour; their intrigue has corrupted the very thought and spirit of many of our people; their sinister and secret diplomacy has sought to take our very territory away from us and disrupt the Union of the States. Our safety would be at an end, our honour forever sullied and brought into contempt were we to permit their triumph. They are striking at the very existence of democracy and liberty.

It is because it is for us a war of high, disinterested purpose, in which all the free peoples of the world are banded together for the vindication of right, a war for the preservation of our nation and of all that it has held dear of principle and of purpose, that we feel ourselves doubly constrained to propose for its outcome only that which is righteous and of irreproachable intention, for our foes as well as for our friends. The cause being just and holy, the settlement must be of like motive and quality. For this we can fight, but for nothing less noble or less worthy of our traditions. For this cause we entered the war and for this cause will we battle until the last gun is fired.

I have spoken plainly because this seems to me the time when it is most necessary to speak plainly, in order that all the world may know that even in the heat and ardour of the struggle and when our whole thought is of carrying the war through to its end we have not forgotten any ideal or principle for which the name of America has been held in honour among the nations and for which it has been our glory to contend in the great generations that went before us. A supreme moment of history has come. The eyes of the people have been opened and they see. The hand of God is laid upon the nations. He will show them favour, I devoutly believe, only if they rise to the clear heights of His own justice and mercy.

3. WAR WITH THE IMPERIAL AND ROYAL AUSTRO-HUNGARIAN GOVERNMENT.

Mr. Flood, from the Committee on Foreign Affairs, submitted the following report:

The Committee on Foreign Affairs, to which was referred the joint resolution (H. J. Res. 169) declaring that a state of war exists between the Imperial and Royal Austro-Hungarian Government and the Government and people of the United States and making provision to prosecute the same, having had the same under consideration, reports it back with amendment, and recommends that the resolution, as amended, do pass. . . .

The President has asked for the declaration that a state of war exists against Austria-Hungary.

In his address, delivered at the joint session of the two Houses of Congress on December 4, he uses this language:

One very embarrassing obstacle that stands in our way is that we are at war with Germany, but not with her allies. I therefore very earnestly recommend that the Congress immediately declare the United States in a state of war with Austria-Hungary.

The accompanying resolution carries out this recommendation of the President.

The enactment of this declaration involved very little readjustment of the affairs between the United States and Austria-Hungary, because a state of war which this declaration declares to exist actually has been a fact for many months. The depredations on American lives and rights by Austrian naval forces have been small compared with that of Germany, but they have been indulged in to an extent to constitute war upon this country, and this fact, taken in connection with other acts of Austria-Hungary, has more and more brought that Government into a position where the American people have realized that she must be included with Germany as an enemy.

ACTIVITIES OF AUSTRIAN AMBASSADOR AND CONSULS

In September, 1915, it was discovered that Ambassador Dumba and Austrian consuls in St. Louis and elsewhere were implicated in instigating strikes in American manufacturing plants engaged in the production of munitions of war. An American citizen named Archibald, traveling under an American passport, had been intrusted with dispatches in regard to this matter from Dumba and Bernstorff to their Governments. These acts were admitted by Dumba. By reason of the admitted purpose and intent of Dumba to conspire to cripple business industries in the United States, and by reason of the flagrant violation of diplomatic propriety in employing an American citizen protected by an American passport as a secret bearer of official dispatches through the lines of an enemy of Austria-Hungary, the Austro-Hungarian Government was requested to recall Dumba.

The Austrian consuls at St. Louis and New York were implicated with Dumba in these transactions, particularly in the circulation of strike propaganda. They were implicated in procuring forged passports from the United States for the use of their countrymen in going home.

Long before the above activities were made public, our Government had evidence that the Austrian diplomatic and consular service was being used in this country for Germany's warlike purposes.

AUSTRIA'S POSITION AS TO SUBMARINE WARFARE

While Austria's submarine warfare has been of a very limited character, they have adopted and adhered to the policy of the ruthless submarine warfare of the Imperial German Government.

After diplomatic relations with Germany had been broken, the department on February 14, 1917, dispatched the following telegram to the American embassy at Vienna, surveying briefly the position of the Austrian Government on submarine warfare:

> In the American note of December 6, 1915, to the Austro-Hungarian Government in the *Ancona* case, this Government called attention to the views of the Government of the United States on the operations of submarines in naval warfare which had been expressed in no uncertain terms to the ally of Austria-Hungary, and of which full knowledge on the part of the Austro-Hungarian Government was presumed. In its reply of December 15, 1915, the Imperial and Royal Government stated that it was not possessed with authentic knowledge of all of the pertinent correspondence of the United States, nor was it of the opinion that such knowledge would be sufficient to cover the *Ancona* case, which was of essentially a different character from those under discussion with the Berlin Government. Nevertheless, in reply to the American note of December 19, 1915, the Austro-Hungarian Government, in its note of December 29, stated:
>
> "As concerns the principle expressed in the very esteemed note that hostile private ships, in so far as they do not flee or offer resistance, may not be destroyed without the persons on board having been placed in safety, the Imperial and Royal Government is able substantially to assent to this view of the Washington Cabinet."

Moreover, in the case of *The Persia*, the Austro-Hungarian Government, in January, 1916, stated in effect that while it had received no information with regard to the sinking of *The Persia*, yet, in case its responsibility were involved, the Government would be guided by the principles agreed to in the *Ancona* case.

> Within one month thereafter, the Imperial and Royal Government, coincidently with the German declaration of February 10, 1916, on the treatment of armed merchantmen announced that "All merchant vessels armed with cannon for whatever purpose, by this very fact lose the character of peaceable vessels," and that, "Under these conditions orders have been given to Austro-Hungarian naval forces to treat such ships as belligerent vessels."

In accordance with this declaration several vessels with Americans on board have been sunk in the Mediterranean, presumably by Austrian submarines, some of which were torpedoed without warning by submarines flying the Austrian flag, as in the cases of the British steamers *Secondo* and *Welsh Prince*. Inquiries made through the American ambassador at Vienna as to these cases have so far elicited no information and no reply.

Again, on January 31, 1917, coincidently with the German declaration of submarine danger zones in waters washing the coasts of the entente countries, the Imperial and Royal Government announced to the United States Government that Austria-Hungary and its allies would from February 1 "prevent by every means any navigation whatsoever within a definite closed area."

From the foregoing it seems fair to conclude that the pledge given in the *Ancona* case and confirmed in the *Persia* case is essentially the same as that given in the note of the Imperial German Government dated May 4, 1916, viz., "In accordance with the general principles of visit and search and destruction of merchant vessels recognized by international law, such vessels, both within and without the area declared as a naval war zone, shall not be sunk without warning and without saving human lives, unless these ships attempt to escape or offer resistance," and that this pledge has been modified to a greater or less extent by the declarations of the Imperial and Royal Government of February 10, 1916, and January 31, 1917. In view, therefore, of the uncertainty as to the interpretation to be placed upon those declarations, and particularly this latter declaration, it is important that the United States Government be advised definitely and clearly of the attitude of the Imperial and Royal Government in regard to the prosecution of submarine warfare in these circumstances.

Please bring this matter orally to the attention of the Austrian Government and request to be advised as to whether the pledge given in the *Ancona* and *Persia* cases is to be interpreted as modified or withdrawn by the declarations of February 10, 1916, and January 31, 1917. If after your conversation it seems advisable, you may hand to the Minister for Foreign Affairs a paraphrase of this instruction, leaving the quoted texts verbatim.

In reply, the Austrian Government, in an aide mémoire of March 2, 1917, after reviewing the illegal blockade measures of the allies, stated that "it now as heretofore firmly adheres to the assurances given by it" in the *Ancona* case.

The Austro-Hungarian Government also stated that Austro-Hungarian submarines had taken no part in the sinking of the British steamers *Secondo* and *Welsh Prince*, and that "the assurance which it gave the Washington Cabinet in the *Ancona* case, and renewed in the *Persia* case, has neither been withdrawn or restricted by its declarations of February 10, 1916, and January 31, 1917."

The Austro-Hungarian note endeavors, through a legal argument, to show consistency between these assurances and its declarations. In this way the Austro-Hungarian Government evades a direct answer to the American inquiry, but in its argument it substantially adheres to the declaration of January 31, 1917, for it states that—

> The entire declaration is essentially nothing else than a warning to the effect that no merchant ship may navigate the sea zones accurately defined in the declaration.

and that—

> The Imperial and Royal Government is, however, unable to accept a responsibility for the loss of human lives which, nevertheless, may result from the destruction of armed ships or ships encountered in the closed zones.

In view of this acceptance and avowal by the Austrian Government of the policy which had led to a breach of relations between the United States and Germany, the Government of the United States found it impossible to receive Dumba's successor, Count Tarnowski. The Government felt that it could not receive a new ambassador from a country which joined Germany in her submarine policy, even though its participation might be by verbal and not physical coöperation. This was communicated to the Austrian Government in a telegram from the department dated March 28, 1917.

In his message to Congress of April 2, 1917, the President said, in respect to the attitude of Austria-Hungary:

> I have said nothing of the Governments allied with the Imperial Government of Germany because they have not made war upon us or challenged us to defend our right and our honor. The Austro-Hungarian Government has, indeed, avowed its unqualified indorsement and acceptance of the reckless and lawless submarine warfare adopted now without disguise by the Imperial German Government, and it has therefore not been possible for this Government to receive Count Tarnowski, the Ambassador recently accredited to this Government by the Imperial and Royal Government of Austria-Hungary; but that Government has not actually engaged in warfare against citizens of the United States on the seas, and I take the liberty, for the present at least, of postponing a discussion of our relations with the authorities at Vienna. We enter this war only where we are clearly forced into it because there are no other means of defending our rights.

The Austrian note of January 31, 1917, proclaimed the same submarine policy as that of Germany, and officially announced her intention, if she saw fit, to pursue the same ruthless submarine policy that Germany had inaugurated.

Many vessels have been sunk by submarines in the Mediterranean —the area in which Austrian submarines operate—by submarines which carried no flag or mark and the nationality of which was unknown. A great many of these undersea craft are believed to have been Austrian submarines or submarines commanded by Austrian officers, or supplied from Austrian bases or by Austrian means.

On April 4, 1917, the American four-masted schooner *Marguerite* was sunk by a submarine 35 miles from the coast of Sardinia, while en route to Spain. The submarine carried no flag or marks to indicate its nationality. It is known, however, that Austrian was the language spoken by the officer of the submarine who came aboard the vessel with the boarding party, and it is believed that the submarine was Austrian.

On November 21, 1917, the *Schuylkill* was sunk off the coast of Algeria by an Austrian submarine; thus Austria is making, whenever opportunity affords, the same ruthless submarine warfare that Germany is making, in disregard of the promises made this Government, in violation of the law of nations and the instincts of humanity, and is as much at war with this country as Germany was after her note of January 31, 1917, and the subsequent sinking of American ships and the drowning of American citizens.

SEVERANCE OF DIPLOMATIC RELATIONS BY AUSTRIA-HUNGARY

Before war was declared to exist between the United States and the Imperial German Government, it was intimated to the United States Government that if war should be declared by the United States upon Germany, Austria-Hungary would be under obligation to break off diplomatic relations with the United States. Consequently after the declaration of war of April 6, 1917, the Austro-Hungarian Government informed the American chargé at Vienna on April 8 that diplomatic relations between the United States and Austria-Hungary were broken and handed him passports for himself and members of the embassy. The following is a translation of the note handed to the American chargé by the Austrian minister for foreign affairs:

IMPERIAL AND ROYAL MINISTRY OF THE
IMPERIAL AND ROYAL HOUSE AND OF FOREIGN AFFAIRS,
Vienna, April 8, 1917.

Since the United States of America has declared that a state of war exists between it and the Imperial German Government, Austria-Hungary, as ally of the German Empire, has decided to break off the diplomatic relations with the United States, and the imperial and royal embassy in Washington has been instructed to inform the Department of State to that effect.

While regretting under these circumstances to see a termination of the personal relations which he has had the honor to hold with chargé d'affaires of the United States of America, the undersigned does not fail to place at the former's disposal herewith the passport for the departure from Austria-Hungary of himself and the other members of the embassy.

At the same time the undersigned avails himself of the opportunity to renew to the chargé d'affaires the expression of his most perfect consideration.

CZERNIN.

To Mr. JOSEPH CLARK GREW,
Chargé d'Affaires of the United States of America.

AUSTRO-GERMAN OPERATIONS AGAINST ITALY

Until the present Austro-German drive in northern Italy, the Austrian forces were gradually being driven back by the forces of the Italian armies. With the assistance of German troops drawn from the Russian front, a very serious catastrophe was inflicted upon the Italian arms, which if it had not been stemmed might have resulted in the total collapse of Italy. Such a result would have been a great blow to those with whom we are associated in this war, and as much to the United States as to any of her cobelligerents.

As a result of this situation the Allies have rushed aid to Italy, and the United States is sending ships, money, and supplies, and will probably soon send troops, who will be facing and making war on Austrian soldiers, and before this takes place there should be a declaration of war, this country against Austria-Hungary.

The Italian situation is of the utmost importance in the present conduct of the war. A declaration of war by the United States against Austria-Hungary will hearten the people of Italy, who have been misled by the mischievous and deluding propaganda engineered by the Germans. It will strengthen from a military point of view the whole allied cause. These are strong reasons for a declaration of war against Austria-Hungary.

These considerations, and the fact that Austria-Hungary is adhering to the illegal and inhumane policy of ruthless submarine warfare, and is, as the committee believes, making war upon American vessels and American citizens upon the high seas, and other reasons which are not deemed necessary to recapitulate here, induced the committee to report unanimously the accompanying resolution declaring that a state of war exists between the Imperial and Royal Austro-Hungarian Government and the Government and people of the United States and making provision to prosecute the same.

The action of the committee was unanimous, and it trusts that the resolution will be adopted unanimously by the House.

4. JOINT RESOLUTION DECLARING THAT A STATE OF WAR EXISTS BETWEEN THE IMPERIAL AND ROYAL AUSTRO-HUNGARIAN GOVERNMENT AND THE GOVERNMENT AND THE PEOPLE OF THE UNITED STATES, AND MAKING PROVISION TO PROSECUTE THE SAME.

Whereas the Imperial and Royal Austro-Hungarian Government has committed repeated acts of war against the Government and people of the United States of America: Therefore be it

Resolved by the Senate and House of Representatives of the United States of America in Congress assembled, That a state of war is hereby declared to exist between the United States of America and the Imperial and Royal Austro-Hungarian Government; and that the President be, and he is hereby, authorized and directed to employ the entire naval and military forces of the United States and the resources of the Government to carry on war against the Imperial and Royal Austro-Hungarian Government; and to bring the conflict to a successful termination all the resources of the country are hereby pledged by the Congress of the United States.

CHAMP CLARK,
Speaker of the House of Representatives,

THOS. R. MARSHALL,
*Vice President of the United States and
President of the Senate.*

Approved, December 7, 1917,
WOODROW WILSON.

INDEX

Abeken, Privy Councillor, xliv, 10
Acteon, The (cited), 245
Acton, Lord (cited), xxiii
Adriatic, The, 17, 26
Ægean, The, 18, 20, 22, 26
Africa, 18, 23
Alexander II, Czar of Russia, 13-16
Alabama, The (Federal cruiser), 81
Alabama, The (Confederate cruiser), 127, 241, 337
Alabama Claims, 313, 337
Alabama Claims, Court of, 338, 339
Albert, Dr., Violation of American neutrality by, 308
Alleganean, The (cited), 343
Allen, Geo. W. (cited), 239
Alsace-Lorraine, 17, 18
Ambrose Channel Light, 112
American trade. *See* Foodstuffs.
Americans, Arrest of, on neutral vessels, 66-73
Ancona, The, Sinking of, 374-375
Annie Larsen, chartered to carry arms to India, 308
Antelope, The (cited), 220
Arabic, The, Attack on, 168-169, 302
Arbitral court, 319-320
Arbitration, 29, 311-325, 331; cases, 313; treaties, 321
Archer, The (cited), 127
Archibald, James J. F., Passport frauds by, 306
Argentina, 321
Arizona, 310
Ariel, The (cited), 241
Armed merchantmen, correspondence concerning status of, 216-264; American circular, 249-250; American rules, 250; British notes, 248-260; American proposal for agreement as to, 258-260; German decrees relative to, 261-262; American proclamation of armed neutrality, 296-298; reply of Allied powers, 360
Armed neutrality, 296-297
Armed neutrality, American proclamation on, 296-297
Armenian, The, Sinking of, 301
Arms and munitions. *See* Munitions of war.
Arndt, Ernst M. (cited), xli, 194-195

Arrest of Americans on neutral vessels, 72; August Piepenbrink, 67
Asia, 18
Atlas Steamship Company, 307
Attacks on ships, 301-304; 374-377
Austria, 2-6, 11, 17-22; ultimatum to Denmark (1864), 3; ultimatum to Servia and reply, 26-36; refused Servia's offer to arbitrate, 27; declared war on Servia, 28, 36; informs Italy of intention to attack Servia (1913), 42; declaration of war by the United States against, 364-379. *See also* Submarine warfare.

Babylonia, 23
Bacon, George Voux, 306
Bagdad Railway, 22, 23
Baltic, The, 211, 344
Balkans, 18, 21
Balkan War (1912), 21, 42
Balkan War (1913), 22; Austria informed Italy of intention to proceed against Servia, 42
Bancroft Treaty, 67
Barboux (cited), 237
Beernaert, Auguste, 191
Belgian Relief Commission, 303-304
Belgium, 23, 28, 29, 184, 190, 193, 303, 326; invasion discussed in 1911, 191-192
Belligerent ships, violations of neutrality by, 110-116
Benedetti, Vincent Count de, French Ambassador to Prussia, xlv-xlvi, 9-12, 334
Benedictus XV, American answer to Peace appeal of, 361-363
Berlin Congress of, 19, 21
Bermuda, The (cited), 85, 89
Bernhardi, Friedrich von (cited), xcii-cxii
Bernstorff, Count von (1871), 238
Bernstorff, Count von, German Ambassador to the United States, 308, 309
See Germany.
Berwindale, The, Sinking of, 302
Bethmann-Hollweg, Theobald, cxiv, 184, 192. *See also* Germany.
Beyens, Baron, 192

381

Bieberstein, Baron Marschall von, German delegate to Hague Conference, 210, 321-324
Bismarck, Herbert Count von, 195
Bismarck, Otto Count von (cited), xliii-xlvii, 1, 21, 195, 238, 317, 334, 335
Black Sea, 18, 344; Russia assumed control, 21
Blatchford Prize Cases (cited), 226
Blockades, 205-215; American proclamation of 1862 declaring blockade, 80; German decree and memorandum, 136-149; North Sea declared war zone, 161; British Note and Orders in Council, 210-215
Bluntschli, Johann Caspar (cited), xlviii-l, 180, 268-270
Boer War, 101, 105-106
Bohemia, 12
Bolles, John A. (cited), 238-240
Bopp, Franz, German Consul-General at San Francisco, 307
Borcke, von, xxix
Bosnia, by treaty of Berlin to be administered by Austria, 19; annexed by Austria, 20, 21
Boxer Rebellion, 78
Boy-Ed, Captain, 306
Brincken, George Wilhelm Baron, 307
Bryan, William J., American Secretary of State, March 4, 1913 to June 9, 1915, 253, 323
Bryan treaties, 323, 324
Buffon, Henri Nadault de, xxiii
Bulgaria, King of, 19-22
Bulmerincq, August von (cited), 269-270
Bülow, von, 192, 318, 320
Bynkershoek, 345, 346

Cables, Censorship of, 57-59
Canal Zone, Panama. *See* Panama Canal Zone.
Canary Islands, Cutting of cable, 57
Cape Argus, The, Sinking of, 242
Caroline Islands, 317
Carranza, General, 309
Cass, Lewis, American Secretary of State, 1860, 147, 198
Catharina Elizabeth, The (cited), 276
Censorship, 57-65
Chakrabarty, Dr., Violation of American neutrality, 305
Charles, King of Roumania, 9, 335
Charles X, King of Sweden, xxxi
Charles XII, King of Sweden, xxxi
Charlotte, The (cited), 238
Chase, Salmon P., Chief Justice of United States, 85, 87

Chiala (cited), 195
China, The, Removal of enemy subjects from *The Laurentic*, 70, 71
Choate, Joseph H., American delegate Hague Peace Conference, 1907, 322
Chihuahua, Mexico, 309
Christian, Prince of Denmark, 3
Churchill, Winston, 247, 248
Citizenship, 116, 117
Citizenship, Case of August Piepenbrink, 66-69
Civil War, American, 313, 336
Clarence, The (cited), 127
Clark, Champ, xxii, 379
Clausewitz, Karl von (cited), xxxix-xli
Coaling of warships in Panama Zone, 128-130; attitude of Great Britain at Hague Conference, 1907, 51
Coburg, House of, 20
Coleridge, Lord Chief Justice of England, 196
Commercen, The (cited), 88
Commission, Belgian Relief, 303
Commission of Inquiry, 327
Communipaw, The, Attack on, 302
Condé, The. August Piepenbrink removed to, 67, 70
Confederacy, 68
Congress of Berlin, 1878, 19, 21
Congress of Vienna, 1815, 2
Congress of Paris, 1856, 21
Constantinople, 17, 18, 19
Contraband, German, French, British decrees relative to, 74-77; Hague Conventions on, 74; Declaration of London, 75; list issued by Secretary of Treasury of United States, May 23, 1862, and American proclamations of April 29, June 15 and June 24 (1865), 77-78
Convention for Pacific Settlement of International Disputes, 314, 329
Conversion of merchant vessels, 247
Copper, Contraband, 77-79
Cornell, Margaret U., Mrs., 307
Cotton, Declaration of Great Britain (August 23, 1915), of Germany (July 22, 1916), 91
Court of arbitral justice, 314-319
Crimean War, 5, 99, 246
Crispi, 195
Cupenberg, Baron von, 306
Cushing, The, Attack on, 150, 301
Cushing vs. United States, 225-226
Czar of Russia, 316

Daeche, Paul, 307
Dalmatia, 17

INDEX

Dana, Richard H. (cited), 88, 266
Dana's Wheaton, 88, 266
Dardanelles, The, 17
Darmstadt, Princess of, xxviii
Davignon, M., Belgian Minister for Foreign Affairs, 191, 192
De Boeck (cited), 228
Declaration of London, Orders and decrees, etc., 50, 68, 74-77, 130-132, 137, 138, 243, 274, 328, 331-333; Germany and Allies willing, but Great Britain and Allies unwilling to accept, 77; failure of United States to protest against British modifications, 130-131
Declaration of Paris, 53, 93, 137, 220-225, 247; Great Britain denied binding force as to the United States, 53
Declaration of St. Petersburg, xlviii
Declaration of war, American against Germany, xxi, xxii, 298-310; against Austria-Hungary, 379
Declarations of war (1914-1917), cxv
Delbrück, Martin Friedrich Rudolf von, 335
Denmark, 2, 4; ultimatum sent by Austria (1864), 3
Department of State War Relief Committee, vi
Depretis, Augustin, Italian Minister of Foreign Affairs, 1882, 195
Desaix, The (cited), 224, 237
Destruction of prizes. *See* Prizes.
Detention camps, 119-120
Deutschland, The, 251
Diplomatic Relations between the United States and Germany severed, 295-297; between the United States and Austria, 378
Draper, Judge, 343
Dual Alliance, Text of, 25
Dumba, Constantin Theodor, Austrian Ambassador, Recall of, 306, 373
Dumont, J. (cited), 267-268
Dumdum bullets, Sale of, 106-110; Hague Conventions relative to, 109; protest of Germany against use, 107
Dutch Gueldre, xxiv

Eagle Point, The, Sinking of, 303
Edward VII, King of England, 25
Eitel Friedrich, The, 255
Elsebe, The (cited), 235
Emden, The, 255
Ems telegram, xliv-xlvi, 9-12
Endymion, The (cited), 236
Enemy property, 237

Englishman, The, Sinking of, 303
Escape of interned officers and men from German ships, 306
Express, The (cited), 242
Eulenberg, Count, xlv
Euphrat, Ernest T., 305

Falaba, The, Sinking of, 150, 158, 255
False colors, Use of, 140, 197-204
Favre, Jules, 16
Fay, Robert, 307
Felicity, The (cited), 236, 238, 244, 245
Field, Justice, 344
Fish, Hamilton, 225
Flag, neutral, 140; correspondence with Great Britain, 201-204; American practice, 199-200; Use by belligerents, 197-204; German authorities on use of, 198
Flood Report on war with Germany, 301-310; with Austria, 372-379
Florida, The (cited), 127
Flotow, von, 192
Foodstuffs, Importation into Germany; Correspondence with Germany and Great Britain, 91-96; Cargo of *Wilhelmina*, 92-94; German Decree, 91; *Modus vivendi* proposed by United States, 93, 96
Force majeure, 237
Foreign Relations Committee. *See* Senate Committee on Foreign Relations.
Foster, John W., 313
France, 2, 5, 12-18, 25, 27, 29, 312, 315, 316; Case of August Piepenbrink, 67-69; *See* Blockades, Censorship, Contraband, Declaration of London, etc.
Francis Joseph, Emperor of Austria and King of Hungary, 11
Franco-Prussian War, xliv-xlvi, 9-12
Frankfort, German representatives met to form empire, 2
Frankfort Peace, xlvii, 2
Franz Ferdinand, Archduke of Austria, assassination of, 26
Frederick the Great (cited), xxii-xxxv
Frederick William IV, King of Prussia (cited), xlii; refused crown offered by Frankfort Assembly, 2
Frederick VIII, The, Removal of mails from, 60
Freedom of the Seas, 336-359
French protest in *Trent* case, 69
French Revolution, 45, 103
Fried, Alfred (cited), 313

Fritzen, charged with plot to blow up Welland Canal, 308
Frye, The. See *William P. Frey, The.*
Fyffe, C. A. (cited), 3, 4, 5

Gastein, Treaty of, 4
Geffcken, Friedrich Heinrich (cited), 271
Geier, The, Internment of, 121-128
Geneva Award, 337
Geneva Convention (Red Cross), 106
Geneva Tribunal (Alabama Claims), 314, 337, 338
German attitude towards arbitration, 314
German charges of unneutral conduct, 54-56
German conceptions of the State, international policy and international law, xxii-cxiv
German Embassy warning to travelers, 151
German Federation, 3
German Minister to Mexico, Zimmermann letter to, 290, 305, 310
German Prize Ordinance, 280-285
German War Book, xci-xcii, 47, 99, 100, 185, 195
Germany, War Book, xci-xcii, 47, 99, 100, 185, 195; prize ordinance, 280-285; embassy warning to travelers, 151; Zimmermann letter, 296, 305, 310; refusal to conclude arbitration treaties with the United States in 1907 and 1914, 324; refused to suspend submarine operations during discussion, 327. *See also* Armed merchantmen, blockades, etc.
Giolotti, Prime Minister of Italy, 42
Goschen, Edward, Sir, 324, 325
Gotter, Count, xxix
Granville, Lord, 21, 224
Gray, George, Justice, 227
Great Britain, proposed a congress to adjust Balkan Question, 21; merchant shipping code, 203. *See also* Armed merchantmen, blockades, etc.
Greece, 21, 22
Greve, Dr., 330
Grey, Sir Edward, 324, 325
Grotius, Hugo (cited), 22, 349-359
Gulflight, The, Attack on, 150, 254, 301
Gustavus Adolphus, King of Sweden, xxxi

Hœlen, The, Attack on, 304
Hague Conventions; rights and duties of neutrals, 58, 120, 122, 125; inviolability of mails, 62; contraband, 74; use of projectiles, 106, 109; war on land, 109, 126; peaceful settlement of international disputes, 166, 314; mines, 208-210
Hague Conventions, ratifications, 109
Hague Peace Conference, 1899, 314
Hague Peace Conference, 1899, 1907, 29, 64, 74, 210, 243, 272, 278, 279, 314, 321, 325
Hall, William Edward (cited), 45, 240
Hamburg-American Line, 307
Hanover, annexation of North German Confederation, 5
Hans Libeau Employment Agency, 308
Harcourt, Sir William Vernon (cited), 341
Harlan, John M., Justice, 339
Hatteras, The (cited), 241
Hawksbury, Lord, 326
Headlam, J. M. (cited), 333
Heffter, August Wilhelm (cited), 265-268, 271
Hegel, Georg W. F. (cited), xxxv
Helgoland, 208
Hensel, Carl Paul, 306
Herzegovina, by treaty of Berlin administered by Austria, 19; annexed by Austria, 21
Hesperian, The, Attack on, 302
Hesse, annexed to North German Confederation, 5
Heynen, Carl, 309
High Seas, 339-347
Hipsang, The (cited), 244
Hired Ships, 223
Historicus, Letters of (cited), 341
Hobbes, Thomas (cited), 161-162
Hohenburg, Duchess of, assassination, 26
Hohenlohe, Prince of, 320, 333
Hohenzollern, House of, 20, 23
Hohenzollern, Prince Karl Anton, xliv-xlv, 334
Hohenzollern, Prince Leopold, xliv-xlv, 334, 335
Hohenzollern-Sigmaringen line, xlv-xlvi, 9-12
Holland, 23, 190
Holls, Frederick, American delegate to Hague Conference, 1899, 318, 320
Holstein, Duchy of, 2, 3, 4
Holtzendorff, Franz J. W. P. von (cited), 266
Holy Roman Empire, 1
Home and Foreign Review (cited), xxiii
Hooper, Admiral, v. United States (cited), 226

INDEX

385

Hope, Captain, 236
Horn, Werner, attempted to blow up bridge at Vanceboro, Me., 307
Hospital Ships, Attacks on, 303
Hovering Warships, 110-116; American ships outside British ports during Civil War, 114; Letters from American Secretary of State (Feb. 3, 1807, May 30, 1807), 111; American proclamation of neutrality (Aug. 22, 1870), 111; American protest against hovering of British warships outside American ports, 110
Huberich, Charles (cited), 280
Humbert-Bazile, xxiii
Hungary, Insurrection, 1850, 5
Hurst, Cecil J. B. (cited), 244

Igel, von Wolf, 306, 308
Ikhona, The (cited), 244
Immunity of private property at sea, *See* Maritime War, Laws of
Indian National Party, 305
Institut de droit International, xlvii, 271, 277
Institute of International Law. *See Institut de droit International*
Instructions to American Armies in the Field, 180
International law, German conceptions of, xxii-cxiv
International policy, German conceptions of, xxii-cxiv
Internment of belligerent ships, 121-128; Hague Conventions relative to, 122-123
Internment of German Ships: *Geier* and *Locksun*, 121-128; *Kronprinz Wilhelm*, escape of interned officers, 306
Internment of tenders to warships, 121-128
Interpretation of treaties with Prussia, 153, 285-289
Isabella, Queen of Spain, 8
Italy, xlvii, 5, 11, 17, 18, 22, 24, 27, 29, 315, 321

Jackson, John P., American Minister to Roumania, ordered to investigate prison camps, 120
Jagow, Herr von, German Secretary of Foreign Affairs, 145, 192, 193, 324, 325
Japan, 11, 290, 310
Jay, John, Chief Justice of the United States, 312, 313
Jay Treaty, 1794, 78, 313
Jecker vs. Montgomery (cited), 85
Jefferson, Thomas, 312

John H. Jarvis, The (cited), 339
Joint State and Navy Neutrality Board (cited), 107-108, 121
Jones, John Paul, 239
Jonge Pieter, The (cited), 84

Kaltenbach, M., 16
Kaltschmidt, Albert, 307
Karlsruhe, The, 255
Kent's Commentaries (cited), 86
Kent, Chancellor (cited), 86, 340, 341
Kiel Canal, 22, 23, 29
King, Richard (cited), 280
King's College, 312
Kirkwall, 60
Kleist, von, Captain, 307
Knight Commander, The (cited), 243, 244
Knowles, Mr., American Minister, 20-21
Koenig, Paul, 307-308
Kopf, Mr., 309
Kriege, Dr., 64-65
Kriegsbrauch in Landkriege (cited), xci-xcii, 47, 99, 100, 185-187, 195
Kronprinz Wilhelm, escape of officers of the, 306
Krum-Hellen, Mr., 309
Kuepper's Administrator (cited), xlii

Labor's National Peace Council, 307
Lafayette, The (cited), 241
Lalaing, Count de, 192
Lancaster, Chancellor of Duchy of, 312
Lanoir, Paul (cited), 12-16
Lansing, Mrs. Robert, vi
Lansing, Robert, Counsellor, Department of State; Secretary of State, ad interim, June 9, Secretary of State, June 23, 1915
Lasson, Adolf (cited), 1-lxx
Lauenberg, Duchy of, 4
Launay, Count de, 195
Laurentic, The, Removal of Austrians, Germans and Turks from, by *The China*, 70-72
Lavalette, Marquis de, 224
Lawrence, William Beach (cited), 88
Lawrence's Wheaton (cited), 88
Leelanaw, The, Attack on, 302
Lena, The (cited), 123-124
Leo, The, Attack on, 302
Leopold, Prince, of Hohenzollern, xliv-xlvi, 9-12
Lieber, Francis (cited), 180
Lincoln, Abraham, 68
Liszt, von Franz (cited), 273
Loans, to belligerents, Change of policy in regard to, 118-119
Localization of Austro-Serbian dispute, 36-42
Locksun, The, Internment of, 121-128

Lombardo-Venetian Kingdom, 5
London Naval Conference. *See* Declaration of London
Louis, Le (cited), 231
Louis Napoleon, 5
Louis Phillippe, King of France, 2
Louis XIV, King of France, xxx
Ludwig, The (cited), 237, 238
Lushington, Dr. (cited), 245
Lusitania, The, Sinking of, 149-168, 172, 184, 253, 254, 256, 301, 308; use of American flag by, 201, 202
Luxembourg, Duchy of, 184, 188
Lyons, Lord (cited), 116

Madison, James, Secretary of State, 111
Mahoney, The, chartered to carry arms to India, 306
Mails, Censorship of, 57-65; American protest against removal of from ships, 60-61; diplomatic pouches, 61; French memorandum, 62; American statement, March 24, 1916, 62, 63; Hague Conventions regarding, 65
Mallina, The, Status of, 128
Malloy, Wm. (cited), 286, 287, 289, 312
Manchester Engineer, The, Sinking of, 303
Manning, J. F. (cited), 339-342
Mansfield, Lord (cited), 162
Manual les lois de la guerre sur terre, xlvii, xlix
Marguerite, The, Sinking of, 377
Maria, The (cited), 232
Marianna Flora, The (cited), 231, 346
Maritime warfare, Rules of, 265-289; immunity of private property withdrawn by Prussia (1870), 224; German authorities on, 265-279; German prize ordinance, 280-285; Prussian-American treaties, 285-289. *See also* Submarine Warfare.
Marshall, John, Chief Justice (cited), 217
Martens, Fedor Fedorovich (cited), 50
Mason and Slidell. *See Trent.*
Matamoras cases (cited), 79-95
Matineés royales ou l'art de régner, Les (cited), xxiii
Maverick, The, chartered to carry arms to India, 308
Mazatlan, The, 306
Mediation proposals, 39, 40, 41
Mediterranean, The, 344

Meneval, Baron de, xxiii
Menzel, Friedrich W., clerk in the Chancellery at Dresden, xxix
Merchant flag, 201-204
Merchant vessels, status of, 216-264; right to arm, 216-229
Meiapan, The, German passengers removed from, 67, 70
Metapan Steamship Company, 70
Mexico, 11, 290, 309, 310
Mines, correspondence with Germany and Great Britain, 205-215; attitude of Germany and Great Britain at Hague Conference, 209; British Orders in Council, 211-212; German memorandum, Feb. 4, 1915, 213
Mirabeau (cited), 146
Mississippi, The, 23
Mohl, Robert von, 266
Moltke, Helmuth, Count von, Prussian chief of staff (cited), xliv, xlvii-xlix, 9, 13, 335
Mommsen, Theodor (cited), xlii-xliii
Monroe Doctrine, 23, 316
Monroe, James, American Minister to England, 111
Montenegro, 19-21
Moore, John Bassett (cited), 116, 198, 313
Morocco, 24
Müller, Max, 100
Munitions of war, correspondence with Germany, 98-105; sale by Germany to Boers, Russia and Turkey, 101; attempt of one Pearson to prevent exports to Great Britain during Boer War, 105-106
Münster, Count, 316-319, 325
Music, The, 339

Napoleon III, 7-9, 12, 13
Napoleonic wars, 1
Nassau, Duchy of, annexation by Prussia, 5
Nationality and citizenship, case of August Piepenbrink, 66-69
Naval Conference. *See* Declaration of London
Nebraskan, The, Attack on, 301
Necessity, law of, 184-196; invasion of Belgium, 184
Nereide, The (cited), 164
Neutral flags, Use by belligerents of, 140, 197-204
Neutrality, 43-135; proclamation of, by United States, 43; appeal by the President of the United States, 48-49; correspondence be-

INDEX

tween Secretary of State to the Senate Committee on Foreign Relations, 54-135; proclamation of, relative to Panama Canal Zone, 128, 129; agreement between United States and Panama, 129

Neutrality of the United States, 43-135

New Amsterdam, The, Removal of mails from, 61

Nicosian, The, Attack on, 302

Niemeyer, Th. (cited), 278

Noncombatants, confinement in detention camps of, 119-121

Noordam, The, Removal of mails from, 61

Noorder Dyke, The, Removal of mails from, 61

Norddeutsche Allgemeine Zeitung, 192

North Atlantic Coast Fisheries Arbitration, 314

North German Confederation, 5, 67, 189, 223, 224, 289

North German Lloyd S. S. Co., 330

North Sea, 23, 161, 210-215; declared war area, 161, 211; British notes and Orders in Council, 210-215

Ocean, The (cited), 83

Oldhamia, The (cited), 244

Olsen, The, chartered to carry arms to India, 306

Oppenheim, Lassa (cited), 279

Orduna, The, Attack on, 302

Origin and extent of modern practice of arbitration, 311-314

Oscar II, The, Removal of mails from, 60

Ottoman Empire. *See* Turkey

Pacific settlement of international disputes, 166, 311-314

Pan-Germanism, 23

Pan-Hellenism, 23

Panama, The (cited), 227, 228

Panama Canal Zone, proclamation of neutrality, Nov. 13, 1914, 128, 129; coaling of warships, 128

Papen, Captain von, 306-308

Parcel post, 62

Paris, Congress of, 21

Paris Exposition, 1867, 13

Parsons, James (cited), 88

Passports, Disregard for American, 116-117; forging of American passports by Austrian consuls, 373; misuse of American passports by J. F. Archibald, 306

Patria, The, Attack on, 302

Patrick Henry, The, 343

Peace, American answer to Peace appeal of Benedictus XV, 361-363

Pearson vs. Parsons (cited), 105-106

Pégou, The (cited), 229

Penal Code of the United States, 43-45

Perels, Ferdinand (cited), 178-180, 198, 199, 272

Permanent Court of Arbitration, 320-321

Persia, The, Attack on, 302, 374-376

Persian Gulf, 22

Peterhoff, The (cited), 79-91, 229

Petrolite, The, Attack on, 302

Phillimore, William (cited), 241

Piepenbrink, August, Arrest of, 66-69

Pigou, The (cited), 229

Pinkney, William, Secretary of United States Treasury, 111

Pistoye et Duverdy (cited), 229

Pitt, William, 311

Podewils, Minister of Frederick the Great (1741), xxii

Poland, xxiv, 1, 5, 13; insurrection, 5

Polly, The, 86

Pope Leo IX, 317

Pomerania, Swedish, xxiv

Portalis (cited), 20, 228-229, 348

Portugal, 23

Posen, 13

Postal union, 322

Prague, 12

President Woodrow Wilson. *See* Wilson, Woodrow.

President, The (cited), 237

Prince Christian, 3

Prince Anton, 9

Prince Leopold, xlv-xlvi, 9-12

Princesse Marie, The (cited), 244

Princip, Gabrilo, assassinated Archduke Franz Ferdinand of Austria and the Duchess of Hohenberg, 26

Prisenordnung (Germany), 200, 280-285

Prize Code of the German Empire, 200, 280-285

Prizes, destruction of, 234-247; German authorities on, 271-273; regulations of *Institut de droit international*, 271; Hague Conventions on, 273; Declaration of London on, 274. *See also* Maritime Law, Rules of

Proclamations of neutrality. *See* United States—Proclamations

Protocol of London, January 17, 1871, 191

Prussia, xxiii-xxxvi, 6, 7; interpretation of treaties with United

States, 153, 285-289; Prussian Volunteer Navy, 223; withdraws immunity of private property at sea (1871), 224
"Prussia was not swallowed up in Germany," lxxxii
Prussian-American treaties, 285-289
Prussian Spy System, 12-16
Prussian Volunteer Navy, 223
Puffendorf, Samuel von, 269
Pultney, Wm., 311-312
Pythagorean theorem, 326

Quintuple treaty of 1839, 189, 190

Reay, Lord, 278
Regina vs. Dudley (cited), 195
Renewal of submarine warfare, 290-294
Reprisals, 177-180; German authorities on, 178
Republican and Cossack, xlvii
Resolutions of the Institute of International Law, 277
Restraints on commerce, 74-97
Retaliation, 181-184; correspondence with Great Britain, 182
Rich vs. United States, 339-342
Ries, Irving Guy, 306
Right of merchant vessel to arm, 216-234
Right of visit and search. *See* Visit and Search
Rights and duties of neutral powers, 58, 120, 122, 125
Rintelin, Franz, Captain, 307, 309
Ritter, Paul, Swiss Minister to the United States, 327
Rockhill, William W., 78
Rode Captain, 307
Roeder, Gustav C., 306
Roon, Count Albrecht Theodor von, Prussian Minister of War, xliv, xlvi, 9-12
Root, Elihu, Secretary of State, 322, 323
Rose, J. Holland (cited), 311, 312
Rotterdam, The, Removal of mails from, 61
Roumania, 19, 20, 22, 315
Rousseau, J. J., 347
Rovigo, Duke of, xxiii
Rules of maritime warfare. *See* Maritime warfare
Rümelin, Gustav (cited), lxx, lxiii
Ruroede, Carl, 306
Rush-Bagot agreement, 313
Russell, Lord Odo, 21, 69, 71
Russell, Lord John, 197
Russia, xxi, 5, 11, 17-19, 21-28, 307, 315, 316, 324

Russo-Japanese War, 91, 243, 246, 247, 272
Russo-Turkish War, 1877-1878, 19, 191

Sadowa, 5, 12
St. Kilda, The (cited), 244
San Jacinto, The (cited), 67, 70
Sanders, Albert, violation of neutrality by, 306
Savary, General, Duke of Rovigo, xxiii
Saxony, xxvii
Schaick, Vice Consul General von, 307
Scheele, Walter T., Dr., 307
Scheldt, The, 23
Schleinitz, 335
Schleswig-Holstein question, 2, 3, 4, 6, 12
Scholts, Walter, 307
Schooner Jane vs. The United States, The (cited), 227
Schramm, Georg (cited), 200
Schuylkill, The, Sinking of, 377
Schurz, Carl (cited), 7-8
Scott, Sir William. *See* Stowell, Lord
Scraps of paper, xlvii, 327
Search, Right of. *See* Visit and Search
Second Hague Peace Conference. *See* Hague Peace Conferences.
Secondo, The, Sinking of, 375
Secretary of State. Correspondence with Senate Committee on Foreign Affairs, 54-135
Semmes, Raphael, Captain (cited), 241
Senate Committee on Foreign Affairs. Correspondence with Secretary of State respecting neutrality, 54-135
Serajevo, 26
Servia, 19, 20, 21, 22, 27, 42; reply to Austrian ultimatum, 27-36; Advised to reply to Austria so as to preserve peace, 41-42
Severance of diplomatic relations with Germany, 295-297; with Austria, 377-378
Seward, William, Secretary of War, 68, 116, 160
Shaw, U. A., xxiii
Silesia, xxiv
Silius, The, Sinking of, 302
Sinking of ships, 301-304, 374-377
Smith, Goldwin (cited), 100-101
Smith, Munroe (cited), 325
Snow, Freeman (cited), 241
Somerfeld, Felix, 309
Spies, Prussian, 12-16
Springbok, The (cited), 79, 89-90
Staal, M. de, President of First Hague Peace Conference, 315, 318
Stahl, Gustav, violation of American neutrality, by, 308

INDEX

Stallforth, violation of American neutrality by, 309
Stert, The (cited), 83
Stieber, Chief of Prussian Spy System, 12-16
Stockholm, The, Removal of mails from, 60
Stone, William, Senator, Letter to Secretary of State from, 54-135
Storstad, The, Sinking of, 304
Story, Justice, 231, 344
Stowell, Lord (cited), 78, 86, 232-236, 245
Streit, Georges (cited), 209
Submarine warfare, Germany, 136, 177-180, 197; renewal of, 290-294; Austria, 374-377
Sumter, The (cited), 241
Sussex, The, Sinking of, 150, 169-176, 263, 303
Switzerland, Minister from, presented memorandum from Germany offering to discuss submarine policy, 327
Syria, xxxiv

Tacony, The (cited), 127
Tarnowsky, Count Adam, xx, 376
Tauscher, Hans, Captain, 308
Tetartos, The (cited), 244
Thea, The (cited), 244
Thile, 335
Thomas Gibbons, The (cited), 226
Thrasher, Leon C., Death of, 150
Three Rules of Treaty of Washington, 337
Trade with Germany, 91-96
Trade with neutrals, 79-91
Trans-shipment of troops, 120-121
Treaties (cited), Treaty of the Pyrenees (1659), 267; United States-Great Britain (1794), 78, 313; Prussia-United States (1799, 1828), 153, 285-289; Treaty of London (1839), 188; Treaty of London (1852), 3, 4; Treaty of Paris (1856), 11, 17, 21; Treaty of Vienna (1864), 3, 4, 6; Treaty of Gastein (1865), 4; Treaty of Prague (1866), 5; Treaty of Nikolsburg (1866), 5; Bancroft Treaty (1868), 67; Treaty of Frankfort (1871), 18; Treaty of London (1871), 190-191; Treaty of Washington (1871), 337; Treaty between Austria and Germany (1878), 6; Treaty of San Stefano (1878), 19; Treaty of Vienna (1879), 25; Great Britain-Russia (1899), 26; Great Britain-France (two in 1904), 26; Great Britain-Russia (1907), 26; Great Britain-France (1907), 26; Treaty of Lausanne (1912), 24; Treaty of Bucharest (1913), 22; Treaty of London (1913), 22; Great Britain-France, Russia (1914), 26; Panama-United States (1914), 129
Treaties are scraps of paper, xlvii
Trietschke, Heinrich (cited), lxxiii-xci
Tremeadow, The, Status of, 128
Trent, The (cited), 67-71, 114
Triepel, Heinrich (cited), 278-279
Triple Alliance, xlvii, 22, 24-26, 29, 42; documents relating to, 26; text, 25, 26; Italy joined (1882), 24
Triple Entente, 25, 26
Troops, transshipment of British, 120, 121; Hague Convention concerning, 120
Tubantia, The, Sinking of, 302
Tuckerton, New Jersey (wireless station), 57
Tunis, 18, 24
Tunisie, The, Attack on, 304
Turkey, 19, 20, 22, 315, 369-370
Turner, Judge (cited), 106
Tuscaloosa, The (cited), 127

Ullmann Emanuel von (cited), 272
Ulrica, Princess, xxviii
Unfriendly acts of United States toward Central Powers, 132-134
Union Metallic Cartridge Company, 107
United States Navy, Order of August 18, 1862, destruction of prizes, 238-240
United States vs. Rodgers (cited), 343
United States, naval war code, 180, 198; penal code, 43-45; proclamations, 77-78, 111, 228; public resolution declaring a state of war to exist with Germany, xxi-xxii; report of House Committee on foregoing, 301-310; public resolution declaring a state of war to exist with Austria, 379; report of House Committee on foregoing, 372-379; circular of Treasury Department on contraband (1862), 77; Treaty with Great Britain (1794), 78, 313; Treaty with Panama (1914), 129; treaties with Prussia (1799, 1828), 285-289, 328, 332

INDEX

Vanceboro, Maine, Attempt to blow up international bridge at, 307
Van del Elst, 192
Vattel, Emmerich de (cited), 233
Vergennes, Count de, 312
Versailles, King of Prussia crowned Emperor of Germany at, 11
Vessels, Attacks on, and sinking of, 301-304, 374-377
Victoria, Queen of England, 11, 25
Vienna, Congress of, 1-2, lxviii
Villa, Francisco, 309
Vinland, The, Stopping of, by British cruiser within three-mile limit, 112
Visit and Search, 230-234
Volunteer Fleet, Prussian, 223
Vorwärts, Der (cited), 238

Walkerville, Canada, 307
War is Prussia's principal industry, 146
Warships, rights and duties of neutral powers relative to, 122-125; treatment in Panama Canal Zone, 128-132; internment of, 123-128
War with Austria, House report, 372-379
War zones, 205-215
Washington, Treaty of 1871. *See* Treaties
Wedell, Hans von, 306
Wehberg, Hans (cited), 274-277
Weingarten, Secretary to Austrian Ambassador to Prussia, xxix
Welch Prince, The, Sinking of, 375
Welland Canal, plot to blow up, 308
White, Andrew D., American delegate to Hague Conference (1899), 315-321

Wheaton, Henry (cited), 88, 228, 266, 341
(Lawrence's and Dana's editions)
Whewell, W. (cited), 22
Whittall, C., xxiii
Whittall, Sir James William, xxiii
Wico, The, Seizure of, 52
Wilhemina, The, Seizure of, 92-96
Wilkes, Charles, Captain, 114
William P. Frye, The, Sinking of, 288, 326-335; application of Prussian-American treaties, 285-289; judgment of prize court, 328; question of indemnity, 329; agreement to arbitrate, 330
William I, King of Prussia and Emperor of Germany, 8, 12, 13, 334
William II, Emperor of Germany, cxiv
William, The (cited), 86
Wilson, Woodrow, xiii-xxi; address of April 2, 1917, xiii-xxi; appeal to people to observe neutrality, 48, 49; address of December 5, 1917, 364-372
Winchester Repeating Arms Company, 107
Windber, The, Arrest of August Piepenbrink on, 67
Windsor, Canada, 307
Wireless, 57
Wolpert, Captain, 307
Wunnonberg, Charles, 306

Yasaka Maru, The, Sinking of, 302

Zanardelli, 195
Zerbst, Princess of, xxvii
Zimmermann, Alfred, letter to German Minister to Mexico, 11, 17, 290, 309, 310
Zinzendorff, xxix
Zorn, Philip (cited), 315, 318

Augsburg Seminary
Library